T0094158

Multimedia Networking and Coding

Reuben A. Farrugia
University of Malta, Malta

Carl J. Debono
University of Malta, Malta

Managing Director:	Lindsay Johnston
Editorial Director:	Joel Gamon
Book Production Manager:	Jennifer Yoder
Publishing Systems Analyst:	Adrienne Freeland
Development Editor:	Austin DeMarco
Assistant Acquisitions Editor:	Kayla Wolfe
Typesetters:	Erin O'Dea, Deanna Jo Zombro
Cover Design:	Nick Newcomer

Published in the United States of America by
Information Science Reference (an imprint of IGI Global)
701 E. Chocolate Avenue
Hershey PA 17033
Tel: 717-533-8845
Fax: 717-533-8661
E-mail: cust@igi-global.com
Web site: http://www.igi-global.com

Library of Congress Cataloging-in-Publication Data

Multimedia networking and coding / Reuben A. Farrugia and Carl J. Debono,
editors.
      pages cm
 Includes bibliographical references and index.
 Summary: "This book covers widespread knowledge and research as well as innovative applications in multimedia communication systems, highlighting recent techniques that can evolve into future multimedia communication systems and showing experimental results from systems and applications"-- Provided by publisher.
  ISBN 978-1-4666-2660-7 (hardcover) -- ISBN 978-1-4666-2691-1 (ebook) -- ISBN 978-1-4666-2722-2 (print & perpetual access) 1. Multimedia communications. 2. Internet programming. I. Farrugia, Reuben A., 1981- editor of compilation. II. Debono, Carl J., 1974- editor of compilation.
 TK5105.15.M825 2013
 006.7'6--dc23
                        2012033551

British Cataloguing in Publication Data
A Cataloguing in Publication record for this book is available from the British Library.

All work contributed to this book is new, previously-unpublished material. The views expressed in this book are those of the authors, but not necessarily of the publisher.

Table of Contents

Section 2
Video Transmission

Section 3
Multimedia Applications

Detailed Table of Contents

Section 1
Video Compression Principles

H. Koumaras, Institute of Informatics and Telecommunications, Greece
M.A. Kourtis, Athens University of Economic and Business, Greece

This chapter presents a general overview of the video coding principles and standards. This chapter launches with a brief explanation of the video coding process, and analyzes its discrete components, using specific examples. It then proceeds to an overall outline of the most important video coding standards by MPEG and their individual profiles/versions, and of the novel video coding standard High Efficiency Video Coding (HEVC). Additionally, this chapter contains a description of the objective and subjective video quality evaluation methods that are widely used in video quality assessment. The chapter concludes with a report on future trends and developments regarding the field of video processing.

Andreas Unterweger, University of Salzburg, Austria

This chapter describes and explains common as well as less common distortions in modern video coding, ranging from artifacts appearing in MPEG-2 Video, MPEG-4 Part 2, H.264, and VC-1 to scalable and multi-view video coding based distortions, including the proposals for next generation video coding (NVC). In addition to a discussion about avoiding these artifacts through encoder-side measures, a state-of-the-art overview of their compensation at the decoder side is given. Finally, artifacts emerging from new sophisticated coding tools in current and upcoming video coding standards are discussed.

Motion estimation is one of the major bottlenecks in real-time performance scalable video coding applications due to high computational complexity of exhaustive search. To address this, researchers so far
focused on low-complexity motion estimation and rate-distortion optimization in isolation. Proliferation of
power-constrained handheld devices with image capturing capability has created demand for much smarter
approach where motion estimation is integrated with rate control such that rate-distortion-complexity
optimization can be effectively achieved. It is indeed crucial to provide such performance scalability
in motion estimation to facilitate complexity management in such devices. This chapter presents an
overview of motion estimation. Beginning with an introduction to the importance of motion estimation,
it systematically examines various motion estimation techniques and their strengths and weaknesses,
focussing primarily on block-based motion search. It then examines the limitation of the existing techniques in accommodating performance scalability, introduces a promising approach, Distance-dependent
Thresholding Search (DTS) motion search, to fill in this gap, and concludes with future research directions in the field. The authors suggest that the content of the chapter will make a significant contribution
and serve as a reference for multimedia signal processing research at postgraduate level.

Chapter 4

The advent of cheaper and more powerful devices with the ability to play, create, and transmit video
content has led to a dramatic increase in the multimedia content distribution on both wireline and
wireless networks. Also, the reduction of cost of digital video cameras along with the development of
user-generated video sites (e.g., iTunes™, YouTube™) stimulated a new user-generated video content
sector and made unprecedented demands for high-quality and low-delay video communication. The
Region-of-Interest (ROI) is a desirable feature in many future scalable video coding applications, such as
mobile device applications, which have to be adapted to be displayed on a relatively small screen; thus,
a mobile device user may wish to extract and track only a predefined ROI within the displayed video.
At the same time, other users having a larger mobile device screen may wish to extract other ROIs to
receive higher video stream resolution. Therefore, to fulfill these requirements, it would be beneficial to
simultaneously transmit or store a video stream in a variety of ROIs, as well to enable efficiently tracking
of the predefined Region-of-Interest. This chapter presents recent advances in Region-of-Interest video
and image processing techniques for multimedia applications, while making a special emphasis on a
scalable extension of the H.264/AVC standard. The detailed observations and conclusions, which are
presented in this chapter, are supported by authors' personal experience in this field, thereby presenting
a variety of experimental results.

Chapter 5

Three-dimensional video (3DV) is expected to be the next multimedia technology that provides depth impression of observed scenery with multi-view videos. In fact, studies on 3D video have a long history, heading back two hundred years; but recently, it has risen as the hottest issue due to rapid progresses of IT technologies. Particularly, 3D video systems are the most promising technology in multimedia area. An extension of typical stereoscopic imaging, realistic and natural 3D video technologies are currently under development. In this chapter, the authors describe overall technologies of 3D video systems from capturing to display, including coding standards. Mainly, the chapter focuses on the recent standardization activities by MPEG (moving picture experts group) associated with 3D video coding.

Chapter 6

Progress in image sensors and computation power has fueled studies to improve acquisition, processing, and analysis of 3D streams along with 3D scenes/objects reconstruction. The role of motion compensation/motion estimation (MCME) in 3D TV from end-to-end user is investigated in this chapter. Motion vectors (MVs) are closely related to the concept of disparities, and they can help improving dynamic scene acquisition, content creation, 2D to 3D conversion, compression coding, decompression/decoding, scene rendering, error concealment, virtual/augmented reality handling, intelligent content retrieval, and displaying. Although there are different 3D shape extraction methods, this chapter focuses mostly on shape-from-motion (SfM) techniques due to their relevance to 3D TV. SfM extraction can restore 3D shape information from a single camera data.

Section 2
Video Transmission

As real-time video streaming moves to the mobile Internet, there is a greater need to protect fragile compressed bit-streams from the impact of lossy wireless channels. Though forward error correction (FEC) has a role, if it is applied without adaptation, it may introduce excessive communication overhead. Alternatively, error resilience methods provide additional protection at the application layer of the protocol stack, without replication of any protection already provided at the data-like layer. In this chapter, a case study shows that these resilience methods can be applied adaptively through stream switching according to channel conditions. Error resilience can work hand-in-hand with error concealment, again applied through source coding. There are many error resilience and concealment methods, which this chapter surveys at a tutorial level. The chapter also includes an overview of video streaming for those unfamiliar with the topic. Though error concealment is a non-normative feature of the H.264/AVC (Advanced Video Coding) codec standard, there is a range of new techniques that have been included within the Standard such as flexible macroblock ordering and stream switching frames. The chapter additionally reviews error concealment provision, including spatial, temporal, and hybrid methods. Results show that there are tradeoffs between the level of protection and the level of overhead, according to the severity of the wireless channel impairment.

Chapter 8

Sunday Nyamweno, McGill University, Canada

Ramdas Satyan, McGill University, Canada

Fabrice Labeau, McGill University, Canada

Motion compensated prediction (MCP) is at the heart of modern video compression standard because of its ability to remove temporal redundancies. However, MCP is responsible for temporal error propagation, which can result in severe quality degradation in lossy environments. In this chapter, the authors present two innovative methods of improving MCP to be more resilient to packet losses. In the first method, the motion trajectory is used to develop a novel distortion weighting technique, and the second method exploits the presence of Intra macroblocks in previously coded frames to develop increase robustness.

Chapter 9

S. Zinger, Eindhoven University of Technology, The Netherlands

L. Do, Eindhoven University of Technology, The Netherlands

P. H. N. de With, Eindhoven University of Technology, The Netherlands

G. Petrovic, Eindhoven University of Technology, The Netherlands

Y. Morvan, Eindhoven University of Technology, The Netherlands

Free-ViewPoint (FVP) interpolation allows creating a new view between the existing reference views. Applied to 3D multi-view video sequences, it leads to two important applications: (1) FVP service provided to the user, which enables the possibility to interactively select the viewing point of the scene; (2) improved compression of multi-view video sequences by using view prediction for inter-view coding. In this chapter, the authors provide an overview of the essential steps for 3D free-view video communication, which consists of the free-viewpoint interpolation techniques, a concept for free-view coding and a scalable free-view video streaming architecture. For facilitating free-view to the user, the chapter introduces the free-viewpoint interpolation techniques and the concept of warping. The authors assume that 3D video is represented by texture and depth images available for each view. Therefore it is possible to apply Depth Image Based Rendering (DIBR), which uses the depth signal as a important cue for geometry information and 3D reconstruction. Authors analyze the involved interpolation problems, such as cracks, ghost contours and disocclusions, which arise from an FVP interpolation and propose several solutions to improve the image quality of the synthesized view. Afterwards, they present a standard approach to FVP rendering used currently by the research community and our FVP interpolation. Additionally, authors show the use of FVP rendering for the multi-view coding and streaming and discuss the gains and trade-offs of it. At the end of the chapter are the state-of-the-art achievements and challenges of FVP rendering and a vision concerning the development of free-viewpoint services.

Chapter 10

Jânio M. Monteiro, ISE, University of Algarve Portugal/INOV, Lisbon, Portugal

Rui S. Cruz, Instituto Superior Técnico/INESC-ID/INOV, Portugal

Charalampos Z. Patrikakis, Technological Education Institute of Piraeus, Greece

Nikolaos C. Papaoulakis, National Technical University of Athens, Greece

Carlos T. Calafate, Universidad Politécnica de Valencia, Spain

Mário S. Nunes, Instituto Superior Técnico/INESC-ID/INOV, Portugal

The Internet as a video distribution medium has seen a tremendous growth in recent years. Currently, the transmission of major live events and TV channels over the Internet can easily reach hundreds or millions of users trying to receive the same content using very distinct receiver terminals, placing both scalability and heterogeneity challenges to content and network providers. In private and well-managed Internet Protocol (IP) networks these types of distributions are supported by specially designed architectures, complemented with IP Multicast protocols and Quality of Service (QoS) solutions. However, the Best-Effort and Unicast nature of the Internet requires the introduction of a new set of protocols and related architectures to support the distribution of these contents. In the field of file and non-real time content distributions this has led to the creation and development of several Peer-to-Peer protocols that have experienced great success in recent years. This chapter presents the current research and developments in Peer-to-Peer video streaming over the Internet. A special focus is made on peer protocols, associated architectures and video coding techniques. The authors also review and describe current Peer-to-Peer streaming solutions.

Section 3
Multimedia Applications

Chapter 11

Simon Denman, Queensland University of Technology, Australia

Frank Lin, Queensland University of Technology, Australia

Vinod Chandran, Queensland University of Technology, Australia

Sridha Sridharan, Queensland University of Technology, Australia

Clinton Fookes, Queensland University of Technology, Australia

The time consuming and labor intensive task of identifying individuals in surveillance video is often challenged by poor resolution and the sheer volume of stored video. Faces or identifying marks such as tattoos are often too coarse for direct matching by machine or human vision. Object tracking and super-resolution can then be combined to facilitate the automated detection and enhancement of areas of interest. The object tracking process enables the automatic detection of people of interest, greatly reducing the amount of data for super-resolution. Smaller regions such as faces can also be tracked. A number of instances of such regions can then be utilized to obtain a super-resolved version for matching. Performance improvement from super-resolution is demonstrated using a face verification task. It is shown that there is a consistent improvement of approximately 7% in verification accuracy, using both Eigenface and Elastic Bunch Graph Matching approaches for automatic face verification, starting from faces with an eye to eye distance of 14 pixels. Visual improvement in image fidelity from super-resolved images over low-resolution and interpolated images is demonstrated on a small database. Current research and future directions in this area are also summarized.

Robert S. H. Istepanian, Medical Information and Network Technologies Research Centre, Kingston University, UK
Ali Alinejad, Medical Information and Network Technologies Research Centre, Kingston University, UK
Nada Y. Philip, Medical Information and Network Technologies Research Centre, Kingston University, UK

It is well known that the evolution of 4G-based mobile multimedia network systems will contribute significantly to future m-health applications that require high bandwidth, high data rates, and more critically better Quality of service and quality of experience. The key to the successful implementation of these emerging applications is the compatibility of emerging broadband wireless networks such as mobile WiMAX, HSUPA, and LTE networks with future m-health systems. Most recently, the concept of 4G-health is introduced. This is defined as the evolution of m-health towards targeted personalized medical systems with adaptable functionalities and compatibility with future 4G communications and network technologies. This new concept represents the evolution of m-health toward 4G mobility. It will have new challenges especially from the next generation of mobile communications and networks perspective and in particular from relevant quality of service and quality of experience issues. This chapter presents some of these challenges and illustrates the importance of the new concepts of medical Quality of Service (m-QoS) and medical Quality of Experience (m-QoE) for 4G-health systems. The chapter also presents a validation scenario of these concepts for medical video streaming application as a typical 4G-health scenario.

Chun-Rong Su, National Taiwan University of Science and Technology, Taiwan
Jiann-Jone Chen, National Taiwan University of Science and Technology, Taiwan

Performing Content-Based Image Retrieval (CBIR) in Internet connected databases through Peer-to-Peer (P2P) network (P2P-CBIR) helps to effectively explore the large-scale image database distributed over connected peers. Decentralized unstructured P2P framework is adopted in our system to compromise with the structured one while still reserving flexible routing control when peers join/leave or network fails. The P2P- CBIR search engine is designed to provide multi-instance query with multi-feature types to effectively reduce network traffic while maintaining high retrieval accuracy. In addition, the proposed P2P-CBIR system is also designed in the way to provide scalable retrieval function, which can adaptively control the query scope and progressively refine the accuracy of retrieved results. To reflect the most updated local database characteristics for the P2P-CBIR users, reconfiguring system at each regular interval time can effectively reduce trivial peer routing and retrieval operations due to imprecise configuration. Experiments demonstrated that the average recall rate of the proposed P2P-CBIR with reconfiguration is higher than the one without about 20%, and the latter outperforms previous methods, i.e., firework query model (FQM) and breadth-first search (BFS) about 20% and 120%, respectively, under the same range of TTL values.

Preface

Recent advances in network infrastructures and multimedia systems have facilitated the introduction of new multimedia services such as Internet Protocol Television (IPTV), Mobile Television, Video on Demand (VoD), Videoconferencing, Tele-medicine, and several other applications. Multimedia-content users are demanding to be always connected to the infrastructure and able to seamlessly access these services from any location and using any device. These services are already consuming around 50% of the Internet traffic and are expected to surpass peer-to-peer file sharing traffic by the end of this year (Cisco, 2011). Moreover, both industries and research communities are pushing towards the introduction of innovative services such as 3D Television (3DTV) and Free View Television (FVTV) which demand a significant increase in bandwidth requirements. Broadcast stereoscopic transmission over DVB-S2 (Digital Video Broadcasting - Satellite) is already with us, with channels like Eurosport 3D and Sky 3D providing such services. These offer a 3D experience by transmitting the left and right eye video side by side using MPEG-4 encoding techniques and MPEG-2 transport stream over satellite links. The received video is then presented to the user on a 3D display and has to wear 3D glasses to view the content. Furthermore, High-Definition Television (HDTV) is becoming common and countries like Japan are experimenting also with Super HDTV services that demand more data to be transmitted. All this increase in content and services has lead Cisco in predicting that the video traffic will reach 62% of the global Internet traffic by the end of 2015 (Cisco, 2011). These predictions indicate that audiovisual services are expected to provide a significant economic value for the coming years (Foster & Broughton, 2011).

The massive bandwidths occupied by video traffic and the huge demand provide several challenges to the service providers who cannot guarantee high quality content over bandwidth-limited channels (Wenger, 2003). Furthermore, the best effort nature of the IP core and unreliability of wireless networks can significantly reduce the quality of the transmitted content (Wenger, 2003), (Stockhammer, Hannuksela, & Wiegand, 2003). Moreover, these services are required on different devices having different resolution, frame rate and quality requirements. All these challenges have inspired both academia and industry to concentrate their research efforts to implement more advanced video compression schemes for both single and multiview video.

In addition, the ITU-T Video Coding Experts Group (VCEG) and the ISO/IEC Moving Picture Experts Group (MPEG) have joined their efforts to try to develop video coding systems which deliver the best video quality at the lowest rates possible. These standardization bodies gave birth to H.264/AVC (ITU-T, 2007), which is the state of the art video coding system that is widely deployed today. They are also expected to draft the High Efficiency Video Coding (HEVC) in 2013, where it is expected to achieve twice the compression efficiency of H.264/AVC at high and ultra high definition television (Sullivan & Ohm, 2010). These developments are also accompanied by the standardization of Multiview Video Coding (MVC) and Scalable Video Coding (SVC), where the first one targets 3DTV and FVTV applications while the latter is targeted for heterogeneous delivery of video content. These are included as extensions to the H.264 standard, H.264/MVC and H.264/SVC. Current standardization work is also being done for Multiview plus Depth Coding (MVD) which is expected to give better performance than MVC in both 3DTV and FVTV applications.

The multimedia signal processing and communication research community has also concentrated its research effort in the design of novel error resilient strategies, quality of experience modeling, cross layer optimization, peer-to-peer video streaming, and specialized multimedia network protocols. In addition to this research, the community has paved the way to the development of novel applications such as telemedicine, real-time intelligent surveillance systems, distributed multimedia retrieval services and several others.

The continuous and fast evolution of this research area has inspired the editors to develop this book, which covers a broad spectrum within the field of multimedia signal processing and communications. The editors felt the need to put the latest research and the future directions in this area together in one book, with the prime purpose to stimulate more research and innovation in multimedia systems. Another major objective of this book was to introduce this research topic to the non-expert readers in order to target this book to a wider audience including engineering and computer science students. The editors have therefore contacted several international experts in the concerned fields who cover different aspects of Multimedia signal processing and communications and were asked to write self-contained chapters about their latest research. The chapters had to be targeted for both expert and non-expert readers, and include future research trends within each field tackled in the chapter.

The book was purposely divided into three sections. The first section focuses on the state of the art video compression schemes and the basic principles deployed by these standards. This section explains the processes adopted by the state of the art codecs such as H.264/AVC, H.264/SVC, H.264/MVC, and those that will be probably deployed by the future H.265/HEVC. These standards will be covered in some depth highlighting the advantages and disadvantages of the architectures and mention future research trends in this area. The theory and future advances in this area are provided in this section. The second section presents the challenges involved when dealing with the transmission of video content over bandwidth-limited and noisy channels. The video artifacts which are produced because of these impairments are discussed in some detail. This section covers the error resilient and error concealment tools adopted by both single and multiview video coding schemes and will present novel solutions which are intended to inspire the readers. This section also treats Peer-to-Peer Video streaming, that is a transmission paradigm which is gaining interest by several companies, especially in China and United States. Peer-to-peer solutions can offer different data paths to a destination and can overcome the asymmetry between uplink and downlink in legacy telecommunication networks such as 3G networks. The third and last section is dedicated towards applications where it presents three promising solutions which may emerge in future technology. These include subject identification using low resolution cameras, the deployment of 4G technology for e-health systems, and image retrieval using Peer-to-Peer networks. Several other applications such as FVTV, 3DTV, layered coding and Peer-to-Peer video streaming were mentioned in other chapters which are incorporated in the other two sections. This list of applications is far from comprehensive and several other applications exist but is representative of the wide possibilities these new technologies are offering.

The first two sections contain introductory material suitable for understanding video compression and transmission systems. These sections are intended to provide an introduction to the basic concepts and methodologies in multimedia signal processing and communications and to develop a foundation that can be used as the basis for further study and research in the respective fields. Therefore, non-expert readers are advised to start reading from the first chapter to the last. On the other hand, expert readers can read each chapter individually as they are self-contained. The knowledge and mathematical complexity presented within this book remains at a level well within the grasp of undergraduate and graduate students who have followed introductory courses in signal processing and communications.

The material in this book is organized as follows.

Chapter 1 describes in detail the basic components which make up any video coding standard available today. These principles are essential for non-experts, since the knowledge delivered in this chapter is essential for the proper understanding of the latter chapters. This book chapter also presents chronologically the complex evolution of video coding standards found today and also briefly introduces the High Efficiency Video Coding (HEVC) standard which is expected to be drafted by the end of 2013. Throughout this chronological representation of the standards the authors highlight the major contribution by each standard. Koumaras and Kourtis present existing subjective evaluation methodologies and explain Reduced reference objective methodology which can model the quality experienced by the end user.

Chapter 2 explains the visual distortions present in modern video communication including but not limited to blocking artifacts, blurring artifacts, ringing artifacts, basis pattern artifacts and others. In this chapter, the author, Unterweger, investigates the artifacts caused by H.264/MVC and Scalable Video Coding and analyzes the effect of distorted depth maps which are used for view rendering for both 3DTV and FVTV applications. The author shows that higher quality can be achieved if the encoder adopts objective metrics which calculate the distortions included by the encoder rather than using the mean absolute error (MAE) adopted by all known video coding standards.

Chapter 3 provides an overview of motion estimation for video coding, which is the major computational complexity bottleneck in existing video encoders. Several motion estimation techniques are analyzed and the drawbacks of the different motion estimation schemes found in literature are pointed out it this chapter. Golam Sorwar and Manzur Murshed demonstrate that the fast motion estimation algorithms are directional and based on the unimodal error surface assumption, which does not always hold true in real world video sequences. The author presents the Distance dependent Thresholding Search (DTS) as a promising alternative solution.

Chapter 4 looks at the possible requirements of Regions-of-Interest (ROI) within video and images. Such a need occurs when a user is only interested in a particular part of the presented media. This is more pronounced in mobile applications where the resources and bandwidth are more limited, suggesting that higher quality video can only be afforded in smaller regions of the video or image. Furthermore, the region-of-interest should be tracked to guarantee a good quality of experience and adapted to the type of display available at the receiver. Grois and Hadar use their experience to show how the scalable video coding extension of H.264 can be used to provide this service. The complexity of the system is also considered in the study to find a good performance-complexity compromise. The authors show through experimental results the advantages of using such a technique and look into future directions in this field.

Chapter 5 delves into the current state of 3D video coding. 3D video is expected to be the next major advancement in multimedia systems that will provide user with a 3D scene immersive experience. This is provided through the depth impression of the observed scenery. 3D video has a long history dating back to concepts proposed in the 19th century but it is only now that technology is reaching the state to provide mass distribution of such content. In this chapter, Lee and Ho describe the overall technologies used in 3D video systemsstarting from the content capturing to their display. The authors focus on the recent standardization activities that were and are undertaken by the MPEGgroup that are associated with the area of 3D video coding.

Chapter 6 focuses on motion estimation in 3D television. As image sensors become smaller and cheaper and computational power increases, more image and video data can be acquired and transmitted. The improvements in computational power allow also better processing tools for the analysis and reconstruction of 3D scenes. Compression plays an important role is transmitting all the generated data. Estrela and Franz tackle the issue of motion compensation/motion estimation in 3D TV. Motion vectors (MVs) can be exploited in a number of sub-systems within the end-to-end 3D video transmission chain. The authors show how motion compensation/motion estimation can be used to improve dynamic scene acquisition, content creation, 2D to 3D conversion, compression, decoding, scene rendering, error concealment, virtual/augmented reality handling, intelligent content retrieval and displaying. Furthermore, the authors argue that since most of the techniques currently applied to 3D are imported from 2D solutions, there is still a lot of room for improvement.

Chapter 7 introduces the different video streaming procedures available. The author describes the network protocols adopted in different video streaming services, and how these protocols can be used to achieve an acceptable level of quality including methodologies that achieve congestion control for video streaming services. This chapter explains in depth the various error resilient mechanisms available in the H.264/AVC video coding system and explains different error concealment strategies that can be used by the decoder to alleviate the effect of transmission errors or packet loss.

Chapter 8 explains how distortions in a frame can propagate in subsequent frames because of the motion compensation prediction process. This chapter explains the rate distortion optimization process adopted by most video compression encoders, and explains how error resilient rate distortion optimization can be used to increase error resilience. The authors propose two novel schemes that can be used which detect the regions which might contain distortions and increases the probability for these regions to be intra encoded, thus stopping the temporal propagation of that particular distortion.

Chapter 9 introduces Free-ViewPoint (FVP) 3DTV and tackles view interpolation, coding, and streaming. Interpolation is a technique used to create a new view in between existing reference views. This gives the user the possibility to interactively select a viewing angle and point of the scene. Moreover, it improves the coding efficiency of multi-view video sequences as the interpolation can be done at the receiver avoiding the transmission of additional streams from the server. Therefore, inter-view coding can be done by exploiting the redundancies within the views. S. Zinger, Do, de With, Pertovic, and Y. Morvan give an overview of the process needed in 3D free-view video communication. This consists of the interpolation techniques, free-view coding, and the introduction of a scalable free-view video streaming architecture. The authors consider a 3D video which is represented by texture and depth images and apply Depth Image Based Rendering (DIBR) for reconstruction of the required viewpoint. The authors analyze the impact of using interpolation to generate intermediate views and propose solutions that can be applied to improve the image quality of the generated view. They give particular attention to the current state-of-the-art interpolation methods for FVP and look at the challenges ahead.

Chapter 10 discusses the application of peer-to-peer solutions to video streaming. Internet has seen high growth in video streaming over the last decade. Most of this delivery is done through unicast links between a server and a number of clients. This implies that the same content is being sent to very distinct receiver terminals, placing a problem to both scalability and heterogeneity in content development and to network providers as the users demanding the service increase. These problems can be mitigated through the use of IP Multicast protocols and Quality of Service (QoS) solutions but not all the networks are equipped with such facilities. Thus the main technology available relies on the best-effort and unicast nature of the Internet. This creates a demand for the development of new protocols and architectures that are capable of supporting the distribution of such large content in an efficient and transparent way. Several Peer-to-Peer protocols have been developed in the last years but these are mainly targeted for file sharing and are not necessarily good for multimedia and need adaptation and improvements. Monteiro, Cruz, Nunes, Patrikakis, Papaoulakis, and Calafate present the current state of research and development in Peer-to-Peer video streaming over the Internet. They focus on available peer-to-peer protocols, the associated architectures and current video coding techniques. Furthermore, they highlight currently funded European project in this area.

Chapter 11 presents a video surveillance application where the system is able to detect particular individuals when using low resolution video sequences. The presented system is able to detect the faces in low resolution video sequences. Object tracking and super-resolution techniques were combined to facilitate person identification. The object detection strategy was used to detect the people of interest, greatly reducing the amount of data for super resolution. A number of instances of these regions were used to obtain a super resolved faces, where improvement of around 7% were achieved for faces having an eye to eye distance of 14 pixels.

Chapter 12 gives details on the possible application of medical video transmission over wireless networks. 4G-based mobile networks are expected to provide higher bandwidth capabilities and thus the transmission of multimedia becomes more accessible and has lower latency than with current solutions. Medical video requires higher resolutions than other video applications since medical professionals need to make accurate diagnostics using this data. Thus 4G networks will be capable of presenting the high bandwidth, high data rates, and better quality of service demanded by such a service. The success of such implementations relies on the compatibility of emerging broadband wireless networks, such as mobile WiMAX and LTE networks, with upcoming m-health and e-health systems. Istepanian, Alinejad, and Philip highlight some of the challenges faced when developing m-health solutions over broadband wireless systems. They show and explain the importance of providing medical Quality of Service (m-QoS) and medical Quality of Experience (m-QoE) concepts when developing 4G-based medical video transmission systems. The authors also present a validation scenario to illustrate the concepts behind a typical medical video streaming application that can be used in a 4G-health system scenario. Furthermore, the authors comment on the need of more work and regulations to make such technology mainstream within the health industry.

Chapter 13 presents the application of peer to peer networks to facilitate content based image retrieval services. This chapter introduces the image features adopted for the application and the MPEG-7 standard descriptors. The author presents a number of similarity measures that can be used and then provide an in depth description of the peer to peer content based image retrieval system where multiple cues are used for the queries. This chapter demonstrates that reconfigurable P2P CIBR achieves the highest retrieval efficiency for different time to lives and thus can be a promising solution for content based image retrieval applications.

Reuben A. Farrugia
University of Malta, Malta

Carl J. Debono
University of Malta, Malta

REFERENCES

Cisco. (2011). *Cisco visual networking index: Forecast and methodology.* Cisco.

Foster, R., & Broughton, T. (2011). *Creative: The audiovisual sector and economic success.* Communications Chambers.

ITU-T. (2007). *ITU-T recommendation h.264: Advanced video coding for generic.* ITU-T.

Stockhammer, T., Hannuksela, M. M., & Wiegand, T. (2003). H.264/AVC in wireless environments. *IEEE Transactions on Circuits and Systems for Video Technology, 13*(7), 657–673. doi:10.1109/TCSVT.2003.815167

Sullivan, G. J., & Ohm, J.-R. (2010). *Recent developments in standardization of high efficiency video coding (HEVC)* (pp. 7798–30). SPIE Applications of Digital Image Processing. doi:10.1117/12.863486

Wenger, S. (2003). H.264/AVC over IP. *IEEE Transactions on Circuits and Systems for Video Technology, 13*(7), 645–656. doi:10.1109/TCSVT.2003.814966

Section 1
Video Compression Principles

Chapter 1
A Survey on Video Coding Principles and Standards

H. Koumaras
Institute of Informatics and Telecommunications, Greece

M.A. Kourtis
Athens University of Economic and Business, Greece

ABSTRACT

This chapter presents a general overview of the video coding principles and standards. This chapter launches with a brief explanation of the video coding process, and analyzes its discrete components, using specific examples. It then proceeds to an overall outline of the most important video coding standards by MPEG and their individual profiles/versions, and of the novel video coding standard High Efficiency Video Coding (HEVC). Additionally, this chapter contains a description of the objective and subjective video quality evaluation methods that are widely used in video quality assessment. The chapter concludes with a report on future trends and developments regarding the field of video processing.

INTRODUCTION

Video coding is defined as the process of compressing and decompressing a raw digital video sequence, which results in lower data volumes, besides enabling the transmission of video signals over bandwidth limited means, where uncompressed video signals would not be possible to be transmitted. The use of coding and compression techniques leads to better exploitation and more efficient management of the available bandwidth.

Video compression algorithms exploit the fact that a video signal consists of sequence series with high similarity in the spatial, temporal and frequency domain. Thus, by removing this redundancy in these three different domain types, it is possible to achieve high compression of the deduced data, sacrificing a certain amount of visual information, which however is not highly noticeable by the mechanisms of the Human Vi-

DOI: 10.4018/978-1-4666-2660-7.ch001

sual System, which in not sensitive at this type of visual degradation.

Thus, the research area of video compression has been a very active field during the last years by proposing various algorithms and techniques for video coding. As we mentioned earlier, video coding techniques compress the data volume of initial raw video signal with the cost of degrading the perceived quality of the video service. By enhancing the encoding algorithms and techniques, the latest proposed coding methods try to perform in a more efficient way both the data compression and the maintenance of the deduced perceived quality of the encoded signal at high levels. In this framework, many of these coding techniques and algorithms have been standardized, encouraging by this way the interoperability between various products designed and developed by different manufactures.

This chapter deals with the evolution of video coding process from the very early standards to the latest one, discussing all the fundamental concepts and ideas behind the video coding evolution. Following the evolution of the video compression efficiency, this chapter presents also the methods for video quality assessment, both subjectively and objectively.

Following this introductory section, the rest of this chapter is organized as follows: Section 2 describes the basic principles of video coding. Section 3 provides an analytical description of the video coding standards evolution, both in ITU-T and MPEG. Section 4 provides information on the video quality assessments methods that are available. Finally, Section 5 provides some future trends, while Section 6 concludes this chapter.

PRINCIPLES OF VIDEO CODING

This section presents the basic principles of video coding procedure, which the reader must understand in order to be able to continue further reading in this book. All forms of video-coding that have

compression as a primary goal, try to minimize redundancy in the media. A video consists of a number of frames, meaning separate pictures, which given the fact that they are projected one after the other at a particular rate, they give the human eye the feeling of continuous movement. This leads us to the fact that we can have two kinds of redundancy; spatial redundancy and temporal redundancy. Spatial redundancy refers to intraframe coding techniques, which means that we use neighboring similar pixels of the same frame to encode it. Temporal redundancy has to do with interframe coding, meaning the usage of past and future frames to encode our current frame.

Therefore, video compression techniques are divided into two categories based on the redundancy type. The temporal phase exploits the similarities between successive frames with the aim to reduce the temporal redundancy in a video sequence. The spatial stage exploits spatial similarities located on the same frame, reducing by this way the spatial redundancy. Then the output parameters of the temporal and spatial stages are further quantized and compressed by an entropy encoder, which removes the statistical redundancy in the data, producing an even more compressed video stream. Thus, all the video coding standards are based on the same basic coding scheme, which briefly consists of the following phases: The temporal, the spatial, the transform, the quantization and the entropy coding phase.

Finally, it must be also noted that in more simplistic systems every frame is coded separately, so the intraframe redundancy method is the best, because the loss of one frame does not affect the coding of the other frames. Due to the simplicity of these systems, this frame specific methodology is not analysed in the chapter, because it is a part of the more complicated coding systems that use both spatial and temporal techniques in order to achieve greater effectiveness and efficiency in video compression ratio.

Compression at the Temporal Plane

As input to the temporal stage of the encoding process, the uncompressed video sequence is used, which contains a lot of redundancy between its successive frames. The scope of this stage is to remove this redundancy by constructing a prediction of each frame based on previous or future frames, enhanced by compensating for fine differences between the selected reference frames. Depending on the prediction level, by which each frame is constructed, each frame is classified to three discrete types, namely: Intra-frame (I), Predictive (P) and Bidirectional predictive (B), widely referred as I, P and B. The I frames are also called Intra frames, while B and P are known as Inter frames. The properties of each type of frame are

- I frames do not contain any prediction from any other coded frame.
- P frames are coded based on prediction from previously encoded I or P frames.
- B frames are coded based on prediction from previously or future encoded I or P frames.

The pattern of successive types of frames like IBBPBBPBBP… forms a Group of Pictures (GOP), whose length is mainly described by the distance of two successive I frames (see Figure 1).

Therefore, in order to perform this temporal compression, two discrete processes are performed at this stage: The motion estimation and motion compensation. Both these processes are usually applied on specific rectangular regions of a frame, called blocks if their size is 8×8 pixels or MBs if they are 16×16 rectangular pixel regions. At the latest standards (i.e. H.264) as Figure 2 depicts, variable block sizes are used for motion compensation depending on the content, achieving better coding efficiency.

During motion estimation, the encoding algorithm searches for an area in the reference frame (past or future frame) in order to find a corresponding matching region. The process of specifying the best match between a current frame and a reference one, which will be used as a predictor of the current frame, is called motion estimation. This is performed by comparing specific rectangular areas (i.e. blocks/MBs) in the reference and current frame, until the best match to be detected. Due to this, their spatial differences are calculated, using the Sum of Absolute Differences (SAD) or Sum of Absolute Errors (SAE), which is defined as:

$$SAD(d_x, d_y) = \sum_{i=0}^{15} \sum_{j=0}^{15} \left| f(i,j) - g(i - d_x, j - d_y) \right|$$

Figure 1. GOP structure

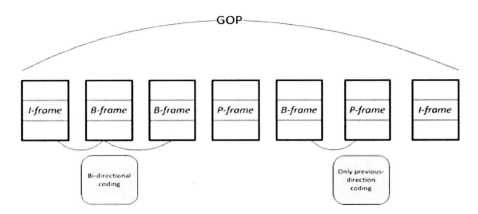

Figure 2. Example of variable block size coding

Figure 3. A frame where motion vectors appear denoting the position of the best matching region

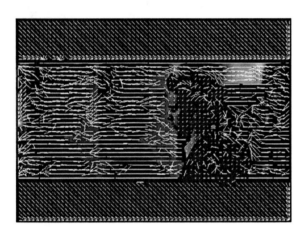

where $f(i,j)$ and $g(i,j)$ denote the luminance pixels of the current rectangular area (in this case a MB) and the reference one respectively. The reference area is relatively defined by the current one using the motion vectors (d_x, d_y), denoting the position of the best matching region as shown in Figure 3.

When the best match is found, then the motion compensation process follows. During this process the selected optimal matching region in the reference frame (i.e. the region that sets the SAD minimum) is subtracted from the corresponding region in the current frame with scope to produce a luminance and chrominance residual block/MB that is transmitted and encoded along with the reference motion vectors. The deduced frame by the motion compensation process is called residual frame, which contains the result of the subtraction of the reference regions from the corresponding ones of the current frame. In the residual frame the static areas correspond to difference equal to zero, while darker areas denote negative differences and lighter areas positive differences respectively. A typical example of a residual frame is represented in Figure 4.

Thus, motion compensation enhances the efficiency of the motion estimation by adding at the predicted frame the fine differences that may contain the motion estimated predicted regions in comparison to the actual frame. Thus, during motion estimation the best matches between

Figure 4. A residual frame (on the left) denoting the differences between two successive frames for the fireman reference sequence (shown on the right)

reference and current frames are detected and this match is further improved by motion compensation, which calculates the residuals of the motion estimated frame and the actual frame. So, adding this motion compensated residual information on the motion estimated frame, an accurate and efficient prediction of the current frame can be performed, using regions of past or future frames.

Compression at the Spatial Plane

Similarly to the temporal stage, where predictive coding is performed between successive frames, a prediction of an image region may be also performed based on samples located within the same image or frame, which is usually referred as Intra coding. At spatial stage, the encoder performs a prediction for a pixel based pattern on combination of previously-coded pixels located on the same frame. Especially for frames that contain homogeneous areas, the spatial prediction can be quite efficient. The process in the terminology of video coding is call intracoding prediction. In the case of a good prediction then the residual

energy is small and the corresponding compression ratio high.

More specifically, the spatial stage predicts the pixels of the current block using reconstructed blocks of neighboring blocks interpolated along different orientations, which try to approximate the current block/MB being encoded. The computational complexity of this process significantly increases because of the number of different block partitioning modes and prediction directions. In order to reduce the computational resources needed, various complexity reduction strategies, along with novel hardware accelerators are used.

Based on the input signal, each frame is divided into Macroblocks (MBs), which are 16×16 pixel areas on Y plane of original frame. Each MB unit consists of 4 Y blocks, 1 Cr block and 1 Cb block. So the steps for Spatial Plane Compression (as it is called Intra Coding Prediction) are depicted on Figure 5 and are the following:

1. Sub-divide picture into 16×16 pixel blocks: Macroblocks

Figure 5. Steps of the intra-coding prediction

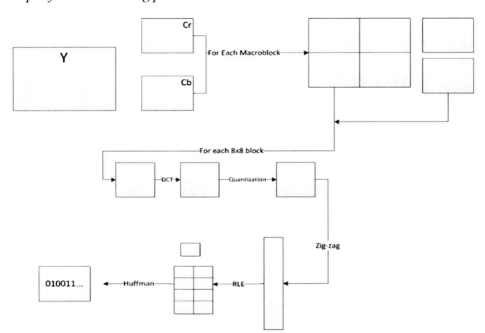

2. Apply DPCM, i.e. intra-prediction of the (16) 4×4 pixel blocks inside one Macroblock

3. Residual transform, quantization and redundancy reduction

In natural sequences, the optimal intraprediction mode usually represents the texture direction in a block. Therefore, the directional prediction can reduce the texture redundancy significantly. H.264/AVC introduces directional intraprediction in the spatial domain. *Intra_4x4* and *Intra_8x8* both have up to nine prediction modes, namely mode 0 - mode 8. Except the DC mode (mode 2), the other eight modes correspond to different prediction directions as illustrated in Figure 6.

An example of intracoding prediction is depicted on Figure 7 (Richardson, 2003), where a specific macroblock identified with white border has been selected to be intracoded predicted. Based on the possible predictions, intracoding algorithm will select the best mode by choosing the one with the smallest SAE. In addition, if multiple modes have the same, smallest SAE, then multiple solutions exist.

Transform Coding Phase

At this stage, the spatially/temporally encoded frames or the motion-compensated residual data are converted into another domain, usually called as the transformed domain, where the optically correlated data become decorrelated. The use of transformation facilitates the exploitation in the compression technique of the various psycho-visual redundancies by transforming the picture to a domain where different frequency ranges with dissimilar sensitivities at the Human Visual System (HVS) can be accessed independently. (Winkler, 2005)

The most commonly used transformation is the Discrete Cosine Transformation (DCT). The DCT operates on an X block of N × N image samples or residual values after prediction and creates Y, which is an N × N block of coefficients. The action of the DCT can be described in terms of a transform matrix A. The forward DCT is given by:

$$Y = AXA^T$$

where X is a matrix of samples, Y is a matrix of coefficients and A is an N × N transform matrix. The elements of A are:

$$A_{ij} = C_i \cos \frac{(2j+1)i\pi}{2N}$$

where

$$C_i = \frac{\sqrt{1/N}, i=0}{\sqrt{2/N}, i>0}$$

Figure 6. H.264/AVC intracoding prediction modes

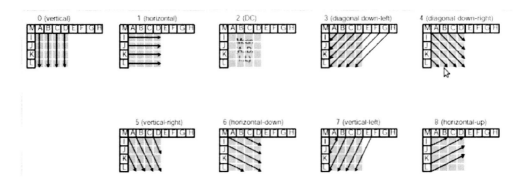

Figure 7. H.264/AVC prediction example

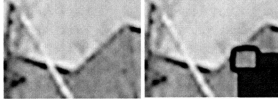

Therefore the DCT can be written as:

$$Y_{xy} = C_x C_y \sum_{i=0}^{N-1} \sum_{j=0}^{N-1} X_{ij} \cos \frac{(2j+1)y\pi}{2N} \cos \frac{(2i+1)x\pi}{2N}.$$

The advantage of the DCT transformation is that it is possible to reconstruct quite satisfactorily the original image, applying the reverse DCT on a subset of the DCT coefficients, without taking

under consideration the rest coefficients with insignificant magnitudes (see Figure 8).

Thus, at the expense of some quality degradation, the original image can be satisfactorily reconstructed with a reduced number of coefficient values. This DCT property is exploited by the following stage where quantization of the DCT coefficients is performed.

Quantization Phase

Quantization is the process of approximating the continuous range of DCT coefficients by a relatively-small set of discrete integer values. The best-known form of quantization is the scalar quantizer, which maps one sample of the input to one quantized output value. A scalar quantization operator $Q()$ can be mathematically represented as

$$Q(x) = g\big(\lfloor f(x) \rfloor\big)$$

where x is a real number, $\lfloor x \rfloor$ is the floor function, and $f(x)$ and $g(i)$ are arbitrary real-valued functions.

Figure 8. Example of DCT efficiency: a) is the source image, while b) is reconstructed using only 1 DCT coefficient, b exploits 4 coefficients, c) uses 8 coefficients, d) uses 12, e) uses 18 and f) 32 out of the 64 total DCT coefficients for each block (i.e. 8x8)

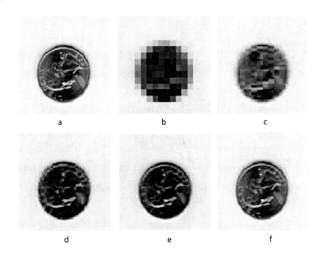

The integer value $i = \lfloor f(x) \rceil$ is the representation that is usually stored or transmitted, but the final interpretation may be further modified using also $g(i)$. Thus, typically during a scalar quantization process, it is performed the rounding of a fractional number to its nearest integer:

$$Y = QP \; round\left(\frac{X}{QP}\right)$$

where QP is the quantization parameter (i.e. quantization step size), X the initial integer value and Y the deduced quantized number. Table 1 depicts some representative examples of the scalar quantization process for various Quantization Parameters.

Applying quantization on the aforementioned DCT coefficients is the main reason for the quality degradation and the appearance of artifacts, like the blockiness effect, at the digitally encoded videos. The blockiness effect refers to a block pattern of size 8×8 pixels in the compressed sequence, which is the result of the independent quantization of individual blocks of block-based DCT. Due to the quantized DCT coefficients, within a block (8×8 pixels), the luminance differences and discontinuities between any pair of adjacent pixels are reduced. On the contrary, for all the pairs of adjacent pixels, which are located across and on both edge sides of the border of adjacent DCT blocks, the luminance discontinuities are increased, by the coding process. This happens because the quantization process is lossy (i.e. not totally reversible) since it is not possible to determine the accurate fractional number from the deduced rounded integer. So it is somewhat equivalent with the case of not exploiting the entire DCT coefficient set for the reconstruction of the original image, as in Figure 4, because some low DCT values may have been quantized to zero.

It must be noted that the quantization stage is the only lossy stage at the described coding chain and is mainly responsible for any visual artifact and quality degradation, which may appear on the deduced coded video signal.

Entropy Coding Phase

At this final stage it is performed a transformation of the video sequence symbols into a compressed stream. The term video sequence symbol stands for all the aforementioned encoding parameters, such as quantization coefficients, motion vectors etc. Basically, two widely known variable length coding techniques are exploited at this stage: The Huffman Coding (Huffman, 1952) and the Arithmetic Coding (Witten et al., 1987). Both methods are briefly analysed hereafter:

Huffman coding technique creates a binary tree of nodes. Each node contains the symbol itself, and the weight (appearance frequency) of the symbol, and optionally a link to a parent node. The internal nodes contain symbol weight, links to their child nodes (two), and a link to the parent node to make the reverse tree reading easier. Usually the bit '0' represents the left child and bit '1' the right child. The basic algorithm to create the Huffman binary tree is:

1. Create a node for every symbol, and place all of them in group.

Table 1. Quantization examples

X	Y		
	QP=1	QP=2	QP=3
0	0	0	0
1	1	0	0
2	2	2	3
3	3	2	3
4	4	4	3
5	5	4	6
6	6	6	6
7	7	6	6
8	8	8	9
9	9	8	9

2. Remove from the group the nodes with the smallest weight, make them children of a new node that will have the weight sum of the two nodes, and place the new node to the group.

3. Repeat recursively step (2) until the group of nodes contains one node containing the weight sum of all nodes.

The decoding afterwards begins by the root of the binary tree and for each symbol we want to encode we memorize the '0,' '1' bits we encounter on the route to the symbol, the string of '0' and '1' we have memorized is the encoded symbol.

Arithmetic coding differs from Huffman coding (Figure 9), because it doesn't separate the input into component symbols and replace each with a code, it encodes the entire message into a single number, a fraction f where $(0.0 \leq f < 1.0)$. Apart from the weight of its symbol arithmetic coding

demands that the terminating symbol does not appear in any other position of the input string. The coding process is the following:

1. All n symbols of input s are sorted, usually in alphabetical order.
2. Every symbol x_i with weight $p(x_i)$ is assigned an interval $[a_i, b_i)$ where $b_i - a_i = p(x_i)$.
3. First symbol is assigned the $[0.0, p(x_1))$ interval.
4. Every next symbol is assigned the $[p(x_1), p(x_1) + p(x_2))$ interval.
5. The last symbol has the interval $[1.0 - p(x_n), 1.0)$.

The algorithm for the arithmetic coding technique is shown in Box 1.

The variable length coding methods assign to each video sequence symbol a variable length code, based on the probability of its appearance.

Figure 9. Huffman coding algorithm

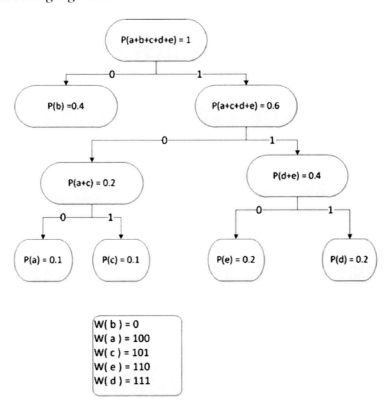

Box 1.

```
LowValue = 0.0;
HighValue = 1.0;
Do {
    inputString s;
    range = HighValue - LowValue;
    HighValue = LowValue + range * highRangeArray[s];
    LowValue = LowValue + range * lowRangeArray[s];
}
While(symbol != '$')
Print any number in [LowValue, HighValue);
```

Symbols appearing frequently are represented with short variable length codes while less common symbols are represented with long variable length codes. Over a large number of encoded symbols, this replacement of video sequence symbols by variable length codes lead to efficient compression of the data. (Held, 1991)

VIDEO CODING STANDARDS EVOLUTION

Till today, all the commonly known video compression methods/standards have been developed and approved either by ITU-T or ISO. The majority of the standards have followed a discrete development phase by either the ITU-T or the MPEG, while some joint standards have been proposed by both bodies. Figure 10 provides a

timeline of the video coding evolution by each standardization body.

The following subsections provide a brief presentation of the standards developed by ITU-T and MPEG respectively, focusing on the new features that each standard developed and introduced in the coding community.

ITU-T Standards

H.261

H.261 is a video standard by ITU-T, ratified in November 1988. It is the first member of the H.26x family of video coding standards in the domain of the ITU-T(VCEG), and was the first video codec that was used in commercial terms. H.261 was originally designed for transmission over ISDN lines on which data rates are multiples

Figure 10. Timeline of video coding standards evolution

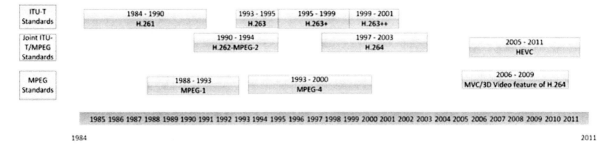

of 64 kbit/s. The coding algorithm was designed to operate at video bit rates between 40 kbit/s and 2 Mbit/s. The standard supports two video frame sizes: CIF (352×288 luma with 176×144 chroma) and QCIF (176×144 with 88×72 chroma) using a 4:2:0 sampling scheme.

The basic processing unit of the design is called a MB and H.261 was the first standard in which the MB scheme appeared. Each MB consists of a 16 × 16 array of luma samples and two corresponding 8x8 arrays of chroma samples, using 4:2:0 sampling and a YcbCr sampling.

The inter-frame prediction reduces temporal redundancy, with motion vectors used to help the codec compensate for motion. Whilst only integer-valued motion vectors are supported in H.261, a blurring filter can be applied to the prediction signal partially mitigating the lack of fractional-sample motion vector precision. Transform coding using an 8x8 discrete cosine transform (DCT) reduces the spatial redundancy. Scalar quantization is then applied to round the transform coefficients to the appropriate precision determined by a step size control parameter, and the quantized transform coefficients are zig-zag scanned and entropy coded (using a "run-level" variable-length code) to remove statistical redundancy. Figure 11 presents the steps of H.261 coding and decoding.

The H.261 standard actually only specifies how to decode the video. Encoder designers were given the liberty to design their own encoding algorithms, as long as their output is properly compatible to be decoded by any decoder implemented according to the standard. Encoders are also left free to perform any pre-processing they want to their input video, and decoders are allowed to perform any post-processing they want to their decoded video prior to display.

One major post-processing feature that was part of the H.261 is the deblocking filter. This technique is applied to blocks in the decoded video to give a more smooth visual texture by reducing the appearance of edgier blocks of the frame, which are caused by the block-based motion compensation and spatial transform of the design. Deblocking filtering has since become an important part of the successor of H.261 the H.264. In which a further post-processing can be done and enhance further the deduced video quality.

Future design optimizations included in later "family" standards have significantly reduced the compression level compared to the H.261, making it out-of-date, although, it is still used in some conferencing systems, internet videos and as a backward-compatibility mode. Despite that, H.261 is indisputably a milestone in the ever-evolving video-coding field.

H.262

The H.262 or MPEG-2 Part 2 (also known as MPEG-2 Video) is a digital encoding and compression standard developed and maintained jointly by ITU-T Video Coding Experts Group (VCEG) and Moving Picture Experts Group (MPEG).

Figure 11. H.261 Coding and decoding steps

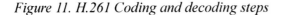

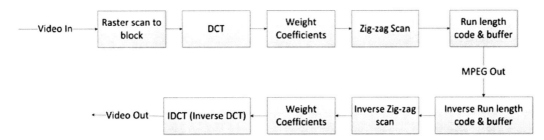

H.262 is very similar to MPEG-2 standard, which will be discussed later, but also provides support for interlaced video. In lower bitrates (less than 1Mbits) H.262 is not very efficient, but outperforms MPEG-1 at bitrates higher than 3 Mbits. All H.262/MPEG-2 conformed standards have full compatibility for MPEG-1 video playback.

H.262 supports a wide range of applications from high quality HD editing to mobile. It's unrealistic or too expensive for several applications to support the entire standard. In order to support these applications too, H.262 defines a set of profiles and levels. A profile defines a set of features i.e compression algorithm, chroma – luma format, etc. A level defines the set of quantitative capabilities i.e maximum frame size, maximum bitrate. The specifications set by an application in terms of profile and level, mean that a given player supports up to main profile and main level, can also playback any MPEG encoded up to this profile and level or less. The set of profiles include SP (Simple profile), MP (Main profile), SNR (SNR scalable profile), HP (High profile), 422 (4:2:2 profile), and MVP (Multi-view profile). Accordingly, the set of levels is LL (Low Level), ML (Main Level), H-14 (High 1440), HL (High Level). Also any given profile – level combination is allowed by the standard.

H.263

H.263 video standard is the successor of H.261 and H.262, it maintains its predecessor's basic structure, but also has additional compression capabilities and error recovery techniques. This makes H.263 suitable for unreliable networks and lower data transfer rates, such as PSTN (public switched telephone network), where we experience high signal to noise ratio.

H.263 can handle very low data transfer rates, supporting SQCIF (sub-QCIF) video frame size. From the aspect of video compression H.263 extends the capabilities of H.261 as it also uses B-frames, which can use both previous and for-

ward frames (I or P frames) for data reference. Additionally, the motion vectors can point to areas that are outside of the reference frame. This can prove very useful particularly in low resolutions supported by H.263.

In the area of error detection and recovery, where H.263 really differs from its predecessor, has the error tracking, the reference picture selection and the independent segment decoding techniques. In the first one when the decoder spots an error on a group of blocks (GOB) sends an error message to the encoder with the ID of the faulty GOB. The encoder uses this information to find the MBs that referenced on the faulty GOB and transmits those MBs with intraframe coding instead of interframe, to stop the error transmission.

The codec in the reference picture selection is able to encode an MB not only from the first past frame, but from a group of past frames. This means that when the decoder finds a faulty GOB and messages accordingly the encoder, the encoder simply excludes that "past" frame from the references and uses "older" frames that have reached the receiver without errors.

The last method for error recovery in H.263 is the independent segment decoding. In this technique the encoder handles every GOB as an independent part of the frame. Meaning intra-frame coded MBs can only refer to MBs that belong to the same GOB. As an example, we encode a frame in QCIF resolution, the frame is separated in 3 different GOBs (parts), and each one is coded as a unique GOB using no reference to the other GOBs, indicating that an error on the first GOB will not affect the other GOBs of the frame on encoding.

H.263+

H.263+ can be referenced as H.263 version 2, as it includes all of H.263 features and decoding and encoding algorithms, but also adds twelve new optional modes for motion image processing quality improvement. The additional modes are:

Annex I, which employs a new VLC table for quantized coefficients encoding for intra MBs. Annex J imports a deblocking filter inside the coding loop, resulting in better prediction and reduction in blocking artifacts. Annex K divides the picture into segments containing numbers of MBs. Annex L provides the decoder supporting features and functionalities within the video bitstream. Annex M uses additional forward and backward predictors that improve P and B frame changes that may occur between pictures. Annex N maintains good picture reproduction by reducing error propagation between corrupted pictures. Annex O specifies techniques for temporal, snr, and spatial scalability capabilities. Annex P provides the algorithm to warp the reference frame prior to its prediction. Annex Q is used for detailed background in highly active motion scenes. Annex R prevents the propagation of errors, which results in efficient error resilience and recovery. Annex S, when enabled, uses the intra VLC table described in Annex I for inter block coding. Annex T has three features. First, rate control methods for increased flexibility in the MB layer quantizer change, second is the chrominance quality enhancement by specifying a finer quantizer step size, and third, improved picture quality by extending the range of representable quantized DCT coefficients. All the aforementioned modes are independent from one another, so according to every case's requirements we could select the best combination.

H.263++

H.263++ can be described best as the H.263 version 3 or the 2000 version. It supports three additional annexes. These and an additional annex (that specified profiles), were originally published separately from the standard's main body. The annexes are: Annex U that provided an improved reference picture selection mode. Annex V introduced the Data-partitioned slice mode, which reduces the error-prone intra frame prediction. Annex W supports additional supple-

mental enhancement information specification, and last, Annex X (originally specified in 2001) provided profile and level specification.

H.264

The intent of the H.264/AVC(Advanced Video Coding) standard was to create a standard capable of providing good video quality at lower bit rates than previous standards (i.e H.263), with and economic design both in terms of complexity and implementation. Another goal of the standard was to be able to be easily applied to a wide variety of applications on a wide variety of networks and systems, including low and high bit rates, low and high resolution video, broadcast, DVD storage, RTP-IP packet networks, and ITU-T multimedia telephony systems.

Due to its wide application on networks and systems H.264 had to be able to provide equal and stable solutions for many of these cases. So it formed a solution based on different profiles, which technically are different configuration files for the encoder. Each profile sets different parameters for the encoder, aiming to provide the suitable solution. H.264 defines a set of three profiles, each supporting a particular set of coding functions and each specifying what is required of an encoder or decoder that complies with the Profile.

The *Baseline Profile* supports intra and inter-coding (using only I-slices and P-slices) and entropy coding with context-adaptive variable-length codes (CAVLC). The *Main Profile* includes support for interlaced video, inter-coding using B-slices, inter coding using weighted prediction and entropy coding using context-based arithmetic coding (CABAC). The *Extended Profile* does not support interlaced video or CABAC, but adds more efficient switching between coded bitstreams (SP- and SI-slices) and is more resilient to errors(Data Partitioning). Potential applications of the Baseline Profile include videotelephony, videoconferencing and wireless communications; potential applications of the Main Profile include television broadcasting and video storage; and the Extended Profile is particularly useful for streaming media applications. A brief analysis of each of the aforementioned profiles follows hereafter.

The Baseline Profile of H.264

The Baseline Profile supports coded sequences containing only I- and P-slices. I-slices contain intra-coded MBs in which each 16×16 or 4×4 luma region and each 8×8 chroma region is calculated and predicted from previously-coded parts of the same slice. P-slices may contain intra-coded, inter-coded or skipped MBs. Inter-coded MBs in a P slice are predicted from a number of previously coded pictures, using motion compensation with quarter-sample (luma) motion vector accuracy.

After prediction, the residual data for each MB is DCT transformed using a 4×4 integer transform and quantised. Quantised transform coefficients are reordered and the syntax elements are entropy coded. In the Baseline Profile, a context-adaptive variable length coding scheme (CAVLC) is used for entropy coding transform coefficients, whereas syntax elements are coded using fixed-length or Exponential-Golomb Variable Length Codes.

Quantised coefficients are scaled, inverse transformed, reconstructed (added to the prediction formed during encoding) and filtered with a de-blocking filter before (optionally) being stored for possible use in reference pictures for further intra- and inter-coded MBs.

A filter similar to H.261 is applied to each decoded MB to reduce block-shaped artifacts. The deblocking filter is applied after the inverse transform in the encoder (right before reassembling and storing the MB for future prediction use) and in the decoder (before reassembling and displaying the MB). The filter creates smoother block edges, improving the appearance of the decoded frames. This is proven to be very beneficial as the filtered image will be used for motion-compensated prediction of future frames and this improves the compression performance because

a more detailed and smoother filtered reference frame is more faithful reproduction of the original frame, than an unfiltered one. Additionally, it is possible for the encoder to alter the filter strength or to disable the filter.

The Main Profile of H.264

The Main Profile is a more complete version of the Baseline Profile, except that multiple slice groups, ASO (Arbitrary Slice Order, i.e no particular frame decoding order) and redundant slices (all supported by the Baseline Profile) are not included. The additional tools provided by Main Profile are B slices (bi-directional prediction slices for greater coding efficiency), weighted prediction (providing increased flexibility in creating a motion-compensated prediction block), support for interlaced video (coding of separate fields as well as frames) and CABAC (an alternative entropy coding method based on Arithmetic Coding). Suitable applications for the Main Profile include (but are not limited to) broadcast media applications such as digital television and stored digital video.

In B slices every MB partition in an intercoded MB can be predicted from one or two reference images, before or after the current picture in temporal order. In relation to the reference pictures stored in the encoder and decoder, this provides the alternative to choose the MB prediction references in a B MB type, for example using: (i) one future and one past, (ii) two past, (iii) two future references to predict a B-frame type image.

Unlike the baseline profile the main profile supports the interlaced video, also used in analog video transmission. The interlaced video is a technique in which we double the perceived video frame rate, efficiently without the cost of extra consumed bandwidth. The interlaced video contains two fields of a video frame shot taken from two different times and it improves the viewer's video perception by reducing flickering and taking advantage of the persistence of vision effect (the phenomenon where the eye by which an afterimage is thought to persist for approx. 1/25 of a sec of the retina). We can achieve this effect by doubling the temporal resolution. In the main profile specifically a specific slice is coded as 'MB pair'. The encoder afterwards will encode each MB either as two frame MBs or two field MBs and can select the optimum pair. Because of that further modification may be required to a several encoding and decoding steps, for example we may need to modify the P and B prediction depending on whether the M Bs are coded in frame or field mode.

The Extended Profile of H.264

The Extended Profile (also known as the X Profile in earlier versions of the draft H.264 standard) can be very helpful in video-streaming applications (H.Schwarz et al 2007). It includes all of the features of the Baseline Profile (i.e. it is a supreme superset of the Baseline Profile, unlike Main Profile), but also uses B-slices, Weighted Prediction and unique features that allow it to be extra-efficient over network stream services such internet video-streaming. SP and SI slices become a helpful tool for switching between different coded streams and 'VCR-like' (the 'SETUP', 'PLAY', 'PAUSE', 'TEARDOWN') functionality and Data Partitioned slices provide improved performance error susceptible data transmission environments.

SP and SI slices are specially-coded slices that allow video decoders to switch efficiently and rapidly between video streams and provide an efficient random access for video decoders. One major requirement for a reliable video stream application is the flexible and quick switching between video streams, to maintain continuous playback. For example, a video stream application in order to provide an uninterrupted video playback has to handle data throughput drop cases, or network traffic issues. A solution this area of problems is to have the same video material in two different coded versions, so when a error occurs, our application should be capable of switching between the high-quality stream to the low-quality one efficiently, this is where SP and SI slices aid with the stream switching.

The decoded data that forms a slice is separated into three Data Partitions supposedly A, B and C, each one contains a part of the coded slice. The slice header and the header data is contained in slice A, B contains coded residual data for intra and SI frame MBs and C the inter-coded MB residual data (bi-directional). Therefore each partition can be put into a different NAL unit and be transported separately. If partition A is lost, it is most likely very difficult or even impossible to reconstruct the slice, which leads to the fact that partition A is very sensitive to transmission errors. However, with a careful choice of parameter we can make partitions B and C independently decodable, thus decoding only A and C or only A and B, gaining flexibility and efficiency in an error-prone environment.

H.265

The High efficiency Video Coding (HEVC) is a standard for video compression, successor of the H.264/MPEG-4 AVC, currently under-development by the MPEG and ITU-T Video Coding Experts Group (VCEG) collaboration team named Joint Collaborative Team on Video Coding(JCT-VC).

The goal of HEVC is to substantially improve coding efficiency compared to AVC High Profile and H.264 extended profile, i.e. improve significantly bitrate to image quality ratio, probably increasing the computational complexity. Depending on the application requirements, HEVC is designed to maintain the balance computational complexity, compression rate against proneness to errors and processing delay time.

HEVC is designed to support next-generation HDTV displays and content capture systems that feature progressive scan frame rates and display resolutions from QVGA (320x240) up to 1080p and Ultra HDTV (7680x4320), as well as techniques that guarantee improved picture quality in terms of noise level, color gamut and dynamic range.

MPEG Standards

In contrast to H.26x standards, which solely covers video-coding, MPEG standards support both video and audio coding and also the multiplexing of several media streams in one.

MPEG-1

MPEG-1 is a video standard designed by Motion Pictures Experts Group (MPEG), which is formed by ISO. It is the first of the MPEG standards family that covers the fields of coding high-quality audio and video, and multiplexing for data storing or network transmission. The first goal of MPEG-1 was the total bandwidth of transmitted audio and video not to exceed 1.2 – 1.5 Mbps (i.e the bandwidth of T-1 transfer line).

MPEG-1 is a more complex variation of H.261, whereas H.261 aimed towards supporting bi-directional symmetric applications, MPEG-1 was designed for multimedia distribution applications. This is because MPEG-1 is usually asymmetrically implemented, as in multimedia distribution applications the time-consuming compression process is performed only once and the video playback constantly.

MPEG-1 Video codec's compression methods significantly reduce the video stream's required data rate. It reduces or disposes information in certain frequencies and areas of the picture that they are not recognized by the human eye. It also exploits temporal (time related) and spatial (area related) redundancy a commonly used method to achieve more efficient compression that would be impossible otherwise.

The first frame category in MPEG-1 is the I-frame that is intra-coded, with no reference to other previous or forward frames. This category fully-supports random access, as the video playback can instantly begin from an I-frame. The second frame category is the P-frame, which coded by using a reference on their previous frame I or P frame. For every P-frame MB the codec searches the corresponding area on the reference frame. The standard does not dictate the search method, but the search range via the motion vector. If no relative area is found, then the frame is intra-coded, just like an I-frame. In an alternate case when the differences between the current and the reference MBs are few the blocks are omitted, otherwise they are DCT transformed, quantised and RLE and entropy coded.

The B-frames are the third frame category, which can use both their next, as well as their previous I or P frame as a reference frame. The reference frame area can also be calculated from the average of a previous and next frame area. The coding of B-frames is almost identical to the P-frame one. P and B frames can use the same quantization parameter array, whereas I-frames use a different array. The fourth frame category is the D-frames that are intra-coded just like I-frames but only using DC and DCT coefficients.

In MPEG-1 standard the entity of frame grouping is reflected upon the picture group (group of pictures – GOP) structure. Every GOP sequence begins with an I-frame and contains all the remaining P and B frames, until the next I-frame. GOP is the main synchronization unit of MPEG-1, since random access is feasible only every I-frame of a GOP. Additionally every GOP is divided into smaller frame groups, which start with an I-frame and end with a P-frame.

MPEG-1 being a full audio and video coding system determines, not only determines the stream of every media type, but also the media multiplexing into a single stream. From the video aspect the media stream is hierarchically ordered and consists of 6 levels. The structure of the steam is: 1.Sequence Header, 2.GOP header, 3.Frame Header, 4.MB Header, 5.Block Header, 6.Block coefficients. The independent media streams are multiplexed into a single stream, which is called pack. The pack contains a timestamp header which assists the codec to remain synchronized with the encoder.

MPEG-2

The MPEG-2 (or H.262) design began, even before the standardization of MPEG-1 was complete. The initial goal was the support of video quality relative to CCIR-601 to support digital television systems, while simultaneously designing MPEG-3 for future use on HDTV. During the development of MPEG-2, MPEG-3 was incorporated, as it was generalized to include the support of HDTV systems.

Due to the wide variety of application support, the MPEG-2 standard states a series of profiles and levels which are related to one another. The profiles cover several complexity categories. Every level states the video parameters, meaning that a level covers a quality category. The levels are the "low level", which supports MPEG-1 television signals with data rate up to 4 Mbps, whilst "main level" supports quality relative to the CCIR-601 video with data rate up to 15-20 Mbps. The "high profile-1440" supports HDTV quality with aspect ratio 4:3 and data rate 60-80 Mbps, and the "high-profile" HDTV quality with aspect ratio 16:9 and data rate 80-100 Mbps.

Profile-wise the "simple profile" is the first one, a simpler version of MPEG-1 aimed for low-cost devices. Next comes the "main profile" which supports all of MPEG-1 capabilities and its common use is on DVDs. The "main profile" characteristics are extended to several "scalable profiles" which support projection devices with different capabilities. The scalability can be achieved in two ways, the signal-to-noise scalability, which allows layered picture coding so that they can be coded in different quality levels, and the spatial scalability which allows the video decoding in different horizontal and vertical resolutions.

In the P and B frame coding, accordingly, three options are provided, the "field mode", in which the MBs are coded by either their next or previous field reference. In the "frame mode" the MBs are coded by either their next or previous same type field reference, meaning the even fields are refer to their previous even field and the odd ones respectively. However in the "mixed mode" the MBs are coded by either their next or previous same type field reference, but taking into consideration which option offers them better compression.

MPEG-2 standard, like MPEG-1, determines the data stream, not only for every individual type of media, but for multiplexed media streams. The difference between the 2 standards is that MPEG-2's media stream can be more complex when used from a scalable profile. Every type of media, including audio and video, is organized into a unique packet stream (PES). In the next level the PES are multiplexed into a single transport stream (TS), and transmitted. Additionally the program stream does not include extra synchronization information, since all the PES derive from the same clock. MPEG-2 specifies that the raw frames are compressed into three types of frames: intra-coded frames (I-frames), predictive-coded frames (P-frames) and bidirectionally-predictive-coded frames (B-frames).

MPEG-4 Part 2

MPEG-4 Part 2 is a video compression standard developed by MPEG, of the MPEG-4 ISO/IEC standards family. Similarly to previous standards MPEG-1 and MPEG-2, it is DCT (Discrete Cosine Transform) based. Popular applications that implement this standard are Divx, Xvid and Nero Digital. It is also H.263 compatible, i.e. a H.263 bit stream can be successfully decoded by an MPEG-4 decoder. MPEG-4 uses 2 video object layer types, the video object layer which fully supports the MPEG-4 functionality and a reduced functionality video object layer with short headers, compatible with baseline H.263.

MPEG-4 focuses on lower bitrates, in which the main goal is the compression efficiency. Since the standard is designed to support different types of terminals with scalable data streams, and error-prone networks with fault detection and recovery techniques, an important service field for MPEG-4 is the mobile telephony.

The quintessential innovation of MPEG-4 differs from its predecessors due to its user-interactive platform support. This enables the user to dynamically interact with the content. In order to achieve this, video and audio signals are handled as single but independent data streams. The content in MPEG-4 is structured as an object-oriented hierarchy, which can be modified by the recipient. The objects can be created uniquely or synthetically, and in their turn consist of simpler objects. Every object is coded according to its type, thus the object hierarchy contributes to low transmission bitrates.

Due to its design MPEG-4 does not only support coding and media multiplexing schemes, but also techniques to build complex scenes from individual objects. In order to achieve efficient media coding MPEG-4 offers various playback options along with coding techniques, unlike MPEG-1 and 2 which coded the video and audio streams integrally.

Every scene in MPEG-4, meaning a sequence of frames with identical content, consists of an audio/visual object (AVO) group. The AVOs are organized hierarchically (i.e. an AVO can consist of simpler AVOs). The scene model used in MPEG-4 is based on the VRML (virtual reality modeling language) with a few modifications like BIFS (binary format for scenes), which is an alternative scene coding method that enables interaction between the user and the AVO, permitting the user to delete or modify any existing AVOs in the scene.

In order to encode every AVO, they separate each of their components so that everyone is com-pressed differently. Every AVO can be projected as a VOP (Video Object Plane), which is composed by an integer-valued sum of MBs in every dimension. VOPs are decoded individually based upon shape, motion and texture. The multiplexer synchronizes every single VOP and AVO accordingly, in order to create a single media stream.

The de-multiplexer from its perspective re-trieves each VOP, the audio data and the pattern of the scene from a single data stream, which can be originated from a network or a storage media object. After that every media is decoded sepa-rately based on its content, and the scene synthesis is performed according to the BIFS information given from the data stream. Optionally the recipi-ent can alter the scene, using the BIFS model, by adding, removing, moving or modifying its ob-jects. Concluding that MPEG-4's main difference from its predecessors is that every media consists of many objects instead of being considered as a single entity during the encoding and decoding.

The MPEG-4 specifications main purpose is the support of several types of bitrate, quality, resolution and service. Since a scene is composed by an object hierarchy, instead of encoding wholes frames, MPEG-4 encodes the object-hierarchy and sends the modifications that need to be performed on every object, based upon the frame motion. The hierarchy itself can change, as new objects enter the scene or current objects exit. If the hierarchy creator allows it, the user can interact with it. Possible interaction cases are the shift of objects, the change in the point of view or the behavioral object modification.

MPEG-4 provides techniques for structure, communication and implementation of the object classes. In order to decode an MPEG-4 media stream, the standard based upon the object's de-coding defines the class structure phase. At the communication phase it transfers the classes that are missing and completing the already installed ones to decode all the objects. When all the class descriptions, including their data structures are transmitted, the standard proceeds to their initialization. In the end all the video and audio objects are de-multiplexed, synchronized and decoded by the recipient according to their relative classes.

The video-object coding supports spatial and temporal scalability, allowing the recipient to decode partially the video-reconstructing data. Scalability allows video decoding with reduced spatial resolution, reduced temporal resolution or both, but with lower quality in exchange. This feature is useful for video transmission applications over networks with limited bandwidth, or for services in which the recipient does not want or is not able to display the video at high resolution and quality. In cases when the screen resolution or the network has limited capabilities, scalability can radically improve the system's efficiency, although subjected to the aforementioned limitations.

MPEG-4 standard provides two technical support solutions for channels with high noise and low bitrates. The first one is the use of fixed-length video packets, which allow the recipient resynchronization at the beginning of the next packet and not at the start of the next part, unlike MPEG-1. Generally every packet contains some MBs, meaning the resynchronization of the decoder is performed at MB level. In order to develop a fault-tolerant system, the packets separate the one packet's motion vectors so that we can exploit the rest of it. The packets can also contain a timestamp, so that the decoder won't dispatch the whole frame in case errors appear at its beginning.

The second fault-tolerant technique is the use of RVLC (reversible variable length codewords). These codewords have the characteristic that their limits can be recognized by reading the data from end to start. During the RVLC procedure for DCT coefficient coding, if the decoder detects errors while reading the frame from start to end, it will not dispatch the entire packet but restart to read it end to start this time. Therefore prior or subsequent to the error codewords are encoded normally, thus affecting the frame only partially, and allowing

the efficient error recovery even from partially destroyed packets.

HEVC (H.265)

High efficiency Video Coding is a standard for video compression, successor of the H.264/MPEG-4 AVC, currently under-development by the MPEG and ITU-T Video Coding Experts Group (VCEG) collaboration team named Joint Collaborative Team on Video Coding (JCT-VC). H.265 is used as a nickname for the standard.

HEVC's goal is to substantially improve coding efficiency compared to AVC High Profile and H.264 extended profile, i.e. improve significantly bitrate to image quality ratio, probably increasing the computational complexity. Depending on the application requirements, HEVC is designed to maintain the balance computational complexity, compression rate against proneness to errors and processing delay time.

HEVC is designed to support next-generation HDTV displays and content capture systems that feature progressive scan frame rates and display resolutions from QVGA (320x240) up to 1080p and Ultra HDTV (7680x4320), as well as techniques that guarantee improved picture quality in terms of noise level, color gamut and dynamic range.

Deblocking filter as we mentioned earlier is the technique that alleviates the blocking artifacts caused by the DCT transform. HEVC employs two filters; the deblocking filter, which is inherited from the H.264 standard, and the Adaptive Loop Filter (ALF) which is used to restore the encoded and degraded frame in entire-frame or MB level, after the deblocking process. The main difference between these 2 filters is that the deblocking filter improves the subjective quality, whereas ALF the objective quality, as a result these two techniques are mutual complements. The spatial redundancy and information loss caused by the deblocking filter is restored at some percentage by ALF.

The HEVC still adopts the block-based hybrid video coding framework, although the MB size is extended to (64x64) compared to H.264. Three units of various sizes are used to describe the overall coding structure, coding unit (CU), prediction unit (PU) and transformation unit (TU). The CU is basically the MB in H.264, it can have various square-shaped sizes. A CU forms a hierarchical tree whose leaves are the PU s, like the H.264 standard two different terms are used to describe the prediction method, PU type and PU splitting. As a result, different PU splittings correspond to different PU types, which consist of skip, intra and inter. This feature enables us to use different prediction techniques in one frame, achieving better quality, while not sacrificing bandwidth for video stream, although costing as in computational resources because of the greater complexity.

In accordance to the CU and PU definitions the TU is defined to transform and quantise. The TU structure resembles the quadtree design of the CU. TU have different splittings for low complexity and high efficiency configurations.

VIDEO QUALITY ASPECTS

The advent of quality evaluation was the application of a pure mathematical error sensitive framework between the encoding and the original/uncompressed video sequence. These primitive methods, although they provided a quantitative approach about the quality degradation of the encoded signal, do not provide reliable measurements of the perceived quality, because they miss out the characteristics and sensitivities of the Human Visual System.

The most widely used primitive methods and quality metrics that used an Error Sensitivity framework are the Peak Signal to Noise Ratio (PSNR) and the Mean Square Error (MSE):

$$PSNR = 10\log 10 \frac{L^2}{MSE}, \qquad (1)$$

where L denotes the dynamic pixel value (i.e. equal to 255 for 8bits/pixel monotonic signal)

$$MSE = \frac{1}{N} \sum_{i=1}^{N} (x_i - y_i)^2, \qquad (2)$$

where N denotes the total pixels and x_i /y_i the ith pixel value in the original/distorted signal

Currently, the evaluation of the PQoS is a matter of objective and subjective evaluation procedures, each time taking place after the encoding process (post-encoding evaluation). Subjective picture/audio quality evaluation processes require large amount of human resources, establishing it as a time-consuming process (e.g. large audiences evaluating video/audio sequences). Objective evaluation methods, on the other hand, can provide PQoS evaluation results faster, but require large amount of machine resources and sophisticated apparatus configurations. Towards this, objective evaluation methods are based and make use of multiple metrics, which are related to the content's artifacts (i.e. tilling, blurriness, error blocks, etc.) resulting during an encoding process. These two categories of PQoS evaluation methods will be analyzed and discussed in the following sections.

Subjective Quality Evaluation Methods

The subjective test methods, which have mainly been proposed by International Telecommunications Union (ITU) and Video Quality Experts Group (VQEG), involve an audience of people, who watch a video sequence and score its quality as perceived by them, under specific and controlled watching conditions. Afterwards, the statistical analysis of the collected data is used for the evaluation of the perceived quality. The

Mean Opinion Score (MOS) is regarded as the most reliable method of quality measurement and has been applied on the most known subjective techniques.

Subjective test methods are described in ITU-R Rec. T.500-11 (2002) and ITU-T Rec. P.910 (1999), suggesting specific viewing conditions, criteria for observers and test material selection, assessment procedure description and statistical analysis methods. ITU-R Rec. The BT.500-11 described subjective methods that are specialized for television applications, whereas ITU-T Rec. P.910 is intended for multimedia applications.

The most know and widely used subjective methods are:

- **Double Stimulus Impairment Scale (DSIS):** This method proposes that observers are shown multiple references and degraded scene pairs. The reference scene is always first. Scoring is on an overall impression scale of impairment: imperceptible, perceptible but not annoying, slightly annoying, annoying, and very annoying. This scale is commonly known as the 5-point scale with 5 being imperceptible and 1 being very annoying.

- **Single Stimulus Methods:** Multiple separate scenes are shown. There are two approaches: SS with no repetition of test scenes and SS where the test scenes are repeated multiple times. Three different scoring methods are used:
  - **Adjectival:** The aforementioned 5-grade impairment scale, however half-grades may be allowed.
  - **Numerical:** An 11-grade numerical scale, useful if a reference is not available.
  - **Non-categorical:** A continuous scale with no numbers or a large range, e.g. 0 100.

- **Stimulus Comparison Method:** Usually accomplished with two well matched monitors, where the differences between scene pairs are scored in one of two ways:
  - **Adjectival:** A 7-grade, +3 to -3 scale labeled: much better, better, slightly better, the same, slightly worse, worse, and much worse.
  - **Non-categorical:** A continuous scale with no numbers or a relation number either in absolute terms or related to a standard pair.

- **Single Stimulus Continuous Quality Evaluation (SSCQE):** According to this method, the viewers watch a program of typically 20–30 minutes without the original reference to be shown. The test program has been processed by the system under test. The subjects/viewers using a slider continuously rate the instantaneously perceived quality on scale from 'bad' to 'excellent', which corresponds to an equivalent numerical scale from 0 to 100.

- **Double Stimulus Continuous Quality Scale (DSCQS):** At DSCQS the viewers watch multiple pairs of quite short (i.e. 10 seconds) reference and test sequences. Each pair appears twice, with random order of the reference and the test sequence. The viewers/subjects are not aware of the reference/test order and they are asked to rate each of the two separately on a continuous quality scale namely ranging from 'bad' to 'excellent', which corresponds to an equivalent numerical scale from 0 to 100. This method is usually used for evaluating slight quality differences between the test and the reference sequence.

The aforementioned methods are described in the ITU-R Rec. T.500-11 document and are mainly indented for television signals. Based on slight modifications and adaptations of these methods, some other subjective evaluation methods (namely Absolute Category Rating (ACR), Degradation Category Rating (DCR) etc.) for multimedia services are described in ITU-T Rec. P.910

Objective Quality Evaluation Methods

The preparation and execution of subjective tests is costly and time consuming and its implementation today is limited to scientific purposes, especially at Video Quality Experts Group (VQEG) experiments.

For this reason, a lot of effort has recently been focused on developing cheaper, faster and easier applicable objective evaluation methods. These techniques successfully emulate the subjective quality assessment results, based on criteria and metrics that can be measured objectively. The objective methods are classified, according to the availability of the original video signal, which is considered to be in high quality.

The majority of the proposed objective methods in the literature requires the undistorted source video sequence as a reference entity in the quality evaluation process, and due to this, these methods are characterized as Full Reference Methods. The methods perform multiple channel decomposition of the video signal, where the proposed objective method is applied on each channel, which features a different weigh factor according to the characteristics of the Human Visual System. The basic block diagram of the full reference methods with multiple channels is depicted on Figure 12. These methods emulate characteristics of the Human Visual System (HVS) using Contrast Sensitivity Functions (CSF), Channel Decomposition, Error Normalization, Weighting and finally Minkowski error pooling for combining the error measurements into single perceived quality estimation (Z. Wang, Sheikh, & Bovik, 2003).

Figure 12. Full reference methods with multiple channels

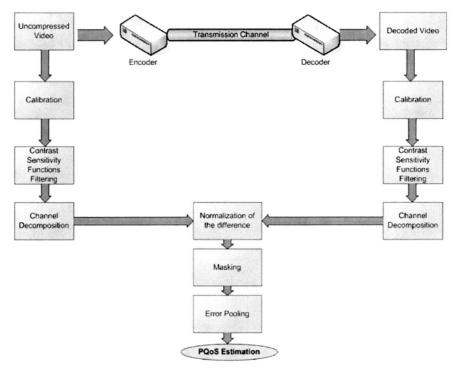

Figure 13. Full reference methods with single channel

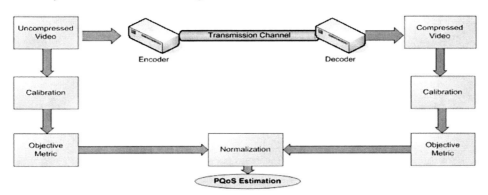

Similarly, in the bibliography it has been proposed full reference methods of single channel, where the proposed objective metric is applied on the video signal, without considering varying weight functions. The block diagram of these methods is depicted on Figure 13. However, it has been reported (VQEG, 2000; Z. Wang, Bovik, & Lu, 2002) that these complicated methods do not provide more accurate results than the simple mathematical measures such as PSNR. Due to this some new full reference metrics that are based on the video structural distortion, and not on error measurement, have been proposed (Z. Wang et al., 2003).

On the other hand, the fact that these methods require the original video signal as reference deprives their use in commercial video service applications, where the initial undistorted clips are not accessible. Moreover, even if the reference clip is available, then synchronization predicaments between the undistorted and the distorted signal (which may have experienced frame loss) make the implementation of the Full Reference Methods difficult and impractical.

Due to these reasons, the recent research has been focused on developing methods that can evaluate the PQoS level based on metrics, which use only some extracted structural features from the original signal (Reduced Reference Methods) (Gunawan & Ghanbari, 2003). The block diagram of the reduced reference methods is depicted on Figure 14, which shows that the RR methods are designed to assess the perceptual quality of distorted images with only partial information about the reference images. Reduced-reference extracted features, which are used in the evaluation procedure, can take several different forms, such as scalar, vector, or matrix. The attractiveness of quality assessment based on reduced-reference approach is the choice of the amount of information required that makes up the reduced-reference overhead data. This amount can be dictated in practice by the accessible bandwidth of the ancillary channel to transmit the reduced-reference data or similarly by the available storage to cache them. For this purpose, it has stated that the bit rates of the reduced-reference channel could be zero (no-reference), 15 kbps, 80 kbps, or 256 kbps. (VQEG, 2007)

Finally, some methods and techniques have been proposed in the bibliography that do not require any reference video signal (No Reference Methods) (Lu, Wang, Bovik, & Kouloheris, 2002). Nevertheless, due to the fact that the 3G/4G vision is the provision of audiovisual content at various quality and price levels (Seeling et al., 2004), there is great need for developing methods and tools that will help service providers to predict quickly and easily the PQoS level of a media clip. These methods will enable the determination of the specific encoding parameters that will satisfy a certain quality level. All the previously men-

Figure 14. Reduced reference methods

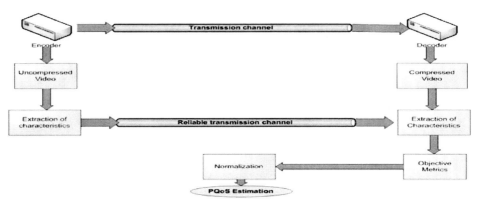

tioned post-encoding methods may require repeating tests in order to determine the encoding parameters that satisfy a specific level of user satisfaction. This procedure is time consuming, complex and impractical for implementation on the 3G/4G multimedia mobile applications.

Towards this, recently it has been performed research in the field of pre-encoding estimation and prediction of the PQoS level of a multimedia service as a function of the selected resolution and the encoding bit rate (Koumaras, Kourtis, & Martakos, 2005; Koumaras et al., 2004). These methods provide fast and quantified estimation of the PQoS, taking into account the instant PQoS variation due to the Spatial and Temporal (S-T) activity within a given encoded sequence. Quantifying this variation by the Mean PQoS (MPQoS) as a function of the video encoding rate and the picture resolution, it is finally used the MPQoS as a metric for pre-encoding PQoS assessment based on the fast estimation of the S-T activity level of a video signal.

CURRENT DEVELOPMENTS AND FUTURE TRENDS

The lately developed multiview video coding (MVC) standard, as an extension profile of H.264/AVC, gains more and more attention due to its high compression ratio and free-viewpoint support.

Besides offering the 3D experience, MVC can also give users full scene perception. However, the multiple-view-point throughput requirement increases the complexity and hardware cost significantly. An MVC encoder requires an optimized system memory bandwidth and processing data throughput of each module.

In real-time HD 3D video communication, three key technologies can make a system feasible. The first one is the multiview capturing and display devices. The second one is the coding standard, and since 3D video contains multiple view angles, alternative and more efficient coding algorithms than the conventional single-view coding standards are required to reduce the bitrate for communication to an acceptable level. Third, in order for the coding speed to meet the real-time constraint advanced and efficient hardware architecture is required. The reason is that the multi-view-angle characteristic, in 3D video, is significantly more demanding regarding the data needed to be processed in a conventional single-view video. Thus, if the conventional architecture is adopted, it dramatically increase the complexity and hardware cost dramatically.

The MVC encodes video data from multiple viewing angles into a single bitstream by hybrid motion and disparity compensated prediction. A camera array captures the multiview video followed by the MVC encoder compressing the multiview video data for storage or transmission.

The decoder from its perspective reconstructs the multiview video, which can be displayed on various displays such as the currently commercialized HDTV. The MVC encoder compresses video frames from the first view channel using a typical H.264/AVC encoder. Furthermore, the bitrate overhead for each view is reduced by the H.264/AVC-based encoding flow. However, the complexity of an MVC encoder is much more increased than the single H.264/AVC encoder given its multichannel characteristic.

Simultaneously with the development of the aforementioned methods and techniques, research has been also focused on developing methods, which determine the adequate quality level for a specific multimedia application, taking under consideration not solely the visual estimations, but also a great number of parameters and metrics that depend on the task nature and the user emotional behavior and psychophysical characteristics (Mullin, 2007). For example the classification of the task as foreground or background in correlation with its complexity (Buxton, 1995) is a parameter that differentiates the quality demands of a multimedia application. On the other hand, the emotional content of a multimedia communication task alters the required quality level of the specific communication service (Olson, 1994). Due to this, various parameters are measured in order to estimate the appropriate minimum quality level of a multimedia application. Such parameters are:

- The user characteristics (i.e. knowledge background, language background, familiarity with the task, age)
- The situation characteristics (i.e. geographical remoteness, simultaneous number of users, distribution of users)
- The user cost (i.e. heart rate, blood volume pulse)
- The user behavior (i.e. eye tracking, head movement)

However, these methods have still some issues to solve on technical, theoretical and practical level. A user that participates in such an assessment procedure is so wired (even on the head may wear the eye tracking equipment), which causes uncomfortable feelings and affects its natural behaviour. Technical issues, such as the eye tracking loss and the manual calibration/correction by a human operator, affect the reliability of the methods in real time environments (Mullin, 2001).

CONCLUSION

This chapter has dealt with the principles of digital video coding and the video coding standards developed by both ITU-T and MPEG standardization group. The chapter has presented the main characteristics of each standard and has discussed the evolution of the video coding compression techniques. Moreover, in this chapter we discussed also the video quality assessment methods, both objective and subjective, analyzing their methodology. Finally future trends have been presented.

REFERENCES

Buxton, W. (1995). Integrating the periphery and context: A new taxonomy of telematics. *Proceedings of Graphics Interface, 1995*, 239–246.

Gunawan, I. P., & Ghanbari, M. (2003). *Reduced-reference picture quality estimation by using local harmonic amplitude information*. London Communications Symposium 2003.

Held, G., & Marshall, T. R. (1991). *Data compression*. Wiley. ISBN 0 471 92941 7

Huffman, D. (1952). A method for the construction of minimum redundancy codes. *Proceedings of the IRE, 40*, 1098–1101. doi:10.1109/JRPROC.1952.273898

ITU-R (1993). *Recommendation H.261 (03/93): Video codec for audiovisual services at p x 64 kbit/s.*

ITU-R (2005). *Recommendation H.263 (01/05): Video coding for low bit rate communication.*

ITU-R (2005). *Recommendation H.264 (03/05): Advanced video coding for generic audiovisual services.*

Koumaras, H., Kourtis, A., Lin, C.-H., & Shieh, C.-K. (2009). A theoretical framework for end-to-end video quality prediction of MPEG-based sequences. *International Journal on Advances in Networks and Services, 1*(1).

Koumaras, H., Kourtis, A., & Martakos, D. (2005). Evaluation of video quality based on objectively estimated metric. *Journal of Communications and Networking, 7*(3).

Koumaras, H., Pallis, E., Xilouris, G., Kourtis, A., Martakos, D., & Lauterjung, J. (2004). *Pre-encoding PQoS assessment method for optimized resource utilization.* 2nd International Conference on Performance Modelling and Evaluation of Heterogeneous Networks, Het-NeTs04, Ilkley, United Kingdom, 2004.

Lu, L., Wang, Z., Bovik, A. C., & Kouloheris, J. (2002). *Full-reference video quality assessment considering structural distortion and no-reference quality evaluation of MPEG video.* IEEE International Conference on Multimedia.

MPEG. (1998). *MPEG-1 ISO/IEC 11172-5:1998: Coding of moving pictures and associated audio for digital storage media at up to about 1,5 Mbit/s.*

MPEG. (2005). *MPEG-2 ISO/IEC 13818-5:2005: Generic coding of moving pictures and associated audio information.*

MPEG. (2005). *MPEG-4 ISO/IEC 14496-5:2001/ Amd.6:2005, MPEG-4 coding of audio visual objects.*

Mullin, J., Smallwood, L., Watson, A., & Wilson, G. (2001). *New techniques for assessing audio and video quality in real-time interactive communications.* Third International Workshop on Human Computer Interaction with Mobile Devices, Lille, France, 2001.

Olson, J. (1994). In a framework about task-technology fit, what are the tasks features. *Proceedings of CSCW '94: Workshop on Video Mediated Communication: Testing, Evaluation & Design Implications,* 1994.

Richardson, I. E. G. (2003). *H.264 and MPEG-4 video compression.* Wiley. doi:10.1002/0470869615

Schwarz, H., Marpe, D., & Wiegand, T. (2007). Overview of the scalable video coding extension of the H.264/AVC standard. *IEEE Transactions on Circuits and Systems for Video Technology, 17*(9), 1103–1120. doi:10.1109/TCSVT.2007.905532

Seeling, P., Reisslein, M., & Kulapala, B. (2004). Network performance evaluation using frame size and quality traces of single layer and two layer video: A tutorial. *IEEE Communications Surveys, 6*(3).

VQEG. (2000). *Final report from the video quality experts group on the validation of objective models of video quality assessment.* Retrieved from http://www.vqeg.org

VQEG. (2007). RRNR-TV group test plan draft version 2. Retrieved from http://www.vqeg.org

Wang, Z., Bovik, A. C., & Lu, L. (2002). Why is image quality assessment so difficult. *Proceedings IEEE International Conference in Acoustics, Speech and Signal Processing,* Vol. 4, (pp. 3313-3316).

Wang, Z., Lu, L., & Bovik, A. C. (2004). Video quality assessment based on structural distortion measurement. *Signal Processing Image Communication, 19*(2), 121–132. doi:10.1016/S0923-5965(03)00076-6

Wang, Z., Sheikh, H. R., & Bovik, A. C. (2003). Objective video quality assessment . In Furht, B., & Marqure, O. (Eds.), *The handbook of video databases: Design and applications* (pp. 1041–1078). CRC Press.

Winkler, S. (2005). *Digital video quality – Vision models and metrics*. Wiley. ISBN 0 470 02404 6

Witten, H., Neal, M., & Cleary, G. (1987). Arithmetic coding for data compression. *Communications of the ACM*, *30*(6), 520–540. doi:10.1145/214762.214771

KEY TERMS AND DEFINITIONS

Bit Rate: A data rate expressed in bits per second. In video encoding the bit rate can be constant, which means that it retains a specific value for the whole encoding process, or variable, which means that it fluctuates around a specific value according to the content of the video signal.

Double Stimulus Continuous Quality Scale (DSCQS): A subjective evaluation method according to which, the viewers watch multiple pairs of quite short (i.e. 10 seconds) reference and test sequences. Each pair appears twice, with random order of the reference and the test sequence.

Frame: Frame is one of the many still images which as a sequence compose a video signal.

Integrated Services Digital Network (ISDN): Is a type of circuit switched telephone network system, designed to allow digital transmission of voice and data over ordinary telephone copper wires, resulting in better quality and higher speeds, than available with analog systems.

International Organization for Standardization (ISO): Is an international standard-setting body composed of representatives from national standards bodies. Founded in 1947, the organization produces world-wide industrial and commercial standards.

Moving Picture Experts Group (MPEG): Is a working group of ISO charged with the development of audiovisual encoding standards. MPEG includes many members from various industries and universities related to audiovisual coding research.

Multimedia: Multimedia can be services, media and content consisting of several different media types (e.g. text, audio, graphics, animation, and video).

Objective Measurement of Perceived Quality: A category of assessment methods that evaluate the PQoS level based on metrics, which can be measured objectively.

Perceived Quality of Service (PQoS): The perceived quality level that a user is experienced by a multimedia service. For video services, PQoS is matched to video quality.

Pixel: Pixel is considered the smallest sample of a digital image or video.

Quality Degradation: The drop of the Perceived Quality to a lower level.

Single Stimulus Continuous Quality Evaluation (SSCQE): A subjective evaluation method according to which, the viewers watch a program of typically 20–30 minutes without the original reference to be shown, and score its quality.

Spatial-Temporal Activity Level: The dynamics of the video content, in respect to its spatial and temporal characteristics.

Video Codec: Video codec is the device or software that enables the compression/decompression of digital video.

Video Coding: Video coding is the process of compressing and decompressing a raw digital video sequence.

Chapter 2
Compression Artifacts in Modern Video Coding and State-of-the-Art Means of Compensation

Andreas Unterweger
University of Salzburg, Austria

ABSTRACT

This chapter describes and explains common as well as less common distortions in modern video coding, ranging from artifacts appearing in MPEG-2 Video, MPEG-4 Part 2, H.264, and VC-1 to scalable and multi-view video coding based distortions, including the proposals for next generation video coding (NVC). In addition to a discussion about avoiding these artifacts through encoder-side measures, a state-of-the-art overview of their compensation at the decoder side is given. Finally, artifacts emerging from new sophisticated coding tools in current and upcoming video coding standards are discussed.

INTRODUCTION

As the coding tools used in modern video coding advanced in the last decades, new compression artifacts emerged, creating the need for sophisticated means of compensation. As the human eye is eventually the final recipient of the coded video, including distortions, artifact compensation based on human visual perception is an important

DOI: 10.4018/978-1-4666-2660-7.ch002

research field, which is faced with new challenges due to new coding tools and the respective new artifacts induced by them.

It is important to be aware of these new artifacts and to analyze their sources in order to be able to compensate for them. As new coding tools are developed, most prominently represented by the current contributions to NVC, a basic understanding of the effects of the artifacts caused by these coding tools as well as their effect on the overall video quality is crucial. Although most of the current research is focused on the compensation of blocking, blurring and ringing artifacts and the development of new coding tools, this book chapter gives an overview of the artifacts caused by existing and new coding tools, focusing on mainstream block-based video coding represented by MPEG-2 Video, MPEG-4 Part 2, H.264, VC-1 and the amendments to H.264 for scalable and multi-view video coding. The interested reader may additionally find an overview of Wavelet-based compression artifacts appearing in Motion JPEG 2000 and others in Watson (1997) and Ramos (2001). Literature on non-mainstream video coding formats like Ogg Theora (Xiph. Org Foundation, 2011) is sparse (Crop, 2010) and therefore out of the scope of this book chapter.

The description of artifacts herein includes a discussion on the impact of new coding tools on artifacts in general and suggestions on how to minimize the appearance of these artifacts, thus eliminating the requirement for compensating them at the decoder side. After summarizing the properties and causes of commonly appearing artifacts such as blocking, blurring and ringing, including a number of artifacts originating from new coding tools, a short outlook on the perception of new artifacts and their connection to quality metrics concludes this chapter.

BACKGROUND

The origins of artifacts in block based transform video coding are, in most cases, directly or indirectly related to quantization errors in the transform domain, which are inevitable when lossily compressing images or sequences thereof. Since the first coding standards of this kind, e.g. JPEG for still image coding and H.261 for video coding, various related visual artifacts have been discussed throughout the literature.

Blocking Artifacts

Perhaps the most "famous" and most widely studied artifacts in today's block based video coding are blocking artifacts which occur due to the division of frames into macroblocks of rectangular shape. All blocks are coded separately from one another despite a possibly existing spatial correlation between them, yielding visible edges at macroblock borders. Due to the equidistant distribution of macroblock borders in JPEG, MPEG-2 Video and MPEG-4 Part 2 which is caused by the constant transform size of 8x8 samples, blocking artifacts are, in most cases, easily spotted by the Human Visual System (HVS) as a regular structure which does not belong to the image (Wu, 2006).

Due to the intense research concerning blocking artifacts, a number of possibilities for their compensation is available, e.g. (Oosa, 1998) and (Triantafyllidis, 2002). As both MPEG-2 Video and MPEG-4 Part 2 do not have an integrated deblocking filter, the artifact compensation has to be performed at the decoder side. In order not to cause a drift between encoder and decoder, deblocking has to be performed as a form of post processing on the decoded pictures which are displayed, but must not be applied to reference pictures which are used for motion compensated prediction.

Simple forms of deblocking involve low pass filtering at or around all macroblock borders, which causes blurring artifacts at borders which do not expose blocking artifacts (see below), whereas advanced approaches use edge detection algorithms to identify visually prominent edges or adaptively adjust the filter strength and/or area of influence, i.e. the number of samples around the macroblock border, based on image properties, quantizers, coding modes etc. The latter approach is incorporated in both H.264 and VC-1 in the form of an in-loop deblocking filter which is applied to all coded pictures before storing them in the reference buffers, yielding filtered references which are used for motion compensation. As experiments have shown that an image or video with blurring artifacts arising from strong deblocking appears more pleasant to a typical viewer than the corresponding unfiltered image or video (Wiegand, 2003), this supports the decision to incorporate in-loop deblocking filters into both video coding standards to improve the perceived quality of the decoded pictures.

Blurring Artifacts

As mentioned above, strong deblocking can expose blurring artifacts due to the loss of high frequencies caused by low pass filtering during the attempt to flatten block edges. However, blurring may also be a result of quantization, if all high-frequency components in the transform domain are quantized to zero, yielding a low-pass-like behavior of the transform and quantization process. Using coarse quantization, i.e. selecting a high quantization parameter, favors blurring as it increases the probability of high-frequency components to be quantized to zero. As the HVS notices the loss of high frequency components to a lower degree than the loss of low-frequency components, the quantization matrices defined by MPEG-2 Video, MPEG-4 Part 2, H.264 and VC-1 cause a coarser quantization of high-frequency components, yielding blurring artifacts for high quantization parameters (Wu, 2006).

All standards mentioned above have no built-in filter to compensate for blurring artifacts and therefore require decoder-side deblurring algorithms, if desired. As the high-frequency components have been quantized to zero at the encoder side, they cannot be restored at the decoder side. Therefore, it is necessary to introduce high frequency components similar to noise, based on the image properties and the number of coefficients quantized to zero. Although sharpening might be an option in some cases, a number of approaches rely on boundary conditions (Ng, 1999) or inverse filtering (Biemond, 2005), yielding oversharpening artifacts or introducing noise. It is important

to note that motion blur causes similar effects in the transform domain but requires different forms of compensation, involving – amongst others – deconvolution (Ben-Ezra, 2004).

In chroma-subsampled images (Kerr, 2009), blurring is often also referred to as color bleeding, as one chroma sample may stretch across multiple luma samples. Thus, the blurred chroma sample(s) spread(s) across a wider area, i.e. multiple luma samples, around an edge or other areas of high frequencies in the chroma planes (Wu, 2006). Although chroma subsampling increases the perceived strength of color bleeding due to the wider area affected, color bleeding can also occur in pictures where there is no chroma subsampling.

Mosquito Noise

At the borders of moving objects, an artifact called mosquito noise or mosquito effect appears, when a block is coded using inter frame prediction, but only a part of the predicted block contains the predicted moving object. The (static) rest of the block, therefore, differs strongly from the prediction, thus accounting for a major part of the total prediction error. As all video coding standards mentioned above use a form of prediction which operates in the transform domain, the quantization error together with the prediction error may yield a high concentration of error energy in the high frequency components due to the attempt to reduce the ringing from the prediction at the object border, thus yielding high frequency noise in the picture domain. The latter is referred to as mosquito noise if it is visible over a number of frames and the conditions described above apply.

Mosquito noise is visually prominent as the prediction error changes from frame to frame, yielding different high frequency noise patterns. It has to be noted that different coding of the same picture region across multiple pictures may also expose mosquito-noise-like artifacts. Another form of mosquito-like noise can be caused by encoder/decoder drift in MPEG-2 Video and

MPEG-4 Part 2, which is due to the finite precision of the floating point operations involved in the transform and inverse transform process, yielding an imperfect reconstruction, differing between encoder and decoder, thus causing a drift between the two which propagates through prediction (Wiegand, 2003).

Ringing Artifacts

Another common form of artifacts which manifest as "halos" around sharp edges is known as ringing (Wu, 2006). As steep edges in general contain a larger range of frequencies, the quantization of blocks with steep edges yields an insufficient reconstruction through the sum of basis functions, forming a less steep slope at the position of the original edge and both over- and undershooting at the samples around the original edge. In one-dimensional Fourier analysis, this is also known as Gibbs Phenomenon. Through the smoother slope of the edge it may appear blurry due to the loss of high frequency components whereas the over- and undershooting typically introduces the "halo"-like effect initially mentioned, creating a silhouette-like shade parallel to the original edge.

Note that the "halo" effect also affects low quantization parameters, i.e. small quantization step sizes, as a higher number of non-zero high frequency basis functions do not necessarily improve the approximation of an edge, thus not always decreasing the amount of ringing around sharp edges. Therefore, ringing may also be present in videos coded with high bit rates.

Although there are multiple approaches available describing how to measure ringing effectively, like (Shen, 1998) and (Liu, 2010), there are currently only two approaches available for compensating ringing artifacts, disregarding approaches optimized for JPEG 2000 and the like (Chang, 2005). Despite a sophisticated approach based on projections onto convex sets (POCS) (Zakhor, 2002) which is also used in the context of compensating blocking artifacts, there is an approach based on edge detection and adaptive filtering (Park, 1999) optimized for MPEG-4 Part 2, but applicable to all DCT and quantization based video coding standards which use a transform size of 8×8 samples, including H.264 with its High profile up to a certain extent.

Stair Case and Basis Pattern Artifacts

Another visual artifact closely related to ringing is the so-called stair case artifact which refers to the incapability of horizontal and vertical basis functions (as building blocks of the DCT and its variations) to accurately represent diagonal edges (similar to steep edges), thus resulting in the visually prominent presence of horizontal or vertical basis functions (Wu, 2006). Across multiple coded macroblocks, the appearance of a diagonal edge may be similar to the pattern of a stair case rather than that of a smooth diagonal connection between two points. Through the influence of blocking, stair case artifacts become visually more prominent as the "stair case step size" equals the size of a macroblock.

High quantization may reduce the number of non-zero coefficients in a transformed block to one, yielding so-called basis pattern artifacts which are similar to stair case artifacts, but exhibit a single basis function with its prominent picture domain representation. Note that this artifact is not limited to the scenarios described for stair case artifacts, but applies in general, when high quantization parameters are used which increase the probability of reducing the number of non-zero coefficients to one. If only the DC coefficient remains non-zero after quantization, a smooth "non-texture" block is coded which exhibits strong blocking and blurring and together with adjacent blocks of equal appearance forms a visual distortion referred to as mosaïking.

Summary

As apparent from the commonly described artifacts above, the causes for most of them are related to distortions through quantization. Some of them share manifestation patterns in terms of the quantization step size range and/or the number of non-zero quantized coefficients, increasing the probability under certain circumstances for artifacts to appear together. Therefore, Table 1 summarizes the quantization-dependent characteristics of these artifacts, together with possible accompanying artifacts. Figure 1 visualizes some of the artifacts described in Table 1. Note that this overview only covers the most relevant artifacts described in the literature. Further artifacts which mostly resemble the artifacts described herein may be found in the subsequent sections and (Wu, 2006).

Figure 1. Common artifacts in video coding caused by high quantization and the H.264 deblocking filter (right image part only): blocking at the ceiling (example marked with 1), blurring through deblocking in the right image part (2), ringing at the window borders on the left (3), stair cases at the screens in the front (4), basis patterns between the screens in the middle (5), mosaïking on the white board in the back (6)

Table 1. Common artifacts in video coding and their causes (hyphens denote that the given artifact does not depend directly or necessarily on a certain value or value range of the respective cause of appearance)

Artifact	Causes of appearance			Coexisting artifacts
	Reason for appearance	**Typical quantization step size (range)**	**Number of non-zero quantized coefficients**	**Possibly appearing together with**
Blocking	Independent coding of spatially correlated adjacent blocks	High, but also depending on quantization step size (difference) of adjacent blocks	-	Mosaïking if neighboring blocks are also affected
Blurring	Loss of high-frequency components	High	Low (or zero) for high-frequency coefficients	Ringing at sharp edges, color bleeding (chroma)
Ringing	Insufficient approximation of steep edges	-	-	Blurring
Stair cases	Insufficient approximation of diagonal edges	-	-	Basis patterns for low quantization step sizes
Basis patterns	Loss of all but one transform coefficients	Very high	1	Stair cases
Mosquito noise	Quantization of high-frequency components and prediction errors	-	High for high-frequency components with a notable amount of total error energy	-

NEW CODING TOOLS, NEW ARTIFACTS

Issues, Controversies, Problems

New Transforms and Transform Sizes

Although most of the artifacts described above have been depicted and explained when MPEG-2 Video was state of the art or prior, they still appear when coding videos with MPEG-4 Part 2, H.264 and VC-1, albeit sometimes with different causes of appearance and probability as explained below. Concerning blocking artifacts, MPEG-4 Part 2 coded videos expose a similar behavior due to its transform size and function which is equal to the transform used in MPEG-2 Video, i.e. an 8×8 DCT (Richardson, 2003). By contrast, both H.264 and VC-1 support a smaller transform size of 4x4 besides 8x8 (VC-1 also supports 8×4 and 4×8, H.264 allows to switch between 4×4 and 8×8), reducing ringing due to the limited space for over- and undershooting within one transformed block (Wiegand, 2003). Smaller transform sizes also increase the probability of blocking as the number of block borders increases, although the transform size may be chosen adaptively. More information on the type of transform used in H.264 and VC-1 as opposed to the DCT may be found below.

Concerning the increase of the probability of blocking, both H.264 and VC-1 apply an in-loop deblocking filter which adaptively smoothens block borders in order to avoid blocking. The strength and area of application is determined by various parameters, like the type and quantization parameter of the involved blocks. As can be seen in the right half of Figure 1, high quantization parameters with in-loop deblocking in H.264 lead to blurring, effectively eliminating blocking artifacts. Although the filter can be turned off, this is not encouraged due to the increased presence of blocking artifacts for high quantization parameters as shown in the left half of Figure 1.

As opposed to MPEG-2 Video and MPEG-4 Part 2, which use a DCT of 8×8 size, both H.264 and VC-1 use an approximation thereof, allowing for implementations with additions, subtractions and logical (barrel) shifts only, thus improving performance on modern CPUs. Although H.264 and VC-1 use different approximations of the DCT, the approximations themselves are similar to one another as they are based on the same transform matrix and were derived through similar operations (Lee, 2008). Therefore, the subsequent paragraphs describe the integer transform used in H.264 for the sake of illustration.

Although H.264 supports both a 4×4 and an 8×8 integer transform since the amendment of the fidelity range extensions, allowing to switch between the two when using the High profile (International Telecommunication Union, 2010), actually two approximations of the DCT are used – one of size 4×4 and one of size 8×8. For the sake of simplicity and illustration, the subsequent paragraph will focus on the 4×4 integer transform whose basis functions are illustrated in Figure 2 and compared to the corresponding DCT basis functions. As can be seen, the integer transform clearly is an approximation of the DCT, with similar basis functions arising from this relationship. The detailed derivation and approximation process may be found in Malvar (2003). It has to be noted that the encoder/decoder drift described above is avoided due to the use of integer operations and the resulting absence of rounding errors.

Even though the basic functions of the 4×4 DCT and the integer transform are similar, they are not the same, thus yielding different transform coefficients and transform coefficient distributions for a number of input signals (disregarding simple cases like DC only blocks whose DC transform coefficient only differs in magnitude due to scaling). Figure 3 illustrates this using a simple input signal which yields eight transform coefficients when using the DCT, but six when using the integer transform used in H.264. Although the two additional coefficients do not contribute much to

Figure 2. Differences between the basic functions of the DCT and the H.264 integer transform: a) 4x4 DCT basis functions, b) H.264 4x4 integer transform basis functions; both derived through inverse transform of single transform coefficients. Black denotes minimum values, white denotes maximum values; picture domain values are within [-128;127].

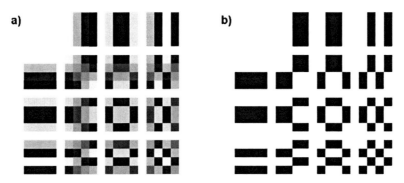

the total signal energy and are likely to be quantized to zero, inverse transform of the quantized coefficients will yield different reconstructed signals for both transforms, considering the small loss of signal energy described.

Although experiments have been carried out to determine new quantization matrices for H.264 due to the new transform (Richardson, 2003), no research is currently focusing on the impact that the new transform may have on type and quantity of distortions. Due to its historical connection to the DCT, the integer transform used in H.264 shares many of its properties, but also yields different transform coefficient distributions due to its different basis functions, as shown above.

Although the speedup through design approximations favoring the capabilities of state-of-the-art CPUs may be convenient, it is necessary to investigate the modified behavior regarding the appearance of artifacts as well as the possible creation of new artifacts which have not been described yet.

The Effect of Macroblock Partitioning

Despite the change in transform size and type, various other new algorithms have been developed for MPEG-4 Part 2, H.264 and VC-1 in order to make coding more efficient or to improve visual quality. Such algorithms are usually referred to

Figure 3. Transform differences between the DCT and the H.264 integer transform: a) original signal, b) 4x4 DCT transform, c) H.264 4x4 integer transform. Black denotes minimum values, white denotes maximum values; picture domain values are within [-128;127].

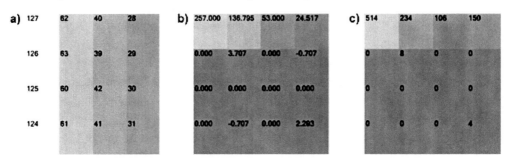

as coding tools. One of them is macroblock partitioning in inter-predictive coding, enabling to perform a separate motion search for each part of a macroblock, allowing finding better matches for each part. While all of the aforementioned standards allow to split a 16×16 inter-predicted block into 4 block partitions of size 8×8 each, H.264 additionally supports 16×8 and 8×16 partitions as well as sub-partitions for 8×8 partitions of sizes 8×4, 4×8 and 4×4, respectively (International Telecommunication Union, 2010).

Such partitioning possibilities not only increase the probability of blocking (without the in-loop deblocking filter) but also favor the appearance of an artifact referred to as motion compensation (MC) mismatch (Wu, 2006). MC mismatch describes an effect during motion compensation where the match found during motion estimation does not belong to the object currently being coded, thus appearing misplaced. When using coarse quantization, the difference to the currently coded macroblock cannot be appropriately compensated for, thus yielding additional blocking and blurring which makes the HVS sensible for the "misplaced" object block. While MC mismatch may be a result of the lack of chroma motion estimation (thus trying to find a matching luma block only), it is also possible that it is due to a purely mathematical error measurement like the sum of squared differences (SSD) or the mean squared error (MSE), yielding a motion estimation match with the minimal mathematical difference, but with a distinct perceptual difference as the match does not belong to the object currently being coded.

As described above, the increasing number of partitions and sub-partitions increases the probability for MC mismatches, which become visually more prominent when surrounded by perceptually adequate matches (Wu, 2006). When using low quantization parameters, this problem quasi disappears as the difference through the MC mismatch can be compensated for by predictive coding. Nonetheless, MC mismatches also favor the appearance of mosquito noise due to the bor-

ders of mismatching objects found during motion estimation. This noise may also be visible at higher bit rates, i.e. lower quantization parameters.

Besides the number and shape of partitions which both increase the probability of certain artifacts as described above, the number of available coding modes to choose from also yield new artifacts. Most prominently, an artifact named flickering or pumping, also known as stationary area fluctuations, appears when the chosen coding modes of one picture area changes over time, i.e. over subsequent frames. As the predicted residuals from intra and inter prediction differ strongly, the form of the coded residual after quantization is different, yielding different errors and thus flickering due to the change of error over time (Chun, 2006).

Although this artifact is often described as having similarities to mosquito noise, its origins are different. As applying temporal smoothing yields side effects when trying to compensate for this artifact during post processing (Wu, 2006), pumping artifacts can be avoided during the coding process by selecting similar modes for co-located regions in subsequent frames as described in Chun (2006). It has to be noted that a similar selection of partitions and sub-partitions is also helpful in order to achieve this, although not all inter predicted partitions have an equivalent intra predicted partition in terms of size. Furthermore, the prediction signals of inter and intra prediction vary strongly, as do the different intra prediction modes, thus requiring careful adaption of quantization parameters in addition to the coding mode selection in order to reduce pumping artifacts effectively.

Multi-View Video Coding

Another current field of research is multi-view video coding (MVC), i.e. the coding of multiple views of a scene in order to either produce a three dimensional rendering of said scene or a part of it, albeit often limited to the number of existing views and the interpolated views between them. The most prominent configuration is stereoscopic coding, i.e. the coding of two views – one for the left eye and one for the right – which enables a three dimensional effect when each view is exposed to the corresponding eye. There are currently multiple technologies (like polarized glasses or active shutter glasses) in order to achieve this (May, 2005). In terms of video coding, there are currently three basic approaches for multi-view video coding, which will be shortly described in the subsequent paragraphs, each together with the artifacts it induces or favors.

Depth Map Quantization Artifacts

The first approach constitutes the coding of a two dimensional image or texture and a so-called depth map indicating the distance from the camera for each pixel. This depth map can either be provided in special cases or is otherwise estimated by the encoder when given one or multiple views (Smolic, 2007). Depth estimation is a research topic of great current interest due to the emerging three dimensional TV sets and the associated technologies (Ohm, 2010). The coding of depth maps is explicitly specified in MPEG-4 part 2. Using transform, quantization and residual coding, depth maps are compressed like textures, thus yielding similar artifacts (Richardson, 2003).

Assuming quasi-lossless compression of textures, the quantization of depth maps yields a number of different artifacts which are related to their counterparts in regular image and video coding, although their appearance to the viewer may be different. One example is so-called depth ringing where ringing artifacts emerge from depth map compression, yielding distortions of the depth map and therefore the perceived depth (Boev, 2008). Figure 4 a) depicts the effects of depth ringing, also referred to as depth bleeding. As its image distortion counterpart, depth ringing is most prominent at steep edges (of the depth map), i.e. the region between the ball and the checkerboard background in Figure 4 a). In general, fluctuations in depth may be perceived easily in some scenes, making MSE, PSNR and similar metrics unsuitable for the quality estimation of multi-view videos which rely on depth map quantization.

Although depth blocking, blurring and similar artifacts may appear when coding depth maps, they have not been described in the literature. Most likely, this is due to the fact that current research efforts are focused on depth estimation and other coding techniques for multi-view video coding. Nonetheless, both depth estimation and harsh quantization may yield an artifact which has been described as card board or puppet theater effect, depicted in Figure 4 b). This refers to a layer-like depth map, similar to the layers of

Figure 4. Depth map compression artifacts: a) depth ringing. © 2008, Mobile3DTV (Boev, 2008). Used with permission; b) card board effect. Lighter colors in the depth map indicate greater depth.

a) b)

objects in a puppet theater, creating the perception of a number of two dimensional layers instead of smooth depth transitions.

Combining the artifacts of depth map and texture coding, a superposition of them may appear. Depending on the severity of artifacts, they may mask each other, making one so visually prominent that the other one is not visible any more (Wu, 2006). This is also true for all other artifacts described herein, although there is currently no research focused on the human visual perception of jointly appearing artifacts. This may change with the number of emerging coding technologies, currently represented by multi-view and scalable video coding, increasing the number of artifacts and therefore the probability of their joint appearance.

Frame Packing Artifacts

The second approach allowing for stereoscopic video coding only is an extension specifically available for H.264, called frame packing (Vetro, 2011). It uses a supplemental enhancement information (SEI) message to signal the frame packing of the pictures in the coded video. Frame packing refers to the coding of both views – left and right – in one single view, with both core encoding and decoding algorithms being possibly unaware of the existence of two separate views, thus maintaining compatibility to the H.264 standard as the core coding tools do not need to be changed. Combining and separating the views before and after coding, respectively, must be performed by the encoder (or a preprocessor) and the decoder (or a postprocessor), respectively as the combination of the two views for coding, the insertion of the SEI message and the separation of the two views for display must be performed.

The latest revision of the H.264 standard (International Telecommunication Union, 2010) specifies a number of frame packing arrangement types depicted in Figure 5. Assuming two views of a size of eight times eight macroblocks each,

both views are either horizontally or vertically subsampled, depending on the arrangement type, and then rearranged in order to form a picture of eight times eight macroblocks containing both views. However, one arrangement type – frame alternation, depicted in Figure 5 f) – does not require spatial subsampling as each view is represented by all even and odd pictures, respectively, i.e. it is temporally subsampled. If subsampling is used, upsampling after decoding is necessary to restore the original picture of each view, thus introducing similar artifacts as upsampling in scalable video coding described below.

In addition to the artifacts caused by subsampling and upsampling – reduced by quincunx sampling of the original samples of both views – crosstalk of artifacts is possible due to the interleaved coding of the two views. Although side-by-side and top-bottom frame packing are only likely to expose these artifacts at the borders between the two views, column and row alternation as well as checkerboard arrangements are expected to introduce crosstalk. As described in Vetro (2011), color bleeding is very likely to propagate across views, mostly when using checkerboards arrangements.

The probability of appearance of mosquito noise, pumping and MC mismatch is also increased due to the interleaving of views, albeit of limited influence to the overall coding performance in terms of PSNR. MC mismatch is favored due to the macroblock size spaced interleaving in most arrangements, causing the motion estimation algorithm to find a match in a macroblock of the other view as the motion estimation search range in most current H.264 encoders is around 16 samples (Jurkiewicz, 2011; Lee, 2008; Richardson, 2003) which equals the size of one macroblock for progressive input.

Using frame alternation arrangements, MC mismatches are even more likely to occur as motion compensation can only be performed on frames which have already been coded, thus disallowing motion compensation in the frame currently being

Figure 5. H.264 frame packing arrangement types: a) side-by-side (horizontal), b) top-bottom (vertical), c) checkerboard, d) column alternation, e) row alternation, f) frame alternation. Light and dark gray depict macroblocks of the left and the right view, respectively.

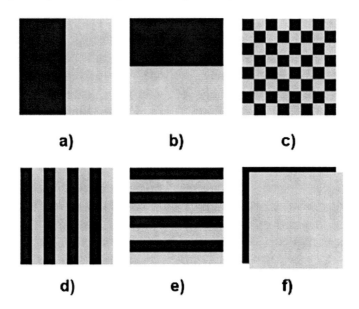

encoded (International Telecommunication Union, 2010). In addition, due to the limited size of the reference lists and practical considerations which limit the number of references used for motion estimation, the number of frames from the other view searched during the motion estimation phase is likely to be greater than the number of frames from the same view that the picture currently being coded belongs to.

Although the artifacts appearing in pictures using frame packing are similar to the artifacts previously described, both subsampling and upsampling have to be considered in terms of the range of artifacts as well as in terms of artifact superposition. Currently, there is only very little research performed in this area, although frame packing is already used intensively by broadcasting and other companies due to its compatibility to H.264 and the frame packing capabilities of the video signal transmission standard HDMI 1.4a.

Due to its increasing popularity in the years 2010 and 2011, more and more H.264 encoders begin to implement support for frame packing (Jurkiewicz, 2011), thus requiring research focused on further coding artifacts due to frame packed coding, including the consideration of the human visual perception of these artifacts when the stereoscopic video is decoded and displayed on a device capable of three-dimensional display using different technologies. As crosstalk and uneven visual quality of the two views are known to influence the perception of depth (Boev, 2008), frame packing requires further investigation regarding these issues.

Artifacts in H.264 MVC

The third approach for coding multiple views is the recent amendment of H.264 named multi-view video coding or MVC for short (Vetro, 2011), extending H.264 in a backwards compatible way. While the first view is coded like a regular H.264 bit stream, all other views use special signaling so that they are ignored by decoders which do not support MVC. In order to improve coding efficiency, all other views may be predicted from the first one or another view of the same access unit, i.e. a view of the same point in time as the view currently being coded (International Telecommunication Union, 2010).

Due to the current widespread use of stereoscopic coding, H.264 MVC defines new Stereo profiles for two views, enabling coding performance similar to the frame packing approach described above, albeit without subsampling and the restrictions imposed thereby (Vetro, 2011). MVC makes use of the similarity of multiple views at any given time instant, referred to as inter-view prediction. As can be seen in Figure 6, the similarity of the left and the right view eases prediction, although predictions from other views may yield a higher amount of MC mismatch artifacts as described above.

Despite the similarity of both views, there are differences due to the different perspective of the depicted objects, mostly notable at the left and right borders. In addition, the illumination of the two views may be slightly different as shown in the left part of both views in Figure 6. Although illumination compensation, i.e. an algorithm to compensate for luminance differences between the coded view and the view used for prediction, had been part of the working drafts of H.264 MVC, it was not included in the final version of the standard as it would require changes of the low level syntax and the corresponding coding

tools. However, notable efforts regarding illumination compensation in terms of the improvement of coding efficiency have been made (Park, 2008) which may be incorporated into future video coding standards (Vetro, 2011).

As the artifacts arising from illumination compensation have not been studied in depth, this leaves room for future research. Other artifacts like crosstalk and different forms of MC mismatches depending on the difference in perspective between the depicted objects in the views used for motion compensation also need a more detailed inspection. Although MPEG-2 Video already included means to encode stereoscopic videos and entailed perceptual considerations of its coding mechanisms (Tseng, 1995), the approach used in MPEG-2 Video and, therefore, its artifacts differ from the approach used in H.264 MVC as the former makes use of the scalability features of MPEG-2, using one view as the base layer and the second one as an enhancement layer, yielding a special form of inter-view prediction based on inter-layer prediction.

Scalable Video Coding

Scalable video coding (SVC) is available in MPEG-2 Video and MPEG-4 Part 2 and has been introduced as an amendment of H.264 in 2007 (Schwarz, 2007). It generally refers to the ability to decode specified parts of the bit stream,

Figure 6. Similarity of the left and the right view of a stereoscopic view. Differences are clearly visible in the form of illumination differences in the left part of both images as well as in differences of perspective at the borders on the left and the right.

yielding a smaller frame rate, spatial resolution or quality than when decoding the whole bit stream. Scalability relies on layers defining temporal scalability in terms of frame rate, spatial scalability in terms of spatial resolution and quality or SNR scalability in terms of fidelity as well as combinations thereof. In general, the overhead of having multiple layers is small, thus allowing for coding performance similar to a stream containing only the highest frame rate, resolution and quality.

Temporal-Scalability-Related Artifacts

H.264 SVC implements temporal scalability similar to prior standards by using backwards compatible B pictures and special signaling. It makes use of hierarchical prediction structures with B pictures using previously coded B pictures within a group of pictures (GOP) for prediction, each B picture hierarchy being equal to one temporal layer. As only the existing concept of B pictures and special signaling is used, no new artifacts originate besides the ones introduced by B pictures themselves, such as mosquito noise, MC mismatch and others (Wu, 2006). In order to avoid pumping artifacts, (Schwarz, 2007) recommends increasing the quantization parameter in higher temporal layers in a predefined pattern when using hierarchical B pictures to achieve temporal scalability, although this results in PSNR fluctuations inside a GOP.

Spatial-Scalability-Related Artifacts

The implementation of spatial scalability differs between MPEG-2 Video, MPEG-4 Part 2 and H.264 SVC, although the basic concept is similar. Higher spatial layers use the coded information of the spatial layer below by upsampling it and using it for prediction, whereas the lowest spatial layer, also called base layer, is coded regularly, i.e. without the use of scalable video coding tools. The upsampled signal from the lower layer can be based on a reconstructed, i.e. decoded, signal (MPEG-2 Video and MPEG-4 Part 2 as well as inter-layer

intra prediction in H.264 SVC) or on transform coefficients of a residual signal (H.264 SVC only, referred to as inter-layer inter prediction).

In H.264 SVC, upsampling also requires the block partitions of the lower layer to be upsampled accordingly, i.e. by a factor of two in each direction when using dyadic differences in resolution between two spatial layers, thereby possibly upsampling blocking artifacts and favoring MC mismatches as motion vectors are scaled accordingly and reference list indices are reused, yielding the same prediction area for motion compensation. In addition, mosquito noise may be upsampled, making it more visible when using higher quantization parameters in the enhancement layer.

The upsampling of transform coefficients in H.264 SVC is performed using a bilinear filter in order to avoid additional signal components due to the in-loop deblocking filter. Inter-layer intra prediction uses a 4-tap FIR filter for the luma samples and a bilinear filter for the chroma samples, albeit based on reconstructed samples instead of transform coefficients. Similar to the required upsampling process in MVC, inter-layer intra prediction upsampling introduces blurring to the prediction signal due to bilinear filtering (Krylov, 2008), thus favoring the appearance of mosquito noise due to the lack of high frequency signal components.

Quality-Scalability-Related Artifacts

Quality scalability is available in a number of different forms throughout the standards mentioned herein. Coarse grain quality scalability in H.264 SVC relies on the same mechanisms as are used for inter-layer inter prediction described above apart from the upsampling operations (the two layers have the same spatial resolution), thus yielding similar artifacts. The difference to be coded is based on the difference between the coarser quantized coefficients in the base layer and the original signal, resulting in finer quantized coefficients in the enhancement layer (Schwarz, 2007).

Medium grain scalability uses the same basic concept as coarse grain scalability, whereas fine grain scalability which has already been supported in MPEG-2 Video and MPEG-4 Part 2 allows for more sophisticated prediction structures between base and enhancement layers.

Although enhancement layers in MPEG-4 Part 2 can only be predicted from the corresponding base layers, MPEG-2 Video allows the prediction of base layers from previously coded enhancement layers, thus introducing a drift between encoder and decoder if enhancement layers are discarded. This has been avoided by a special key picture concept in H.264 SVC which is described in detail in International Telecommunication Union (2010) and Schwarz (2007). Although the aforementioned drift differs from the drift of MPEG-2 Video encoders and decoders described above, no research has been conducted so far in order to explore the visual effects of drift-based distortions.

SOLUTIONS AND RECOMMENDATIONS

Encoder-Side Artifact Awareness

As can be seen from the descriptions in the previous section, new coding tools tend to introduce new forms of artifacts or to modify the presence or number of existing artifacts. Therefore, it is important to know the sources of these new artifacts and to develop strategies to avoid or compensate for them. Taking MC mismatch as a prominent example from the previous section, avoiding the resulting artifacts might be a better idea than trying to compensate for them as both detection and compensation may be difficult. This may be the reason why currently neither is described in the literature.

Modifying the encoder may therefore be a better option in order to avoid or at least reduce MC mismatch significantly. Chroma motion estimation, for example, may assist regular luma

motion estimation by supplying additional information to consider when calculation the SSD or MSE in order to avoid MC mismatches, albeit more time consuming than luma-only motion estimation. Another option would be to replace the mathematical functions for difference and error measurement by functions which reflect the properties of the HVS better. This would allow avoiding MC mismatches as well as other artifacts up to a certain extent, incorporating properties of the HVS during coding.

Most current video encoders make use of rate distortion optimization (RDO), i.e. testing multiple possible modes and selecting the mode with the smallest cost. The smallest cost is defined as the mode with the best rate-distortion tradeoff, subject to a predefined relation between rate and distortion in order to calculate these costs for all modes. As distortion is mostly measured in a mathematical sense in these calculations as described below, it may be favorable to replace it with distortion measures which are aware of some important properties of the HVS, considering the most common artifacts and their effect on the human visual perception.

Development and Application of New Quality Metrics

Although a number of multiple similar distortion measurements have been discussed in the literature, each with its own strengths and weaknesses, the structural similarity (SSIM) index developed by Wang (2004) has proven to be a distortion measure that correlates well with the human visual perception subject to certain restrictions (Sheikh, 2006). By measuring the structural similarity in terms of variance and covariance of two images on a per-block (8×8) basis, the structural similarity index is capable of considering blurring, ringing, basis patterns and stair cases as well as other forms of image distortions, albeit unable to detect blocking artifacts with blocks of the size of the SSIM block size (8x8).

A first approach to incorporate SSIM indices as distortion measures has been proposed in Mai (2005). Therein, a subset of an H.264 encoder has been modified to use SSIM indices as a distortion measure for RDO during intra mode decision. As may be anticipated from a classical (peak signal to noise ratio, PSNR) point of view, the PSNR performance of the encoded pictures decreases compared to an unmodified encoder, while the perceptual quality increases. If this approach was extended to all RDO-amenable decisions involving new coding tools, the impact of new artifacts or the (re)appearance of classical artifacts might be reduced significantly, favoring coding modes with a reduced presence of artifacts. For motion estimation and similar coding tools, SSIM block matching may not only help to avoid MC mismatches, but also to find structurally more similar blocks than existing approaches, making the arising differences perceptually easier to encode.

The awareness of the perceptual influence of decisions during coding (mode decision, motion estimation etc.) is crucial. Therefore, it is necessary to include facilities into encoders which are aware of the perceptual impact of these decisions, helping to improve the perceived quality by design. As PSNR and other purely mathematical measures of difference give a general hint of the degree of quality degradation, they have proven insufficient when masking effects of the HVS and small or imperceptible differences come into play (Wang, 2004).

Although the computational complexity and ease of comparability of PSNR and the like is convenient for the purposes of state-of-the-art video coding, it is not in terms of the correlation between this metric and a typical human viewer rating video quality. Instead of sacrificing computational power (and therefore time) for new coding tools which improve the PSNR of a given configuration by a small amount, it is conceivable to sacrifice this time to design an HVS-aware quality metric for use within the encoder (perhaps even in form of a new coding tool) in order to improve the overall quality of the encoded pictures, thus also enabling perceptually aware coding control units which can distribute more bit rate to perceptually critical areas of a picture, thereby reducing the number and strength of perceived artifacts at the same bit rate.

Approaches to switch to a different metric for the measurement of differences and errors have also already been proposed by others, e.g. Ohm (2010), although there is currently no concrete direction observable in terms of a concrete metric to choose. SSIM may be an intermediate approach on the way to a new metric, albeit imperfect as it does not cover all important aspects of the human visual perception and does not correlate well with the HVS at low bit rates (Hofbauer, 2010). Despite its incapability to detect certain types of artifacts as discussed above, its high correlation throughout a wide range of bit rates with the HVS would make it a good choice to replace PSNR in the short or medium term, leaving potential for design optimizations in form of a new or different metric in the long term.

FUTURE RESEARCH DIRECTIONS

Next Generation Video Coding

As the future of video coding and its arising artifacts is closely related to the new coding tools designed, the current development of next generation video coding (NVC) based on H.264's coding tools, also referred to as high efficiency video coding (HEVC), gives an insight into the new coding tools and artifacts that will have to be dealt with in the future. At the time of this writing, a preliminary version (1.0) of the future reference software "HM" (HEVC testing model) has been made available to the public (https://hevc.hhi. fraunhofer.de/svn/svn_HEVCSoftware/), implementing most of the new coding tools selected for detailed evaluation after their approval in the call for proposals for NVC.

As the number of new coding tools compared to the latest revision of the H.264 standard (International Telecommunication Union, 2010) increased significantly and the release date of the preliminary reference software did not allow for thorough testing at the time of writing of this book chapter, those of the new coding tools which will probably have the strongest impact on artifacts will be discussed, considering that the current version of the reference software is not the final one and the continuing evaluation process may exclude coding tools described herein as well as include new ones.

A major change in terms of video coding is the macroblock size which is now 64×64 luma samples and referred to as a coding unit (CU) with accompanying concepts for prediction units (PU) and transform units (TU), allowing partitioning and sub-partitioning over four hierarchy levels (down to 4×4) as opposed to the two hierarchy levels in H.264 inter prediction (McCann, 2010). Although the number of partitions does not necessarily change the probability of the appearance of artifacts (the smallest size is still the same as in H.264), the introduction of a 16×16 integer transform might lead to a more significant appearance of ringing artifacts compared to the 4×4 and 8×8 transform sizes in H.264 due to the increased number of coefficients and samples available for over- and undershooting as described in the previous section. Transform sizes of 32×32 and 64×64, which are also being evaluated, yet increase the probability of ringing artifacts.

Besides the change in transform size, which also requires thorough inspection as described above for integer transforms in general, the interpolation filter for subsamples in the motion estimation and compensation process may be changed, too. The proposed improvements describe the use of a 6-tap directional filter or a 12-tap DCT based interpolation filter, replacing the Wiener and bilinear filter used in H.264 for subsample interpolation. As both approaches change the signal characteristics of the interpolated subsamples and therefore the likeliness to expose artifacts, future research will have to show how this affects the perceptual quality and artifact propagation.

In addition to the coding tools described, an extension of the number of available intra prediction modes has been proposed and modified (Min, 2010), introducing angular intra prediction in contrast to the nine 4×4 and four 16×16 prediction modes in H.264 making use of a limited number of horizontal, vertical and diagonal prediction. With a total of 17 modes for 4x4 PUs, 34 for 8x8, 16x16 and 32x32 PUs and 5 for 64x64 PUs, requiring the interpolation of predicted samples up to an accuracy of 1/32 of a sample, the new intra prediction modes will increase the probability of pumping artifacts further, apart from increasing the number of modes for RDO and therefore computational complexity significantly.

Analysis of Existing Artifacts

Despite the fact that future research related to HEVC which will have to wait until the reference software and the HEVC specification are finalized, the evaluation of artifacts arising from the emerging SVC and MVC standards will offer a number of opportunities for artifact research. As described above, there are multiple coding tools whose effects on existing and new artifacts have not yet been examined in depth, thus requiring further inspection and analysis.

Furthermore, the superposition of different artifacts and their effect on the HVS becomes more relevant as the number of known artifacts is already high and yet keeps increasing through the introduction of new video coding standards and amendments thereof. Studying which artifacts are visually prominent when appearing in certain constellations with other artifacts might not only provide a clearer perspective on the perception of artifact superpositions, but also on masking effects originating from the HVS in general.

Artifact-Aware Encoder Design

Overall, the consideration of the human visual perception in video encoder design is an important issue to take into account. If the artifact-related properties of the HVS are already considered in the design process of new coding tools and in the encoder, future research can focus on artifact avoidance instead of compensation. Furthermore, the encoder-side awareness of the presence of artifacts could be used to apply artifact compensation algorithms on both, the encoder and the decoder side, more selectively, reducing the post-processing complexity on the latter side through encoder-generated artifact signaling.

In addition, new metrics can be developed which represent the human visual perception better than existing ones, allowing for improved encoder decisions. Such metrics can also be used for the difference and distortion measurements in general, making artifact detection easier. If, in addition, artifact propagation is analyzed in the encoder, video quality can be estimated more precisely, eventually enabling artifact-aware video coding.

CONCLUSION

Despite the increasing rate of improvement in terms of compression efficiency in modern video coding, the avoidance and compensation of coding artifacts are currently not getting the attention they deserves. The development of new coding tools decreases bit rates compared to previous standards at the cost of increased computational complexity and a lack of awareness of the impact of these new coding tools on the appearance of known or new artifacts. It is important to be aware of the artifacts arising from improvements in video coding algorithms, enabling a broader understanding of the human visual perception besides the classical artifacts, such as blocking, ringing, blurring and the like.

Although it might not be the final solution, the consideration of different quality metrics like SSIM for difference and error measurement as well as RDO can be a step towards the awareness of certain artifacts during the encoding process. Be it in form of a new coding tool as an integral part or as an addition to the core coding tools of a video encoder, the consideration of the human visual perception during the coding process can help to improve the perceptual quality of encoded videos in current and future video coding standards. It may also help to gain a better understanding of the influence of new coding tools regarding their vulnerability to induce artifacts.

In doing so, the need for decoder side artifact detection and compensation would also diminish, thus requiring less attention than currently, allowing future research to concentrate on the development of new metrics for quality measurement on the encoder side rather than sophisticated artifact compensation algorithms on the decoder side. Therefore, it is indispensable to focus future research efforts on artifact avoidance at the encoder side or (even before) in the design process of new coding tools. In the end, it is the casual user, unaware of the mere existence of the most sophisticated coding tools, who judges the visual quality and the visibility of coding artifacts.

REFERENCES

Ben-Ezra, M., & Nayar, S. K. (2004). Motion-based motion deblurring. *IEEE Transactions on Pattern Analysis and Machine Intelligence*, *26*(6), 689–698. doi:10.1109/TPAMI.2004.1

Biemond, J., Lagendijk, R. L., & Mersereau, R. M. (1990). Iterative methods for image deblurring. *Proceedings of the IEEE*, *78*(5), 856–883. doi:10.1109/5.53403

Boev, A., Hollosi, D., & Gotchev, A. (2008). *Classification of stereoscopic artifacts*. Retrieved February 1, 2011, from http://sp.cs.tut.fi/mobile3dtv/results/tech/D5.1_Mobile3DTV_v1.0.pdf

Chang, Y.-W., & Chen, Y.-Y. (2005). *Alleviating-ringing-artifact filter using voting scheme*. Paper presented at the ICGST International Conference on Graphics, Vision and Image Processing, Cairo, Egypt.

Chun, S. S., Kim, J. R., & Sull, S. (2006). Intra prediction mode selection for flicker reduction in H.264/AVC. *IEEE Transactions on Consumer Electronics, 52*(4), 1303–1310. doi:10.1109/TCE.2006.273149

Crop, J., Erwig, A., & Selvaraj, V. (2010). *Ogg video coding*. Retrieved September 21, 2011, from http://people.oregonstate.edu/~cropj/uploads/Classes/577finalreport.pdf

Hofbauer, H., & Uhl, A. (2010). *Visual quality indices and low quality images*. Paper presented at the IEEE 2nd European Workshop on Visual Information Processing, Paris, France.

International Telecommunication Union. (2010). *Recommendation ITU-T H.264 – Advanced video coding for generic audiovisual services (03/2010)*. Geneva, Switzerland: International Telecommunication Union.

Jurkiewicz, A., et al. (2011). *X264 settings*. Retrieved February 1, 2011, from http://mewiki.project357.com/wiki/X264_Settings

Kerr, D. A. (2009). *Chrominance subsampling in digital images*. Retrieved February 1, 2011, from http://dougkerr.net/pumpkin/articles/Subsampling.pdf

Krylov, A., & Nasonov, A. (2008). Adaptive total variation deringing method for image interpolation. *Proceedings of the 15th IEEE International Conference on Image Processing 2008*, (pp. 2608–2611).

Lee, J.-B., & Kalva, H. (2008). *The VC-1 and H.264 video compression standards for broadband video services*. New York, NY: Springer Science+Business Media LLC.

Liu, H., Klomp, N., & Heynderickx, I. (2010). *A no-reference metric for perceived ringing*. Paper presented at the Fourth International Workshop on Video Processing and Quality Metrics for Consumer Electronics, Scottsdale, Arizona.

Mai, Z.-Y., Yang, C. L., & Xie, S. L. (2005). Improved best prediction mode(s) selection methods based on structural similarity in H.264 I-frame encoder. *IEEE International Conference on Systems, Man and Cybernetics*, Vol. 3, (pp. 2673–2678).

Malvar, H. S., Hallapuro, A., & Karczewicz, M., & Louis Kerofsky. (2003). Low-complexity transform and quantization in H.264/AVC. *IEEE Transactions on Circuits and Systems for Video Technology, 13*(7), 598–603. doi:10.1109/TCSVT.2003.814964

May, P. (2005). *A survey of 3D display technologies*. Retrieved February 1, 2011, from http://www.ocuity.co.uk/Ocuity_white_paper_Survey_of_3D_display_technologies.pdf

McCann, K., Han, W.-J., & Kim, I. K. (2010). *Samsung's response to the call for proposals on video compression technology (JCTVC-A124)*. Retrieved February 1, 2011, from http://wftp3.itu.int/av-arch/jctvc-site/2010_04_A_Dresden/JCTVC-A124.zip

Min, J.-H., Lee, S., Kim, I.-K., Han, W.-J., Lainema, J., & Ugur, K. (2010). *Unification of the directional intra prediction methods in TMuC (JCTVC-B100)*. Retrieved February 1, 2011, from http://wftp3.itu.int/av-arch/jctvc-site/2010_07_B_Geneva/JCTVC-B100.zip

Ng, M. K., Chan, R. H., & Tang, W.-C. (1999). A fast algorithm for deblurring models with Neumann boundary conditions. *SIAM Journal on Scientific Computing, 21*(3), 851–866. doi:10.1137/S1064827598341384

Ohm, J.-R. (2008). *Recent, current and future developments in video coding.* Retrieved February 1, 2011, from http://wiamis2008.itec.uni-klu.ac.at/keynotes/ohm.pdf

Oosa, K. (1998). *A new deblocking filter for digital image compression.* Retrieved February 1, 2011, from http://www.nsc.co.jp/en/tech/report/pdf/7716.pdf

Park, G. H., Park, M. W., Lim, S. C., Shim, W. S., & Lee, Y. L. (2008). Deblocking filtering for illumination compensation in multiview video coding. *IEEE Transactions on Circuits and Systems for Video Technology, 18*(10), 1457–1461. doi:10.1109/TCSVT.2008.2002890

Park, H. W., & Lee, Y. L. (1999). A postprocessing method for reducing quantization effects in low bit-rate moving picture coding. *IEEE Transactions on Circuits and Systems for Video Technology, 9*(1), 161–171. doi:10.1109/76.744283

Ramos, M. G., & Hemami, S. S. (2001). Suprathreshold wavelet coefficient quantization in complex stimuli: Psychophysical evaluation and analysis. *Journal of the Optical Society of America. A, Optics, Image Science, and Vision, 18*(10), 2385–2397. doi:10.1364/JOSAA.18.002385

Richardson, I. E. G. (2003). *H.264 and MPEG-4 video compression.* Chichester, UK: John Wiley & Sons Ltd. doi:10.1002/0470869615

Schwarz, H., Marpe, D., & Wiegand, T. (2007). Overview of the scalable video coding extension of the H.264/AVC standard. *IEEE Transactions on Circuits and Systems for Video Technology, 17*(9), 1103–1120. doi:10.1109/TCSVT.2007.905532

Sheikh, H. R., Sabir, M. F., & Bovik, A. C. (2006). A statistical evaluation of recent full reference image quality assessment algorithms. *IEEE Transactions on Image Processing, 15*(11), 3440–3451. doi:10.1109/TIP.2006.881959

Shen, M. Y., & Kuo, C.-C. J. (1998). Review of postprocessing techniques for compression artifact removal. *Journal of Visual Communication and Image Representation, 9*(1), 2–14. doi:10.1006/jvci.1997.0378

Smolic, A., Müller, K., Stefanoski, N., Ostermann, J., Gotchev, A., & Akar, G. B. (2007). Coding algorithms for 3DTV—A survey. *IEEE Transactions on Circuits and Systems for Video Technology, 17*(11), 1606–1621. doi:10.1109/TCSVT.2007.909972

Triantafyllidis, G. A., Tzovaras, D., & Strintzis, M. G. (2002). Blocking artifact detection and reduction in compressed data. *IEEE Transactions on Circuits and Systems for Video Technology, 12*(10), 877–890. doi:10.1109/TCSVT.2002.804880

Tseng, B. L., & Anastassiou, D. (1995). *Perceptual adaptive quantization of stereoscopic video coding using MPEG-2's temporal scalability structure.* Paper presented at the International Workshop on Stereoscopic and Three Dimensional Imaging 1995, Santorini, Greece.

Vetro, A., Wiegand, T., & Sullivan, G. J. (2011). Overview of the stereo and multiview video coding extensions of the H.264/AVC standard. *Proceedings of IEEE, Special Issue on "3D Media and Displays", 99*(4), 626–642.

Wang, Z., Bovik, A. C., Sheikh, H. R., & Simoncelli, E. P. (2004). Image quality assessment: from error visibility to structural similarity. *IEEE Transactions on Image Processing, 13*(4), 600–612. doi:10.1109/TIP.2003.819861

Watson, A., Yang, G. Y., Solomon, J., & Villasenor, J. (1997). Visibility of wavelet quantization noise. *IEEE Transactions on Image Processing*, *6*(8), 1164–1175. doi:10.1109/83.605413

Wiegand, T., Sullivan, G. J., Bjøntegaard, G., & Luthra, A. (2003). Overview of the H.264/AVC video coding standard. *IEEE Transactions on Circuits and Systems for Video Technology*, *13*(7), 560–576. doi:10.1109/TCSVT.2003.815165

Wu, H. R., & Rao, K. R. (Eds.). (2006). *Digital video image quality and perceptual coding*. Boca Raton, FL: CRC/Taylor & Francis.

Xiph.Org Foundation. (2011). *Theora specification*. Retrieved September 21, 2011, from http://theora.org/doc/Theora.pdf

Zakhor, A. (2002). Iterative procedures for reduction of blocking effects in transform image coding. *IEEE Transactions on Circuits and Systems for Video Technology*, *2*(1), 91–95. doi:10.1109/76.134377

ADDITIONAL READING

Boujut, H., Benois-Pineau, J., Hadar, O., Ahmed, T., & Bonnet, P. (2011). Weighted-MSE based on saliency map for assessing video quality of H.264 video streams. *Proceedings of the SPIE – Image Quality and System Performance VIII, 7867*.

Brooks, A. C., Zhao, X., & Pappas, T. N. (2008). Structural similarity quality metrics in a coding context: Exploring the space of realistic distortions. *IEEE Transactions on Image Processing*, *17*(8), 1261–1273. doi:10.1109/TIP.2008.926161

Carballeira, P., Tech, G., Cabrera, J., Müller, K., Jaureguizar, F., Wiegand, T., & García, N. (2010). *Block based rate-distortion analysis for quality improvement of synthesized views*. Paper presented at the 3DTV-Conference: The True Vision - Capture, Transmission and Display of 3D Video 2010, Tampere, Finland.

Farrugia, R. A., & Debono, C. J. (2010). A hybrid error control and artifact detection mechanism for robust decoding of H.264/AVC video sequences. *IEEE Transactions on Circuits and Systems for Video Technology*, *20*(5), 756–762. doi:10.1109/TCSVT.2010.2045808

Goldmann, L., De Simone, F., Dufaux, F., Ebrahimi, T., Tanner, R., & Lattuada, M. (2010). *Impact of video transcoding artifacts on the subjective quality*. Paper presented at the Second International Workshop on Quality of Multimedia Experience 2010, Trondheim, Norway.

Hewage, C. T. E. R., Worrall, S. T., Dogan, S., & Kondoz, A. M. (2008). Prediction of stereoscopic video quality using objective quality models of 2-D video. *Electronics Letters*, *44*(16), 963–965. doi:10.1049/el:20081562

Hoffmann, H., Itagaki, T., Wood, D., Hinz, T., & Wiegand, T. (2008). A novel method for subjective picture quality assessment and further studies of HDTV formats. *IEEE Transactions on Broadcasting*, *54*(1), 1–13. doi:10.1109/TBC.2008.916833

Hwang, Y., & Park, J. (2003). *Reduction of compression artifacts (blocking artifacts, ringing artifacts) using POSC*. Retrieved February 1, 2011, from http://homepages.cae.wisc.edu/~ece533/project/f04/hwang_park.pdf

Kim, W. S., Ortega, A., Lai, P. L., Tian, D., & Gomila, C. (2009). *Depth map distortion analysis for view rendering and depth coding*. Paper presented at the 16th IEEE International Conference on Image Processing 2009, Cairo, Egypt.

Le Meura, O., Ninassib, A., Le Calletc, P., & Barbac, D. (2010). Do video coding impairments disturb the visual attention deployment? *Signal Processing Image Communication*, *25*(8), 597–609. doi:10.1016/j.image.2010.05.008

Lee, J., & Park, H. W. (2011). A new distortion measure for motion estimation in motion-compensated hybrid video coding. *Signal Processing Image Communication*, *26*(2), 75–84. doi:10.1016/j.image.2010.12.002

Liu, T., Wang, Y., Boyce, J. M., Yang, H., & Wu, Z. (2009). A novel video quality metric for low bit-rate video considering both coding and packet-loss artifacts. *IEEE Journal of Selected Topics in Signal Processing*, *3*(2), 280–293. doi:10.1109/JSTSP.2009.2015069

Merkle, P., Morvan, Y., Smolic, A., Farin, D., Müller, K., de With, P. H. N., & Wiegand, T. (2008). The effects of multiview depth video compression on multiview rendering. *Signal Processing Image Communication*, *24*(1), 73–88. doi:10.1016/j.image.2008.10.010

Shao, L., & Kirenko, I. (2007). Coding artifact reduction based on local entropy analysis. *IEEE Transactions on Consumer Electronics*, *53*(2), 691–696. doi:10.1109/TCE.2007.381747

Shao, L., Zhang, H., & Liu, Y. (2011). A generalized coding artifacts and noise removal algorithm for digitally compressed video signals. *Lecture Notes in Computer Science*, *6523*, 1–9. doi:10.1007/978-3-642-17832-0_1

Sugimoto, O., Naito, S., Sakazawa, S., & Koike, A. (2009). *Objective perceptual video quality measurement method based on hybrid no reference framework*. Paper presented at the 16th IEEE International Conference on Image Processing 2009, Cairo, Egypt.

Suk, J.-Y., Lee, G. W., & Lee, K.-I. (2005). Effective blocking artifact reduction using classification of block boundary area. *Lecture Notes in Computer Science*, *3768*, 606–616. doi:10.1007/11582267_53

Unterweger, A., & Thoma, H. (2007). *The influence of bit rate allocation to scalability layers on video quality in H.264 SVC*. Paper presented at the Picture Coding Symposium 2007, Lisboa, Portugal.

van den Branden Lambrecht, C. J., & Verscheure, O. (1996). Perceptual quality measure using a spatio-temporal model of the human visual system. *Digital Video Compression: Algorithms and Technologies*, *2668*, 450–461.

Vo, D. T., & Nguyen, T. Q. (2009). *Optimal motion compensated spatio-temporal filter for quality enhancement of H.264/AVC compressed video sequences*. Paper presented at the 16th IEEE International Conference on Image Processing 2009, Cairo, Egypt.

Wang, Z., Bovik, A. C., & Lu, L. (2002). *Why is image quality assessment so difficult?* Paper presented at the IEEE International Conference on Acoustics, Speech, & Signal Processing 2002, Orlando, Florida.

Winkler, S., & Mohandas, P. (2008). The evolution of video quality measurement: From PSNR to hybrid metrics. *IEEE Transactions on Broadcasting*, *54*(3), 660–668. doi:10.1109/TBC.2008.2000733

Wu, H. R., & Yuen, M. (1997). A generalized block-edge impairment metric for video coding. *IEEE Signal Processing Letters*, *4*(11), 317–320. doi:10.1109/97.641398

Yang, J., & Wu, H. (2010). Robust filtering technique for reduction of temporal fluctuation in H.264 video sequences. *IEEE Transactions on Circuits and Systems for Video Technology*, *20*(3), 458–462. doi:10.1109/TCSVT.2009.2035850

Zhang, Z. L., Shi, H., & Wan, S. (2009). *A novel blind measurement of blocking artifacts for H.264/AVC video*. Paper presented at the Fifth International Conference on Image and Graphics 2009, Xi'an, China.

KEY TERMS AND DEFINITIONS

Artifact: Image distortion induced by side effects of a coding tool and/or quantization.

Block: Rectangular unit of image samples grouped for coding.

Blocking: Artifact caused by independent coding of neighboring blocks.

Blurring: Artifact caused by loss of high frequency components, making the block appear fuzzy.

Coding Tool: Distinct set of algorithms within a video encoder to improve compression or picture quality.

Macroblock: Synonym for a block or a group thereof (depending on the context).

Ringing: Artifact related to Gibbs Phenomenon in Fourier analysis, creating a "halo" consisting of over- and undershooting samples as well as blurring parallel to steep edges due to the insufficient approximation of the original edge by the quantized coefficients in the transform domain.

Chapter 3
Performance Scalable Motion Estimation for Video Coding:
An Overview of Current Status and a Promising Approach

Golam Sorwar
Southern Cross University, Australia

Manzur Murshed
Monash University, Australia

ABSTRACT

Motion estimation is one of the major bottlenecks in real-time performance scalable video coding applications due to high computational complexity of exhaustive search. To address this, researchers so far focused on low-complexity motion estimation and rate-distortion optimization in isolation. Proliferation of power-constrained handheld devices with image capturing capability has created demand for much smarter approach where motion estimation is integrated with rate control such that rate-distortion-complexity optimization can be effectively achieved. It is indeed crucial to provide such performance scalability in motion estimation to facilitate complexity management in such devices. This chapter presents an overview of motion estimation. Beginning with an introduction to the importance of motion estimation, it systematically examines various motion estimation techniques and their strengths and weaknesses, focussing primarily on block-based motion search. It then examines the limitation of the existing techniques in accommodating performance scalability, introduces a promising approach, Distance-dependent Thresholding Search (DTS) motion search, to fill in this gap, and concludes with future research directions in the field. The authors suggest that the content of the chapter will make a significant contribution and serve as a reference for multimedia signal processing research at postgraduate level.

DOI: 10.4018/978-1-4666-2660-7.ch003

INTRODUCTION

Digital video technology has been facing by an exponential growth in the last few years driven by new and fundamental applications such as videoconferencing, net-meeting, video e-mail, video over mobile phone (3G), wireless multimedia applications and video streaming over personal digital assistants. These new and emerging multimedia applications have driven the need for more advanced video coding standards. Currently, there are several video standards, such as H.261/3/4/ AVC established for a variety of multimedia applications. Video encoding, however, involves a huge amount of computations and hence, there is significant interest and need to speed up the processing of video encoders. Video coding exploits temporal redundancy in order to reduce the bandwidth while preserving the quality of the receiver-reconstructed images. This has resulted in many motion based video compression strategies which have become an integral part of multimedia applications for both communication and entertainment purposes. Most work in this area has been mainly focused on the fast motion estimation algorithms and attempted to optimise only *rate-distortion* performance on scalable video coding. However, it is indeed crucial to provide performance scalability in motion estimation in facilitating complexity management in video coding, especially in real-time software-only low bit rate video CODECs (Coder and Decoder) or low-power video CODECs for mobile or hand-held computing platforms which particularly require a more flexible trade-off between complexity and quality (Richardson, 2002).

In this chapter, we present an overview of motion estimation techniques, providing a snapshot of its current status, focussing primarily on block-based motion estimation algorithms (BMAs). We identify the limitations of BMAs in accommodating performance scalability in real-time video coding applications and then present a promising approach, *Distance-dependent Thresholding*

Search (DTS) motion search, to fill in this gap. Finally the chapter concludes with future research directions in the field.

BACKGROUND

A video sequence is a much richer source of visual information than a still image, due to the capture of motion. While a single image provides a snapshot of a scene, a sequence of images (widely termed as frames) register the dynamics within it. The registered motion is a very strong cue for human vision to recognise objects as soon as they move even if they are inconspicuous when still. Motion is, therefore, the most obvious and effective feature to provide global and local understanding as well as describing the dynamic content within a video sequence. The extraction of motion information from sequences of time-varying images has numerous applications in a wide range of areas especially computer vision and image processing. Perhaps the most important application of motion is in video data compression. In the evolving digital technology era, video compression has become an integral part of multimedia applications for both communication and entertainment purposes. As the diversity of these applications indicate, *Motion estimation* (ME) has been the focus of extensive research over many years, and this is reflected in the plethora of motion estimation and analysis techniques that have been proposed. Existing motion estimation techniques may be broadly classified into three distinct classes which will be discussed briefly below.

Gradient-Based Motion Estimation

Pixel-based motion estimation is a gradient-based method (Aggarwal & Nandhakumar, 1988; Lucas & Kanade, 1981; Barron et al., 1994) which focuses on estimating the apparent motion of intensity patterns in a video sequence, known as *optical flow,* based on two assumptions. Firstly, that the brightness of an object stays constant over time and secondly that pixels in a given small image neighbourhood are likely to correspond to points on the same 3-dimensional (3-D) surface, the so called spatial coherence assumption. Since the projected motion of points on a 3-D surface usually varies gradually, a correspondence of this assumption is to impose a smoothness constraint on the *optical flow*. These techniques have the following drawbacks:

- They require estimation of spatial and temporal gradients which is often noise sensitive.
- The intensity derivatives are numerically approximated. This requires local spatio-temporal linearity of intensity. In image sequences with high motion, local linearity is violated (Kearney et al., 1887).
- OFE is ambiguous of the projected motion; that motion can only be defined in a direction perpendicular to a gradient means that the gradient-basedmethods suffer from *aperture* problems (Tekalp, 1995).

From video coding perspective, there are also two other fundamental drawbacks:

- The smoothness constraint leads to increased prediction error energy.
- The dense motion field requires large information overhead.

Pel-Recursive Motion Estimation

Pel–recursive methods (Robbins & Netravali, 1983; Boroczky, 1991). can be considered as a subset of gradient-based methods, and have been developed for image-sequence coding. They obtain a dense optical flow by raster scanning, that is, they start the estimation at the top-left pixel and end at the bottom-right pixel. The luminance of pixel x in the current image is predicted from the reference image by means of the correspondence

vector found at the previous pixel in the current image, by recursively minimising some prediction error criteria, commonly known as the *Block Distortion Measure* (BDM). It is assumed that the previous vector is a good estimator of the new vector and thus, only small changes are allowed between the two vectors. There are however, a number of disadvantages when applying these methods to video compression applications:

- The first of the above advantages is obtained at a cost of increased complexity at the decoder, as the encoder has also to estimate the motion field (Dufaux & Moscheni, 1995).
- The causality constrains these algorithms and reduces their prediction capability compare with non-causal methods.
- As the error function to minimise generally contains many local minima, the iterative procedure may converge to a local rather than the global minima. In particular, these algorithms are very sensitive to noise.
- Large displacements and discontinuities in the motion field cannot be efficiently processed.
- The pel-recursive motion estimation technique (with recursion on pel) is not compatible with transform coding of BDM, as in this case the decoder is unable to reconstruct the motion vector.

To address the shortcomings of both the gradient-based and pel-recursive methods, the obvious alternative is to consider a block of pixels, rather than estimating motion on a pixel-by-pixel basis.

Block-Based Motion Estimation

Block-based methods represent, in certain respects, an opposite philosophy from the previously discussed gradient-based estimation techniques where larger analysis windows are used to avoid some of the problems identified in previous sections. Besides the *data constancy constraint*, these methods also assume that objects move in a translation movement for at leas, a few frames. Based on this assumption, the idea in block-matching algorithms is that the image sequence consists of a set of regions each undergoing a single motion between frames. Each frame is divided into a set of non-overlapped, equally spaced, fixed size, small rectangular blocks called macroblocks; and the translation motion within each block is assumed to be uniform. The motion vector of each block is then found by searching for the corresponding blocks in the reference frame by minimising some matching criteria, such as the *mean absolute error* (MAE), between the gray levels. Such block-based motion estimation methods are popularly termed *block-matching algorithms* (BMAs).

BMAs have a number of advantages compared to other techniques:

- They are very simple, straightforward, and yet very efficient.
- Their regular structure and causality allow for efficient implementation.
- They are less sensitive to *aperture* problems since, with a suitable block size; each block is likely to contain several image gradients. In general, block-matching methods will also be less sensitive to noise since more image data is used in the motion estimation process.
- They outperform other methods in capturing *true* motion in high motion video sequences (Shi & Sun, 2000).
- Although the simple BMA model considers translation motion only, other types of motion, such as rotation and zooming of large objects, may be closely approximated by the piecewise translation of these small blocks, provided the blocks are small. This important observation, originally made by Jain & Jain (1984), has been frequently confirmed (Shi & Sun, 2000).

These advantages are counterbalanced by two key limitations:

- During motion estimation, a single motion vector is considered for all pixels within one block and the motion vectors of partitioned blocks are estimated independently of each other, which leads to picture artifacts.
- The fixed block size also imposes a limit on the accuracy of the estimated motion field since the regions are unable to adapt to the underlying image data.

To address these shortcomings, one extension to the basic block-matching algorithm is to consider sub-pel (half-pel or quarter-pel) accuracy in motion estimation which leads to a significant improvement when compared to integer pel accuracy (Richardson, 2002; Chang & Leou, 2006).

From this discussion, it can be concluded that among all different motion estimation techniques, the BMA is the most effective for video coding point of view and for this reason has been adopted by all the international video coding standards including the newest video compression standard H.264/ AVC (Wiegand et al., 2003).

BLOCK-BASED MOTION ESTIMATION TECHNIQUES

Block matching is a correlation technique that searches for the best match between the current image block and candidates in a confined area of the reference frame. In a typical use of this method, images are partitioned into non overlapped rectangular blocks. Each block is viewed as an independent object and it is assumed that the motion of pixels within the block is uniform. The *Motion Vector* (MV) is the by-product when the new location of the object (block) is identified. The size of the block affects the performance of motion estimation. Small block sizes afford good approximation of the natural objects' boundaries and to real motion, which is now approximated by piecewise translation movement. However, small block sizes produce a large amount of raw motion information, which increases the number of transmission bits or the required data compression complexity, to condense this motion information. The international video transmission standards, such as H.261-4 and MPEG-4, all adopt the block size of 16x16 pixels. The basic operation of block matching is selecting a candidate block and calculating the matching function (usually a nonnegative function of the intensity difference) between the candidate and the current block. This operation is repeated until all candidates have been processed and the best match identified. The relative distance between the best candidate and the current block is the estimated MV.

Several parameters are involved in the searching process and all have an impact on both accuracy and complexity:

- The number of search points (candidate blocks).
- The matching function.
- Search order of candidates.

Assume that the maximum displacement of a motion vector is $\pm d$ in both horizontal and vertical directions as shown in Figure 1. Throughout this chapter, pixels of a frame are numbered using the Cartesian coordinate system with the origin starting in the upper-left corner.Except for the blocks at the image boundaries, the size of the search space is $(N+2d+1)\times(N+2d+1)$, where the macroblock size is $N\times N$, and therefore a MV(u,v) is obtained by finding a matched block within the above mentioned search space in the reference frame by using a predetermined matching criterion, where the number of possible search points is $(2d+1)\times(2d+1)$ for the best match of the current block, and (k,l) represents the x and y coordinate of the upper left pixel position of the current macroblock in current frame, (u,v)

represents the x and y components of MV where the directions of x and y in Figure 1.

This single motion vector assumption may not always be true because an image block may contain more than one moving object. In image sequence coding however, prediction errors due to imperfect motion compensation are coded and transmitted. Hence, because of its simplicity and small overhead the block-based motion estimation-compensation method is widely adopted in real video coding system.

The algorithm, which examines all these locations, is called the *Exhaustive Search*, or *Full Search* (FS). If more than one block generates a minimum BDM, the FS algorithm selects the block whose MV generates the smallest error, to exploit the centre-biased motion vector distribution characteristics of real video sequences (Li et al., 1994; Po & Ma, 1996). To achieve this, checking points trace a spiral trajectory starting at the centre of the search space. This trajectory is used by the FS algorithm with the example of a maximum displacement $d=\pm7$ shown in Figure 2. The centre of the search window is equal to the location of the searching block (current block) of the current frame.

Figure 1. Search space of block-matching algorithms

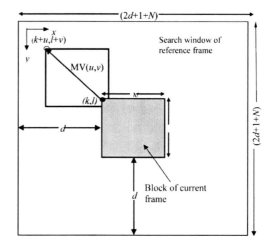

Figure 2. The spiral trajectory of the checking points in the FS algorithm

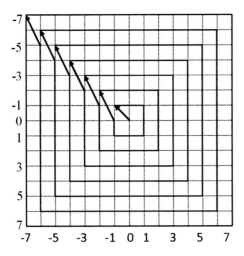

Block-Matching Criteria

It is necessary to choose an appropriate matching function in the process of searching for the best matching block. The selection of the matching function has a direct impact on computational complexity and coding efficiency. Several popular matching functions that appear in the literature are *Mean Absolute Error* (MAE), *Mean Square Error* (MSE), *Cross Correlation Function* (CCF), and Matching *Pel-Count* (MPC).

If $F_n(i,j)$ denotes the intensity of the pixel with coordinates (i,j) for the current frame, then the MAE, MSE, CCF, and MPC matching criteria are defined as follows:-

Mean Absolute Error (MAE): In this criterion, the pixels from each block in the current frame n, are compared with the corresponding candidate

block in the search area in the reference frame, $n-1$ and their absolute differences are summed and averaged. The MAE criterion is given as follows:

$$MAE_{(k,l)}(u,v) = \frac{1}{N^2} \sum_{i=0}^{N-1} \sum_{j=0}^{N-1} |F_n(k+i,\ l+j)$$
$$- F_{n-1}(k+u+i,l+v+j)|$$
$$\text{for} -d \leq u,v \leq d \tag{1}$$

where $F_{n-1}(u,v)$ is a candidate block in the search space in the reference frame, and (u,v) is a motion vector representing the search location. The search space is specified by $u = (-d, +d)$ and $v = (-d, +d)$. The candidate block with the minimum MAE is considered to give the best match. The MAE is also known as *Mean Absolute Difference* (MAD).

Mean Square Error (MSE): This is similar to the MAE function, except that the difference between pixels is squared before addition. The MSE function is defined as:

$$MSE_{(k,l)}(u,v) = \frac{1}{N^2} \sum_{i=0}^{N-1} \sum_{j=0}^{N-1} [F_n(k+i,l+j)$$
$$- F_{n-1}(k+u+i,l+v+j)]^2$$

$$\tag{2}$$

The candidate block with the minimum MSE is considered to give the best match. The *Mean Square Error* (MSE) function is also known as the *Mean Square Difference* (MSD).

Cross Correlation Function (CCF): The Cross Correlation Function (CCF) for the block-matching criterion is derived from Equation 3 in Box 1.

Box 1. Equation 3

$$CCF_{(k,l)}(u,v) = \frac{\sum_{i=0}^{N-1} \sum_{j=0}^{N-1} F_n(k+i,l+j)F_{n-1}(k+u+i,l+v+j)}{\sqrt{\sum_{i=0}^{N-1} \sum_{j=0}^{N-1} F_n^2(k+i,l+j)} \sqrt{\sum_{i=0}^{N-1} \sum_{j=0}^{N-1} F_{n-1}^2(k+u+i,l+v+j)}}$$

Table 1. Average MSE per pixel and SP per motion vector of the FS, TSS, NTSS, DS, HEXBS, and EHEXBS algorithms for football and flower garden video sequences

	Football			Flower Garden		
BMA	**MSE**	**PSNR[dB]**	**SP**	**MSE**	**PSNR[dB]**	**SP**
FS	218.9	24.4	160.1	208	24.9	209.7
TSS	240.8	24.3	25.6	243.0	24.3	31.2
NTSS	239.2	24.3	26.9	213.3	24.8	29.0
DS	237.0	24.4	24.9	219.7	24.7	22.8
HEXBS	241.0	24.3	21.0	226.2	24.6	20.2
EHEXBS	246.7	24.2	19.9	229.2	24.5	18.6

The candidate block with the maximum value of CCF is considered to give the best match.

Matching Pel-Count(MPC): The Matching Pel-Count (MPC) function compares each pixel of the target block of the current frame n with the corresponding pixel block within the search space of the reference frame $n-1$. If the pixels are similar to each other, the pixel pair is classified as a matching pixel; if not, then it is a mismatching pixel. The matching and the mismatching classifications are done with respect to a pre-defined threshold value. The MPC criterion is as follows:

$$MPC(u,v) = \sum_{i=1}^{N} \sum_{j=1}^{N} P(u,v,i,j) \text{ for } -d \leq u, v \leq d$$

(4)

where $P(u,v,i,j)$ is the binary representation of the pixel difference defined as Equation 5 in Box 2 where T_p is a pre-defined threshold value. For a matching pixel $P = 1$, while for a mismatching pixel $P = 0$. The greater the number of matching pixels, the better the match.

Among the above matching criteria, MSE and CCF require multiplication and accumulations while MAE and MPC require comparison and accumulation, and a multiplication is always more computationally expensive than either a comparison or accumulation. Although MPC is computationally less expensive compared with the MAE, its performance is highly sensitive to the choice of the threshold value T_p (Lim & Ho, 1998). The optimum threshold selection is a difficult task which entirely depends on the video sequence, and therefore, its performance is not guaranteed.

Table 2. Prediction error adaptation for the football video sequence (345 frames)

Target Quality		Calculated Quality		Search Point (SP)
MSE	**PSNR [dB]**	**MSE**	**PSNR [dB]**	
230	24.51	232.04	24.48	49.18
235	24.42	234.70	24.43	32.25
240	24.32	241.00	24.31	19.87
250	24.15	252.13	24.11	16.56

Box 2. Equation 5

$$P(u,v,i,j) \begin{cases} = 1 & if \left| F_n(k+i, l+j) - F_{n-1}(k+u+i, l+v+j) \right| \leq T_p \\ = 0 & \text{otherwise} \end{cases}$$

Among the various matching criteria therefore, MAE is the most popular and widely used in block motion estimation due to its low complexity, while its performance is comparable to that of MSE.

Motion Estimation Algorithm Complexity

Motion estimation algorithm optimisation has been widely studied because of their fundamental impact on compression efficiency and its high requirements in both processing power and data bandwidth.

In this section, a complexity analysis of motion estimation is reviewed. At the same time, the advantages and disadvantages of the different approaches, both in terms of compression quality and processing speed efficiency are characterised. Figure 1 showed the motion estimation process for the current macroblock of size $N \times N$ within a search range of $+/- d$ (horizontally and vertically) in the reference frame. To find a motion vector with minimum BDM for this current macroblock, the computational complexity of performing the motion estimation is given by:

$$Complx_{MB} = SP \times \left[\left(N \times N \right) \times Complx_p \right]$$

(6)

This shows that the complexity $Complx_{MB}$ is proportional to the number of *search points* SP, the number of pixels used to perform the matching ($N \times N$), and the complexity involved in evaluating one pixel match $Complx_p$. To illustrate the complexity, consider a typical application of a $\pm d$ pixels maximum displacement used for a video sequence with frame size $\left[N_h, N_v \right]$ and frame rate f fps (frames per second). The total number of integer arithmetic operations per second required for an MAE-based FS algorithm is

$$\left(\frac{N_h \times N_v}{N^2} \right) \times (2d + 1)^2 \times 3N^2 \times f$$

(7)

For example, for a typical MPEG-1 application of a 15×15 pixels search space used for a video sequence with SIF format (352×240 pixels) and 30 fps, based on (7), the FS algorithm requires about 1.71 billion integer arithmetic operations per second, which can consume up to 90% of the computational power of the whole encoding system (Moschetti, 2001). When considering applications which require encoding at higher resolutions and at higher quality, it is evident that the use of the FS algorithm becomes forbidding for a real-time implementation.

Fast Search Motion Estimation Algorithms

Most fast algorithms have been devised to save computation complexity of the FS algorithm at the price of impaired quality performance. The most common approach is to lower the search computation by reducing the number of Search Point (SP)in (6) insidethe defined search space. Normally, a fast search algorithm starts with a rough search, computing a set of scattered points. The distance between two nearby search points is called the search *step size*. After the first step is completed, the search moves to the most promising search point and continues with a next step. This process will be continued until satisfaction with some predefined conditions for motion estimation is established.

Jain & Jain (1984) first used a block-matching motion estimation for an interframe coding structure and proposed a fast search algorithm to reduce computation. Extensive work has been undertaken to extend their method. A number of fast block ME algorithms have been proposed to lower the computation complexity, for example, the 2-D logarithmic search (2DLOG) (Jain & Jain, 1984), the three-step search (TSS) (Koga et al., 1981), the new three-step search (NTSS) (Li et al., 1994), the advanced center biased search (Nisar & Choi, 2000), the four-step search (FSS) (Po & Ma, 1996), the cross-search (Ghanbari,

1990), the prediction search (Luo et al., 1997), the diamond search (DS) (Zhu & Ma, 2000), and the hexagon-based search (HEXBS) (Zhu et al., 2002; Zhu et al., 2004).

Most of the fast search algorithms assume that either the error surface is *unimodal* over the entire search area (i.e. there is only one global minimum) or the MV is centre-biased which will be elaborated later. These assumptions essentially require that either the BDM increases monotonically as the search point moves away from the global minimum position, or the MV is centrally distributed.

In reviewing the general attributes of the fast search algorithms, the following conclusions can be drawn.

The main advantages include:

- All existing fast BMAs reduce computational complexity in terms of the number of search points the FS algorithm takes to estimate motion vectors.
- Most have good regularity in terms of motion vector generation.

There are, however, a number of limitations associated with these fast BMAs:

- Lower complexity is achieved only by sacrificing the accuracy of the prediction.
- All are directional search techniques whose performance depends on the *unimodal error surface assumption* (USEA). There is a probability of falling into a local minimum if this assumption does not hold true always.
- The complexity factor increases with search area. The number of steps increases linearly with d so increasing the probability of falling into local minima.
- Application dependent. For example, TSS performs reasonably well on uniformly distributed motion video sequences but has very poor performance with centre-biased low motion video sequences. On the other

hand, the NTSS performs better with centre-biased motion distributed sequences (low motion) only.

- There is no single mechanism or parameter to provide any flexibility in controlling the quality as well as the complexity for motion estimation in different applications. None of the fast BMAs can satisfy any prescribed level of *Quality of Service* (QoS) in terms of prediction image quality or processing speed.
- Not suitable for real time software-only or low power video coding, which requires a more flexible approach to the trade-off between quality and complexity.

The various examples that have been included in this section used integer-pel accuracy motion estimation. While fast algorithms reduce computational complexity in terms of the number of search points by sacrificing image quality, the prediction quality of these search algorithms can be improved by considering sub-pel (Richardson, 2002; Chang & Leou, 2006) accuracy motion estimation.

Variants of Block Matching Algorithms

The fast search algorithms, based on UESA, described in previous sections, are designed to reduce computation in the process of finding the best matching block in the search window. There are some approaches which can in general be integrated into the BMAs mentioned in the previous sections so as to further improve the search efficiency. These algorithms are based on using the concept of *inter-block motion correlation* (Xu et al., 1999, Armanito & Schafer, 1996; Hsieh et al., 1990; Luo et al., 1997; Cheung et al., 1998; Lai & Wong, 2002; Lim & Choi, 2001; Feng et al. 2001; Nam et al., 2000), considering a subset of pels (pixel subsampling) inside the image blocks when computing the matching function (Liu & Zaccarin, 1993; Cao & Wei, 1997), and a multiresolution approach (Han & Hwang, 1998; Lim & Ra, 1997). There also exist some different fast-matching motion estimation techniques (Huang & Hung, 1997; Moshnyaga, 2001; Cheung & Po, 2000; Cheung & Po, 2001) which can also be integrated into the FS algorithm to improve its search efficiency by reducing the computational cost in the number of operations.

In the following section the different existing types of BMAs are described based on the above different options to improve the search efficiency for computational cost minimisation without or with low quality degradation.

Inter-Block (Spatio-Temporal) Correlation

The motion estimation search strategies previously described imply a fixed initial starting point that can be centered on the origin of the search window. However, the spatio/temporal correlation of the motion vector fields are often high and can be used to predict a better starting point, other than the centre of the search window, which reflects the current block's motion trend, and therefore, may lead to obtaining motion vectors with less BDM using fewer search points (Armanito & Schafer, 1996).

Indeed, usually the objects span over several macroblocks and move mostly uniformly from frame to frame. The motion correlation, in both spatial and/or temporal domain, among the neighbouring blocks can be used to predict a better starting point, other than the centre of the search window, which reflects the current block's motion trend, and therefore, may lead to obtain motion vectors with less BDM using fewer search points. Considering this, a motion tracking algorithm proposed in (Luo et al., 1997) used the previous frames' motion vectors in the neighborhood of the current block to form an initial estimate of the current block motion vector. Hsieh et al. (1990); Lai & Wong (2002); Lim & Choi (2001); Feng et al.(2001); Nam et al.(2000); Nisar & Choi (2009); Ishfaq et al. (2006); Luo et al. (2008) and Jiang et al. (2009)used spatial as well as temporal motion vector correlation as an offset vector to

track the motion vector of the current block. Luo et al. (1997) proposed an algorithm utilising the linear weighting of the motion vectors of the three adjacent blocks to obtain a prediction motion vector, namely the initial search point. Xu et al (1999); Cheung et al (1998) and Wen Jing Hao et al. (2012) used the spatial relation to predict the initial search centre and then used the centre-biased block matching algorithm (Hsieh et al., 1990; Luo et al., 1997) to refine the final motion vectors. Xie et al. (2012) proposed a fast algorithm considering spatio-temporal correlation to predict the search starting point and dynamically adjust the search range and pattern to improve the search efficiency. All these approaches have the following advantages and disadvantages:

These methods provide the following advantages

- Incorporating these schemes in any fast search algorithms reduces the computational cost and motion vector overhead.
- It also increases the possibility of finding the global minima.

However, the major disadvantages:

- In case of acceleration or moving object boundaries, this technique may become trapped in local minima due to inaccurate initial estimates.
- Temporal correlation requires a large memory buffer to keep the previous frame motion vectors in the decoder.

Although this technique has the abovementioned limitations, these only apply for temporal, not spatial, correlation.

Pixel Subsampling

Since block-matching is based on the assumption that all pixels move in the same way, a good estimate can be obtained by using only a fraction of the pixels in the block to be matched. As this approach only considers a subset of the pixels in the matching macroblock, it reduces overall computational complexity in terms of the number of operations required for motion vector estimation.

A straightforward approach to pixel subsampling is to adopt a fixed chess-board like pattern with subsampling factors ranging from two to eight with an equivalent saving in complexity. An example of this class of fast algorithm is the simple 4:1 pixels subsampling technique (Liu & Zaccarin, 1993; Cao & Wei, 1997).However, since only a uniform fraction of the pixels are used in the matching computation, the use of these standard subsampling techniques can seriously affect the accuracy of motion vector detection, and the computational cost is only reduced by four compared to the FS algorithm. Liu & Zaccarin (1993) propose a popular subsampling algorithm referred to as alternating pixel subsampling. This corresponding 4:1 pixel subsampling pattern consists of alternating over the locations searched so that all pixels of a block contribute to the computation of the motion vector. Figure 3 shows a block of 8×8 pixels with each pixel labeled as a,b,c, or d in a regular pattern. This method considers all four subsampling patterns, but only one at each location of the search area, and in a specific alternating manner. The one that has minimum BDM among the four is selected as the motion vector for the block. Alternating between these patterns allows using all the pixels of the current block and all the pixels of the search area. Though the performance is better than the standard 4:1 subsampling method, the computational complexity of the FS algorithm is also reduced only by a factor of four. In 1997, Chan *et al.* propose an adaptive pixel subsampling technique instead of the regular pixel pattern in (Liu & Zaccarin, 1993), where a lesser number of pixels are considered with uniform intensity blocks, and more pixels are considered with high active blocks for the BDM calculation. Li & Salari (1995) address a successive elimination algorithm (SEA) to obtain the best-matched block by successive eliminating the positions in

computing the SAD. Based on SEA, Chen et al. (2008) give a successively elimination algorithm with integral frame (SEAIF), which further improves the performance of conventional SEA. The above mentioned subsampling algorithms have the following advantages and disadvantages:

- **Advantages:**
  - All the macroblock positions in the search area are covered.
  - Regular data flow and easy generation of candidate motion vectors, while pixels extraction complexity is dependent on the algorithm used.
- **Disadvantages:**
  - Only a small complexity reduction factor is achieved (typically four to eight) which is often inadequate for real-time applications.
  - High probability of falling into local minimum if a scene contains a lot of spatial detail.
  - The special structure of alternating pixels subsampling makes it difficult to embed within algorithms such as TSS and NTSS.

Figure 3. Alternating patterns of pixels used for computing the matching criterion with a 4 to 1 subsampling ratio

a	b	a	b	a	b	a	b
c	d	c	d	c	d	c	d
a	b	a	b	a	b	a	b
c	d	c	d	c	d	c	d
a	b	a	b	a	b	a	b
c	d	c	d	c	d	c	d
a	b	d	b	a	b	a	b
c	d	c	d	c	d	c	d

Hierarchical Block Matching Algorithm

A different approach, the *hierarchical block-matching* proposed in (Han & Hwang, 1998; Lim & Ra; 1997), can improve the prediction performance of the BMA. The basic principles are similar and can be summarised as follows. A large block size is chosen at the beginning to obtain a rough estimate of the motion vector. By considering a large block, the ambiguity problem – blocks of similar content – can often be eliminated. However, motion vectors estimated from large blocks are not accurate. It is then possible to refine the estimated motion vectors by decreasing the block size and the search region. A new search with smaller block size starts from an initial motion vector that is the best matched motion vector in the previous stage. As the pels in a small block are more likely to share the same motion vector, the reduction of block size typically increases the motion vector accuracy. In hierarchical block matching (multiresolution), the basic idea is to perform motion estimation at each level successively, starting with the lowest resolution level. The estimate of the motion vector at a lower resolution level is then passed onto the next higher resolution level as an initial estimate. The motion estimation at the higher levels refines the motion vector at the lower one. This technique has the following properties:

- **Advantages:**
  - All the blocks in the searching area are likely to be covered.
- **Disadvantages:**
  - Memory requirement is increased because of subsampling and pre-stage filtering and the need to store images at several resolutions.
  - Lower accuracy because of the high probability of local minima when the scene contains a lot of spatial details (depends on subsampling factors).

The above discussion leads to the conclusion that although there are a number of block-based motions estimation algorithms available, there still remain many challenges. Amongst the key issues are directionality, application dependency, performance scalability for QoS, and flexibility for real time software or low power video coding applications.

This therefore, motivates the development of a general system, which can be used under all conditions; is non-directional; is scalable for any level of quality of services; and provides flexibility in performance management for real time video coding applications, especially software-only and low power video coding, where available resources are restricted. This will be discussed in the following section

Distance-Dependent Thresholding Search Algorithm: A Promising Approach

In this section, a non-directional *Distance-dependent Thresholding Search* (DTS) block motion estimation algorithm is presented that employs the novel concept of distance dependent thresholds. This algorithm is based on one key finding from real world video sequences—this is that the distortion of an object in any video frame increases with its velocity, as well as camera zoom and pan factors. To accommodate this key finding, the DTS algorithm uses a "parametric" thresholding function to terminate the search even at relatively high BDM values, especially when the length of the motion vector tends to increase. The DTS algorithm encompasses both the FS and very fast searching modes. Different threshold settings can provide different QoS levels and therefore the DTS algorithm provides a general solution for all types of video sequences and coding demands. This unique feature provides good flexibility in controlling performance, especially the computational complexity required for motion estimation in real-time video coding applications.

Moreover, the non-directional nature of the DTS algorithm means it does not suffer from potential difficulties due to the UESA. Parts of this work were published in Sorwar et al. (2007).

Rationale in Distance-Dependent Thresholding

Before introducing the full DTS algorithm, a series of key definitions are provided.

Definition 1: Consider two points with Cartesian coordinates (x_1, y_1) and (x_2, y_2). The Euclidean distance, City-block distance, and City-block-max distance between these two points are calculated as $\sqrt{\left(x_1 - x_2\right)^2 + \left(y_1 - y_2\right)^2}$, $\left|x_1 - x_2\right| + \left|y_1 - y_2\right|$, and $\max\left(\left|x_1 - x_2\right|, \left|y_1 - y_2\right|\right)$ respectively.

It is interesting to note that the trajectory of a point maintaining constant Euclidean distance, City-block-max distance, or City-block distance from a fixed point traces a circle, a square, and a diamond shape respectively.

Definition 2 (Search Squares SS_τ): The search space with maximum displacement $\pm d$, centred at pixel $p_{cx,cy}$, can be divided into $d+1$ mutually exclusive concentric search squares SS_τ, such that a checking point at pixel $p_{x,y}$, representing motion vector $(x - cx, y - cy)$, is in SS_τ if, and only if, the city-block-max distance (Definition 3.1) of the motion vector is $\max\left(\left|x - cx\right|, \left|y - cy\right|\right) = \tau$, for all $-d + cx \leq x \leq d + cx$, $-d + cy \leq y \leq d + cy$, and search square index $\tau = 0, 1, \ldots, d$.

It can be readily verified that the number of checking points in search square SS_τ,

$$\left|SS_\tau\right| = \begin{cases} 1, & \tau = 0 \\ 8\tau, & \tau = 1, 2, \ldots, d \end{cases} \qquad (8)$$

and SS_τ represents the motion vectors of city-block-max distance τ that translates to a conventional Euclidean distance (Definition 1) in the range of $[\tau, \tau\sqrt{2}]$ for all $0 \leq \tau \leq d$. The checking points used in the first three search squares, SS_0, SS_1, and SS_2 are shown in Figure 4.

Figure 4. DTS search squares SS_0, SS_1, and SS_2

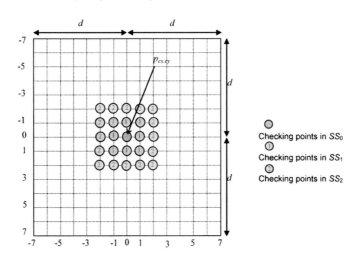

Definition 3 (Cumulative Probability): Consider a continuous probability function $f(t)$ in the range of fully ordered events $0 \leq t \leq T$ such that $\int_{0}^{T} f(t)dt = 1$. The cumulative probability function $F(t)$ of this probability function $f(t)$ is defined as

$$F(t) = \int_{0}^{t} f(x)dx \qquad (9)$$

for all $0 \leq t \leq T$.

The cumulative probability of an event represents the probability of all possible events up to and including that event, and it can be verified that $F(t_1) \leq F(t_2)$ if and only if $t_1 \leq t_2$ and $F(T) = 1$.

Now consider that the average MAE per pixel of a macroblock is used as the BDM in the FS algorithm. For each macroblock, the FS algorithm looks for the minimum MAE per pixel value in the range of $[0,2^b-1]$ for a b-bit gray scale image.

In Lim & Ho (1998) and Feng et al. (1998) it was proved that the magnitude of a motion vector is proportional to the magnitude of the BDM. This observation has been explored further on a number of standard and non-standard video sequences covering a wide range of object and camera motions. In Figure 5, the cumulative probabilities of minimum MAE are plotted for a search squares on a Football sequence. The minimum MAE is calculated for each search square of macroblocks in the first 80 frames. In each search square, the probability of each distinct minimum MAE is calculated based on the frequency, and cumulative probability using (9).

To interpret these graphs, consider the cumulative probability of finding a minimum MAE of 20 or less in individual search square of the video sequence. It can easily be followed that the cumulative probability gradually decreases from 0.64 to 0.13 and then to 0.01 as the city-block-max distance of a motion vector increases from 0 to 1 and then to 7. This means as the motion vector length increases, so does the probability of terminating the FS algorithm at a higher MAE value. This observation can be enhanced further by the horizontal extension shown in Figure 5 at a cumulative probability of 0.64, which reveals that the minimum MAE increases from 20 to 43 and 54 as the city-block-max distance of a motion vector increases from 0 to 1 and then to 7. Figure 5 therefore, reveals the following:

Figure 5. The cumulative probability of minimum MAE for different search squares on the first 80 frames of football video sequences

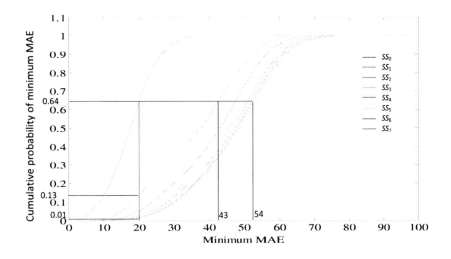

- The cumulative probability of having a particular minimum MAE decreases as the motion vector length increases.
- The minimum MAE, at which the cumulative probability first reaches the value 1, increases as the motion vector length increases.

Both these findings reveal that the probability of terminating the FS algorithm at a higher MAE value increases with the length of the motion vector.

Based on these observations, the key finding is that the distortion of an object in a video frame increases with its velocity, as well as the zoom and pan factors of the camera. As the length of the motion vector grows, so does the distortion error. It can be therefore concluded that locating a block with a minimum prediction error but with a motion vector of high length, is not only ineffectual in the prevailing distorted search space, but may lead to *false* motion vectors being erroneously selected.

This elegantly leads to a potential solution to the challenge raised in the background section of developing a non-directional search algorithm which is comparable in terms of speed to the other fast directional search algorithm, while providing improved image quality. A non-directional search can be effectively made faster if the search is not only directed by the sole desire of reaching the global minima unconditionally but also terminated for a relatively high BDM once the current minimum BDM exceeds a threshold value, which also increases as the search moves away from the centre.

By making the thresholding function distance-dependent, the search can be controlled by a user defined parameter, so this new search algorithm can be transformed from the qualitatively best, but slow, FS algorithm to extremely fast searches which trade-off quality for search speed. This search technique thus provides an effective control

mechanism for performance scalability and QoS by trading between predicted image quality and processing time in motion estimation.

Being non-directional and incorporating a relationship between distortion, object velocity and camera factors, this new *Distance-dependent-Thresholding Search* (DTS) algorithm affords the potential of capturing more *true* object motion vectors compared with other directional fast search algorithms and non-directional FS algorithm.

The DTS algorithm is now presented in detail with an analysis of the influence of using linear and non-linear thresholding functions.

The Distance-Dependent Thresholding Search (DTS) Algorithm

Definition 4: $MAE_{(cx,cy)}(u,v)$ denotes the Mean Absolute Error per pixel of the macroblock centred at pixel $p_{cx,cy}$ in the current frame with respect to the block centred at pixel $p_{cx+\mathbf{u},cy+\mathbf{v}}$ in the reference frame.

The Algorithm

Like all block-base motion estimation search techniques, the DTS algorithm starts at the centre of the search space. The search then progresses outwards by using search squares, SS_r in order while monitoring the current minimum MAE. A parametric thresholding function, *Threshold*(r,C), is used to determine the various thresholds to be used for the search involving each SS_r, where the parameter C is set at the start of each search and acts as a control parameter as alluded above. After searching each SS_r, the current minimum MAE is compared against the threshold value of that specific search square and the search is terminated if this MAE value is not higher than the threshold value. The DTS algorithm is formally presented in Figure 6.

Figure 6. The DTS algorithm

- **Parameter** C
- **Precondition:** Pixel $p_{cx,cy}$ is the centre of the search space with maximum displacement d.
- **Initialisation:**
  $MAE_{min} = MAE_{(cx,cy)}(0,0)$ (Definition 4)
  $MV = (0,0)$
- **Main Algorithm:**
  If $MAE_{min} > 0$ Then
      For $\tau = 1, 2, ..., d$
        For each checking point $p_{x,y}$ in SS_{τ}
          $e = MAE_{(cx,cy)}(x\text{-}cx, y\text{-}cy)$
          If $e < MAE_{min}$ Then
            $MAE_{min} = e$
            $MV = (x\text{-}cx, y\text{-}cy)$
        If $MAE_{min} \leq Threshold(\tau, C)$ Then STOP
- **Postcondition:** MV contains the motion vector and MAE_{min} contains the distortion error of the respective block.

Characteristics of the Thresholding Function

To make sure that the DTS algorithm can be transformed to an exhaustive FS algorithm, the threshold value for SS_0 is always assumed to be 0. As the maximum MAE value using a b-bit gray level intensity is 2^b-1, threshold values for all other search squares can at most be 2^b-1. However, to ensure the algorithm includes the entire search space, all but the outermost threshold value must be less than 2^b-1. Moreover, to make the thresholding function distance dependent, the function must be monotonically increasing.

The DTS algorithm therefore assumes the following general properties of the thresholding function:

$$Threshold(0, C) = 0 \qquad (10)$$

$$Threshold(1, C) \leq Threshold(2, C)$$
$$\leq ... \leq Threshold(d, C) \qquad (11)$$

$$Threshold\,(\tau, C) < 2^b - 1, \text{ for all}$$
$$\tau = 1, 2, ..., d-1 \qquad (12)$$

$$Threshold(d, C) \leq 2^b - 1 \qquad (13)$$

Parameter C plays a significant role in the DTS algorithm by allowing users to define different sets of monotonically increasing threshold values based on specific values of C. Obviously, a set of larger threshold values terminates a search earlier than a set of smaller values. C therefore, provides a control mechanism to allow trading-off between the computational complexity in terms of search points and prediction image quality.

The monotonic increasing function requirement means the DTS algorithm could use a linear, exponential, or any other complex analytic function to control C. In the next two sections, linear and exponential thresholding functions within the DTS algorithm will be explored.

Linear Thresholding (LT) Function

A linear thresholding function can be defined as follows:

$$Threshold(\tau, C_L) = C_L \times \tau, \text{ for all}$$
$$\tau = 0, 1, ..., d \qquad (14)$$

The above notation uses subscript L for the parameter C to specify linear thresholding, while in the next section, subscript E is used to indicate exponential thresholding.

It can be verified that the above definition satisfies conditions (10) and (11) if $C_L \geq 0$. In order to satisfy the remaining two properties in (12) and (13), $C_L \times d \leq 2^b - 1$, i.e., $C_L \leq \dfrac{2^b - 1}{d}$.

So, the range of values for parameter C_L is

$$0 \leq C_L \leq \frac{2^b - 1}{d} \qquad (15)$$

Exponential Thresholding (ET) Function

An exponential thresholding function can be defined as follows:

$$Threshold(\tau, C_E) = \begin{cases} 0 & \text{if } \tau = 0 \\ 2^{\tau/C_E} & \text{otherwise} \end{cases} \qquad (16)$$

The above definition satisfies conditions (10) and (11) if $C_E > 0$. In order to satisfy the remaining two properties in (12) and (13), $2^{d/C_E} \leq 2^b - 1$, i.e., $C_E \geq \dfrac{2^b - 1}{\log_2(2^b - 1)}$. So, the range of values for parameter C_E is

$$\frac{d}{\log_2(2^b - 1)} \leq C_E \leq \infty \qquad (17)$$

Selecting the Thresholding Control Parameter

The values of C_L and C_E have a significant influence on the level of computation, the quality of the motion vector, and the prediction error. In the previous section, the upper and lower limits on the values of C_L and C_E were defined. To clarify the nomenclature, the DTS algorithm using the linear thresholding parameter C_L and exponential thresholding parameter C_E are denoted as LT(C_L) and ET(C_E) respectively in this chapter.

The choice of C_L involves a trade-off between the quality of the motion estimation and the computational complexity. When LT(0) in (14), the search terminating threshold value of any search square (SS) is zero. In this case, the DTS algorithm translates into the exhaustive FS algorithm as there is no threshold to terminate the search until all possible locations in the search space have been visited. Conversely, when C_L is very high in

(14), the DTS algorithm is fast as the probability of getting the minimum BDM within the search terminating threshold limit is high, especially around the search centre. In case of low motion video sequences, such as *Salesman* and *Miss America,* where MV distribution is centre-biased a high C_L performs well with low computation. Conversely, for high motion video sequences, such as *Football* and *Flower Garden,* where the motion vector distribution is not centre-biased, a high C_L may stop the search with an inaccurate motion vector and high prediction error.

The effect of the exponential control parameter will now be considered. ET with low value, the DTS algorithm will be faster than the FS algorithm. If the value of C_E is higher, for example ET(7), the threshold value for all search squares, except the centre, becomes a maximum of 2. In this case, the likelihood of a BDM being within this small range is low for most types of video sequence, especially if it is non-stationary. Therefore, a high value of C_E means the DTS algorithm moves towards the original FS algorithm.

Empirical results indicated that the LT function provides full flexibility in controlling the computational complexity for real-time video coding applications, and since complexity management is crucial for such applications, only linear thresholding has been considered in the proposed algorithm.

Computational Complexity of the DTS Algorithm

The computational complexity of a motion estimation algorithm is usually expressed in terms of either the number of search points or operations that the algorithm requires to calculate the motion vectors. The complexity of the DTS algorithm is analysed in terms of the average number of search points considered for calculating the best matching block for each candidate block. However, since the DTS process calculates the motion vectors by considering all pixels of the current and candidate block, the number of operations is directly proportional to the number of search points. As stated earlier that only the LT function will be considered for the DTS algorithm, so consequently the complexity of the LT-based DTS algorithm will be discussed.

Consider a motion estimation system with the following parameters: frame size = $[N_h, N_v]$; macroblock size = $N \times N$; maximum motion vector displacement = $\pm d$; and temporal frequency = f frames per second. If there are Ω number of operations required for BDM calculation of one search point, then the FS algorithm requires a maximum $\psi = \Omega(2d + 1)^2 \varsigma$ operations per second using integer-pel accuracy, where ς is the total number of macroblocks per second,

$$\varsigma = \left(\frac{N_h N_v}{N^2}\right) f.$$

The DTS algorithm requires extra d operations to compare the current minimum BDM with the predefined threshold of each search square, for each macrboblock, while searching the entire search space. The total number of extra operations required per second is therefore $d\varsigma$.

Hence, for the LT function DTS algorithm with control parameter $C_L = 0$ (the FS case), the number of operations required per second is: -

$$\psi + d\varsigma \tag{18}$$

which is the upper computational bound, and thus the worst case scenario for computational complexity.

Conversely, using a very high threshold value, when only the corresponding centre of the search space is checked, only one operation is required to compare the BDM found at the search centre with a predefined threshold for each macroblock. So, the number of extra operations required per second is ς, and the total number of operations required per second is:-

$$\varsigma(\Omega + 1) \tag{19}$$

which forms the lower bound. From (18) and (19), the computational complexity based on user-defined levels is always bounded between $\varsigma(\Omega + 1)$ and $\psi + d\varsigma$ operations per second for the DTS algorithm using an LT function.

When half-pel accuracy is used for motion estimation, eight neighbouring half-pel positions around the current minimum point, obtained with integer-pel accuracy, are checked. In this case, the upper and lower bound of computational complexity of the DTS algorithm increase by another $8\varsigma\Omega$ operations per second.

Experimental Analysis of the DTS Algorithm

The purpose of this section is to present the results of experiments to demonstrate the DTS algorithm's performance scalability and the searching efficiency. To compare the searching efficiency, its performance is compared against a number of well-known fast search algorithms such as FS, TSS, NTSS, DS, HEXBS, and EHEXBS in terms of quality-speed measurement where quality and speed are measured as MSE per pixel and SP per motion vector respectively. All algorithms were implemented to compute the block-based inter-frame motion vectors from the luminance (Y-component) signal of a number of high and low motion standard test video sequences such as *Football* (320 × 240 pixels, 345 frames), *Flower Garden* (352 × 240 pixels, 150 frames), *Salesman* (352 × 288 pixels, 150 frames), *Miss America* (176 × 144 pixels, 150 frames), *Tennis* (352 × 240 pixels, 150 frames), and *Foreman* (176 × 144 pixels, 298 frames). DTS performed consistently well for all of them, results of the two most challenging sequences, *Football* and *Flower Garden* with heavy object motion and camera panning respectively, are presented in this section.

All sequences were uniformly quantised to an 8-bit gray level intensity. The block size dimensions $[N, N]$ and maximum displacement d were considered as [16,16] and ±7 respectively throughout the experiments. A maximum of $(2d+1)^2 = 225$ checking points were used, and the MAE distortion measure was used as the matching criterion. In all cases, the centre of the search window was examined first, and if the MAE = 0, then the search was immediately terminated without checking any further points.

To isolate improvement due to motion search technique only, motion estimation was carried out differently than is done for video coding so that any influence of rate-distortion optimisation (Sullivan & Wiegand, 1998) and error propagation can be avoided. For each pair of successive frames, motion was estimated for the second frame using the original version of the first frame (not the motion compensated version of that frame as is used for video coding) as the reference and MSE per pixel was averaged using the first frame and the motion compensated second frame. As no entropy coding was used to compress the residual, this MSE measure was higher than what could be achieved by a video coder with residual encoding. However, this MSE measure correlates highly with residual compression and thus still represents quality of the image, if rate-distortion trade off is factored in. All the results are shown with half-pel accuracy motion estimation.

Average MSE per pixel values and average search point numbers per motion vector for different non-adaptive algorithms are summarised in Table 1. While FS achieves the maximum quality with the minimum average MSE per pixel for each sequence, the speed gain of DS, HEXBS and EHEXBS over TSS is clearly evident.

The performance of the DTS algorithm was tested and evaluated for quality and speed adaptation as follows.

Quality Adaptation

The performance of the DTS algorithm for quality adaptation is presented in Tables 2 and 3 for a number of different target values for the *Football* and *Flower Garden* sequences. From these tables,

it can be seen that the DTS algorithm achieved all target demands in terms of predicted image quality and processing speed. For example, targets were set to estimate motion with an average 230 MSE or 24.51 dB PSNR image quality for the *Football* sequence and 215 MSE or 24.81dB PSNR image quality for the *FlowerGarden* sequence. It is shown that the DTS algorithm satisfied these demands providing MSE or PSNR very close to targets such as 232.04 MSE or 24.48 dB PSNR for the *Football* sequence, and 214.41 MSE or 24.82 dB PSNR for the *Flower Garden* sequence, with average search points 49.18 and 24.54, respectively. The flexibility of the DTS algorithm for QoS demand was investigated by setting different targets, for example, a target of average 250 MSE or 24.15 PSNR for the *Football* sequence, and 225 MSE or 24.61 PSNR for the *Flower Garden* sequence. Tables 2 and 3 show that the DTS algorithm, again, satisfied these demands by calculating motion with 252.13 MSE or 24.11PSNR for the *Football* sequence, and 222.79 MSE or 24.65 PSNR for the *Flower Garden* sequence, while reducing computational cost almost 3 and 1.6 times respectively compared to previous demand. These settings reveal that the DTS algorithm is able to reach any bounded target level of quality, with the implicit assumption that the minimum target error obtained by FS is the lower bound. Note that if a target is set so high that the resultant C_l exceeds $C_{l_{max}}$ to achieve the target, the DTS algorithm will fail. However, defining such a high target is very unlikely, as it will produce an extremely poor quality output.

Search Point Adaptation

The performance of the DTS algorithm for computational scalability in terms of the average number of search points (SP) per motion vector was tested with a number of targets, i.e., average search points considered. Table 4 shows some of

Table 3. Prediction error adaptation for the flower garden video sequence (150 frames)

Target Quality		Actual Quality		Search Point (SP)
MSE	PSNR [dB]	MSE	PSNR [dB]	
210	24.91	212.80	24.85	34.95
215	24.81	214.41	24.82	24.58
220	24.71	218.62	24.73	16.65
225	24.61	222.79	24.65	15.21

these targets and the actual values obtained by the DTS algorithm for the *Football* and *Flower Garden* video sequences.

Table 4 indicates that the DTS algorithm can satisfy all user demand for different computational complexity in terms of the average number of search points. For example, consider the target search points of average 20 SP, for the *Football* sequence, and 15 SP for the *Flower Garden* sequence, per motion vector. From Table 4, it can be observed that the DTS algorithm satisfied these demands by estimating motion vector with an average 20.10 and 15.52 SP, where the prediction image quality in terms of PSNR was average 24.27 and 24.70 dB for the *Football* and *Flower Garden* sequences, respectively. Another example, with the targets of average 30 SP for the *Football* sequence, and 25 SP for the *Flower Garden* sequence is in Table 4, which demonstrates that the DTS algorithm satisfied the demands of the target estimating motion vector with an average 29.89 and

24.69 SP, with 24.41 and 24.81 dB PSNR, respectively.

From Tables 1, 2, 3, and 4, it is clear that the DTS algorithm not only satisfied any user defined targets, but also showed better error performance with computational complexity. For the *Football* sequence, while DTS outperformed TSS and NTSS in terms of both quality and speed adaptations, its performance is comparable to DS, HEXBS, and FHEXBS algorithms. Conversely, for the *Flower Garden* sequence, DTS maintained the same performance as NTSS and provided superior results over all other fast algorithms for both adaptations.

This is because the DTS algorithm adaptively selects the threshold control parameter to limit the search for different frames with different content, whereas a directional fast algorithm, such as TSS, always searches for 25 points irrespective of the content variation. It is shown by certain authors (Li et al., 1994; Po & Ma, 1996; Zhu & Ma, 2000; Luo et al., 1997;Cheung et al., 1998) most of the macroblocks in a video sequence are stationary or quasi-stationary in nature. In this case, the DTS algorithm stopped searching after using a smaller number of search points with similar error performance. No other existing fast directional algorithm provides such a level of flexibility in trading off predicted image quality and computational complexity, whereas the DTS algorithm demonstrates considerable flexibility in providing target-driven services, especially in terms of computational complexity.

Table 4. Speed adaptation for the football and flower garden video sequences (345, and 150 frames respectively)

Football sequence				Flower Garden sequence			
Target SP	Actual SP	Actual Error		Target SP	Actual SP	Actual Error	
		MSE	PSNR [dB]			MSE	PSNR [dB]
20	20.10	243.00	24.27	15	15.52	220.54	24.70
25	24.99	237.82	24.37	20	19.68	216.27	24.78
30	29.89	235.32	24.41	25	24.69	214.85	24.81
40	39.08	230.22	24.51	30	29.68	214.19	24.82

If *rate-distortion* (RD) optimisation technique (Sullivan & Wiegand, 1998) is embedded into a motion search algorithm, longer motion vectors are less likely to be selected as they incur more bits to encode. Our experimental results reveal that DTS used on average no more than 25 search points per MV to achieve the target MSE per pixel compared with the DS or HEXBS algorithms, so it can be reasonably concluded that majority of the motion vectors selected by DTS were bounded by the search diamond SD_3 with motion vectors being no longer than three pixels, which is in fact less than one third of the maximum feasible length of $7\sqrt{2} \approx 10$ pixels. While DS and HEXBS used a similar number of search points, being directional no similar conclusion can be drawn on the length of their motion vectors, so RD optimisation will therefore affect DTS no more than it does affect DS and HEXBS.

CONCLUSION AND FUTURE RESEARCH DIRECTIONS

In this chapter, a comprehensive review of various motion estimation techniques, especially different block-matching motion estimation techniques has been provided. It is clear that a number of key issues in block motion estimation remain to be resolved in accommodating performance scalability in real-time video coding applications. In particular, none of the existing techniques can be seen as a complete solution for all types of motion video sequences. All the fast algorithms are directional and based on the *unimodal error surface assumption (UESA)*, which does not always hold true in real world video sequences. Moreover, these fast algorithms are not designed to provide any flexibility for performance management in motion estimation for QoS in terms of prediction image quality or computational complexity (processing speed). To address the issues with existing algorithms, a promising approach, *Distance-dependent*

Thresholding Search (DTS) motion search, has been presented for performance management block-based motion estimation in real-time video coding applications. The key feature of this approach is the progressive adjusting of the required threshold control value by an adaptive process based on the previous frames information for achieving any specified user demand in terms prediction quality or processing speed. This flexibility has considerable potential for exploitation in a wide range of applications ranging from low-bit rate video conferencing, through to adaptive high-quality video coding. This adaptive algorithm is especially important for complexity management in software-only video coding or low power coding (mobile or handheld computing platform), which requires more flexible approach in trading off between predicted image quality and computational complexity. This would extend the capabilities of the H.264/AVC design to address the needs of applications to make video coding more flexible for use in highly heterogeneous and time –varying environments.

Recently, Distributed Source Coding (DSC) based video coding has gained research attention due to its ability of flexibly transferring computational complexity from the encoder to the decoder by performing the motion search at the decoder (Ali & Murshed, 2010). A computationally light video encoder is desirable in power-constrained devices such as handheld devices and microminiaturized edible cameras to capture and transmit real-time video without draining its battery power too fast. Such an encoder has to rely on a computationally heavy decoder capable of performing motion search to exploit temporal correlation. In absence of the current block at the decoder, it has to perform motion estimation using already decoded neighbouring blocks. This will ultimately compromise the quality of motion search. To achieve two-way video conferencing between two power-constrained devices, it is also important to keep the complexity of the decoder in check. So, the three-way rate-distortion-complexity optimization we have introduced in DTS will be even more important in this context. We aim to explore the effectiveness of DTS in future DSC-based video coding.

REFERENCES

Aggarwal, J. K., & Nandhakumar, N. (1988). On the computation of motion from sequences of images-A review. *Proceedings of the IEEE, 76,* 917–935. doi:10.1109/5.5965

Ali, M., & Murshed, M. (2010). Motion compensation for block-based lossless video coding using lattice-based binning. In the *Proceedings of International Symposium on Circuits and Systems,* (pp. 2183-2186).

Armanito, R., & Schafer, R. (1996). Motion vector estimation using spatio-temporal prediction and its application to video coding. In the *Proceedings of International Conference of SPIE- Digital Video Compression,* San Jose, CA, Vol. 2668, (pp. 290-301).

Barron, J. L., Fleet, D. J., & Beauchemin, S. S. (1994). Performance of optical flow techniques. *International Journal of Computer Vision, 12,* 43–77. doi:10.1007/BF01420984

Boroczky, L. (1991). *Pel-recursive motion estimation for image coding.* Delft University of Technology.

Cao, N., & Wei, B. W. Y. (1997). A 4:1 checkerboard algorithm for motion estimation. In the *Proceedings of International Conference of SPIE- the International Society for Optical Engineering,* Vol. 2847, (pp. 408-412).

Chan, Y.-L., Hui, W.-L., & Siu, W.-C. (1997). A block motion vector estimation using pattern based pixel decimation. In the *Proceedings of IEEE International Symposium on Circuits and Systems,* Hong Kong, Vol. 2, (pp. 1153-1156).

Chang, J. F., & Leou, J. J. (2006). A quadratic prediction basedfractional-pixel motion estimation algorithm for H.264. *Journal of Visual Communication and Image Representation, 17,* 1074–1089. doi:10.1016/j.jvcir.2006.01.001

Chen, V. W., Hsiao, M. H., Chen, H. T., Liu, C. Y., & Lee, S. Y. (2008). Content-aware fast motion estimation algorithm. *Journal of Visual Communication and Image Representation, 19,* 256–296. doi:10.1016/j.jvcir.2008.01.002

Cheung, C.-H., & Po, L.-M. (2001). A fast block motion estimation using progressive partial distortion search. In the *Proceedings of International Symposium on Intelligent Multimedia, Video and Speech Processing,* Hong Kong, (pp. 406-409).

Cheung, C.-K., & Po, L.-M. (2000). Normalized partial distortion search algorithm for block motion estimation. *IEEE Transactions on Circuits and Systems for Video Technology, 10,* 417–422. doi:10.1109/76.836286

Cheung, P. Y. S., Chung, H. Y., & Yung, N. H. C. (1998). Adaptive search center non-linear three step search. In the *Proceedings of International Conference on Image Processing (ICIP '98),* (pp. 191-194).

Dufaux, F., & Moscheni, F. (1995). Motion estimation techniques for digital TV: A review and a new contribution. *Proceedings of the IEEE, 83,* 858–876. doi:10.1109/5.387089

Feng, J., Liu, T. Y., Lo, K. T., & Zhang, X. D. (2001). Adaptive motion tracking for fast block motion estimation. In the *Proceedings of IEEE International Symposium on Circuits and Systems,* Sydney, NSW, Australia, Vol. 5, (pp. 219-222).

Feng, J., Lo, K.-T., Mehrpour, H., & Karbowiak, A. E. (1998). Adaptive block matching algorithm for video compression. *IEE Proceedings. Vision Image and Signal Processing, 145,* 173–178. doi:10.1049/ip-vis:19981916

Ghanbari, M. (1990). The cross-search algorithm for motion estimation (image coding). *IEEE Transactions on Communications, 38*(7), 950–953. doi:10.1109/26.57512

Han, T.-H., & Hwang, S. H. (1998). A novel hierarchical-search block matchingalgorithm and VLSI architecture considering the spatial complexity of the macroblock. *IEEE Transactions on Consumer Electronics, 44*, 337–342. doi:10.1109/30.681947

Hsieh, C.-H., Lu, P., Shyn, J.-S., & Lu, E.-H. (1990). Motion estimation algorithm using interblock correlation. *Electronics Letters, 26*, 276–277. doi:10.1049/el:19900183

Huang, H.-C., & Hung, Y.-P. (1997). Adaptive early jump-out technique for fast motion estimation in video coding. *Graphical Models & Image Processing, 59*, 388–394. doi:10.1006/gmip.1997.0449

Ishfaq, A., Weiguo, Z., Jiancong, L., & Ming, L. (2006). A fast adaptive motion estimation algorithm. *IEEE Transactions on Circuits and Systems for Video Technology, 16*(3), 420–438. doi:10.1109/TCSVT.2006.870022

Jain, J. R., & Jain, A. K. (1984). Displacement measurement and its application in inter frame image coding. *IEEE Transactions on Communications, 29*, 1799–1808. doi:10.1109/TCOM.1981.1094950

Jiang, W., Latecki, L. J., Liu, W., Liang, H., & Gorman, K. (2009). A video coding scheme based on joint spatiotemporal and adaptive prediction. *IEEE Transactions on Image Processing, 8*(5), 1025–I036. doi:10.1109/TIP.2009.2016140

Kearney, J. K., Thomson, W. B., & Boley, D. L. (1987). Optical flow estimation: An error analysis of gradient-based methods with local optimization. *IEEE Transactions on Pattern Analysis and Machine Intelligence, 9*, 229–244. doi:10.1109/TPAMI.1987.4767897

Koga, T., Iinuma, K., Hirano, A., Iijima, Y., & Ishiguro, T. (1981). Motion compensated inter frame coding for videoconferencing. In *Proceedings of the National Telecommunications Conference*, New Orleans, LA, December (pp. G5. 3.1–G5.3.5).

Lai, K. C., & Wong, S. C. (2002). A fast motion estimation using a three-dimensional reference motion vector. *International Conference on Acoustics, Speech, and Signal Processing (ICASSP 2002)*, Vol. 4, (pp. 3429-3432).

Li, R., Zeng, B., & Liou, M. L. (1994). A new three-step search algorithm for block motion estimation. *IEEE Transactions on Circuits and Systems for Video Technology, 4*, 438–442. doi:10.1109/76.313138

Li, W., & Salari, E. (1995). Successive elimination algorithm for motion estimation. *IEEE Transactions on Image Processing, 4*(1), 105–107. doi:10.1109/83.350809

Lim, D.-K., & Ho, Y.-S. (1998). A fast block matching motion estimation algorithm based on statistical properties of object displacement. In the *Proceedings of IEEE Region 10 International Conference on Global Connectivity in Energy, Computer, Communication and control*, Vol. 1, (pp. 138-141).

Lim, J.-H., & Choi, H.-W. (2001). Adaptive motion estimation algorithm using spatial and temporal correlation. In the *Proceedings of IEEE Pacific Rim Conference on Communications, Computers and Signal Processing*, Piscataway, NJ, USA, Vol. 2, (pp. 473-476).

Lim, K., & Ra, J. B. (1997). Improved hierarchical search block matching algorithm by using multiple motion vector candidates. *Electronics Letters, 33*, 1771–1772. doi:10.1049/el:19971222

Liu, B., & Zaccarin, A. (1993). New fast algorithms for the estimation of block motion vectors. *IEEE Transactions on Circuits and Systems for Video Technology, 3*, 148–157. doi:10.1109/76.212720

Liu, L. K., & Feig, E. (1996). A block-based gradient descent search algorithm for block motion estimation in video coding. *IEEE Transactions on Circuits and Systems for Video Technology, 6*, 419–422. doi:10.1109/76.510936

Lu, J., & Liou, M. L. (1997). A simple and efficient search algorithm for block-matching motion estimation. *IEEE Transactions on Circuits and Systems for Video Technology, 7*, 429–433. doi:10.1109/76.564122

Lucas, B., & Kanade, T. (1981). An iterative image registration technique with an application to stereo vision. In the *Proceedings of DARPA Image Understanding Workshop*, (pp. 121-130).

Luo, J., Ahmad, I., Liang, Y., & Swaminathan, V. (2008). Motion estimation for content adaptive video compression. *IEEE Transactions on Circuits and Systems for Video Technology, 18*(7), 900–909. doi:10.1109/TCSVT.2008.923423

Luo, L., Zou, C., Gao, X., & Zhenya, H. (1997). A new prediction search algorithm for block motion estimation in video coding. *IEEE Transactions on Consumer Electronics, 43*(1), 56–61. doi:10.1109/30.580385

Moschetti, F. (2001). *A statistical approach to motion estimation*. Ecole polytechnique Federale De Lausanne, PhD Thesis.

Moshnyaga, V. G. (2001). A new computationally adaptive formulation of block-matching motion estimation. *IEEE Transactions on Circuits and Systems for Video Technology, 11*, 118–124. doi:10.1109/76.894295

Nam, J.-Y., Seo, J.-S., Kwak, J.-S., Lee, M.-H., & Yeong, H. H. (2000). New fast-search algorithm for block matching motion estimation using temporal and spatial correlation of motion vector. *IEEE Transactions on Consumer Electronics, 46*, 934–942. doi:10.1109/30.920443

Nisar, H., & Choi, T.-S. (2000). An advanced center biased search algorithm for motion estimation. In the *Proceedings of International Conference on Image Processing (ICIP '00)*, Vol. 1, (pp. 832-835).

Nisar, H., & Choi, T. S. (2009). Multiple initial point prediction based search pattern selection for fast motion estimation. *Pattern Recognition, 42*, 475–48. doi:10.1016/j.patcog.2008.08.010

Po, L.-M., & Ma, W.-C. (1996). Novel four-step search algorithm for fast block motion estimation. *IEEE Transactions on Circuits and Systems for Video Technology, 6*, 313–317. doi:10.1109/76.499840

Richardson, I. E. G. (2002). *Video codec design*. John Wiley & sons, ltd. doi:10.1002/0470847832

Robbins, J. D., & Netravali, A. N. (1983). Recursive motion compensation: A review . In *Image sequence processing and dynamic sconce analysis* (pp. 76–103). Springer-Verlag. doi:10.1007/978-3-642-81935-3_3

Shi, Y. Q., & Sun, H. (2000). *Image and video compression for multimedia engineering: Fundamentals, algorithms, and standards*. Boca Raton, FL: CRC Press.

Sorwar, G., Murshed, M., & Dooley, L. S. (2007). A fully adaptive distance-dependent thresholding search (FADTS) algorithm for performance-management motion estimation. *IEEE Transactions on Circuits and Systems for Video Technology, 17*(4), 429–440. doi:10.1109/TCSVT.2006.888816

Sullivan, G. J., & Wiegand, T. (1998). Rate-distortion optimization for video compression. *IEEE Signal Processing Magazine, 15*, 74–90. doi:10.1109/79.733497

Tekalp, A. M. (1995). *Digital video compression.* Prentice Hall PTR.

Wen, J. H., Li, C. Z., & Yan, N. W. (2012). Cross-diamond search algorithm for motion estimation based on projection. *Advanced Materials Science and Information Technology, 433-440*, 3713-3717.

Wiegand, T., Sullivan, G., Bjontegaard, G., & Luthra, A. (2003). Overview of the H.264/Avc video coding standard. *IEEE Transactions on Circuits and Systems for Video Technology, 3*(7), 560–576. doi:10.1109/TCSVT.2003.815165

Xie, L. Y., Su, X. Q., Zhang, S., & Xu, Z. G. (2012). A Novel adaptive fast motion estimation algorithm for video compression. In the *Proceedings of International Conference in Electrics, Communication and Automatic Control*, (pp. 241-250).

Xu, J.-B., Po, L.-M., & Cheung, C.-K. (1999). Adaptive motion tracking block matching algorithms for video coding. *IEEE Transactions on Circuits and Systems for Video Technology, 9*, 1025–1029. doi:10.1109/76.795056

Zhu, C., Chau, L.-P., & Lin, X. (2002). Hexagon-based search pattern for fastblock motion estimation. *IEEE Transactions on Circuits and Systems for Video Technology, 12*(5), 349–355. doi:10.1109/TCSVT.2002.1003474

Zhu, C., Lin, X., Chau, L., & Po, L.-M. (2004). Enhanced hexagonal searchfor fast block motion estimation. *IEEE Transactions on Circuits and Systems for Video Technology, 14*(10), 1210–1214. doi:10.1109/TCSVT.2004.833166

Zhu, S., & Ma, K.-K. (2000). A new diamond search algorithm for fast block-matching motion estimation. *IEEE Transactions on Image Processing, 9*, 287–290. doi:10.1109/TIP.2000.826791

KEY TERMS AND DEFINITIONS

Block-Based Motion Estimation: Block-based motion estimation methods are the most common motion estimation techniques used for video coding applications. In this technique, the image sequence consists of a set of regions each undergoing a single motion between frames. Each frame is divided into a set of non-overlapped, equally spaced, fixed size, small rectangular blocks called macroblocks; and the translation motion within each block is assumed to be uniform. The motion vector of each block is then found by searching for the corresponding blocks in the reference frame by minimising some matching criteria as stated above. Such block-based motion estimation methods are popularly termed *block-matching algorithms* (BMAs).

Block Distortion Measure: It is the technique used to measure the similarity or dissimilarity of a block of pixels of a current frame compared to a candidate block of the reference frame. There are, mainly, three matching cost functions are used and that are: *Mean Square Error* (MSE), *Mean Absolute Error* (MAE) and *Cross Correlation Function* (CCF).

Distance-Dependent Thresholding Search (DTS) Algorithm: A newblock based motion estimation algorithm based on one key characteristic of real world video sequences—this is that the distortion of an object in any video frame increases with its velocity, as well as camera zoom and pan factors. To accommodate this key characteristic, the DTS algorithm uses a "parametric" thresholding function to terminate the search even at relatively high *Block Distortion* values, especially when the length of the motion vector tends to increase. The DTS algorithm encompasses both the Full Search and very fast searching modes. Different threshold settings can provide different QoS levels and therefore the DTS algorithm provides a general solution for all types of video sequences and coding demands. This unique feature provides good flexibility in controlling performance, especially the computational complexity required for motion estimation in real-time video coding applications.

Motion Vector: The offset of two positions of a same object between two/more successive frames is called the *motion vector* (MV), which defines how to move the object in the reference frame to its new position in the current frame. The motion vector can be estimated for either each pixel or for a block of pixels (block-based) in a given frame.

Unimodal Error Surface Assumption: The block distortion measured between a block of a current frame and a candidate block of a reference frame increases monotonically as the search point moves away from the global minimum. Most of the first algorithms are based on this assumption, however this assumption does not hold true for most real world video sequences as there may have many local minima due to the non-stationary characteristics of the video signal. As a consequence, it is unlikely that conventional fast search algorithms, which use few directional candidates, would ever converge to the global minima. In other words, the search could easily be trapped in a local minimum instead of the global minima and generate a higher prediction error.

Chapter 4
Advances in Region–of–Interest Video and Image Processing

Dan Grois
Ben-Gurion University of the Negev, Israel

Ofer Hadar
Ben-Gurion University of the Negev, Israel

ABSTRACT

The advent of cheaper and more powerful devices with the ability to play, create, and transmit video content has led to a dramatic increase in the multimedia content distribution on both wireline and wireless networks. Also, the reduction of cost of digital video cameras along with the development of user-generated video sites (e.g., iTunes™, YouTube™) stimulated a new user-generated video content sector and made unprecedented demands for high-quality and low-delay video communication. The Region-of-Interest (ROI) is a desirable feature in many future scalable video coding applications, such as mobile device applications, which have to be adapted to be displayed on a relatively small screen; thus, a mobile device user may wish to extract and track only a predefined ROI within the displayed video. At the same time, other users having a larger mobile device screen may wish to extract other ROIs to receive higher video stream resolution. Therefore, to fulfill these requirements, it would be beneficial to simultaneously transmit or store a video stream in a variety of ROIs, as well to enable efficiently tracking of the predefined Region-of-Interest. This chapter presents recent advances in Region-of-Interest video and image processing techniques for multimedia applications, while making a special emphasis on a scalable extension of the H.264/AVC standard. The detailed observations and conclusions, which are presented in this chapter, are supported by authors'personal experience in this field, thereby presenting a variety of experimental results.

DOI: 10.4018/978-1-4666-2660-7.ch004

INTRODUCTION

The number of video applications has been dramatically increased in the last decade, due to many reasons, such as rapid changes in the video coding standardization process driven by the increase of the computing power and significant developments of network infrastructures. Nowadays, the most common video applications include wireless and wired Internet video streaming, high-quality video conferencing, High-Definition (HD) TV broadcasting, HD DVD storage and Blu-ray storage, while employing a variety of video transmission and storage systems (e.g., MPEG-2 for broadcasting services over satellite, cable, and terrestrial transmission channels, or H.320 for conversational video conferencing services (Schwarz et al., 2007)).

The H.264/AVC (ISO/IEC MPEG-4 Part 10) video coding standard (Wiegand & Sullivan, 2003), which was officially issued in 2003, has become a challenge for real-time video applications. Compared to the MPEG-2 standard, it gains about 50% in bit rate, while providing the same visual quality. In addition to having all the advantages of MPEG-2 (ITU-T & ISO/IEC JTC 1, 1994), H.263 (ITU-T, 2000), and MPEG-4 (ISO/IEC JTC 1, 2004), the H.264 video coding standard possesses a number of improvements, such as the content-adaptive-based arithmetic codec (CABAC), enhanced transform and quantization, prediction of "Intra" macroblocks, and others. H.264/AVC is designed for both constant bit rate (CBR) and variable bit rate (VBR) video coding, useful for transmitting video sequences over statistically multiplexed networks, the Ethernet, or other Internet networks. This video coding standard can also be used at any bit rate range for various applications (e.g., typically from 100kb/sec to 15Mb/sec), varying from wireless video phones to high definition television (HDTV) and digital video broadcasting (DVB). In addition, H.264 provides significantly improved coding efficiency and greater functionality, such as rate scalability, "Intra" prediction and error resilience in comparison with its predecessors, MPEG-2 and H.263. However, H.264/AVC is much more complex in comparison to other coding standards and to achieve maximum quality encoding, high computational resources are required (Grois et al., 2010c; Kaminsky et al., 2008).

Most access networks are usually characterized by a wide range of connection qualities, and a wide range of end-user devices with different capabilities, starting from cell phones/mobile devices with relatively small displays and limited computational resources to powerful Personal Computers (PCs) with high-resolution displays (Schwarz et al., 2007). As a result, due to the continuous need for scalability, much of the attention in the field of video processing and coding is currently directed to the Scalable Video Coding (SVC), which was standardized in 2007 as an extension of H.264/AVC (Schwarz et al., 2007), since the bit-stream scalability for video is currently a very desirable feature for many multimedia applications (e.g., video conferencing, video surveillance, telemedical applications, etc.). The need for the scalability arises from the need for spatial formats, bit-rates or power (Wiegand & Sullivan, 2003; Grois & Hadar, 2011a; Grois & Hadar, 2011b). To fulfill these requirements, it would be beneficial to simultaneously transmit or store video in a variety of spatial/temporal resolutions and qualities, leading to video bit-stream scalability. Major requirements for the Scalable Video Coding are to enable encoding of a high-quality video bitstream that contains one or more subset bitstreams to provide video services with lower temporal or spatial resolutions, or to provide reduced reliability, while retaining reconstruction quality that is highly relative to the rate of the subset bitstreams. Therefore, Scalable Video Coding provides important functionalities, such as the spatial, temporal and fidelity/quality (i.e. Medium Grained Scalability (MGS) and Coarse Grain Scalability (CGS)) scalabilities (Schwarz et al., 2007; Schierl et al., 2007), as schematically

Figure 1. Schematic representation of the SVC bitstream: the resolution is increased with the increase of the layer index, while the base-layer (layer 0) has the lowest bitsream resolution (Schierl et al., 2007)

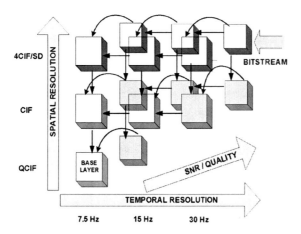

only a predefined Region-of-Interest within the displayed video). At the same time, other users having a larger mobile device screen may wish to extract other ROI(s) to receive higher video stream resolution (Grois & Hadar, 2011c; Grois & Hadar, 2011d). Therefore, to fulfill these requirements, it would be beneficial to simultaneously transmit or store a video stream in a variety of Regions-of-Interest, as well to enable efficiently tracking the predefined Region-of-Interest.

This chapter is organized as follows: first, recent Region-of-Interest detection and tracking techniques are described in detail, while presenting the pixel-domain approach and compressed-domain approach, and further providing various models and techniques, such as the visual attention model, object detection, face detection, skin detection. Second, recent advances in ROI transmission techniques are discusses, emphasizing the ROI-based error-resilience transmission. After that, the ROI image processing methods are described in detail by using JPEG2000. Then, the ROI coding for the H.264/SVC (Schwarz et al.,

presented in Figure1. In turn, these functionalities lead to enhancements of video transmission and storage applications.

SVC has achieved significant improvements in coding efficiency compared to the scalable profiles of prior video coding standards due to the largely increased flexibility and adaptability (e.g., SVC provides a graceful degradation in lossy transmission environments as well as in the bit-rate and power adaptation). Also, in addition to the temporal, spatial and fidelity/quality scalabilities, the SVC supports ROI scalability, thereby enabling to define a particular portion of each picture/frame as a desired ROI, as schematically presented in Figure2, which shows two possible ways to define the desired ROIs, and then encoding the whole SVC video sequence accordingly (e.g., encoding the ROI as a Base-Layer/*Layer 0*).

The ROI is a desirable feature in many future scalable video coding applications, such as mobile device applications, which have to be adapted to be displayed on a relatively small screen (thus, a mobile device user may wish to extract and track

Figure 2. (a, b) Two possible ways for defining the desired ROIs with different spatial resolutions (e.g., QCIF, CIF, SD/4CIF resolutions) to be provided within a Scalable Video Coding stream

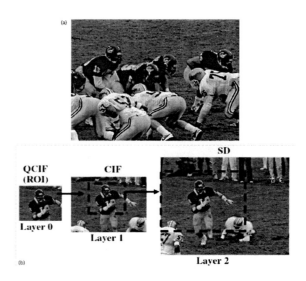

2007) standard is presented, including the ROI scalability by performing cropping and the ROI scalability by using Flexible Macroblock Ordering (FMO) technique (Lambert et al., 2006), followed by the bit-rate control techniques for the ROI coding. After that, the complexity-aware ROI scalable video coding by performing pre-processing is discussed in detail, while focusing on the complexity-aware SVC bit allocation and presenting a comparison between the Medium Grained Scalability (MGS) and Coarse Grain Scalability (CGS) of the Scalable Video Coding. Finally, this chapter is concluded by presenting future research directions.

Region of Interest Detection and Tracking

In order to successfully perform the ROI coding, it is important to accurately detect, and then correctly track, the desired Region-of-Interest. There are mainly two methods for the ROI detection and tracking: (a) the pixel-domain approach; and (b) the compressed-domain approach. The pixel-domain approach is more accurate compared to the compressed-domain approach, but it requires relatively high computational resources. On the other hand, the compressed-domain approach does not consume many resources since it exploits the encoded information (such as DCT coefficients, motion vectors, macroblock types which are extracted in a compressed bitstream, etc.) (Manerba et al., 2008; Kas & Nicolas, 2009; Hanfeng et al., 2001; Zeng et al., 2005). However, the compressed-domain approach results in a relatively poor performance due to many reasons, such as unreliability of the encoded information, sparse assignment of the block-based data; also, it is mainly applicable to simple scenarios and is poorly applicable for abrupt appearance changes and occlusions. Also, for the same reason, the compressed-domain approach has significantly fast processing time and is adaptive to compressed videos.

Both the pixel-domain and compressed-domain approaches are explained in detail in the following sections.

Pixel-Domain Approach

Generally, the main research on object detection and tracking has been focused on the pixel domain approach since it can provide a powerful capability of object tracking by using various technologies. The pixel-domain detection can be classified into the following types:

- **Region-based methods:** "According to these methods, the object detection is performed according to ROI features, such as motion distribution and color histogram. The information with regard to the object colors can be especially useful when these colors are distinguishable from the image background or from other objects within the image" (Vezhnevets, 2002).
- **Feature-based methods:** "According to these methods, various motion parameters of feature points are calculated (the motion parameters are related to affine transformation information, which in turn contains rotation and 2D translation data)" (Shokurov et al., 2003).
- **Contour-based methods:** "According to these methods, the shape and position of objects are detected by modeling the contour data" (Wang et al., 2002).
- **Template-based methods:** "According to these methods, the objects (such as faces) are detected by using predetermined templates" (Schoepflin et al., 2001).

As mentioned above, the pixel-domain approach is, generally, more accurate than the compressed-domain approach, but has relatively high computational complexity and requires further additional computational resources for decoding compressed video streams. Therefore, the desired ROI can be predicted in a relatively accurate manner by defining various pixel-domain models, such as visual attention models, object detection models, face detection and skin detection models, as presented in detail in the following sub-sections.

Visual Attention

The visual attention models refer to the ability of a human user to concentrate his/her attention on a specific region of an image/video. This involves selection of the sensory information by the primary visual cortex in the brain by using a number of characteristic, such as intensity, color, size, orientation in space, and the like (Hu et al., 2008). Actually, the visual attention models simulate the behavior of the Human Visual System (HVS), and in turn enable detection of the Region-of-Interest within the image/video, such as presented in Figure 3.

Several research investigations have been conducted with this regard in order to achieve better ROI detection performance, and in turn improve the ROI visual presentation quality. Thus, for example Cheng et al. (2005) present a frame-

Figure 3. An example of concentrating the attention on a specific region of an image, based on the behavior of the human visual system (HVS)

work for automatic video Region-of-Interest determination based on a user attention model, while considering the three types of visual attention features, i.e. intensity, color and motion. The contrast-based intensity model is based on the fact that particular color pairs, such as red-green and blue-yellow possess high spatial and chromatic opposition; the same characteristics exist in high difference lighting or intensity pairs. Thus, according to Cheng et al. (2005), the intensity, red-green color and blue-yellow color constant models should be included into the user attention representation module. Also, when there is more than one ROI within the frame (e.g., a number of football players), then a saliency map is used which shows the ability to characterize the visual attraction of the image/video. The saliency map, which represents visual saliency of a corresponding visual scene, is divided into *n* regions, and ROI is declared for each such region, thereby enabling to dynamically and automatically determine ROI for each frame-segment.

Also, Sun et al. (2010) propose a visual attention based approach to extract texts from a complicated background in camera-based images. Firstly, the approach applies the simplified visual attention model to highlight the ROI in an input image and to yield a map consisting of the ROIs. Secondly, an edge map of image containing the edge information of four directions is obtained by Sobel operators; character areas are detected by connected component analysis and merged into candidate text regions. Finally, the map consisting of the ROIs is employed to confirm the candidate text regions.

Further, other visual attention models have been recently proposed to improve the ROI visual presentation quality, such as (Engelke et al., 2009), which discusses two ways of obtaining subjective visual attention data that can be subsequently used to develop visual attention models based on the selective region-of-interest and visual fixation patterns. Chen et al. (2010) disclose a model of the focus of attention for detecting the attended regions in video sequences by using the similarity between the adjacent frames, establishing the gray histogram, selecting the maximum similarity as a predicable model, and finally obtaining a position of the focus of attention in the next fame. Li et al. (2010) present a three-stage method that combines the visual attention model with target detection by using the saliency map, covering the region of interest with blocks and measuring the similarity between the blocks and the template. Kwon et al. (2010) show a ROI based video preprocessor method that deals with the perceptual quality in a low-bit rate communication environment, further proposing three separated processes: the ROI detection, the image enhancement, and the boundary reduction in order to deliver better video quality at the video-conferencing application for use in a fixed camera and to be compatible as a preprocessor for the conventional video coding standards. Duchowski (2000) presents a wavelet-based multiresolution image representation method for matching the human visual system (HVS) spatial acuity within multiple regions of interest. ROIs are maintained at high (original) resolution, while peripheral areas are gracefully degraded.

As seen from the above observations, the visual attention approach has recently become quite popular among researchers, and many improved techniques have been lately presented. In the following sub-section, main issues with regard to the object detection are discussed on detail.

Object Detection

Automatic object detection is one of the important steps in image processing and computer vision (Bhanu et al., 1997; Lin & Bhanu, 2005). The major task of object detection is to locate objects in images and extract the regions containing them (the extracted regions are ROIs). The quality of object detection is highly dependent on the effectiveness of the features used in the detection. Finding or designing appropriate features to capture the characteristics of objects and building the

feature-based representation of objects are the key to the success of detection. Usually, it is not easy for human experts to figure out a set of features to characterize complex objects, and sometimes, simple features directly extracted from images may not be effective in object detection.

The ROI detection is especially useful for medical applications (Liu et al., 2006). Automatic detection of an ROI in a complex image or video, like endoscopic neurosurgery video, is an important task in many processing applications such as an image-guided surgery system, real-time patient monitoring system, and object-based video compression. In telemedical applications, object-based video coding is highly useful because it produces a good perceptual quality in a specified region, i.e., a region-of-interest, without requiring an excessive bandwidth. By using a dedicated video encoder, the ROI can be coded with more bits to obtain a much higher quality than that of the non-ROI which is coded with fewer bits.

In the last decade, various object detection techniques have been proposed. For example, Han & Vasconcelos (2008) present a fully automated architecture for object-based ROI detection, based on the principle of discriminant saliency, which defines as salient the image regions of strongest response to a set of features that optimally discriminate the object class of interest from all the others. It consists of two stages, saliency detection and saliency validation. The first detects salient points, the second verifies the consistency of their geometric configuration with that of training examples. Both the saliency detector and the configuration model can be learned from cluttered images downloaded from the web.

Also, Wang et al. (2008) describe a simple and novel algorithm for detecting foreground objects in video sequences using just two consecutive frames. The method is divided into three layers: sensory layer, perceptual layer, and memory layer (short-term memory in conceptual layer). In the sensory layer, successive images are obtained from one fixed camera, and some early computer vision processing techniques are applied here to extract the image information, which are edges and visually inconsistent spliced regions. In the perceptual layer, moving objects are extracted based on the information from the sensory layer, and may request the sensory layer to support with more detail. The detected results are stored in the memory layer, and help the perceptual layer to detect the temporal static objects.

In addition, Jeong et al. (2006) proposes an object image detection system based on the ROI. The system proposed by Jeong et al. (2006) excels in that ROI detection method is specialized in object image detection. In addition, a novel feature consisting of weighted Scalable Color Descirptor (SCD) based on an ROI and skin color structure descriptor is presented for classifying objects in an image. Using the ROI detection method, Jeong et al. (2006) can reduce the noisy information in an image and extract more accurate features for classifying objects in an image.

Further, Lin & Bhanu (2005) use genetic programming (GP) to synthesize composite operators and composite features from combinations of primitive operations and primitive features for object detection. The motivation for using GP is to overcome the human experts' limitations of focusing only on conventional combinations of primitive image processing operations in the feature synthesis. GP attempts many unconventional combinations that in some cases yield exceptionally good results. Compared to a traditional region-of-interest extraction algorithm, the composite operators learned by GP are more effective and efficient for object detection. Still further, Kim & Wang (2009) propose a method for smoke detection in outdoor video sequences, which contains three steps. The first step is to decide whether the camera is moving or not. While the camera is moving, the authors skip the ensuing steps. Otherwise, the second step is to detect the areas of change in the current input frame against the background image and to locate ROIs by connected component analysis. In the final step, the

authors decide whether the detected ROI is smoke by using the k-temporal information of its color and shape extracted from the ROI.

Face Detection

Face detection can be regarded as a specific case of object-class detection. In object-class detection, the task is to find the locations and sizes of all objects in an image that belong to a given class (such as pedestrians, cars, and the like). Also, face detection can be regarded as a more general case of face localization. In face localization, the task is to find the locations and sizes of a known number of faces (usually one). In face detection, one does not have this additional information.

Early face-detection algorithms focused on the detection of frontal human faces, whereas recent face detection methods aim to solve the more general and difficult problem of multi-view face detection. Face detection from an image video is considered to be a relatively difficult task due to a plurality of possible visual representations of the same face: the face scale, pose, location, orientation in space, varying lighting conditions, face emotional expression, and many others (as presented for example, in Figure 4). Therefore, in spite of the recent technological progress, this field still has many challenges and problems to be resolved.

Generally, the challenges associated with face detection can be attributed to the following factors (Yang et al., 2002):

- **Facial expression:** The appearance of faces is directly affected by a person's facial expression.
- **Pose:** The images of a face vary due to the relative camera-face pose (frontal, 45 degree, profile, upside down), and some facial features such as an eye or the nose may become partially or wholly occluded.
- **Occlusion:** Faces may be partially occluded by other objects. In an image with a

Figure 4. An example of a plurality of possible visual representations of the same face, which has an influence on the accurate face detection. Although the accuracy of face detection systems has dramatically increased during the last decade, such systems still have many challenges and problems to be resolved, such as varying lighting conditions, facial expression, presence or absence of structural components, etc.

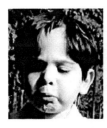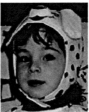

group of people, some faces may partially occlude other faces.

- **Image orientation:** Face images directly vary for different rotations about the camera's optical axis.
- **Imaging conditions:** When the image is formed, factors such as lighting (spectra, source distribution and intensity) and camera characteristics (sensor response, lenses) affect the appearance of a face.
- **Presence or absence of structural components:** Facial features such as beards, mustaches, and glasses may or may not be present and there is a great deal of variability among these components including shape, color, and size.

During the last decade, many researchers around the world tried to improve the face detection and develop an efficient and accurate detection system. For example, Mustafah et al. (2009) propose a design of a face detection system for a real-time high resolution smart camera, while making an emphasis on the problem of crowd surveillance where the static color camera is used to monitor a wide area of interest, and utilizing a background subtraction method to reduce the ROI to areas where the moving objects are located. Another work was performed by Zhang et al. (2009), in which a ROI based H.264 encoder for videophone with a hardware macroblock level face detector

was presented. The ROI definition module operates as a face detector in a videophone, and it is embedded into the encoder to define the currently processed and encoded ROI macroclocks, while the encoding process is dynamically controlled according to the ROI (the encoding parameters vary according to the ROI).

Further, other face detection techniques have been recently proposed to improve the face detection, such as: Micheloni et al. (2005) present an integrated surveillance system for the outdoor security; Qayyum & Javed (2006) disclose a notch based face detection, tracking and facial feature localization system, which contains two phases: visual guidance and face/non-face classification; and Sadykhov & Lamovsky (2008) disclose a method for real-time face detection in 3D space.

Skin Detection

The successful recognition of the skin ROI simplifies the further processing of such ROI. The main aim of traditional skin ROI detection schemes is to detect skin pixels in images, thereby generating skin areas. According to Abdullah-Al-Wadud & Oksam (2007), if the ROI detection process misses a skin region or provides regions having lots of holes in it, then the reliability of applications significantly decreases. Therefore, it is important to maintain the efficiency of the human-computer interaction (HCI) based systems.

In turn, Abdullah-Al-Wadud & Oksam (2007) present an improved ROI selection method for skin detection applications. This method can be applied in any explicit skin cluster classifier in any color space, while not requiring any learning or training procedure. The proposed algorithm mainly operates on a grayscale image (DM), but the processing is based on color information. The scalar distance map contains the information of the vector image, thereby making this method relatively simple to implement.

Also, Yuan & Mu (2007) present an ear detection method, which is based on skin-color and contour information, while introducing a modified Continuously Adaptive Mean Shift (CAMSHAFT) algorithm for rough and fast profile tracking. The aim of profile tracking is to locate the main skin-color regions, such as the ROI that contains the ear. The CAMSHIFT algorithm is based on a robust non-parameter technique for climbing density gradients to find the peak of probability distribution called the mean shift algorithm. The mean shift algorithm operates on a probability distribution, so in order to track colored objects in video sequence, the color image data has to be first represented as the color distribution. According to Yuan & Mu (2007), the modified CAMSHIFT method is performed as follows:

- Generating the skin-color histogram on training set skin images.
- Setting the initial location of the 2D mean shift search window at a fixed position in the first frame such as the center of the frame.
- Using the generated skin-color histogram to calculate the skin-color probability distribution of the 2D region centered at the area slightly larger than the mean shift window size.
- Calculating the zeroth moment (area of size) and mean location (the centroid).
- For the next frame, centering the search window at the calculated mean location

and setting the window size using a function of the zeroth moment. Then the previous two steps are repeated.

In addition, Chen et al. (2003) present a video coding H.263 based technique for robust skin-color detection, which is suitable for real time videoconferencing. According to Chen et al. (2003), the ROIs are automatically selected by a robust skin-color detection which utilizes the Cr and RGB variance instead of the traditional skin color models, such as YCbCr, HSI, etc. The skin color model defined by Cr and RGB variance can choose the skin color region more accurately than other methods. The distortion weight parameter and variance at the macroblock layer are adjusted to control the qualities at different regions. As a result, the quality at the ROI can be significantly improved.

In the following two sub-sections, the recent advances in the compressed-domain detection and region-of-interest tracking are presented.

Compressed-Domain Detection

The conventional compressed domain algorithms exploit motion vectors or Discrete Cosine Transform (DCT) coefficients instead of original pixel data as resources in order to reduce computational complexity of object detection and tracking (You, 2010).

In general, the compressed domain algorithms can be categorized as follows: the clustering-based methods and the filtering-based methods.

The clustering-based methods (Benzougar et al., 2001; Babu et al., 2004; Ji & Park, 2000; Jamrozik & Hayes, 2002) attempt to perform grouping and merging all blocks into several regions according to their spatial or temporal similarity. Then, these regions are merged with each other or classified as background or foreground. The most advanced clustering-based method, which handles the H.264/AVC standard, is the region growing approach, in which several seed fragments grow spatially and temporally by merging similar neighboring fragments (Porikli & Sun, 2005).

On the other hand, the filtering-based methods (Aggarwal et al., 2006; You et al., 2007; You et al., 2009) extract foreground regions by filtering blocks, which are expected to belong to background or by classifying all blocks into foreground and background. Then, the foreground region is split into several object parts through a clustering procedure.

Region-of-Interest Tracking

Object tracking based on a video sequence plays an important role in many modern vision applications such as intelligent surveillance, video compression, human-computer interfaces, sports analysis (Haritaoglu et al., 2000). When an object is tracked with an active camera, traditional methods such as background subtraction, temporal differencing and optical flow may not work well due to the motion of camera, tremor of camera and disturbance from the background (Xiang, 2009).

Some researchers propose methods of tracking a moving target with an active camera, yet most of their algorithms are too computationally complex due to their dependence on accurate mathematical model and motion model, and can't be applied to real-time tracking in the presence of fast motion from the object or the active camera, irregular motion and un-calibrated camera. Xiang (2009) makes a great effort to find a fast, computationally efficient algorithm, which can handle fast motion, and can smoothly track a moving target with an active camera, by proposing a method for real-time follow-up tracking fast moving object with an active camera. Xiang (2009) focused on the color-based Mean Shift algorithm which shows excellent performance both on computationally complexity and robustness.

Wei & Zhou (2010) present a novel algorithm that uses the selective visual attention mechanisms to develop a reliable algorithm for object tracking that can effectively deal with the relatively big

influence of external interference in a-priori approaches. To extract the ROI, it makes use of the "local statistic" of the object. By integrating the image feature with state feature, the synergistic benefits can bring following obvious advantages:

- It doesn't use any a-priori knowledge about blobs and no heuristic assumptions must be provided;
- The computation of the model for a generic blob doesn't take a long processing time.

According to Wei & Zhou (2010), during the detection phase, there are some false-alarms in tracking an object in any actual image. To reduce the fictitious targets as much as possible, a method needs to identify the extracted ROI, while the tracing target can be defined by the following characteristics:

- The length of boundary of the tracing target in the ROI.
- **Aspect ratio:** The length and the width of the target can be expressed by the two orthogonal axes of minimum enclosing rectangle. The ratio between them is the aspect ratio.
- **Shape complexity:** The ratio between the length of the boundary and the area.

The ROI, whose parameters accord with the above three features, can be considered as the ROI including the real target.

Further, there are many other recent tracking methods, such as: Mehmood, (2009) implements kernel tracking of density-based appearance models for real-time object tracking applications; Wang et al. (2009) disclose a wireless, embedded smart camera system for cooperative object tracking and event detection; Sun & Sun (2008) present an approach for detecting and tracking dynamic objects with complex topology from image sequences based on intensive restraint topology adaptive snake mode; Wang & Zhu (2008) present a sensor platform with multi-modalities, consisting of a dual-panoramic peripheral vision system and a narrow field-of-view hyperspectral fovea; thus, only hyperspectal images in the ROI should be captured; Liu et al., 2006 present a new method that addresses several challenges in automatic detection of ROI of neurosurgical video for ROI coding, which is used for neurophysiological intraoperative monitoring (IOM) system. According to (Liu et al., 2006), the method is based on an object tracking technique with multivariate density estimation theory, combined with the shape information of the object, thereby by defining the ROIs for neurosurgical video, this method produces a smooth and convex emphasis region, within which surgical procedures are performed. Abousleman, 2009 present an automated region-of-interest-based video coding system for use in ultra-low-bandwidth applications.

In the following section, recent advances in a field of the Region-of-Interest transmission are presented, while making a special emphasis on the recent ROI-based error-resilient techniques.

Region of Interest Transmission over the Network

The advent of cheaper and more powerful devices, such as mobile devices, which have the ability to play, create, and transmit video content, has led to a dramatic increase in the multimedia content distribution on both wireline and wireless networks. Also, the reduction of cost of digital video cameras along with the development of user-generated video sites (e.g., iTunes™, YouTube™) stimulated a new user-generated video content sector and made unprecedented demands for the high-quality and low-delay video communication/transmission. For example, Figure 5 presents a sample live streaming scheme by using the scalable extension of the H.264/AVC standard (Schwarz et al., 2007), in which the Base-Layer can be defined as the desired Region-of-Interest (Grois & Hadar, 2011c; Grois & Hadar, 2011d).

It should be noted that conventional row-by-row image transmission usually decreases the transmission efficiency and increases the time period for browsing the images. In turn, the image progressive transmission (Gong et al., 2003; Zheng et al., 2007; Lim et al., 2010) can improve the efficiency. First of all, the image contour is transmitted. Then, the image details are transmitted. Once the image data is received, it can be decoded immediately. Also, users can select one or more ROIs, in order to prioritize the transmission of particular image regions, and also can arbitrarily terminate and continue image transmission according to their various requirements. In addition, many of image coding algorithms, which support progressive transmission, are related to

Figure 5. Live SVC-based streaming scheme

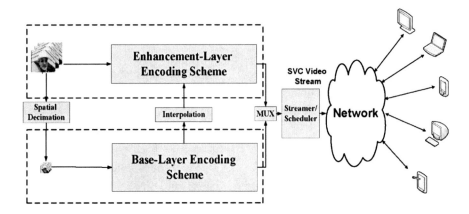

the wavelet subband coding (Park K., & Park H., 2008). With this regard, Zheng et al., (2007) propose a progressive image transmission algorithm based on ROI using the properties of the Integer Wavelet Transform (IWT) and Multiresolution Analysis, which improves the conventional ROI progressive image transmission algorithm (Bradley & Stentiford, 2002). According to Zheng et al., (2007), first, all ROI data is transmitted; afterwards, the data of the background image is dynamically transmitted, while considering aspects of the human vision system. As a result, the displayed images are relatively smooth and have better visual quality, when compared to the image progressive transmission tecnique.

Also, additional techniques, such as the offset based leaky prediction, have been recently proposed in this field of research. According to Luo et al. (2009), an enhanced leaky prediction enables the image ROI to gently recover from a frame, which immediately succeeds the erroneous one, in favor of the better human perception quality. Also, an optimized offset compensation technique is designed by Luo et al. (2009) to improve the coding performance.

In the following section, the recent advances in the ROI-based error-resilience techniques are discussed.

ROI-BASED ERROR-RESILIENCE TECHNIQUES FOR IMAGE/ VIDEO TRANSMISSION

Motion compensation is usually employed to achieve high coding efficiency in conventional compression and communication applications (Li & Gao, 2011). However, it increases the de-pendency of neighboring frames and makes the compressed video to be relatively sensitive to various transmission errors. Once an error occurs in a frame, it propagates to subsequent frames along the prediction loop, which in turn results in severe degradation of the reconstructed video quality. As a result, many research efforts have been recently directed towards the development of the error-resilient video coding (Li & Gao, 2011).

One of the known error-resilient techniques is Forward Error Correction (FEC), which can protect video content from the congestive packet loss, according to the packet importance. The FEC is an error control method for data transmission, which allows the receiver to correct errors without the retransmission from the sender, in contrast to the Automatic Retransmission ReQuest (ARQ) retransmission operations. One advantage of FEC is that a back-channel is not required or that retransmission of data can often be avoided in a congested network scenario. A simple example of the FEC is to transmit each data bit three times, which is known as a (3,1) repetition code. Thus, through a noisy channel, a receiver might see eight versions of the output, as presented in the Table 1.

This allows an error in any one of the three samples above, to be corrected by a "majority vote". The FEC schemes can be generally classified into two classes. In the first class, the so-called static FEC, a fixed number of redundant data is added to the transmitted data. However, static FEC algorithms can create a large overhead even when no error occurs. Thus, static FEC can degrade the performance of the system by poorly matching their overhead to the degree of the underlying channel error, especially when the channel path rate fluctuates widely (Ke et al., 2006). In the second class, depending on the packet loss condi-

Table 1. Simple example of the FEC: eight versions of the output through a noisy channel

Triplet received	000	001	010	100	111	110	101	011
Interpreted as	0 (error free)	0	0	0	1 (error free)	1	1	1

tion and the channel state, the dynamic FEC has a different number of redundant data. According to the FEC approach, the source node transmits parity packets along with the original data packets. The receiver can accurately recover any lost data packets less than the parity packets. The amount of the parity packets is determined at the time of FEC encoding. Although eliminating the need for time-consuming acknowledgement and retransmission operations of ARQ, FEC consumes more bandwidth.

With this regard, Xue et al., (2010) present an error-resilient scheme called Wyner-Ziv Error-Resilient (WZER), based on a receiver driven layered Wyner-Ziv (WZ) coding framework. The WZER purposely emphasizes the protection of the ROI area in the frame, in order to achieve better tradeoff between the bandwidth usage and error-resilience. WZER is designed to work for the scenario of wavelet based video coding over packet erasure channel, where several techniques, including automatic ROI detection, ROI mask generation, Rate Distortion Optimization (RDO) quantization, WZ coding with layer design, and packet level Low Density Parity Check (LDPC), are used.

In addition, Shanableh et al., (2008) proposes a frequency-domain and a compressed-domain transcoder for improving the error resilience of the pre-encoded video streams by using distributed source coding techniques. In both above-mentioned transcoders, it is proposed to identify the ROIs in the pre-encoded video streams. In the compressed-domain transcoder, the ROIs are retained as they are, while in the frequency-domain

transcoder, such regions are reproduced at a lower fidelity by requantization or low pass filtering.

Further, Duong & Zepernick (2008) propose a ROI-based scheme for image transmission over wireless cooperative/relay fading channels, in which the ROI resilience is increased without using any FEC. According to Duong & Zepernick (2008), both the ROI and image background are extracted to be transmitted on different links. In particular, cooperative communications with three terminals, i.e., source, relay, and destination, is considered. In the first-hop transmission, the source broadcasts the ROI to both the relay and destination. In the second-hop transmission, the source sends the background image to the destination, while the relay assists to enhance the quality of ROI at the destination by forwarding the ROI, which was received during the first-hop transmission. Within this transmission scheme, the relay does not consume the power used to transmit the background image. Therefore, to satisfy the total power constraint, the relay can allocate more power for the ROI-based image transmission by using the remaining power reserved for the background image.

Also, Jerbi et al. (2004) and Jerbi et al. (2005), propose a non-linear transform that increases the redundancy of macroblock (MB) rows within the ROI by generating MB pairs to achieve the ROI quality improvement, as schematically shown in Figure 6. It should be noted that the authors suppose that the ROI is not changed within the entire video sequence, which can be especially relevant to video conferencing applications with the above-mentioned "head and shoulder" video content type.

Figure 6. The scheme, as proposed by Jerbi et al. (2005)

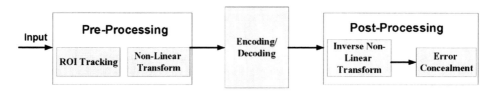

The pre-processing module of Figure 6 above contains a ROI tracking mechanism, according to the block-based motion estimation of the source frames: every ROI macroblock in the previous frame is compared with macroblocks in the current frame, based on the sum of absolute difference (SAD). Then, the non-linear transform doubles a number of macroblocks in the ROI of the source frame, thereby generating identical macroblock pairs. In other words, each macroblock in the ROI is duplicated in the vertical direction of the frame. The motivation behind this is based on the fact that the video coding is usually performed on a macroblock level. Therefore, upon generating a macroblock pair, the corresponding reconstructed macroblock pair resulting from the encoding and decoding will look similar to each other, but not necessarily exactly the same. This is due to the fact that the same macroblocks in the source frame may not undergo similar mode decisions during the encoding process. In order to quantify the level of similarity between decoded macroblocks in a macroblock pair within the ROI, Jerbi et al. (2005) utilize a correlation coefficient. Finally, the inverse nonlinear transform is applied on the decoded image at the post-processing stage, and then the error concealment is performed to minimize an impact of the packet loss on the visual presentation quality.

Another research perspective is to introduce the human visual system (HVS) into the the coding scheme (Li & Gao, 2011). These approaches are based on the fact that in many applications clients pay more attention to an area, in which they are interested in. For example, the "head and shoulder" video content type is usually encoded during the real-time video communication/conferencing, and the corresponding ROI is usually a human face. Therefore, for both the encoder and decoder, more resources including bits and computational power should be allocated to the human face region to improve the overall visual quality. As a result, a concept of the ROI is an efficient tool for the image classification, i.e. it can be used to divide an image into several areas with varying importance (Liu et al., 2008). By this way, the overall visual presentation quality can be optimized. With this regard, Liu et al., (2008b) propose an ROI-based bit-rate allocation scheme for conversational video communication of H.264/AVC, according to which the ROI mask is first determined with the direct frame difference and skin-tone information. Then, more resources including bits and computational power, are allocated to the ROI, and several coding parameters (e.g., quantization parameter (QP), MB candidate modes, etc.) are adaptively adjusted at the MB level according to the ROI mask. In this way, the visual quality of the area, which is more sensitive to the HVS, is emphasized, and the overall visual quality is improved.

In addition, Luo & Chen (2008) propose a ROI-based Flexible Macroblock Ordering (FMO) method by using the FMO mechanism of H.264/AVC (Lambert et al., 2006; Katz et al., 2007). It should be noted that one of the basic elements of an H.264/AVC video sequence is a slice, which contains a group of macroblocks. Each picture can be subdivided into one or more slices and each slice can be provided with increased importance as the basic spatial segment, which can be encoded independently from its neighbors (the slice coding is one of the techniques used in H.264/AVC for transmission) (Chen et al., 2008; Liu et al., 2005; Ndili & Ogunfunmi, 2006; Kodikara et al., 2006). Usually, slices are provided in a raster scan order with continuously ascending addresses; on the other hand, FMO is an advanced tool of H.264 that defines the information of slice groups and enables to allocate different macroblocks to slice groups according to mapping patterns.

Each slice of each picture/frame is independently intra predicted, and the macroblock order within a slice must be in the ascending order. In the H.264 standard, FMO consists of seven slice group map types (*Type 0* to *Type 6*), six of them are predefined fixed macroblock mapping types (interleaved, dispersed, foreground, box-out, raster scan and wipe-out, as illustrated in Figure 7),

Figure 7. Six fixed FMO types, where each color represents a slice group

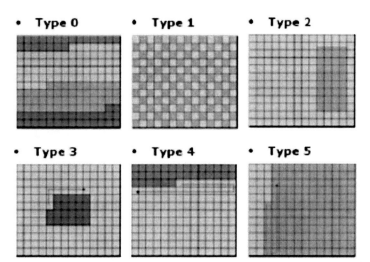

which can be specified through picture parameter setting (PPS), and the last one is a custom type, which allows the full flexibility of assigning macroblock to any slice group.

With this regard, according to Luo & Chen (2008), the ROI and non-ROI are separated into different slice groups, and the ROI is bounded in one or more rectangular areas. Each rectangular area is further divided into several sub-slice groups. Then, some bits are inserted into the video streams, e.g., in the Picture Parameter Set (PPS) to indicate the ROI location, the number of sub-slice groups in each ROI region, and also the type of the sub-slice groups.

The PPS syntax is modified as shown in Box 1 (Luo & Chen, 2008).

For this, a new slice group map *Type 7* is defined (i.e. *slice_group_map_type == 7*), and then it is added to the PPS syntax. Luo & Chen, 2008 suggest that the attention area of a frame should be marked with one or more rectangles. Also, the frame is divided into several ROIs (excluding the background), and the number of the ROIs is specified by "num_slice_groups_minus1" parameter. For each ROI, three parameters are used to define its property: top_left[i] and bottom right[i] specify the top-left and bottom-right rectangle corners, respectively, which are positions of the

Box 1.

```
if(slice_group_map_type == 0){
…
}else if…
…
}else if (slice_group_map_type == 7){
  for(iGroup = 0;iGroup<num_slice_groups_minus1; iGroup++){
  top_left[iGroup]
  bottom_right[iGroup]
  sub_num_slice_groups_minus1[iGroup]
}
```

slice group map unit in a picture raster scan, and the parameter "sub_num_slice_groups_minusl" specifies the number of sub-slice groups for the rectangular area (or ROI) inside a frame (Luo & Chen, 2008).

In addition, Li & Gao (2011) propose an error resilient coding scheme for conversational video communication, which combines the ROI segmentation and Long Term Reference (LTR) frame coding. The main idea of Li & Gao (2011), is to provide the ROIs with more accurate predictive coding by using the LTR frame coding. The scheme, which is proposed by Li & Gao (2011), can be integrated into the H.264/AVC encoder, thereby enabling to efficiently improve the video quality of the predefined ROIs.

Further, Phadikar & Maity (2010) present a compressed domain object-based image error concealment scheme that recovers lost data of the ROI. The scheme integrates the Quantization Index Modulation (QIM) into the JPEG2000 coding pipeline and finds the ROI by using threshold-based image segmentation and morphological operations. The scheme proposed by Phadikar & Maity (2010) uses the Integer Wavelet Transform (IWT) for data embedding to take various benefits over the traditional Discrete Wavelet Transform (DWT).

In the following section, the ROI image processing with regard to the JPEG-2000 is discussed.

Region of Interest Image Processing by Using JPEG-2000

JPEG2000 was introduced in 2000 by ISO/IEC JTC1/SC20/WG1 as a new image compression standard. When comparing it with the previous commonly-used *JPEG* compression standard, the JPEG2000 supports numerous attractive features, which were not available in *JPEG*, and in most of the previous image coding standards. Such features include (Liu et al., 2009):

- State-of-the-art low bit rate compression performance;
- Lossy to lossless compression;
- Progressive transmission by quality, resolution, component, or spatial locality;
- Random access to particular regions of an image, without decoding the entire code stream;
- Region of interest coding by progression;
- Error resilience; and
- A more flexible file format.

In order to achieve the features mentioned above, the JPEG2000 standard makes use of many new image processing and compression technologies. JPEG2000 adopts the *discrete wavelet transform* (DWT) as the image transformation algorithm, and the *embedded block coding with optimization truncation* (EBCOT) as the entropy coding algorithm. The functional block diagram of the baseline JPEG2000 encoder is presented in Figure 8 (Liu et al., 2009).

According to Figure 8, the image pre-processing stage contains three optional functions: first tiling, then Direct Current (DC) level shifting, followed by the multi-component transformation for color image. On the other hand, the compression phase is mainly divided into three sequential steps: (1) image transformation; (2) quantization; and (3) entropy coding (Liu et al., 2009). In the first step, Discrete Cosine Transform (DCT) in previous JPEG standard is replaced by the Discrete Wavelet Transform (DWT). The DWT essentially decomposes each component into a number of sub-bands in different resolution levels. Each sub-band is then independently quantized by a parameter, in case of lossy compression (Liu et al., 2009).

The default performance metric for JPEG2000 is an optimization of the objective quality versus bit-rate. However, for high compression applications, it would be more appropriate that ROI is prioritized for obtaining better visual quality (Nguyen et al., 2003).

Figure 8. A block diagram of the baseline JPEG2000 encoder (Liu et al., 2009)

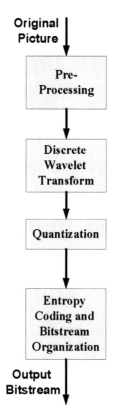

The ROI is supported in JPEG2000, which adopted DWT to perform a compression where ROI image can be coded with the better visual presentation quality compared to the background (Xue et al., 2008). For this, in general, two main methods are defined, which are the scaling-based and maximum-shift ROI coding methods. The principle of the scaling-based method is to scale up ROI coefficients so that the corresponding bits are placed in higher bit-planes. As any scaling value is allowed, an ROI mask is required at the decoder, because small scaling values can cause an overlapping between the ROI and background. In the final bitstream, these scaled-up bit-planes appear prior to any bit-planes associated with the background. Therefore, the entire ROI has to be decoded prior to the rest of the image (Quast & Kaup, 2008). Therefore, since the scaling-based method needs a ROI mask representing the corresponding ROI coefficients at the time of encoding, it is not compatible with the aspect of a user defined ROI, as can be used for example, for video surveillance. In the video surveillance system, as shown for example in Figure 9, a user defined ROI cannot be selected before the operator saw at least a low resolution image of the scene.

Since the ROI mask is also required for decoding, it has to be also transmitted, which results in an increasing bit-rate that is another drawback of the JPEG2000 scaling-based method (Quast & Kaup, 2008). For this, Chen & Chen (2004) and Chen & Chen (2007) propose to apply a rate-distortion function to automatically determine the

Figure 9. A video surveillance system, which supports one or more user-defined ROIs (Quast & Kaup, 2008)

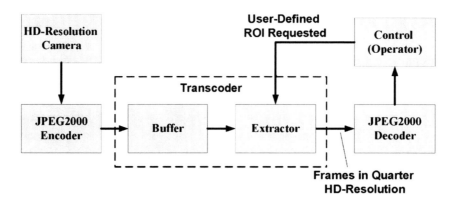

optimized ROI mask. The rate-distortion optimization techniques, with regard to JPEG2000, were also proposed by Bartrina-Rapesta et al. (2008), who present a ROI coding method with fine-grain accuracy. The second method, i.e. the maximum-shift method, is similar to the scaling-based method, but it shifts up the ROI coefficients well above the background. Thus, according to the maximum-shift method, the ROI mask doesn't have to be transmitted since no mask is required at the decoder side. However, the ROI has still to be known at the time of encoding. Therefore, the maximum-shift ROI coding is also not suitable for the video surveillance. With this regard, Quast & Kaup (2008) propose a method for spatial scalable ROI transcoding of JPEG2000 images for video surveillance applications, according to which the HD images are transcoded into quarter HD images with a ROI in HD resolution (the transcoding method proposed by Quast & Kaup (2008) is based on the "empty packet" property of the JPEG2000 standard): the transcoder extracts all packets, which belong to the ROI or to the lower resolution of the background, and then all non-ROI packets of higher resolution levels are deleted and replaced by empty-packets. The above-mentioned "empty packet" property is also used in the fast ROI transcoding method, which is proposed by Kong et al. (2005).

Actually, the principle of both scaling-based and maximum-shift ROI coding methods is similar, according to which upon performing the wavelet transform, the resulting coefficients, which do not relate to the ROI, are scaled down so that the ROI-associated bits are placed in the higher bit plane. During embedded encoding process, the bits in the higher bit plane will be sent earlier than those bits in the lower bit plane. To carry out this process, a ROI mask is generated to indicate all the wavelet coefficients, which are related to the ROI (Xue et al., 2008). Such mask generated, is schematically shown in Figure 10, in which shaded regions correspond to the ROI, while non-shaded regions correspond to the background. The extent of the ROI region in the wavelet domain depends on the length of the synthesis wavelet filters and the number of wavelet decomposition levels (Nguyen et al., 2003).

According to Nguyen et al. (2003), the above-mentioned scaling-based (the "implicit") and maximum-shift ROI coding methods have both advantages and disadvantages relative to another, and the decision, which ROI coding method should be used, depends on the particular application requirements. Thus, for example, the maximum-shift ROI coding method is found to be more appropriate when it is desirable to have the ROI received as early as possible, while the implicit ROI coding method should be used to suppress the background in a variable manner. The implicit ROI coding weights of importance, which are specified for the ROI and the background region, can be adjusted to obtain the desired visual presentation quality ratings for both the ROI

Figure 10. Derivation of ROI bit-mask from ROIs identified in the spatial domain (Nguyen et al., 2003)

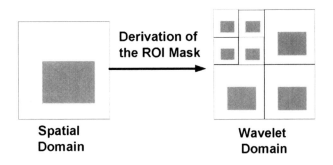

and background, under given bit-rate conditions (Nguyen et al., 2003).

With this regard, several methods for improving the JPEG2000 ROI coding have been proposed, such as the ROI mask generation method of Xue et al., (2008), according to which the ROI-related coefficients are identified but they are not scaled; instead, the ROI-related coefficients are sent to the Wyner-Ziv (WZ) codec for transmission, leading to obtaining better visual presentation quality.

Also, Signoroni et al. (2003) propose a technique to extend the ROI coding within the JPEG2000 framework by focusing on the image quality decrease between the ROI and the background. According to the conventional JPEG2000 ROI coding method, the reconstructed image quality sharply drops along the ROI boundary; however this effect may be considered as objectionable in some situations. As a result, Signoroni et al. (2003) propose a quality-decay management, which makes use of concentric ROI with different scaling factors. It should be noted that generally, the objective quality between the reconstructed and original images is usually measured by either Peak Signal to Noise Ratio (PSNR) or Structural Similarity (SSIM), as follows. The PSNR metrics is measured in Decibels [dB] and is calculated by the following equation (Bharti et al., 2009):

$$PSNR = 10 \log_{10} \left(\frac{255^2}{MSE} \right) \tag{1}$$

where MSE is a Mean Square Error, which is defined as follows:

$$MSE = \frac{1}{M \cdot N} \sum_{m=0}^{M-1} \sum_{n=0}^{N-1} | x(m,n) - \tilde{x}(m,n) |^2 \tag{2}$$

where $\tilde{x}(m,n)$ is a reconstructed image, $x(m,n)$ is an original image, $M \cdot N$ are the original image dimensions, and m and n are variables (pixels) values. On the other hand, the SSIM index is a

method for measuring the similarity between two images. The SSIM index, as well as the PSNR, is a full reference metrics, i.e. the image quality measurements are based on the initial uncompressed or distortion-free image as a reference. The SSIM index is a decimal value between "-1" and "1", and the value of "1" is only reachable in the case of two identical sets of data (images). The SSIM is calculated on various windows of an image. The measure between two windows x and y of the common size $N \times N$ is:

$$SSIM(x,y) = \frac{(2\mu_x \mu_y + c_1) \cdot (2\sigma_{xy} + c_2)}{(\mu_x^2 + \mu_y^2 + c_1) \cdot (\sigma_x^2 + \sigma_y^2 + c_2)} \tag{3}$$

where μ_x is an average of x, μ_y is an average of y, σ_x^2 is a variance of x, σ_y^2 is a variance of y, σ_{xy}^2 is a covariance of x and y, $c_1 = (k_1 \cdot L)^2$ and $c_2 = (k_2 \cdot L)^2$ are variables used to stabilize the division with a weak denominator, while L is a dynamic range of the pixel values and k_1=0.01, k_2=0.03, by default.

There are three major drawbacks of the general scaling-based JPEG2000 method. First, it is not convenient to deal with different wavelet sub-bands in different ways, which is sometimes desired by the users Wang & Bovik (2002). For example, the users may like to treat all the coefficients equally at some low-frequency sub-bands and differently at the high frequency sub-bands (better quality at ROIs than at the background). Second, it needs to encode and transmit the shape information of the ROIs. In turn, this significantly increases the complexity of encoder/decoder implementations. Third, if arbitrary ROI shapes are desired, then shape coding will consume a large number of bits, which significantly decreases the overall coding efficiency.

The JPEG2000 Part II standard attempts to avoid this problem and only defines rectangle and ellipse shaped ROIs, which can be coded with a small number of bits. However, this limits the application scope of ROI coding because in real-world applications, ROIs are usually associated with certain objects in the image, which generally have arbitrary shapes. With this regard, Wang & Bovik (2002) propose a bitplane-by-bitplane shift method, which supports both arbitrary ROI shape and arbitrary scaling without shape coding. In addition, the more recent work of Yao & Xu (2010) present a plane shift method, called PBShift (instead of the conventional method in JPEG2000), which supports arbitrary shaped ROI coding. According to Yao & Xu (2010), this method has four primary advantages:

1. It can get the ROI dynamically without defining the ROI in advance;
2. It supports arbitrarily shaped ROI coding without coding the shape;
3. It allows different wavelet sub-bands, which can have different ROI definitions; and
4. It have a smoother ROI boundary.

JPEG2000 exhibits a highly structured codestream organization, as shown in Figure 11. It consists of a main header followed by a sequence of tile-streams. The main header, which contains the global information necessary to correctly decode the image, is the most important part of the code-stream (Yatawara et al., 2005). Transmission errors in the main header can result in the failure

of the entire decoding process. Each tile-stream contains information required to decode its associated tile and consists of a tile header followed by a pack-stream. The packstreams comprise of a sequence of packets which contains the actual encoded image data. Moreover, the information required for correctly decoding a JPEG2000 code-stream is contained within special identifiers called markers and marker segments. A two byte end of codestream (EOC) marker is used to signal the end of the code-stream.

The hierarchical nature of the ROI coded JPEG2000 images suggests a use of the Unequal Error Protection (UEP) that provide a varying amount of error protection according to the importance of the transmitted data. With this regard, Yatawara et al. (2005) focuses on UEP schemes in improving the ROI quality and reducing the computational complexity, thereby providing increased resilience against the effects of transmissionerrors over a wireless communications channel. Figure 12 presents the two-level UEP scheme, as proposed by Yatawara et al. (2005).

In Figure 12, the packets containing ROI image information, along with the data contained within the JPEG2000 blocks and the JPEG2000 main header, are protected using a stronger code, while the packets related to the background, are protected by using a weaker code.

Further, there are many other works in the field of the JPEG2000 ROI coding. For example, Raj

Figure 11. The organization of the JPEG2000 code-stream (Yatawara et al., 2005)

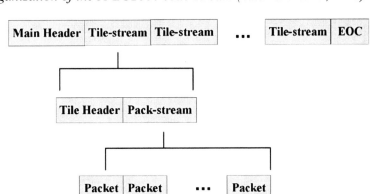

Figure 12. The two-level UEP scheme, as proposed by Yatawara et al. (2005)

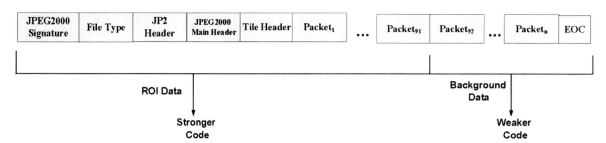

et al. (2008) propose a Fuzzy C-Means clustering approach for generating an arbitrary shape mask in order to cluster images into regions of varying homogeneity - in turn, homogenous ROIs can be coded at a lower bitrate than the high detail regions, and this ensures that the target recognition process is not affected by the compression process; Liu &Fan (2002) present a ROI coding method, called Partial Significant Bitplanes Shift (PSBShift) that combines advantages of both JPEG2000 scaling-based and maximum-shift ROI coding methods, thereby not only supporting arbitrarily shaped ROI coding without coding the shape, but also enabling the flexible adjustment of compression quality in both ROI and background; Sanchez et al. (2004) propose to encode multiple Regions-of-Interest in the JPEG2000 image-coding framework by presenting an algorithm that is based on the rearrangement of packets in the code-stream to place the regions of interest prior to the background coefficients.

In the following section, the recent research directions in the SVC Region-of-Interest coding are discussed in detail.

REGION OF INTEREST CODING IN H.264/SVC STANDARD

Region-of-Interest coding is a desirable feature in the future SVC applications, especially in applications for the wireless networks, which have a limited bandwidth. However, the H.264 standard does not explicitly teach as how to perform the ROI coding.

The ROI coding is supported by various techniques in the H.264/AVC standard (Wiegand & Sullivan, 2003) and the SVC (Schwarz et al., 2007) extension. Some of these techniques include quantization step size control at the slice and macroblock levels, and are related to the concept of slice grouping, also known as Flexible Macroblock Ordering (FMO). For example, Lu et al. (2005a) handle the ROI-based fine granular scalability (FGS) coding, in which a user at the decoder side requires to receive better decoded quality ROIs, while the pre-encoded scalable bit-stream is truncated. Lu et al. (2005a) present a number of ROI enhancement quality layers to provide fine granular scalability. In addition, Thang et al. (2005) present a ROI-based spatial scalability scheme, concerning two main issues: overlapped regions between ROIs and providing different ROIs resolutions. However, Thang et al. (2005) follow the concept of slice grouping of H.264/AVC, considering the following two solutions to improve the coding efficiency:

- Supporting different spatial resolutions for various ROIs by introducing a concept of virtual layers; and
- Enabling the avoidance of the duplicate coding of overlapped regions in multiple ROIs by encoding the overlapped regions such that the corresponding encoded regions can be independently decoded.

Further, Lu et al. (2005b) present an ROI-based coarse granular scalability (CGS), using a perceptual ROI technique to generate a number of quality profiles, and in turn, to realize the CGS. According to (Lu et al., 2005b), the proposed ROI based compression achieves better perceptual quality and improves coding efficiency. Moreover, Lambert et al. (2006) relate to extracting the ROIs (i.e., of an original bit-stream by introducing a description-driven content adaptation framework. According to Lambert et al. (2006), two methods for ROI extraction are implemented:

1. The removal of the non-ROI portions of a bit-stream; and
2. The replacement of coded background with corresponding placeholder slices.

In turn, bit-streams that are adapted by this ROI extraction process have a significantly lower bit-rate than their original versions. While this has, in general, a profound impact on the quality of the decoded video sequence, this impact is marginal in the case of a fixed camera and static background. This observation may lead to new opportunities in the domain of video surveillance or video conferencing. According to Lambert et al. (2006), in addition to the bandwidth decrease, the adaptation process has a positive effect on the decoder due to the relatively easy processing of placeholder slices, thereby increasing the decoding speed.

It should be noted that several works with regard to the Multiview Video Coding (MVC) have been also recently presented. The Multiview Video (MVV) has attracted considerable attention since it is capable of providing users with three-dimensional perception and interactive functionalities. However, the Multiview Video data require large amount of storage and bandwidth during the network transmission. In turn, Zhang et al., (2010) present a novel Depth Perceptual Region-of-Interest (DP-ROI) based Multiview Video Coding (RMVC) scheme to extensively improve data compression efficiency by exploiting redundancies in depth perception. Firstly, Zhang et al., (2010) define DP-ROI according to the three-dimensional depth sensation of human visual system. Then, a framework of RMVC is developed to improve compression efficiency by properly segmenting the MVV into different macroblock-wise DP-ROIs and encoding them separately. After that, Zhang et al., (2010) propose three fast depth based DP-ROI extraction and tracking algorithms by jointly using motion, texture, depth as well as previous extracted DP-ROIs.

Further, a dynamically adjustable and scalable ROI video coding scheme is presented by Grois et al., (2010a) and Grois et al., (2010b). The technique enables adaptively and efficiently setting the desirable ROI location, size, resolution and bit-rate, according to the network bandwidth (especially, if it is a wireless network in which the bandwidth is limited), power constraints of resource-limited systems (such as mobile devices/servers) where low power consumption is required, and according to end-user resource-limited devices (such as mobile devices, PDAs, and the like), thereby effectively selecting best encoding scenarios suitable for most heterogeneous and time-invariant end-user terminals (i.e., different users can be connected each time) and network bandwidths.

In the following two sub-sections, the evaluation of different ROI scalability types is presented (Grois et al., 2010a; Grois et al., 2010b): the ROI scalability by performing cropping, and ROI scalability by employing the FMO technique.

ROI Scalability by Performing Cropping

According to the first method for the ROI video coding, and in order to obtain a high-quality ROI on resource-limited devices (such as mobile devices), the ROI is cropped from the original image, and it is used as a base layer (or other low enhancement layers, such as *Layer 1* or *2*), as schematically illustrated in Figure 13 (Grois

Figure 13. An example of ROI dynamic adjustment and scalability (e.g., for mobile devices with different spatial resolutions) by using a cropping method

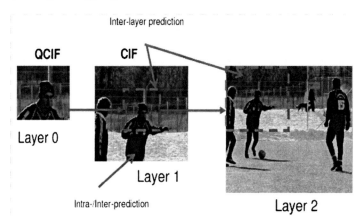

et al., 2010a). Then, an Inter-layer prediction is performed within similar sections of the image, i.e., in the cropping areas. As a result, a significantly low bit-rate overhead can be achieved.

Prior to cropping the image, the location of a cropping area in the successive layers of the image is determined (in Layer *1*, and then in *Layer 2*, as shown on Figure 13). For this, an ESS (Extended Spatial Scalability) method can be employed that introduces cropping and non-dyadic scaling modes, according to which the picture width and height of successive spatial layers can have any possible configuration (Francois & Vieron, 2006; Shoaib & Anni, 2010). In addition, a Group-of-Pictures (GOP) for the SVC is defined as a group between two I/P frames, or any combination thereof (Grois et al., 2010a; Grois et al., 2010b).

In addition, Table 2 presents R-D (Rate-Distortion) experimental results for the variable-layer coding with different cropping spatial resolutions, while using the Inter/Intra-layer prediction (*"SOCCER"* video sequence; 30 f/sec; 300 frames; GOP size 16; QPs varying from 22 to 34). Particularly, the Table 2 presents the R-D (Rate-Distortion) experimental results for the three-layer coding (QCIF-CIF-SD) with the QCIF-CIF cropping versus single layer coding.

As is clearly seen from this table, there is significantly low bit–rate overhead of only 4.7% to 7.9%, compared to the conventional single layer coding, for the same visual quality (in terms of the PSNR), which is especially important for transmitting over limited-bandwidth networks, such as wireless networks.

Table 2. Three-layer (QCIF-CIF-SD) spatial scalability coding vs. single layer coding ("SOCCER" video sequence, 30 fp/s, 300 frames, GOP size 16)

Quantization Parameters	Single layer		QCIF-CIF-SD		Bit–Rate Overhead (%)
	PSNR [dB]	Bit-Rate [kb/sec]	PSNR [dB]	Bit-Rate [kb/sec]	
22	41.0	5663.3	41.0	5940.6	4.7
26	38.8	3054.9	38.8	3248.1	6.0
30	36.8	1770.2	36.8	1894.9	6.6
34	34.8	1071.3	34.8	1163.6	7.9

It is clearly seen from the above experimental results that when using the Inter/Intra-layer prediction, the bit-rate overhead is very small and is much less than 10%.

ROI Scalability by Using Flexible Macroblock Ordering

The second method refers to ROI dynamic adjustment and scalability (Grois et al., 2010a) by using the FMO in the scalable baseline profile (not for *Layer 0*, which is similar to the H.264/AVC baseline profile without the FMO). With this regard, the ROI can be defined as a separate slice in the FMO *Type 2* (as previously presented in Figure 7), which enables defining slices of rectangular regions, and then the whole sequence can be encoded accordingly, while making it possible to define more than one ROI (these definitions should be made in the SVC configuration files, according to the JSVM 9.19 reference software manual (JSVM, 2009)).

Table 3 presents experimental results for four layers spatial scalability coding versus six layers

coding of the "*SOCCER*" sequence (30 fp/s; 300 frames; GOP size is 16), where four layers are presented by one CIF layer and three SD layers having the CIF-resolution ROI in an upper-left corner of the image. In turn, the six layers are presented by three CIF layers (each layer is a crop from the SD resolution) and three 4CIF/SD layers (Grois et al., 2010a; Grois et al., 2010b).

Further, Table 4 presents R-D (Rate-Distortion) experimental results for the HD video sequence "*STOCKHOLM*" by using four-layer coding (640×360 layer and three HD layers having two ROIs (CIF and SD resolution, respectively) in the upper-left corner of the image) versus six-layer coding (three CIF and three SD layers).

As it is clearly observed from Tables 3 and 4, there are very significant bit-rate savings – up to 39%, when using the FMO techniques.

In the following section, recent advances in the ROI bit-rate control techniques are discussed.

Table 3. FMO: Four-layer spatial scalability coding vs. six-layer coding ("SOCCER" video sequence, 30 fp/s, 300 frames, GOP size 16)

Quantization Parameters	4 Layers (CIF and three SD layers)		Six Layers (three CIF layers and three SD layers)		Bit-Rate Savings (%)
	PSNR [dB]	Bit-Rate [kb/sec]	PSNR [dB]	Bit-Rate [kb/sec]	
32	36.0	2140.1	36.0	2290.1	6.6
34	35.1	1549.4	35.1	1680.1	7.8
36	34.0	1140.1	34.0	1279.4	10.9

Table 4. FMO: Four-layer coding vs. six-layer coding ("STOCKHOLM", 30 fp/s, 96 frames, GOP size 8)

Quantization Parameters	Four Layers (640×360, and three HD layers)		Six Layers (three CIF layers and three SD layers)		Bit–Rate Savings (%)
	PSNR [dB]	Bit-Rate [Kb/sec]	PSNR [dB]	Bit-Rate [Kb/sec]	
32	34.5	2566.2	34.5	3237.0	19.3
34	33.9	1730.2	33.9	2359.1	29.7
36	33.3	1170.0	33.3	1759.0	39.9

BIT-RATE CONTROL FOR REGION OF INTEREST CODING

Bit-rate control is crucial in providing desired compression bit-rates for H264/AVC video applications, and especially for Scalable Video Coding, which is an extension of H264/AVC.

Bit-rate control has been intensively studied in existing single-layer coding standards, such as MPEG 2, MPEG 4, and H.264/AVC (Li et al., 2003). According to the existing single-layer rate-control schemes, the encoder employs the rate control as a way to control varying bit-rate characteristics of the coded bit-stream. Generally, there are two objectives of the bit-rate control for the single-layer video coding: one is to meet the bandwidth that is provided by the network, and another is to produce high-quality decoded pictures (Li et al., 2007). Thus, the inputs of the bit-rate control scheme are: the given bandwidth; usually, the statistics of a video sequence (e.g., the Mean Squared Error (MSE) or Mean Absolute Deviation (MAD) between macroblocks in two sequential frames); and a header of each predefined unit (e.g., a basic unit, macroblock, frame, slice). In turn, the outputs are a quantization parameter (QP) for the quantization process and another QP for the rate-distortion optimization (RDO) process of each basic unit, while these two quantization parameters, in the single layer video coding, are usually equal in order to maximize the coding efficiency.

In the current JSVM reference software (JSVM, 2009) there is no rate control mechanism, besides the base-layer rate control, which does not consider enhancement layers. The target bit-rate for each SVC layer is achieved by coding each layer with a fixed QP, which is determined by a logarithmic search (JSVM, 2009; Liu et al., 2008a). Of course, this is very inefficient and time-consuming. To solve this problem, only a few works have been published during the last few years, trying to provide an efficient rate control mechanism for the SVC. However, none

of them handles scalable bit-rate control for the ROI coding. Thus, in Xu et al. (2005), the rate distortion optimization (RDO) involved in the step of encoding temporal subband pictures is only implemented on low-pass subband pictures, and rate control is independently applied to each spatial layer. Furthermore, for the temporal subband pictures obtained from the motion compensation temporal filtering (MCTF), the target bit allocation and quantization parameter selection inside a GOP make a full use of the hierarchical relations inheritance from the MCTF. In addition, (Liu et al., 2008) proposes a switched model to predict the mean absolute difference (MAD) of the residual texture from the available MAD information of the previous frame in the same layer and the same frame in its "Base-Layer". Further, Anselmo and Alfonso (2010) describe a constant quality variable bit-rate (VBR) control algorithm for multiple layer coding. According to Anselmo & Alfonso (2010), the algorithm allows the achievement of a target quality by specifying the memory capabilities and the bit-rate limitations of the storage device. In the more recent work of Roodaki et al. (2010), the joint optimization of layers in the layered video coding is investigated. The authors show that spatial scalability, like the fidelity/quality scalability, does benefit from joint optimization, though not being able to exploit the relation between the quantizer step sizes. Also, (Chi et al., 2008) present a fuzzy logic controller, which can adaptively adjust the weighting factor for corresponding quantization parameters (QPs) by the distortion variation in the macroblock layer. Also, a linear prediction formula, derived from the rate variation, is proposed by (Chi et al., 2008) to allocate appropriate bits for each ROI macroblock and maintain the target bit rate and buffer fullness.

Further, Grois et al. (2010b) present a method and system for the efficient ROI Scalable Video Coding, according to which a bit-rate that is very close to the target bit-rate is achieved, while being able to define the desirable ROI quality (in term of QP or Peak Signal-to-Noise Ratio (PSNR)) and while adaptively changing the background region quality (the background region excludes the ROI), according to the overall bit-rate. In order to provide the different visual presentation quality to at least one ROI and to the background (or other less important region of the frame), Grois et al. (2010b) divide each frame into at least two slices, while one slice is used for defining the ROI and at least one additional slice is used for defining the background region, for which fewer bits should be allocated.

In the following section, a novel complexity-aware ROI pre-processing scheme for the Scalable Video Coding is presented and discussed in detail.

COMPLEXITY AWARE REGION OF INTEREST SCALABLE VIDEO CODING BY PERFORMING PRE-PROCESSING

A novel method and system for an efficient adaptive spatial ROI pre-processing/pre-filtering for the Scalable Video Coding (Grois & Hadar, 2011c; Grois & Hadar, 2011d) is presented. This scheme is based on an adaptive SVC Computational Complexity-Rate-Distortion (SVC C-R-D) model, which is discussed in detail in the following section (the C-R-D model was extended from the authors' previous research (Kaminsky et al., 2008; Grois et al., 2010c) to support SVC systems).

The SVC spatial pre-filtering scheme enables to decrease the motion activity of the background region (or other less important regions within the video sequence), thereby decreasing overall quantization fluctuations. As a result, smaller quantization parameters can be used for encoding the ROIs, which leads to obtaining the high-quality visual presentation quality of the ROIs, while keeping the overall bandwidth substantially the same. Thus, the device computational resources are employed in an optimal manner, leading to the optimal video presentation quality even for

devices with very limited computational resources (e.g., mobile/cellular devices).

The pre-filter, which should be preferably used in the adaptive ROI SVC pre-processing system of Figure 14, is a Gaussian filter due to its relatively low computational complexity, in term of the CPU processing time (i.e. the CPU clocks). According to the simulation results, which are further presented in Table 5, the pre-processing of the Gaussian filter wastes relatively few computational complexity/power resources in term of the CPU processing time (CPU clocks), and also it lasts for a relatively short period of time, comparing to the Wiener or Wavelet filters.

Table 5 presents the simulation comparison results for pre-processing the *"SUNFLOWER"* video sequence, having various spatial resolutions: 1080p, 720p, and 4CIF (SD), by means of Gaussian, Wiener and Wavelet filters. In addition, the values of the Gaussian standard deviation parameter (σ) are varied from 2 to 8 (the test platform is: Intel® Core 2 Duo CPU, 2.33 GHz, 2GB RAM with Windows® XP Professional® operating system, version 2002, Service Pack 3). As clearly seen from Table 5, the pre-processing performed by the Gaussian filter wastes much less computational resources, when compared to the Wiener or Wavelet filters. Also, the PSNR and Structural Similarity (SSIM) values of the pre-processed video sequences remain relatively high, which is sufficient for pre-processing the background (or other predefined less important) regions. In such a way, it is ensured that the computational complexity for the pre-processing stage remains relatively low, and the CPU resources are not wasted.

It should be noted that the pre-filtering scheme of Grois & Hadar (2011c) and Grois & Hadar (2011d) is adaptively implemented for each layer of the Scalable Video Coding, according to the layer scalability (e.g., according to a particular spatial scalability such as the CIF or HD resolution). As a result, the pre-filtering process for each layer varies according to the above particular layer scalability; the pre-filter standard deviation σ and

Figure 14. Block-diagram of the proposed adaptive pre-filtering scheme for the ROI scalable video coding. For simplicity, only two layers (base-layer/layer 0 and enhancement layer/layer 1) are presented, while the layers' relationship is previously shown in Figure 13

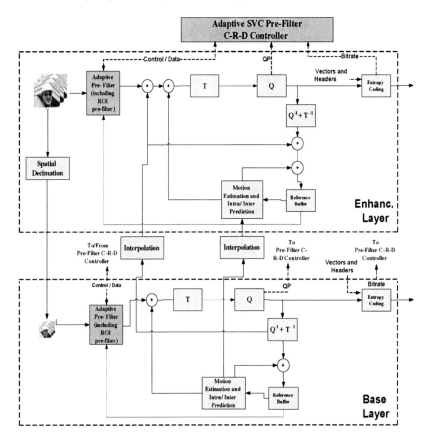

other parameters (e.g., the kernel matrix size) are adaptively adjusted by the Adaptive SVC Pre-Filter C-R-D Controller (as illustrated in Figure 14), according to the C-R-D analysis, which is discussed in the following section.

In addition, Table 6 shows the influence of the varying kernel matrix size (varying from 3×3 to 15×15) on the computational complexity of the pre-filtering process in term of the CPU processing time. The tested sequence is "*FOREMAN*", QCIF - *Layer 0*, CIF - *Layer 1*, 300 frames, 30 fp/s. Further, Table 6 presents, sample 3×3 Gaussian filter kernel matrices for different standard deviation (σ) values (varying from σ=0.5 to σ=1.5). As is observed from Table 6, the Gaussian kernel matrices having larger sizes lead to obtaining larger

computational complexity values. Therefore, in order to save computational resources, small-size Gaussian matrices should be used.

According to the pre-processing scheme of Figure 14, the Adaptive SVC Pre-Filter C-R-D Controller performs the C-R-D analysis of the input scalable video sequence, and adaptively determines the Gaussian filter standard deviation for pre-filtering the background region (or other predefined less important region) of each input sequence layer in order to optimally encode the video sequence in term of visual presentation quality. The bits which are removed from the background region due to the pre-filtering process, are reallocated according to the C-R-D model to the ROI, and as a result, the high-quality ROI

Table 5. Comparison results for pre-processing of "SUNFLOWER" video sequences having 1080p, 720p, and 4CIF spatial resolutions (80 frames, 30 fp/sec)

Reso-lution	Pre-Filter Type	Processing Time |sec|	Average PSNR Y |dB|	PSNR U |dB|	PSNR V |dB|	Y-SSIM	U-SSIM	V-SSIM
1080p	Gaussian (σ=2)	119.9	39.7	40.6	40.6	0.99	0.99	0.99
	Gaussian (σ=3)	119.9	36.5	37.3	39.0	0.99	0.99	0.98
	Gaussian (σ=5)	90.5	33.9	34.6	37.5	0.97	0.97	0.97
	Gaussian (σ=8)	90.3	32.8	33.6	37.0	0.96	0.96	0.96
	Wiener	177.4	37.0	38.1	40.9	0.97	0.97	0.97
	Wavelet	341.0	42.9	44.2	41.8	0.99	0.99	0.99
720p	Gaussian (σ=2)	59.2	36.6	37.3	40.5	0.99	0.99	0.98
	Gaussian (σ=3)	59.6	33.1	33.8	38.2	0.96	0.97	0.96
	Gaussian (σ=5)	48.2	30.4	31.2	36.5	0.93	0.93	0.93
	Gaussian (σ=8)	48.0	29.4	30.2	35.9	0.90	0.91	0.92
	Wiener	84.9	33.4	34.5	40.0	0.93	0.92	0.95
	Wavelet	145.2	41.8	42.8	42.8	0.99	0.99	0.99
4CIF	Gaussian (σ=2)	30.7	32.8	33.5	38.1	0.96	0.96	0.95
	Gaussian (σ=3)	30.7	29.5	30.2	36.0	0.90	0.91	0.92
	Gaussian (σ=5)	25.5	27.1	27.7	34.6	0.82	0.83	0.88
	Gaussian (σ=8)	25.6	26.2	27.0	34.1	0.78	0.80	0.87
	Wiener	40.6	29.7	31.1	38.1	0.90	0.90	0.91
	Wavelet	63.9	38.4	39.1	40.5	0.99	0.99	0.97

visual presentation is achieved. The ROI can be defined either as a separate SVC layer (e.g., the Base-Layer: *Layer 0*) or as a portion of any SVC layer (either the Base or Enhancement Layer).

Table 6. Gaussian kernel matrix size vs. computational complexity of the "foreman" video sequence (QCIF - layer 0, CIF -layer 1)

Standard Deviation (σ)	Gaussian Kernel Matrix Sizes/ Computational Complexity in Terms of CPU Processing Time (sec.)			
	3×3	7×7	11×11	15×15
σ=0.5	132.5	241.3	264.9	382.9
σ=1	129.1	250.0	302.2	342.0
σ=1.5	142.2	233.7	312.2	333.9
σ=2.0	117.9	230.8	301.4	305.1
σ=2.5	135.6	217.7	308.7	362.3

In addition, Figure 15 is an example of using the adaptive ROI SVC pre-processing scheme of Figure 14. The ROI is defined as a rectangular region including upper parts of the crew member bodies.

As already noted, the adaptive pre-processing is performed for each layer of the Scalable Video Coding, and the adaptive ROI SVC pre-processing system (Figure 14) enables to adaptively updates various parameters, such as a particular SVC layer scalability, filter standard deviation σ, filter kernel matrix size, etc.

Further, a transition region between the ROI and background can be provided, as shown in Figure 16. The Gaussian filters are used for the low-pass filtering of the background and transition regions of each frame within each SVC layer (except for *Layer 0*, where the ROI is provided

Figure 15. a) the original frame of the "CREW" SVC sequence (CIF resolution, 30fp/sec) b) the decoded frame of the "CREW" video sequence (layer 1; initial QP of layer 1 is 28; CIF resolution; 30fp/sec; PSNR (ROI) = 39.1; average PSNR=30.6; σ=1.5), which was pre-filtered and encoded by the adaptive ROI SVC pre-processing system of Figure 14

(a)   (b)

as a whole frame). The bits which are removed due to the pre-filtering process, are reallocated according to the C-R-D analysis to the ROI (Grois et al., 2011b; Grois et al., 2011c), and as a result, the high-quality ROI visual presentation is achieved. The ROI can be defined either as a separate SVC layer (e.g., the *Base-Layer: Layer 0*) or as a portion of any SVC layer (either the *Base or Enhancement Layer*). It should be noted that automatically determining and tracking of the exact ROI region can be performed according to many conventional techniques and algorithms (You et al., 2007).

In order to ensure a smooth transition from the ROI to the background, a transition region around the ROI is *adaptively* and *dynamically* defined for each SVC spatial layer, as schematically illustrated inFigure 16. The dynamic transition region of each SVC layer contains a variable number of filtered straps (e.g., from 5 to 20 filtered straps, where each strap has a width of a predefined number of pixels) around the ROI, while the closer the strap is located with respect to the ROI, then the higher visual quality it should have. For varying the visual quality of the straps, each strap can be pre-filtered by means of a Gaussian filter with a different standard deviation σ.

It should be noted that a gradual transition of the visual quality from the ROI toward the background is discussed in Karlsson & Sjostrom (2005) and Gopalan (2009). However, Karlsson & Sjostrom (2005) and Gopalan (2009) do not provide a solution for the scalable video coding, where different adaptive gradual transitions are required for each layer, according to a particular layer scalability (e.g., according to a particular spatial resolution, such as the CIF, HD or a particular temporal resolution, and at 15, 30 or 60 frames per second).

Figure 16. Providing a dynamic transition region for gradual transition from ROI to the background of an SVC video sequence

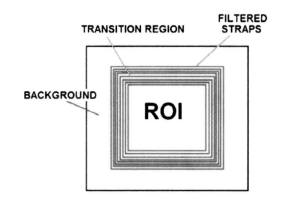

The corresponding computational complexity for providing the pre-filtered transition region with a varying number of Gaussian straps is summarized in Table 7, which refers to the pre-filtering of *Layer 1* of the following video sequences: "*FOREMAN*", "*CREW*", and "*MOBILE*" (the standard deviation range is 1-1.5; 100 frames; 30 fp/sec; Gaussian kernel matrix size is 3×3; *Layer 0* is the ROI (a crop of *Layer 1*)). As seen from Table 7, the more Gaussian filters are used, the greater is the CPU processing time of the pre-filtering process. Also, according to the experimental results of Grois et al.(2011b) and Grois et al. (2011c), in order to save computational resources, the small-size Gaussian kernel matrices should be used (e.g., the kernel matrix size of 3X3).

Further, Figure 17 presents PSNR values of the ROI region as a function of a varying number of Gaussian filters (from 5 to 15 filters) provided for pre-filtering the transition region.

As seen from Figure 17, the PSNR values are not influenced too much by increasing a number of Gaussian filters, and therefore, in order to save computational resources, only 5 pre-filtered straps can be used, while still obtaining substantially optimal visual presentation quality (Grois & Hadar, 2011c; Grois & Hadar, 2011d).

In the following section, the recent adavances in the complexity-aware bit allocation for the ROI Scalable Video Coding are further discussed.

COMPLEXITY AWARE BIT ALLOCATION FOR THE REGION OF INTEREST SCALABLE VIDEO CODING

There are several attempts to provide a solution for the complexity issues with regard to the Scalable Video Coding. Lin et al. (2010) present a computation control motion estimation method, which can perform motion estimation adaptively under different computation or power budgets, further evaluating the impact of different tools (such as key picture, etc.) on the performance of an SVC decoder. Also, Tan et al. (2009) propose a singularly parameterized complexity-scalable scheme for designing power-aware H.264 video encoders. However, traditional solutions, which consider the computational complexity constraints, are not related to the Region-of-Interest scalable video coding for providing the ROI high-quality visual presentation.

According to the novel complexity-aware adaptive ROI SVC pre-filtering scheme of Grois et al. (2011b) and Grois et al. (2011c), in addition to calculating the target bit-rate, the authors calculate the target encoding computational complexity that is required for encoding the current frame (and in turn, for encoding each macroblock within the frame) at each layer of the Scalable Video Coding. The target encoding computa-

Table 7. Computational complexity for pre-filtering the transition region with a different number of gaussian filters (100 frames, 30 fp/sec.)

No. of Pre-Filters	Video Sequences		
	FOREMAN [sec]	CREW [sec]	MOBILE [sec]
Pre-Processing only the Background	1.24	1.19	1.19
Pre-Processing also the Transition Region with 5 Gaussian Pre-Filters (5 straps)	1.90	1.76	1.73
Pre-Processing also the Transition Region with 10 Gaussian Pre-Filters (10 straps)	3.17	2.91	2.92
Pre-Processing also the Transition Region with 15 Gaussian Pre-Filters (15 straps)	4.24	4.07	4.13

Figure 17. PSNR values as a function of a varying number of Gaussian filters (from 5 to 15 pre-filters) provided for pre-filtering the transition region. Each Gaussian filter is used for pre-filtering a single transition region strap (which has a predefined width), as illustrated in Figure 16.

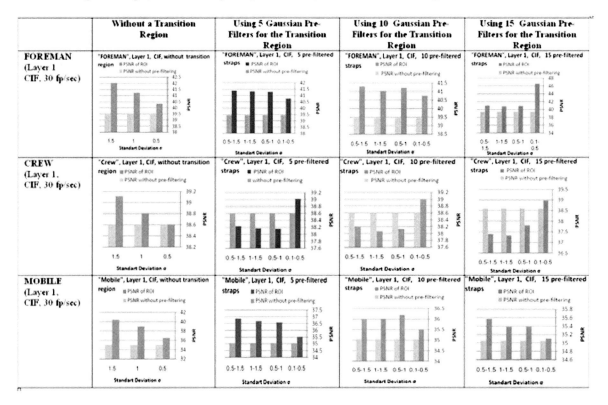

tional complexity $C_t^{Layer}(i)$ (Kaminsky et al., 2008; Grois et al., 2009; Grois et al., 2010c) for the frame i in each SVC layer should be a weighted combination of the remaining computational complexity for encoding the remaining frames, and the target encoding computational complexity allocated for frame i, which is formulated as:

$$C_t^{Layer}(i) = \alpha \cdot \tilde{C}_r^{Layer}(i) - (1-\alpha) \cdot \hat{C}_t^{Layer}(i) \tag{4}$$

where α is a weight coefficient; $\tilde{C}_r^{Layer}(i)$ is the remaining computational complexity for encoding the current frame i; and $\hat{C}_t^{Layer}(i)$ is the target encoding computational complexity allocated for frame i in the current GOP. $\tilde{C}_r^{Layer}(i)$ and $\hat{C}_t^{Layer}(i)$ are represented by the following expressions:

$$\tilde{C}_r^{Layer}(i) = \frac{C_r^{Layer}(i)}{N_r} \tag{5}$$

and

$$\hat{C}_t^{Layer}(i) = \frac{\dfrac{C_r^{Layer}(i)}{N_r} \cdot \Theta^2(i)}{\dfrac{1}{N - N_r} \sum_{j=1}^{N-N_r} \Theta^2(j)} \tag{6}$$

where, N_r is the number of remaining frames; and N is the total number of frames in the current GOP; $C_r^{Layer}(i)$ is the remaining computational complexity for encoding the remaining frames; $\Theta(i)$ is the predicted Mean Absolute Deviation (MAD) of the current frame i; and $\Theta(j)$ is the actual MAD of the previous frame. By using a linear prediction model, the target encoding complexity allocated for the *i* frame in the current GOP can be determined based on the predicted MAD of the current frame and the actual MADs of the previous frames. In turn, the bit-rate control C-S-R and R-Q-C models (Kaminsky et al., 2008; Grois et al., 2010c), for each SVC layer are as follows:

$$C^{SVC\_Layer}(S,R) = A_{C_1} \cdot S^{-1} + A_{C_2} \cdot S^{-2} + A_{C_3} \cdot R^{SVC\_Layer}$$
(7)

and

$$R^{SVC\_Layer}(Q,C) = A_{R_1} \cdot Q^{-1} + A_{R_2} \cdot Q^{-2} + A_{R_3} \cdot C^{SVC\_Layer}$$
(8)

where A_{C_1}, A_{C_2}, A_{C_3} and A_{R_1}, A_{R_2}, A_{R_3} are corresponding coefficients that are calculated for each SVC layer regressively, according to a linear regression method (Kaminsky et al., 2008; Grois et al., 2010c); *S* is the complexity step for selecting a corresponding group of coding modes for each SVC layer (e.g., Inter-Search16X8, Inter-Search8X16, Inter-Search8X8, Inter-Search8X4 modes); C^{SVC_Layer} is a computational complexity of encoding each SVC layer; R^{SVC_Layer} is the bit-rate for each SVC layer; and *Q* is the corresponding quantization step-size for performing the RDO for each macroblock in the current frame.

According to a buffer occupancy constraint, due to the finite reference SVC buffer size, the buffer at each SVC layer should not be full or empty (i.e. overloaded or underloaded, respectively). The formulation of the optimal buffer control (for controlling the buffer occupancy for each SVC layer) can be given by (Grois et al., 2009):

$$\min_{\{r(i)\}}\{\sum_{i=1}^{N} e(i)\}, \text{subject to } B^{Layer}_{max} \geq B^{Layer}(i) \geq 0$$
for $i = 1, 2, ..., N$
(9)

where $e(i)$ is a distortion for basic unit *i*; $B^{Layer}(i)$ is a buffer size and B^{Layer}_{max} is the maximal buffer size. The state of the buffer occupancy can be defined as:

$$B^{Layer}(i+1) = B^{Layer}(i) + r^{Layer}(i) - r^{Layer}_{out}$$
(10)

where $r^{Layer}(i)$ is the buffer input bit-rate with regard to each SVC layer and r^{Layer}_{out} is the output bit-rate of buffer contents.

It should be noted that the optimal buffer control approach is related to the following optimal bit allocation formulation:

$$\min_{\{r(i)\}}\{\sum_{i=1}^{N} e(i)\}, \text{ subject to } \sum_{i=1}^{n} r^{Layer}(i) \leq R^{Layer}$$
for $i = 1, 2, ..., N$
(11)

and is schematically presented in Figure 18.

For overcoming the buffer control drawbacks and overcoming buffer size limitations, thereby preventing underflow/overflow of the buffer, and significantly decreasing the buffer delay, the computational complexity (such as a number of CPU clocks) and bits of each basic unit within a video sequence can be dynamically allocated, according to its predicted MAD. In turn, the optimal buffer control problem can be solved by implementing the C-R-D analysis of (Grois et al., 2009) for each SVC layer.

As a result, the modified SVC encoder is capable of allocating computational complexity and bit-rate resources for each SVC layer for obtaining much better coding efficiency with improved processing speed in term of processing time. It should be noted that the computational complexity is mainly presented in term of the CPU processing time since the processing time can be easily tracked for updating the bit-rate control models and for the parameter adjustments on any computing platform.

Figure 18. (a) Each block (1...B$_N$) in the sequence has different R-D characteristics (for a given set of quantizers (1...Q$_M$) for blocks in the sequence, R-D (Rate-Distortion) points (r$_{N1}$, r$_{N2}$, r$_{N3}$ and d$_{N1}$, d$_{N2}$, d$_N$, etc.) can be obtained to form composite characteristics); and (b) R at t$_2$ is not a feasible solution to the selected maximum buffer size B$_{MAX}$

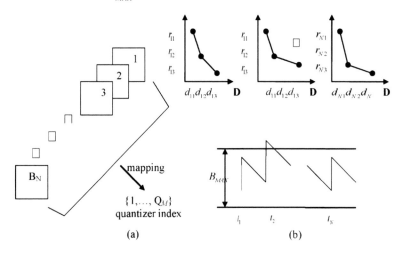

(a) (b)

For evaluating and testing the presented complexity-aware bit-rate control for the ROI scalable video coding, the following test platform was used: Intel® Core 2 Duo CPU, 2.33 GHz, 2GB RAM with Windows® XP Professional® operating system, version 2002, Service Pack 3. The general conditions for evaluating the presented adaptive ROI SVC pre-processing scheme are as follows: QP for *Layer 0* is 30; QP for *Layer 1* varies from 20 to 30; Spatial Resolution for *Layer 0* is QCIF or CIF, and for *Layer 0* is CIF or 4CIF/SD; 30fp/sec for either *Layer 0* or *Layer 1*; Motion Vector (MV) search range is 16; Number of coded frames is from 100 to 300; Fast Search is ON, GOP structure is IPPP.

Table 8 presents the PSNR and bit-rate values for the SVC video sequences ("*FOREMAN*", "*CREW*", and "*MOBILE*") encoded by a conventional JSVM reference encoder (JSVM 9.19).

On the other hand, Table 9 presents the encoding of the same SVC video sequences ("*FOREMAN*", "*CREW*", and "*MOBILE*") by using the novel adaptive ROI SVC pre-filtering scheme of (Grois et al., 2011b; Grois et al., 2011c) with varying standard deviation σ and with varying quantization parameters (QPs). The size of the Region-of-Interest in *Layer 1* (which has the 4CIF/SD resolution) is about 25% of the frame size. It is noted that the *Layer 0* (CIF resolution) is not shown in Table 9, since it represents only the Region-of-Interest (without the background).

As is clearly seen from Table 9, there is a significant improvement - *approximately, up to 7 dB* for the ROI region in *Layer 1*, when compared to results of Table 8, which are based on the JSVM 9.19 reference software (JSVM, 2009). The Gaussian filter standard deviation σ values are varied from 0.5 to 1.5, and the bit-rate remains substantially the same.

Table 8. Bit-rate and PSNR values for encoding SVC video sequences on JSVM 9.19

Tested Video Sequences (on JSVM 9.19)		Bit-Rate (Kb/sec)	Average PSNR of the ROI
FOREMAN	Layer 1	2695.5	**39.5**
CREW	Layer 1	2689.3	**38.6**
MOBILE	Layer 1	6801.0	**33.0**

Table 9. Bit-rate and PSNR comparison of various test sequences, according to the proposed SVC pre-filtering scheme of Figure 14

Tested Video Sequences		Bit-Rate (Kb/sec)	Average PSNR [dB]	Average PSNR of the ROI *in Layer 1* [dB]
FOREMAN (0.5<σ<1)	Layer 1	2719.5	37.9	**41.8**
FOREMAN (1<σ<1.5)	Layer 1	2674.4	37.4	**42.3**
CREW(0.5<σ<1)	Layer 1	2772.7	37.6	**38.8**
CREW(1<σ<1.5)	Layer 1	2621.3	37.3	**39.1**
MOBILE(0.5<σ<1)	Layer 1	7207.0	33.8	**39.0**
MOBILE(1<σ<1.5)	Layer 1	7258.1	34.0	**40.4**

Also, Figure 19 presents experimental results for performing the C-R-D analysis (on frame and macroblock levels) for pre-processing and encoding the "FOREMAN", "SOCCER", and "CREW" video sequences (1 or 5 Reference Frames; GOP size is 16; GOP type is IPPP*)*. As it is seen from Figure 19, when implementing the C-R-D analysis on either frame or macroblock levels, there is a very significant improvement in the encoding time and also in PSNR values, compared to JSVM 9.19 reference software (JSVM, 2009).

Figure 19. a) Experimental results for the "FOREMAN", "FOOTBALL", "CREW", and "SOCCER" video sequences (GOP size is 16; GOP type is IPPP)

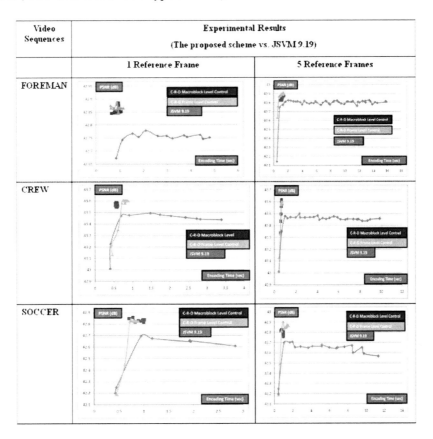

In the following section the SVC Medium Grained Scalability (MGS) and SVC Coarse Grain Scalability (CGS) comparison is presented.

MEDIUM GRAINED SCALABILITY AND COARSE GRAIN SCALABILITY COMPRESSION

The quality/fidelity scalability of H.264/SVC can be considered as a special case of the spatial scalability with identical picture sizes for base and enhancement layer (Schwarz et al., 2007). This case is supported by the general concept for spatial scalable coding, and it is also referred to as coarse-grain quality scalable coding (CGS). The same inter-layer prediction mechanisms as for spatial scalable coding are employed, but without using the corresponding upsampling operations and the inter-layer deblocking for intra-coded reference layer macroblocks. Furthermore, the inter-layer intra- and residual-prediction are directly performed in the transform domain (Schwarz et al., 2007).

When utilizing inter-layer prediction for coarse-grain quality scalability in SVC, a refinement of texture information is typically achieved by requantizing the residual texture signal in the enhancement layer with a smaller quantization step size relative to that used for the preceding CGS layer. However, this multilayer concept for quality scalable coding only allows a few selected bit rates to be supported in a scalable bit stream. In general, the number of supported rate points is identical to the number of layers. Switching between different CGS layers can only be done at defined points in the bit stream (Schwarz et al., 2007). Therefore, for increasing the flexibility of bit stream adaptation and error robustness, and also for improving the coding efficiency for bit streams that have to provide a variety of bit rates, a variation of the CGS approach, which is also referred to as medium-grain quality scalability (MGS), is provided in the SVC standard. The differences to the CGS concept are a modified high-level signaling, which allows a switching

between different MGS layers in any access unit. With the MGS concept, any enhancement layer NAL unit can be discarded from a quality scalable bit stream, and thus packet-based quality scalable coding is provided (Schwarz et al., 2007).

With this regard, the performance of the JSVM 9.19 reference software (JSVM, 2009) was compared with the adaptive bit-rate control method of Grois et al. (2010b) with regard to the Medium Grained Scalability (MGS) and Coarse Grain Scalability (CGS) of the Scalable Video Coding. For this, In JSVM 9.19, three quality layers of QCIF, CIF and SD resolutions (*"STOCKHOLM"* video sequence) were used. On the other hand, in the proposed adaptive bit-rate control method, only two quality layers of CIF and SD resolutions were used. Then, the quality and bit-rate of the Base-Layer (*Layer 0*) and Enhancement Layer (*Layer 1*) were compared.

As it is clearly seen from the MGS scalability comparison presented in Tables 10 and 11, the proposed bit-rate control scheme of Grois et al. (2010b) provides, for each layer, much better results in terms of the bit-rate and in terms of the PSNR (the PSNR degradation, when it exists, is negligible). Further, Figures 20 and 21 present additional MGS comparison results, respectively with Tables 10 and 11.

Further, Figure 22 presents a ratio of the MGS and CGS scalabilities with regard to the adaptive bit-rate control of Grois et al. (2010b).

As it is seen from *Figure 22*, the MGS and CGS of the Base-Layer (*Layer 0*) are the same, and the MGS of the Enhancement Layer (*Layer 1*) provides better results in term of the PSNR values.

This chapter is concluded by presenting the following future research directions.

FUTURE RESEARCH DIRECTIONS AND CONCLUSION

The *research* in 3D video coding is limited, and the issues, such as the 3D ROI detection and

Table 10. MGS comparison of the JSVM 9.19 reference software with the adaptive bit-rate control method of Grois et al. (2010b)- 3 layers of JSVM 9.19 vs. 2 layers of the rate control method of Grois et al. (2010b)

Layer 0 –proposed Rate Control		Layer 0 - JSVM 9.19	
Bit-Rate [kb/sec]	Average PSNR [dB]	Bit-Rate [kb/sec]	Average PSNR [dB]
56.5	33.6	87.0	32.4
71.5	34.4	102.8	35.2
119.8	35.8	156.4	37.9
Layer 1 – proposed Rate Control		Layer 1 - JSVM 9.19	
Bit-Rate [kb/sec]	Average PSNR [dB]	Bit-Rate [kb/sec]	Average PSNR [dB]
158.4	34.2	279.0	33.4
178.7	34.7	325.6	35.8
239.2	35.7	548.0	37.9

Table 11. Additional MGS comparison of the JSVM 9.19 reference software with the adaptive bit-rate control method of Grois et al. (2010b) - 4 layers of JSVM 9.19 vs. 2 layers of the rate control method of Grois et al. (2010b)

Layer 0 – proposed Rate Control		Layer 0 - JSVM 9.19	
Bit-Rate [kb/sec]	Average PSNR [dB]	Bit-Rate [kb/sec]	Average PSNR [dB]
356.5	33.6	89.4	32.4
71.5	34.4	105.2	35.2
119.8	35.8	158.7	37.9
Layer 1 –proposed Rate Control		Layer 1 – JSVM 9.19	
Bit-Rate [kb/sec]	Average PSNR [dB]	Bit-Rate [kb/sec]	Average PSNR [dB]
158.4	34.2	281.4	33.4
178.7	34.7	327.9	35.8
239.2	35.4	550.3	37.9

Figure 20. MGS scalability comparison of the JSVM 9.19 reference software versus the proposed bit-rate control method (3 layers of JSVM 9.19 vs. 2 layers of the proposed rate control method). The tested QP values for each layer are: 30, 35, and 40.

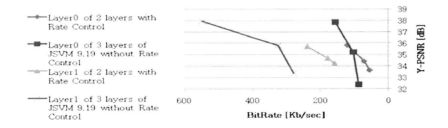

Figure 21. Additional MGS scalability comparison of the JSVM 9.19 reference software versus the proposed bit-rate control method (4 layers of JSVM 9.19 vs. 2 layers of the proposed rate control method). The tested QP values for each layer are: 30, 35, and 40.

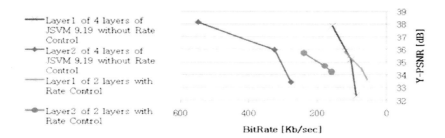

tracking, 3D object/face detection and recognition, and the like, are very challenging, especially when used in surveillance systems. In addition, both in 2D and 3D, the ROI temporal filtering for scalable video coding should be handled in a more appropriate manner in order to improve the overall visual presentation quality (which is reduced due to the filtering of the background in a temporal domain). A possible solution for this can be performing "intelligent" post-filtering at the decoder end in order to at least partially recover the lost temporal information.

Also, there is still a need to reduce the computational complexity for processing and coding videos with one or more regions-of-interest, especially for real-time/live systems, and in turn, to

decrease the end-to-end delay in order to improve the user visual experience.

Further, techniques mentioned in this chapter (such as the ROI complexity-aware bit allocation, ROI cropping, ROI coding by using the FMO, bit-rate control for the ROI coding, etc.) should be evaluated and tested in detail with regard to the emerging High Efficiency Video Coding (HEVC) standard, which is expected to be officially declared during the next year, and which is expected to widely penetrate the multimedia market due to its significantly improved coding efficiency (e.g., currently provides up to 50% bit-rate savings).

This chapter covered the Region-of-Interest processing and coding for video applications, making a special emphasis on the relatively new

Figure 22. CGS/MGS scalability comparison of the adaptive bit-rate control of Grois et al. (2010b). The tested QP values for each layer are: 30, 35, and 40.

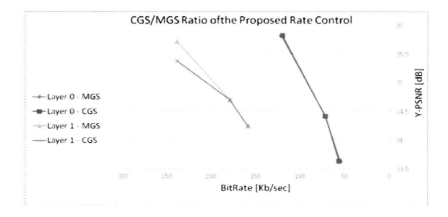

Scalable Video Coding standard, which introduced various scalability domains, such as spatial, temporal and fidelity/quality domains. First of all, the authors presented the Region-of-Interest detection and tracking techniques, while discussing various approaches, such as the visual attention model, object detection, face detection, and skin detection. Second, recent advances in ROI transmission techniques were discusses, emphasizing the ROI-based error-resilience transmission. Then, the ROI image processing methods using JPEG2000 were described in detail. After that, the ROI coding for the H.264/SVC standard was presented, including the ROI scalability by performing cropping and the ROI scalability by using the FMO technique. Then, the bit-rate control techniques for the ROI coding were discussed, followed by the detailed discussion of the complexity-aware ROI scalable video coding, while focusing on the complexity-aware SVC bit allocation, and presenting a comparison between the Medium Grained Scalability and Coarse Grain Scalability of the Scalable Video Coding. All observations and conclusions were supported by a variety of experimental results, which were further compared to the SVC reference software (JSVM 9.19).

ACKNOWLEDGMENT

This work was supported by the NEGEV consortium, MAGNET Program of the Israeli Chief Scientist, Israeli Ministry of Trade and Industry under Grant 85265610. The authors thank Guy Azulay, Adir Atias, Ronen Varfman, Idan Ori, Ron Heiman, Ran Dubin, Aviad Hadarian, Igor Medvetsky, Evgeny Kaminsky and Alexander Samochin for their assistance in evaluation and testing.

Also, the authors thank anonymous reviewers for their valuable comments and suggestions.

REFERENCES

Abdullah-Al-Wadud, M., & Oksam, C. (2007). Region-of-Interest selection for skin detection based applications. *International Conference on Convergence Information Technology*, 2007, (pp. 1999-2004). 21-23 Nov. 2007.

Abousleman, G. P. (2009). Target-tracking-based ultra-low-bit-rate video coding. *Military Communications Conference, MILCOM 2009*, IEEE, (pp. 1-6).

Aggarwal, A., Biswas, S., Singh, S., Sural, S., & Majumdar, A. K. (2006). *Object tracking using background subtraction and motion estimation in MPEG videos. ACCV 2006, LNCS* (Vol. 3852, pp. 121–130). Heidelberg, Germany: Springer.

Anselmo, T., & Alfonso, D. (2010). Constant quality variable bit-rate control for SVC. *2010 11th International Workshop on Image Analysis for Multimedia Interactive Services* (WIAMIS), (pp. 1-4).

Babu, R. V., Ramakrishnan, K. R., & Srinivasan, S. H. (2004). Video object segmentation: A compressed domain approach. *IEEE Transactions on Circuits and Systems for Video Technology*, 14(4), 462–474.

Bartrina-Rapesta, J., Serra-Sagrista, J., & Auli-Llinas, F. (2009). JPEG2000 ROI coding with fine-grain accuracy through rate-distortion optimization techniques. *Signal Processing Letters*, 16(1), 45–48.

Benzougar, A., Bouthemy, P., & Fablet, R. (2001). MRF-based moving object detection from MPEG coded video. In *Proceedings of the IEEE International Conference on Image Processing, 2001*, Vol. 3, (pp. 402-405).

Bhanu, B., Dudgeon, D. E., Zelnio, E. G., Rosenfeld, A., Casasent, D., & Reed, I. S. (1997). Guest editorial introduction to the special issue on automatic target detection and recognition. *IEEE Transactions on Image Processing, 6*(1), 1–6. doi:10.1109/TIP.1997.552076

Bradley, A. P., & Stentiford, F. W. M. (2002). JPEG2000 and region of interest coding. *Digital Image Computing: Techniques and Applications* (DICTA'02), Melbourne, Australia, (pp. 303-308). Jan. 2002.

Chen, C.-C., & Chen, O. T.-C. (2004). Region of interest determined by perceptual-quality and rate-distortion optimization in JPEG 2000. *Proceedings of the 2004 International Symposium on Circuits and Systems, ISCAS '04*, Vol. 3, (pp. III- 869-72).

Chen, H., Han, Z., Hu, R., & Ruan, R. (2008). Adaptive FMO selection strategy for error resilient H.264 coding. *International Conference on Audio, Language and Image Processing, ICALIP 2008*, July 7-9, (pp. 868-872). Shanghai, China.

Chen, M.-J., Chi, M.-C., Hsu, C.-T., & Chen, J.-W. (2003). ROI video coding based on H.263+ with robust skin-color detection technique. *2003 IEEE International Conference on Consumer Electronics, ICCE 2003*, (pp. 44-45).

Chen, O. T.-C., & Chen, C.-C. (2007). Automatically-determined region of interest in JPEG 2000. *IEEE Transactions on Multimedia, 9*(7), 1333–1345. doi:10.1109/TMM.2007.906572

Chen, Q.-H., Xie, X.-F., Guo, T.-J., Shi, L., & Wang, X.-F. (2010). The study of ROI detection based on visual attention mechanism. *2010 6th International Conference on Wireless Communications Networking and Mobile Computing (WiCOM)*, (pp. 1-4).

Cheng, W.-H., Chu, W.-T., Kuo, J.-H., & Wu, J.-L. (2005). Automatic video region-of-interest determination based on user attention model. In *Proceedings of IEEE International Symposium on Circuits and Systems* (ISCAS '05), (pp. 3219-3222).

Chi, M.-C., Chen, M.-J., Yeh, C.-H., & Jhu, J.-A. (2008). Region-of-interest video coding based on rate and distortion variations for H.263+. *Signal Processing Image Communication, 23*(2), 127–142. doi:10.1016/j.image.2007.12.001

Duchowski, A. T. (2000). Acuity-matching resolution degradation through wavelet coefficient scaling. *IEEE Transactions on Image Processing, 9*(8), 1437–1440. doi:10.1109/83.855439

Duong, T. Q., & Zepernick, H.-J. (2008). On the performance of ROI-based image transmission using cooperative diversity. *IEEE International Symposium on Wireless Communication Systems, ISWCS '08*, (pp. 340-343).

Engelke, U., Zepernick, H.-J., & Maeder, A. (2009). Visual attention modeling: Region-of-interest versus fixation patterns. *Picture Coding Symposium, PCS 2009*, (pp. 1-4).

Francois, E., & Vieron, J. (2006). Extended spatial scalability: a generalization of spatial scalability for non dyadic configurations. *2006 IEEE International Conference on Image Processing*, (pp. 169-172).

Fukuma, S., Ikuta, S., Ito, M., Nishimura, S., & Nawate, M. (2003). An ROI image coding based on switching wavelet transform. *Proceedings of the 2003 International Symposium on Circuits and Systems, ISCAS '03*, Vol. 2, (pp. II-420- II-423).

Gong, W., Rao, K. R., & Manry, M. T. (1993). Progressive image transmission. *IEEE Transactions on Circuits and Systems for Video Technology, 3*(5), 380–383. doi:10.1109/76.246089

Gopalan, R. (2009). *Exploiting region-of-interest for improved video coding.* Department of Electrical and Computer Engineering, Ohio State University, Thesis, 2009.

Grois, D., & Hadar, O. (2011a). Efficient adaptive bit-rate control for scalable video coding by using computational complexity-rate-distortion analysis. *2011 IEEE International Symposium on Broadband Multimedia Systems and Broadcasting* (BMSB), (pp. 1-6). Nuremberg, Germany, 8-10 Jun. 2011.

Grois, D., & Hadar, O. (2011b). Recent advances in region-of-interest coding . In Del Ser Lorente, J. (Ed.), *Recent advances on video coding* (pp. 49–76). Intech. doi:10.5772/17789

Grois, D., & Hadar, O. (2011c). Complexity-aware adaptive bit-rate control with dynamic ROI pre-processing for scalable video coding. *2011 IEEE International Conference on Multimedia and Expo* (ICME), (pp. 1-4). Barcelona, Spain, 11-15 Jul. 2011.

Grois, D., & Hadar, O. (2011d). *Complexity-aware adaptive spatial pre-processing for ROI scalable video coding with dynamic transition region.* International Conference on Image Processing (ICIP 2011), Brussels, Belgium, 11-14 Sep. 2011.

Grois, D., Kaminsky, E., & Hadar, O. (2009). Buffer control in H.264/AVC applications by implementing dynamic complexity-rate-distortion analysis. *IEEE International Symposium on Broadband Multimedia Systems and Broadcasting, BMSB '09,* (pp. 1-7).

Grois, D., Kaminsky, E., & Hadar, O. (2010a). ROI adaptive scalable video coding for limited bandwidth wireless networks. *2010 IFIP Wireless Days* (WD), (pp. 1-5).

Grois, D., Kaminsky, E., & Hadar, O. (2010b). Adaptive bit-rate control for region-of-interest scalable video coding. *2010 IEEE 26th Convention of Electrical and Electronics Engineers in Israel* (IEEEI), (pp. 761-765).

Grois, D., Kaminsky, E., & Hadar, O. (2010c). Optimization methods for H.264/AVC video coding . In Angelides, M. C., & Agius, H. (Eds.), *The handbook of MPEG applications: Standards in practice.* Chichester, UK: John Wiley & Sons, Ltd. doi:10.1002/9780470974582.ch7

Han, S., & Vasconcelos, N. (2008). Object-based regions of interest for image compression. *Data Compression Conference, DCC 2008,* (pp. 132-141).

Hanfeng, C., Yiqiang, Z., & Feihu, Q. (2001). Rapid object tracking on compressed video. In *Proceeding of the 2nd IEEE Pacific Rim Conference on Multimedia,* Oct. 2001, (pp. 1066-1071).

Haritaoglu, I., Harwood, D., & Davis, L. S. (2000). W4: real-time surveillance of people and their activities. *IEEE Transactions on Pattern Analysis and Machine Intelligence, 22*(8), 809–830. doi:10.1109/34.868683

Hu, Y., Rajan, D., & Chia, L. (2008). Detection of visual attention regions in images using robust subspace analysis. *Journal of Visual Communication and Image Representation, 19*(3), 199–216. doi:10.1016/j.jvcir.2007.11.001

Jamrozik, M. L., & Hayes, M. H. (2002). A compressed domain video object segmentation system. In *Proceedings of the IEEE International Conference on Image Processing, 2002,* Vol. 1, (pp. 113-116).

Jeong, C. Y., Han, S. W., Choi, S. G., & Nam, T. Y. (2006). An objectionable image detection system based on region of interest. *2006 IEEE International Conference on Image Processing,* (pp.1477-1480).

Jerbi, A., Jian, W., & Shirani, S. (2004). Error-resilient ROI coding using pre- and post-processing for video sequences. *Proceedings of the 2004 International Symposium on Circuits and Systems, ISCAS '04,* Vol.3, (pp. 757-60).

Jerbi, A., Jian, W., & Shirani, S. (2005). Error-resilient region-of-interest video coding. *IEEE Transactions on Circuits and Systems for Video Technology, 15*(9), 1175–1181. doi:10.1109/TCSVT.2005.852619

Ji, S., & Park, H. W. (2000). Moving object segmentation in DCT-based compressed video. *Electronics Letters, 36*(21). doi:10.1049/el:20001279

JSVM. (2009). *JSVM software manual*, ver. JSVM 9.19 (CVS tag: JSVM_9_19), Nov. 2009.

Kaminsky, E., Grois, D., & Hadar, O. (2008). Dynamic computational complexity and bit allocation for optimizing H.264/AVC video compression. *Journal of Visual Communication and Image Research, 19*(1), 56–74. doi:10.1016/j.jvcir.2007.05.002

Karlsson, L. S., & Sjostrom, M. (2005). Improved ROI video coding using variable Gaussian pre-filters and variance in intensity. *IEEE International Conference on Image Processing, ICIP 2005*, Vol. 2, (pp. 313-16).

Kas, C., & Nicolas, H. (2009). Compressed domain indexing of scalable H.264/SVC streams. *Signal Processing Image Communication (2009), Special Issue on Scalable Coded Media beyond Compression,* 484-498.

Katz, B., Greenberg, S., Yarkoni, N., Blaunstien, N., & Giladi, R. (2007). New error-resilient scheme based on FMO and dynamic redundant slices allocation for wireless video transmission. *IEEE Transactions on Broadcasting, 53*(1), 308–319. doi:10.1109/TBC.2006.889694

Ke, C.-H., Chilamkurti, N., Dudeja, G., & Shieh, C.-K. (2006). *A new adaptive FEC algorithm for wireless LAN networks.* The IASTED International Conference on Networks and Communication Systems, March 29-31, 2006, Chiang Mai, Thailand.

Kim, D.-K., & Wang, Y.-F. (2009). Smoke detection in video. *2009 WRI World Congress on Computer Science and Information Engineering,* Vol. 5, (pp. 759-763).

Kodikara Arachchi, H., Fernando, W. A. C., Panchadcharam, S., & Weerakkody, W. A. R. J. (2006). Unequal error protection technique for ROI based H.264 video coding. *Canadian Conference on Electrical and Computer Engineering,* (pp. 2033-2036).

Kong, H.-S., Vetro, A., Hata, T., & Kuwahara, N. (2005). Fast region-of-interest transcoding for JPEG 2000 images. *IEEE International Symposium on Circuits and Systems, ISCAS 2005*, Vol. 2 (pp. 952- 955).

Kwon, H., Han, H., Lee, S., Choi, W., & Kang, B. (2010). New video enhancement preprocessor using the region-of-interest for the video-conferencing. *IEEE Transactions on Consumer Electronics, 56*(4), 2644–2651. doi:10.1109/TCE.2010.5681152

Lambert, P., Schrijver, D. D., Van Deursen, D., De Neve, W., Dhondt, Y., & Van de Walle, R. (2006). *A real-time content adaptation framework for exploiting ROI scalability in H.264/AVC* (pp. 442–453). Advanced Concepts for Intelligent Vision Systems. doi:10.1007/11864349_40

Li, F., & Gao, Y. (2011). ROI-based error resilient coding of H.264 for conversational video communication. *2011 7th International Wireless Communications and Mobile Computing Conference* (IWCMC), (pp. 1719-1723).

Li, Z., Pan, F., Lim, K. P., Feng, G., Lin, X., & Rahardja, S. (2003). *Adaptive basic unit layer rate control for JVT.* In Joint Video Team (JVT) of ISO/IEC MPEG and ITU-T VCEG (ISO/IEC JTC1/SC29/WG11 and ITU-T SG16 Q.6), Doc. JVT-G012, Pattaya, Thailand, Mar. 2003.

Li, Z., Zhang, X., Zou, F., & Hu, D. (2010). Study of target detection based on top-down visual attention. *2010 3rd International Congress on Image and Signal Processing* (CISP), Vol. 1, (pp.377-380).

Li, Z. G., Yao, W., Rahardja, S., & Xie, S. (2007). New framework for encoder optimization of scalable video coding. *2007 IEEE Workshop on Signal Processing Systems*, (pp. 527-532).

Lim, N.-K., Kim, D.-Y., & Lee, H. (2010). Interactive progressive image transmission for realtime applications. *IEEE Transactions on Consumer Electronics*, *56*(4), 2438–2444. doi:10.1109/TCE.2010.5681125

Lin, W., Panusopone, K., Baylon, D. M., & Sun, M.-T. (2010). A computation control motion estimation method for complexity-scalable video coding. *IEEE Transactions on Circuits and Systems for Video Technology*, *20*(11), 1533–1543. doi:10.1109/TCSVT.2010.2077773

Lin, Y., & Bhanu, B. (2005). Object detection via feature synthesis using MDL-based genetic programming. *IEEE Transactions on Systems, Man, and Cybernetics. Part B, Cybernetics*, *35*(3), 538–547. doi:10.1109/TSMCB.2005.846656

Liu, B., Sun, M., Liu, Q., Kassam, A., Li, C.-C., & Sclabassi, R. J. (2006). Automatic detection of region of interest based on object tracking in neurosurgical video. *27th Annual International Conference of the Engineering in Medicine and Biology Society, IEEE-EMBS 2005*, (pp. 6273-6276).

Liu, L., & Fan, G. (2003). A new JPEG2000 region-of-interest image coding method: Partial significant bitplanes shift. *Signal Processing Letters*, *10*(2), 35–38. doi:10.1109/LSP.2002.807867

Liu, L., Zhang, S., Ye, X., & Zhang, Y. (2005). Error resilience schemes of H.264/AVC for 3G conversational video services. *The Fifth International Conference on Computer and Information Technology*, (pp. 657- 661).

Liu, Y., Li, Z. G., & Soh, Y. C. (2008a). Rate control of H.264/AVC scalable extension. *IEEE Transactions on Circuits and Systems for Video Technology*, *18*(1), 116–121. doi:10.1109/TCSVT.2007.903325

Liu, Y., Li, Z.-G., & Soh, Y.-C. (2008b). Region-of-Interest based resource allocation for conversational video communication of H.264/AVC. *IEEE Transactions on Circuits and Systems for Video Technology*, *18*(1), 134–139. doi:10.1109/TCSVT.2007.913754

Liu, Z., Chai, Z., & Xing, P. (2009). ROI auto-detecting and coding method for MRI images transmission. *ICME International Conference on Complex Medical Engineering*, (pp. 1-4).

Lu, Z., Lin, W., Li, Z., Pang Lim, K., Lin, X., Rahardja, S., et al. (2005b). *Perceptual region-of-interest (ROI) based scalable video coding.* JVT-O056, Busan, KR, 16-22 Apr., 2005.

Lu, Z., Peng, W.-H., Choi, H., Thang, T. C., & Shengmei, S. (2005a). *CE8: ROI-based scalable video coding.* JVT-O308, Busan, KR, 16-22 April, 2005.

Luo, R., & Chen, B. (2008). A hierarchical scheme of flexible macroblock ordering for ROI based H.264/AVC video coding. *10th International Conference on Advanced Communication Technology, ICACT 2008*, Vol. 3, (pp. 1579-1582).

Luo, Z., Li, S., & Shibao, Z. (2009).Offset based leaky prediction for error resilient ROI coding. *IEEE International Conference on Multimedia and Expo, ICME 2009*, (pp. 145-148).

Manerba, F., Benois-Pineau, J., Leonardi, R., & Mansencal, B. (2008). Multiple object extraction from compressed video. *EURASIP Journal on Advances in Signal Processing, 2008*, 231930. doi:10.1155/2008/231930

Mehmood, M. O. (2009). Study and implementation of color-based object tracking in monocular image sequences. *2009 IEEE Student Conference on Research and Development* (SCOReD), (pp. 109-111).

Micheloni, C., Salvador, E., Bigaran, F., & Foresti, G. L. (2005). An integrated surveillance system for outdoor security. *IEEE Conference on Advanced Video and Signal Based Surveillance, AVSS 2005* (pp. 480- 485).

Mustafah, Y. M., Bigdeli, A., Azman, A. W., & Lovell, B. C. (2009). Face detection system design for real time high resolution smart camera. *Third ACM/IEEE International Conference on Distributed Smart Cameras, ICDSC 2009* (pp. 1-6).

Ndili, O., & Ogunfunmi, T. (2006). On the performance of a 3D flexible macroblock ordering for H.264/AVC. *Digest of Technical Papers International Conference on Consumer Electronics, 2006,* (pp. 37-38).

Nguyen, A., Chandran, V., Sridharan, S., & Prandolini, R. (2003). Interpretability performance assessment of JPEG2000 and part 1 compliant region of interest coding. *IEEE Transactions on Consumer Electronics, 49*(4), 808–817. doi:10.1109/TCE.2003.1261159

Niu, Y., Wu, X., & Shi, G. (2009). Edge-based dynamic ROI coding with standard compliance. *IEEE International Workshop on Multimedia Signal Processing, MMSP '09*, (pp. 1-6).

Park, K.-H., & Park, H.-W. (2002). Region-of-interest coding based on set partitioning in hierarchical trees. *IEEE Transactions on Circuits and Systems for Video Technology, 12*(2), 106–113. doi:10.1109/76.988657

Phadikar, A., & Maity, S. P. (2009). ROI based error concealment of object based image using data hiding in JPEG 2000 coding pipeline. *2009 Annual IEEE India Conference* (INDICON), (pp. 1-4).

Phadikar, A., & Maity, S. P. (2010). ROI based error concealment of compressed object based image using QIM data hiding and wavelet transform. *IEEE Transactions on Consumer Electronics, 56*(2), 971–979. doi:10.1109/TCE.2010.5506028

Porikli, F., & Sun, H. (2005). *Compressed domain video object segmentation.* Technical Report TR2005-040, Mitsubishi Electric Research Lab, 2005.

Qayyum, U., & Javed, M. Y. (2006). Real time notch based face detection, tracking and facial feature localization. *International Conference on Emerging Technologies, ICET '06*, (pp. 70-75).

Quast, K., & Kaup, A. (2008). Spatial scalable region of interest transcoding of JPEG2000 for video surveillance. *IEEE Fifth International Conference on Advanced Video and Signal Based Surveillance, AVSS '08*, (pp. 203-210).

Raj, K. C. E., Venkataraman, S., & Varadan, G. (2008). A fuzzy approach to region of interest coding in JPEG 2000 for automatic target recognition applications from high-resolution satellite images. Sixth Indian Conference on Computer Vision, Graphics & Image Processing, ICVGIP '08, (pp. 193-200).

Reichel, J., & Nadenau, M. J. (2000). How to measure arithmetic complexity of compression algorithms: A simple solution. *2000 IEEE International Conference on Multimedia and Expo, ICME 2000*, Vol. 3, (pp. 1743-1746).

Roodaki, H., Rabiee, H. R., & Ghanbari, M. (2010). Rate-distortion optimization of scalable video codecs. *Signal Processing Image Communication, 25*(4), 276–286. doi:10.1016/j.image.2010.01.004

Sadykhov, R. K., & Lamovsky, D. V. (2008). Algorithm for real time faces detection in 3D space. *International Multiconference on Computer Science and Information Technology, IMCSIT 2008*, (pp. 727-732).

Sanchez, V., Basu, A., & Mandal, M. K. (2004). Prioritized region of interest coding in JPEG2000. *IEEE Transactions on Circuits and Systems for Video Technology, 14*(9), 1149–1155. doi:10.1109/TCSVT.2004.833168

Schierl, T., Hellge, C., Mirta, S., Gruneberg, K., & Wiegand, T. (2007). Using H.264/AVC-based scalable video coding (SVC) for real time streaming in wireless IP networks. *IEEE International Symposium on Circuits and Systems, ISCAS 2007*, (pp. 3455-3458).

Schoepflin, T., Chalana, V., Haynor, D. R., & Kim, Y. (2001). Video object tracking with a sequential hierarchy of template deformations. *IEEE Transactions on Circuits and Systems for Video Technology, 11*, 1171–1182. doi:10.1109/76.964784

Schwarz, H., Marpe, D., & Wiegand, T. (2007). Overview of the scalable video coding extension of the H.264/AVC standard. *IEEE Transactions on Circuits and Systems for Video Technology, 17*(9), 1103–1120. doi:10.1109/TCSVT.2007.905532

Shanableh, T., May, T., & Ishtiaq, F. Applications of distributed source coding to error resiliency of pre-encoded video. *2008 IEEE International Conference on Multimedia and Expo*, (pp. 597-600).

Shoaib, M., & Anni, C. (2010). Efficient residual prediction with error concealment in extended spatial scalability. *Wireless Telecommunications Symposium* (WTS), 2010, (pp. 1-6).

Shokurov, A., Khropov, A., & Ivanov, D. (2003). Feature tracking in images and video. In *International Conference on Computer Graphics between Europe and Asia* (GraphiCon-2003), (pp. 177-179).

Signoroni, A., Lazzaroni, F., & Leonardi, R. (2003). Exploitation and extension of the region-of-interest coding functionalities in JPEG2000. *IEEE Transactions on Consumer Electronics, 49*(4), 818–823. doi:10.1109/TCE.2003.1261160

Sun, Q., Lu, Y., & Sun, S. (2010). A visual attention based approach to text extraction. *2010 20th International Conference on Pattern Recognition* (ICPR), (pp. 3991-3995).

Sun, Z., & Sun, J. (2008). Tracking of dynamic image sequence based on intensive restraint topology adaptive snake. *2008 International Conference on Computer Science and Software Engineering*, Vol. 6, (pp. 217-220).

Tai, H.-M., Long, M., He, W., & Yang, H. (2002). An efficient region of interest coding for medical image compression. *Proceedings of the Second Joint Annual Fall Meeting of the Biomedical Engineering Society*, Vol. 2, (pp. 1017- 1018).

Tan, Y. H., Lee, W. S., Tham, J. Y., Rahardja, S., & Lye, K. M. (2009). Complexity control and computational resource allocation during H.264/SVC encoding. In *Proceedings of the Seventeenth ACM international conference on Multimedia*, Beijing, China, (pp. 897-900).

Thang, T. C., Bae, T. M., Jung, Y. J., Ro, Y. M., Kim, J.-G., Choi, H., & Hong, J.-W. (2005). *Spatial scalability of multiple ROIs in surveillance video*. JVT-O037, Busan, KR, 16-22 April, 2005.

Vezhnevets, M. (2002). Face and facial feature tracking for natural human-computer interface. In *International Conference on Computer Graphics between Europe and Asia* (GraphiCon-2002), (pp. 86-90).

Wang, H., Leng, J., & Guo, Z. M. (2002). *Adaptive dynamic contour for real-time object tracking.* In Image and Vision Computing New Zealand (IVCNZ2002), Dec. 2002.

Wang, J.-M., Cherng, S., Fuh, C.-S., & Chen, S.-W. (2008). Foreground object detection using two successive images. *IEEE Fifth International Conference on Advanced Video and Signal Based Surveillance, AVSS '08*, (pp. 301-306).

Wang, Y., Casares, M., & Velipasalar, S. (2009). Cooperative object tracking and event detection with wireless smart cameras. In *Proceedings of the 2009 Sixth IEEE International Conference on Advanced Video and Signal Based Surveillance* (AVSS '09), Washington, DC, USA, (pp. 394-399).

Wei, Z., & Zhou, Z. (2010). An adaptive statistical features modeling tracking algorithm based on locally statistical ROI. *2010 International Conference on Educational and Information Technology* (ICEIT), Vol. 1, (pp. 433- 437).

Wiegand, T., & Sullivan, G. (2003). *Final draft ITU-T recommendation and final draft international standard of joint video specification* (ITU-T Rec. H.264 ISO/IEC 14 496-10 AVC). In Joint Video Team (JVT) of ITU-T SG16/Q15 (VCEG) and ISO/IEC JTC1/SC29/WG1, Annex C, Pattaya, Thailand, Mar. 2003, Doc. JVT-G050.

Xiang, G. (2009). Real-time follow-up tracking fast moving object with an active camera. *2nd International Congress on Image and Signal Processing, CISP '09*, (pp. 1-4).

Xie, Y., & Han, G.-Q. (2005). ROI coding with separated code block. *Proceedings of 2005 International Conference on Machine Learning and Cybernetics*, Vol. 9, (pp. 5447-5451).

Xu, L., Ma, S., Zhao, D., & Gao, W. (2005). Rate control for scalable video model. In *Proceedings of the SPIE, Visual Communications and Image Processing*, Vol. 5960, (p. 525).

Xue, Z., Loo, K.-K., & Cosmas, J. (2008). Bandwidth efficient error resilience scheme for wavelet based video transmission. *2008 IEEE International Symposium on Broadband Multimedia Systems and Broadcasting*, (pp. 1-6).

Xue, Z., Loo, K.-K., Cosmas, J., Tun, M., Feng, L., & Yip, P.-Y. (2010). Error-resilient scheme for wavelet video codec using automatic ROI detection and Wyner-Ziv coding over packet erasure channel. *IEEE Transactions on Broadcasting, 56*(4), 481–493. doi:10.1109/TBC.2010.2058371

Yang, M.-H., Kriegman, D. J., & Ahuja, N. (2002). Detecting faces in images: A survey. *IEEE Transactions on Pattern Analysis and Machine Intelligence, 24*(1), 34–58. doi:10.1109/34.982883

Yao, Z.-W., & Xu, X. (2010). Dynamic region of interest extract method for JPEG2000 coding. *2010 International Conference on Computer and Communication Technologies in Agriculture Engineering* (CCTAE), Vol. 2, (pp. 150-153).

Yatawara, Y., Caldera, M., Kusuma, T. M., & Zepernick, H.-J. (2005). Unequal error protection for ROI coded images over fading channels. *Proceedings Systems Communications, 2005*, 111–115.

You, W. (2010). *Object detection and tracking in compresses domain.* Retrieved from http://knol.google.com/k/wonsang-you/object-detection-and-tracking-in/3e2si9juvje7y/7#

You, W., Sabirin, M. S. H., & Kim, M. (2007). *Moving object tracking in H.264/AVC bitstream. MCAM 2007, LNCS (Vol. 4577*, pp. 483–492). Heidelberg, Germany: Springer.

You, W., Sabirin, M. S. H., & Kim, M. (2009). Real-time detection and tracking of multiple objects with partial decoding in H.264/AVC bitstream domain . In Kehtarnavaz, N., & Carlsohn, M. F. (Eds.), *Proceedings of SPIE* (pp. 72440D–72440D, 12). San Jose, CA: SPIE. doi:10.1117/12.805596

Yuan, L., & Mu, Z.-C. (2007). Ear detection based on skin-color and contour information. *2007 International Conference on Machine Learning and Cybernetics*, Vol. 4, (pp. 2213-2217).

Zeng, W., Du, J., Gao, W., & Huang, Q. (2005). Robust moving object segmentation on H.264/AVC compressed video using the block-based MRF model. *Real-Time Imaging, 11*(4), 290–299. doi:10.1016/j.rti.2005.04.008

Zhang, T., Liu, C., Wang, M., & Goto, S. (2009). Region-of-interest based H.264 encoder for videophone with a hardware macroblock level face detector. *IEEE International Workshop on Multimedia Signal Processing, MMSP '09* (pp. 1-6).

Zhang, Y., Jiang, G., Yu, M., Yang, Y., Peng, Z., & Chen, K. (2010). Depth perceptual region-of-interest based multiview video coding. *Journal of Visual Communication and Image Representation, 21*(5-6), 498–512. doi:10.1016/j.jvcir.2010.03.002

Zheng, J.-M., Zhou, D.-W., & Geng, J.-L. (2007). ROI progressive image transmission based on wavelet transform and human visual specialties. *International Conference on Wavelet Analysis and Pattern Recognition, ICWAPR '07*, Vol. 1, (pp. 260-264).

Zhou, W., & Bovik, A. C. (2002). Bitplane-by-bitplane shift (BbBShift) - A suggestion for JPEG2000 region of interest image coding. *Signal Processing Letters, 9*(5), 160–162. doi:10.1109/LSP.2002.1009009

ADDITIONAL READING

Bae, T. M., Thang, T. C., Kim, D. Y., Ro, Y. M., Kang, J. W., & Kim, J. G. (2006). Multiple region-of-interest support in scalable video coding. *ETRI Journal, 28*(2), 239–242. doi:10.4218/etrij.06.0205.0126

Bing, L., Mingui, S., Qiang, L., Kassam, A., Li, C.-C., & Sclabassi, R. J. (2006). Automatic detection of region of interest based on object tracking in neurosurgical video. *27th Annual International Conference of the Engineering in Medicine and Biology Society, IEEE-EMBS 2005*, (pp. 6273-6276).

Chiang, T., & Zhang, Y.-Q. (1997). A new rate control scheme using quadratic rate distortion model. *IEEE Transactions on Circuits and Systems for Video Technology, 7*(1), 246–250. doi:10.1109/76.554439

Cuhadar, A., & Tasdoken, S. (2003). Multiple arbitrary shape ROI coding with zerotree based wavelet coders. *Proceedings 2003 International Conference on Multimedia and Expo, ICME '03*, Vol. 3, (pp. 157-60).

Dai, W., Liu, L., & Tran, T. D. (2005). Adaptive block-based image coding with pre-/post-filtering. *Proceedings of DCC 2005*, March 2005, (pp. 73-82).

Foo, B., Andreopoulos, Y., & Van der Schaar, M. (2008). Analytical rate-distortion-complexity modeling of wavelet-based video coders. *IEEE Transactions on Signal Processing, 56*, 797–815. doi:10.1109/TSP.2007.906685

Hadar, O., Stern, A., & Koresh, R. (2001). Enhancement of an image compression algorithm by pre- and post-filtering. *Optical Engineering (Redondo Beach, Calif.), 40*, 193–199. doi:10.1117/1.1339203

Hannuksela, M. M. (2001). Syntax for supplemental enhancement information. *VCEG 14th Meeting*, Santa Barbara, CA, USA, September 2001, (pp. 24-27).

He, Z., Cheng, W., & Chen, X. (2008). Energy minimization of portable video communication devices based on power-rate-distortion optimization. *IEEE Transactions on Circuits and Systems for Video Technology, 18*, 596–608. doi:10.1109/TCSVT.2008.918802

He, Z., Liang, Y., Chen, L., Ahmad, I., & Wu, D. (2005). Power-rate-distortion analysis for wireless video communication under energy constraints. *IEEE Transactions on Circuits and Systems for Video Technology, 15*(5), 645–658. doi:10.1109/TCSVT.2005.846433

Itti, L. (2004). Automatic foveation for video compression using a neurobiological model of visual attention. *IEEE Transactions on Image Processing, 13*, 1304–1318. doi:10.1109/TIP.2004.834657

Jiang, M., & Ling, N. (2006). Lagrange multiplier and quantizer adjustment for H.264 frame-layer video rate control. *IEEE Transactions on Circuits and Systems for Video Technology, 16*(5), 663–668. doi:10.1109/TCSVT.2006.873159

Kannangara, C. S., Richardson, I. E. G., & Miller, A. J. (2008). Computational complexity management of a real-time H.264/AVC encoder. *IEEE Transactions on Circuits and Systems for Video Technology, 18*(9), 1191–1200. doi:10.1109/TCSVT.2008.928881

Kim, S. D., & Ra, J. B. (2003). Efficient block-based video encoder embedding a Wiener filter for noisy video sequences. *Journal of Visual Communication and Image Representation, 14*(1), 22–40.

Kwon, D.-K., Shen, M.-Y., & Kuo, C.-C. J. (2007). Rate control for H.264 video with enhanced rate and distortion models. *IEEE Transactions on Circuits and Systems for Video Technology, 17*(5), 517–529. doi:10.1109/TCSVT.2007.894053

Richardson, I. E. G. (2010). *The H.264 advanced video compression standard* (2nd ed.). Chichester, UK: John Wiley & Sons. doi:10.1002/9780470989418

Schaar, M., & Andreopoulos, Y. (2005). Rate-distortion-complexity modeling for network and receiver aware adaptation. *IEEE Transactions on Multimedia, 7*(3), 471–479. doi:10.1109/TMM.2005.846790

Song, B. C., Kim, N. H., & Chun, K. W. (2005). Transform-domain wiener filtering for H.264/AVC video encoding and its implementation. *IEEE ICIP, 3*, 529–532.

Su, L., Lu, Y., Wu, F., Li, S., & Gao, W. (2009). Complexity-constrained H.264 video encoding. *IEEE Transactions on Circuits and Systems for Video Technology, 1*, 477–490.

Tran, T. D., Liang, J., & Tu, C. (2003). Lapped transform via time-domain pre- and post-filtering. *IEEE Transactions on Signal Processing, 51*, 1557–1571. doi:10.1109/TSP.2003.811222

Vanam, R., Riskin, E. A., & Ladner, R. E. (2009). H.264/MPEG-4 AVC encoder parameter selection algorithms for complexity distortion tradeoff. *Proceedings of Data Compression Conference, 2009*, (pp. 372-381).

Wiegand, T., & Girod, B. (2001). Parameter selection in Lagrangian hybrid video coder control. *Proceedings of International Conference on Image Processing*, Vol. 3, Thessaloniki, Greece, (pp. 542-545).

Wiegand, T., Schwarz, H., Joch, A., Kossentini, F., & Sullivan, G. J. (2003). Rate-constrained coder control and comparison of video coding standards. *IEEE Transactions on Circuits and Systems for Video Technology, 13*(7), 688–703. doi:10.1109/TCSVT.2003.815168

Wiegand, T., Sullivan, G., Reichel, J., Schwarz, H., & Wien, M. (2006). *Joint draft 8 of SVC amendment.* ISO/IEC JTC1/SC29/WG11 and ITU-T SG16 Q.6 9 (JVT-U201), 21st Meeting, Hangzhou, China, Oct. 2006.

Wu, S., Huang, Y., & Ikenaga, T. (2009). A macroblock-level rate control algorithm for H.264/AVC video coding with context-adaptive MAD prediction model. *Proceedings of the International Conference on Computers and Modeling Simulation, 2009,* (pp. 124-128).

Zhan, C. Q., & Karam, L. J. (2003). Wavelet-based adaptive image denoising with edge preservation. *Proceedings of the ICIP, 1,* 97–100.

KEY TERMS AND DEFINITIONS

Flexible Macroblock Ordering (FMO): One of the basic elements of the H.264 video sequence is a slice, which contains a group of macroblocks. Each picture can be subdivided into one or more slices and each slice can be provided with increased importance as the basic spatial segment, which can be encoded independently from its neighbors. FMO is an advanced tool of H.264 that defines the information of slice groups and enables to employ different macroblocks to slice groups of mapping patterns.

H.264/AVC (Advanced Video Coding/AVC): H.264/AVC is a video coding standard of the ITU-T Video Coding Experts Group and the ISO/IEC Moving Picture Experts Group, which was officially issued in 2003. H.264/AVC has achieved a significant improvement in rate-distortion efficiency relative to prior standards.

H.264/SVC (Scalable Video Coding/SVC): SVC is an extension of H.264/AVC video coding standard; SVC enables the transmission and decoding of partial bit streams to provide video services with lower temporal or spatial resolutions or reduced fidelity, while retaining a reconstruc- tion quality that is high relative to the rate of the partial bit streams.

High Efficiency Video Coding (HEVC): Is a high-definition video compression standard, which is developed by a Joint Collaborative Team on Video Coding (JCT-VC) formed by ITU-T VCEG and ISO/IEC MPEG. The HEVC standard is intended to provide significantly better com- pression capability than the existing AVC (ITU-T H.264 | ISO/IEC MPEG-4 Part 10) standard.

Mean Absolute Difference (MAD): Is one of the most popular block matching criterions, according to which corresponding pixels from each block are compared and their absolute dif- ferences are summed.

Motion Compensation: Is a technique em- ployed for video compression, which describes a picture in terms of the transformation of a refer- ence picture to the current picture. The reference picture may be a previous or future picture.

Motion Estimation: Is a process of determin- ing motion vectors that describe the transformation from one image to another; usually, from adjacent frames in a video sequence. The motion vectors may relate to the whole image or to particular image portions, such as rectangular blocks, etc.

Peak Signal-To-Noise Ratio (PSNR): Is the ratio between the maximum possible power of a signal and the power of corrupting noise that affects the fidelity of the signal representation.

Scalability: In video coding, the term scal- ability relates to providing different qualities in various domains, such as in the spatial domain (by varying the video resolution), temporal domain (by varying the frame rate), and fidelity domain (by varying the fidelity/quality), which are embedded into a single SVC bit stream.

Structural Similarity (SSIM) Index: Relates to a method for measuring the similarity between two images. The SSIM index is a full reference metric, in other words, the measuring of image quality based on an initial uncompressed or distortion-free image as a reference.

Chapter 5
Technical Challenges of 3D Video Coding

Cheon Lee
Gwangju Institute of Science and Technology, Republic of Korea

Yo-Sung Ho
Gwangju Institute of Science and Technology, Republic of Korea

ABSTRACT

Three-dimensional video (3DV) is expected to be the next multimedia technology that provides depth impression of observed scenery with multi-view videos. In fact, studies on 3D video have a long history, heading back two hundred years; but recently, it has risen as the hottest issue due to rapid progresses of IT technologies. Particularly, 3D video systems are the most promising technology in multimedia area. An extension of typical stereoscopic imaging, realistic and natural 3D video technologies are currently under development. In this chapter, the authors describe overall technologies of 3D video systems from capturing to display, including coding standards. Mainly, the chapter focuses on the recent standardization activities by MPEG (moving picture experts group) associated with 3D video coding.

INTRODUCTION

A new generation for three-dimensional video (3DV) has arrived. Countless 3D films have been produced since the record-breaking success of *Avatar* by *J. Cameron* in 2009; many 3D items such as 3D-TV are released continuously reflecting the market demands. Simultaneously, worldwide major broadcasting channels are testing 3D-TV services while 3D contents are under production.

In fact, researches on 3D imaging have a long history from studies of stereopsis. It is the process in human visual system leading to the perception of depth impression from two slightly different projections of the world onto retinas of the two eyes; it was first described by *Charles Wheatstone* in 1838 (Wheatstone, 1838). He invented a stereoscope to show that stereopsis can be realized by creating illusion of depth from flat pictures that includes differences in horizontal disparity. Stereopsis became popular during *Victorian* times with the invention of prism stereoscope by *David*

DOI: 10.4018/978-1-4666-2660-7.ch005

Brewster. It is used for stereoscopic photography to generate stereograms. In 1970s, stereoscopic films were produced by anaglyph images; depth cues can be seen with red and blue films. In recent years, research efforts have been strengthened due to the advanced IT technologies, e.g., multi-view camera arrays, 3D scene representation, coding and transmission applied to capturing, calibration, rendering and 3D display (Benoit, 2008), (Smolic, 2007), (Lang, 2008), (Pesquet-Popescu, 2009), (Milani, 2011), (Maitre, 2008), (Maitre, 2010), (Kubota, 2007).

In terms of content production, the 3D content provider considers how to implement depth cues to the video data and how to transmit them efficiently. Since the amount of 3D data is greater than a single viewpoint video, an efficient video coding for 3D video contents is highly required; it is a core technology in 3D video service. Recently, the moving picture experts group (MPEG), which is working group to set standards for audio and video compression and transmission, started activities on 3D video systems since 2001 (Smolic, 2006). As a first step, they explored various technologies related to 3D video in the name of 3D audio-visual (3DAV). After exploring related technologies, the multi-view video coding (MVC) was developed for compressing multiple viewpoint video data under the team named JVT (joint video team) in 2007; it was the first phase of FTV (free-viewpoint TV) work. Right after, as a second phase of FTV work, the standardization activity on 3D video coding (3DVC) started in 2008. The primary goal of 3DVC is to define a data format and associated compression technologies to enable high-quality reconstruction of synthesized views for various types of 3D displays(ISO/IEC JTC1/ SC29/WG11, 2011).

Since MPEG 3DVC group considers future 3D video systems as well as coding standards, it is easy to understand what core technologies are related to 3D video systems. In this chapter, we describe the general framework for 3D video systems and their elemental technologies in detail.

We also explain the related video coding methods on 3D video coding according to the history of standardization activities in MPEG.

Technologies of 3D Video Systems

The 3D video system employs multi-view video to render various viewpoint images of a scene to provide realistic and natural depth impression to users. Since it uses more than two viewpoint images for 3D effects differently from the single viewpoint video, there are many constraints for achieving a successful system such as capturing conditions, distortions between views, generating supplementary data for rendering, and efficient 3D rendering. Therefore, each part of technologies may determine the feasibility of 3D video systems. In this section, we describe the generic 3D video system and its related technologies.

FRAMEWORK FOR 3D VIDEO SYSTEMS

As we mentioned above, the future 3D video systems involve multi-view videos to support advanced stereoscopic displays and auto-stereoscopic displays. The most popular data format for these systems is the multi-view video plus depth data (MVD), where the depth information is used for rendering an arbitrary viewpoint video using view synthesis algorithms. This data format allows generating any virtual viewpoint image; hence a certain type of display can render 3D scenery by selecting proper viewpoint images. In detail, if a certain display is a typical 2D display, it can render only one viewpoint image; in general, 3D video systems support backward compatibility. For the stereoscopic display, a pair of viewpoint images are selected and rendered on the display. In the case of the auto-stereoscopic display, more than two viewpoint images, e.g., 9-views, are rendered by generating sufficient viewpoint images with the reconstructed data.

In order to support such various 3D functionalities, MPEG 3D video coding ad Hoc group have described a signal processing chain for 3D video as shown in Figure 1 (ISO/IEC JTC1/SC29/WG11, 2010). At acquisition, many pre-processing methods can be involved, e.g., capturing with multiple camera, camera calibration, multi-view image rectification, and color correction between views. At the encoder, depth estimation and converting multi-view video data into 3D representations and video compressions are involved, where the 3D coding method can be used as a mean of coding standards, e.g., 3D video coding under developing by MPEG or other standards. After receiving the bit-stream, the decoder reconstructs the 3D video data and renders the 3D scene by selecting proper viewpoint images; if the number of reconstructed views is not enough or the baseline is not proper for rendering, view synthesis can be exploited for generating additional views.

Depth Cues

Human visual systems perceive the depth of an object and the world in three dimensions by various *depth cues*. We can categorize them into monocular cues and binocular cues. The monocular cues are perceived by viewing a scene with one eye (Goldstein, 2002). There are many factors of monocular cues: motion parallax, aerial perspective, and linear perspective. When the observer moves, the apparent motion of several stationary objects against the background gives hints about their relative distance; this is the motion parallax. If information about the discretion and velocity of movement is known, motion parallax can provide absolute depth information. This effect can be seen clearly when driving a car. Nearby objects pass quickly, while far-off objects appear stationary. The aerial perspective appears by light scattering by the atmosphere. In detail, objects at a great distance away have lower luminance contrast and less color saturation. Object differing only in their contrast with a background appear to be at different depths. The linear perspective is the property of parallel lines converging at infinity. This allows us to reconstruct the relative distance of two parts of objects.

The binocular cue is the basic principle of perceiving depth impression from two slightly different viewpoint images as described in Figure 2 (Howard, 1996). Since human eyes are distanced by 50mm to 65mm in general, one projected image to the left eye is different from that of the right eye. It can be explained by using the disparity which refers to the relative difference of position in two images. A near object to the camera has large disparity and a far object from the camera has a small disparity. Human brain perceives that the object with large disparity is the closer one and the object with small disparity is farther. We can generate a comfort and effective 3D scene with this binocular cue.

Figure 1. 3D video processing chain

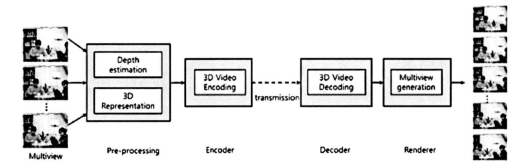

Figure 2. Stereopsis by slightly different viewpoint images

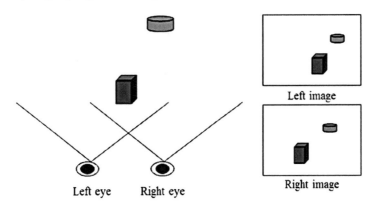

Left image

Right image

Left eye   Right eye

3D Video Cameras

3D cameras (or stereo cameras) are designed by exploiting the binocular depth cues efficiently. The most common and general stereo camera is a form of 1D parallel, which has two cameras pointing at the same directions. The advanced 3D camera employs convergence functions to provide efficient binocular depth cues. Recently, multiple cameras are being investigated to enlarge the limited viewing angle and support auto-stereoscopic displays. If there are multi-view videos reconstructed at the decoder for stereoscopic display, two optimal viewpoint images providing comfortable depth cues are chosen and rendered. For this reason, recent multiple camera systems are arranged with regular grid.

Figure 3 shows multiple camera systems for these objectives. The first type is a form of 1D-parallel multiple cameras which employ multiple cameras with a unified baseline and the same camera model (ISO/IEC JTC1/SC29/WG11, 2008). The captured multi-view videos have only horizontal disparities between cameras according to distances of objects from the camera. Using this property, depth data of each viewpoint can be obtained easily by searching the corresponding pixels between views in horizontal direction. The second type is a hybrid-multiple camera system which employs the TOF (time-of-flight) camera

and multiple cameras simultaneously (Kim, 2008). Since the TOF camera can capture depth images in real-time, many research topics are related to this camera system. The 2D cross type and 2D parallel type, as shown in Figure 3(c), can capture wider angle beyond 1D type (Free Viewpoint TV). In the case of 1D arc type, as shown in Figure 3(d) and all viewing directions are pointing at a certain convergence point (Zitnick, 2004). Figure 3(e) shows 3D cameras with two cameras, which can adjust convergence and baseline. This camera type can give better depth cues for a scene than 1D parallel, while it is hard to estimate disparity information between views. One important issue for capturing process is synchronization between cameras. Generally, a sync-generator, which triggers a signal to all cameras simultaneously, is used for capturing. Sooner or later, these systems will be a basic form of 3D broadcasting systems because its feasibility and capability.

Pre-Processing for Multi-View Video

Although we captured the multi-view video data using mechanically well-aligned multi-view camera rigs, there exist significant distortions between views such as geometrical distortions and color mismatches. In order to correct the geometrical distortion, we need to find the geometrical camera information, i.e., camera parameters. The *camera*

Figure 3. Multi-view camera systems: (a) 1D multi-view cameras, (b) hybrid camera, (c) 2D multi-view camera, (d) arc multi-view camera, (e) stereo cameras

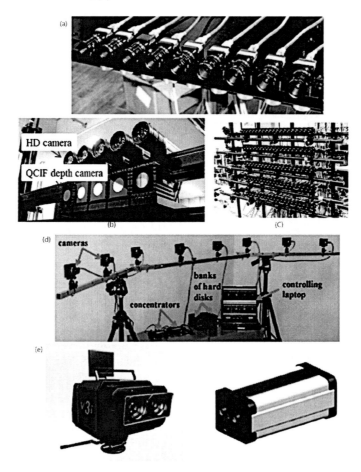

calibration is a process of finding true parameters of the camera that took the scene simultaneously. This process is used primarily in robotic applications, and when modeling scenes virtually based on real input. The most popular scheme of camera calibration is to use a calibration objects with a known pattern image, e.g., a chess board by calculating direction, relative position, focal length, and optical offset values of a camera (Zhang, 2000).

The geometric errors between views are caused by misalignment of multiple cameras on the multi-view camera array. These errors induce serious problems in 3D video processing such as depth estimation and 3D rendering. Therefore, we need to correct geometrical mismatches between views using *image rectification*(Fusiello, 2000).

In general, the image rectification process makes epipolar lines become parallel. Given a pair of stereo images, we determine a plane transformation of each image such that pairs of conjugate epipolar lines become collinear and co-planar in parallel (usually the horizontal one). By transforming two images each other, we can obtain two rectified images which can be thought of as captured by a new stereo rig, i.e., ideally aligned cameras. The important advantage of rectification is that computing stereo correspondences is made simpler, because search is done along the horizontal lines of the rectified images. Figure 4 shows the comparisons of the original images and the rectified images, respectively. As shown in Figure 4(a), each object has different horizontal

Figure 4. Result of image rectification: (a) original, (b) rectified

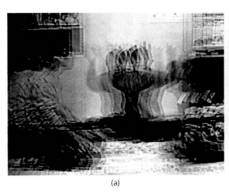
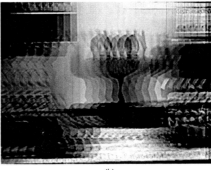

(a) (b)

positions relative to each other. However, in the right image, every object is aligned perfectly in horizontal axis.

Independently on geometrical distortions, a color mismatch between views is also a serious problem in multi-view video. The color characteristics of multi-view images depend not only on the reflectance properties of objects, but also the properties of each camera. Hence, even though we capture a scene with the same type of cameras, the color of the object in each image can be different. These variations come from the different properties of image sensors in each camera, jitter of shutter speed and aperture, or the variation of angle between objects and camera. Therefore, *color correction* plays an important role in 3D video systems (Yamamoto, 2007). Many researchers have made efforts to overcome this color mismatch problem.

Color correction algorithms can be categorized by the usage of a known object when capturing. Most algorithms use a known object, e.g., color chart or color bar, to compare the color distribution of the multi-view images. Ilie *et al.* have improved inter-camera consistency using iterative closed-loop calibration (Ilie, 2005). Joshi *et al.* have proposed an automated calibrating camera arrays to improve color consistency (Chen, 2006). However, due to the high cost and limited color samples with a narrow intensity range, it is not practical. On the other hand, other algorithms use

only common-features between views. Gangyi *et al.* proposed a region correspondence based color correction algorithm by means of a statistical model (Jiang, 2006). Yamamoto *et al.* proposed an energy function with dynamic programming (Yamamoto, 2007). Although the use of common-features between views is popular, it has limitations due to the difficulties of finding the accurate corresponding points between views. Recently, Jung *et al.* have proposed a multiview color correction algorithm using camera characteristics. Figure 5 shows the results of color correction using camera characteristics (Jung, 2012).

DEPTH ESTIMATION

The depth information directs the distance between camera and objects in a scene. Using this property, we can define geometrical relations between an image and a real scene. Eventually, the depth data can be used for 3D video systems as supplementary data to assist virtual view generation. Therefore, estimating depth information from the multi-view image is a very important issue in 3D content production. Figure 6 shows the generation of depth data via *depth estimation*. In this section, we describe the general principal of depth estimation and some methodologies which are implemented in the depth estimation reference software (DERS).

Figure 5. Results of color correction: (a) original left image, (b) original right image, (c) color corrected right image

Figure 6. Generation of depth data: (a) process of multi-view depth map generation, (b) principle of disparity in stereoscopic images

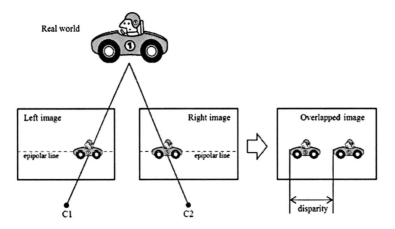

The basic principle of all depth estimation approaches is to estimate the relative positions of corresponding pixels in the left and right images. These corresponding pixels generally lie along epipolar lines, which are the basics of the stereo camera geometry and can be derived by intrinsic and extrinsic camera parameters. For instance, as shown in Figure 6(b), if the camera rig is 1D parallel, the epipolar lines are aligned with the horizontal axis in both stereo images. This makes easier to determine the correspondence between views by finding it along a horizontal line when we capture a scene with stereo camera. The *disparity* is determined by the relative difference of positions between views, as illustrated in Figure 6(b). Therefore, the closer object to camera has larger disparity, and vice versa. Although there

are many algorithms on depth estimation, we can categorize them into four steps as (Scharstein, 2006):

- Matching cost computation
- Cost aggregation
- Disparity computation (optimization)
- Disparity refinement

According to the pre-defined search range, every disparity value for a target pixel in the reference image calculates the cost values with a certain matching method, e.g., MAD (mean absolute difference). After determining all cost values, we aggregate them by summing matching cost over square windows with constant disparity; where selecting the size of window is another important issue in depth estimation. The disparity of a pixel in the reference image can be determined by disparity computation step. In other words, we call this process disparity optimization. The most and fast disparity optimization method is WTA (winner-take-all) which determines the disparity having the minimum cost, but it generates a lot of noisy disparities. However, a global method shows relatively good performance at the expense of high complexity. Among various global optimization methods, belief propagation and graph-cuts are the most prominent methods giving the best accuracy. Using the Markov network, the disparity map is determined by maximizing a posteriori (MAP) estimation using belief propagation (Sun, 2003). The graph-cuts based stereo matching algorithm uses local energy minimization via graph-cuts (Boykov, 2003).

As a work of MPEG 3DV activity, a depth estimation tool named DERS(depth estimation reference software) has been developed by proponents (DERS). It employs three viewpoint images generating the center view's depth map with the graph-cutsmethod for disparity optimization (see Figure 7). To execute the software, all intrinsic and extrinsic parameters are required. Figure 8 shows a simplified flow diagram for three main modes of DERS(ISO/IEC JTC1/SC29/WG11, 2010).

The basic flow of each estimation mode is similar to each other. First, cost values for all possible disparities are calculated by a simple block matching. Second, the cost values are adjusted by helping other information, e.g., the edge map. For the final step, the graph-cuts algorithm determines the optimal depth map for the center view. In the case of segmentation mode, image segmentation is performed before block matching. This segment information is used for selecting the disparity value during graph-cuts and plane fitting. In the case of semi-automatic mode, three

Figure 7. DERS flow diagrams: (a) automatic mode, (b) segmentation mode, (c) semi-automatic mode

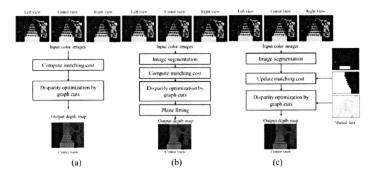

Figure 8. Results of depth estimation on 'newspaper' sequence: (a) original view, (b) automatic mode, (c) segmentation mode, (d) semi-automatic mode

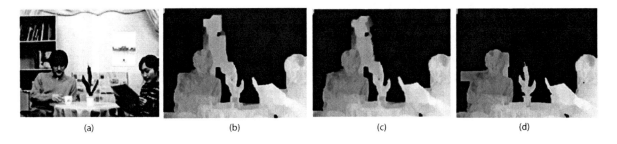

manual data, i.e., initial disparity map, static map, and edge map, are used. Referring to the static map, depth values for the static objects are fixed during whole frames; it keeps temporal consistency. Referring to the initial disparity map, unnecessary matching costs are declined. Referring to the edge map, sharp and accurate depth values are determined during disparity optimization process. Figure 8 demonstrates estimated depth maps by DERS. The automatic mode generates high-accuracy depth map, while some background regions have false depth values. The segmentation mode shows similar results with automatic mode, whereas some segments have slanted depth values. The most accurate depth maps are generated by the semi-automatic mode.

View Synthesis

Using the generated depth maps, additional views can be generated by interpolating pixel values from reference images. For this process, we employ the 3D image warping method which maps the pixels from one reference view to another 'virtual view' utilizing the depth values. If there are holes in the rendered images due to occlusions, they can be filled by referring to neighboring pixels, e.g., using in painting algorithms. An overview of depth-image based rendering (DIBR) could be found in (Fehn, 2004).In this section, we describe the whole processes of *view synthesis* from the principal of the 3D image warping to generating the final virtual image (Figure 9).

Generating a virtual viewpoint image using multi-view videos and the associated depth data utilizes the multiple view geometry between views(Lee, 2011). Therefore, we need to understand the basic camera geometry in conjunction with camera parameters. Camera parameters describe the relationship between camera coordinates and world coordinates. They consist of one intrinsic parameter $\mathbf{A}$ and two extrinsic parameters: the rotation matrix $\mathbf{R}$ and the translation vector $\mathbf{t}$. If a point $\mathbf{X}$ in the real world is pro-

jected to the pixel $\mathbf{x}$ of an image, we formulate it using a projective matrix as $\mathbf{P}=\mathbf{A}[\mathbf{R}|\mathbf{t}]$.

Assuming that all multi-view cameras are calibrated, i.e., all camera parameters are given; we can define the pixel correspondences for all images captured by multiple cameras. In detail, when a point $\mathbf{M}_W$ in the world coordinates is projected to the camera coordinates, a pixel $\tilde{m}$ in the image can be found by:

$$\tilde{m} = \mathbf{P}\tilde{M} = \mathbf{A}\left[\mathbf{R} \mid \mathbf{t}\right]\tilde{M} \qquad (1)$$

where a single point $\tilde{M} = \begin{bmatrix} X & Y & Z & 1 \end{bmatrix}^T$ in world coordinates is a homogeneous form of $\mathbf{M}_W$ and a projected point $\tilde{m} = \begin{bmatrix} x & y & 1 \end{bmatrix}^T$ represents the form of a homogeneous pixel position. When we find corresponding pixels between the reference and target viewpoint images, we put a pixel $\mathbf{m}_r$ in the reference image back to the world coordinates by

$$\mathbf{M}_r = \mathbf{R}_r^{-1} \cdot \mathbf{A}_r^{-1} \cdot \mathbf{m}_r \cdot d(\mathbf{m}_r) - \mathbf{R}_r^{-1} \cdot \mathbf{t}_r \qquad (2)$$

where $\mathbf{A}_r$, $\mathbf{R}_r$, and $\mathbf{t}_r$ stand for camera parameters of the reference view, and $d(\mathbf{m}_r)$ is a depth value of the position $\mathbf{m}_r$ of the reference image. After

Figure 9. Stereo correspondence of a 3D point in the world coordinate system

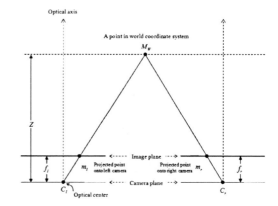

this backward projection, we project $\mathbf{M}_r$ into the camera coordinates of the virtual viewpoint using Equation (3). As a result, we can find the relationship between two positions $\mathbf{m}_r$ and $\mathbf{m}_v$ as follows.

$$\tilde{\mathbf{m}}_r = \mathbf{A}_v \left[\mathbf{R}_v \mid \mathbf{t}_v \right] \tilde{\mathbf{M}}_\mathbf{r} \qquad (3)$$

A popular depth representation is the 8-bit mono-channel image. Hence, the total area of depth-of-field is divided into 256 levels, i.e., the range of representative depth values is from 0 to 255. Based on this depth format, we can find 256 homography matrices by defining pixel correspondences between adjacent views. A homography matrix is formed by a 3x3 matrix having eight degrees of freedom (DOF); hence we can determine it with four corresponding pixels for one depth level. Equation (4) explains relationship between two corresponding pixels with a homography matrix. $\mathbf{H}_d$ represents the homography matrix for a certain depth value d.

$$\tilde{\mathbf{m}}_t = \mathbf{H}_d \tilde{\mathbf{m}}_r \qquad (4)$$

Since the 3D warping technique uses corresponding pixels between views, we can synthesize a virtual image by mapping all corresponding pixels between the virtual view and reference view images. Practically, we use the backward warping technique to map the pixel correspondences between views. In detail, instead of warping the reference color image to the virtual view directly, we obtain the virtual depth map at the virtual view using the 3D warping method by exploiting the reference depth map itself. The backward warping method is composed of two steps. First, we obtain the depth map of virtual view by forward warping to the virtual viewpoint, and then, we fill small holes using a simple interpolation filter or a median filter. Next, we map intensity values of the virtual view image using the obtained depth map. As a first step, we obtain the depth map for

the virtual view using the forward depth warping as described above. Let $\mathbf{D}_{v,l}$ be the depth map of the virtual view warped from left, then it can be obtained by:

$$\begin{cases} \mathbf{D}_{v,l}(\mathbf{m}_{v,l}) = \alpha_{v,l}(\mathbf{m}_{v,l}) \cdot \mathbf{D}_l(\mathbf{m}_l) \\ \mathbf{m}_{v,l} = \mathbf{H}_{D_l} \cdot \mathbf{m}_l \end{cases} \qquad (5)$$

where the alpha value is a binary value representing the visibility of the pixel in the virtual viewpoint. In the same manner, we can obtain the warped depth image $\mathbf{D}_{v,r}$ warped from the right reference view as:

$$\begin{cases} \mathbf{D}_{v,r}(\mathbf{m}_{v,r}) = \alpha_{v,r}(\mathbf{m}_{v,r}) \cdot \mathbf{D}_r(\mathbf{m}_r) \\ \mathbf{m}_{v,r} = \mathbf{H}_{D_r} \cdot \mathbf{m}_r \end{cases} \qquad (6)$$

In the second step, we obtain virtual view images using warped depth maps, $\mathbf{D}_{v,l}$ and $\mathbf{D}_{v,r}$, respectively. The intensity value of a point $\mathbf{m}_v$ in virtual view is determined by referring to a point $\mathbf{m}_{l,v}$ in the left reference view. Similar to the forward warping, small holes appear in the warped depth maps due to rounding truncation error during warping. Likewise, two adjacent pixels in the reference view may have identical pixel position in virtual view. Conversely, some pixels cannot be mapped to the reference view even though those are visible in virtual view. We call these holes small holes hereinafter. Since small holes are visible in the virtual view, we fill them with an interpolation filter or a median filter. Consequently, we obtain modified depth maps, $\tilde{D}_{v,l}$ and $\tilde{D}_{v,r}$, and modified alpha maps representing pixel's visibility, i.e., $\tilde{\alpha}_{v,l}$ and $\tilde{\alpha}_{v,r}$. Using those depth map and alpha maps, we can generate two synthesized images for the virtual view referring to the left and right, respectively, as:

$$\begin{cases} \mathbf{I}_{v,l}(\mathbf{m}_v) = \tilde{\alpha}_{v,l}(\mathbf{m}_v) \cdot \mathbf{I}_l(\mathbf{m}_{v,l}) \\ \mathbf{m}_{v,l} = \mathbf{H}_{\tilde{D}_{v,l}} \cdot \mathbf{m}_l \end{cases} \quad (7)$$

$$\begin{cases} \mathbf{I}_{v,r}(\mathbf{m}_v) = \tilde{\alpha}_{v,r}(\mathbf{m}_v) \cdot \mathbf{I}_r(\mathbf{m}_{v,r}) \\ \mathbf{m}_{v,r} = \mathbf{H}_{\tilde{D}_{v,r}} \cdot \mathbf{m}_r \end{cases} \quad (8)$$

The most important issue in view synthesis for the 3D video system is dealing with the hole area which is the newly exposed area in the virtual viewpoint. If we have only one reference view (there is no available alternative texture), we fill holes with an inpainting method (Telea, 2004) or by referring to neighboring pixels in general. However, if we have more than two reference views, since 3D video system has enough viewpoints, we can find alternative textures for the hole referring to the other reference view. In detail, for example, the hole area is revealed at the virtual view when the reference view is left, then the alternative texture exists in the right reference view in most cases. Consequently, we can get two synthesized images as Equation (9) and Equation (10), respectively.

$$\begin{aligned} \mathbf{I}_{v,l}(m_v) = \tilde{\alpha}_{v,l}(m_v) \cdot \mathbf{I}_l(m_{v,l}) \\ + (1 - \tilde{\alpha}_{v,l}(m_v)) \cdot \mathbf{I}_r(m_{v,r}) \end{aligned} \quad (9)$$

$$\begin{aligned} \mathbf{I}_{v,r}(m_v) = \tilde{\alpha}_{v,r}(m_v) \cdot \mathbf{I}_r(m_{v,r}) \\ + (1 - \tilde{\alpha}_{v,l}(m_v)) \cdot \mathbf{I}_l(m_{v,l}) \end{aligned} \quad (10)$$

If both alpha values for a pixel are all zeros, we use an inpainting method alternatively.

By determining all pixel correspondences for the virtual view, we obtained two virtual views. Then we need to blend those images to make one resultant virtual image $\mathbf{I}_v$. The blending method uses weighted summing regarding the baseline distance. Let l_L be the baseline distance between the left reference view and the virtual view, and l_R be the baseline distance between right reference

view and virtual view. Then the weighting factor for synthesized view from left can be defined as $\beta_L = l_R / (l_L + l_R)$, while the weighting factor for synthesized view from right is defined by $\beta_R = l_L / (l_L + l_R)$. Using two factors, we can obtain the blended image as:

$$\mathbf{I}_v(m_v) = \beta_L \cdot \mathbf{I}_{v,l}(m_{v,l}) + \beta_R \cdot \mathbf{I}_{v,r}(m_{v,r}) \quad (11)$$

The whole processes above are implemented in the view synthesis reference software (VSRS) developed by MPEG 3DV ad Hoc group (VSRS), which is distributed in the MPEG SVN server. Figure 10 describes flows of view synthesis in VSRS. With two color reference views and their corresponding depth maps, we first warp the depth map to the virtual viewpoint using 3D warping, and then we obtain the warped depth maps with Equation (5) and (6), as shown in Figure 10(c). We fill small holes with a 3x3 median filter. With the warped depth maps and the original reference color images, we obtained two synthesized images using Equation (7) and (8), as shown in Figure 10(d). Next, we fill the hole regions using Equation (9) and (10). Finally, we obtain the synthesized image by blending two synthesized images.

There is error robust view synthesis method, i.e., the boundary noise removal. If the object boundaries between the color and depth images are not matched, boundary noises may exist in the synthesized images as shown in Figure 11(b). To remove such noises, extend the hole regions toward background by referring to the warped depth data, and then fill the holes. Figure 11 demonstrates the results of view synthesis with or without boundary noises. Figure 11(a) is the existing original image for the target view, and the rest images are the resultant synthesized images. With the proposed method, the boundary noises are perfectly removed from the synthesized image (ISO/IEC JTC1/SC29/WG11).

Figure 10. Overall procedure of view synthesis: (a) two original reference images, (b) depth maps corresponding two reference images, (c) generated depth maps using 3D warping and small hole filling, (d) synthesized images on the virtual viewpoint, (e) hole filled images by referring to other synthesized image, (f) boundary noise removed images

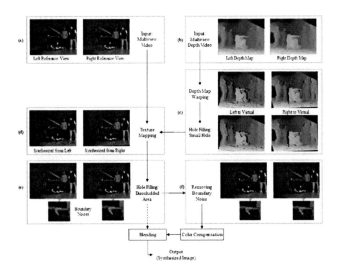

Figure 11. Results of view synthesis using 'ballet' sequence: (a) original image, (b) synthesized image with boundary noises, (c) boundary noise removed synthesized image

Coding Standards on 3D Video

3D Audio-Visual (3DAV)

As a first step of developing coding standards on 3D video systems, various 3D technologies have been investigated in MPEG 3D audio-visual (3DAV) ad Hoc group since 2001. In the beginning, diverse applications and technologies have been discussed in relation to the term 3D video. The common feature of these applications is selectivity of viewpoint by users; the users can choose viewpoint or direction in dynamic real audio-visual scene. In this sense, 3DAV was classified into three main application scenarios, omni-directional video, free-viewpoint video (FTV) and interactive stereo video.

MPEG has standardized many coding standards regarding to the stereoscopic video coding such as the parallel multi-view video coding in MPEG-2(ISO/IEC 13818-2) and the 3D mesh coding in MPEG-4(ISO/IEC 14496-2). Beyond capabilities of existing coding standards, demands for the new coding technology on 3D video had been raised. MPEG group has started the standard activity to develop related technologies of 3DAV since December 2001. From many exploration experiments (EE), four representative technologies were investigated(ISO/IEC JTC1/SC29/WG11, 2003). For EE1, the omni-directional video was investigated that provides 360 degrees panoramic image by capturing a special camera as shown in Figure 12 (ISO/IEC JTC1/SC29/WG11, 2003). Recently, many internet services with this omni-directional video are on service such as *Street view at Google Earth.* The key technology of EE1 was how to compress the huge amount of image data captured by omni-directional camera. As a result, they selected the coding method that the captured data is transformed into mesh data and then reconstruct a 3D video. For EE2, the free-viewpoint TV (FTV) system was investigated, which provides any viewpoint image from the ray-space data. The ray-space data, which is proposed by Nagoya University, is a kind of transformed data from multi-view video. For EE3, the stereoscopic video coding using MAC (multiple auxiliary components) was investigated. In order to support backward compatibility, they considered compatibility to use the existing coding standard as MAC. Instead of coding two views simultaneously and independently each other, they encode the base view, e.g., the left view, using MPEG-2 encoder, and then encode a disparity map between two views. The right view can be reconstructed at the decoder by shifting the left view using the decoded disparity map. For EE4, depth/disparity coding methods using various types of filters were investigated. To improve the quality of the reconstructed image in EE3, they considered deblocking filters and the median filters.

Multi-View Video Coding (MVC)

After exploring many technologies in 3DAV group, experts have agreed with starting the standardization activity on multi-view video coding since the multi-view video is the basic input data of 3D video systems. In order to set the experimental environment, MPEG MVC ad Hoc group gathered many multi-view test sequences. During standardization activities, many technologies were investigated: prediction structures, illumination compensation methods, and motion skip method. In this section, we will describe those technologies in detail.

Prediction Structure

A single viewpoint video is coded with the conventional compression codec such as H.264/AVC, which utilizes temporal, spatial, and statistical redundancies(Sullivan, 2004). In the case of multi-view video, there is additional redundancy: inter-view redundancy. To use these redundancies, MVC employs inter-view/temporal prediction structure as well as the hierarchical B coding method, as shown in Figure 13. Here are the details of the prediction structure. To encode three views, for example, we select one base view for the backward compatibility; we call this view as I-view, e.g. S_0, since every first frame of GOP (group of pictures) is coded with I picture coding. We call the first frame of GOP the anchor frame. The in-between frames of anchor frames are the non-anchor frames, which are coded with the hierarchical B picture coding. After encoding one GOP of I-view, encoder conducts encoding one GOP of S_2. The first frame of S_2 is coded with P picture coding referring to the adjacent frame of

Figure 12. Omni-directional camera

I-view T_0S_0; hence this view is called P-view. The in-between frames of P-view are coded with the hierarchical B picture coding as well as I-view. After coding two GOPs for both I-view and P-view, encoding one GOP of intermediate view, i.e., S_1, is followed; hence we call this view as B-view. The anchor frame of B-view is coded with the B picture coding referring to the reconstructed two inter-view frames, e.g., T_0S_0 and T_0S_2. The other intermediate frames are coded with the hierarchical B picture coding referring to both temporal direction and inter-view direction. Here, there are four reference frames for the intermediate frames of B-view: two frames from temporal direction and two frames from inter-view direction. The coding order of picture is indexed in gray circle at every picture when we encode only 9 frames.

Illumination Compensation

The input data of MVC is the multi-view videos captured by multiple camera arrays. Although their cameras use the same model, the color distributions of each view are different from the other; we already mentioned this phenomenon in Figure 5. If a set of multi-view video includes this color mismatches between views, the coding performance would be lower than that of the results using color corrected data. In order to reduce such effects and improve the coding efficiency, ETRI/

Sejong and Thomson/USC proposed the illumination compensation method (Lee, 2006)]. They considered that the global illumination differences and local illumination changes between views. They proposed the illumination compensation method that the encoder sends DVIC (difference value of illumination change) to the decoder with a flag bit indicating whether a macroblock used the IC mode or not. For all prediction blocks having 16x16, e.g., P-SKIP, P_16x16, B_SKIP, B_Direct, B_16x16, this IC mode is tested for coding. In terms of RD (rate-distortion) optimization, if the cost is lower than the other prediction modes, this IC mode is selected for coding.

Here are the detailed procedures of DVIC searching method. Instead of using the conventional searching criteria, i.e., SAD (sum of absolute difference) as described in Equation (12), the IC mode uses the advanced measure, MR_SAD (mean-removed SAD) as described in Equation (13).

$$SAD(x,y) = \sum_{i=m}^{m+S-1} \sum_{j=n}^{n+T-1} \left| f(i,j) - r(i+x, j+y) \right|$$

$$(12)$$

where M_{cur} and M_{ref} stand for the current block to be encoded and the reference block of the reference frame, respectively, and $f(i,j)$ and $r(i,j)$ stand for

Figure 13. Inter-view/temporal prediction structure of multi-view video coding

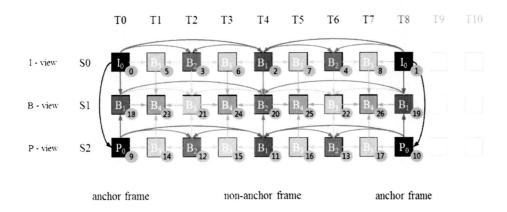

Equation 13

$$MR\_SAD(x,y) = \sum_{i=m}^{m+S-1} \sum_{j=n}^{n+T-1} \left| \left\{ f(i,j) - M_{cur} \right\} - \left\{ r(i+x, j+y) - M_{ref}(m+x, n+y) \right\} \right|$$

the pixel positions of the current frame and the reference frame, respectively. Using MR_SAD, we can find the optimal block by removing color changes between views. Figure 14 describes the signal flows of the illumination compensation method(Lee, 2006).

Motion Skip Mode

The multi-view videos have high correlations between views since those are captured by multiple camera arrays simultaneously. The motion skip mode is designed by LG/Thomson for exploiting inter-view correlations efficiently (Koo, 2008) . Particularly, they assumed that the coding characteristics between views are very similar; hence they utilized them for improving coding efficiency. The key idea of the motion skip mode is sharing coding information with that of already coded view as shown in Figure 15. For example,

let P_0 and P_0' be the corresponding blocks of two neighboring views, then the motion vector of the current block mv_{cur} will be very similar to the motion vector of neighboring view mv_{nbr}. Therefore, if we can find the corresponding block between two views, we can refer to the motion vector for the neighboring view; this is one example of motion vector sharing.

The motion skip mode has two steps: finding corresponding block and deriving the motion vector information from the neighboring view. Finding corresponding block is to calculate *dv* in Figure 14 [38] in every anchor frame as Equation 14 where *img0* and *img1* stand for two anchor frames of the current view and the neighboring view, and *R* is the overlapped area of two frames. The calculated GDV can have a multiple of 16 since the block size of macroblock is 16, and it is coded as header information in the bit-stream. The GDV value for the non-anchor frame is determined by referring to that of the anchor frames.

Figure 14. Macroblock level illumination compensation method

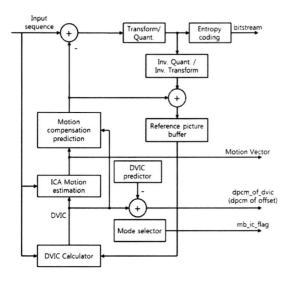

Figure 15. Coding correlations between views

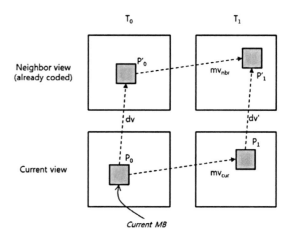

Equation 14

$$GDV(x,y) = \min_{x,y} \left[\frac{\sum_{i,j \in R} \left| img0(i,j) - img1(i - 16 \times x, j - 16 \times y) \right|}{R} \right]$$

By referring to the calculated GDV values, the current block finds the corresponding macroblock from the neighboring frame and shares the motion information. To determine the best mode, the motion skip mode competes with the conventional prediction modes in terms of RD optimization. If the motion skip mode is selected as an optimal mode, the encoder sends a flag bit defined as *motion_skip_flag* to distinguish the motion skip mode from the conventional modes and the rest of information, e.g., block type, reference index, and motion vector, are not coded in the bit-stream because those information can be derive from the neighboring view. This coding method is implemented in JMVM4.0. The improved coding performance of the motion skip mode was 0.18 dB on average.

3D Video Coding (3DVC)

After finalizing the standardization of MVC, activities on 3D video coding started in 2007 as the second phase of FTV works. The objective of MPEG activity of 3D video coding is achieving a new coding standard dealing with 3D video data. The new standard of 3D video will enable stereo devices to cope with various display types and sizes, and different viewing preferences. For the new coding standards on 3D video coding, experts of MPEG 3D video coding are considering multi-view video sequences and associated depth data as inputs because those data can provide a wide angle of a scene. However, since the amount of input data increases proportionally to the number of cameras, an efficient coder for multi-view video and its depth data is necessary. Currently, the format of 3D video is not determined yet but the depth data should be encoded simultaneously as well as multi-view videos. In addition, an important requirement for the new standard is backward compatibility with existing standards, such as H.264/AVC and MVC. In this chapter, we describe the upcoming standard on 3D video coding; requirements and coding conditions.

Vision on 3D Video

In January 2008, MPEG declared a vision on 3D video that a new 3D video format to be standardized goes beyond the capabilities of existing standards to enable both advances stereoscopic display processing and improved support for auto-stereoscopic *N*-view displays, while enabling interoperable 3D services (ISO/IEC JTC1/SC29/WG11, 2009). Basically, the 3D video format supports conventional stereoscopic displays and the advanced type of stereoscopic displays such as auto-stereoscopic displays and head-tracked stereoscopic displays; these systems can adjust the baseline distance for comfort 3D viewing. MPEG experts expect that the market of 3D displays will grow fast in the next few years; hence there is a demand for a new coding framework to enable the generation of high-quality intermediate views from a limited amount of input data, e.g., stereo and depth. Figure 16 shows the data format of 3D video coding supporting various types of displays (ISO/IEC JTC1/SC29/WG11, 2009).

Test Materials for 3D Video Coding

In order to establish the coding environments of core experiments, MPEG 3DV ad Hoc group

Figure 16. Target of 3D video format

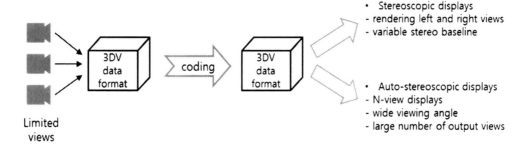

gathered many test sequences that satisfies various requirements for 3D video coding (ISO/IEC JTC1/SC29/WG11, 2008). The followings are some important requirements for providing test sequences as:

- **Camera setting:** 1D parallel camera arrangement with a baseline distance between cameras on the order of 5 cm.
- **Synchronization:** All captured views should be aligned in temporal synchronization.
- **Camera calibration:** Accurate camera parameters should be provided.
- **White balancing, color consistency:** Color consistency among the multiple views should be adjusted.
- **Image Rectification:** All views should be rectified in parallel

After two meetings from call for test materials, 10 test sequences were provided by four institutes. Two years later, the 3DV group called another shooting with various scenarios as well as moving scene. Finally, 19 test sequences were contributed from many proponents. As well as the multi-view video coding, the associated depth data are the basic inputs of 3D video coding, hence they need to be generated by any means of depth estimation. In order to support these requirements, MPEG group has developed the depth estimation reference software (DERS), as we mentioned above. Along with the depth estimation software, the

view synthesis reference software (VSRS) was developed by MPEG 3D video group. Similar to DERS, many techniques were investigated and integrated into the VSRS software. All reference software are distributed in the MPEG SVN server.

Call for Proposal on 3D Video Coding

In the 96th MPET meeting, held in Geneva, the 'Call for Proposal on 3D Video Coding' has been distributed (ISO/IEC JTC1/SC29/WG11, 2011). As we mentioned in Introduction, the primary goal of 3D video coding is to determine the data format for 3D video system which supports reconstruction of the arbitrary viewpoint images using multi-view video data and to develop an efficient compression method. Table 1 describes the test sequences of 3D video coding. Only three views are used for testing with corresponding depth data. Among them, 'Undo_Dancer' and 'GT_Fly' sequences are captured by computer graphics; hence their depth data correspond to ground truth. Other sequences have estimated depth data via DERS.

There are two test scenarios: 2-view and 3-view configurations. 2-view configuration consists of two texture views and their corresponding depth data, where the prediction structure is I-P structure. When multi-view video is coded with I-P structure, the base view is coded with I-view coding and the dependent view is coded with P-view coding. Similarly, the data of 3-view configuration is coded with P-I-P structure; the base view at cen-

Table 1. Test sequences of 3D video coding

Test Sequence	Views	Frames	Provider	Frame size
Poznan_Hall2	9	250	PoznanUniversity	
Poznan_Street	9	250	PoznanUniversity	
Undo_Dancer	9	250	Nokia	1920x1088
GT_Fly	9	250	Nokia	
Kendo	7	300	NagoyaUniversity	
Balloons	7	300	NagoyaUniversity	1024x768
Newspaper	9	300	GIST	

ter is coded with I-view and the rest dependent views are coded with P-view coding.

The current 3D video coding is under development with two different coding standards: AVC-compatible and HEVC-compatible coding methods. The first one is to design a 3D video coding compatible with the conventional coding standard, i.e., H.264/AVC. The last one is to design a 3D video coding compatible with the HEVC (high-efficiency video coding) which is under standardization by JCT-VC (Joint Collaborative Team on Video Coding).

Technical Challenges in 3D Video Coding

As a response to the call for proposal on 3D video coding, many institutes have proposed various compression methods on 3D video data. Every proposal employed the inter-view prediction structure to utilize the inter-view correlations. In particular, HEVC-compatible methods modified the HM (HEVC test model) reference software to achieve the inter-view prediction. Although there exist some differences between proposed methods, texture coding refers to the adjacent reconstructed texture view and depth coding refers to the adjacent reconstructed depth view, respectively. Figure 17 demonstrates the data flow of 3D video system. Using the state-of-the-art 3D video coding standards, MVD data are compressed. Then the receiver reconstructs the target data according to the type of displays. Currently, various CEs(core experiments) are under progress

Figure 17. Data flow diagram of 3D video system

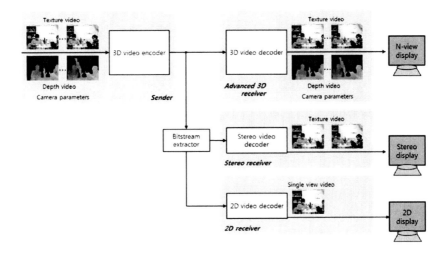

to evaluate proper methods on 3D video coding (ISO/IEC JTC1/SC29/WG11, 2012).

On CE1, view synthesis prediction method sare under investigation. The view synthesis prediction method uses a synthesized image using the reconstructed adjacent video data both texture and depth. The synthesized image can be used as an additional reference frame in the encoder and decoder, and it can be used for coding using proposed 'VSP_SKIP' mode. Samsung, Mitsubishi, and Nokia, etc. have developed various methods on view synthesis prediction. Since these methods need the view synthesis process at the decoder, complexity problem is one of issue for standardization.

On CE2, the depth representation and coding methods are under investigation. PoznanUniversity has proposed a non-linear representation for depth information, where the depth values are determined by considering the human visual system. For depth coding, Samsung has proposed an adaptive depth coding method by controlling the quantization parameter (QP) along depth boundary. Figure 18 shows the encoder structure via adaptive quantization method (ISO/IEC JTC1/SC29/WG11, 2011).

On CE3, in-loop depth resampling methods are under investigation. Under the assumption that the depth map has rather simple texture, depth map can be down-sampled before compression. Figure 19 shows the coding process with down-sampled depth data (ISO/IEC JTC1/SC29/WG11, 2012). Before encoding the depth data, depth down-sampling process is conducted. The decoder reconstructs the down-sampled depth data and up-sample them using a proposed up-sampling method. Since the quality of depth data determines the synthesized images, efficient up-sampling method is required.

On CE4, in-loop depth filtering methods are under investigation. The depth map filtering is conducted after deblocking filter of depth map to enhance the quality of synthesized image. The coding errors on depth data may affect the quality of synthesized images, adaptive filtering on depth boundaries is required. Samsung, AachenUniversity, and ETRI&KWU are participating in this CE.

Figure 18. Adaptive quantization method for depth video coding

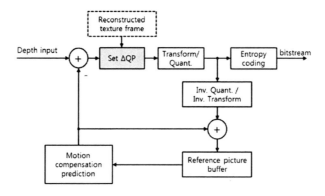

Figure 19. Coding process via down-sampled depth map

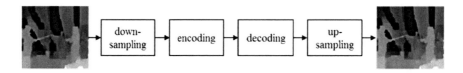

Figure 20. Coding parameter sharing

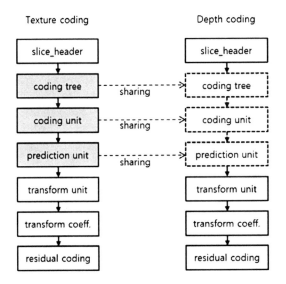

On CE5, prediction parameter coding methods for motion data are under investigation. Since the 3D video data employs multi-view, the coding parameters between views or texture-to-depth can be shared for coding. Figure 20 describes the concept of sharing coding parameters in HEVC-compatible coding (ISO/IEC JTC1/SC29/WG11, 2011). After compressing texture data, their corresponding coding parameters for encoding depth data can be shared; the shared data are not transmitted to decoder.

On CE6, depth intra prediction methods are under investigation. ZhejianUniversity has proposed a gradient-based intra prediction method which is compatible with AVC. Samsung uses image segmentation for intra prediction and sends representative values of a block to decoder. Similarly, NTT uses the mean and the variation values of a block to decoder to distinguish the foreground and background.

On CE8, RD (rate-distortion) optimization methods are under investigation. When the encoder selects the best prediction mode, RD optimization is used in both AVC and HEVC standards. With the conventional coding method, the distortion term is calculated with the distortion of reconstructed depth data. However, the proposed RD optimization method in CE8 uses different distortion calculation. Since the distortion of depth map affects the quality of synthesized image, the distortion term is replaced with the synthesis distortion. Figure 21 shows an example of depth distortion and synthesis result (ISO/IEC JTC1/SC29/WG11, 2012). In Case 1, if the color image have no texture around the object boundaries, the reconstructed depth data containing serious coding error shows no synthesis error.

Ghent University have compared the coding performance of various type of 3D video coders, as shown in Figure 22 (ISO/IEC JTC1/SC29/

Figure 21. Example of depth distortion at different texture regions

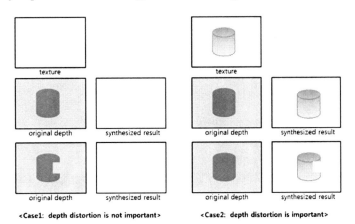

143

Figure 22. Comparison of coding performance of 3D video coders: (a) 'Kendo' sequence, (b) 'Poznan_Hall2' sequence

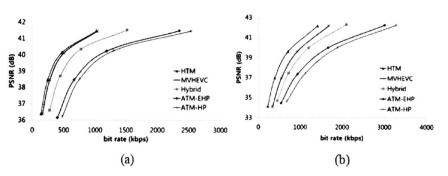

(a)   (b)

WG11, 2012). First, ATM-HP is a simple MVC extension for 3D video coding. Since MVC is intended for multi-view videos, the depth coding has not been considered. Second, ATM-EHP is an extended version of MVC, hence several proposed methods for 3D video coding are included such as depth re-sampling, view synthesis prediction and etc. Third, there is a hybrid coder by combining AVC coder and HEVC coder together; the texture videos are coded with AVC coder and the depth videos are coded with HEVC coder. Fourth, MVHEVC is a simple extension of HEVC to predict inter-view prediction; hence there are no changes on sub-LCU. The last one is HTM that includes several proposed coding methods such as wedgelet-based depth coding, view synthesis prediction and view synthesis optimization. All these coders are not fixed and under development by MPEG 3D video coding group. Therefore, the coding efficiency can be different with the final version of 3D video coder.

CONCLUSION

The future multimedia technology will be occupied by 3D video processing as well as ultra-definition image processing. By extending dimensions of viewing with depth, 3D video will draw IT technology into new research area. Hitherto, the conventional stereoscopic image and displays have used the exact viewpoint images as captured with stereo cameras. Therefore, if two viewpoints are inappropriate for viewing, a user may feel discomfort. Furthermore, most of stereoscopic displays use special glasses for 3D viewing, but auto-stereoscopic displays can render a 3D scene without 3D glasses using multi-view images. Generating additional view with depth data can be the best solution for comfortable rendering on stereoscopic displays and auto-stereoscopic displays. Therefore, depth estimation and view synthesis techniques are very important for 3D video systems. Based on these technologies, MPEG has investigated many coding technologies related on 3D video systems. Recently, the multi-view video coding (MVC) was established for encoding multiple view video utilizing inter-view correlations. As a next step, 3D video coding is being investigated by MPEG 3DVC (3D video coding) adHoc group. From the standard activities, various coding techniques for 3D video and application models are under discussion. However, there is no flag on the top of the mountain in the field of 3D video yet, anyone can reach and get the honor of frontier.

ACKNOWLEDGEMENT

This work was supported by the National Research Foundation of Korea (NRF) grant funded by the Korea government (MEST) (No. 2012-0009228)

REFERENCES

Benoit, A., Le Callet, P., Campisi, P., & Cousseau, R. (2008). Quality assessment of stereoscopic images. *EURASIP Journal on Image and Video Processing, 2008*, 659024. doi:10.1155/2008/659024

Boykov, Y., Veksler, O., & Zabih, R. (2001). Fast approximate energy minimization via graph cuts. *IEEE Transactions on Pattern Analysis and Machine Intelligence, 23*, 1222–1239. doi:10.1109/34.969114

Chen, Y., Chen, J., & Cai, C. (2006). *Luminance and chrominance correction for multi-view video using simplified color error model.*

DERS. (n.d.). *Depth estimation reference software.* Retrieved from http://wg11.sc29.org/svn/repos/MPEG-4/test/trunk/3D/depth_estimation/DERS/DERS

Fehn, C. (2004). Depth-image-based rendering (DIBR), compression and transmission for a new approach on 3D-TV. In *Stereoscopic Displays and Virtual Reality Systems XI*, (pp. 93-104).

Fusiello, A., Trucco, E., & Verri, A. (2000). Compact algorithm for rectification of stereo pairs. *Machine Vision and Applications, 12*, 16–22. doi:10.1007/s001380050120

Goldstein, E. B. (2002). *Sensation and perception.* Pacific Grove, CA.

Howard, I. P., & Rogers, B. J. (1996). *Binocular vision and stereopsis.* Oxford. doi:10.1093/acprof:oso/9780195084764.001.0001

Ilie, A., & Welch, G. (2005). Ensuring color consistency across multiple cameras. *Proceedings of the IEEE International Conference on Computer Vision*, (pp. 1268-1275).

ISO/IEC JTC1/SC29/WG11. (2003). *Report on 3DAV exploration.* MPEG output document N5878, July 2003.

ISO/IEC JTC1/SC29/WG11. (2008). Call for contributions on 3D video test material (update). MPEG output document N9595, Jan. 2008.

ISO/IEC JTC1/SC29/WG11. (2008). *Multiview video test sequence and camera parameters.* MPEG intput document m15419, April 2008.

ISO/IEC JTC1/SC29/WG11. (2009). *View synthesis method without blending.* MPEG input document M16091, Feb. 2009.

ISO/IEC JTC1/SC29/WG11. (2009). *Vision on 3D video.* MPEG output document N10357, Jan. 2009.

ISO/IEC JTC1/SC29/WG11. (2010). *Report on experimental framework for 3D video coding.* MPEG output document N11631, Oct. 2010.

ISO/IEC JTC1/SC29/WG11. (2011). *Applications and requirements on 3D video coding.* MPEG output document N11829, Jan. 2011.

ISO/IEC JTC1/SC29/WG11. (2011). *Call for proposals on 3D video coding technology.* MPEG output document N12036, March 2011.

ISO/IEC JTC1/SC29/WG11. (2011). *Description of AVC compatible 3D video coding technology by Samsung.* MPEG input document M22632, Nov. 2011.

ISO/IEC JTC1/SC29/WG11. (2011). *Descriptions of 3D video coding proposal* (HEVC-compatible category). MPEG input document M22566, Nov. 2011.

ISO/IEC JTC1/SC29/WG11. (2012). *3D-AVC-CE06 results on in-loop depth resampling by Mitsubishi.* MPEG input document M23774, Feb. 2012.

ISO/IEC JTC1/SC29/WG11. (2012). *3D-AVC-CE7 results on: Joint RDO for depth coding of 3D video by ZJU.* MPEG input document M23627, Feb. 2012.

ISO/IEC JTC1/SC29/WG11. (2012). *Description of core experiments in 3D video coding*. MPEG output document N12561, Feb. 2012.

ISO/IEC JTC1/SC29/WG11. (2012). *Overview of the coding performance of 3D video architectures*. MPEG input document M24968, April 2012.

Jiang, G., Shao, F., Yu, M., Chen, K., & Chen, X. (2006). New color correction approach to multi-view images with region correspondence. *LNCS, 4113*, 1224–1228.

Jung, J.-I., & Ho, Y. S. (2012). (in press). Color correction algorithm based on camera characteristics for multi-view video coding. *Signal Image and Video Processing*. doi:10.1007/s11760-012-0341-1

Kim, S. Y., Lee, E. K., & Ho, Y. S. (2008). Generation of ROI enhanced depth maps using stereoscopic cameras and a depth camera. *IEEE Transactions on Broadcasting, 54*, 732–740. doi:10.1109/TBC.2008.2002338

Koo, H. S., Jeon, Y. J., & Jeon, B. M. (2007). *MVC motion skip mode*. JVT of ISO/IEC MPEG & ITU-T VCEG JVT-W081, April 2007.

Lang, M., Hornung, A., Wang, O., Poulakos, S., Smolic, A., & Gross, M. (2010). *Non-linear disparity mapping for stereoscopic 3D*. Presented at the ACM SIGGRAPH 2010, July 2010.

Lee, C., Choi, B. H., & Ho, Y. S. (2011). Efficient multiview depth video coding using depth synthesis prediction. *Optical Engineering (Redondo Beach, Calif.), 20*.

Lee, Y. L., Hur, J. H., Lee, Y. K., Han, K. H., Cho, S. H., Hur, N. H … Gomila, C. (2006). *CE11: Illumination compensation*. JVT of ISO/IEC MPEG & ITU-T VCEG JVT-U052, Oct. 2006.

Maitre, M., Shinagawa, Y., & Do, M. N. (2008). Wavelet-based joint estimation and encoding of depth-image-based representations for free-viewpoint rendering. *IEEE Transactions on Image Processing, 17*, 946–957. doi:10.1109/TIP.2008.922425

Milani, S., Zanuttigh, P., Zamarin, M., & Forchhammer, S. (2011). *Efficient depth map compression exploiting segmented color D*. 2011.

Onural, L. (2010). Signal processing and 3DTV. *IEEE Signal Processing Magazine, 27*, 144+141-142.

Pesquet-Popescu, B., Daribo, I., & Tillier, C. (2009). Motion vector sharing and bitrate allocation for 3D video-plus-depth coding. *EURASIP Journal on Advances in Signal Processing*.

Scharstein, D., & Szeliski, R. (2002). A taxonomy and evaluation of dense two-frame stereo correspondence algorithms. *International Journal of Computer Vision, 47*, 7–42. doi:10.1023/A:1014573219977

Smolić, A., Mueller, K., Merkle, P., Fehn, C., Kauff, P., Eisert, P., & Wiegand, T. (2006). 3D video and free viewpoint video - Technologies, applications and MPEG standards. *Proceedings of IEEE ICME*, Canada, (pp. 2161-2164).

Smolic, A., Mueller, K., Stefanoski, N., Osteraiann, J., Gotchev, A., & Akar, G. B. (2007). Coding algorithms for 3DTV - A survey. *IEEE Transactions on Circuits and Systems for Video Technology, 17*, 1606–1620. doi:10.1109/TCSVT.2007.909972

Sullivan, G. J., Topiwala, P., & Luthra, A. (2004). *The H.264/AVC advanced video coding standard: Overview and introduction to the fidelity range extensions*. Presented at the SPIE Conference on Applications of Digital Image Processing XXVII, 2004.

Sun, J., Zheng, N. N., & Shum, H. Y. (2003). Stereo matching using belief propagation. *IEEE Transactions on Pattern Analysis and Machine Intelligence, 25,* 787–800. doi:10.1109/TPAMI.2003.1206509

Telea, A. (2004). An image inpainting technique based on the fast marching method. *Journal Graphics Tools, 9,* 25–36.

Test Sequence Download Page, M. P. E. G.-F. T. V. (n.d.). *Free-viewpoint TV.* Retrieved from http://www.tanimoto.nuee.nagoya-u.ac.jp/~fukushima/mpegftv/

VSRS. (n.d.). *View synthesis reference software.* Retrieved from http://wg11.sc29.org/svn/repos/MPEG-4/test/trunk/3D/view_synthesis/VSRS

Wheatstone, C. (1838). On some remarkable, and hitherto unobserved, phenomena of binocular vision. *Philosophical Transactions of the Royal Society of London, 54,* 196–199.

Yamamoto, K., Kitahara, M., Kimata, H., Yendo, T., Fujii, T., & Tanimoto, M. (2007). Multiview video coding using view interpolation and color correction. *IEEE Transactions on Circuits and Systems for Video Technology, 17,* 1436–1449. doi:10.1109/TCSVT.2007.903802

Zhang, Z. (2000). A flexible new technique for camera calibration. *IEEE Transactions on Pattern Analysis and Machine Intelligence, 22,* 1330–1334. doi:10.1109/34.888718

Zitnick, C. L., Kang, S. B., Uyttendaele, M., Winder, S., & Szeliski, R. (2004). High-quality video view interpolation using a layered representation. *Proceedings of ACM SIGGRAPH,* (pp. 600-608).

KEY TERMS AND DEFINITIONS

3D Video Coding: A coding standard under developing by MPEG that compresses the 3D video data consisted of multi-view video and their associated depth data.

Advanced Stereoscopic Display: A 3D display device that renders the stereoscopic images by choosing proper two viewpoint images among provided multi-view images.

Auto-Stereoscopic Display: A 3D display device that renders multi-view images without glasses.

Depth Estimation: A depth map acquisition process that determines disparity values of stereoscopic or multi-view images.

Depth Estimation Reference Software (DERS): That is provided by MPEG 3D video coding group. It uses three views to estimate the center view's depth map.

Multi-View Video Coding: A coding standard established by MPEG that compresses the multi-view video data using interview prediction based on H.264/AVC standard.

View Synthesis: A process that generates an additional viewpoint image using supplementary data, i.e., depth map.

View Synthesis Reference Software (VSRS): That is provided by MPEG 3D video coding group. It generates any virtual view point image using two color images and two depth maps.

Chapter 6
State-of-the Art Motion Estimation in the Context of 3D TV

Vania V. Estrela
Universidade Federal Fluminense, Brazil

A. M. Coelho
Instituto Federal de Ed., Ciencia e Tecn. do Sudeste de Minas Gerais, Brazil

ABSTRACT

Progress in image sensors and computation power has fueled studies to improve acquisition, processing, and analysis of 3D streams along with 3D scenes/objects reconstruction. The role of motion compensation/motion estimation (MCME) in 3D TV from end-to-end user is investigated in this chapter. Motion vectors (MVs) are closely related to the concept of disparities, and they can help improving dynamic scene acquisition, content creation, 2D to 3D conversion, compression coding, decompression/decoding, scene rendering, error concealment, virtual/augmented reality handling, intelligent content retrieval, and displaying. Although there are different 3D shape extraction methods, this chapter focuses mostly on shape-from-motion (SfM) techniques due to their relevance to 3D TV. SfM extraction can restore 3D shape information from a single camera data.

INTRODUCTION

Technological convergence has been prompting changes in 3D image rendering together with communication paradigms. It implies interaction with other areas, such as games, that are designed for both TV and the Internet. Obtaining and creating perspective time varying scenes are essential for 3D TV growth and involve knowledge from multidisciplinary areas such as image processing, computer graphics (CG), physics, computer vision, game design, and behavioral sciences (Javidi & Okano, 2002). 3D video refers to previously recorded sequences. 3D TV, on the other hand, comprises acquirement, coding, transmission, reception, decoding, error concealment (EC), and reproduction of streaming video.

DOI: 10.4018/978-1-4666-2660-7.ch006

This chapter sheds some light on the importance of motion compensation and motion estimation (MCME) for an end-to-end 3D TV system, since motion information can help dealing with the huge amount of data involved in acquiring, handing out, exploring, modifying, and reconstructing 3D entities present in video streams. Notwithstanding the existence of many methods to render 3D objects, this text is concerned with shape-from-motion (SfM) techniques.

Applying motion vectors (MVs) to an image to create the next image is called motion compensation (MC). This text will use the term "frame" for a scene snapshot at a given time instant regardless of the fact that it is 2D or 3D video. Motion estimation (ME) explores previous and/or future frames to identify unchanged blocks. The combination of ME and MC is a key part of video compression as used by MPEG 1, 2 and 4 in addition to many other video codecs.

Human beings get 3D data from several cues via parallax. In binocular parallax, each eye captures its view of the same object. In motion parallax, different views of an object are obtained as a consequence of head shift. Multi-view video (MVV) refers to a set of N temporally synchronized video streams coming from cameras that capture the same real world scenery from different viewpoints and it is widely used in various 3D TV and free-viewpoint video (FVV) systems where stereo ($N = 2$) is a special case. Some issues regarding 3D TV that need further developments to turn this technology mainstream are

- Availability of a broad range of 3D content;
- Suitable distribution mechanisms;
- Adequate transmission strategies;
- Satisfactory computer processing capacity;
- Appropriate displays;
- Proper technology prices for customers; and
- 2D to 3D conversion allowing for popular video material to be seen on a 3D display.

Video tracking is an aid to film post-production, surveillance and estimation of spatial coordinates. Information is gathered by a camera, combined with the result from the analysis of a large set of 2D trajectories of prominent image features and it is used to animate virtual characters from the tracked motion of real characters. The majority of motion-capture systems rely on a set of markers affixed to an actor's body to approximate their displacements. Next, the motion of the makers is mapped onto characters generated by CG (Deng, Jiang, Liu, & Wang, 2008).

3D video can be generated from a 2D sequence and its related depth map by means of depth image-based rendering (DIBR). As a result, the conversion of 2D to 3D video is feasible if the depth information can be inferred from the original 2D sequence (Fehn, 2006; Kauff, et al., 2007).

Light field refers to radiance as a function of location and direction of areas without occlusion. The final objective is to get a time-varying light field that hits a surface and is reflected with negligible delay. An example of a feasible dense light field acquisition system is one using optical fibers with a high-definition camera to obtain multiple views promptly (Javidi & Okano, 2002). For the most part, light field cameras allow interactive navigation and manipulation of video and per-pixel depth maps to improve the results of light field rendering.

Video restoration is crucial to 3D TV and it continues to call for research because of difficulties such as nonstationarities and discontinuities in spatio-temporal signals as well as the need to minimize the error between the unknown original sequence and the restored one. Denoising can benefit from ME to manage large displacements due to camera motion.

At least two video streams captured by different cameras synchronized in time are necessary to show 3D content. A 3D TV system should offer an adequate amount of viewpoints and this trait is called FVV by the MPEG Ad-Hoc Group on 3D Audio and Video (3DAV) (Smolic & McCutchen,

2004). A high number of pixels per viewpoint also helps rendering 3D scenarios. Current developments in hardware point towards a completely distributed design for acquisition, compression, transmission, and representation of dynamic scenes as well as total scalability when it comes to the implementation of all stages.

Figure 1 illustrates a typical 3D TV system. The acquisition step has arrangements of synchronized cameras connected to the computers (producers) that generate/assemble the 3D video content. The producers combine several image sources from live, uncompressed streams and then, code them. Next, the compressed dynamic scenes are sent to distinct channels with the help of a broadcast network. Individual video streams are decompressed by decoders at the receiver side. The decoders are networked to a cluster of consumer computers in charge of rendering the proper views and direct them to a 3D display. A dedicated controller may transmit virtual view parameters to decoders and consumers. It can also be connected to cameras located in the viewing region for automatic display calibration. Scalability in the amount of captured, broadcast, and presented views can be achieved if a completely distributed processing is used.

A possible system realization applies a one-to-one mapping of cameras to projectors, provided images are rectified (camera calibration) to correct aligned. Because cameras must be uniformly spaced, this mapping lacks flexibility and it fails if the number of cameras differs from the amount of projectors. However, it scales fine.

Another flexible scheme is an image-based rendering to synthesize views at the correct virtual camera positions where the geometric proxy for the scene is a single plane arbitrarily set.

Lately, academia and industries have paid a lot of attention to multimedia communications over networks. Video applications can be conversational (video telephony or teleconference) and streaming. In talkative applications, a peer-to-peer connection is created and both sides execute identical tasks, such as coding and decoding. Video streaming generally employs client-server architecture. The client queries the server for a particular video stream, and then a specific quantity of information is reserved. Subsequently, the server sends video so that the client is able to decode and display dynamic scenes in real-time. If packets are lost, the preliminary lag caused by the pre-rolling process typically permits the client to request some retransmissions; nevertheless a remaining rate of packet losses persists. Error concealment (EC) algorithms encompassing spatial, temporal, and spatiotemporal interpolation soothe damages caused by losses as seen in (Belfiore, Grangetto, Magli, & Olmo, 2003; Coelho, Estrela, & de Assis, 2009; Coelho, & Estrela, 2012b).

This chapter is organized as follows: section A.2 provides the necessary background on MCME; section A.3 explains how MCME aid all stages of an end-to-end 3D TV. Recommendations for future research are suggested in a separate section, which is followed by a final one compiling the major conclusions on MCME in the context of 3D TV.

Figure 1. End-to-end 3D TV system

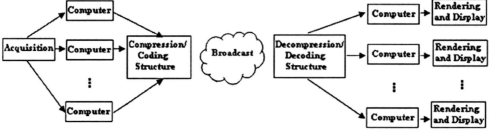

Background and Definitions

Motion Compensation/Motion Estimation (MCME)

Motion analysis is necessary to understand visual surrounds as well as to improve coding, vision, object segmentation, tracking, and so on. In addition, MCME and depth data are strongly related in 3D TV.

Tracking significant objects in video is the basis of many applications like video production, remote surveillance, robotics, interactive immersive games and comprehension of large video datasets. It helps to trim down the work required for a task and thus facilitating the development of 3D TV systems

Motion detection (MD) is the ability of a system to perceive motion and gather important occurrences. An MD algorithm senses motions, prompts the surveillance system to start acquiring a scene and it can evaluate the motion to take a course of action. So far, the intricacy of MV detection does not permit real-time realizations of this procedure. MEMC schemes based on the H.264 standard use a fixed block-size matching procedure. The motion of an object is directly proportional to its distance from the camera. Thus, the depth map is approximated by a constant associated to the estimated motion. Regrettably, this only holds for a small fraction of videos with camera panning across a stationary scene or with a still camera (Figure 2).

MVs may be related to global motion or to local motion of specific regions. The MVs may be represented by: 1) a translational model only; 2) models that can approximate the motion of a real camera; 3) feature-oriented methods such as the Harris corner detector, so as to locate a set of points that work as a signature of an object; and 4) feature-matching methods that find all corresponding features between frames. The most popular classes of motion estimation algorithms are described in the next 3 paragraphs.

The consistency of local grey-level patterns in successive images is an important assumption for optical flow (OF) estimation. Redundancy between adjoining frames can be used for compression where a frame is chosen as a reference and the next frames are predicted from this reference by means of ME (*interframe coding*). So, each frame can be predicted by considering the previous frame and the estimated motion. Optical Flow (OF) is the perceptible displacement of objects and special features in a scene caused by dislocation of image intensities (pixel grey levels) in a scene. There is a close relationship between ME, and stereo disparity measurement (Estrela, & Galatsanos, 2000; Garbas et al., 2006; Coelho & Estrela, 2012b). Lots of advances in ME and video compression have resulted from OF research, because it yields a dense motion field, and it helps estimating the 3D structure of its constituents. 3D Optical Flow (3D OF) is more sensible when it comes to motion awareness and mental maps generation of the environment. A typical approach

Figure 2. Simplified view of an end-to-end 3D TV system

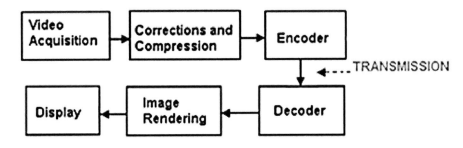

for 3D OF is to compute time-varying depth maps using stereo algorithms, followed by the computation of range or scene flow from data. In practice, stereo is used to obtain depth maps and compute range flow. An interesting application of stereo is 3D scene generation for CG and 3D tracking (Wedel et al. 2008) (Figure 3).

A Block Matching Algorithm (BMA) locates matching blocks between video frames in order to estimate motion, that is, it picks up MVs compliant with the best correlation between pairs of blocks contained in successive frames. Hence, BMA takes advantage of the concept of temporal redundancy in the video sequence, which aims at increasing the effectiveness of interframe video compression and it has been adopted in MPEG-2 motion estimation (ME) due to its simplicity and effectiveness (Furht, 2008). However, the lack of contrast, noise and illumination changes can impair ME an lead to inverse problems. Once the MVs are found, they can be used to describe the transformation from one image to another. Algorithms for implementing ME are carried out by the codec.

Phase Correlation (PC) uses the Fourier Transform (FT) of adjacent or similar images to estimate the relative offset between them. PC is more robust to rotation and deformation of objects than other methods which turn it easier the identification of frequency signatures related to MVs. The FT represents only the inter-frame changes in terms of frequency distribution; hence there exists less data to be processed. Each motion corresponds to a peak in the 3D frequency spectrum given by the FT. So, the computer has just to track the peaks and assign the right MVs to them. Once the dominant motion has been estimated, then filtering along the motion direction can be performed (Lucchese, Doretto, & Cortelazzo, (2002))

High compression and high coding efficiencies result from taking advantage of both spatial and temporal redundancies. A coder configuration using the closed-loop ME is called as a predictive video encoder.

H.264/MPEG-4 Part 10 or AVC (Advanced Video Coding) is an extremely popular standard for video compression, and for high definition sequences. This standard has a codec that relies on a BMA MC.

Scalable Video Coding (SVC) allows bitstreams that contain sub-bitstreams, where both conform to the standard. The base layer can be decoded by an H.264/AVC that does not support SVC. A subset bitstream can represent a lower spatial resolution, or a lower temporal resolution, or a lower quality video signal compared to the bitstream it is derived from. There are four possible types of scalability:

Figure 3. A general 3D video coding architecture

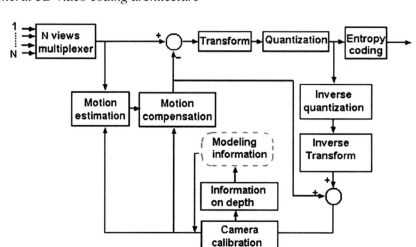

- Temporal (frame rate) scalability structures the MC dependencies, so that complete frames can be removed from the bitstream.
- Spatial (frame size) scalability is related to the fact that dynamic sequences are coded at various spatial resolutions. The information and decoded samples from lower resolutions can be used to predict data or samples of higher resolutions aiming at decreasing the bit rate necessary to code the higher resolutions.
- SNR/Quality/Fidelity scalability is concerned with coding at a particular spatial resolution but with different image qualities. The information and decoded samples corresponding to lower qualities can be used to estimate data or samples from higher qualities to lessen the bit rate used to code the higher qualities.
- All scalability defined above can be combined.

MVV Coding (MVC) permits the creation of bitstreams corresponding to several views of a scene, which facilitates the implementation of stereoscopic 3D video coding. The Multi-view High Profile supports multiple views, and the Stereo High Profile is dedicated to stereoscopic video (two views).

Broadcasting problems can be alleviated by means of efficient coding and compression strategies. 3D TV broadcasting calls for the transmission of all views to multiple clients at the same time. The quantization can be described as a mapping of a continuous set of values (or a very large set of possible discrete values) to a relatively small discrete and finite set. The resulting quantized signal should be possible to represent with fewer bits than the original since the range of values is smaller. The process is lossy (*i.e.* not reversible). Many transforms have been proposed to trim down redundancies and the amount of data to be coded, such as the Principal Component analysis

(PCA), Singular Value Decomposition (SVD), the Discrete Wavelet Transform (DWT), and the discrete cosine transform (DCT). Since most compression techniques are lossy, compression-induced distortion metrics are needed to appraise video coding algorithms. In practice, MSE and PSNR have been extensively used due to their clear physical meanings and simplicity, but they are far from portraying perception as the HVS.

The DCT is omnipresent in all video compression standards because it is well fitted with the BMA structure. Non-zero DCT coefficients of a translating area (global, constant-velocity, translational motion) are situated on a folded plane in the spatio-temporal frequency space and this fact helps to estimate motion in a 3D block of pixels.

Most visual coding standards (MPEG-1, MPEG-2, MPEG-4 Visual, H.261, H.263 and H.264) are based on predictive DPCM/DCT design (Hewage, Karim, Worrall, Dogan, & Kondoz, 2007; Richardson& al., 2003; Schwarz, Marpe, & Wiegand, 2006). An MPEG image consists of slices of a contiguous sequence of pixel macro-blocks (MB). In MPEG, a sequence is divided into groups of pictures (GOP) providing random access as well as errorresiliencyand including three types of pictures:

1. Intra coded pictures, or I-pictures use only information present in the picture itself, and provide potential random access points and error robustness inside the video sequence. They use only spatial transform coding without motion data. The first picture inside GOP must be an I-picture, since it allows decoding at the start of any GOP.
2. Predicted pictures, or P-pictures are coded with respect to some previous I-picture or P-picture (forward prediction). They use MC to improve compression efficiency and serve as prediction reference for B-pictures as well as future P-pictures.

3. Bi-directional pictures use both a past and future frames as a reference (bi-directional prediction). So, their best compression comes from using past and future frames as reference increasing computational cost and delay.

An efficient transmission format for 3D TV sends one color video view with a per-pixel depth map. The depth data helps rendering virtual views in which the objects of the monoscopic color video have been shifted to positions and captured by a virtual camera parallel to the real one. Depth map represented as a grayscale video can be better compressed than the corresponding color video while preserving good quality (Ozaktas & Onural, 2008). Stereo video is the most important special case of MVV with N = 2 views. Compression of conventional stereo video has been studied for a long time and the corresponding standards are available.

In this text, the problem of allocating bits to color and depth information when using H.264/AVC video codec is considered, because of the strong relationship between MCME and depth information in 3D TV. The quality of 3D videos stored as video plus depth map is affected by the number of bits used for coding color and depth when using baseline H.264.

Motion video plus depth (MVD) standards are still under examination by the JVT. The MPEG-C Part 3 and the MVC specifications do not handle well the MVD data representation and they may require extensions or combinations of other characteristics (Ozaktas & Onural, 2008).

Video Quality Metrics

There has been a growing interest for better video quality metrics to automatically predict the perceptual improvement of video streams, video databases and numerous other applications. Motion-JPEG – where each frame is stored with the JPEG format - extends the JPEG standard to video.

Visual metrics are crucial in quality monitoring/assessment for broadcasting, compression, coding, EC and resiliency and they influence the entire design of video systems. There are two broad classes of quality measures: objective and subjective.

Objective video quality metrics rely on meaningful mathematical procedures without viewer panels and they are classified as follows: (1) Full-Reference (FR) metrics have full access to the original (reference) signal; (2) No-Reference (NR) metrics help when the reference signal is not completely accessible; and (3) Reduced Reference (RR) metrics use features from the original video and send them as side information to the receiver to help evaluating distorted video.

Subjective metrics try to imitate human vision, leading to improved methodologies since human beings are the ultimate video receivers. Nevertheless, a deficient human vision system (HVS) comprehension and difficulty in learning from physiological/psychological data degrade the performance of this class of metrics (Furht, 2008). Human vision is exceptional, but it seems to give unequal consideration to all data/cues, tending to center on some image parts. Visual awareness is central to the HVS and it is helps signaling saliencies amid objects in a scene (Kienzle, Schölkopf, Wichmann, & Franz, 2007). Progress achieved on subjective 3D quality evaluation have limitations and should be applied to specific features (for instance, compression artifacts) due to the required computational costs and processing time. The mean opinion score (MOS) i.e. has been regarded as the most reliable quality metric (Wang & Bovik, 2006), but it is cumbersome, and time consuming.

Spatial information (SI) features are related to the standard deviation of edge-enhanced images and it presupposes that compression will alter the edge statistics in the frames. Temporal information (TI) features are related to the standard deviation of the difference amid frames. Relationships between the reference and the distorted videos are derived from SI and TI features.

Many simple objective image metrics such as the PSNR have been used, but they fall short from the human perception of the differences involving frames. PSNR is also extremely sensitive to depth map errors. Perceptually-guided rendering focuses on fast photo-realistic algorithms to reduce the number of unnecessary computations. It is difficult to recognize 3D objects, because they can be represented in numerous ways such as polygonal meshes, parametric surfaces and discrete models.

Validation is an important step towards successful development of practical video quality metrics because it is indispensable to build a video database with subjective evaluation scores associated with each of the video sequences in the database. MCME methods require several evaluation metrics to help assessing and correcting dynamic scenes. Subjective and objective quality metrics are very correlated in 3D video. Hence, individual objective appraisals of 3D video can replace subjective procedures for most parameter alterations. These potential objective metrics are FR methods where the receiver needs the original 3D stream for quality assessment of the rendered video (Brunnström & al, 2009; Starck, Kilner, & Hilton, 2008).

Visual attention metrics encompass schemes to lessen the computational cost of the searching processes inherent to visual perception algorithms and they are modeled after a bottom-up process (BuP) based in image traits stimuli or a top-down task/comprehension (TDT) strategies. For a BuP, saliency levels are constrained by image characteristics/stimuli rather than visual information and, thus, creating a saliency map. The resulting sum of BuP responses can be nonlinear due to miscellaneous stimuli sources. The corresponding analysis has been done by subjective tests and modeled accurately for combinations of cues such as orientation, motion, luminance, color and contrast (Furht, 2008; Kienzle, Schölkopf, Wichmann, & Franz, 2007).

THE ROLE OF MCME IN AN END-TO-END 3D TV SYSTEM

This section shows how MCME can improve all parts of an end-to-end 3D TV system, namely: image acquisition/creation, video coding/compression, broadcasting, reception, decoding/decompression, EC, and display/rendering.

Acquisition and Content Generation

Single Camera and 2D to 3D Conversion

The available techniques for 3D extraction from single-camera sequences are useful for conversion of the legacy mono-view video to 3D TV. The compatibility with conventional 2D TV to ensure a gradual transition to 3D is referred to as backward-compatibility. 2D to 3D conversion suffers due to scarce information on depth and it relies on multiple cues from monoscopic video such as motion parallax and texture. Depth extraction methods must be content-adaptive and the most successful is 3D stereo video generation by the DIBR technique (Cheng, Li, &Chen, 2010). The translation of 2D material to 3D plays an important role in the implementation of 3D TV and it involves a backward-compatible system. The concept of depth maps takes advantage of the HVS ability to merge reduced disparity data that situated largely on boundaries where depth cues create an improved depth sensation over legacy 2D images.

Depth estimation based on displacement data may have uncertainties thanks to the simultaneous dislocation of objects and camera and to the accuracy of H.264-estimated MVs. ME in H.264/AVC and other standards rely on maximizing compression efficiency at the expense of the accuracy of object displacement estimates. Hence, not all MVs can be used to correctly estimate depth, but only those MVs that correspond to the object displacement (Pourazad, Nasiopoulos, & Ward, 2009).

In case of depth uncertainty, an object with larger motion than others is not unavoidably close to the camera, because its direction in relation to an object may have changed. If there is camera panning, then the predicted MVs corresponding to stationary regions are equal to the camera motion. These stationary regions are repeatedly classified by the H.264/AVC motion rating procedure such as the 'Skip Mode'. The transformed coefficients and the displacements are not transmitted once a block is omitted. Thus, the median of the MVs of the nearby blocks - identified as predicted MV - is used as the block MV. Besides panning, camera zooming can also cause depth ambiguity. If the MVs are biased, then the estimated MVs are scaled accordingly. Zooming in/out may reverse depth or may cause eye weariness if not corrected during depth estimation. Nonlinear scaling models can be used for the reason that there is a nonlinear relation involving visual depth perception and the distance of an object. The suggested scaling factor reduces as the object distance increases – with superior depth sensitivity – and, hence, boosts the distinction amid depth values. The estimated depth map combined with the 2D video stream can facilitate the recovery of stereoscopic pairs via a DIBR algorithm in order to handle occlusion.

The low-cost single-camera technique solves the problems in mono-view video content and shows potential as a link between the available conventional video sequences and the 3D displays. The SfM scheme is considered the finest single-camera method for acquiring real life video. SfM is also adequate to human face and body capture. However, implementing synchronized multi-camera acquisition increases hardware complexity and makes the 3D TV system more expensive. Several algorithms have been proposed for creation of dynamic scene representations from the data acquired from the multi-view points. In this aspect, the virtual FVV generation from arbitrarily chosen viewing angles is an important step for 3D TV displays.

Techniques to retrieve 3D video such as monoscopic video, multi-view or stereoscopic vision result in ill-posed problems due to the conversion procedures. Although there is no ideal solution to this extraction problem, SfM is very popular and it tries to identify the 3D geometry involving camera and objects. Feature correspondences obtained from two (or more) video frames are required to establish geometrical relationships, to estimate camera calibration parameters or to infer scene structure (Schmid, Mohr, & Bauckhage, 2000). The converted 3D TV lacks the camera intrinsic structural parameters (Hartley & Zisserman, 2003). Structure and motion problems require a camera array with high precision and resolution thanks to the nonlinearity of the rendering process. Thus, formulations robust to motion variations should be favored.

Multi-Camera Systems

The majority of multi-camera systems for 3D TV and 3D reconstruction are intended for telepresence, telemedicine and teleconferencing. This type of capture system requires software and/or hardware synchronization (Yang, Everett, Buehler, & Mcmillan, 2002) as well as calibration. The last step involves a more complex correspondence problem, since there are multiple parameters to be found (a set of parameters for each camera). A dense camera mesh captures better the light field; however high-quality reconstruction filters could be used, provided the light field is undersampled (Stewart, Yu, Gortler, & Mcmillan, 2003).

Model-Based Systems

Various views from a camera array can be used to interpolate 3D image in order to render it properly in the synthesis stage (Carranza, Theobalt, Magnor, & Seidel, 2003; Fehn, et al., 2002; Zitnick, Kang, Uyttendaele, Winder, & Szeliski, 2004). Throughout rendering, the MVV can be combined with a mathematical and/or computational model to build better quality surfaces (Carranza, Theobalt, Magnor, & Seidel, 2003). Real-time capture of high definition video relying on models is complex due to needs such as extra storage and transmission bandwidth.

The multiple-frame structure from motion (MFSfM) involves more than three frames obtained with a monocular single-camera which circles the desired subjects. The MFSfM requires the existence of causality and temporal continuity constraints, so that there is a small disparity between frames. Temporal redundancy is of limited use, without excellent feature tracking and inter-frame correspondence. Although linear algorithms give straightforward solutions, the SfM problem is intrinsically nonlinear and dependent on linearization assumptions (Kanatani, 1990). In a multi-frame context, the main algorithms rely on the fact that image measurements can be expressed as a product of two matrices, representing the motion and the structure. Nonlinear algorithms also depend on iterative minimization of a cost function on both structure and motion parameters. Nonlinear methods rely on an iterative cost function minimization of a cost function on both structure and motion parameters. Local minima, nonguaranteed convergence and dependency on good parameters initialization are some limitations of these algorithms.

Linear and nonlinear cost functions can be proposed to complete absent entries, handle occlusions and unreliable features (Jebara & Pentland, 1999). Fusion methods estimate structure by combining intermediate reconstructions resulting from smaller subsets of the sequence. Another strategy for SfM considers state estimation for dynamical systems with new constraints and reducing the solution space (Oliensis, 2000).

The use of 3D images and model databases is growing, but fall short to match users' expectations. Efficient data recovery from collections of images and videos involves offline and online processes for 3D model indexing. Offline processes use performance descriptors that are invariant to particular transformations. In online processes, the end-user queries the search engine using similarity metrics to compare 3D objects, for a given model description (Stoykova, et al., 2007). Possible descriptors are:

- Statistical approaches focus on the probability distributions of 3D local and global model descriptions.
- Structural approaches look for high-level structure, such as a graph, from a 3D mesh.
- To handle 3D shapes in other domains with the help of transformations.
- To represent a 3D model by a set of 2D-decribed characteristic views.

Many 3D applications are limited to human face or full body processing. They involve face and facial feature detection; capturing of 3D structure of the face; analysis of global face motion/mimic; 3D modeling; kinematics and motion analysis; and motion recognition. Algorithms can be more efficient with a priori knowledge about 3D structure and motion of human faces and bodies which is extremely necessary for the development of 3D visualization technology. In 3D visualization and 3D display systems, robust detection and tracking of the observer's eyes and the observer's view point is necessary to render the correct view according to the observer position.

3D Compression and Coding

When it comes to high-quality rendering of 3D video and FVV, MPEG has been revised to include more possibilities (Smolic & McCutchen, 2004), because of the existing challenges (Bourges-Sevenier & Jang, 2004). MPEG-C Part 3 handles video plus depth data (ISO/IEC JTC1/SC29/WG11, 2007). Transmission and 3D TV with video plus depth can be also be found in (ITU-T Recommentation H.264 & ISO/IEC 14496-10 AVC, 2005). Additionally, H.264/AVC express depth through its auxiliary picture syntax (Martinian, Behrens, Xin, Vetro, & Sun, 2006). Figure 4 depicts a general 3D TV content producer.

Figure 4. Stages from the 3D TV producer

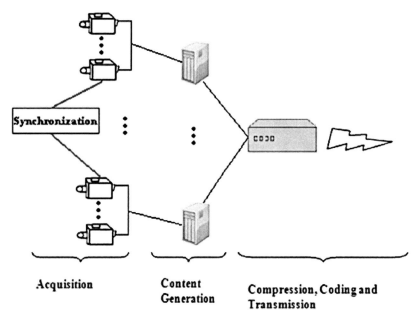

Acquisition   **Content Generation**   **Compression, Coding and Transmission**

The latest H.264/MPEG-4 AVC standard incorporate features from the MPEG-2 codec with a mixture of temporal and spatial estimation (Micallef, Debono, & Farrugia, Sep. 2010) characteristics, as follows: temporal prediction with variable block sizes, multiple reference frames, intra prediction, adaptive entropy coding, and filters to reduce the blocking effect. Moreover, it uses more efficiently the spatio-temporal correlation between adjacent MBs with the SKIP mode (predictive P-slices) and the DIRECT mode (bi-predictive B-slices) (Schwarz, Marpe, & Wiegand, 2006). Compression and prediction of 3D OFF can reuse past coded MVs. If there is some motion information that can been skipped without compromising image retrieval at the decoder side, then the bitrate savings may be higher.

The MPEG-7 standard provides mechanisms to represent audiovisual data in multimedia systems (Manjunath, Salembier, & Sikora, 2002; Sikora, 2001): descriptors (D), description schemes (DS), description definition language (DDL) and additional features. Descriptors symbolize parts of the syntax and the semantics of each attribute representation (Manjunath, Salembier, & Sikora, 2002). DS, schemes detail structure, semantics and the relationships among components (D and DS). DDL allows the DS and maybe descriptors creation/modifications; system tools to support multiple descriptions; synchronization; transmission methods; file formats; etc...

Multimedia descriptions encompass still pictures, video, graphics, audio, 3D models and their relationship. It is desirable that a 3D descriptor also supports any 2D descriptors - such as contour shape, color or texture –used to render real-world objects; c.g. (ITU-T H.264 & ISO/IEC 14496-10 AVC, 2005).

Unmistakably, excellent MVV coding is vital to 3D TV. The simplest way to solve the multi-view coding problem is to code video streams independently in time and transmit each of the views, entitling the use of current video coding standards and codecs. Conversely, the coding efficiency is for the most part lower than with other multi-view coding methods.

MVV compression has habitually focused on static light fields e.g., (Magnor, Ramanathan, & Girod, 2003). There is a need to research in compression and transmission of MVV in real-time (Yang, Everett, Buehler, & Mcmillan, 2002). Most systems compress the MVV offline and focus on providing interactive decoding and display (Javidi & Okano, 2002). MC in time is called temporal encoding, and disparity prediction between cameras is called spatial encoding (Tanimoto & Fuji, 2003). Combining temporal and spatial encoding also leads to good results (Zitnick, Kang, Uyttendaele, Winder, & Szeliski, 2004). An extra approach to MVV compression, endorsed by the ATTEST project (Fehn, et al., 2002), is to condense the data to a single view with per-pixel depth map, compressing these data in real-time and broadcasting them as an MPEG enhancement layer. At the receiver, stereo or multi-view images are created using image-based rendering, but high-quality output is impaired by occlusions or high disparities in the scene (Chen & Williams, 1993). Furthermore, one view is not enough to capture view-dependent effects, such as reflections and highlights.

In high-quality 3D TV distribution, all views are sent to many users at once. For compression and transmission of dynamic MVV data, either the data from multiple cameras is compressed using spatial or spatio-temporal coding, or each video stream is compressed by temporal coding. The first option gives higher compression, due to the high coherence between the views, but it requires the compression of multiple video streams by a centralized computer, which is not scalable, since inserting extra views surpasses the coder bandwidth.

An extra benefit of using existing 2D coding standards is that the codecs are well established and broadly accessible. Tomorrow's 3D TV could include one or many decoders, depending on the amount of views available for an object or scene. A system should be complaint with several 3D TV compression algorithms, allowing for multiple views in all its stages.

In order to design 3D video (3DV) and FVV, the entire 3D processing chain needs to be considered (Ozaktas & Onural, 2008), because of the existing dependence among its elements. For instance, an interactive display requiring random access to 3D data will shape the performance of a coding scheme based on data prediction. There are several different 3D scene representations, which result in numerous data types.

Since both stereo pair images are very similar, one image can help predicting the other. The second image can be predicted from the one already coded, similarly to the way temporally related images can be motion-compensated in video compression. The samples of both images relate to each other through the 3D scene geometry and camera properties, including positions and internal camera properties such as the focal length. The displacement or disparity of each sample in one image with respect to the other is equivalent to a dense motion field in between consecutive images of a video sequence. Thus, MEMC helps disparity estimation and disparity compensation in image prediction followed by coding of the prediction error or residual.

Some differences between motion compensation and disparity compensation exist due to the dissimilarity between the statistics of disparities and MVs. Disparities are biased and larger than MVs. Then, small disparity means large depth of the corresponding point in 3D. 3D points close to the camera may have a very large disparity value which calls for modifications of entropy coding of the disparity vectors. Additionally, temporally adjacent video images tend to be more alike than views of a stereo pair at realistic frame rates. In general, disocclusion effects are more apparent in a stereo pair than in two video frames next in time. Moreover, some differences in a stereo pair result from erroneous white and color balance, but also due to scene lighting and surface reflectance effects.

The combination of inter-view and temporal prediction is the central idea behind effcient stereo video compression ruled by the standard defined in ITU-T Rec. H.262 | ISO/IEC 13818-2 MPEG-2 Video, the Multi-view Profile (Garbas, Fecker, Troger, & Kaup, 2006).Typically, the increase in compression performance compared to independent coding using both video streams is not noteworthy, because temporal prediction efficiency is already admirable. In general, if time prediction is excellent further inter-view prediction does not boost coding efficiency a lot. Images adjacent in time tend to have more similarities than spatial adjacency.

I pictures are coded without reference to other temporally adjacent images in the dynamic sequence; a great gain can be accomplished by inter-view prediction. Inter-view prediction coding increases compression efficiency considerably compared to coding this picture as I picture.

Compression of stereo video may include optimum joint bit allocation for both channels, in detriment of backward compatibility to plan better inter-view prediction structures. Algorithms for modern video codecs must take into account new and current standards such as MPEG-4 Visual and H.264/AVC along with HVS understanding and stereo perception.

Compression of video plus depth data is as an option to typical stereo video, where the stereo pair is generated by view interpolation. This format increases compression performance and depth can be considered as a signal with just monochromatic and luminance information. Figure 5 shows a 2D color image with its corresponding depth map. The depth ranges from *Depth*$_{Min}$ (close to the viewer) and *Depth*$_{Max}$ (far away from the viewer) as a gray scale image with linear distribution from 255 to 0 in that order. These gray values can be inputted to the luminance channel and the chrominance can be made constant. Hence, the resultant signal can be handled by any video codec. This format has been investigated by the European ATTEST project with several state-of-the-art video codecs (MPEG-2, MPEG-4, H.264/AVC). Depth can be coded at high quality with merely 10–20% of the bit rate because the depth data statistics is smoother and less structured than color data. Indeed, even strong depth-image coding problems such as blocking artifacts do not correspond to perceptible distortions in the rendered views.

Both 3DV and FVV systems use multiple views of the same scene that have to be sent to the user. A simple solution would be to code all signals independently using a state-of-the-art video codec like H.264/AVC. MVV contains lots of inter-view statistical dependencies because all cameras capture a scene from different viewpoints. These can be exploited for combined temporal/inter-view prediction images are not only predicted from temporally neighboring images but also from corresponding images in adjoining views. Investigations in MPEG have shown that MVC algorithms surpass independent coding with gains of more than 2 dB for the same bit rate.

Figure 5. Video plus depth format for the interview sequence consisting of (a) a 2D color frames with (b) a depth frame. Depth is code with 8 bits.

(a)　　　　(b)

Any video coding standard must have a high compression efficiency. For MVC, the performance should be higher than when independent compression is employed. Small computational costs, error robustness, support for different pixel/color resolutions and low delay are also important requirements. A standard mechanism called *Profiles* may help satisfying these application prerequisites.

MVC requires temporal random access which can be obtained with the help of I frames. Scalability is a sought-after attribute for most video coding standards, because a decoder can access part of a bitstream to output a low-quality video which reduces temporal or spatial resolution, or a reduced video quality. For MVC, extra view scalability is necessary by using a bit stream fraction in order to yield a limited number out of the N views. Also backward compatibility is vital for MVC. Thus, one bitstream corresponding to one view that is extracted from the MVC bitstream shall be compliant to H.264/AVC. It should be feasible to fine-tune coding to equalize quality over all views. Parallel processing allows for a great coder realization and resource management. Both extrinsic and intrinsic camera parameters should be sent with the bitstream to provide intermediate view interpolation at the decoder.

The key MVC aspiration is to boost compression in contrast to coding all video data separately. It is a common practice to code all views with H.264/AVC independently and to use the result for objective and subjective performance assessments. Coding can be done using common settings and parameters. As a rule, illumination and color inconsistencies can be reduced by taking into account light variations over multi-view images thanks to the illumination circumstances. The fundamental idea is to modify MC on macroblock level, assuming locally constant illumination and color. Prior to subtracting the sample values of the block to be coded and the reference block, their means are compensated. Illumination correction has been adopted by the Joint MVV Model (JMVM) (Vetro, Su, Kimata, & Smolic, 2006) as an option. Other strategies are working on macroblock level at the coding stage and pre-processing prior to coding. Since algorithms for light compensation are well-known, then the corrected data can be assigned to a typical coder without the need to project a new coder/decoder and bitstream syntax.

Disparity coding may improve inter-view prediction. An alternative to improve disparity estimation is to treat it like motion, although its statistical properties can differ from MVs and to take geometric properties and constraints into account. Specific coding modes for MVC such as the inter-view direct mode are also under research (Guo, Lu, Wu, & Gao, 2006).

High-level syntax is required to indicate the properties of a MVC bitstream to a decoder. Extra high-level syntax is under improvement to permit resourceful random access, buffer supervision, and parallel processing. Additional paths in MVC analysis like combining scalability and MVC are under investigation, but in general scalability lessens compression efficiency.

Suitable video coding schemes for compression and transmission that are based on the 3D video formats are discussed in this part of the text. Since pictures from a stereo video sequence are very similar, then they are well suited for compression with one predicting the other.

An alternative to MVV compression is to diminish the data to a single view with a per-pixel depth map in order to send them out using the MPEG enhancement layer. Stereo or multi-view frames rendered at the receiver may be impaired by view-dependent effects, occlusions and/or high-valued disparities. The 3D ATTEST chain can set apart distortions in video coding, depth quantization, and geometry. The MPEG committee has been examining numerous contributions to the video plus depth issue and techniques were proposed to allow for estimation over time and across space.

Constant translational motion in video corresponds to a planar Fourier spectrum, i.e., non-zero Fourier-transform amplitudes are located on a plane passing through the origin of the frequency space and orthogonal to the movement direction. This allows for the use of a speed voting strategy or filtering. When it comes to the discrete Fourier transform (DFT) similar behavior occurs.

In the case of a stereo system, a multi-view profile (MVP) has been defined in MPEG-2 standard, which allows the transmission of two video signals for stereoscopic TV applications. One of the main features of the MVP is the use of scalable coding tools to guarantee the backward compatibility with the MPEG-2 Main Profile. The MVP relies on a multilayer representation such that one view is designed as the base layer and the other view is assigned as the enhancement layer. Also, the MVP conveys the camera parameters (i.e. geometry information, focal length, etc.) in the bitstream. The base layer is encoded in conformance with the Main Profile, while the enhancement layer is encoded with the scalable coding tools.

Temporal prediction only is used on the based layer, while temporal prediction and inter-view prediction are simultaneously performed on the enhancement layer. As a consequence, backward compatibility with legacy 2D decoders is achieved, since the the base layer represents a conventional 2D video sequence.

Stereo video information has to be organized, so that the decoder can distinguish the left and right view inside the bitstream. The stereo video supplemental enhancement information (SEI) message defined in H.264/MPEG-4 AVC fidelity range extensions (FRExt) helps implementing this mechanism.

The MPEG-C Part 3 (aka ISO/IEC 23002-3) standardizes video-plus-depth coding based on the coding of 3D content inside a conventional MPEG-2 transport stream, which includes texture, depth and some auxiliary data. This solution provides interoperability of the content, display technology independence, capture technology independence, backward compatibility, compression performance and the ability of the user to control the global depth range without increasing the bandwidth too much.

An additional coding tool for video-plus-depth data is the multiple auxiliary components (MAC) defined in version 2 of MPEG-4. The MAC is not only used to describe transparency of video objects, but can also describe shape, depth or texture. Therefore, the depth plus video can use the auxiliary components. MAC coding uses motion compensation and DCT like it is done with the MVs of the 2D video. This coding scheme represents the disparity vector field, the luminance and the chrominance data by 3 components.

Some CG research resulted in the animation framework extension (AFX) of MPEG-4 which keeps backward compatibility. Three tools of interest in the scope of 3D video are depth image-based rendering, point rendering and view-dependent multi-texturing.

The general case for two or more views appears in the draft MVC specification that provides new ways to improve coding efficiency, to reduce decoding complexity and to diminished memory consumption for various applications. The compressed multi-view bitstream include a base layer stream that could be easily extracted and used for compatibility with legacy 2D devices.

For each camera, view dependencies are transmitted using the sequence parameter sets (SPS) MVC syntax which improves MVV content compression exploiting redundancies among the inter-pictures of one camera and the inter-view pictures of other cameras, and leads to an additional coding gain compared to the H.264/MPEG-4 AVC simulcast.

DECODING/DECOMPRESSION

The receiver generates all potential views (the entire light field) to the user all the time. The display controller asks for one or more virtual views by stating the virtual cameras parameters. The decoders receive compressed video, and store the decoded frame in a buffer (see Figure 4). There is a virtual video buffer (VVB) for each end user with data from all received source frames. A user watches a rendered scene generated after processing pixels from several frames in the VVB. Due to bandwidth and processing restrictions, each end user cannot obtain the entire source frames from all the decoders. This also decreases the system scalability.

When views are decoded from an MVC bitstream, some views may not be displayed, but are needed for inter-view compensation and decoding of the target views. The single loop decoding (SLD) method from the MVC requires partial decoding of reference views and it relies on the inter-view SKIP mode. Then, decoding temporal non-key pictures in reference views equals to not fully decode MBs, but to storing motion information to decode the corresponding MBs in the target views.

Error Concealment (EC)

The consequences of spatial impairment and the use of multiple reference picture estimation in both spatial and temporal dimensions are still being examined (Farrugia & Debono, 2010). EC mechanisms exploiting the spatial and temporal coherences among views are needed in order to: (i) attain the best possible efficiency in coding/ compression, (ii) correct light and color, (iii) lessen residual errors caused by spatial estimates (Coelho, Estrela, & de Assis, 2009), and (iv) account for cameras uncertainties (Stoykova, et al., 2007). H.264/AVC finds displacements by favoring compression efficiency over displacement precision. So, two blocks with identical MVs may not belong to the same object or part of the object under analysis which leads to errors in disparity and MV estimation (Micallef, Debono, & Farrugia, Sep. 2010).

Joint-source and channel-coding strategies developed for video transmission over channels can alleviate packet losses in streaming video due to limited bandwidth. Nevertheless, EC methods are needed at the receiver to reduce the observed damages caused by these losses. In general, if a packet is lost, then the entire video frame is affected and this is a very notorious drawback in video streaming. The onward MVs of the last received frame can be estimated via methods that exploit knowledge from precedent frames. That is, EC uses MVs to improve the quality of the damaged frame by inferring the missing blocks and rendering an approximation of the real frame.

Conversational applications have benefited from EC algorithms a lot. However, video streaming applications have been less successful when it comes to error remediation up to now. If a packet vanishes, probably a complete video frame is lost, so that the majority of the EC algorithms fail (Micallef, Debono, & Farrugia, 2010). The most relevant problems related to EC are the following: i) Lost MVs cannot be estimated from neighboring blocks, if the corresponding MVs are not available; ii) Without nearby MVs adjoining MBs do not help to re-estimate the MVs via block matching with respect to a reference frame; iii) one cannot use the nearby MBs to test the side boundary match of a candidate substitute MB; iv) partial decoding of DCT coefficients is not offered; v) syntax-based repairs are not useful as a result of the bursty nature of the errors; vi) even spatial EC is not feasible because no neighboring MBs is available. So, video streaming applications need an EC algorithm that can handle loss of entire frames.

EC algorithms tailored for video streaming should estimate whole missing frames of a sequence and exploit the multiple reference frame buffer provided by H.264 to reduce the recovered video error. Specifically, the algorithm is based on the estimation of the absent frame MV field, the previous received frames, and on the previous frame projection on the missing one founded on this estimated data.

The difference among viewpoints inside a MVV may provoke illumination changes between sequences. Inter-view illumination changes between the pictures can be balanced by means of illumination change-adaptive MC (ICA MC). The MVC extension uses the multiple reference frames feature of H.264/MPEG-4 AVC.

Inter-view correlations combine motion/disparity compensated estimation, where a predictive frame is created from temporally adjoining frames. As an extension of the traditional temporal SKIP mode, inter-view SKIP mode comes from the idea of exploiting the relationship between MVs between neighboring views. So, the motion data of the current MB is derived from the corresponding MB in the image at the same temporal index of the neighboring view.

The Role of MCME in 3D Image Rendering

Multi-View Scene Reconstruction

Multi-camera systems capture dynamic scenes from numerous viewpoints. Multi-view scene reconstruction can be performed by: 1) minimization of a cost function related to the 3D volume; 2) iterative evolution of a surface, where the rendering quality is associated to cost-function optimization; 3) mixing individual views together; 4) reconstruction from feature points (surface fitting); and 5) reconstruction from silhouettes.

3D TV implies depth impression of the observed scenery and FVV allows interactive choice of viewpoint and direction in a certain range as well-known from CG. They can be combined in a single system, provided they are based on a suitable 3D scene representation. If a stereo pair can be rendered, then 3DV is feasible. If a camera view not normally accessible (virtual view) related to a random viewpoint can be rendered, then FVV is viable.

The definition of a 3D representation format is essential to improve rendering algorithms, navigation range, quality, interactivity, compression and broadcast for 3D TV and FVV. Image-based representations call for dense camera arrays in order to render properly virtual views.

Photo-realistic 3D scene and object modeling is often difficult and time consuming. An automatic 3D object and scene reconstruction implies camera geometry estimation, depth structures, and 3D shapes. All these methods introduce geometric rendering errors. Another challenge in 3D scene representation is image-based modeling which requires intermediate virtual views obtained from the interpolation of available camera views and/or dense sampling with several camera views.

3D is perceived because the information from each eye about a slightly different viewpoint of an object is combined by the brain and it creates the sensation of depth. This property is used to design 3D displays. Two cameras capture scenes from distinct viewpoints as if each of them was an eye. If a display allows each eye to see only its related view, then a 3D impression is created and it can be captured in stereo or converted from existing 2D video allowing for 2D to 3D conversion.

The FVV (Figure 6) functionality makes possible to implement depth-based stereo rendering. A video signal and a depth map are transmitted to the user, helping rendering a stereo pair. Depth and disparity estimation can only be solved up to a residual error probability because data is in general incomplete. Estimation errors affect the quality of the generated views. One method is to use a stereo camera for acquiring and estimating depth/disparity from correspondences or from motion as well as other single view video properties.

FVV offers the same 3D functionality as CG, that is, the user can select a viewpoint and viewing direction within a visual scene, meaning interactive free navigation. The figure above illustrates the complexity associated to these features. The red arc shows the amplitude of the observer's perception in a plane parallel to the ground, but the viewer can actually change his/her viewpoint in a 3D framework. A perfect viewing experience would require lots of scene interpolations and would slow down rendering in order to allow a natural 3D impression of the object whose orthographic views are shown above.

Figure 6. FVV with interactive selection of virtual viewpoint and viewing directions. An object in shown with 5 radically different views (N=5).

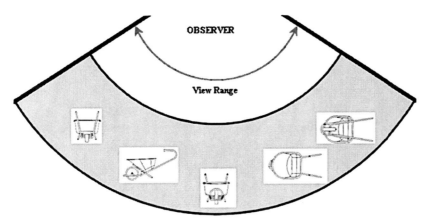

Virtual/Augmented Reality

Because of convergence, future TV sets will permit navigation through a scene and will be able of handling more than movies and games. There are also several situations where either the application or the extent of the terrain under scrutiny demand distance measurements. Bearing these issues in mind, range imaging is an option, since each range image pixel has a property corresponding to a sensor that can be given in physical units. Distance and other properties can be tracked and mapped in real time which will improve considerably environmental and disaster remediation (Fernandes, do Carmo, Estrela, & Assis, 2009). The use of this type of equipment combined with photogrammetry can be valuable in remote sensing and surveillance (Gokturk, Yalcin, & Bamji, 2005) (Vlasic, et al., 2009).

It is easier to measure distance/depth with a time-of-flight (TOF) sensor than with stereo and triangulation. A small amount of processing power is used because the software required by a smart sensor is simple. Hence, computational effort can be put on more demanding tasks such as classification and target location. As TOF images can be obtained in real time, tracking human beings and their interaction with games/ simulators is simplified. In automation, mobile robots can map their surroundings in order to evade obstacles or track a person or vehicle. TOF techniques can also replace radar or LIDAR with a smaller computational load.

Motion capture technologies help rendering augmented-reality views because the output of a 3D camera can be combined with live creatures in CG environments (Sorbier, Takaya, Uematsu, Daribo, & Saito, 2010). Because TOF cameras capture a whole 3D scene with dedicated image sensors, the hardware complexity decreases (Gokturk, Yalcin, & Bamji, 2005).

SOLUTIONS AND RECOMMENDATIONS

High spatial resolution as well as efficient coding of depth and texture are technological challenges in 3D TV. Coding/compression performance advances can result from the strong correlation between the color video and the depth map sequences. The amount of information used to describe textured video motion with depth map and a common MV field need to be compacted in order to make the overall system behave as close as possible of real time. The bitrate control scheme should depend on the content of each sequence instead of having a fixed percentage range.

Handling 3D scenes poses a severe computational burden. When color is added to 3D video, the scenario becomes even more complicated. Hence, new formats to describe color objects and more efficient metrics to evaluate color distortion and geometry are needed.Depth pre-processing along with depth-aided in-painting can diminish the occlusion/disocclusion effects.

It is indispensable to trim down temporal and inter-view redundancies of frames with joint motion/disparity field estimation in MVV while keeping motion and compression artifacts to a minimum. Segmentation and coding based on ratio distortion (RD) can replace the block-based motion/disparity estimation stage in the MVC extension, thus improving RD efficiency (Vetro, Su, Kimata, & Smolic, 2006). The coding performance vs. bitrate impasse for high-quality rendering needs further research (He, Yu, Yang, & Jiang, 2008). Furthermore, the stereo-motion consistency constraint means that all displacement vector fields are greatly correlated. Hence, they can benefit from interfield compression (Guo, Lu, Wu, & Gao, 2006). Several multi-view-based video compression schemes exploiting the intrinsic correlation in MVV need to be considered.

Since 3D video involves several views they can be coded independently which increases bandwidth compared to established coding techniques. However, prediction across views can improve compression performance. Bitrate requirements for 3D services can be considerably reduced if the HVS is taken into account. For instance, different views can be coded differently without spoiling the 3D sensation in way that resembles in the HVS asymmetric view. Hence, understanding the asymmetric coding will perk up the quality of asymmetrically coded video.

Better distortion models to describe the quality of the rendered views will also improve 3D video codecs. Since 3D perception quality is very important, ignoring the HVS poses grave problems. All stages of a 3D end-to-end system can also benefit from research on domain transformations.

FUTURE RESEARCH DIRECTIONS

It seems quite impossible to acquire and to render high quality 3D TV content without combining computer vision and computer graphics. Hence, it is probable that the frontier between these areas of knowledge disappears and it will give birth to a new one encompassing convergence issues.

It seems that convergence is a much broader and more complicated issue than simply combining technologies. There is a need for "knowledge convergence" as well. Just to site an example, we have a tendency to think about images in the visual part of the frequency spectrum due to the fact that we as human beings "see" the world using our eyes only. However, the internet of the future will carry multispectral and hyperspectral images. Moreover, the existence of tactual and olfactory data should not be forgotten.

Standards help developing better video systems from capture to display, although it is not possible to establish them and believe they can be always "extended" to adapt changes. Other standards must be studied/proposed in conjunction with the existent ones, since there is always the risk that too many amendments can compromise other technological solutions that may become more viable in the long term.

Interactivity needs to be handled not only from the event-driven point of view, but depending on the application, it has to take into consideration the end user's psychological responses to "change". Is the offline-to-online digital shift going to occur more often? Or maybe the right question would be "Is the offline-to-online digital shift going to happen?" Our point is, shall the end user be the only entity responsible for the content s(he) is exposed? We think that at some point in time real life will have to be encouraged.

Next-generation video infrastructure will rely on cloud computing. Ubiquitous access and the necessity of high quality video pose network restrictions such as computing ability, storage and optimal bandwidth.

CONCLUSION

It is clear from the literary reviews in this chapter that 3D technology demands more improvement. Video systems for 3D are complex and have room for lots of progress. Besides the obvious issues related to transmission and reception of such content, both acquisition and reception suffer with the lack of fast and efficient algorithms, adequate structures for capturing and displaying images as well as more intelligent computation units.

Independently from the technology used, it seems that all stages do need better ways of summarizing information without sacrificing quality. This text tackles this problem looking from the visualization and content generation perspectives.

Motion data play an important role in all stages of an end-to-end 3D TV system. The tight relationship between motion and depth impacts these stages because 3D information can be recovered from these cues, and they help optimizing the performance of all algorithms and standards from different parts of 3D system.

Current 3D video coding standards are mostly extensions of present 2D standards. There is still room for lots of research on 3D video data representations since more standards for interactive 3D video services need to be established. Global motion field estimation, coding and compression can exploit the correlation between sequences and carry out a better bit allocation strategy. View quality can benefit from knowledge about the compression impact on the rendered scene and the influence of depth in video compression.

Depth pre-processing helps lessen geometric distortion for small baselines. On the other hand, large baselines amplify geometric distortions. A post-processing approach to handle large baselines and disoccluded regions has been suggested by (Daribo, Miled, & Pesquet-Popescu, 2010). Image inpainting (Furht, 2008) fills in pixels in image regions where they are absent or distorted with the help of the neighboring data and relates to error

concealment. Since the depth map is a 2D representation of a 3D scene, it is relevant to appraise the depth compression-induced artifacts on the 3D warping process. Preserving discontinuities is essential in depth data compression, because lots of 3D image effects demand robustness to abrupt changes in the depth map. The impact of depth map compression on rendering is analyzed by the MPEG 3DAV AHG activities (Schuur, Fehn, Kauff, & Smolic, 2002) with an MPEG-4 compression scheme. They applied decoding combined with a median filter to limit the coding-induced artifacts typical of view synthesis.

Depth map coding in MVV sequences decomposed with motion-compensated wavelet decomposition and multiple auxiliary components from MPEG-4 MAC are not closed problems and need more developments.

The joint MV field is part of the MPEG-2 texture stream for backward-compatibility purposes. Transmitting the correlation among MVs with both texture and depth streams can enforce error resiliency of a video-plus-depth sequence, because the lost data in one stream can be compensated by the information from the other.

Dense disparity estimation followed by block-based segmentation and coding in MVC generally produces a smooth disparity field which increases precision. Enforcing the smoothness constraint to these estimates improves SKIP prediction, and consequently, coding performance. It is indispensable to enforce displacement vectors consistency in a stereo/multi-view sequence for joint motion/disparity estimation. The resulting model can be solved using convex optimization. An H.264-based codec can split each dense motion/disparity subfield into variable block sizes, while keeping the RD cost minimum.

Temporal/inter-view redundancies of key and non-key frames need to be reduced and disparity estimation and joint motion/disparity estimation are very useful. A possibility is to estimate dense motion/disparity fields followed by RD-driven segmentation and coding. This could replace the block-based motion/disparity estimation stage in MVC extension, improving the overall RD performance. Research on coding improvement in terms of bitrate and the quality of the synthesized image will result in better depth map quantization procedures.

DIBR helps synthesizing new virtual views from the video-plus-depth data. DIBR main bottleneck is the occlusion/disocclusion problem. This calls for efficient smoothing of the sharp depth changes near object edges. Geometric distortions and the computation time can be reduced by means of uniform filtering of the depth video. Large disocclusions can be handled by post-processing using depth data combined with inpainting techniques. High-dynamic range imaging is a promising research area to help reducing the computer load related to 3D TV.

REFERENCES

Belfiore, S., Grangetto, M., Magli, E., & Olmo, G. (2003). An error concealment algorithm for streaming video. *IEEE International Conference on Image Processing 2003* (ICIP 2003), Vol. 22, (pp. 649-652).

Bourges-Sevenier, M., & Jang, E. (2004). An introduction to the MPEG-4 animation framework extension. *IEEE Transactions on Circuits and Systems for Video Technology, 14*, 928–936. doi:10.1109/TCSVT.2004.830662

Brunnström, K. (2009). VQEG validation and ITU standardization of objective perceptual video quality metrics. *IEEE Signal Processing Magazine, 96.* doi:10.1109/MSP.2009.932162

Carranza, J., Theobalt, C., Magnor, M., & Seidel, H. (2003). Free-viewpoint video of human actors. *ACM Transactions on Graphics, 22*(3), 569–577. doi:10.1145/882262.882309

Chen, S., & Williams, L. (1993). View interpolation for image synthesis. *SIGGRAPH 93 Proceedings*, (pp. 279–288).

Cheng, C., Li, C., & Chen, L. (2010). A 2D to 3D conversion scheme based on depth cues analysis for MPEG videos. *IEEE Transactions on Consumer Electronics, 56*(3), 1739–1745. doi:10.1109/TCE.2010.5606320

Coelho, A., Estrela, V. V., & de Assis, J. (2009). *Error concealment by means of clustered blockwise PCA.* Picture Coding Symposium, Chicago, IL: IEEE.

Coelho, A. M., & Estrela, V. V. (2012a). Data-driven motion estimation with spatial adaptation. *International Journal of Image Processing, 6*(1), 53-67. Retrieved May 7, 2012, from http://www.cscjournals.org/csc/manuscript/Journals/IJIP/volume6/Issue1/IJIP-513.pdf

Coelho, A. M., & Estrela, V. V. (2012b). EM-based mixture models applied to video event detection. In P. Sanguansat (Ed.), *Principal component analysis - Engineering applications*, (pp. 102-124). Intech. Retrieved in May 7, 2012 from http://www.intechopen.com/books/principal-component-analysis-engineering-applications/em-based-mixture-models-applied-to-video-event-detection

Daribo, I., Miled, W., & Pesquet-Popescu, B. (2010). Joint depth-motion dense estimation for multiview video coding. *JVCI Special Issue on Multi-Camera Imaging, Coding and Innovative Display: Techniques and Systems.*

Deng, X., Jiang, X., Liu, Q., & Wang, W. (2008). Automatic depth map estimation of monocular indoor environments. *2008 International Conference on Multimedia and Information Technology (MMIT 2008)*, (pp. 646-649).

Estrela, V. V., & Galatsanos, N. (2000). Spatially-adaptive regularized pel-recursive motion estimation based on the EM algorithm. *SPIE/IEEE Proceedings of the Electrical Imaging 2000 (EI00)*, (pp. 372-383). San Diego, CA, USA.

Farrugia, R., & Debono, C. (2010). Resilient digital video transmission over wireless channels using pixel-level artefact detection mechanisms. In De Rango, F. (Ed.), *Digital video* (pp. 71–96). Intech.

Fehn, C. (2006). *Depth-image-based rendering (dibr), compression, and transmission for a flexible approach on 3DTV. (B.M.* Berlin, Germany: TechnicalUniversity, Ed.

Fehn, C., Kauff, P., De Beeck, M., & Ernst, F. Ijssel- Steijn, W., Pollefeys, M., et al. (2002). An evolutionary and optimised approach on 3D-TV. *Proceedings of International Broadcast Conference*, (pp. 357–365).

Fehn, C., Kauff, P., De Beeck, M., Ernst, F., Ijssel-Steijn, W., & Javidi, B. (2002). *Three-dimensional television, video, and display technologies*. Springer-Verlag.

Fernandes, S. R., do Carmo, F., Estrela, V. V., & Assis, J. (2009). Using the SIFT (scale invariant feature transform) to determine pairs of image points for using in the SITH (3D hybrid imaging system). *Proceedings of the XII Workshop on Computer Modeling (XII EMC)*. Volta Redonda, RJ, Brazil.

Flierl, M., Mavlankar, A., & Girod, B. (2006). Motion and disparity compensated coding for video camera arrays. *IEEE Proceedings of Picture Coding Symposium (PCS2006)*. Beijing, China.

Furht, B. (2008). *Encyclopedia of multimedia*. Springer. doi:10.1007/978-0-387-78414-4

Garbas, J., Fecker, U., Troger, T., & Kaup, A. (2006). 4D scalable multi-view video coding using disparity compensated view filtering and motion compensated temporal filtering. *Proceedings of the IEEE International Workshop on Multimedia Signal Processing 2006 (MMSP06)*. Victoria, Canada.

Gokturk, S., Yalcin, H., & Bamji, C. (2005). A time-of-flight depth sensor - System description, issues and solutions. *IEEE Computer Society Conference on Computer Vision and Pattern Recognition Workshops 2004* (pp. 35-45). IEEE.

Guo, X., Lu, Y., Wu, F., & Gao, W. (2006). Inter-view direct mode for multiview video coding. *IEEE Transactions on Circuits and Systems for Video Technology*, *16*(12), 1527–1532. doi:10.1109/TCSVT.2006.885724

Hartley, R., & Zisserman, A. (2003). *Multiple view geometry in computer vision*. Cambridge, UK: Cambridge University Press.

He, R., Yu, M., Yang, Y., & Jiang, G. (2008). Comparison of the depth quantification method in terms of coding and synthesizing capacity in 3DTV system. *Proceedings of the 9th International Conference on Signal Processing (ICSP) 2008*, (pp. 1279–1282). Leipzig, Germany.

Hewage, C., Karim, H., Worrall, S., Dogan, S., & Kondoz, A. (2007). Comparison of stereo video coding support in MPEG-4 MAC, H.264/AVC and H.264/SVC. *Proceedings of IET Visual Information Engineering-VIE07*.

ITU-T Recommention H.264 & ISO/IEC 14496-10 AVC. (2005). *Advanced video coding for generic audio-visual services, version 3*.

Javidi, B., & Okano, F. (2002). *Three-dimensional television, video, and display technologies*. Springer-Verlag.

Jebara, T. A., & Pentland, A. (1999). 3-D structure from 2-D motion. *IEEE Signal Processing Magazine, 16*(3), 66–84. doi:10.1109/79.768574

Kanatani, K. (1990). *Group-theoretical methods in image understanding (Vol. 20)*. Springer Series in Information Sciences. doi:10.1007/978-3-642-61275-6

Kauff, P., Atzpadin, N., Fehn, C., Muller, M., Schreer, O., Smolic, A., et al. (2007). Depth map creation and image based rendering for advanced 3DTV services providing interoperability and scalability. *Signal Processing: Image Communication, Special Issue on 3DTV, 22*(2), 217-234.

Kienzle, W., Schölkopf, B., Wichmann, F., & Franz, M. (2007). How to find interesting locations in video: A spatiotemporal interest point detector learned from human eye movements. *Pattern Recognition (DAGM 2007)* (pp. 405-411). Darmstadt, Germany: Springer, LNCS.

Lucchese, L., Doretto, G., & Cortelazzo, G. M. (2002). A frequency domain technique for 3D view registration . *IEEE Transactions on Pattern Analysis and Machine Intelligence, 24*(11), 1468–1484. doi:10.1109/TPAMI.2002.1046160

Magnor, M., Ramanathan, P., & Girod, B. (2003). Multi-view coding for image-based rendering using 3-D scene geometry. *IEEE Transactions on Circuits and Systems for Video Technology, 13*(11), 1092–1106. doi:10.1109/TCSVT.2003.817630

Manjunath, B., Salembier, P., & Sikora, T. (2002). *Introduction to MPEG-7: Multimedia content description language*. John Wiley & Sons.

Martinian, E., Behrens, A., Xin, J., Vetro, A., & Sun, H. (2006). Extensions of H.264/AVC for multiview video compression. *Proceedings of IEEE International Conference on Image Processing (ICIP 2006)*. Atlanta, GA, USA.

Micallef, B., Debono, C., & Farrugia, R. (Sep. 2010). Error concealment techniques for H.264/MVC encoded sequences. *IEEE Proceedings of International Conference of Electrotechnical and Computer Science (ERK)*. Portoroz, Slovenia.

Micallef, B. W., Debono, C., & Farrugia, R. (2010). Exploiting depth information for fast multi-view video coding. *IEEE Proceedings of International Picture Coding Symposium 2010 (PCS 2010)*. Nagoya, Japan.

Morvan, Y., Farin, D., & de With, Peter H. N. (2006). Design considerations for view interpolation in a 3D video coding framework. *27th Symposium on Information Theory in the Benelux*, Vol. 1, Noordwijk, The Netherlands.

Oliensis, J. (2000, Nov.). A critique of structure from motion algorithms. *Computer Vision and Image Understanding, 80*(2), 172–214. doi:10.1006/cviu.2000.0869

Ozaktas, H., & Onural, L. (2008). *Three-dimensional television capture, transmission, display*. Springer-Verlag.

Pourazad, M., Nasiopoulos, P., & Ward, R. (2009, May). An H.264-based scheme for 2D to 3D video conversion. *IEEE Transactions on Consumer Electronics, 55*(2), 742–748. doi:10.1109/TCE.2009.5174448

Richardson, E. (2003). *H.264 and MPEG-4 video compression: Video coding for next-generation multimedia*. Chichester, UK: John Wiley & Sons Ltd. doi:10.1002/0470869615

Schmid, C., Mohr, R., & Bauckhage, C. (2000). Evaluation of interest point detectors. *International Journal of Computer Vision, 37*(2), 151–172. doi:10.1023/A:1008199403446

Schuur, K., Fehn, C., Kauff, P., & Smolic, A. (2002). *About the impact of disparity coding on novel view synthesis, MPEG02/M8676 doc.* Klagenfurt.

Schwarz, H., Marpe, D., & Wiegand, T. (2006). Analysis of hierarchical B pictures and MCTF. *Proceedings of IEEE International Conference on Multimedia and Expo (ICME 2006).* Toronto, Ontario, CA.

Sikora, T. (2001). The MPEG-7 visual standard for content description – an overview. *IEEE Transactions on Circuits and Systems for Video Technology, 11*(6), 696–702. doi:10.1109/76.927422

Smolic, A., & McCutchen, D. (2004). 3DAV exploration of video-based rendering technology in MPEG. *IEEE Transactions on Circuits and Systems for Video Technology, 14*(3), 348–356. doi:10.1109/TCSVT.2004.823395

Sorbier, F. D., Takaya, Y., Uematsu, Y., Daribo, I., & Saito, H. (October 2010). *Augmented reality for 3D TV using depth camera input.* IEEE VSMM 2010, Seoul, Korea.

Starck, J., Kilner, J., & Hilton, A. (2008). Objective quality assessment in free-viewpoint video production. *IEEE Proceedings of 3DTV08,* (pp. 225–228).

Stewart, J., Yu, J., Gortler, S., & Mcmillan, L. (2003). A new reconstruction filter for undersampled light fields. *Eurographics Symposium on Rendering, ACM International Conference Proceeding Series,* (pp. 150–156).

Stoykova, E., Alatan, A., Benzie, P., Grammalidis, N., Malassiotis, S., & Ostermann, J. (2007). 3D time varying scene capture technologies - A survey. *IEEE Transactions on Circuits and Systems for Video Technology, 17*(11), 1568–1586. doi:10.1109/TCSVT.2007.909975

Tanimoto, M., & Fuji, T. (2003). *Ray-space coding using temporal and spatial predictions.* ISO/IEC JTC1/SC29/WG11 Document M10410 .

Vetro, A., Su, Y., Kimata, H., & Smolic, A. (2006). *Joint multi-view video model.* Joint Video Team, Doc. JVT-U207, Hangzhou, China.

Vlasic, D., Peers, P., Baran, I., Debevec, P., Popovic, J., & Rusinkiewicz, S. (2009). Dynamic shape capture using multi-view photometric stereo. *ACM Transactions on Graphics, 28*(5). doi:10.1145/1618452.1618520

Wang, Z., & Bovik, A. (2006). *Image quality assessment.* New York, NY, USA.

Yang, J., Everett, M., Buehler, C., & Mcmillan, L. (2002). A real-time distributed light field camera. *Proc. of the 13th Eurographics Workshop on Rendering,* (pp. 77–86).

Zitnick, C., Kang, S., Uyttendaele, M., Winder, S., & Szeliski, R. (2004, August). High-quality video view interpolation using a layered representation. *ACM Transactions on Graphics, 23*(3). doi:10.1145/1015706.1015766

ADDITIONAL READING

Balasubramanian, R., Das, S., & Swaminathan, K. (2003). Simulation studies for the performance analysis of the reconstruction of a line in 3-D from two arbitrary perspective views using two plane intersection method. *International Journal of Computer Mathematics, 80*(5), 559–571. doi:10.1080/0020716021000038974

Basha, T., Moses, Y., & Kiryati, N. (2010). Multiview scene flow estimation: A view centered variational approach. *Proceedings of CVPR, 2010.*

Ben-Ari, R., & Sochen, N. (2009). A geometric framework and a new criterion in optical flow modeling. *Journal of Mathematical Imaging and Vision, 33*(2), 178–194. doi:10.1007/s10851-008-0124-z

Chiuso, A., & Soatto, S. (2000). Motion and structure from 2-D motion causally integrated over time: Analysis. *IEEE Transactions on Robotics and Automation, 24*, 523–535.

Cyganek, B., & Siebert, J. P. (2009). *An introduction to 3D computer vision techniques and algorithms.* John Wiley & Sons. doi:10.1002/9780470699720

Dahmen, H., Franz, M. O., & Krapp, H. (2001). Extracting egomotion from optic flow: limits of accuracy and neural matched filters. In Zanker, J., & Zeil, J. (Eds.), *Motion vision: Computational, neural and ecological constraints* (pp. 143–168). Berlin, Germany: Springer. doi:10.1007/978-3-642-56550-2_8

Daribo, I., Kaaniche, M., Miled, W., Cagnazzo, M., & Pesquet-Popescu, B. (2009). *Dense disparity estimation in multiview video coding. IEEE MMSP09.* Rio de Janeiro: RJ, Brazil.

Favaro, P., & Soatto, S. (2007). *3-D shape estimation and image restoration-exploiting defocus and motion blur.* Springer-Verlag.

ISO/IEC JTC 1. (2001). *Coding of audio-visual objects – Part 2: Visual.* ISO/IEC 14496-2 (MPEG-4 visual version 1), April 1999; Amd. 1 (ver. 2), February, 2000; Amd. 2, 2001, Amd. 3, 2001, Amd. 4 (streaming video profile), Amd 1 to 2nd ed. (studio profile).

ITU-T and ISO/IEC JTC 1. (1994). *Generic coding of moving pictures and associated audio information – Part 2: Video.* Recommendation H.222.0 and ISO/IEC 13818-2 (MPEG-2 Video).

Jurie, F., & Dhome, M. (2002, February). Real time tracking of 3D objects: An efficient and robust approach. *Pattern Recognition, 35*(2), 317–328. doi:10.1016/S0031-3203(01)00031-0

Kumar, S., Sukavanam, N., & Balasubramanian, R. (2006) Reconstruction of quadratic curves in 3D from two or more arbitrary perspective views: Simulation studies. *Proceedings of the SPIE Vision Geometry XIV, IS&T/SPIE International Symposium on Electronic Imaging - 2006,* Vol. 6066, (pp. 180-190). San Jose, California, USA.

Levin, A., Fergus, R., Durand, F., & Freeman, W. T. (2007). Image and depth from a conventional camera with a coded aperture. *Proceedings of SIGGRAPH,* ACM.

Ma, Y., Soatto, S., Kosecka, J., & Sastry, S. S. (2003). *An invitation to 3-D vision.* Springer.

Martens, J. (2002). Multidimensional modeling of image quality. *Proceedings of the IEEE, 90,* 133–153. doi:10.1109/5.982411

Matusik, W., & Pfister, H. (2004). *3D TV: A scalable system for real-time acquisition, transmission and autostereoscopic display of dynamic scenes* (pp. 814—824).

Neumann, J., Fermuller, C., & Aloimonos, Y. (2003). Polydioptric camera design and 3D motion estimation. *Proceedings of CVPR,* 2003.

Smolic, A., & Kauff, P. (2005). Interactive 3D video representation and coding technologies . *Proceedings of the IEEE, 93*(1), 98–110. doi:10.1109/JPROC.2004.839608

Tam, W., Soung Yee, A., Ferreira, J., Tariq, S., & Speranza, F. (2005). Stereoscopic image rendering based on depth maps created from blur and edge information. *Stereoscopic Displays and Applications XII, 5664,* 104–115.

Tam, W., Speranza, F., Zhang, L., Renaud, R., Chan, J., & Vazquez, C. (2005). Depth image based rendering for multiview stereoscopic displays: Role of information at object boundaries. *Three-Dimensional TV, Video, and Display IV, 6016*, 75–85.

Vedula, S., Rander, P., Collins, R., & Kanade, T. (2003). *Three-dimensional scene flow*. PAMI.

VQEG. (March 2000). *Final report from the video quality experts group on the validation of objective models of video quality assessment-Phase I.* Retrieved from http://www.vqeg.org/

VQEG. (2003). *Final report from the video quality experts group on the validation of objective models of video quality assessment-Phase II.* http://www.vqeg.org/.

Wang, Z., & Bovik, A. (2009). Mean squared error: Love it or leave it. *IEEE SP Magazine, 98*.

Wildeboer, M., Fukushima, N., Yendo, T., Panahpour Tehrani, M., Fujii, T., & Tanimoto, M. (2010). A semi-automatic multi-view depth estimation method. In P. Frossard, H. Li, F. Wu, B. Girod, S. Li, & G. Wei (Eds.), *Proceedings of the SPIE, Visual Communications and Image Processing, 7744*, (pp. 77442B-77442B-8.)

Wöhler, C. (2009). *3D computer vision: Efficient methods and applications*. Springer Verlag.

Zhu, C., Zhao, Y., Yu, L., & Tanimoto, M. (2012). *3D-TV system with depth-image-based rendering: Architectures, techniques and challenges*. Springer Verlag.

Section 2
Video Transmission

Chapter 7
Source Coding Methods for Robust Wireless Video Streaming

Martin Fleury
University of Essex, UK

Sandro Moiron
University of Essex, UK

Mohammad Altaf
University of Essex, UK

Nadia Qadri
COMSATS Institute of Information Technology, Wah Cantt, Pakistan

Mohammed Ghanbari
University of Essex, UK

ABSTRACT

As real-time video streaming moves to the mobile Internet, there is a greater need to protect fragile compressed bit-streams from the impact of lossy wireless channels. Though forward error correction (FEC) has a role, if it is applied without adaptation, it may introduce excessive communication over-head. Alternatively, error resilience methods provide additional protection at the application layer of the protocol stack, without replication of any protection already provided at the data-like layer. In this chapter, a case study shows that these resilience methods can be applied adaptively through stream switching according to channel conditions. Error resilience can work hand-in-hand with error concealment, again applied through source coding. There are many error resilience and concealment methods, which this chapter surveys at a tutorial level. The chapter also includes an overview of video streaming for those unfamiliar with the topic. Though error concealment is a non-normative feature of the H.264/AVC (Advanced Video Coding) codec standard, there is a range of new techniques that have been included within the Standard such as flexible macroblock ordering and stream switching frames. The chapter additionally reviews error concealment provision, including spatial, temporal, and hybrid methods. Results show that there are tradeoffs between the level of protection and the level of overhead, according to the severity of the wireless channel impairment.

DOI: 10.4018/978-1-4666-2660-7.ch007

INTRODUCTION

Video compression efficiency improves with each successive codec, with each bit carrying more information. Consequently, a video bit-stream becomes more error sensitive, resulting in significant quality degradation in error-prone channels. This is especially the case for the extension of video services such as *Internet Protocol TV (IPTV)* (Park & Jeong, 2009)to mobile, broadband wireless networks. The efficiency is also a problem both for sensor networks and mobile ad hoc networks, because of the risk of routing link failures. This Chapter presents source coding methods to combat these errors, resulting in robust video streaming in such networks.

We have considered source coding approaches to providing robust video streaming. The aim of source coding is to reduce the bit-rate of the uncompressed video by exploiting redundancies or correlations within the uncompressed video. Source coding algorithms are organized within a codec. A codec consists of an encoder/decoder pair corresponding to the sender/receiver in a transmission path. Suppose one takes the smallest of spatial resolutions commonly now employed, *Common Intermediate Format (CIF)* (352 × 288 pixel/picture) with 8-bit precision for each luminance and chrominance component (with half resolution for each chrominance component to account for the reduced sensitivity to color information of the *human visual system (HVS)*). Taking a typical frame rate of 25 frame/s then the raw video data-rate is 30 Mbps. The most common capacity of the widely-deployed *Asymmetric Digital Subscriber Line (ADSL)* form of access network is typically 1.25 Mbps. Therefore, even if it were commercially prudent to stream raw video, there are practical limits, due to the potential bottleneck at the access network. Moreover, a one-minute uncompressed video would occupy 225 Mbytes of storage, which explains why even short range transmission of uncompressed video (as in *High-Definition Multimedia Interface (HDMI)*)

effectively employs streaming. Of course, apart from being employed in networked and broadcast communication of video, codecs are also necessary for storage of video on digital media such as DVDs.

Standard hybrid video codecs (Ghanbari, 2003) exploit various forms of redundancy to achieve efficient data compression. The correlation of the three color signals output from a video camera is reduced prior to codec processing by conversion into a different color space (for example, RGB to recommendation CCIR-601). Perceptual coding is not generally exploited for video compression, though it may have a future role (Tan & Wu, 2006). In fact, there are basically two forms of source-coded video picture, depending on whether spatial or temporal redundancy is exploited. Both these forms of compression are 'lossy' in the sense that the original video picture cannot be exactly reproduced after decoding. However, as the viewer is not normally aware of the exact nature of any natural scenes captured by a camera and as the HVS does not hold an exact representation of natural scenes, loss of fidelity can be tolerated.

Of these two forms of redundancy, still-image codecs such as JPEG2000 (Taubman & Marcellin, 2002) only exploit spatial redundancy. However, it is intuitively obvious that the similarity between successive video pictures (except when there are scene cuts or rapid motion of the camera or objects within the scene) in a video sequence can potentially lead to large reductions in bit rate. Another form of redundancy, statistical redundancy, is exploited through entropy coding at the output stage of both still-image and video codecs. Entropy coding is a lossless form of compression. Therefore, it is particularly susceptible to data loss, as each successive codeword depends on the preceding sequence of codewords since the last reset point. On the other hand, due to the tolerance of the HVS to some loss of spatio-temporal information it is possible to replace lost data with similar data, for example by blocks of data from the previous picture. In fact, error resilience together with error concealment, the topics of this Chapter can both act to help restore a video picture after data is lost or arrives in corrupted form at a wireless receiver.

Intra-coded video data relies on spatial reference within the video picture and, hence, is unaffected by the corruption of previous pictures. I-pictures are completely spatially coded. This is in contrast to inter-coded video data which takes reference from past (predictively-coded P-pictures) or even future video pictures in bi-predictively-coded B-pictures. In both these forms of coding (intra and inter), it is the difference image (or residual data) that is processed in subsequent stages of a hybrid video encoder. For networked TV, I-pictures can serve as a point at which the TV channel can be switched or zapped. For streaming of live video, periodic I-pictures can also act as the point in time of joining the broadcast stream. Pseudo-*video cassette recorder (VCR)* functions (otherwise known as trick modes) such as fast forward, rewind and so on, can also be based on I-pictures. Thus, though I-pictures are not as efficiently coded as P- or B-pictures, which mostly exploit temporal redundancy, they or their equivalent are required within a compressed video stream. I-, P-, and B-pictures are the basic frame types introduced into the first standard codecs (Ghanbari, 2003), and current codecs have added to the variety, without changing the underlying exploitation of the two forms of redundancy. For detailed examination of codecs the reader is referred to treatments such as Richardson (2010) or Shi & Sun (2008). The topic of frame structure organization is returned to in the next Section.

Though *Forward Error Correction or Control (FEC)* (Hamzaoui et al., 2007) can be applied to protect a vulnerable bitstream, there is a risk of duplicating protection at the physical and/or data-link layers of the wireless protocol stack. FEC can also be an unnecessary overhead when channel conditions improve, whereas error resilience, the principle form of source-coding protection, may impose a limited burden. However, this depends on which form(s) of error resilience are chosen,

as some such as data-partitioning have a low overhead whereas others do not. Error concealment can effectively be combined with some forms of error resilience such as *Flexible Macroblock Ordering (FMO)* (Lambert et al., 2006). Consequently, error concealment is topic that is related to error resilience. Many error concealment methods have been proposed (Wang & Zhu, 1998) but there is an issue over computational complexity. In addition, channel coding can be combined with some forms of error resilience, especially in combination with data-partitioning (Stockhammer & Bystrom, 2004).

Error-resilience methods are a way of responding to 'lossy' wireless channels through source coding, i.e. at the video codec level. When transmission errors occur, pixels represented in the packetized bit-stream cannot be decoded and are replaced by concealed versions of previously received pixels (Wah et al., 2000). In order to combat transmission errors, the H.264/AVC (Advanced Video Coding) standard (Wiegand et al., 2003) has incorporated a number of error resilient techniques which have at their core the ability to encode pictures into self-contained sub-units called slices (Stockhammer & Zia, 2007). Slicing itself is an error resilience technique, as each slice resynchronizes the entropy decoder, thus limiting the scope of error propagation. An H.264/AVC codec can use up to 16 previously-coded frames as references (Wiegand et al., 1999) for the current frame being encoded (known as inter frame prediction). This not only increases the compression efficiency but also the inter-frame dependency. Hence, errors in a distorted frame will propagate to the following frames, as error concealment may not clear some distorted parts. To prevent temporal error propagation intra-coded *macroblocks (MBs)* are normally used to refresh damaged areas. Besides periodic intra-refresh, which is most suitable for broadcast video, there are other intra-refresh patterns (Schreier & Rothermel, 2006)) more suitable for wireless networks, as they do not result in sudden increases in the data-rate and can be adapted to gradual decoder refresh. Moreover, periodic intra-refresh can cause unnecessary delays, which are a threat to low-delay applications such as video telephony.

There are many subtleties associated with these protection methods. For example, though data-partitioning in H.264/AVC (Dhondt et al., 2007) appears to separate the different types of coding data into self-contained units, dependencies between two of the partitions cannot be completely removed. The overhead of some methods such as FMO can be greater than others. However, the protection afforded may well be better when using FMO in worsening channel conditions than it is when there are relatively fewer errors. The effectiveness of some techniques can vary with the level of compression. Another dimension to the solution is the relationship between content type and the effectiveness of protection. Content type chiefly manifests itself in source coding complexity (Ghanbari, 2003), either spatial or temporal complexity, both resulting in reduced coding efficiency but with temporally complex content more at risk from temporal error propagation.

However, it would create a misleading impression to suggest that there is one single error resilience method that will suffice. In fact, an appropriate error resilience strategy (Liu et al, 2009) combining several techniques can be chosen. For example, in support of the scalable video coding extension of H.264, the authors (Liu et al., 2009) compared error concealment protection on its own at the receiver's decoder with two strategies for 3G cellular phone transmission of video. For interactive video streaming, slice structuring with error concealment was employed, while for a multicast video messaging service, a combination of FEC, redundant slices (including duplicate lower quality slices), error concealment, and supplementary messaging was employed. The research considered different wireless error patterns and different video content. Its main conclusion was that error resilience strategies worked for 3G video transport compared to neglecting error resilience.

When source coding error resilience is employed packet loss can be compensated for and temporal error propagation can be alleviated. However, as there is a proliferation of error resiliency methods now available, the challenge is to select an appropriate method or methods according to the error conditions, both the intensity of errors and their pattern of occurrence. The Chapter now introduces video streaming. It then goes on to survey error resilience techniques and error concealment at a tutorial level. The Chapter considers the relative performance of the techniques as the level of errors increases. A case study introduces adaptive stream switching according to whether error resilience is required or not. Finally, after considering future developments in this field, the Chapter draws some conclusions.

VIDEO STREAMING PRINCIPLES

This Section is intended as a working guide to video streaming. It cannot possibly consider all aspects of this rich topic, each aspect of which probably deserves a separate chapter. The reader is referred to the additional reading section, for example to Schaar & Chou (2007), to follow up on these topics.

Distribution Methods

Networked video applications are sometimes divided into three categories (Wenger, 2003) according to latency constraints. These categories are:

- **Video file download:** The download of complete pre-encoded video streams before decoding has no latency implications other than the user response to excessive start-up delay. As a reliable application-layer protocol such as FTP or HTTP can be used, the main issue is that of compression efficiency. Therefore, this form of video streaming presents no risk of errors, though there is the problem of providing sufficient data storage on the target device. Thus, because of the high start-up delay, this form of streaming is unsuitable for any but the shortest of video clips. Codec design research mainly addresses this form of downloading, which is why it is beyond the scope of this Chapter.

- **Interactive or conversational video applications:** Such as video phone and video conferencing have very strict end-to-end latency constraints. These result from the need to synchronize responses at either end of a connection (point-to-point applications such as video phone) or connections (point-to-multipoint applications such as video conferencing). Ideally a one-way latency of 100 ms should be aimed at so as to fall below the level of human consciousness. Though such a constraint on many network paths is unobtainable, still latency should be minimized. Thus, if errors occur error control, through some form of *Automatic Repeat reQuest (ARQ)*, should be limited to one request or not used at all. Codec design for this type of streaming is concerned with minimizing computational latency, as video is not pre-encoded. Thus, multiple reference or even bi-reference frames are unsuitable.

- **Video-on-demand:** Streaming applications can be sub-divided into two sub-types depending on whether the video is pre-encoded or not. Traditional video-on-demand applications of pre-encoded video rely on a single server, which supplies videos on a one-to-one basis or as a form of multicast. However, IPTV may offer live streaming of video such as in the networked broadcast of sports events. This may take the form of true multicasting (see next Section) or pseudo-multicasting, in which a copy of the same stream is sent to multiple recipients. For all these methods

of distribution, as delivery is one way, latency constraints can be relaxed compared to conversational applications of streaming. For non-live applications around 10 s of start-up delay can be tolerated by the user. Input buffering can subsequently absorb network packet jitter to ensure a continuous stream at video rate at the display. (Though notice that there is usually a decoder buffer placed between the input buffer and the display.) Live broadcasts potentially present more of a problem, as it is possible for different streams of the same broadcast to arrive at co-located places at offset instances in time. For example, for world cup football the cheers of the crowd after a goal might be heard at different times, which could affect the anticipation of the viewer. However, as there is a brief delay before output, while editors check live video streams for problems, it is unclear whether this issue is addressed at present.

Unicast and Multicast

Video streaming is generally employed to avoid the need to reserve large amounts of storage at the receiver device. Direct access to streamed data by the processor is also possible, by-passing intermediate storage. Content providers also benefit, as access to the complete video is not possible without special de-streaming procedures. In video streaming, a video is intended to be displayed in real-time on the end-user's device. In this context 'real-time' (or video rate) means at the same rate as it was originally captured, though there generally will be a short (and hopefully imperceptible) start-up delay. This Chapter is mostly about true streaming. True streaming may be employed for on-demand streaming in which a user requests pre-recorded content. Pre-recorded content is normally pre-encoded and stored on a disc system or some other form of secondary storage. True video streaming is also suitable for live streaming in which a copy of the same video is sent to every viewer at the same time. The Chapter considers single-stream or unicast streaming but it is obviously possible to multicast a video stream across a network, with potential saving in bandwidth. However, multicasting is a large topic that deserves a separate treatment such as that provided in Wittman & Zitterbart (2001).

Compared to unicast distribution, multicast improves bandwidth efficiency by sharing video packets delivered through a network. However, multicasting over a wireless network is subject to a physical channel that is error-prone and time-varying. Consequently, users signed up to a multicast service in such a network can often suffer (Liu et al., 2007) from diverse channel conditions. With multicast streaming there is a risk of a feedback implosion at the server, an overload of network resources due to the attempts of many receivers trying to send repair requests for a single packet. The risk increases with the size of the multicast group. A number of approaches exist to avoid this implosion effect such as randomized timers, local recovery, whereby receivers can also send repair packets, and hierarchical recovery (Tan & Zakhor, 2001). However, while such approaches are effective, providing reliability without implosion, they can result in significant and unpredictable delays, making them unsuitable in practice for real-time applications. Other studies such as that of Rubenstein et al. (1998) have been devoted to hybrid schemes, combining FEC and ARQ to reliably deliver data, with an emphasis on reducing delay and meeting real-time delivery constraints. However, there is a risk of unnecessary repair data being sent to those mobile receivers not affected by localized channel errors, such as through the effect of overlapped multipath reception.

Optimized Streaming

At a cost in computational complexity, it is possible to optimize streaming (Chou & Miao, 2006) according to rate-distortion analysis. For streaming of pre-encoded video it may be possible to absorb the latencies, especially if the time window over which optimization takes place is shortened. In fact, rate-distortion analysis is embedded in the H.264/AVC encoder so that a Lagrangian cost function is optimized according to a desired mean rate. For example, different modes of block matching in predictive coding can be selected in order to optimize the objective video quality (*Peak Signal-to-Noise Ratio (PSNR)*). In the extension of rate-distortion analysis to network transport, a packet dropping policy, π, is adopted in order to dynamically optimize the sending rate. The policy can be specified as a dropping pattern that reflects the relative importance of packets, as determined by the frame type of the video data in the payload. (Frame type importance is returned to in the next Section.) The Lagrangian cost function is now:

$$J(\pi) = D(\pi) + \lambda R(\pi), \qquad (1)$$

where λ is the Lagrangian multiplier, with D and R the distortion and rate functions respectively. The rate is affected by the number of dropped packets within a given window of time. Distortion is affected by the packet error pattern and the delay-dependent distortion. In respect to the latter, a packet may arrive late and, consequently, not contribute to the display but still contribute to the data rate. It is also possible for a packet to not contribute to the display but still be employed as reference for subsequent frames.

Network Protocols for Video Streaming

In contrast to true video streaming, according to the 'download and play' approach, the whole compressed video file is transported across the network and stored on a user's device. In other words, the complete video file is downloaded before it is decoded and displayed. This allows a reliable transport protocol to be employed (such as *Transmission Control Protocol (TCP)*), which can improve coding efficiency in error-prone networks, as no error resilience measures are required. As TCP is a connection-oriented protocol, it is easy to manage at a firewall. However, all of the content is stored on the end device, exposing the content owners to multiple copies of their digital media. Another obvious disadvantage of download and play is that large files (such as for two-hour movies) not only result in a long start-up time but despite compression may overwhelm the storage at an end-user's device.

Progressive download and display or pseudo-streaming is a compromise between true video streaming and download and play. In basic terms, the content is split into separate physical or logical files, each of which contains a chunk or segment of compressed video. The chunks are then transported by a reliable transport protocol (normally TCP). As reliability implies the possibility of an unbounded delivery delay in best-effort IP networks or error-prone mobile networks, pseudo-streaming is unsuitable for interactive video streaming.

Direct streaming employing TCP transport without chunking can also be applied to pre-encoded or stored video. However, to do so successfully (Wang et al., 2004) requires available bandwidth to be about twice the peak video rate and several seconds buffering is required. Successful streaming implies (Wang et al., 2004) no more than 10^{-4} of packets are delayed beyond their play-out deadline, for a start-up penalty of 10 s. However, even a few seconds of buffering are a potential problem for click-and-view services such as YouTube, while the bandwidth requirements are onerous for high-quality video.

Direct streaming with TCP has other detractions: such as the need for a feedback channel; and the sawtooth rate fluctuations that occur in response to packet loss events. Nonetheless, TCP emulators (Widmer et al., 2001) for video transport over the *User Datagram Protocol (UDP)* (to avoid unbounded delivery delay) do include feedback of a packet loss factor in their models.

Congestion control mechanisms for streaming such as Rate-Adaptive Protocol (RAP) (Rejaie et al., 1999), TCP-Friendly Rate Control (TFRC) (Handley et al., 2003), Loss-Delay Adaptation algorithm (LDA+) (Sisalem & Wolisz, 2000) and TCP Emulation at Receivers (TEAR) (Rhee et al, 2000) have in some measure based themselves on TCP's bandwidth probing mechanism, which results in packet loss before the rate is reduced. However, all of these mechanisms aim to reduce the bit-rate fluctuations that are a feature of TCP congestion control.

Whether a UDP packet stream is delivered under the control of a congestion controller or not, due to the primitive facilities provided by UDP, it is likely to be encapsulated in a *Real-time Transport Protocol (RTP)* (Perkins, 2003) packet. RTP is not itself a control mechanism in the sense that a protocol such as TCP is. Instead, it specifies a packet format with a header containing sequence numbers and time stamps. As an aid to RTP, the *Real-time Transport Control Protocol (RTCP)* is available to provide feedback messages containing quality-of-service statistics. Streaming may also mean the inclusion of any associated audio streams. In which case, a multimedia container such as MPEG2 *Transport Stream (TS)* or the MPEG-4 container (Bing, 2010) can be employed or indeed the RTP packets themselves can carry associated audio streams. RTP can also transport MPEG2-TS packets as sub-packets within an RTP packet. Synchronization between video and audio can be provided within MPEG2-TS or RTP. However, because audio normally consumes much less bandwidth than video but has different characteristics, it is usually treated separately and this Chapter will be no different.

In respect to pre-encoded video, the commercial world has largely opted for simulcast (Conklin et al., 2001) as the means of adjusting the streaming rate delivered across access networks to the user's display. In simulcast, a number of pre-encoded streams at different data rates are stored at the server. According to available bandwidth the server can then switch between the streams at anchor frames. However, because the user chooses just one rate at streaming start-up, this method can result in service interruptions. To cope with changing conditions, variants of HTTP live streaming (Stockhammer, 2011) have been introduced and are on the point of standardization, for example as *Dynamic Adaptive Streaming over HTPP (DASH)* (Stockhammer et al., 2011). These adaptive forms of streaming differ from the push mechanism associated with server-based streaming, because now the client device pulls video data from the server.

Client-Server Streaming

In simple *Client-Server (CS)* streaming, the client initiates a connection with the video source address and the server at that address streams the content to the client. This asymmetric arrangement avoids potential deadlocks. However, as all the content is located at and provided by a single central entity, any failure of that entity may interrupt the video streaming to the server's clients. Power cuts and denial-of-service attacks are just two ways that a video server can be disabled. Sudden bursts of content requests can quickly overwhelm the resources of the server and force it to begin dropping connections. To address those problems, system designers built processor banks, which were highly secured against network intruders. However, such systems are difficult to scale, require specialized staff to operate them, and are costly (Liu et al., 2008). They remain vulnerable to 'flash' crowds. This prompted the design of distributed architectures, in particular *Content Delivery Networks (CDNs)* (Pallis & Vakali, 2006). CDNs still employ CS streaming but the video content is cached locally to reduce access time and to reduce the risk of server overload.

CDNs employ many strategically-placed video servers on the network edge. Any video is delivered by the closest server to the requesting client. Initially, a central server distributes its content to outlying servers. Clients access a content server, usually the central server. If that server is not the closest one the request is redirected to the 'nearest' server to the client. This arrangement also reduces network traffic, as streams tend to take the shortest path to the client. YouTube (user-created content), MySpace™ (social network), and Veoh (IPTV network) distribute content (Hossfeld & Leibnitz, 2008) through a CDN, whereas Akamai and Limelightare well-known multimedia CDN providers. However, though the costs involved in maintaining a massive centralized server facility are reduced, distributing video content to multiple, smaller servers introduces higher costs in terms of design and maintenance. Traffic monitoring is required in order to select a CDN server location. The servers must be maintained in many countries, all with differing regulations and requirements. Thus, system management outsourcing is preferred by providers, though this comes at a cost. This situation has led to the search for a content distribution system in which the users or peers themselves can assist in video streaming.

Peer-to-Peer Streaming

Peer-to-Peer (P2P) networks are distribution network overlays that are constructed on top of and decoupled from the underlying physical network. The P2P concept has been developed into several commercial P2P streaming systems, such as Joost (Fu et al., 2007), Sopcast, Zattoo, PPlive, and Coolstream (Zhang et al., 2005). P2P streaming architectures can be categorized according to their distribution mechanisms. The various approaches to P2P streaming have been surveyed by (Liu et al. 2008). Two principle topologies have emerged, namely: tree-based (Padmanabhan et al., 2003) and mesh-based P2P (for a comparison see Sentinelli et al. (2007)). Mesh-P2P streaming is flexible and can be managed easily in comparison to a tree-based topology. Consequently, mesh-based distribution is becoming more widespread than tree-based distribution and has been adopted by most successful P2P streaming systems (Fu et al., 2008) (Zhang et al., 2005) (Reza, 2006).

In the tree-based architecture, the peers are ordered hierarchically by the source, known as the parent. The parent node, in turn, sends data packets to intermediate nodes, and these nodes relay them iteratively until leaf nodes are reached. An example of a tree-based streaming application is Peercast (Zhang et al., 2008), which is open-source software for streaming both audio and video. A feature of Peercast is that any node can specify the maximum number of incoming connections allowed. Despite introducing a good level of parallelism and distribution, this approach suffers from several limitations. The root, or data source, is a single point of failure, limiting the robustness of the system. The other problem is that if peers join and leave frequently the tree has to be rebuilt too often, which has a negative impact on signaling overheads, latency, and stability.

The very successful BitTorrent P2P file distribution protocol (Shah & Pâris, 2007) has been the inspiration behind mesh-P2P streaming. In the all-to-all connectivity of a mesh, the overlay network supporting the stream distribution incorporates the swarm-like content delivery introduced by BitTorrent. To deliver a video stream, the video is divided into chunks or blocks in such a way that allows a peer to receive portions of the stream from different peers and assemble them locally, leading to the delivery of good quality streams to a large number of users. The original video stream from a source is distributed among different peers (Jurca et al., 2007). A peer joining the mesh retrieves video chunks from one or more source peers. The peer also receives information about the other receiver peers from the same sources that serve the video chunks. Each peer periodically reports its newly available video chunks to all its neighbors. The chunks requested by each peer from a neighbor are determined by a packet scheduling algorithm based on available content and bandwidth from its neighbors (Jurca et al., 2007). This approach is more robust than the tree-based architecture, because, when a stream comes from various sources, communication does not breakdown if a small subset of peers disconnect.

Multi-Sender Video Streaming

P2P streaming (Lee, 2010) is an example of a multi-sender streaming system. Compared to the client-server model, multi-sender systems (Nguyen & Zakhor, 2004) do not present a single distribution bottleneck at a centralized server. This in turn allows the streaming system to become scalable. It also allows the effect of congestion to be ameliorated by transmitting over diverse paths in the wired Internet. Similarly the impact of wireless channel errors might be reduced if multiple senders distribute a video over an ad hoc network. Sensor networks are static wireless ad hoc networks to which media streaming can be applied (Akyildiz et al., 2007; Melodia & Akyildiz, 2011). *Mobile ad hoc networks (MANETs)* (Qadri et al., 2009) or even *Vehicular Ad Hoc Networks (VANETs)* also have employed P2P video streaming (Qadri et al., 2012). However, P2P streaming itself has weaknesses, as it may assume that identical copies of the same video are first distributed from a central source to the senders. If the same video is distributed from multiple senders bandwidth consumption increases, unless some form of layered video or multi-description coding is applied (Lee, 2010). The alternative is to partition the distribution so that each sender supplies part of the video. However, that approach leads to the problems of how best to partition the video stream data and how to synchronize streaming across the multiple senders (and receivers).

One way that these problems might be addressed is through network coding (Fragouli & Sljanin, 2007). Network coding is a relatively simple technique, whereby packets are combined at intermediate nodes, sometimes by an exclusive OR (XOR) operation. The XOR operation is its own inverse. Suppose two packets, $p1$ and $p2$, are to be sent to a number of destinations. Forming a new packet as $p1 \oplus p2$ and transmitting it to a destination allows the destination to recover the packet it has not received by an operation $(p1 \oplus p2) \oplus p2$ or $(p1 \oplus p2) \oplus p1$. In a network with limited link capacity, this property potentially enables throughput to be increased across the network as a whole (Ahleswede et al., 2000), as only the XORed packet need be sent across part of the network. As the XOR operation is non-linear knowing $p1 \oplus p2$ does not allow either p1 or p2 to be recovered unless one of the two is known separately. Therefore, network coding can build in some measure of network security, as it requires all network links to be monitored simultaneously by an intruder. Monitoring in this way is difficult to achieve in a network such as a MANET or VANET. Network coding also potentially enables lost packets to be recovered through erasure coding at an intermediate network node. Because recovery is performed at an intermediate node, if packets continue to be at risk of loss at the next node in the network path, the overall probability of loss across a network path is reduced, compared to simply apply erasure recovery procedures at the destination. Network coding can reduce the delay from these intermediate operations, thus enabling real-time delivery of video streams.

In addition, as pointed out in Nguyen et al. (2011), network coding has some advantages in respect to pull-based streaming. CS systems are push-based in the sense that the video server pushes video according to the display schedule determined at the encoder. Pull-based streaming is more common in P2P streaming (Zhang et al., 2005), as it overcomes the problem of a peer leaving the network but still having data streamed to it. In principle, pull-based streaming also allows control by the receiver of what video data is received by the peer. This allows the peer to reduce overlap arising from the same video data being delivered by multiple senders. However, if more than one peer requests the same video data duplication can

still occur. Each sender contacted by a peer must also have a complete copy of the video stream. The receiving peer is then able to select from which senders it receives particular segments of the video stream. In Nguyen et al. (2011), layered video was combined with network coding to overcome these issues. Packets were formed according to a hierarchical scheme, whereby more important packets only contain data from the essential base layer. Less important packets contain video data from the base layer and one or more enhancement layers. The more enhancement layers included the less important a packet was. This hierarchical scheme was combined with a probabilistic request scheme. In addition, packets are network coded so that there is a good chance of receiving and reconstructing all base-layer packets at a given time. However, strangely TCP was used with this scheme, which seems to negate the protection properties of network coding. Thus, network coding was used to allow a random selection of packets to be employed to reconstruct the video stream to a good quality but successful receipt of all packets was also guaranteed by means of a reliable protocol. Though the authors' simulations demonstrate relatively low latency, there is always a risk from using TCP on a wireless network of increased latencies.

Cross-Layer Design for Video Streaming

Multimedia applications with real-time constraints and limited tolerance of data loss such as video streaming can significantly benefit from cross-layer design and optimization (Schaar, 2007). A cross-layer approach allows the exchange of information across protocol-layer boundaries and, in some cases the approach allows system-wise optimization of performance. For example, sensor networks benefit from system-wise optimization (Jurdak, 2007), as they usually run dedicated applications such as video surveillance. The same applies to ad hoc networks in general, where video streaming can benefit (Setton et al., 2005) from cross-layer design. Widening the remit, IEEE 802.11 wireless LANs (Schaar et al., 2003) have also proved a fertile ground for multimedia applications of cross-layer design.

Cross-layer design can be applied to *Personal Area Networks (PANs)*, which enable short-range wireless communication between desk-top or office devices. This includes cable replacement for single link communication. The video streaming should be protected across a volatile wireless channel when there is PAN congestion. This protection can be performed in a cross-layer manner: firstly through a form of adaptive modulation at the physical layer in a way that favors the more important video data originating at the application layer; and secondly through data-link control of a transmit buffer that is partitioned according to video frame type. PANs originally came to prominence through the success of the Bluetooth technology and in Razavi et al. (2008) such a cross-layer scheme for Bluetooth is described in detail.

ERROR RESILIENT TECHNIQUES

Early video codecs had a very limited range of error-resiliency features, as they were intended for storage of compressed video. However, in later versions of the H.263 codec, namely H.263+ and H.263++, and MPEG-4, a number of resiliency tools were introduced such as a form of in-packet data-partitioning and *reversible variable-length codes (RVLC)* (Cote et al., 2001).H.264/AVC along with its efficient compression has strong error resilience features (Wenger, 2003), though notice that RVLC was not included in H.264/AVC,because it was assumed that physical-layer FEC would correct for bit errors. Error resilience introduces limited delay and as such is suitable for real-time, interactive video streaming, especially video-telephony, and video conferencing. It is also suitable for one-way streaming over cellular wireless networks and broadband wireless access

networks to the home. As data-link-layer FEC is normally already present, application-layer FEC may duplicate its role if applied at the bit level. The exception is if application-layer FEC can be designed to act as an outer code after inner coding at the data-link layer, in the manner of concatenated channel coding. Various forms of *Automatic Repeat reQuest (ARQ)* are also possible (Wicker, 1995) but care must be taken to avoid additional delay.

It is also possible to apply application-layer channel coding or FEC as a form of erasure coding to protect against packet losses. In a binary erasure channel, a packet is either received or lost. For example, in a wireless network this may occur because the signal strength of the received packet falls below a receiver's sensitivity threshold. Alternatively, in a binary symmetric channel, individual bits of a packet are received but they may be randomly flipped in value. Thus, the bits are received in error rather than lost. Though these models are commonly employed in communications theory, a more common reality (Rappaport, 2002) is that errors in a wireless channel occur in bursts due to the impact of slow fading. Nevertheless, the two forms of binary channel illustrate the distinction between the roles of application-layer channel coding and data-link layer channel coding.

In recent years, an effective form of application-layer channel coding has been introduced that is known as rateless coding. The coding is rateless because the redundant to information data ratio can be dynamically varied, which is not easily possible for traditional codes such as Reed-Solomon codes (Lin & Costello, 2004). Consequently, rateless codes are now attracting applications in video streaming. For example, in Ahmad et al. (2007) rateless coding was applied to packets in unicast video streaming over the Internet. In Rahnavard et al. (2007), rateless coding was selected for reasons of reduced decode computational complexity in an energy reduction scheme for wireless mesh networks. The fact that one member of the family of rateless codes has linear complexity means that it may be selected for that reason rather than its rateless properties. That member, Raptor coding (Shokrollahi, 2006), can also be made systematic, allowing reduced processing if no errors occur. Window-growth codes (Vukobratovic et al., 2008) are an extension of rateless codes, which allow the amount of protection to be incrementally scaled. As such they can allow prioritized protection of the more important of the partitions. In Samek et al. (2011), this concept was applied to data-partitioned video streaming (see below), allowing protection to be varied in a practical manner.

Differential protection of video data through FEC is one of a number of unequal error protection (UEP) methods. In general, UEP applies to data that can be arranged in a nested set of priorities. Thus, if the highest priority data are not received then lower-priority data are no longer useful, as occurs in *Priority-Encoding Transmission (PET)* schemes (Albanese et al., 1996). In PET, parity symbols of a systematic code are included in successive packets such that high-priority segments can be recovered even if a large number of packets are erased. Lower priority segments will be lost if a few packets amongst the interleaved group are erased. PET is capable of refinement in a rate-distortion manner (Mohr et al., 2000) but a problem with all packet-interleaving methods is the risk of increased latency if the decoder has to wait for all the packets in an interleaved group to arrive before reconstruction can take place.

Technical Preliminaries

Video compression or video coding refers to the reduction in the quantity of data used to represent video sequences. In the standard video method, compression is based on spatial and temporal redundancy reduction along with entropy coding[1] (static or dynamic Huffman, or Arithmetic) (MacKay, 2003). Spatial redundancy reduction results in Intra (I) frames, within which each block of the picture is predicted from its neigh-

boring coded blocks without reference to any other frame. The difference or residue between the two blocks is typically transformed by means of the *Discrete Cosine Transform (DCT)*[2], which removes correlations. As a natural image can be respesented as an order-one Markov field, pixel correlation quickly drops off after a few pixels are traversed. The wavelet transform has also found favor in the BBC's Dirac codec. The orthogonal frequency transform (or bi-orthogonal in the case of the wavelet) is followed by quantization of the transform coefficients and subsequent entropy coding. As intra coded frames do not rely on other frames, they are used for a number of operations, typically for random access (video cassette recorder functionality) and confining temporal error propagation errors due to corruption during transmission.

Inter frames exploit the temporal redundancy between frames. In this process (Richardson, 2010), the movements of objects between reference frames are modeled by means of motion vectors. However, MB-based coding is employed in most standard codecs. This can reduce memory requirements and enables parallel processing. A motion-compensated frame is subsequently subtracted from its reference frame to form a residue image. In the case of B-frames or multiple reference frames, each MB may be subtracted from the reference frame of a different reference frame. This process reduces the dynamic range of the pixels in the residue image. The residue is transformed to the frequency domain (as in intra coding) in order to de-correlate the image. After quantization the transform coefficients are entropy coded (as in Intra coding). Other symbols such as motion vectors are also entropy coded and take their place in the output bitstream. Inter frames can be further categorized as Predictive (P) frames and Bi-predictive (B) frames. In P-frames the prediction is made from earlier P- or I-frames, while in B-frames the prediction can be made from an earlier and/or later I- and/or P-frame, but not from a B-frame. In an H.264/AVC codec this

Figure 1. A general diagram of a GOP

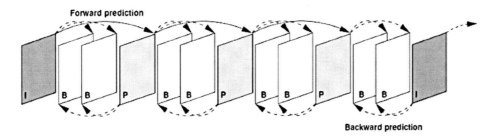

restriction is removed and a B-frame can be used as reference for predicting other frames (Flierl & Girod, 2003) A sequence of frames grouped between two I frames is referred to as a Group of Pictures (GOP)as shown in Figure 1.

Intra-MB/IDR Frames

Intra-frames or intra-coded MB placement in slices is used to confine temporal propagation errors (Osterman et al., 2003). An H.264/AVC codec supports two types of intra picture, the *Instantaneous Decoding Refresh (IDR)*and the intra-coded I-frame. Furthermore, it also supports intra-coded MBs (known as intra-refresh MBs) within inter-coded frames (Wenger, 2003). Both I-frames and IDR-frames are intra-coded frames, without reference to any other frames. The difference between the two is that the IDR picture invalidates all short-term reference memory buffers and, thus, can completely confine drift errors arising from the loss of previous frames. On the other hand, an I-frame does not invalidate the reference memory buffers and, thus, can confine drift error at that frame position only. If future frames refer to any picture older than the intra picture then drift error can occur again. The insertion of intra-coded MBs into frames normally encoded through motion-compensated prediction allows temporal error propagation to be arrested for matching MBs in a previous frame are lost. However, notice that temporal error propagation can give rise to spatial errors if a previously correct spatial MB references a temporally corrupted MB.

Flexible reference frames in H.264/AVC allow (Wiegand et al., 1999) MBs in a single picture to reference different frames. This can reduce the need for sending intra-coded data. Another possibility is for inter-prediction through different subsequences of prior frames. Another possibility is to use switching frames, which allow a smooth transition between video streams encoded at different qualities (assuming *Variable BitRate (VBR)* encoding), as a form of error resilience or method of adaptation (Stockhammer et al., 2006) to channel conditions. It is also possible to vary the Intra-Refresh (IR) rate according to scene type or channel conditions (Liang et al, 2006). For example, in a scene with rapid motion then predictive reference will be more severely affected by data loss. Therefore, the distance to the next anchor frame can be shortened by increasing the rate of insertion of I-pictures. Motion is detected by a count of the number of non-zero motion vectors included in the compressed version of a frame.

Slicing

The simplest form of error resilience is through slicing. Compressed picture data is often split into a number of slices each consisting of a set of MBs. Slice resynchronization markers ensure that if a slice is lost then the entropy decoder is still able to continue without loss of synchronization. An advanced feature of later codecs (MPEG-4 and H263) is *Reversible Variable Length Coding (RVLC)* (Jeong et al., 2004), which allows partial decoding of a slice even if part of it is damaged.

Asymmetric RVLC produces better results but requires two look-up tables rather than the one needed for symmetric RVLC. Returning to slicing, in the MPEG-2 codec, slices could only be constructed from a single row of MBs. Later codecs such as H.261 relaxed this requirement (Ghanbari, 2003), allowing contiguous MBs to form a slice. In H.264/AVC, *Arbitrary Slice Ordering (ASO)* allows the decoder to reconstruct a picture if the slices arrive in a different order to the encoding order. A slice is a unit of error resilience and it is normally assumed that one slice forms a packet, after packing into a *Network Abstraction Layer unit (NALU)* in H.264/AVC. Each NALU is normally encapsulated in a *Real Time Protocol (RTP)* packet, though other transport options such as MPEG-2 *transport stream (TS)* are possible. For a given picture or frame, the more slices the picture is broken up into, the smaller the packet size and the less risk of packet loss through bit errors. However, header overhead grows unless header compression (Pelletier and Sandlund, 2008) is applied. The latter is common within wireless networks.

H.264/AVC can divide a frame into slices, whose size can be as small as a MB and as large as one complete frame. MBs are assigned to slices in raster-scan order, unless FMO is used. Figure 2 shows a frame representation with three slices (Sullivan & Wiegand, 2005). Intra prediction across the slice boundaries is not allowed making slices self-contained units that can be decoded without referring to other slices of the frame and, thus, can prevent error propagation. However the non-availability of intra prediction across the slice boundaries reduces the compression efficiency, which can further decrease with an increase in the number of slices per frame. Slices can be decoded independently. However, some information from other slices may be needed when applying de-blocking filters. A de-blocking filter smoothes sharp edges, which can form at MB boundaries.

Data Partitioning

In the video bitstream some syntax elements are more important than the others and thus, the error robustness can be enhanced by separating these data from one another and protecting it unequally based on their importance (Sullivan & Wiegand, 2005). Data partitioning in H.264/AVC, Figure 3, separates the compressed bitstream into: A) configuration data and motion vectors; B) intra-coded transform coefficients; and C) inter-coded coefficients. This data form A, B, and C partitions which are packetized as separate NALUs (Kumar et al., 2006). The arrangement allows a frame to be reconstructed even if the inter-coded MBs in partition C are lost, provided that the motion vectors in partition-A survive. Partition-A is normally strongly protected at the application layer or physical layer protection may be provided such as the hierarchical modulation scheme in Barmada et al. (2005) for broadcast TV. Notice that in codecs prior to H.264/AVC, data partitioning was also applied but no separation into NALUs occurred. The advantage of integral partitioning is that additional resynchronization markers are available that reset entropy encoding. This mode of data partitioning is still available in H.264/AVC and is applied to I-frames.

The H.264/AVC codec standard conceptually separates the *Video Coding Layer (VCL)* from the NAL. The VCL specifies the core compression

Figure 2. Picture partitioned into slices (no FMO used) with MBs shown

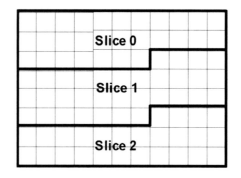

Figure 3. H264/AVC data-partitioning in which a single slice is split into three NAL units (types 2 to 4). The relative size of the C partition will depend on the quantization parameter (QP), with a lower QP leading to higher quality and a larger C partition.

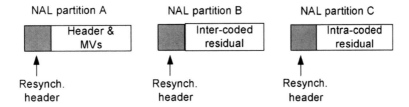

features, while the NAL supports delivery over various types of network. This feature of the standard facilitates easier packetization and improved video delivery. The NAL facilitates the delivery of the H.264 VCL data to the underlying transport layers such as RTP/IP, H.32X and MPEG-2 transport systems. Each NAL unit could be considered as a packet that contains a header and a payload. The 8-bit header shown in Figure 4 specifies the NALU payload type (nal_unit_type) and the relative importance of the NALU (nal_ref_idc), while the payload contains the compressed video data.

The concept of the NAL, together with the error resilience features in H.264/AVC, allows communication over a variety of different channels. Table 1 is a summarized list of different NAL unit types. NAL units 1 to 5 contain different VCL data that will be described later. NAL units 6 to 12 are non-VCL units containing additional information such as parameter sets and supplemental information.

As previously mentioned, each frame can be divided into several slices; each of which contains a flexible number of MBs. *Variable Length Coding (VLC)* that is entropy coding of the compressed data takes place as the final stage of the hybrid codec. In H.264/AVC, arithmetic coding replaced other forms of entropy coding in earlier codecs. In each slice, the arithmetic coder is aligned and its predictions are reset. Hence, every slice in the frame is independently decodable. Therefore, they can be considered as resynchronization points

that prevent error propagation to the entire picture. Each slice is placed within a separate NAL unit (see Table 1). The slices of an IDR- or I-picture are located in type 5 NAL units, while those belonging to a non-IDR or I-picture (P- or B-pictures) are placed in NAL units of type 1, and in types 2 to 4 when data partitioning mode is active, as now explained.

In type 1 and type 5 NALs, MB addresses, motion vectors and the transform coefficients of the blocks, are packed into the packet, in the order they are generated by the encoder. In Type 5, all parts of the compressed bitstream are equally important, while in type 1, the MB addresses and motion vectors are much more important than the transform coefficients. In the event of errors in this type of packet, the fact that symbols appearing earlier in the bit-stream suffer less from errors than those which come later[3] means that bringing the more important parts of the video data (such as headers and MVs) ahead of the less important data or separating the more important

Table 1. NAL unit types

NAL unit type	Class	Content of NAL unit
0	-	Unspecified
1	VCL	Coded slice
2	VCL	Coded slice partition A
3	VCL	Coded slice partition B
4	VCL	Coded slice partition C
5	VCL	Coded slice of an IDR picture
6-12	Non-VCL	Suppl. info., Parameter sets, etc.
13-23	-	Reserved
24-31	-	Unspecified

data altogether for better protection against errors can significantly reduce channel errors. Thus, in the standard video codecs prior to H.264/AVC, it is this that is known as data partitioning.

However, in H.264/AVC when data partitioning is enabled, every slice is divided into three separate partitions and each partition is located in either of type 2 to type-4 NAL units, as listed in Table 1. A NAL unit of type 2, also known as partition A, comprises the most important information of the compressed video bit stream of P- and B-pictures, including the MB addresses, MVs and essential headers. If any MBs in these pictures are intra-coded, their transform coefficients are packed into a type-3 NAL unit, also known as partition B. Type 4 NAL, also known as partition C, carries the transform coefficients of the motion-compensated inter-picture coded MBs.

In order to decode partition-B and -C, the decoder must know the location from which each MB was predicted, which implies that partitions B and C cannot be reconstructed if partition-A is lost. Though partition-A is independent of partitions B and C, *constrained intra prediction* (CIP) should be set (Dhondt et al., 2007) to make partition-B independent of partition-C. By setting this option, partition-B MBs are no longer predicted from neighboring inter-coded MBs, the prediction residuals of which reside in partition-C. As discussed in Section I this has a by-product of increasing packet sizes due to a reduction in compression efficiency.

There is another dependency (Dhondt et al., 2007) arising from *Context-Adaptive VLC (CAVLC)* entropy coding, because the number of non-zero coefficients in one MB are predicted from the number in a neighboring MB. By design, setting CIP also results in setting the number of non-zero coefficients in data-partitioned inter-coded MBs to zero when CAVLC is in operation to code intra-coded MBs. Thus, partition-B can be made independent of partition-C. It is not possible to employ the alternative *Context Adaptive Binary Arithmetic Coding (CABAC)* as this option

is not supported in the Extended profile of H.264/AVC, though this is the only profile in which data-partitioning is supported. As CAVLC still predicts from intra-coded MBs when coding partition-C's inter-coded MBs, partition-C cannot normally be made independent of partition-B.

Redundant Slices/Frames

To enhance error robustness in H.264/AVC, the encoder sends duplicate copies of some or all parts of a picture. Redundant frames (Bacchichet et al., 2006) (or strictly redundant slices making up a frame) are coarsely quantized frames (or slice) that can avoid sudden drops in quality marked by freeze frame effects if a complete frame (or slice) is lost. Methods to refine the selection of redundant slices (Ferré et al., 2010) have also been designed. The main weakness of the redundant frame solution is that these frames are discarded if not required but are still a more efficient solution than including extra I-frame synchronization, as redundant frames are predictively coded and require fewer bits as compared to I-frames. A subsidiary weakness of this scheme is the delay in encoding and transmitting redundant frames, making it more suitable for one-way communication. If the redundant frame/slice replaces the lost original frame/slice there will still be some mismatch between encoder and decoder. This is because the encoder will assume the original frame/slice was used. However, the impact of this substitution will be much less than if no substitution took place.

A possibility (Zhu et al., 2006) is to use correctly-received reference pictures for reconstruction of redundant pictures rather than the reference pictures used by primary pictures. The decoder is able to select from a set of potential replacement redundant pictures according to the possibility of correct reconstruction. Alternatively, in Ferré et al. (2010), MBs were selected for their relative impact on reconstruction and placed within Flexible Macroblock Ordering (FMO) slices.

FMO (Flexible Macroblock Ordering)

FMO allows different arrangements of MBs in a slice by utilizing the concept of slice groups. The MBs may be arranged in a slice in a different order to that of the scan order, enhancing the error resilience. In each slice group, the MBs are arranged according to an MB to slice group map. In H.264/AVC, by varying the way in which the MBs are assigned to a slice (or rather group of slices), FMO gives a way of reconstructing a frame even if one or more slices are lost.

Within a frame up to eight slice groups are possible. H.264/AVC provides different MB classification patterns. Assignment of MBs to a slice group can be general (type 6) but the other six types pre-define an assignment formula. The latter reduces the coding overhead arising from providing a full assignment map. Pre-defined assignments in the *Joint Model (JM)* implementation of the H.264/AVC codec are: interleaved, checkerboard (or dispersed), foreground, box out, raster scan and wipe (Thomos et al., 2005). Figure 4 shows these different FMO assignments with the number of the slice group type as indicated: type 0 is interleaved, type 1 is checkerboard, type 2 is foreground and back ground map, type 3 is box out, type 4 is raster and type 5 is wipe. In type 0 it is only necessary to specify run-lengths, because assignment of macroblocks to a slice group proceeds in raster scan order. The type 1 example in Figure 5 is just one example of assignment by a mathematical function, which must be specified in advance at the encoder and decoder. Type 2 requires a mapping in order to

specify rectangular regions of interest. Types 3 to 5 allow the growth of a slice group over a cycle of frames in the directions indicated. An isolated region evolves (Hannuksela et al., 2004) in this way across successive frames. In the explicit case, type 6, the parameter "slice_group_id" is transmitted for each MB in the picture specifying the slice group to which it belongs.

The checkerboard type stands apart from other types, as it does not employ adjacent MBs as coding references, which decreases its compression efficiency and the relative video quality after decoding. However, if there are safely decoded MBs in the vicinity of a lost packet, error concealment can be applied. Consequently, the rate of decrease in video quality with an increase in loss rate is lower than for the other pre-set types.

Arranging MBs in multiple slice groups' increase error resilience, for example if one of the slice groups in the dispersed map is 'lost' due to buffer overflow, the missing slice can be concealed by interpolation from the available slices. Experiments show (Son and Jeong, 2008) that at a loss rate of 10% in case of video conferencing, the impairments due to losses can be kept so small that it is very difficult to be observed. In FMO, the possible errors are scattered across the whole frame to avoid their accumulation in a limited area. In this way, the distance between the correctly recovered block and the erroneous block is reduced. Consequently, the distortion is less in the recovered block (Kumar et al., 2006). Therefore it is easier to conceal scattered errors as compared to the errors concentrated in a region.

Figure 4. NAL unit format

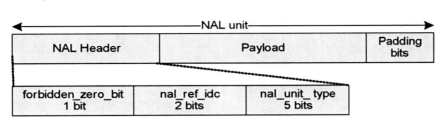

Figure 5. Different types of FMOs

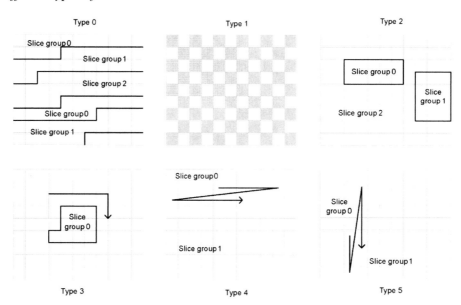

Switching Frames

In H.264/AVC, new types of frame, namely Switching Predictive/Intra frames (SP/SI-frame), were defined. SP- and SI-frames were originally proposed by Karczewiz & Kurceren (2003). These frames were designed to support different applications such as stream-switching between bitstreams at different coding rates, random access, VCR functionality such as fast forwarding, error resiliency and error recovery, as well as splicing between different sequences and switching between bitstreams coded at different frame rates. The aim of the SP/SI frames (Karczewiz & Kurceren, 2003) is to "enable reconstruction of identical frames using different reference frames". Thus, in stream switching between bitstreams encoded at different rates, the reconstructed frame after the switching frame is the same as if it was reconstructed in the normal manner without switching. Stream switching also enables switching between streams encoded with differing forms of error resiliency (Altaf et al., 2011), according to measured wireless channel conditions. In the Chapter case study, this possibility is demonstrated.

ERROR CONCEALMENT TECHNIQUES

Technical Preliminaries

Error concealment allows superior reconstruction of video in the event of packet loss, especially if checkerboard FMO is used. Error concealment is a non-normative feature of H.264/AVC (Vars & Hannuksela, 2001) in the sense that its form is not specified in the standard but left to implementers. In fact, error concealment can give rise to computational complexity issues at the decoder. For error concealment in H.264/AVC, the MVs of correctly received slices (or prior concealed slices) are used in boundary-matching MV recovery (Lam et al., 1993) if the average motion activity is sufficient (more than a quarter pixel). Research in Vars & Hannuksela (2001) gives details of which MV to select to give the smoothest block transition. It is also possible to select the intra-coded frame method of spatial interpolation, which provides smooth and consistent edges at an increased computational cost through weighted pixel-value averaging (Salama et al., 1998). According to measured picture continuity, the error-concealment method that best reduces 'blockiness' at MB boundaries is dynamically selected by the decoder. Rather than simple replacement from the previous frame, the potential role of error concealment, in improving video quality was highlighted in Stockhammer et al. (2003).

Error concealment is a non-standardized decoder-only technique which tries to hide or minimize the effects of packet loss in order to improve the final subjective video quality. When decoding a loss affected bit stream the decoder goes into error-concealment mode every time a packet number discontinuity is detected. The concealment process starts with the detection and localization of the affected MBs by the lost packet. Afterwards, error-concealment techniques come into place to minimize the negative impact of errors by reconstructing a frame as similar as possible to the original frame. The closer to the original, the smaller subsequent temporal error drifts.

Concealing lost MBs is a complex procedure due to the lack of information about the lost picture details. Fortunately, video frames are usually highly correlated, simplifying the reconstruction process. In order to reconstruct the affected areas, error concealment uses the available decoded data such as motion information, texture and shape. Depending on the type of information used, error-concealment techniques can be classified into three categories: spatial, temporal and spatio-temporal error concealment.

Spatial Concealment

Techniques that follow the spatial approach to reconstruct the missing areas make use of the correctly decoded information from the current frame being concealed. The lost areas are reconstructed by pixel interpolation from the available neighbor MBs. This obviously implies that the frame being reconstructed has multiple slices and that not all of them were lost. Otherwise, pixel interpolation is not possible. Despite its simplic-

ity, this approach provides good results for small and homogeneous areas. If the original area being concealed is highly detailed then the concealed area will differ much from the original, resulting in poor quality concealment. Hence, this technique is used best to conceal small and homogeneous areas. This occurs usually in low resolution frames, where each slice represents a small portion of the whole image area and is relatively homogeneous.

Temporal Concealment

In order to overcome the limitations of spatial error concealment, several techniques were developed to exploit temporal similarities between consecutive frames. These techniques make use of available data from other previously decoded frames in order to estimate the current one. Most videos have a high inter-frame correlation which means that the video content has a smooth flow and continuity as time progresses. There can be a static scene (e.g. two persons having a chat on a table) or an object with constant motion (e.g. a car passing by on the street). In both examples, the temporal activity is constant and it is possible to estimate the next frame with good accuracy. This type of concealment works best the closer the available frame is to the frame being concealed as the inter-frame correlation is higher for consecutive frames. Some exceptions might also occur such as the case of a scene change. In this case, the inter-frame correlation is very low and the concealed frame has low similarity to the original version.

Spatio-Temporal (Hybrid) Concealment

Most sophisticated methods combine both spatial and temporal error concealment features in a hybrid manner. These schemes can use spatial interpolation in some cases, temporal interpolation in other cases or even a mixture of both at the same time. Overall, spatial and temporal concealment can be used to verify the accuracy of each other and help to find the closest estimate to the original data. Selecting the best concealment without the original data to compare with as a test of similarity is quite challenging. However, numerous video features can be exploited. Despite the use of block-based video compression, block edges usually match between adjacent blocks.

Error Concealment Algorithms

Performing error concealment is a challenging task where the decoder has to use as much as possible of the available data in order to reconstruct the missing areas with the highest similarity to the original. Selecting the best approach depends significantly on the type of frame being concealed, as well as on the available information and its reliability. A reliability index is stored into a matrix and is generated as follows.

The first step is to decode all error-free slices and to identify the affected MBs by the lost slices. Immediately, all MBs from correctly-received slices are marked as "Correctly Received", while those MBs belonging to lost slices are marked as "Lost". During the concealment process, MBs are processed column-by-column from the edges of the frame to the center and are marked as "Concealed" when processing is complete. This MB classification serves as a reliability index for the error concealment algorithm, when "Correctly Received" has a higher reliability index than

"Concealed" in terms of accuracy of the information represented.

Figure 6 shows the status of the reliability matrix during the concealment process where some MB have already been processed and marked as "Concealed" in the matrix. Once again, the concealment technique depends on the frame type as described next.

Intra-Frame Error Concealment Algorithms for a Decoder

Reconstructing lost areas in intra-coded frames is usually done using spatial-error concealment. This frame type is not only used periodically to provide synchronization points during the video stream but also at scene cuts. In the latter case, the correlation between the intra-frame being concealed and the previous frame is very low and temporal error concealment techniques are not recommended. Instead, lost slices are concealed by weighted pixel interpolation from correctly decoded slices as illustrated in Figure 7. The central pixel is reconstructed based on a weighted average of the four surrounding pixels shown. The weight for each of the four contributing pixels can be determined based on its inverse distance from the central pixel that is being concealed.

An exception is when streaming video over low bit-rate channels such as 3G mobile networks. Then each video frame is fairly small and is usually encapsulated into a single packet to minimize

Figure 6. MB status map at the decoder

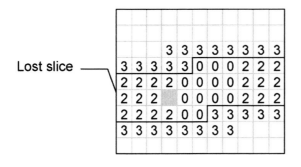

194

Figure 7. Spatial concealment based on weighted pixel averaging (Varsa et al., 2001)

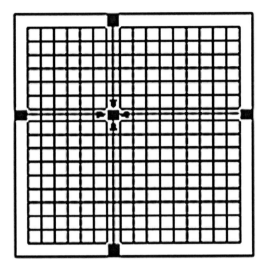

packetization overheads (Bandyopadhyay et al., 2006). In this case, a packet loss corresponds to a lost frame making the concealment of the lost frame area much harder, due to the lack of spatial neighbors from the same frame to assist the reconstruction. Thus, inter-frame error concealment techniques are applied as a last resort to reconstruct the lost frame.

Inter-Frame Error Concealment Algorithms for a Decoder

Concealment in inter-frame is usually more flexible in terms of the available options to reconstruct the missing slices. Previously decoded frames are used to predict the slice being concealed, assuming that there is a high inter-frame correlation.

Frame copy is the most basic and least computational intensive method of concealing errors. The lost slice is reconstructed by simply copying each pixel value from the co-located position of the closest available frame. While being simple to implement, its use should be carefully considered. This method does not take into account any motion activity, therefore it is only recommended for sequences with static and/or low motion activity.

For sequences with higher motion activity, methods exploiting the available motion information data should be used instead.

Motion copy is an enhanced error concealment technique that uses motion data from previous decoded frames to estimate the one being concealed. In a simple approach (Bandyopadhyay et al., 2006)the motion vectors of the correspondent co-located blocks from the nearest available frame are copied to the slice being concealed. Motion vector scaling based on the temporal distance between the frames should also be applied when needed. Then motion compensation is applied to reconstruct the slice. Figure 8 shows the comparison between "Frame Copy" and "Motion Copy" for the *Foreman* test sequence when subject to a 3% packet loss rate.

Other schemes (Varsa et al., 2001) are more elaborate and can also take motion data from correctly received MBs from the frame being concealed. In this case, multiple concealment options exist and only one has to be selected. The best candidate is then selected based on the one which results in the smallest luminance change at the block edges.

ASSESSMENT OF ERROR RESILIENCE TECHNIQUES

Tests were carried out by the authors based on the *Foreman* and *Coastguard* sequences. *Foreman* is a typical sequence taken from a handheld camera, as might appear in YouTube, with a close-up sequence followed by a rapid pan. *Coastguard* is a view of a speeding coastguard boat as might be taken from a surveillance camera. Therefore, both of these sequences illustrate common applications of video streaming, namely the communication of user-generated content from one mobile device to another via a server; and streaming of video from a security camera. These sequences additionally present significant temporal coding complexity, which is a test for any error resilience method,

Figure 8. Comparison of "frame copy", "motion vector copy" and no error cases with "foreman" sequence for average packet loss = 3% (Bandyopadhyay et al., 2006)

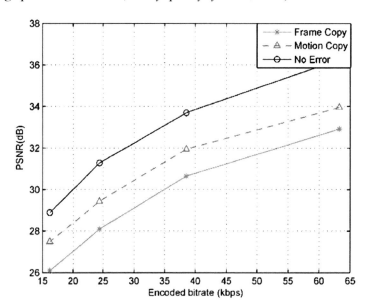

compared to a sequence with limited coding complexity. Both the sequences are of *Quarter Common Intermediate Format (QCIF)* resolution ((176 × 144 pixel/frame) at a frame rate of 15 frames per second (fps) using the JM reference software for H.264/AVC. The CBR target bitrate was 64 kbps, which is a typical rate for 3G systems (Stockhammer et al., 2003).

The relative merits of the error resilience techniques are discussed in this Section. In Figure 9, these techniques are compared against no error resilience (No-Res) for random losses. Clearly, no error resilience is inferior, except when there is a zero packet loss rate, as then the lack of coding overhead for an equivalent datarate results in good quality. Notice that PSNR between 30 and 25 dB is weaker than would normally be accepted in wired Internet streaming but that this quality is generally accepted (Sadka, 2002) by users of mobile devices. Below 25 dB plots are included to show trends but these levels of PSNR would normally be unacceptable for viewing.

When error resilience is added one technique at a time then simple three slices per frame gener-

ally result in the worst quality. Adding intra-coded macroblocks (Int-MB) results in an improvement with two slice checkerboard FMO (FMO-Check) being better still. Two-slice checkerboard FMO combined with intra-coded macroblocks has the best performance followed by three slices combined with intra-coded macroblocks. Again ordering at zero packet loss reflects the relative coding overhead from each technique. In general, it is best to combine at least two error resilience techniques. For random errors, it is important to notice that in these circumstances utilizing checkerboard FMO with larger packet sizes is better than smaller packet sizes with more slices.

CASE STUDY: ERROR RESILIENT STREAM-SWITCHING

Error robustness and high compression are two opposing concepts; increasing one may decrease the other. Therefore, in an adaptive solution, applying error resiliency should be limited to periods

Figure 9. Different error resiliency schemes with random losses for (a) foreman, (b) coastguard video sequences

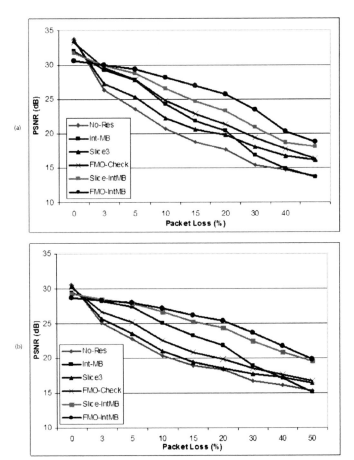

of poor channel conditions in order to increase the average quality of the overall streaming session. To guarantee continuous playback of an acceptable quality, this case study introduces the concept of adaptive selection of robust streams according to packet loss conditions.

Figure 10 is a diagram of the robust adaptive switching system. At the streaming server, a set of pre-encoded videos are stored with varying degrees of error protection through resiliency. After adaptively switched selection of the stream, generic data-link layer FEC is applied before IP packetization and transmission over the wireless packet loss channel. IP packets are aggregated or fragmented into their coding units (see next paragraph) before error detection of remaining errors.

At this point in time, packets are declared lost. If a packet is lost then the process of error concealment (Error Con. in Figure 10) takes place at the decoder, using a previously decoded frame. If no error concealment is possible because of multiple lost frames, previous frame replacement takes place. Otherwise, the usual decoding processes of variable length decoding, de-quantization (Deq.) and inverse transformation applied to the residual predication data.

If a frame is inter-coded then *motion compensation prediction (MCP)* from a previously decoded frame takes place using motion vectors to match the decoded residual data with a previously decoded frame. Upon detection of packet loss, a feedback route exists to the server in the

Figure 10. Switched video stream system for packet loss wireless channels

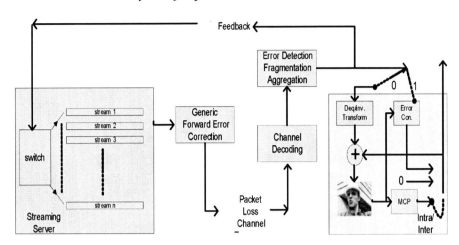

event of a stream switch being required. An application-layer *Negative Acknowledgment (NACK)* from the receiving device to the server is sent.

Tests were carried out again based on the *Foreman* and *Coastguard* sequences. For simulation purposes, the feedback time threshold before switching back to a non-error resilient stream was taken to be five frames or 33 ms for a sequence with 15 fps, though in an implementation this value could be decided by the service provider. When there was no error resiliency or error resiliency without switching then the frame structure was IPPPPP, that is an initial I-frame followed by all P-frames.

In comparing the relative impact of randomly occurring bit errors, a comparison was made between: 1) streaming with no error resilience; 2) streaming with the best of the schemes in Figure 9, FMO with intra-macroblock refresh; and 3) switching ('Switch' in Figure 10) from no error resilience at the start of poor channel conditions to option 2) with error resilience. A period of poor channel conditions with a rate of 10% random packet losses was created. To compare results the same pattern of losses was replicated for all three tests. In Figure 11, the graph is divided into three regions: 1) before a stream switch at frame 50, as no errors occur until frame 45 but there is

a short lag before the switch; 2) after frame 50 when random packet loss occurs; and 3) after frame 100 when no errors occur. The bitrate for all three streams was the same.

Before frame 45, the video quality plots in Figure 11 for no-resilience and switching are identical, with video quality declining once the effect of the initial I-frame has faded. Using error resilience during this period results in worst coding efficiency, because of the overhead involved in providing resilience. When the first packet loss occurs, both the no resilience and switching curves drop in quality but as a result of a switch at frame 50, the video quality of the switched stream recovers. The decoder is resynchronized as a result of the switching frame and consequently the quality becomes equivalent to the protected stream without switching. On entering the good period after frame 100, the video is resynchronized at the decoder. However, the no-resilience stream does not recover in quality for some time, due to error drift caused by the loss of packets during the period of poor channel conditions.

FUTURE RESEARCH DIRECTIONS

There are a number of studies, for example in Lambert et al. (2006) and Dhondt et al., (2007),

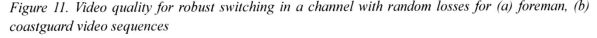

Figure 11. Video quality for robust switching in a channel with random losses for (a) foreman, (b) coastguard video sequences

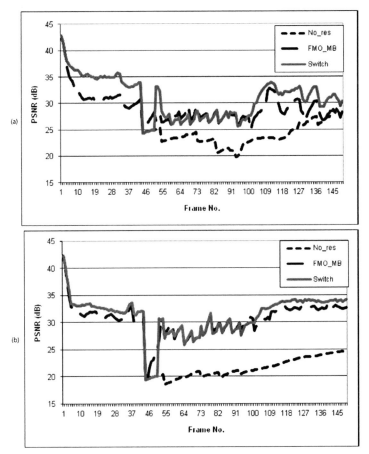

that treat each data partitioning technique on an individual basis. While this approach presents a detailed analysis of the source coding aspects of these techniques it tends to disguise the need to combine the techniques in an error resilience strategy. It is important also to note that choice of error resilience should take into account computational complexity on the mobile device. Another practical issue is whether the codec profile supports a particular error-resilience or error-concealment technique. It is possible to emulate a lower-level profile by a higher-level profile keeping a more complex technique but, otherwise, only employing lower-level techniques. However, this pre-supposes that a higher-level profile such as H.264/AVC's Extended profile has actually been implemented

on the target device. In summary, future research on error resilience can take a holistic approach in which the type of video streaming, the type of target device, and the correct combination of techniques are all considered.

This Chapter has considered single-layer streaming but protection of scalable, multi-layer video is also necessary and provides an interesting future research topic. The *Scalable Video Coding (SVC)* extension to the H.264 standard codec (Schwarz et al., 2007) includes quality or *Signal-to-Noise Ratio (SNR)* scalability, as well as temporal, and spatial scalability. In the case of redundant pictures, H.264/SVC allows the simple duplication of the primary pictures. To indicate the frequency of generating such pictures a *Supplemental Enhancement Information* (SEI) message can be generated within the bitstream. This in turn allows a network node to generate a redundant picture or discard unwanted redundant pictures. Other research also considers generation of reduced resolution redundant pictures using *polyphase downsampling(PD)* (Jia et al., 2007). In (Liu et al., 2009), PD for redundant pictures was combined with SEI messaging with spatial scalability. This resulted in a significant gain in video quality for a full decode with an enhancement layer at CIF resolution and a QCIF resolution base layer. However, application-layer FEC was also applied.

The successor codec to H.264/AVC, known as *High Efficiency Video Codec (HEVC)* (Sullivan and Ohm, 2010), is under active development. It promises significant gains, perhaps eventually over 50%, in coding efficiency over H.264/AVC. At the time of writing, high-definition (1024 × 768 pixel/frame progressive at 24 frame/s) broadcast quality video, i.e. with intra refresh, is reported (Li et al., 2011) as having an average coding gain of 44%, low-delay coding gain for the same resolution is reported to be on average 48% better, while all-Intra frame coding gain is 26%. However, as yet HEVC development has concentrated on compression efficiency and not network aspects, which will no doubt be added by the target finalization date of November 2013. In (Nightingale et al., 2012), a prototype, the Test Model under Consideration (TMuC HM4.0), was evaluated with some additional resiliency features and simple error concealment at the decoder, in a streaming environment in order to establish a benchmarking framework. Improved coding gain increases the need to protect the video stream during streaming if some form of adaptive HTTP streaming is not used. For applications such as video call and video conferencing it is likely that true streaming will be preferred, which increases the need for effective adaptive streaming. For stored video the increased coding efficiency of HEVC implies that higher quality video can be

transported directly by TCP. This is because if TCP needs approximately twice the available bandwidth as its maximum rate to be delivered at video rate, then improved coding efficiency implies high-quality video can be transported in a satisfactory manner, without delays.

CONCLUSION

Far from seeing the demise of broadcast TV, this period in time has seen the growth of networked TV, which implies video streaming. Though multicast and broadcast varieties of TV exist as baseline services, unicast streaming is a greater commercial interest, as it supports value added services such as video-on-demand and TV-on-demand. In the UK, the BBC's iPlayer supports catch-up TV (time-shifted TV) and start-over TV (live programs started at the beginning) as part of its public service. Though, current services use a form of pseudo-streaming in which video is broken up into individual blocks. A block is downloaded while a previous block is displayed. This can lead to interruptions if a block is not ready even when streaming over wired digital subscriber lines (at the end of the network path). The industry appears to have retreated from fully managed IP networks and is again supporting the best-effort Internet. This suggests that better quality video will result from true-streaming schemes which present a continuous bitstream to the target device. When that target device is mobile then extra problems arise in support of robust wireless video streaming.

These developments indicate a greater need for protection against errors. In the H.264/AVC standard, as the Chapter makes clear, a range of error resilience techniques have been thoughtfully provided for this purpose. Error concealment is left as an implementation feature in an H.264/AVC codec but there is no doubt that error concealment works in close cooperation with error resilience. Spatial, temporal, and hybrid methods of error concealment were all considered. The Chapter has reviewed the different methods (data-partitioning, slice structuring, FMO, intra-refresh macroblocks, redundant pictures, SEI messages), showing the relative advantages of each. The intention is that implementers will be able to craft a solution to the undoubtedly heavy error rates that occur during wireless streaming. In fact, the ability to cope with errors may be used to advantage, because the UDP-Lite protocol allows a payload checksum to be turned off so that a decoder can cope with errors as best it can. With the variety of mobile devices, with differing display rates, screen resolutions, memory, and processing capabilities, scalable video seems a likely next step in consumer electronics. Data dependencies exist between the layers due to a compromise made between flexibility and bitrate. This suggests a greater need for error resilience protection in H.264/SVC and investigations are ongoing.

REFERENCES

Ahlswede, R., Cai, N., Li, S.-Y. R., & Yeung, R. W. (2000). Network information flow. *IEEE Transactions on Information Theory*, *46*(4), 1204–1216. doi:10.1109/18.850663

Ahmad, S., Hamzaoui, R., & Al-Akaidi, M. (2007). Robust live unicast video streaming with rateless codes. In *Proceedings of the 16th International Packet Video Workshop*, (pp. 78–84).

Akyildiz, I. F., Melodia, T., & Chowdhury, K. R. (2007). A survey on wireless multimedia sensor networks. *Computer Networks*, *51*, 921–960. doi:10.1016/j.comnet.2006.10.002

Albanese, A., Blömer, J., Edmonds, J., Luby, M., & Sudan, M. (1996). Priority encoding transmission. *IEEE Transactions on Information Theory*, *42*(6), 1737–1744. doi:10.1109/18.556670

Altaf, M., Fleury, M., & Ghanbari, M. (2011). Error resilient video stream switching for mobile wireless channels. *International Journal of Mobile Multimedia*, *7*(3), 216–235.

Baccichet, P., Shantanu, R., & Girod, B. (2006). Systematic lossy error protection based on H. 264/AVC redundant slices and flexible macroblock ordering. *Springer Journal of Zhejiang University-Science A*, *7*(5), 900–909. doi:10.1631/jzus.2006.A0900

Bandyopadhyay, S. K., Wu, Z., Pandit, P., & Boyce, J. M. (2006). An error concealment scheme for entire frame losses for H. 264/AVC. In *IEEE Sarnoff Symposium*, (pp. 1–4).

Barmada, B., Ghandi, M. M., Jones, E. V., & Ghanbari, M. (2005). Prioritized transmission of data-partioned H. 264 video with hierarchical modulation. *IEEE Signal Processing Letters*, *12*(8), 577–580. doi:10.1109/LSP.2005.851261

Bing, B. (2010). *3D and HD broadband video networking*. Norwood, MA: Artech House.

Chao, P. A., & Miao, Z. (2006). Rate-distortion optimized streaming of packetized media. *IEEE Transactions on Multimedia*, *8*(2), 390–404. doi:10.1109/TMM.2005.864313

Conklin, G., Greenbaum, G., Lillevold, K., Lippman, A., & Reznik, Y. (2001). Video coding for streaming media delivery over the Internet. *IEEE Transactions on Circuits and Systems for Video Technology*, *11*(3), 269–281. doi:10.1109/76.911155

Cote, G., Kossentini, F., & Wenger, S. (2001). Error resiliency coding . In Sun, M.-T., & Reibmen, A. R. (Eds.), *Compressed video over networks*. New York, NY: Marcel Deck Inc.

Dhondt, Y., Mys, S., Vermeirsch, K., & Van de Walle, R. (2007). Constrained inter prediction: Removing dependencies between different data partitions. In *Advanced Concepts for Intelligent Visual Systems*, (pp. 720-731).

Ferré, P., Agrafiotis, D., & Bull, D. (2010). A video error resilience redundant slices algorithm and its performance relative to other fixed redundancy schemes. *Image Communication*, *25*(3), 163–178.

Flierl, M., & Girod, B. (2003). Generalized B pictures and the draft H. 264/AVC video compression standard. *IEEE Transactions on Circuits and Systems for Video Technology, 13*(7), 587–597. doi:10.1109/TCSVT.2003.814963

Fragouli, C., & Soljanin, C. (2007). Network coding fundamentals. *Foundations and Trends in Networking, 2*(1), 1–133. doi:10.1561/1300000003

Fu, X., Lei, J., & Shi, L. (2007). *An experimental analysis of Joost peer-to-peer VoD service. Technical Report*. Institute of Computer Science, University of Goettingen.

Ghanbari, M. (2003). *Standard codecs: Image compression to advanced video coding*. London, UK: Institution of Engineering and Technology.

Hamzaoui, R., Stanković, V., & Xiong, Z. (2007). Forward error control for packet loss and corruption . In van der Schaar, M., & Chou, P. A. (Eds.), *Multimedia over IP and wireless networks* (pp. 271–292). Burlington, MA: Academic Press. doi:10.1016/B978-012088480-3/50010-2

Handley, M., Floyd, S., Padhye, J., & Widmer, J. (2003). *TCP friendly rate control (TFRC) protocol specification*. IETF, RFC 3448.

Hannuksela, M. M., Wang, Y.-K., & Gabboj, M. (2004). Isolated regions in video coding. *IEEE Transactions on Multimedia, 6*(2), 259–267. doi:10.1109/TMM.2003.822784

Hossfeld, T., & Leibnitz, K. (2008). A qualitative measurement survey of popular Internet-based IPTV systems. *Second International Conference on Communications and Electronics*, (pp. 156-161).

Jeong, W.-H., Yoon, Y.-S., & Ho, Y.-S. (2004). *Design of asymmetrical reversible variable-length codes and comparison of their robustness*. In European Signal Processing Conference.

Jia, J., Choi, H.-C., Kim, J.-G., Kim, H.-K., & Chang, Y. (2007). Improved redundant picture coding using polyphase downsampling. *ETRI Journal, 29*(1), 18–26. doi:10.4218/etrij.07.0106.0159

Jurdak, R. (2007). *Wireless ad hoc and sensor networks: A cross-layer design perspective*. Berlin, Germany: Springer Verlag.

Karczewicz, M., & Kurceren, R. (n.d.). (J2003). The SP- and SI-frames design for H. 264/AVC. *IEEE Transactions on Circuits and Systems for Video Technology, 13*(7), 637–644. doi:10.1109/TCSVT.2003.814969

Kumar, S., Xu, L., Mandal, M., & Panchanathan, S. (2006). Error resiliency schemes in H. 264/AVC standard. *Journal of Visual Communication and Image Representation, 17*, 425–450. doi:10.1016/j.jvcir.2005.04.006

Lam, W. M., Reibman, A. R., & Liu, B. (1993). Recovery of lost or erroneously received motion vectors. In *IEEE International Conference on Acoustics, Speech, and Signal Processing* (pp. 417–420).

Lambert, P., de Neve, W., Dhondt, Y., & van de Walle, R. (2006). Flexible macroblock ordering in H. 264/AVC. *Journal of Visual Communication, 17*, 358–375.

Lee, I. (2010). A scalable P2P video streaming framework. In A. -E. Hassanien, et al. (Eds.), *Pervasive computing: Innovations in intelligent multimedia and applications* (pp. 341-363), London, UK: Springer Verlag.

Li, B., Sullivan, G. J., & Xu, J. (2011). Comparison of compression performance of HEVC working draft 4 with AVC high profile. In *Proceedings of 7th Meeting of Joint Collaborative Team on Video Coding JCT-VC*, (document no JCTVC-G399-r2).

Lin, S., & Costello, D. J. (2004). *Error control coding* (2nd ed.). Upper Saddle River, NJ: Prentice Hall.

Liu, Y., Guo, Y., & Liang, C. (2008). A survey on peer-to-peer video streaming systems. *Peer-to-Peer Networking and Applications*, *1*(1), 18–28. doi:10.1007/s12083-007-0006-y

Liu, Y., Zhang, S., Xu, S., & Zhang, Y. (2009). H. 264/SVC error resilience strategies for 3G video service. In *International Conference on Image Analysis and Signal Processing*, (pp. 207-211).

Liu, Y., Zhang, S., Xu, S., & Zhang, Y. H. (2005). H. 264/AVC error resilience tools suitable for 3G mobile video services. *Journal of Zhejiang University*, *6*(1), 41–46. doi:10.1631/jzus.2005.AS0041

Liu, Z., Wu, Z., Liu, H., & Stein, A. (2007). A layered hybrid-ARQ scheme for scalable video multicast over wireless networks. In *Proceedings of the Asilomar Conference on Signals, Systems and Computers*, (pp. 914-919).

MacKay, D. (2003). *Information theory, inference, and learning algorithms*. Cambridge, UK: Cambridge University Press.

Melodia, T., & Akyildiz, I. F. (2011). Research challenges for wireless multimedia sensor networks . In Bhahu, B. (Eds.), *Distributed Video Sensor Networks* (pp. 233–246). Berlin, Germany: Springer Verlag. doi:10.1007/978-0-85729-127-1_16

Mohr, A. E., Riskin, E. A., & Ladner, R. E. (2000). Unequal loss protection: Graceful degradation of image quality over packet erasure channels through forward error correction. *IEEE Journal on Selected Areas in Communications*, *18*(6), 819–828. doi:10.1109/49.848236

Nguyen, K., Nguyen, T., & Cheung, S. (2010). Video streaming with network coding. *Journal of Signal Processing Systems for Signal, Image, and Video Technology*, *57*(3), 319–333. doi:10.1007/s11265-009-0342-7

Nguyen, K., & Zakhor, A. (2004). Multiple sender distributed video streaming. *IEEE Transactions on Multimedia*, *6*(2), 315–326. doi:10.1109/TMM.2003.822790

Ostermann, J., Bormans, J., List, P., Marpe, D., Narroschke, M., & Pereira, F. (2004). Video coding with H. 264/AVC: Tools, performance and complexity. *IEEE Circuits and Systems Magazine*, *4*, 7–28. doi:10.1109/MCAS.2004.1286980

Padmanabhan, V., Wang, H., & Chou, P. (2003). Resilient peer-to-peer streaming. *Proceedings of 11th IEEE International Conference on Network Protocols*, (pp. 16- 27).

Pallis, G., & Vakali, A. (2006). Content delivery networks. *Communications of the ACM*, *49*(1), 101–106. doi:10.1145/1107458.1107462

Park, S., & Jeong, S.-H. (2009). Mobile IPTV: Approaches, challenges, standards and QoS support. *IEEE Internet Computing*, *13*(3), 23–31. doi:10.1109/MIC.2009.65

Pelletier, G., & Sandlund, K. (2008). *Robust header compression version 2 (ROHCv2): Profiles for RTP, UDP, IP, ESP and UDP-Lite*. Internet Engineering Task Force, RFC 5225.

Perkins, C. (2003). *RTP: Audio and video for the internet*. Boston, MA: Addison Wesley.

Qadri, N., Fleury, M., Altaf, M., & Ghanbari, M. (2009). Emergency video multi-path transfer over ad hoc wireless networks. *The Journal of Communication*, *4*(5), 324–338.

Qadri, N., Fleury, M., Rofoee, B., Altaf, M., & Ghanbari, M. (2012). Robust P2P multimedia exchange within a VANET. *Wireless Personal Communications, 63*, 561–577. doi:10.1007/s11277-010-0150-1

Rahnavard, N., Vellambi, B. N., & Fekri, F. (2007). Efficient broadcasting via rateless coding in multihop wireless networks with local information. In *Proceedings of the International Wireless Communications and Mobile Computing Conference*, (pp. 85–95).

Rappaport, T. S. (2002). *Wireless communications: Principles and practice* (2nd ed.). Upper Saddle River, NJ: Prentice Hall.

Razavi, R., Fleury, M., & Ghanbari, M. (2008). Unequal protection of video streaming through adaptive modulation with a tri-zone buffer over Bluetooth Enhanced Data Rate. *EURASIP Journal on Wireless Communications and Networking*. Article ID 658794, 16 pages. doi:10.1155/2008/658794

Rejaie, R., Handley, M., & Estrin, D. (1999). RAP: An end-to-end rate-based congestion control mechanism for realtime streams in the Internet. In *Proceedings of the IEEE INFOCOM*, (pp. 1337–1345).

Reza, R. (2006). Anyone can broadcast video over the internet. *Communications of the ACM, 49*(11), 55–57. doi:10.1145/1167838.1167863

Rhee, I., Ozdemir, V., & Yi, T. (2000). *TEAR: TCP emulation at receivers*. Department of Computer Science, NCSU, Technical Report.

Richardson, I. E. G. (2010). *The H. 264 advanced video compression standard*. Chichester, UK: J. Wiley & Sons. doi:10.1002/9780470989418

Rubenstein, D., Kurose, J., & Towsley, D. (1998). *Real-time reliable multicast using proactive forward error correction*. Technical Report 98-19, Dept. of Computer Science, University of Massachusetts, Amherst, MA, 32 pages.

Sadka, A. (2002). *Compressed video communications*. Chichester, UK: J. Wiley & Sons. doi:10.1002/0470846712

Salama, F., Shroff, N. B., & Delp, E. J. (1998). Error concealment in encoded video . In *Image recovery techniques for image compression applications*. Norwell, MA: Kluwer.

Samek, H., Fleury, M., & Ghanbari, M. (2011). Robust video communication for ubiquitous network access. *Journal of Personal and Ubiquitous Computing, 15*(8), 811–820. doi:10.1007/s00779-011-0367-3

Schreier, R. M., & Rothermel, A. (2006). Motion adaptive intra refresh for low-delay video coding. In *International Conference on Consumer Electronics* (pp. 453-454).

Schwarz, H., Marpe, D., & Wiegand, T. (2007). Overview of the scalable video coding extension of the H. 264/AVC standard. *IEEE Transactions in Circuits and Systems for Video Technology, 17*(9), 1103:1120.

Sentinelli, A., Marfia, G., Gerla, M., Kleinrock, L., & Tewari, S. (2007). Will IPTV ride the peer-to-peer stream? *IEEE Communications Magazine, 45*(6), 86–92. doi:10.1109/MCOM.2007.374424

Setton, E., Yoo, T., Xhu, X., Goldsmith, A., & Girod, B. (2005). Cross-layer design of ad-hoc networks for realtime video streaming. *IEEE Wireless Communications Magazine, 12*(4), 59–65. doi:10.1109/MWC.2005.1497859

Shah, P., & Pâris, J. F. (2007). *Peer-to-peer multimedia streaming using BitTorrent* (pp. 340–347). IEEE International Performance, Computing, and Communications Conference.

Shi, Y. Q., & Sun, H. (2008). *Image and video compression for multimedia engineering: Fundamentals, algorithms, and standards* (2nd ed.). Boca Raton, Fl: CRC Press. doi:10.1201/9781420007268

Shokorallahi, A. (2006). Raptor codes. *IEEE Transactions on Information Theory*, *52*(6), 2551–2567. doi:10.1109/TIT.2006.874390

Sisalem, D., & Wolisz, A. (2000). LDA+ TCP-friendly adaptation: A measurement and comparison study. In *Proceedings of the 10th International Workshop on Network and Operating Systems Support for Digital Audio and Video*, (pp. 25-28).

Son, N., & Jeong, S. (2008). An effective error concealment for H. 264/AVC. In IEEE *8th International Conference on Computer and Information Technology Workshops* (pp. 385-390).

Stockhammer, T. (2011). Dynamic adaptive streaming over HTTP – Design principles and standards. In *Proceedings of the Second Annual ACM Conference on Multimedia Systems* (pp. 133-144).

Stockhammer, T., & Bystrom, M. (2004). H. 264/AVC data partitioning for mobile video communication. In *IEEE International Conference on Image Processing* (pp. 545-548).

Stockhammer, T., Hannuksela, M. M., & Wiegand, T. (2003). H. 264/AVC in wireless environments. *IEEE Transactions on Circuits and Systems for Video Technology*, *13*(7), 657–673. doi:10.1109/TCSVT.2003.815167

Stockhammer, T., & Zia, W. (2007). Error-resilient coding and decoding strategies for video communication . In van der Schaar, M., & Chou, P. A. (Eds.), *Multimedia over IP and wireless networks* (pp. 13–58). Burlington, MA: Academic Press. doi:10.1016/B978-012088480-3/50003-5

Sullivan, G., & Wiegand, T. (2005). Video compression — From concepts to the H. 264/AVC standard. *Proceedings of the IEEE*, *93*, 18–31. doi:10.1109/JPROC.2004.839617

Sullivan, G. J., & Ohm, J.-R. (2010). Recent developments in standardization of high efficiency video coding (HEVC). In *Proceedings of SPIE Applications of Digital Image Processing XXXIII*, *7798*, paper no. 7798-30.

Tan, D. M., & Wu, H. R. (2006). Perceptual image coding . In Wu, H. R., & Rao, K. R. (Eds.), *Digital image quality and perceptual coding*. Boca Raton, FL: CRC Press.

Tan, W., & Zakhor, A. (1999). Multicast transmission of scalable video using layered FEC and scalable compression. *IEEE Transactions on Circuits and Systems for Video Technology*, *11*(3), 373–386. doi:10.1109/76.911162

Taubman, D. S., & Marcellin, M. W. (2002). *JPEG2000: Image compression fundamentals, standards, and practice*. Boston, MA: Kluwer. doi:10.1007/978-1-4615-0799-4

Thomos, N., Argyropoulos, S., Boulgouris, N., & Strintzis, M. (2005). Error-resilient transmission of H. 264/AVC streams using flexible macroblock ordering. In *Second European Workshop on the Integration of Knowledge, Semantic, and Digital Media Techniques* (pp. 183-189).

van der Schaar, M. (2007). Cross-layer wireless multimedia . In van der Schaar, M., & Chou, P. A. (Eds.), *Multimedia over IP and wireless networks* (pp. 337–408). Burlington, MA: Academic Press. doi:10.1016/B978-012088480-3/50013-8

van der Schaar, M., Krishnamachari, S., Choi, S., & Xu, X. (2003). Adaptive cross-layer protection strategies for robust scalable video transmission over 802. 11 WLANs. *IEEE Journal on Selected Areas in Communications*, *21*(10), 1751–1763. doi:10.1109/JSAC.2003.815231

Varsa, V., Hannuksela, M. M., & Wang, Y. K. (2001). *Non-normative error concealment algorithms*. VCEG-N62, 14th Meeting: Santa Barbara, CA, USA, 21-24 September, 2001.

Vukobratovic, D., Stankovic, V., Sejdinovic, D., Stankovic, L., & Ziong, Z. (2008). Expanding window Fountain codes for scalable video multicast. In *Proceedings of IEEE International Conference on Multimedia and Expo*, (pp. 77–80).

Wah, B. W., Su, X., & Lin, D. (2000). A survey of error concealment schemes for real-time audio and video transmissions over the Internet. In *IEEE International Symposium on Multimedia Software Engineering* (pp. 17-24).

Wang, B., Kurose, J. F., Shenoy, P. J., & Towsley, D. F. (2004). Multimedia streaming via TCP: An analytic performance study. In *Proceedings of ACM Multimedia Conference* (pp. 908-915).

Wang, Y., & Zhu, Q. (1998). Error control and concealment for video communication: A review. *Proceedings of the IEEE, 86*, 974–997. doi:10.1109/5.664283

Wenger, S. (2003). H. 264/AVC over IP. *IEEE Transactions on Circuits and Systems for Video Technology, 13*(7), 645–656. doi:10.1109/TCSVT.2003.814966

Wicker, S. (1995). *Error control systems for digital communication and storage*. Upper Saddle River, NJ: Prentice Hall.

Widmer, J., Denda, R., & Mauve, M. (2001). A survey on TCP-friendly congestion control. *IEEE Network, 15*(3), 28–37. doi:10.1109/65.923938

Wiegand, T., Färber, N., Stuhlmuller, K., & Girod, B. (2003a). Error resilient video transmission using long-term memory motion compensated prediction. *IEEE Journal on Selected Areas in Communications, 18*(6), 1050–1056. doi:10.1109/49.848255

Wiegand, T., Sullivan, G. J., Bjontegaard, G., & Luthra, A. (2003). Overview of the H. 264/AVC video coding standard. *IEEE Transactions on Circuits and Systems for Video Technology, 13*(7), 560–576. doi:10.1109/TCSVT.2003.815165

Wiegand, T., Zhang, X., & Girod, B. (1999). Long-term memory motion-compensated prediction. *IEEE Transactions on Circuits and Systems for Video Technology, 9*(1), 70–84. doi:10.1109/76.744276

Witterman, R., & Zitterbart, M. (2001). *Multicast communication: Protocols and applications*. San Francisco, CA: Morgan Kaufmann.

Zhang, J., Liu, L., Ramaswamy, L., & Pu, C. (2008). PeerCast: Churn-resilient end system multicast on heterogeneous overlay networks. *Journal of Network and Computer Applications, 31*(4), 821–850. doi:10.1016/j.jnca.2007.05.001

Zhang, X., Liu, J., Li, B., & Yum, Y.-S. P. (2005). CoolStreaming/DONet: A data-driven overlay network for peer-to-peer live media streaming. *Proceedings of the 24th Annual Joint Conference of the IEEE Computer and Communications Societies (INFOCOM)*, (pp. 2102-2111).

Zhu, C., Wang, Y. K., Hannuksela, M., & Li, H. (2006). Error resilient video coding using redundant pictures. In *IEEE International Conference on Image Processing* (pp. 801–804).

ADDITIONAL READING

Fleury, M., & Qadri, N. (Eds.). (2012). *Streaming media with peer-to-peer networks: Wireless perspectives*. Hershey, PA: IGI Global. doi:10.4018/978-1-4666-1613-4

Hantanong, W., & Aramvith, S. (2005). Analysis of macroblock-to-slice group mapping for H. 264 video transmission over packet-based wireless fading channel. *45th Mid-West Symposium on Circuits and Systems*, (pp. 1541-1544).

Ho, T., & Lun, D. S. (2009). *Network coding: An introduction*. Cambridge, UK: Cambridge University Press.

Lee, J. B., & Kalva, H. (2008). *The VC-1 and H. 264 video compression standards for broadband video services*. New York, NY: Springer Verlag. doi:10.1007/978-0-387-71043-3

Marpe, D., Wiegand, T., & Sullivan, G. V. (2006). The H. 264/MPEG4 advanced video coding standard and its applications. *IEEE Communications Magazine, 44*(8), 134–142. doi:10.1109/MCOM.2006.1678121

Ngan, K. N., Yap, C. W., & Tan, K. T. (2001). *Video coding for wireless communication systems.* New York, NY: Marcel Dekker Inc.

Schaar, van der S., & Chou, P. A. (Eds.). (2007). *Multimedia over wireless networks: Compression, networking, and systems.* Burlington, MA: Academic Press.

Wang, Y., Ostermann, J., & Zhang, Y.-Q. (2002). *Video processing and communications.* Upper Saddle River, NJ: Prentice Hall.

ENDNOTES

1. Entropy coding is a lossless form of data compression.
2. The DCT is now replaced by a reversible integer transform in an H.264/AVC codec to avoid arithmetical inaccuracies during the inverse transform.
3. Because of the cumulative effect of VLC, symbols nearer the slice synchronization marker suffer less from errors than those that appear later in a bitstream.

Chapter 8
Resilient Video Coding via Improved Motion Compensated Prediction

Sunday Nyamweno
McGill University, Canada

Ramdas Satyan
McGill University, Canada

Fabrice Labeau
McGill University, Canada

ABSTRACT

Motion compensated prediction (MCP) is at the heart of modern video compression standard because of its ability to remove temporal redundancies. However, MCP is responsible for temporal error propagation, which can result in severe quality degradation in lossy environments. In this chapter, the authors present two innovative methods of improving MCP to be more resilient to packet losses. In the first method, the motion trajectory is used to develop a novel distortion weighting technique, and the second method exploits the presence of Intra macroblocks in previously coded frames to develop increase robustness.

INTRODUCTION

Digital video communication is a rapidly growing industry accelerated by increased consumer mobility. Robust video compression that potentially withstands varied network conditions has been at the forefront of research in both academia and industry. H.264/AVC is the latest international video coding standard(Wiegand, Sullivan, Bjontegaard, & Luthra, 2003; Richardson, 2003). It has achieved a significant improvement in compression performance compared to the previous standards (up to 50% higher compression efficiency) and provides a network friendly representation of video for a variety of applications including, video telephony, broadcasting and storage. When transmitting H.264/AVC compressed bitstreams through unreliable channels, a mismatch between the encoder and decoder predictions caused by packet losses results in errors spreading both spatially and temporally due to Motion Compensated Prediction (MCP). Error resilient tools are

DOI: 10.4018/978-1-4666-2660-7.ch008

therefore necessary to mitigate the effects of the spatio-temporal error spread.

In this chapter we study the behavior of a motion-compensated predictive video encoder, with the aim of improving its error resilience. After reviewing the principles of error resilience in video communications over lossy networks as well as some existing techniques, we will suggest two methods of improving the performance of compressed video in error prone environments. The first method is a procedure for weighting the distortion used in rate-distortion optimized video coding and the second method alters the reference frames used in predictive coding to generate a bitstream that is robust to transmission errors. Through simulations, we demonstrate that the weighted distortion technique is able to achieve performance comparable to current state of the art techniques, but without the assumptions made by existing schemes. Our second method improves on the performance of current reference frame altering techniques by up to 1.0 dB and also presents subjective video quality improvements.

BACKGROUND

Error Resilient (ER) video coding approaches can be classified into 3 broad categories: encoder, decoder and encoder/decoder co-operation techniques, which are summarized below,

1. **Encoder:** These methods involve adding redundancy at source coder, channel coder or both. Bitstream prioritization (Turletti & Huitema, 1996; Zhu, 1997; Sun & Zdepsky, 1994), and Forward Error Correction (FEC) (Chou, Mohr, Wang, & Mehrotra, 2001; Tan & Zakhor, 2001; R. Zhang, Regunathan, & Rose, 2001) fall into this category. Also some interesting work has been done on error resilient techniques that exploit channel characteristics. The main technologies are based on path diversity (Apostolopoulos,

Wong, Tan, & Wee, 2002; Nguyen & Zakhor, 2002; Padmanabhan, Wang, & Chou, 2003), network coding (Chou, Wu, & Jain, 2003; Wu, Chou, & Kung, 2005) and cross-layer design/optimization (Wu, Chou, Zhang, et al., 2005; Setton, Yoo, Zhu, Goldsmith, & Girod, 2005).

2. **Decoder:** These methods are also known as error concealment. Despite the use of encoder techniques to protect the video bitstream, some errors or losses may escape/penetrate encoder protections and cause a perceptual degradation of received video quality. Hence it is necessary for the decoder to perform error concealment. Most of these techniques exploit either spatial (Aign & Fazel, 1995; Wang, Zhu, & Shaw, 1993; Sun & Kwok, 1995) or temporal correlations (Aravind, Civanlar, & Reibman, 1996; Wang & Zhu, 1998; Wang, Wenger, Wen, & Katsaggelos, 2000; Lam, Reibman, & Liu, 1993; Lu, Lieu, Letaief, & Chuang, 1998) in order to predict the erroneous pixels.

3. **Encoder/Decoder:** ARQ methods fall into this category (Podolsky, McCanne, & Vetterli, 2001; Chou & Miao, 2006; Miao & Ortega, 2002). A better approach adjusts the encoder prediction upon receiving channel feedback to send a correcting signal that is able to update the decoder prediction to match that in the encoder (Girod & Farber, 1999; Chang & Lee, 2000). These methods may not be suitable for low delay applications such as video telephony.

This chapter is focused on improved source coding, which falls in the "Encoder" category defined above. Therefore, we now highlight the error resilient tools present in the H.264/AVC standard, followed by a discussion of rate distortion optimized (RDO) video coding, along with an exploration of current state-of-the-art end-to-end RDO techniques.

ERROR RESILIENCY TOOLS IN H.264/AVC

When transmitting through unreliable channels, a mismatch between the encoder and decoder predictions due to packet losses causes the error to extend as prescribed by motion vectors. Error resilient tools are therefore necessary to mitigate the effects of the spatio-temporal error spread due to motion vectors. H.264/AVC includes the following tools to combat transmission errors:

1. Intra Updating
2. Picture segmentation (slices)
3. Multiple reference frames
4. Redundant slices (RS)
5. Flexible macroblock ordering (FMO)
6. Data partitioning

These tools are discussed in detail in the following sections. It is important to note that while these tools offer some level of protection to the compressed bitstream, they do not fundamentally change the encoding process to be error resilient. In Section 3, we will present two methods that improve the encoding process to be robust to network losses.

Intra Updating

Intra coding is one of the most effective ways of terminating the error spread because it does not rely on information contained in previous frames (Girod & Farber, 1999). Therefore, error resilience can be achieved by using more Intra macroblocks (or I MBs) in a video frame. For example, an extreme case would be coding the entire frame as an Intra frame (all MBs coded as Intra) which would stop the error propagation instantly. This approach is not advisable because it would result in an enormous increase in bitrate. A better approach is to code only a percentage of the MBs in a frame as Intra. This technique is commonly referred to as Intra Updating or Intra Refresh.

One of the new features in H.264/AVC that improves compression efficiency is intra coding using spatial prediction. This feature allows Intra MBs to predict from nearby Inter MBs (or P MBs). However, in an error prone environment errors in Inter MBs can propagate into Intra MBs. This eliminates the ability of an Intra macroblock to terminate error propagation. The work presented in this chapter and similar work that relies on Intra MBs to eliminate error propagation disable this feature[1](Stockhammer, Hannuksela, & Wiegand, 2003; Hannuksela, 2009).

Slice Structuring

Picture segmentation is achieved by grouping an integer number of MBs together to form a slice. Each slice may contain an entire frame or only one MB and is usually transmitted independently in a packet. The primary reason for implementing slices is to allow for the adaptation of the coded slice size to the maximum transmission unit (MTU) size of the network (Wiegand et al., 2003). This allows H.264/AVC to easily adapt to different network conditions.

For transmission of video in wireless environments it is common to encode a row of macroblocks in one slice (Y. Zhang, Gao, Lu, Huang, & Zhao, 2007; He & Xiong, 2006). This method is preferred to encoding an entire frame in one slice because the loss of a packet will result in only a portion of the frame rather than the entire frame being corrupted. H.264/AVC also provides provisions for *slice interleaving*. This means that slices from different frames will arrive in an order other than the display order. Slice interleaving is useful in the presence of burst errors as it would spread the error across multiple frames(Kumar, Xu, Mandal, & Panchanathan, 2006). However, this incurs a delay at the decoder as it waits for out of order slices and therefore is ill-suited for low-delay applications.

Multiple Reference Frames

H.264/AVC uses multiple reference frames for improving the compression efficiency, but it is also useful as an error resilience tool. The presence of older reference frames has been used in a feedback system for error resilience. In this scheme, the decoder sends back positive (ACK) or negative (NACK) acknowledgments allowing the encoder to select older acknowledged frames for reference (Wiegand, Farber, Stuhlmuller, & Girod, 2000). Multiple reference frames have also been used for error resilience in multi-hypothesis motion compensated prediction (MHMCP). MHMCP uses a linear combination of multiple signals or MBs (also termed hypotheses) to predict an MB. It was originally developed to improve the compression efficiency compared to single hypothesis MCP (Girod, 2000). It has an inherent resilience property, whereby error propagation is reduced by performing prediction from several hypothesis.

Redundant Slices (RS)

Redundant slices permit the insertion of one or more duplicate representations of the same macroblocks in one slice directly into the bitstream. The difference between this approach and packet repetition at the link layer is that the redundant representation can be coded at a lower fidelity. For example, the primary slice may be generated using a lower quantization parameter (QP) (good quality) and the redundant slice can be coded at a higher QP (low quality) (Stockhammer et al., 2003). When the primary slices of a frame are received correctly, the decoder discards all the redundant slices in the bitstream associated with the frame. On the other hand, if any of the primary slices contains error or is lost, the decoder can use a correctly decoded redundant slice to replace the corrupted slice, thus minimizing the drifting phenomenon. It should be noted that this approach cannot completely eliminate error propagation, unless the redundant slice are coded at the same fidelity as the primary slice and both primary and redundant slices are not lost.

Flexible Macroblock Ordering (FMO)

The macroblock to slice mapping is usually selected in raster scan fashion. FMO allows for different MB to slice mappings that can help the error resiliency of H.264/AVC. The spatial distribution of MBs suggested by FMO means that when a slice is lost, errors are spread over the entire frame, thereby avoiding error accumulation in certain regions. This improves the error concealment performance if the MBs surrounding a lost MB are received correctly. New MB to slice mappings are constantly being developed that show some improvement to those specified in the H.264/AVC standard (Katz, Greenberg, Yarkoni, Blaunstien, & Giladi, 2007; Ogunfunmi & Huang, 2005). FMO basically rearranges MB locations, and does not fundamentally change the encoding process as proposed in this chapter.

Data Partitioning

All the information necessary to decode a MB is usually contained in a single bitstream. Data partitioning places this data in three separate partitions: A, B and C.

- **Partition A:** Contains header information for the slice and for all MBs in the slice. This includes MB types, motion vectors, quantization parameters, etc.
- **Partition B:** Contains residual data for I MBs.
- **Partition C:** Contains residual data for P MBs.

Partition A is the most important because both Partitions B and C require this header information. It is therefore common to offer extra protection to Partition A through Unequal Error Protection

(UEP) (Ghandi, Barmada, Jones, & Ghanbari, 2006; Harmanci & Tekalp, 2004). Partition B is also more important than Partition C because I MBs are able to eliminate error propagation along the motion prediction path as mentioned in Section 2.1.1. Data Partitioning allows for higher quality decoder reconstruction if Partitions A or B have a higher probability of arriving uncorrupted.

RATE DISTORTION OPTIMIZATION FOR VIDEO

For the remainder of this chapter, we will refer to $F(n,i)$ as the i'th pixel in the n'th frame of the original video sequence. $\hat{F}(n,i)$ will refer to the reconstructed value of the pixel at the encoder. This is the same as the decoder reconstruction when there are no transmission errors. $\tilde{F}(n,i)$ will refer to the decoder reconstructed value (possibly with transmission errors). $D_s(n)$ will refer to the source coding distortion and $D_t(n)$ will refer to the transmission distortion. Mean squared error (MSE) will be used as the distortion criterion. The transmission distortion and source distortion are defined as

$$D_t(n) = E\{[\hat{F}(n,i) - \tilde{F}(n,i)]^2\}$$

and

$$D_s(n) = E\{[F(n,i) - \hat{F}(n,i)]^2\}$$

respectively. The end-to-end expected distortion per pixel is defined as

$$D(n,i) = E\{|F(n,i) = \tilde{F}(n,i)|^2\} \qquad (1)$$

The rate-distortion efficiency of today's video compression schemes is based on a sophisticated interaction between a variety of coding choices. The encoder has to choose from coding options

such as motion vector, quantization level, block size, prediction mode, reference frame, etc. Coding mode selection is complicated by the fact that different coding choices have varying efficiency at different bitrates or reproduction quality. Different scene content require different coding options. For example, static background would benefit from the SKIP[2] coding option while finer motion activity may require smaller block sizes and several motion vectors. The encoder's task can thus be summarized as: *Minimize distortion D, subject to the constraint R_c on number of bits R* (Sullivan & Wiegand, 1998). This is a constrained minimization problem

$$\min D \text{ subject to } R < R_c \qquad (2)$$

commonly solved using Lagrangian optimization. Each macroblock therefore undergoes Lagrangian minimization to find the optimal coding mode o^*, according to

$$o^* = \arg \min_{o \in O} D(o) + \lambda \cdot R(o) \qquad (3)$$

where O is the set of all coding options, {modes, motion vectors, reference frames, block-sizes}. Calculating (2) for all possible combinations of coding options O is not practical. In the H.264/AVC test model, this problem is simplified by breaking down the Lagrangian minimization into 2 steps: motion estimation followed by mode decision (Stockhammer et al., 2003).

During motion estimation, motion vectors are selected to minimize the Lagrangian cost functional

$$J_{me} = D_{SAD} + \lambda_{me}(QP) \cdot R \qquad (4)$$

where $\lambda_{me}(QP)$ is the Lagrange multiplier that depends on the quantization parameter QP and R_{mv} denotes the number of bits required to code the motion vectors and D_{SAD} is the sum of absolute difference distortion measure between the reference and current MB. Two other distortion measures are available in the reference software for motion estimation: 1) Sum of squared errors (SSE) and 2) Sum of Absolute Transformed/Hadamard Differences (SATD), with SAD offering reduced complexity compared to SSE and SATD ((JVT), 2009). Motion estimation is a very time consuming operation as the motion vectors have to be calculated for different block sizes. It is common to restrict the spatial search range to a certain radius in order to speed up the operation. Even faster motion estimation algorithms have been proposed that use novel search patterns to narrow the number of candidate motion vectors (Zhu, Lin, & Chau, 2002).

Once optimal motion vectors are determined, the encoder then selects the best coding mode (with different block sizes) {inter4x4, inter8x8,...,inter16x16, skip, intra4x4,...,intra16x16} according to

$$J_{md} = D_{SSD} + \lambda_{md}(QP) \cdot R \qquad (5)$$

where the sum of squared differences (D_{SSD}) is used as the distortion measure and the Lagrangian multiplier for mode decision is given by,

$$\lambda_{me}(QP) = 0.85 \times 2.0^{(QP-12)/3}$$

The Lagrange multiplier for motion estimation is given by

$$\lambda_{me}(QP) = \sqrt{\lambda_{md}(QP)} \ .$$

Selecting coding options in this manner is optimal only if the distortion used in the encoder is identical to that used in the decoder. When transmission errors occur, a mismatch exists between the encoder and decoder predictions, therefore the encoder and decoder distortions do not match and rate distortion optimization (RDO) as described above is no longer optimal. The quest for RDO techniques specifically designed for

video in lossy environments has ushered a field of research in *error robust - rate distortion optimization* (ER-RDO) (Stockhammer, Kontopodis, & Wiegand, 2002; Cote, Shirani, & Kossentini, 2000; Stockhammer et al., 2003; Y. Zhang et al., 2007; Harmanci & Tekalp, 2007; R. Zhang, Regunathan, & Rose, 2000; Wan & Izquierdo, 2007). The main premise behind ER-RDO techniques is to obtain a suitable estimate of the overall end-to-end distortion. Once a suitable end-to-end distortion estimate D_{est} is found, three options have been proposed: replacing D_{SSD} in (4) with D_{est}, replacing D_{SAD} in (3) with D_{est}, or both. The Lagrangian parameter λ may also be adjusted to reflect the channel's lossy nature (Stockhammer et al., 2002; Harmanci & Tekalp, 2007).

ER-RDO Mode Decision

We mentioned in Section 2.1.1 that inserting Intra MBs is an effective way of terminating error propagation, therefore finding the optimal allocation of Intra MBs has historically been the focus of most of the ER-RDO schemes. Numerous error-resilient RDO methods have been proposed for mode decision (Stockhammer et al., 2002; Cote et al., 2000; R. Zhang et al., 2000; Y. Zhang et al., 2007) and will be discussed in Section 2.3. In these instances, RD optimized mode decision is performed with a suitable estimate of the end-to-end distortion. Mode decisions will therefore take into account the potential loss of packets. These methods are considerably simpler to implement than ER-RDO Motion Estimation techniques because there are fewer options to go through.

ER-RDO Motion Estimation

It is important to also look at the RD optimization of motion vectors because Inter modes usually offer increased compression efficiency compared to Intra modes and the fact that Inter prediction is responsible for error propagation. This makes finding effective motion vectors in lossy environments very important.

Motion vector optimization in lossy environments has been studied by Yang and Rose (Yang & Rose, 2005) and later by Wan and Izquierdo (Wan & Izquierdo, 2007). Both methods use the recursive optimal per-pixel estimate (ROPE) (R. Zhang et al., 2000) to estimate the end-to-end distortion. Due to the random nature of transmission errors, ROPE treats the decoder reconstructed pixels as random variables and attempts to model the transmission distortion at the encoder in a statistical sense. This value of distortion is then used to optimize the motion vectors in an RD framework. ROPE is discussed in greater detail in Section 2.3.3. In contrast, our weighted distortion method looks forward at the impact of each MB in future frames, and uses this information in a novel manner to improve the motion vector selection.

END-TO-END DISTORTION ESTIMATION

Most of the existing work on error resilient video coding is based on the encoder estimating the expected distortion incurred at the decoder, and using this distortion for RD optimized coding mode selection. The main challenge in accurately determining the distortion incurred at the decoder due to losses is developing an accurate model of the transmission errors at the encoder. In this section, we present the available techniques for estimating end-to-end distortion.

Block Weighted Distortion Estimate (BWDE)

BWDE by Cote et al. (Cote et al., 2000) represents some of the earliest work in obtaining an estimate of the overall end-to-end distortion. The distortion estimate is computed recursively on an MB basis, as a weighted average of the concealment distortion. It should be noted that this method assumes

that the current block is received accurately and considers whether the previous block was lost and concealed. This simple technique ignores the error propagation associated with temporal error concealment and is therefore not very accurate.

K-Decoders

This is a highly complex but accurate distortion estimation procedure that relies on implementing K decoders in the encoder (Stockhammer et al., 2002) and has been incorporated in the H.264/AVC test model ((JVT), 2009; Stockhammer et al., 2003) for addressing ER-RDO. It assumes the encoder has K copies of the random variable channel behavior, $C(k)$, and averages these to determine the end-to-end distortion.

$$D(n,i) = \frac{1}{K} \sum_{k=1}^{K} \left| F(n,i) - \left(\tilde{F}(n,i) \mid C(k) \right) \right|^2$$

(6)

As $K \to \infty$ the encoder is able to obtain the expected distortion at the encoder. However, the complexity of this method increases as K increases. It has been suggested that $K=30$ is suitable for most applications and very accurate results have been reported for $K=500$ (Y. Zhang et al., 2007). The computational complexity and implementation cost prevent this method from being used in practice, especially for large values of K.

Recursive Optimal Per-Pixel Estimate (ROPE)

ROPE was initially developed to determine the optimal Intra rate for an error prone environment (R. Zhang et al., 2000) and is widely cited as an industry benchmark in the field of distortion estimation. ROPE works by tracking the distortion at the pixel level. Due to the random nature of transmission errors, this method treats the decoder reconstructed value as a random variable and attempts to model the transmission distortion at the encoder in a statistical sense (R. Zhang et al., 2000). By expanding (1) as follows,

$$D(n,i) = [F(n,i)]^2 + 2F(n,i) \\ + E\{\tilde{F}(n,i)\} + E\{[\tilde{F}(n,i)]^2\} \tag{7}$$

ROPE develops estimates for the first order $E\{\tilde{F}(n,i)\}$ and second order moments $E\{[\tilde{F}(n,i)]^2\}$. These estimates result in accurate distortion estimate when motion vectors with integer accuracy are used. However it is computationally intensive since it involves tracking the two moments at every pixel. It is also not applicable to subpixel motion estimation used in H.264/AVC. Improvements to the ROPE algorithm for subpixel motion estimation have been made using cross-correlation estimates (Yang & Rose, 2010) and using a 6-tap filter on the first moment and on the square root of the second moment of the reconstructed pixel value (Y. Zhang et al., 2007).

Distortion Map

Another recursive approach based on creating an error propagation distortion map has been suggested by Zhang et. al. (Y. Zhang et al., 2007). A distortion map D_{ep} is defined for each frame on a block basis. Since Intra macroblocks terminate error propagation, Intra pixel i, of frame n have a $D_{ep}(n,i)$ value of zero. The first frame is coded as an Intra frame and therefore has $D_{ep} = 0$ and subsequent Inter frames obtain their D_{ep} value recursively from the previous frames D_{ep}:

$$D_{ep}(n,i) = (1-p)D_{ep}(ref, j) + pD_{ec\_r}(n,i) + \\ pD_{ep}(n-1, k) \tag{8}$$

where *ref* is the reference frame index, and $D_{ec\_r}(n,i)$ is the reconstructed frame error concealment, which is the MSE between the reconstructed and error concealment pixel at the encoder. Complete derivations of these quantities can be found in (Y.

Zhang et al., 2007). This method has been included in the H.264/SVC[3] JSVM reference software as the ER-RDO technique of choice ((JVT), 2010).

Stochastic Frame Buffers (SFB)

Recursion is the common theme in all the solutions presented thus far, and the stochastic frame buffer approach of Harmanci and Tekalp (Harmanci & Tekalp, 2007) follows suit. The derivation of this method is identical to ROPE in Section 2.3.3, except that this method does not store the actual pixel values of the reference frame. In ROPE, the end-to-end distortion estimate is obtained from the 1st and 2nd moments of each pixel and used in mode decision only. In contrast, this method stores these moments in stochastic frame buffers and uses them for residual calculation, motion estimation and mode decision. The SFB replaces the regular frame buffer, therefore the actual pixel values are no longer needed.

Residual-Motion-Propagation-Correlation (RMPC) Distortion Estimation

Recently the importance non-linear clipping noise in distortion estimation has been investigated. Transmission errors cause the decoder to approximate pixel values at the decoder which may include clipping noise that may be ignored by other distortion estimation methods (Chen & Wu, 2010)

RMPC was developed for estimating frame level transmission distortions (RMPC-FTD) and pixel level transmission distortions (RMPC-PTD) at the encoder as a non-linear time variant function of frame statistics, system parameters and channel statistics (Chen & Wu, 2010) In deriving their model, Chen and Wu assume that data partitioning is employed so that residual information is sent separate packets from motion vector information. Using UEP in order to improve the likelihood of receiving motion vector packets can potentially improve the error resilience performance as it allows the decoder to perform better error concealment. This approach is slightly different from the methods described above, which assume residual information is lost along with motion vector information. The resulting end to end distortion for RMPC-PTD takes on the following general form.

$$D(n,i) = D_{RCE}(n,i) + D_{MVCE}(n,i) + D_{prop}(n,i) + D_{corr}(n,i) \qquad (9)$$

where $D_{RCE}(n,i)$ is the residual concealment error (RCE), $D_{MVCE}(n,i)$ is the motion vector concealment error MVCE, $D_{prop}(n,i)$ is the propagated error plus clipping noise, and $D_{corr}(n,i)$ represents correlations between RCE and MCVE. This distortion decomposition facilitates the derivation of a simple closed-form formula for each of the four distortion terms.

This is different than the ROPE algorithm which estimates the first and second moments of the decoder reconstructed pixel mainly because it considers clipping noise at the decoder when estimation $D(n,i)$. Clipping noise in the distortion estimation process is shown by the authors to have a significant impact on the distortion estimate.

REFERENCE FRAME MODIFICATION

Similar to prior video coding standards, H.264/AVC standardizes only the decoding process by imposing restrictions on the bitstream and syntax. This gives the designer maximum freedom in encoder implementation and guarantees that every conforming decoder will produce similar output when given an H.264/AVC compliant bitstream (Wiegand et al., 2003). The end-to-end distortion estimation techniques presented in Section 2.3 and our weighted distortion technique presented in Section 3.1 are encoder based techniques and therefore result in a standard compliant bitstream. However, given the freedom to redesign both the encoding and decoding process, significant error

resilient performance is possible. Reference Frame Modification (RFM) achieves this by introducing some predictability (or leakage) into the prediction mechanism. In the following sub-section we will review two existing RFM techniques: Leaky Prediction and Generalized Source Channel Prediction (GSCP).

Conventional Prediction

Video coding standards generally adopt the classical predictive quantization framework. Therefore the reference frame used to predict the next frame, $n + 1$ can be described as

$$\tilde{F}_n = \hat{F}_n \qquad (10)$$

where $\hat{F}_n$ represents the encoder reconstruction of frame n and $\tilde{F}_n$ represents the reference for input video frame $n + 1$.

This ensures that the encoder and decoder reference frames are identical during error free transmission. In addition, using only the previous reconstructed frame as the reference provides for high coding efficiency and low complexity video compression. However, during transmission in error prone networks an appropriate amount of error resilience is required to combat channel errors effectively. The methods presented below make predictive coding less susceptible to errors by modifying the reference frame $\tilde{F}_n$.

Leaky Prediction

Leaky prediction achieves error resilience by introducing a scaling factor to the current reconstructed frame. The use of scaled prediction coefficients enables exponential decay of propagated errors. The general description for leaky prediction is given as

$$\tilde{F}_n = \hat{F}_n + (1 - \alpha)K \qquad (11)$$

where α is the leaky factor which scales the reconstructed frame $\hat{F}_n$ and K is a constant. The constant K is often assumed zero but for video coding where pixels range from 0 to 255, the mid-gray signal level 128 is a typical choice (Yang & Rose, 2006). The leaky factor α takes a value between 0 and 1. The scaling of the reconstructed frame by α implies that errors introduced in earlier video frames $\hat{F}_{n-j}$ get scaled by α^j which lead to an exponential decay of past errors (Huang, Wang, & Chiang, 2002).

The leaky factor controls the trade off between coding efficiency and error resilience. Due to the high correlation between consecutive video frames it has been observed that prediction with a leaky factor which is significantly below 1 generally compromises the overall performance as predicting from a constant value K is less efficient than predicting from a similar signal. There is a high bitrate penalty with an insufficient gain in PSNR. This is shown in Figure 1, where for different values of α the increase in bitrate is plotted against the gain obtained in PSNR. The sequences and all subsequent simulations were encoded using the *IPPP...* format, where the first frame is Intra coded, and all subsequent frames are Inter coded. We can observe that a tradeoff exists between resilience and efficiency, as lower values of α result in increased error resilience performance at the expense of higher bit rates. α usually takes a value around 0.9 to 0.95. For values of α less than 0.9, the bitrate increase is unjustifiable.

Figure 1. Gain in PSNR vs. percentage increase in bitrate curves for (a) foreman and (b) mother daughter QCIF sequences at 15 fps and a packet loss rate of 5% and for (c) Stefan and (d) coastguard CIF sequences at 30 fps and packet loss rate of 3% using H.264/AVC modified to incorporate leaky prediction. Each plot also shows the initial PSNR and bitrates for the case when $\alpha = 1$.

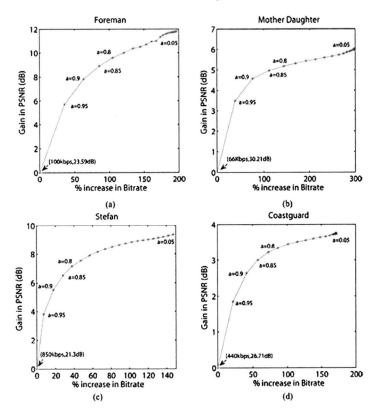

However, we propose in Section 3 to use leaky prediction selectively for those MBs in a video frame that provide a good trade-off between error resilience and coding efficiency.

Generalized Source Channel Prediction (GSCP)

Generalized Source Channel Prediction generates a prediction reference for the next frame as a weighted sum of the current frame reconstruction and the prediction reference of the previous frame (Yang & Rose, 2006) according to

$$\tilde{F}_n = \alpha \hat{F}_n + (1 - \alpha)\tilde{F}_{n-1} \qquad (12)$$

where α is the weighting parameter. This equation is used both at the encoder and the decoder. This equation implies that if $\alpha = 1$, then it is equivalent to conventional prediction (very good coding efficiency) as described above and if $\alpha = 0$ then prediction for all the frames is done from the first I-frame (excellent error resilience). Therefore α controls the error resilience and coding efficiency trade off.

From equations (7) and (8) we can observe that the difference between leaky and GSCP prediction is the second term where the constant K has been replaced by the prediction reference of the last frame. This has resulted in

1.   Higher coding efficiency than leaky prediction due to better prediction performance;
2.   More importantly increased error resilience because GSCP efficiently exploits the inherent Intra pixels present in the past frames thus reducing error propagation effect in the future frames.

Yang and Rose (Yang & Rose, 2006) suggested the value of α to be

$$\alpha = 1 - p - H \qquad (13)$$

where p is the average packet loss rate and H is a constant in the range of 0.1 to 0.2. Since (8) is being applied both at the encoder and decoder, it is assumed that p is available at both ends and it is not necessary to transmit α to the decoder. In Figure 2, we plot PSNR for different values of α at a fixed bitrate to validate the choice for α. We observe that different test sequences have a peak performance at different values of α but conform to (9) and the range of H. Thus (9) does not guarantee an optimal value but a good choice for practical purposes.

IMPROVED MOTION COMPENSATED PREDICTION

In this chapter, we investigate the nature of error propagation in a predictive coding framework in order to build a more robust encoding system. Unlike current techniques that emphasize the statistical nature of transmission errors, our methods are flexible to changing channel conditions and do not rely on accurate channel estimation. In addition, we make improvements to existing Reference Frame Modification techniques by exploiting some of their shortfalls. Our weighted distortion technique is able to improve MCP in a standard compliant way, and the proposed enhancements to RFM improve MCP when given the freedom to redesign the decoding procedure.

Weighted Distortion

Motivated by the fact that motion vectors directly impact error propagation, we study the influence an MB has along its propagation path and devise a weighting mechanism to appropriately bias the distortion values used in rate distortion optimization (RDO). In order to mitigate the negative effects of macroblock (MB) loss, we have to first determine what influence an MB has along the motion propagation path. Our proposed method tracks motion vectors to determine problematic

Figure 2. PSNR vs. α for GSCP scheme using H.264/AVC for (a) foreman (b) mother daughter QCIF sequences at 15 fps, 80 kbps, random intra updating of 10% and a packet loss rate of 10% and for (c) Stefan (d) coastguard CIF sequences at 30 fps, 500 kbps, random Intra updating of 10% and a packet loss rate of 5%

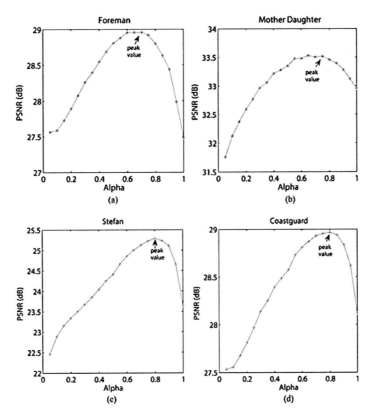

areas in a video sequence (Nyamweno, Satyan, Solak, & Labeau, 2008; Nyamweno, Satyan, & Labeau, 2009).

As presented in Section 2.3, ER-RDO video coding schemes (Stockhammer et al., 2002; Cote et al., 2000; R. Zhang et al., 2000; Y. Zhang et al., 2007) replace the source coding distortion with an end-to end distortion estimate for RDO coding mode selection. Our approach diverges from this distortion modelling paradigm, but instead addresses the error propagation aspect that is due to motion compensated prediction.

ER-RDO techniques look backwards and given a certain loss probability p, try to and determine the likelihood that errors have propagated to a particular region. In contrast, our method looks forward at the motion trajectory and uses this to improve the encoders' performance in error prone scenarios.

A major advantage of our method is that we do not require an estimate of the channel's packet loss probability p, which all the distortion modelling methods discussed in Section 2.3 need. Obtaining accurate channel loss estimates requires feedback and can be problematic in the case of rapidly changing channel conditions.

Our method is shown to improve performance across a variety of channel conditions without requiring an explicit estimate of p. Our solution addresses the drawbacks of the distortion modelling methods by introducing a bias that penalizes the distortion of MBs that have a greater influence on error propagation. We apply this technique to motion estimation and to mode decisions as well.

In addition, we will show how this technique can be used to improve the performance of the redundant slice feature present in the H.264/AVC specification.

Weighted Distortion for Motion Estimation and Mode Decision

By weighting the D_{SAD} of (3) in proportion to an MB's influence on the motion propagation path, we are able to mitigate the detrimental effects of error propagation. Equation (3) becomes,

$$J_{me} = w_{me} \cdot D_{SAD} + \lambda_{me}(QP) \cdot R \qquad (14)$$

where w_{me} is the weighting factor for motion estimation and a function of the candidate prediction region. w_{me} will be described in detail in Section 3.1.2.

Equation (10) is motivated by the fact that the more future frames depend on a particular block, the less we want to predict from it. This weighting of the source distortion allows the encoder to select motion vectors from regions that have a smaller impact in the future. As a result, the motion trajectory will now be sparser, removing the long prediction chains that cause motion propagation errors to linger in future frames. While selecting motion vectors in this manner will ultimately reduce the source coding efficiency, it will result in improved error resilient performance. Our simulation results will demonstrate that this weighting strategy is able to achieve a good balance between efficiency and resilience.

Significant gains can be achieved by only performing weighted distortion for motion estimation only. Furthermore, additional gains can be realized when weighted distortion is applied to mode decisions as well. Therefore, we also modify (4) to take into account a MB's sensitivity to losses as follows,

$$J_{md} = w_{md} \cdot D_{SSD} + \lambda_{md}(QP) \cdot R \qquad (15)$$

where w_{md} is the weighting factor for mode decision and is derived from motion vectors. This will be described in Section 3.1.3.

When there is a strong dependence on a particular block in future frames, making these blocks Intra can help reduce the error propagation effect. The purpose of w_{md} is to favour the selection of Intra MBs for those MBs that affect many pixels in the future. This is a desirable outcome because Intra MBs do not propagate any errors, making them "safer" to predict from. However, we should not forget that Intra MBs usually require a higher bitrate, and that RD optimization allows finding a trade-off between bitrate and reproduction quality.

What we introduce by using w_{md} in RD optimized mode decisions is added consideration to the resilience offered by using Intra MBs, while still paying attention to the bitrate and quality implications. The result is a prediction region with a reduced chance of containing propagated errors, thereby reducing the error propagation effect in the event of the MB's loss. Selecting the appropriate weighting factor is crucial to this method's success. In the upcoming sections we describe how w_{me} and w_{md} are obtained.

Motion Estimation Weighting Factor

In order to obtain the weighting factor used in (10) and (11), we track the influence an MB has along the motion propagation path using its motion vectors. This process entails a two-pass encoding process where in the first pass the motion vectors are computed according to (3), and the influence of each MB is tracked. The tracking reveals the number of pixels in future frames that would be affected by the loss of each MB. We then use this information in the second pass to optimize the motion vector selection according to (10).

A graphical representation of the tracking procedure is depicted in Figure 3, where the trajectory of two macroblocks 'A' and 'B' is highlighted. Macroblock 'A' affects many pixels in the future, while macroblock 'B' is referred to by only one macroblock in frame $n + 1$. Our algorithm will therefore penalize macroblock '**A**' more than macroblock '**B**'. In the first pass, the weight for '**A**' and '**B**' in frame n is determined, with '**A**' being much higher than '**B**'. In the second pass, while encoding frame $n + 1$, the weights of '**A**' and '**B**' are used to determine J_{mc} of (10) resulting in MBs with lower weights (such as '**B**') being preferred over MBs with higher weights (such as '**A**').

Intuitively, this is a reasonable approach because if an MB is used by many pixels in the future, then we expect it to be highly sensitive to transmission errors. By tracking MB dependencies we capture the future impact of each MB, allowing us to identify which areas are referred to often in the future. Our method reduces the usage of these sensitive MBs for prediction, thereby lowering their susceptibility to errors. The number of future frames to search, N, is a design criterion that trades off computation time and algorithm effectiveness.

Table 1 shows the motion vector tracking algorithm used to determine the number of future pixels that are affected by the loss of an MB. The value of w_{me} in (10) used in our simulations is derived from the C value obtained by the algorithm described in Table 1. In this work, we only consider integer-pel accuracy for simplicity, however, it is possible to apply motion vector tracking to fractional-pel accuracy by adjusting the number of pixels affected according to the interpolation filter used.

Once the C value of each MB has been determined, the error resilient motion estimation process can begin. The weight w_{me} takes into account any overlapping MBs in the previous frame. If the candidate motion vector (MV) points to a region in the previous frame that overlaps a number of MBs, w_{me} is computed in proportion to the overlap area as depicted in Figure 4.

Therefore if C_i represents the *counter* from MB i, A_i is the area of MB i and a_i is the overlap

Figure 3. Tracking the number of pixels that are affected by the loss of an MB over N frames

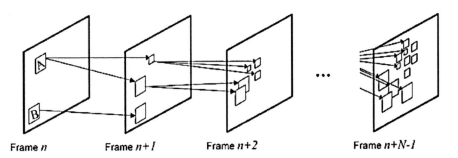

Frame n Frame $n+1$ Frame $n+2$ Frame $n+N-1$

Table 1. Motion vector tracking procedure

1)	Compute the motion vectors for all the MBs in the chosen N frames using (3)
2)	For an MB in the current frame search for the MB/sub MB(s) in the next frame which reference this MB.
3)	A counter, C, is incremented for each pixel that references the current MB.
4)	The MB/ sub MB(s) which was referenced is chosen and a search is performed in the consecutive frame to obtain MB/ sub MB (s) which references these and Step 3 is repeated.
5)	Step 4 is performed for all the MBs in the current frame. Thus a counter, C, is generated for every MB in the frame.
6)	Proceed to next frame and repeat Steps 2 to 5 for all the N frames considered.

Figure 4. Obtaining weight w_{me} from counter C during overlap

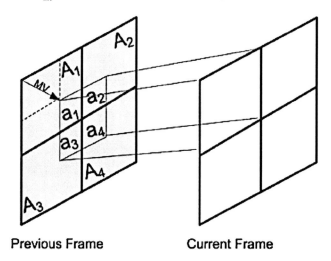

Previous Frame   **Current Frame**

area in MB i as shown in Figure 4, the weight will be given by;

$$w = \sum_{i=1}^{4} \frac{a_i}{A_i} C_i \qquad (16)$$

This proportional representation of weight is necessary to ensure the proper bias is given to each MB.

Mode Decision Weighting Factor

Coding a macroblock as either Inter or Intra has significant and conflicting implications on the error resilience and coding efficiency of a video compression scheme. In this section, we enhance the performance achieved from weighted motion estimation by finding a weighting strategy for mode decision that addresses the tradeoff between resilience and rate.

We stated in Section 2.1.1 that Intra MBs generally have a higher bitrate compared to Inter MBs because they do not remove temporal redundancy. We also stated that from an error resilience standpoint, the fact that they do not employ temporal prediction means that they do not cause error propagation.

We present a weighting strategy that is applied to Intra modes only, with the intention of reducing their distortion value in proportion to the number of future pixels they affect. To that end we develop a weight factor w_{md} for the Intra mode based on the *counter* value C_i of MB i according to

$$w_{md} = T - \frac{C_i}{C_{max}} \qquad (17)$$

where C_i/C_{max} is the *counter* value for an MB normalized by the maximum *counter* value of the frame C_{max}. T is a threshold value that allows for increased error resilience performance. We select $0 < T \leq 1$, to ensure a fractional reduction in the distortion and prevent negative distortion values. Negative distortion values would put unfair emphasis on rate alone in determining the coding options.

The rationale behind selecting this value for w_{md} is similar to that of w_{me} in that we want to favour Intra mode selection for the MBs that are referenced often in the future. In addition, our mode decision method ensures that the sensitive MBs are error-free by coding them as Intra rather than Inter. This allows these areas to be safely used in the future by reducing the risk of error propagation. It is important to note that w_{md} does not simply code MBs that affect numerous pixels in the future as Intra. Its application in (11) will ensure that if coding as Intra would require a prohibitively large rate, Inter mode will be used. Our proposed method therefore takes into account the rate-distortion tradeoff as well as error resilience in making decisions.

This weighting method for mode decision can be viewed as an Intra updating scheme similar to those presented in Section 2.1. It is more robust than Random Intra updating because it is able to adapt the Intra updating strategy according to sequence specific characteristics. By using information from the motion trajectory for mode decision and motion estimation we are able to distinguish our technique from the error resilience tools included in H.264/AVC presented in Section 2.1 because we combine efficient Intra updating with efficient motion vector selection within the RD framework.

Simulation results verifying the effectiveness of our weighted distortion methods are presented in Section 4. We should mention that the 2-pass encoding process proposed for weighted distortion can be computationally intensive. The complexity can be managed by moderating the number of future frames N that are searched. We showed in some of our earlier work that searching $N =$ 3 or $N = 5$ frames ahead can be very effective (Nyamweno et al., 2008).

IMPROVED REFERENCE FRAME MODIFICATION SCHEMES

Our proposed techniques improves on the GSCP scheme presented in Section 2.4.3 by effectively exploiting the inherent resilience of Intra MBs in previous reconstructed frames, during the formation of the reference frame. As mentioned in Section 2.1.1, Intra MBs stops error propagation in hybrid video compression schemes. We exploit this knowledge by putting greater emphasis on Intra

MBs during the formation of reference frames, resulting in improved error resilience. We also reintroduce the leaky factor into one of our proposed schemes. Since the use of leaky prediction decreases the coding efficiency substantially, we use the leaky factor judiciously on an MB basis thus keeping the bitrate increase at a minimum and achieving significant performance gains (Satyan, Nyamweno, & Labeau, 2010).

Improved GSCP (IGSCP)

In developing Improved GSCP we use the fact that GSCP does not effectively exploit Intra MBs of the previous frame reconstruction $(\hat{F}_{n-1})$ during the formation of the reference frame. We also recognize that GSCP applies the weight α at a frame level which is not efficient because channel loss affects each MB within a frame differently depending on the video sequence and the coding mode. Hence changing α at a MB level would be beneficial.

IGSCP pays special attention to Intra MBs present in the previous reconstructed frame. GSCP provides emphasis on the Intra pixels present in the past frames due to their ability to terminate error propagation. Our technique maintains this emphasis and gives further importance to Intra MBs present in the previous reconstructed frame. This technique of adding redundancy results in a reference frame that has more Intra pixels. Intra pixels are important in limiting error propagation because they do not rely on information contained in previous frames. Correctly received Intra MBs therefore represent the most reliable information. We exploit this fact by copying the Intra MBs to the reference frame and applying GSCP to the rest of the MBs in the frame. Equation (8) is now treated at a MB level and is given by

$$\tilde{F}_n^m = \begin{cases} \tilde{F}_{n-1}^m & \text{if } \hat{F}_{n-1}^m \text{ is Intra} \\ \alpha \tilde{F}_n^m + (1-\alpha)\tilde{F}_{n-1}^m & \text{otherwise} \end{cases}$$
$$\text{for } m = 1...M$$

$$(18)$$

where the indices $_n{}^m$ refer to a MB m in frame n, and M is the total number of MBs in a frame.

The utilization of (14) at a MB level helps to create a reference frame with more Intra MBs and thus provides increased error resilience. Due to the Intra MB's ability to eliminate error propagation, prediction from Intra MBs is more reliable.

Modified Weighted Prediction (MWP)

Weighted Prediction is used by the H.264/AVC Standard for coding fade to black scenes. It is also used in improving the coding efficiency of B-Pictures whereby the reference frame is formed by averaging together two reconstructed frames (Boyce, 2004). The significance of exploiting the available Intra MBs of the previous reconstructed frame in the formation of the reference frame can be extended to weighted prediction. The modified weighted prediction can be defined as

$$\tilde{F}_n^m = \begin{cases} \hat{F}_{n-1}^m & \text{if } \hat{F}_{n-1}^m \text{ is Intra} \\ \alpha\hat{F}_n^m + (1-\alpha)\hat{F}_{n-1}^m & \text{otherwise} \end{cases}$$
for $m = 1...M$
$$\qquad\qquad\qquad\qquad\qquad\qquad (19)$$

The difference between IGSCP and MWP is that the reference frame is formed in the former by a weighted sum of a reconstructed frame and a reference frame and, in the latter, by a weighted sum of two consecutive reconstructed frames. MWP offers an improvement in coding efficiency compared to IGSCP because it uses two recent reconstructed frames. MWP outperforms GSCP in error prone scenarios which validate the importance of exploiting Intra MBs in the reference frame. However, IGSCP has better error resilience than MWP due to the fact that it makes use of historical information of Intra pixels present in the past frames (due to the use of past reference frame). These results will be shown in the next section.

Leaky IGSCP

The choice for α in (9) is not optimal for all types of video sequences. We have seen through extensive experiments that medium and fast moving video sequences have a better end-to-end rate distortion (RD) performance when α is changed adaptively. We propose to use a different α for each MB in a video frame so as to maximize the error resilience property. In doing so we propose to compute for each MB the mean square error (MSE) between the current reconstructed frame and the previous reconstructed frame given by

$$MSE_{mb}(m) = \sum_{i=1}^{256}\left(\hat{F}_n^m(i) - \hat{F}_{n-1}^m(i)\right)^2 \quad ,\qquad (20)$$
for $m = 1...M$

where $\hat{F}_n^m(i)$ is a pixel value of the MB m in the reconstructed frame n, 256 is the total number of pixels in a MB and M denotes the total number of MBs in a frame.

MSE_{mb} gives an indication of the activity level on a MB basis. If a MB has a high MSE_{mb} value then it suggests that there is presence of new information in the current frame MB compared to the previous frame. This implies that using more of the current MB in the formation of the reference frame would give a higher coding efficiency. Since coding efficiency and error resilience function inversely, this suggests MBs which have a high MSE_{mb} must be used to a lesser extent in the formation of the reference frame to get more robustness against channel errors. This has been verified through simulations by choosing an appropriate threshold for MSE_{mb} and the idea of using a different α based on the above criteria results in a better rate distortion performance than IGSCP in error prone scenarios. This will be denoted by mod_IGSCP scheme in the next section. mod_IGSCP technique is the same as IGSCP technique with an adaptive α. The promising result of mod_IGSCP technique

Equation 21

$$\tilde{F}_n^{m} = \begin{cases} \hat{F}_{n-1}^{m} & \text{if } \hat{F}_{n-1}^{m} \text{ is Intra} \\ \alpha\hat{F}_n^{m} + (1-\alpha)\tilde{F}_{n-1}^{m} & \text{if } \hat{F}_{n-1}^{m} \text{ is Inter and } MSE_{mb} < T_h \\ (\alpha-\beta)\hat{F}_n^{m} + (1-\alpha)\tilde{F}_{n-1}^{m} & \text{if } \hat{F}_{n-1}^{m} \text{ is Inter and } MSE_{mb} > T_h \end{cases}$$

for $m = 1...M$

has prompted us to reintroduce leaky prediction as explained below.

By decreasing α (using smaller weight for current frame reconstruction) smartly at an MB level with the use of (16) would lead to a more robust bit-stream in an IGSCP setup. We propose to form the prediction for the reference frame by incorporating a leaky factor into the IGSCP framework for those MBs in a frame which have a good resilience efficiency trade-off. Thus Leaky IGSCP framework can be stated as Equation 21 where β is the leaky factor, C is a constant chosen as the mid range of pixel values i.e. 128 for pixels ranging from 0 to 255 and T_h is an appropriate threshold.

In (17), the first two equations are the same as IGSCP and the third equation is the incorporation of leaky prediction. The advantages of using Leaky IGSCP are that

1. It exploits the inherent Intra MBs in present and past frames effectively through the use of GSCP and IGSCP schemes.
2. It has a minimum robustness as that of IGSCP, for those MBs which have the MSE between the current frame reconstruction and previous frame reconstruction less than a threshold T_h.
3. Error propagation is mitigated exponentially by using the leaky factor for all MBs which have the MSE_{mb} greater than a threshold T_h.

It has been experimentally seen that slow moving sequences (Figure 1) do not have much performance gain with the use of leaky prediction.

Video sequences which have very slow motion will generally have small activity between any two consecutive frames. This suggests that most of the MBs will have a small value of MSE_{mb} and will fall below the threshold T_h. However, medium and fast moving video sequences will generally have a lot of activity and more MBs will have a large value of MSE_{mb}. The percentage of MBs with MSE_{mb} values greater than a threshold ($T_h = 2$) for various video sequences is shown in Table 2. Hence our proposed technique applies leaky prediction to only those MBs which have a good error resilience and efficiency tradeoff. Resilience for the rest of the MBs is obtained through IGSCP. Thus the bit rate penalty of using leaky prediction is kept to a minimum.

It is important to note that all the methods discussed in Section 3.2 require that both the encoder and decoder have access to the packet loss probability p. This is a reasonable assumption for point-to-point applications, but may be dif-

Table 2. Comparison of MSE_{mb} values for different sequences

QCIF Sequence	% of MBs having MSE_{mb} greater than a threshold ($T_h = 2$)
NBA	87.2
Football	57.9
Stefan	50.7
Foreman	14.4
Car	6.6
Mother Daughter	1.7
Akiyo	0.6

ficult to achieve in a broadcast scenario. A practical version would e.g. have just a few quantized values of loss to choose from on each side, which could rather easily be transmitted with high probability of correct decoding.

Once transmission errors occur, encoder-decoder mismatch is inevitable. The use of (16) for computing the leaky factor gives rise to a possible drift error between the encoder and decoder. These effects will be discussed in detail in the next section. We reemphasize that the techniques proposed only modify the reference frame used for prediction to bring about better error resilience in the compressed bitstream. The motion compensation mechanism for all the techniques presented here remains unchanged.

SIMULATION RESULTS

We implemented all the new methods discussed in Section 3 by modifying the JM 15.1 reference software ((JVT), 2009). The first frame was coded as Intra frame and the rest of the frames as Inter frames. For each frame, a row of MBs was placed in a slice, which formed an RTP packet. Assuming RTP/UDP/IP transmission, lost or damaged packets were discarded without retransmission.

Weighted Distortion

In this section, we combine Equations (10) and (11) to show the benefit of weighting the distortions used in both motion estimation and mode decision. We use (13) in (11) on Intra modes only in order to penalize MBs that have a long prediction trail. Applying w_{md} in (11) reduces the distortion value used in RD mode decisions for Intra MBs, thereby favoring their selection, while still paying attention to the bitrate implications. Some comparisons between ROPE and K-decoders (Stockhammer et al., 2002; Y. Zhang et al., 2007) suggest little or no difference in the resultant error resilience performance of these

methods at fixed bitrates. Therefore, in order to compare our proposed method with current *state of the art* error resilient strategies, the K-decoders method (with $K = 30$) gives us a fair comparison.

The threshold value T, described in Section 3.1.3 permits the designer to improve the error

Figure 5. RD curves for football and NBA sequences (CIF format) in a channel with 10% packet loss rate for weighted mode decision and motion estimation compared to K-decoders. K dec 3 is the K decoders method designed for a channel with 3% packet loss while K dec 10 has 10% channel loss. Rand Intra 20 is 20% intra updating and w_{me} & w_{me} T is the weighted procedure applied to both mode decision and motion estimation with a threshold value of T.

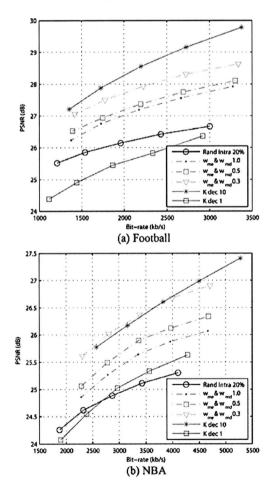

(a) Football

(b) NBA

Table 3. Δ PSNR and Δ bitrate incurred by using various RD optimization methods when compared to random intra 20 in an error free environment. T is the threshold value in (13)

Methods	Football		NBA	
	Δ PSNR	Δ rate(%)	Δ PSNR	Δ rate(%)
K dec 10	1.42	16.73	2.67	20.53
K dec 3	0.39	4.67	1.20	10.88
w_{me} **only**	0.19	2.04	0.33	2.75
w_{me} & w_{md} T=1.0	0.37	3.92	0.46	3.87
w_{me} & w_{md} T=0.5	0.59	6.16	0.71	5.97
w_{me} & w_{md} T=0.3	0.86	8.72	1.12	9.11

resilience performance of our weighted procedure while maintaining a modest increase in bitrate. For illustrative purposes, we show results for $T = 1.0$, $T = 0.5$ and $T = 0.3$. These decreasing values of T mean that the Intra mode distortion values are decreasing, resulting in an increase in error resilience performance. We avoid negative values of w_{md} since they would put unfair emphasis on bitrate alone in determining coding options.

Figure 5 displays the rate-distortion curves resulting from the combination of Weighted Mode Decision and Motion Estimation. It is clear from Figure 5 that our proposed method outperforms 20% Random Intra Updating by up to 2.1 dB with a threshold of $T = 0.3$. Our method also performs better than K-decoders with erroneous channel estimation. The addition of w_{md} improves on the use of w_{me} alone because it results in Intra MBs for those regions that are referenced often. As mentioned earlier, obtaining accurate estimates of channel loss rates is difficult in practice, therefore mismatch between actual and estimated channel performance is of practical concern. Figure 5 also shows that our method with different values of T performs better than the K-decoder method with a channel encoding mismatch. Though Figure 5 shows the result for a CIF sequence in a 10% packet loss channel only, our method however is able to perform well under different channel conditions and video resolutions. This is witnessed in Figure 6, which shows the PSNR vs loss rate for QCIF sequences with a fixed bitrate.

After discussing the improved error resilient performance afforded by employing our technique, we draw your attention to the slight increase in resources required by our technique in an error

Figure 6. PSNR vs loss percentage; football and NBA QCIF sequences with fixed bitrate. K dec 3 is the K-decoders method designed for a channel with 3% packet loss while K dec 10 has 10% channel loss. Rand intra 20 is 20% intra updating and w_{me}&w_{md}T is the weighted procedure applied to both mode decision and motion estimation with a threshold value of T.

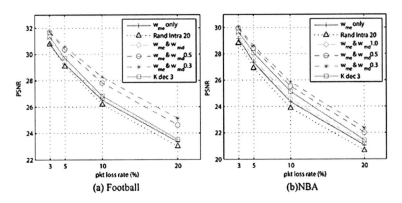

(a) Football   (b)NBA

Table 4. Complexity comparison of the various weighted distortion techniques

	Computation complexity per pixel	Storage (bits/pixel)	Encoding time (min for 80 frames)
Standard H.264	-	-	18.90
K decoders K=30	810 ADD & 600 MUL	240	29.18
K decoders K=100	2700 ADD & 2000 MUL	800	37.03
Weighted distortion	1 ADD & 20+S MUL	32	40.82

free channel. There is a slight increase in bitrate incurred by using our method in an error free environment. By comparing the RD curves of the error frees case using the Bjøntegard formula (Bjøntegaard, 2001), we get the results tabulated in Table 3. It is worth noting that while K dec 3 requires a 10% bitrate increase, our method with $T = 0.5$ only requires a 5% bit rate increase and still outperforms K dec 3 in a lossy environment.

Complexity Analysis

In this section we compare the complexity of our forward tracking method with the K decoders method used in the simulations. The K-decoders involves reconstructing pixel values for inter-modes which would require 1 ADD and calculation the E2E distortion would require 1 ADD and 1 MUL. Intra modes do not need pixel reconstruction therefore only require 1 ADD and 1 MUL

Figure 7. Rate distortion curves for (a) coastguard (b) Stefan QCIF sequences at 15 fps, 10% intra updating for a packet loss rate of 10% and (c) foreman (d) football CIF sequences at 30 fps, 10% intra updating for a packet loss rate of 5% for various techniques

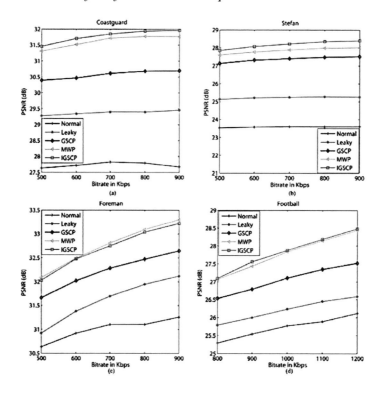

Table 5. Average end-to-end PSNR for various QCIF sequences at 15 fps, 500 kbps and at a packet loss rate of 10% and 10% Intra updating

Sequence	NBA	Football	Flower	Car	Akiyo
Normal	19.65	22.99	21.99	33.0	41.54
Leaky	20.86	24.14	23.29	34.61	42.26
GSCP	22.90	25.65	25.14	35.02	42.58
MWP	23.47	26.62	25.44	36.24	43.49
IGSCP	23.65	26.90	25.70	36.16	43.43

(Chen & Wu, 2010). Given that H.264 has 7 inter-modes and 13 intra-modes, this means that the K-decoders method would need $27 \cdot K$ ADDS and $20 \cdot K$ MULs. Storage for all the K simulated decoders is also required.

The forward tracking method of Chapter 3 would require 1 ADD in the first pass to accumulate the Count value, 2 MULs to generate the weight value in (16). The second pass requires 1 MUL for all the motion vectors within the search range, S and 1 MUL for all the modes in (5). This means a total of 1 ADD and $20+S$ MULs are required for the forward tracking methods. Storage for the Count values of every MB is also required, along with more time to perform the tracking.

The encoding times for the various methods in Table 4 were obtained from an Intel i5 2.8Ghz PC running a 32 bit version of a modified JM reference software. It is important to note that speed tuning was not performed on the implemented algorithms and further performance improvements can be made by implementing the tracking algorithm in assembler.

Reference Frame Modification

We present some results from employing our reference frame modification techniques in Figure 7 which shows the rate distortion curves for the Coastguard and Stefan QCIF sequences for a packet loss rate of 10% and Foreman and Football CIF sequences for a packet loss rate of 5% with 10% Intra Updating. 10% Intra Updating indicates

that 10% of the MBs in a frame are randomly chosen to be coded as Intra. The rate control algorithm present in the JM reference software is used to achieve constant bitrates. Leaky prediction uses $\alpha = 0.95$ and α for GSCP, MWP and IGSCP is chosen according to (9) with $H = 0.1$. In all the Figures "normal" refers to encoding using H.264/AVC reference software with no modifications (i.e. conventional prediction). From the curves we can observe that GSCP outperforms normal and leaky techniques. MWP and IGSCP methods

Figure 8. Subjective results for football frame 30 with 10% intra refresh rate and 10% packet loss rate

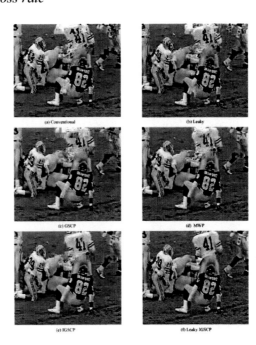

perform better than all the competing techniques. Amongst them IGSCP has the best rate distortion performance. This highlights the importance of efficient exploitation of Intra MBs in the formation of the reference frame.

These improved results are witnessed in a variety of test sequences as displayed in Table 5, which shows the average end-to-end PSNR using different techniques (normal, leaky, GSCP, MWP and IGSCP) at 500 kbps, for a packet loss rate of 10% and 10% random Intra updating. Leaky prediction uses $\alpha = 0.95$ and α for GSCP, MWP and IGSCP is chosen to be 0.8 as in (9). For all the sequences MWP and IGSCP outperform GSCP on average by 0.8 dB and 1.0 dB respectively.

To gain a better understanding on how this affects the decoded video quality, we present subjective performance comparison for all the prediction schemes discussed in Section 2.4 in Figure 8. Looking at the figure we see an improvement in reproduction quality by going from conventional, to Leaky, to GSCP, to IGSCP and finally to Leaky IGSCP. Thus Leaky IGSCP has the best performance in comparison to all competing techniques. These subjective results further demonstrate the importance of efficiently suppressing error propagation in video coding.

CONCLUSION

In this chapter we investigated motion compensated prediction (MCP) and presented two methods of improving the performance of compressed video over unreliable links. In our first method we were able to use prediction dependencies inherent in MCP to bias the source distortion values. This is in contrast to current state of the art error resilient strategies which rely on an estimate of the end-to-end distortion, allowing us to achieve resilience without the need for reliable channel estimation.

The second method presented significant enhancement to current reference frame modification techniques. We showed that modified

prediction techniques based on providing greater emphasis on Intra pixels during the formation of reference frames provide improved end-to-end performance in error prone networks. IGSCP and MWP schemes outperform GSCP scheme by around 1 dB in most testing scenarios. The use of leaky prediction judiciously in a source channel prediction framework can provide substantial performance improvements in error prone scenarios. We have observed that Leaky IGSCP outperforms IGSCP scheme for medium and fast moving video sequences with gains of around 1.5 dB. This improvement provides a good reproduction video quality during transmission over unreliable networks with a modest bitrate penalty.

REFERENCES

Aign, S., & Fazel, K. (1995, June). Temporal and spatial error concealment techniques for hierarchical mpeg-2 video codec. *Proceedings of IEEE ICC*, *3*, 1778–1783. doi:10.1109/ICC.1995.524505

Apostolopoulos, J. G., Wong, T., Tan, W., & Wee, S. J. (2002, Nov.). On multiple description streaming with content delivery networks. *Proceedings - IEEE INFOCOM*, *3*, 1736–1745.

Aravind, R., Civanlar, M. R., & Reibman, A. R. (1996, Oct.). Packet loss resilience of MPEG-2 scalable video coding algorithms. *IEEE Transactions on Circuits and Systems for Video Technology*, *6*(5), 426–435. doi:10.1109/76.538925

Bjøntegaard, G. (2001, Apr.). *Calculation of average psnr differences between rd-curves*. ITU-T Q.6/SG16 VCEG, VCEG-M33.

Boyce, J. (2004, May). Weighted prediction in the H.264/MPEG AVC video coding standard. In *Proceedings IEEE International Symposium on Circuits and Systems (ISCAS'04)* (Vol. 3, pp. 789-792). Nagoya, Japan.

Chang, P.-C., & Lee, T.-H. (2000, June). Precise and fast error tracking for error-resilient transmission of h.263 video. *IEEE Transactions on Circuits and Systems for Video Technology, 10*(4), 600–607. doi:10.1109/76.845005

Chen, Z., & Wu, D. (2010, November). Prediction of transmission distortion for wireless video communication: Algorithm and application. *Journal of Visual Communication and Image Representation, 21*, 948–964. doi:10.1016/j.jvcir.2010.09.004

Chou, P. A., & Miao, Z. (2006, April). Rate-distortion optimized streaming of packetized media. *IEEE Transactions on Multimedia, 8*(2), 390–404. doi:10.1109/TMM.2005.864313

Chou, P. A., Mohr, A. E., Wang, A., & Mehrotra, S. (2001, March). Error control for receiver-driven layered multicast of audio and video. *IEEE Transactions on Multimedia, 3*(1), 108–122. doi:10.1109/6046.909598

Chou, P. A., Wu, Y., & Jain, K. (2003). Practical network coding. In *Proceedings of Allerton Conference on Communication, Control and Computing.*

Cote, G., Shirani, S., & Kossentini, F. (2000, Jun.). Optimal mode selection and synchronization for robust video communications over error-prone networks. *IEEE Journal on Selected Areas in Communications, 18*(6), 952–965. doi:10.1109/49.848249

Ghandi, M., Barmada, B., Jones, E., & Ghanbari, M. (2006, May). Unequally error protected data partitioned video with combined hierarchical modulation and channel coding. *Proc. of ICASSP '06, 2*, (pp. 529-531).

Girod, B. (2000, Feb.). Efficiency analysis of multihypothesis motion-compensated prediction for video coding. *IEEE Transactions on Image Processing, 9*(2), 173–183. doi:10.1109/83.821595

Girod, B., & Farber, N. (1999, Oct.). Feedback-based error control for mobile video transmission. *Proceedings of the IEEE, 87*(10), 1707–1723. doi:10.1109/5.790632

Hannuksela, M. (2009). *Error-resilient communication using the h.264/avc video coding standard.* Unpublished doctoral dissertation, Tampere University of Technology, Tampere, Finland.

Harmanci, O., & Tekalp, A. (2004, Oct.). Optimization of H.264 for low delay video communications over lossy channels. *Proceedings of ICIP '04*, Vol. 5, (pp. 3209-3212).

Harmanci, O., & Tekalp, A. M. (2007, March). A stochastic framework for rate-distortion optimized video coding over error-prone networks. *IEEE Transactions on Image Processing, 16*(3), 684–697. doi:10.1109/TIP.2006.891047

He, Z., & Xiong, H. (2006, Sept.). Transmission distortion analysis for real-time video encoding and streaming over wireless networks. *IEEE Transactions on Circuits and Systems for Video Technology, 16*(9), 1051–1062. doi:10.1109/TCSVT.2006.881198

Huang, H., Wang, C., & Chiang, T. (2002, Jun.). A robust fine granularity scalability using trellis-based predictive leak. *IEEE Transactions on Circuits and Systems for Video Technology, 12*(6), 372–385. doi:10.1109/TCSVT.2002.800314

J. V. T. (2009, Apr.). *H.264/AVC reference software (ver JM 15.1).* Retrieved from http://iphome.hhi.de/suehring/tml/

J. V. T. (2010, Jan.). *H.264/SVC reference software (jsvm 9.19) and manual.* Retrieved from garcon.ient.rwth-aachen.de

Katz, B., Greenberg, S., Yarkoni, N., Blaunstien, N., & Giladi, R. (2007, Mar.). New error-resilient scheme based on FMO and dynamic redundant slices allocation for wireless video transmission. *IEEE Transactions on Broadcasting, 53*(1), 308–319. doi:10.1109/TBC.2006.889694

Kumar, S., Xu, L., Mandal, M. K., & Panchanathan, S. (2006, Apr.). Error resiliency schemes in H.264/AVC standard. *Journal of Visual Communication and Image Representation, 17*(2), 425–450. doi:10.1016/j.jvcir.2005.04.006

Lam, W. M., Reibman, A. R., & Liu, B. (1993, Apr.). Recovery of lost or erroneously received motion vectors. *Proceedings of IEEE ICASSP, 5,* 417–420.

Lu, J., Lieu, M. L., Letaief, K. B., & Chuang, J. I. (1998, June). Error resilient transmission of H.263 coded video over mobile networks. In *Proceedings of IEEE International Symposium on Circuits and Systems* (Vol. 4, p. 502-505).

Miao, Z., & Ortega, A. (2002, Apr.). Expected run-time distortion based scheduling for delivery of scalable media. In *Proceedings of packet video workshop.*

Nguyen, T., & Zakhor, A. (2002, Jan.). Distributed video streaming over the internet. In *Proceedings of SPIE Conference on Multimedia Computing and Networking* (pp. 186-195).

Nyamweno, S., Satyan, R., & Labeau, F. (2009, July). Error resilient video coding via weighted distortion. *Proceedings of ICME, 09,* 734–737.

Nyamweno, S., Satyan, R., Solak, S., & Labeau, F. (2008, Oct.). Weighted distortion for robust video coding. *Proceedings of ASILOMAR, 08,* 1277–1281.

Ogunfunmi, T., & Huang, W. (2005, May.). A flexible macroblock ordering with 3D MBAMAP for H.264/AVC. *IEEE International Symposium on Circuits and Systems, ISCAS 2005,* Vol. 4, (pp. 3475-3478).

Padmanabhan, V. N., Wang, H. J., & Chou, P. A. (2003). Resilient peer-to-peer streaming. *Microsoft Research Technical Report* (MSR-TR-2003-11)

Podolsky, M., McCanne, S., & Vetterli, M. (2001). Soft ARQ for layered streaming media. *Journal of VLSI Signal Processing Systems, 27*(1-2), 81–97.

Richardson, I. E. (2003). *H.264 and mpeg-4 video compression: Video coding for next-generation multimedia.* Chichester, UK: John Wiley & Sons, Inc. doi:10.1002/0470869615

Satyan, R., Nyamweno, S., & Labeau, F. (2010). Novel prediction schemes for error resilient video coding. *Signal Processing Image Communication, 25*(9), 648–659. doi:10.1016/j.image.2010.05.001

Setton, E., Yoo, T., Zhu, X., Goldsmith, A., & Girod, B. (2005, Aug.). Cross-layer design of ad hoc networks for real-time video streaming. *IEEE Wireless Communications, 12*(4), 59–65. doi:10.1109/MWC.2005.1497859

Stockhammer, T., Hannuksela, M. M., & Wiegand, T. (2003, Jul.). H.264/AVC in wireless environments. *IEEE Transactions on Circuits and Systems for Video Technology, 13*(7), 657–673. doi:10.1109/TCSVT.2003.815167

Stockhammer, T., Kontopodis, D., & Wiegand, T. (2002). Rate-distortion optimization for JVT/H.26L video coding in packet loss environment. In *Proceedings of Packet Video Workshop 2002.* Pittsburg, PA.

Sullivan, G., & Wiegand, T. (1998, November). Rate-distortion optimization for video compression. *IEEE Signal Processing Magazine, 15*(6), 74–90. doi:10.1109/79.733497

Sun, H., & Kwok, W. (1995, April). Concealment of damaged block transform coded images using projections onto convex sets. *IEEE Transactions on Image Processing, 4*(4), 470–477. doi:10.1109/83.370675

Sun, H., & Zdepsky, J. (1994, February). Error concealment strategy for picture header loss in MPEG compressed video. In *Proceedings of SPIE Conference of High-Speed Networking and Multimedia Computing* (Vol. 2188, pp. 145-152).

Tan, W., & Zakhor, A. (2001, March). Video multicast using layered FEC and scalable compression. *IEEE Transactions on Circuits and Systems for Video Technology, 11*(3), 373–386. doi:10.1109/76.911162

Turletti, T., & Huitema, C. (1996). *RTP payload format for h.261 video streams*. United States: RFC Editor.

Wan, S., & Izquierdo, E. (2007, May). Rate-distortion optimized motion-compensated prediction for packet loss resilient video coding. *IEEE Transactions on Image Processing, 16*(5), 1327–1338. doi:10.1109/TIP.2007.894230

Wang, Y., Wenger, S., Wen, J., & Katsaggelos, A. K. (2000, July). Error resilient video coding techniques. *IEEE Signal Processing Magazine, 17*(4), 61–82. doi:10.1109/79.855913

Wang, Y., & Zhu, Q. F. (1998, March). Error control and concealment for video communication: A review. *Proceedings of the IEEE, 86*(5), 974–997. doi:10.1109/5.664283

Wang, Y., Zhu, Q. F., & Shaw, L. (1993). Maximally smooth image recovery in transform coding. *IEEE Transactions on Communications, 41*(10), 1544–1551. doi:10.1109/26.237889

Wiegand, T., Farber, N., Stuhlmuller, K., & Girod, B. (2000, June). Error-resilient video transmission using long-term memory motion-compensated prediction. *IEEE Journal on Selected Areas in Communications, 18*(6), 1050–1062. doi:10.1109/49.848255

Wiegand, T., Sullivan, G., Bjontegaard, G., & Luthra, A. (2003, July). Overview of the h.264/avc video coding standard. *IEEE Transactions on Circuits and Systems for Video Technology, 13*(7), 560–576. doi:10.1109/TCSVT.2003.815165

Wu, Y., Chou, P. A., & Kung, S. Y. (2005, November). Minimum-energy multicast in mobile ad hoc networks using network coding. *IEEE Transactions on Communications, 53*(11), 1906–1918. doi:10.1109/TCOMM.2005.857148

Wu, Y., Chou, P. A., Zhang, Q., Jain, K., Zhu, W., & Kung, S. Y. (2005). Network planning in wireless ad hoc networks: A cross-layer approach. *IEEE Journal on Selected Areas in Communications, 23*(1), 136–150. doi:10.1109/JSAC.2004.837362

Yang, H. (2007, July). Advances in recursive per-pixel end-to-end distortion estimation for robust video coding in H.264/AVC. *IEEE Transactions on Circuits and Systems for Video Technology, 17*(7), 845–856. doi:10.1109/TCSVT.2007.897116

Yang, H., & Rose, K. (2005, March). Rate-distortion optimized motion estimation for error resilient video coding. In *Proceedings of ICASSP '05* (Vol. 2, pp. 173-178). Philadelphia, PA.

Yang, H., & Rose, K. (2006, May). Generalized source-channel prediction for error resilient video coding. *Proceedings of ICASSP '06*, Vol. 2, (pp. 533-536).

Yang, H., & Rose, K. (2010, January). Optimizing motion compensated prediction for error resilient video coding. *IEEE Transactions on Image Processing, 19*, 108–118. doi:10.1109/TIP.2009.2032895

Zhang, R., Regunathan, S. L., & Rose, K. (2000, June). Video coding with optimal inter/intra-mode switching for packet loss resilience. *IEEE Journal on Selected Areas in Communications, 18*(6), 966–976. doi:10.1109/49.848250

Zhang, R., Regunathan, S. L., & Rose, K. (2001, November). End-to-end distortion estimation for RD-based robust delivery of pre-compressed video. In *Proceedings of 35th Asilomar Conference on Signals, Systems and Computers* (Vol. 1, pp. 210-214).

Zhang, Y., Gao, W., Lu, Y., Huang, Q., & Zhao, D. (2007, Apr.). Joint source-channel rate-distortion optimization for h.264 video coding over error-prone networks. *IEEE Transactions on Multimedia, 9*(3), 445–454. doi:10.1109/TMM.2006.887989

Zhu, C. (1997, Mar.). *RTP payload format for H.263 video streams.* IETF draft.

Zhu, C., Lin, X., & Chau, L.-P. (2002, May). Hexagon-based search pattern for fast block motion estimation. *IEEE Transactions on Circuits and Systems for Video Technology, 12*(5), 349–355. doi:10.1109/TCSVT.2002.1003474

ENDNOTES

1. In the H.264/AVC JM reference software this feature is disabled by setting the UseConstrainedIntraPred flag in the encoder.

2. SKIP is a special Inter mode where no residue or motion vectors are sent. It is commonly used for stationary background or motionless objects.

3. H.264/SVC (Scalable Video Coding), is the scalable extension to the H.264/AVC video coding standard.

Chapter 9
Free–Viewpoint 3DTV:
View Interpolation, Coding, and Streaming

S. Zinger
Eindhoven University of Technology,
The Netherlands

P. H. N. de With
Eindhoven University of Technology,
The Netherlands

L. Do
Eindhoven University of Technology,
The Netherlands

G. Petrovic
Eindhoven University of Technology,
The Netherlands

Y. Morvan
Eindhoven University of Technology,
The Netherlands

ABSTRACT

Free-ViewPoint (FVP) interpolation allows creating a new view between the existing reference views. Applied to 3D multi-view video sequences, it leads to two important applications: (1) FVP service provided to the user, which enables the possibility to interactively select the viewing point of the scene; (2) improved compression of multi-view video sequences by using view prediction for inter-view coding. In this chapter, the authors provide an overview of the essential steps for 3D free-view video communication, which consists of the free-viewpoint interpolation techniques, a concept for free-view coding and a scalable free-view video streaming architecture. For facilitating free-view to the user, the chapter introduces the free-viewpoint interpolation techniques and the concept of warping. The authors assume that 3D video is represented by texture and depth images available for each view. Therefore it is possible to apply Depth Image Based Rendering (DIBR), which uses the depth signal as a important cue for geometry information and 3D reconstruction. Authors analyze the involved interpolation problems, such as cracks, ghost contours and disocclusions, which arise from an FVP interpolation and propose several solutions to improve the image quality of the synthesized view. Afterwards, they present a standard approach to FVP rendering used currently by the research community and our FVP interpolation. Additionally, authors show the use of FVP rendering for the multi-view coding and streaming and discuss the gains and trade-offs of it. At the end of the chapter are the state-of-the-art achievements and challenges of FVP rendering and a vision concerning the development of free-viewpoint services.

DOI: 10.4018/978-1-4666-2660-7.ch009

INTRODUCTION

Three-dimensional (3D) video is nowadays broadly considered to succeed existing 2D HDTV technologies (Smolic, 2011). The depth in a 3D scene can be created with e.g. stereo images or by explicitly sending a depth signal or map, as an addition to the texture image. This means that the viewer can perceive depth while looking at a stereoscopic screen. Many movies are already recorded in a stereoscopic format today, and commercially available stereoscopic displays are strongly emerging. It is expected that stereoscopic 3D video will first establish its place in the market while standards for 3D extensions will emerge in parallel, thereby paving the way for more advanced forms of 3D imaging. One of those advanced interesting forms in 3D imaging is to virtually move through the scene in order to create different viewpoints. This feature, called multi-view video has become a popular topic in coding and 3D research. Viewing a scene from different angles is an attractive feature for applications, such as medical imaging (Zinger *et al.*, 2009; Ruijters & Zinger, 2009), multimedia services (Kubota *et al.*, 2007) and 3D reconstruction (Leung & Lovell, 2003). Since the number of cameras is practically limited and consequently also the number of viewing angles, research has been devoted to interpolate views between the cameras.

The chosen free-viewpoint may not only be selected from the available multi-view camera views, but also any viewpoint between these cameras. It will be possible to watch a soccer game or a concert from the viewpoint preferred by the user, where the viewpoint can be changed at any time. This interactivity adds complexity to the 3D TV system because it requires a smart rendering algorithm that allows free- viewpoint view interpolation.

To create an interactive free-viewpoint 3D TV system, several challenges have to be addressed: multi-view texture and depth acquisition, multi-view coding, transmission and decoding, and multi-view rendering (see Figure 1).

Each block of the diagram in Figure 1 represents an essential processing stage of active research in 3D vision. Let us briefly discuss these stages. With respect to data generation, there are various ways to create multi-view 3D video content. For example, a set of stereo-cameras may be installed around the scene. Multi-view 3D video can also be acquired by cameras that can produce depth maps for their views.

In multi-view video, a scene is captured by several cameras, which are typically positioned along an arc with the optical axis pointing to the center of the scene. For accurate free-viewpoint generation, the parameters that define the position and orientation (intrinsic and extrinsic) of each camera need to be extracted. This process is well known and called camera calibration,

Figure 1. Block diagram of a free-viewpoint 3DTV system

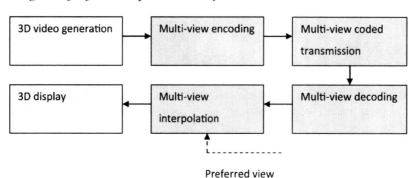

The positioning of cameras is an open question because it influences not only the viewing experience, but also the approach to multi-view coding and view interpolation. This influence changes per scene, it depends on the scene complexity and geometry. When the captured views are far enough from each other, the redundancy in information that they contain will decrease, therefore the performance of coding and interpolation relying on the inter-view redundancy will be reduced similarly. 3D Display technology has been under development for several years and now it is introduced to the consumers. Various technologies are applied for 3D displays: stereoscopic vision with active or passive glasses, autostereoscopy with different number of views presented to the user. Even though the algorithms for virtual view creation discussed in this chapter aim at one virtual view, it is easy to extend them to stereo images that better fit the current 3DTV displays. These extensions to stereo output are introduced by Do *et al.* (2010b). The remaining four processing stages – free-viewpoint (multi-view) interpolation, multi-view coding and streaming – will be the subject of discussion in the sequel of this chapter.

Free-Viewpoint Interpolation Concepts

DIBR Steps and Warping

Depth Image Based Rendering (DIBR) algorithms are based on warping (McMillan & Pizer, 1997) a camera view to another view. Warping is essentially a recomputation of one camera view into another perspective, where the depth signal plays a vital role for the 3D signal reconstruction at the new view.

For obtaining a high free-viewpoint rendering quality, the two nearest reference cameras are used for warping to a virtual viewpoint. Disocclusions, i.e. the areas invisible from the reference cameras, are compensated and textures of the virtual image are blended from the reference cameras. Figure 2(a) shows how the virtual image is warped from the left and right reference cameras.

The basic idea of most DIBR rendering methods is to perform 3D warping to the virtual viewpoint using texture and depth information of the reference cameras. Artifacts are removed by post-processing the projected images. These images are then blended together and the remaining disocclusions are filled in by inpainting techniques. The basic diagram of most DIBR methods for free-viewpoint interpolation is depicted in Figure 3.

Figure 2. DIBR virtual view point reconstruction using two reference cameras

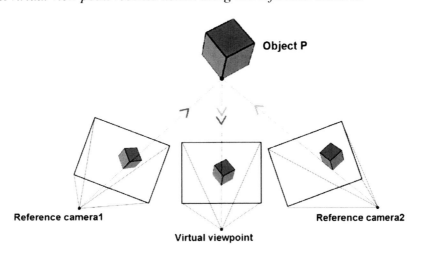

Figure 3. Basic diagram of free-viewpoint DIBR methods

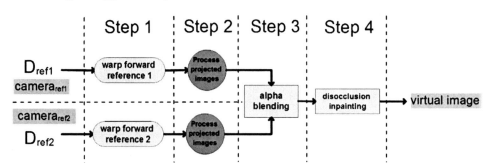

In the first step, the left and right reference cameras are warped to the virtual viewpoint using the reference depth maps. In Step 2, the projected images are processed to cope with artifacts. The most perceptually relevant artifacts are empty pixels (cracks) caused by sampling and ghost contours, resulting from ill-defined borders in depth maps. The projected texture maps are blended in Step 3. The blending process determines, for every pixel, whether the virtual image should take the left and/or right projected textures. By comparing the projected depth maps, we can guarantee that foreground objects will always be visible. The last Step 4 processes and closes the disocclusions that still exist as a result of the geometry of the scene. Various inpainting techniques can be exploited to fill in the disocclusions by using colors from the edges of the disoccluded areas (Bertalmio *et al.*, 2003; Telea, 2004).

Let us now explain warping in more detail, where we provide the essential model and equations involved with the processing. At first, we consider the pinhole camera model that helps us to introduce the notations needed for defining the warping procedure. Then, we consider the warping equation on which the DIBR algorithms are based (Figure 3).

The pinhole camera model has been broadly accepted as a fundament and is illustrated in Figure 4. It is the simplest and the ideal model of a (camera) viewpoint and can be used to define mappings of 3D objects to a 2D plane, also known

as perspective projection (Carlbom & Paciorek, 1978). Let $P_c = (X_c, Y_c, Z_c)$ be a 3D point in the rotation field of the pinhole camera (Figure 4), then $p = (x, y, 1)$ is the projection of P_c onto the image plane. From Figure 4(b), we can calculate that the perspective scaling leads to

$$x = f\frac{X_c}{Z_c} + c_x$$

and

$$y = f\frac{Y_c}{Z_c} + c_y.$$

Rewriting these two equations in the matrix form, we obtain

$$\lambda p = KP_c \qquad (1)$$

$$\lambda \begin{pmatrix} x \\ y \\ 1 \end{pmatrix} = \begin{bmatrix} f & 0 & c_x \\ 0 & f & c_y \\ 0 & 0 & 1 \end{bmatrix} \begin{pmatrix} X_c \\ Y_c \\ Z_c \end{pmatrix},$$

where λ is relative depth of point $P_c = Z_c$.

We suppose that the pinhole camera is located at position C, rotated with a rotation matrix R with respect to the axis of the 3D world and 3D point $P = (X, Y, Z)$. Equation (1) can then be rewritten into

Figure 4. Pinhole camera model with 3D orientation and perspective scaling

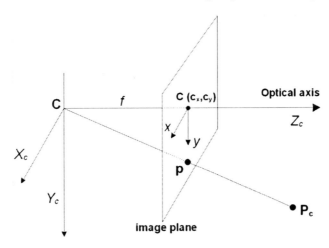

(a) pinhole camera 3D view

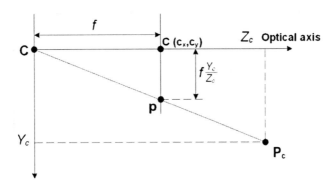

(b) pinhole camera, 2D view

$$\lambda p = K[R - RC]P = K[R\ t]P, \qquad (2)$$

where $P_c = [R\ t]P$. From Equation (2), we can see that a viewpoint is completely defined by three variables, namely K, R and t, where K and $[Rt]$ are called the intrinsic and extrinsic parameters of the camera, respectively. Equation (2) forms the basis for 3D warping, which is performed in two steps. First, an image point p_1 from the reference image is projected to the real world 3D point P. Then, P is projected back to image point p_2 of the virtual image (Figure 5).

From Equation (2) follows that

$$\lambda_2 p_2 = K_2[R_2\ t_2]P = K_2 R_2 P + K_2 t_2,$$

where $P = [K_1 R_1]^{-1} \lambda_1 p_1 + C_1$. Equation (3) below describes the resulting 3D warping formulation:

$$\lambda_2 p_2 = K_2 R_2 [K_1 R_1]^{-1} \lambda_1 p_1 + K_2 R_2 C_2 + K_2 t_2. \qquad (3)$$

Imperfections of DIBR and Artifact Reduction

In this section, imperfections from the DIBR algorithms are explained in detail and we present several solutions for each of them (Zinger *et al.*, 2010, Do *et al.*, 2010a). Different combinations of these solutions lead to various rendering algorithms. Depending on the quality and the

Figure 5. Warping from the existing (reference) image to the virtual image at the free-viewpoint

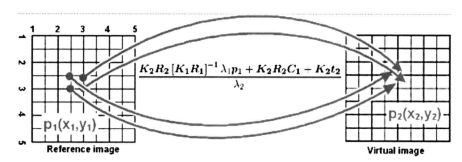

implementation issues, such as hardware, software running on a GPU, a specific rendering algorithm may be adopted.

Cracks and Holes Due to Sampling Rate

The first problem we have to overcome is the occurrence of cracks in the reconstructed image due to sampling in the x and y-direction of the reference image. Figure 6 explains an example of the variable object size depending on the viewpoint. In Figure 6, the angle of surface S with the reference viewpoint is smaller than that with the virtual viewpoint.

To reconstruct surface S at the virtual viewpoint, we have to sample the visible part of S in the reference image and warp it to the virtual image. When the sampling rate is the same as the image resolution, we see that the number of samples (area of S') at the reference image for surface S is 25 pixels, while the area of S' at the virtual image is 40 pixels. So, for the virtual image, we have to reconstruct an area of 40 pixels with only 25 data samples. If every data sample contains one pixel, there will be empty areas, or cracks, at the virtual image. A visualization of this phenomenon can be seen in Figure 7. The large empty areas, appearing as shadows at the right side of each person, are disocclusions. The small

Figure 6. Warping of a surface: object sizes change at different viewpoints

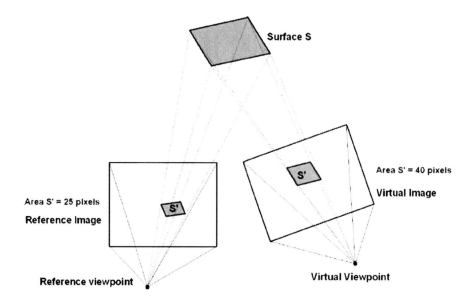

Figure 7. Cracks after warping

vertical stripes in the background are cracks. Let us now consider the possible solutions for this problem.

The simplest solution to cope with cracks is oversampling, or supersampling, the image space. When we sample the reference image, in the x and y direction, with a sampling rate that is twice the resolution, most cracks will disappear. However, the disadvantage is that we have to perform warping four times, which is a costly operation. In our earlier experiments, we have concluded that it is too expensive to perform oversampling only to fill in the cracks, which consist of usually less than 3% of the image. Another way to fill in the cracks is to model the warping of a reference pixel to the virtual image as a light beam that travels from one viewpoint to another viewpoint. When we enlarge the warp beam that hits the virtual image, the cracks will be automatically filled in. The disadvantage of this method is that we have to copy every warped pixel several times, for example, eight times, to the virtual image. Another downside is that some neighboring warped pixels will have the wrong value because the beam is too large. The third solution is to label the cracks and perform an inverse warping of the labeled pixels to retrieve

the textures. First, we process the projected depth map with a median filter. Depth maps consist of smooth regions with sharp edges, so filtering with a median will not degrade the quality. Afterwards, we compare the input and output of the median filter and perform an inverse warping when pixels have changed. Do et al. (2011) perform an in-depth study of this issue.

Ghost Contours Due to High Discontinuities in Depth Maps

Inaccuracy in depth maps causes textures to be warped to wrong places in the virtual image. This is most visible at edges of objects, where the discontinuities in depth maps are high. In depth maps, these edges are sharp and only one pixel wide, while in texture maps, they cover usually two to three pixels. This results in foreground textures at the edges, which are warped to the background. When we do not remove these pixels, the resulting rendered image will have a ghost contour of the foreground objects. This principle is shown in Figure 8.

We notice that ghost contours at the projected images occur at borders of disocclusions. One solution to remove the contours is to dilate the

Figure 8. Ghost contour within the virtual image due to ill-defined borders

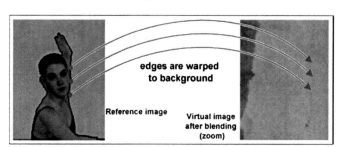

disocclusions. An important drawback of this method is that not only ghost contours will be removed, but also correct texture pixels. An alternative solution is to remove only the warped pixels at the edges of high discontinuities, but this approach is restricted to edges at the background side in order to avoid distortions at the foreground objects. After a projection of the reference image to the virtual image, we find the edges at high discontinuities, warp them again and erase them from the virtual image. Because we know that the edges cover two to three pixels, the neighboring pixels are also erased. The advantage of this method is that only ghost contours are erased. However, we need an additional processing step to find the high discontinuities. We now briefly explain how this is accomplished. The objective is to find background pixels that have a neighboring foreground pixel. In general, we have to compare every pixel with its eight surrounding neighbors to verify if there is a high discontinuity. However, it is sufficient to label a pixel as a ghost contour, if only one of its neighbors is a foreground pixel. So for every pixel, we check the following condition that the difference between neighbors and central pixel is larger than a threshold, so that

$$\forall_{x,y} \in S, \quad \sum_{i=-1}^{1} \sum_{j=-1}^{1} D\big(x+i, y+j\big) - 9 \cdot D\big(x,y\big) > T_d, \tag{4}$$

where S is the image space, D denotes the depth map of the reference camera and T_d is a predefined threshold. If the above condition is true, then pixel $D(x,y)$ is labeled as a ghost contour. We warp the labeled pixels and erase them from the background.

If we zoom in at high discontinuity edges, we observe that the textures of those edges are a mixture of both the foreground and background. Therefore, it is better to fully omit the warping of those edges. Based on this observation, our third method is to warp only pixels that are not labeled as ghost contour pixels. For every pixel, we verify with Equation (4), whether the pixel should be warped or not. The advantage is that we do not have to erase the ghost contour in a separate pass. However, because the edges cover usually two pixels, we have to expand the labeled edges by one pixel.

Disocclusion Inpainting

After blending the two projected images, disocclusions may still occur. These are areas that cannot be viewed from both reference cameras simultaneously. Most inpainting techniques are developed to reconstruct small regions of an image. These regions can be inpainted by textures from the edges of the disocclusions, while maintaining the structure of the textures. Although these techniques are good, the resulting inpainted regions contain a certain amount of blurring. In our case, the disocclusions are not just random regions of an image. They are newly uncovered areas of background without texture information, and certainly not part of the foreground objects. When we assume that the disocclusions should be background, we may use the depth information at the edges of the disoccluded region for inpainting with more accurate textures. This method is illustrated in Figure 9 and consists of several steps.

First, we search for every pixel in the disoccluded region in eight directions for the nearest edge pixel. Then, we only take into account the edge pixels with the lowest depth value. With these pixels, we calculate a weighted average according to the following equation:

$$\forall_{u,v} \in O, \qquad P\left(u,v\right) = \frac{\sum_{i=1}^{N} d_i^{-2} * t_i}{\sum_{i=1}^{N} d_i^{-2}}, \qquad (5)$$

where O is the disoccluded region, N represents the number of edge pixels at the background, d is the distance of empty pixel P to the edge of the disoccluded region, t is the texture value of an edge pixel. The advantage of our method is that there is no blurring between foreground and background textures. The drawback is that the inpainted region becomes a low-frequency patch, when the disoccluded region is very large. The last picture of Figure 9 shows that blurring of foreground and background textures occurs when we do not consider depth information for inpainting.

Our inpainting algorithm is based on a weighted interpolation from neighboring pixels that do contain texture values. This method is similar to recently published work of Oh *et al.* (2009), but the authors had to first define the disoccluded regions and their boundaries. The disoccluded regions are inpainted using the computationally expensive method of Telea (2004), which requires analyzing the whole boundary region around disoccluded pixels. We process each pixel in the disoccluded region separately, in order to achieve a high-quality resulting image, while keeping our algorithm simple and fast.

FREE-VIEWPOINT 3D VIDEO: ALGORITHM, CODING, AND STREAMING

FVP Interpolation Algorithm

For the free-viewpoint interpolation, the virtual camera is normally placed between the two existing views. For producing a video at a virtual viewpoint, the camera parameters for both the existing and virtual views are needed. Since we rely on DIBR for creating a new video, we also need a depth map for each existing view. First experiments with DIBR for 3D video are performed by Morvan (2009).

We have further developed a novel view synthesis algorithm (Do *et al.*, 2010a) for 3D video in such a way that it suits both applications:

Figure 9. Inpainting with and without depth information

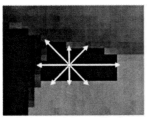 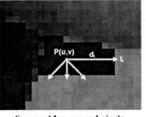  

find nearest edge pixel   disregard foreground pixels   result of inpainting with depth information   result of inpainting without depth information

free-viewpoint 3DTV and interview prediction for Multi-View Coding (MVC). Our algorithm has a number of key aspects that differ from the state-of-the-art approaches. We describe these aspects by comparing our algorithm with the recently published rendering algorithm of Mori *et al.* (2009).

The first key aspect is that Mori first creates a complete depth map prior to rendering. In our case, we warp the reference image, but copy both the texture and depth values to the virtual image at the same time. This almost halves the amount of warping operations. In addition, the amount of errors is also reduced, as every warping iteration causes rounding errors.

The second key aspect is that ghost contours are removed by dilating the disoccluded regions. Dilation also removes some correct pixels and therefore it is not considered as a feasible technique for implementation. Instead, we label the edge pixels that cause ghost contours and omit those pixels from warping.

The third key aspect involves inpainting disocclusions. Mori *et al.*(2009)fill every disoccluded pixel by textures from a boundary region, while our algorithms only consider boundary pixels that are part of the background. Using depth information for inpainting disocclusions, we ensure that blurring between foreground and background objects is avoided.

Let us now describe the steps of our free-viewpoint interpolation algorithm.

Warping Depth Maps and Copying Texture Values to the Corresponding Locations

This step is the Step 1 in Figure 3. We warp depth maps and create textures for the new viewpoint by copying the texture values to the pixel locations, defined by depth map warping. The warping is specified by

$$[D_{warped1}; T_{warped1}] = Warp(\sim HD(D_{ref1})), \qquad (6)$$

$$[D_{warped2}; T_{warped2}] = Warp(\sim HD(D_{ref2})), \qquad (7)$$

where D_{ref1} and D_{ref2} are depth maps of the first and second reference cameras, respectively, Warp is a warping operation, $D_{warped1}$ and $D_{warped2}$ are depth maps, warped from D_{ref1} and D_{ref2}, respectively. Parameters $T_{warped1}$ and $T_{warped2}$ are textures at the new viewpoint. Pixels at high discontinuities are first labelled with the function HD as shown in Equation (4) and only the non-labelled pixels are warped. The advantage is that we do not need an additional step for erasing ghost contours.

Median Filtering and Defining Changed Pixels

We apply median filtering to the images $D_{warped1}$ and $D_{warped2}$ and find the indexes $Index_{to\ warp1}$ and $Index_{to\ warp2}$ of pixels whose values have changed. This index computation is specified by

$$Index_{to\ warp1} = Cracks(Median(D_{warped1})), \qquad (8)$$

$$Index_{to\ warp2} = Cracks(Median(D_{warped2})), \qquad (9)$$

where Median is a median filter with a 3x3 window, and Cracks is a function detecting pixels that have changed during median filtering. In Figure 3, this and the following step are combined in Step 2.

Texture Crack Filling by Inverse Warping

The cracks on warped textures are filled in by inverse warping, which is warping from the new view to the reference camera views. This covers the following relations:

$$[D_{warped1}; T_{warped1}] = Warp^{-1}(Index_{to\ warp1}), \qquad (10)$$

$$[D_{warped2}; T_{warped2}] = Warp^{-1}(Index_{to\ warp2}). \qquad (11)$$

Create the texture for the new view.

The two warped textures are blended with the function Blend and disocclusions inpainting of the resulting image gives a new image according to

$$[D_{new}; T_{new}] = Inpaint(Blend(T_{warped1}; T_{warped2})),$$
(12)

where Inpaint defines the inpainting procedure described in the previous section. Blending and inpainting are represented in Figure 3 as Step 3 and Step 4.

Our free-viewpoint rendering algorithm does not only provide a good quality, but it also considers occlusions and is of limited complexity. The limited complexity will lead to reduced computation times for multi-view encoding and decoding. For free-viewpoint 3DTV, the reduced complexity is needed for real-time implementation.

MULTI-VIEW CODING AND FVP

A comprehensive overview of 3D MVC is provided by Morvan (2009) and by Vetro *et al.* (2011). We discard the straightforward solution to encode multiple views independently, as in simulcast coding, because it is not efficient. Motion- and Disparity-Compensated (MaDC) prediction can be employed to benefit from the redundancy in both neighboring views and over time.

Figure 10 presents a diagram where each camera view is a column where the video frames are coded over time in the vertical direction using motion-compensated predictive coding. The horizontal arrows indicate the dependent coding between neighboring camera views where the scene change resulting from the changed viewing angle is modeled as a disparity. This leads to motion- and disparity-compensated coding. Figure 10 shows that for each view, MaDC coding is possible along the time axis and similarly between views (Smolic *et al.*, 2007). Various prediction structures are possible (Morvan, 2009), but common elements for suitability and efficiency are that a few reference views are encoded over time and some neighboring views are reconstructed from those reference views. With respect to robustness, it is required that the coded multi-view stream offers sufficient access points to (re-)start decoding both in time and in place. The problem of the above prediction schemes is that the coding between views is less efficient because differences between the views are larger than with time-based coding. Disparities depend on the baseline distance between the cameras and on the depth of the object in the scene. These values can be rather large and additionally, light variations and object disocclusions may occur.

Morvan (2009) showed that the advantage of MaDC is obvious only when the baseline between cameras is small. MaDC does not necessarily yield a coding gain when the baseline between cameras increases.

Figure 10. Visualization of motion- and disparity-compensated prediction

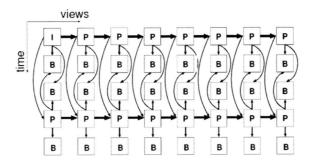

Figure 11(a) shows the quality of these two coding approaches for different bit rates for the "Ballet" video. Simulcast is slightly better in most of the cases. From Figure 11(a) we observe that MaDC (MVC) offers no gain, especially for the case when the baselines are large. The reason for this is that the translational motion model employed by the block-based motion-compensated scheme is not sufficiently accurate to predict the motion of objects with different depths. We observe on Figure 11(b) the quality of these two coding approaches for different bit rates for the Breakdancers video. MaDC coding is slightly better in most of the cases. For example, the PSNR improved with 0.2 dB at 700 kbit/s.

A more sophisticated prediction scheme than the system in Figure 10 employs hierarchical B-frames. This concept is used in the current standard proposal for MVC encoding from the MPEG group. According to Merkle *et al.* (2007), this MVC yields a coding improvement of 0.25 dB and 0.05 dB for the Breakdancers and Ballet sequences, respectively. When the baseline becomes larger, MVC yields hardly any compression gain. Therefore, alternative methods are needed such as view synthesis prediction coding.

Figure 12 presents an architecture diagram of an adaptive H.264 encoder incorporating view synthesis prediction. H264 encoding in this figure is performed using Disparity Compensated Prediction (DCP) and View Synthesis Prediction (VSP). View synthesis can be performed through relief-texture mapping or another rendering method. This adaptive encoding employs the following important steps:

1. The VSP provides an approximation of the predicted view using a selected image rendering technique;

2. The DCP refines the view synthesis prediction using a block-based disparity-compensated prediction;
3. The prediction scheme is carried out adaptively, using a rate-distortion criterion for an optimal prediction-mode selection for each image block.

The advantage of this approach is that large baseline coding is possible. The disadvantage is that the cameras must be fully calibrated and the depth maps must be known. A study is performed on the effect of depth compression on the rendering quality (Merkle *et al.*, 2009). In the scheme in Figure 12, it can be noticed that the depth map and camera parameters are used to compute the predictive picture.

3D MULTI-VIEW VIDEO STEAMING

3D video systems allow a user to perceive depth in the viewed scene and to display the scene from arbitrary viewpoints interactively and on-demand. Here we discuss a prototype implementation of a 3D-video streaming system using an IP network. The architecture of our streaming system is layered, where each information layer conveys a single coded video signal or coded scene-description data. We demonstrate the benefits of a layered architecture with two examples: (a) stereoscopic video streaming, (b) monoscopic video streaming with remote multiple-perspective rendering. Our experimental architecture confirms that prototyping 3D-video streaming systems is possible with today's software and hardware. Furthermore, the proposed architecture concept enables that highly heterogeneous clients can coexist in the system, ranging from auto-stereoscopic 3D displays to resource-constrained mobile devices.

Figure 11. Experimental results with motion- and disparity-compensated prediction for the ballet (a) and breakdancers (b) video sequences

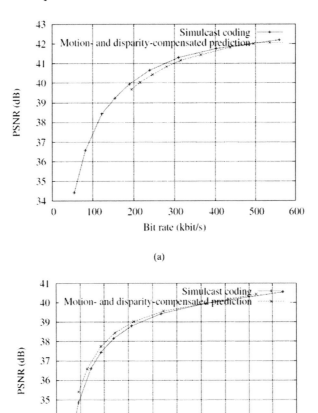

(a)

(b)

Streaming System with Depth (Disparity) Maps and Layered Streaming

3D-Video rendering algorithms as discussed earlier in this chapter are adopted for the 3D video streaming system. This involves the use of DIBR and the depth maps for all reference views, so that new views can be computed.

Information layering is a well-known design guideline for the content representation in adaptive streaming systems. It is commonly used to simplify the problem of receiver heterogeneity by allowing the system to select the number of layers to transmit based on receiver preferences or capabilities. As a result, representation scalability is achieved, where the rendering quality depends on the selected number of layers (e.g., scalable video coding).

Application of the information layering concept in our system means that each information layer conveys a single video stream or a scene-description stream. This design decision is based on two observations related to the 3D-video rendering process. First, the usage of scene-geometry description for rendering (e.g., depth maps in DIBR,

Figure 12. Architecture of an H.264/MPEG-4 AVC encoder that adaptively employs a block-based disparity-compensated prediction (DCP) or view synthesis prediction (VSP), followed by a prediction-refinement. The main view and the synthesized view are denoted Ref and W(Ref), respectively.

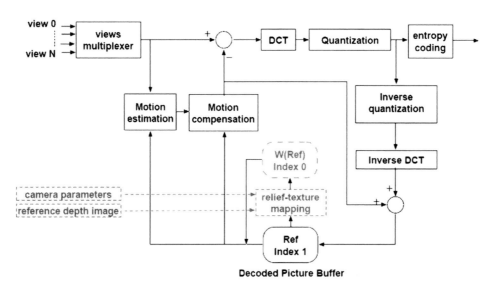

occlusion information in view interpolation) is a norm in computer graphics, but is uncommon in video streaming. It is therefore useful only to the receivers supporting this rendering option. Second, the quality of interpolated virtual frames depends on the number of original frames and depth maps that are blended together.

In view of a large number of possible combinations, we believe that optimized decisions are best implemented at run-time, for each individual streaming session independently. Following the layering principle, the number of layers used can be extended to include multiple viewpoints, which we call a multiple-view streaming system. The user can select the number of different camera streams to receive simultaneously. Similarly, in the scene-descriptive case, the number of layers can be increased to improve the quality by sending additional descriptive data, such as occlusion or objects masks. As an example of a combined scheme, it is possible to transmit several camera streams and a selection of supporting depth maps, where the depth maps can be located at intermediate positions. In its optimal form, the actual transmission scheme at any given time will be adaptively determined by the view interpolation algorithm, taking into account the user navigation patterns and the resources available.

Another important system aspect is the inherent interactivity. In the envisaged system, some camera streams will be transmitted frequently, and others not at all, entirely driven by the user interest. Therefore, an on-demand transmission is desired to reduce the overall bandwidth cost. As our initial implementation experiences suggest, these bandwidth savings appear sufficient to implement 3D-video streaming systems in today's networks.

Our prototype implementation includes software modules that demonstrate both aspects of 3D-video streaming: (a) stereoscopic video streaming, (b) monoscopic video streaming with remote multiple-view rendering. For the experimental implementation of stereoscopic video streaming, we instantiate two layers. Depending on the stereoscopic image-rendering algorithm available at the receiver end, either a depth stream and a texture stream (either left or right), or both the left and the right camera streams are transmitted (Figure 13).

Figure 13. Example of a dual-layer stereoscopic video streaming system

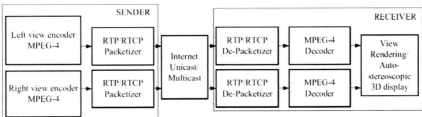

The presented streaming architecture supports these two 3D-video modalities as separate applications. We can only report on the implementation for the case where all the data required by the view interpolation is locally available. Therefore, our current multiple-view streaming prototype can be thought of as a client-server application in which the server creates the interpolated views, compresses and streams them to the client in real time (Figure 14).

Multiple-View Streaming and Viewpoint Control

The viewpoint control to support interactive scene viewing is implemented using standard PC input-devices. The user sends a request for a viewpoint change by moving the mouse pointer inside of the video display window. The generated events are transmitted to the sender, including the current pointer position in display window coordinates.

The sender maintains a mapping between the client's display window coordinates and the coordinates of the capturing cameras. A routine in the "listening thread" at the sender determines if the receiver coordinates match one of the original cameras and if so, transmits its video stream. Otherwise, it starts the view interpolation procedure.

The intermediate views are interpolated in the rectified coordinate system, using the disparity estimates, and projected back into the original coordinate system prior to display. Carrying out the interpolation on rectified images has the advantage that only horizontal pixel shifts are involved. The interpolation consists of compensating for both the translational and the rotational motion of the virtual camera. We compensate for the translational motion using the estimated

Figure 14. Multi-view video streaming

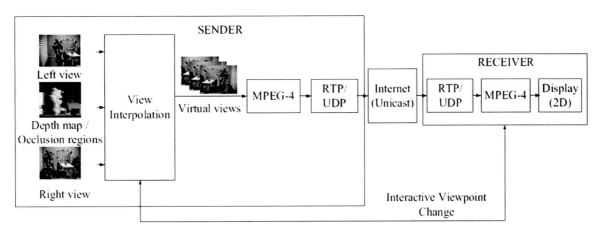

disparities. The compensation of the rotational component is simulated by gradually interpolating the rectification transforms.

As only a monoscopic video stream (containing a sequence of virtual and/or original frames) is transmitted, the receiver application can be any media-player with streaming support. Our choice of remote rendering design is geared towards enabling multiple-view video on receivers, which are constrained in bandwidth and rendering resources. The proposed concepts and ideas have been evaluated in an experimental system using standard PC components (Petrovic *et al.*, 2008).

FUTURE RESEARCH DIRECTIONS

The future work in the areas highlighted in this chapter consists of several directions. For the FVP interpolation, the quality of the resulting picture still needs to be studied and improved. The quality metrics for the interpolated images are also a research area. Recently, several metrics for 3D video quality evaluation have been proposed but a broadly accepted approach for subjective and objective evaluation is still under study. Furthermore, the perception of 3D video needs to be investigated. Another direction of future work in this area concerns the real-time implementation of the FVP algorithms. This is necessary for most of the practical applications and the research is needed to make the algorithms feasible.

For 3D multi-view video coding, more research is needed for the automatic and real-time choice of coding parameters for insuring the optimal coding performance. In the case that the FVP interpolation is performed at the receiver side of the FVP system, the expected quality of the interpolated picture should also be taken into account when choosing streaming and encoding parameters.

CONCLUSION

Depth-based video technology captures the reality of the world which is in 3D. With the increasing popularity of 3DTV, new research and development questions arise. In this chapter, we have discussed multi-view 3D video rendering and coding algorithms and an IP-based streaming system for 3D video communication.

An essential part in 3D multi-view rendering is the view interpolation algorithm exploiting camera reference views. It has been shown that with DIBR rendering, the depth maps of each reference view provide important information about the geometry borders of the objects in the texture image. We have presented an algorithm that simultaneously warps texture and depth into the new view. Additionally, we present simple and effective processing of the artifacts that occur after warping. The primary artifact reduction steps are removal of cracks and ghost contours in the background and depth-based inpainting.

This chapter discussed the application of motion- and disparity-based predictive coding and concepts for adaptive free-viewpoint inter-view coding. It has been shown that an H.264-based coding system can be employed for camera reference view coding and it forms also a basis for an adaptive coding system. In that system, view synthesis prediction can be used to improve the coding efficiency by exploiting redundancy between multiple views.

We have presented a scalable architecture for the delivery of 3D-video streaming, allowing both multi-view and stereoscopic viewing. First, we have cast the multi-view transmission as an on-demand layered streaming problem and implemented a stereoscopic streaming prototype using standard transport protocols and compression techniques. Second, we have addressed the continuous navigation requirement of 3D-video systems by incorporating an interactive view rendering and interpolation algorithm at the sender end. The streaming architecture setup enables that heterogeneous clients coexist in the system, ranging from auto-stereoscopic 3D displays to resource-constrained mobile devices.

Our review provided in this chapter shows that the areas mentioned above are still research subjects and more effort is needed for elaborating specific points. However, the presented results cover an experimental 3DTV communication system and contribute to the optimal and adaptive parameters for free-viewpoint, compression and streaming.

REFERENCES

Bertalmio, M., Vese, L., Sapiro, G., & Osher, S. (2003). Simultaneous structure and texture image inpainting. *IEEE Transactions on Image Processing, 12*, 882–889. doi:10.1109/TIP.2003.815261

Carlbom, I., & Paciorek, J. (1978). Planar geometric projections and viewing transformations. *ACM Computing Surveys, 10*(4), 465–502. doi:10.1145/356744.356750

Do, L., Zinger, S., & de With, P. H. N. (2010a). Quality improving techniques for free-viewpoint DIBR. *IS&T/SPIE Electronic Imaging, Vol. 7524, SDA XXI*, San Jose, USA.

Do, L., Zinger, S., & de With, P. H. N. (2010b). Conversion of free-viewpoint 3D multi-view video for stereoscopic displays. *IEEE International Workshop on Hot Topics in 3D, in conjunction with International Conference on Multimedia & Expo (ICME)*, (pp. 1730-1734). Singapore.

Do, L., Zinger, S., & de With, P. H. N. (2011). *Warping error analysis and reduction for depth image based rendering in 3DTV*. San Francisco, USA: IS&T / SPIE Electronic Imaging, Stereoscopic Displays and Applications XXI. doi:10.1117/12.873384

Kubota, A., Smolic, A., Magnor, M., Tanimoto, M., Chen, T., & Zhang, C. (2007). Multiview imaging and 3DTV. *IEEE Signal Processing Magazine, 24*(6), 10–21. doi:10.1109/MSP.2007.905873

Leung, C., & Lovell, B. C. (2003). 3D reconstruction through segmentation of multi-view image sequences. *Workshop on Digital Image Computing,* Vol. 1, (pp. 87–92).

McMillan, L., & Pizer, R. S. (1997). *An image based approach to three-dimensional computer graphics*. Technical Report TR97-013, University of North Carolina at Chapel Hill.

Merkle, P., Morvan, Y., Smolic, A., Farin, D., Muller, K., de With, P. H. N., & Wiegand, T. (2009). The effects of multiview depth video compression on multiview rendering. *Signal Processing Image Communication, 24*(1-2), 73–88. doi:10.1016/j.image.2008.10.010

Merkle, P., Smolic, A., Mueller, K., & Wiegand, T. (2007). Experiments on coding of multi-view video plus depth. *Joint Video Team of ISO/IEC MPEG & ITU-T VCEG, Doc. JVT-X064*, Geneva, Switzerland.

Mori, Y., Fukushima, N., Yendo, T., Fujii, T., & Tanimoto, M. (2009). View generation with 3D warping using depth information for FTV. *Image Communication, 24*(1-2), 65–72.

Morvan, Y. (2009). *Acquisition, compression and rendering of depth and texture for multi-view video*. Ph.D. thesis, Eindhoven, the Netherlands: Eindhoven University of Technology.

Oh, K.-J., Sehoon, Y., & Ho, Y.-S. (2009). *Hole-filling method using depth based in-painting for view synthesis in free viewpoint television (FTV) and 3D video*. Picture Coding Symposium (PCS), Chicago, USA.

Petrovic, G., Farin, D., & de With, P. H. N. (2008). Toward 3D-IPTV: Design and implementation of a stereoscopic and multiple-perspective video streaming system. *SPIE Stereoscopic Displays and Applications (SDA 2008),* Vol. 6803 (pp. 505-512). San Jose, USA.

Ruijters, D., & Zinger, S. (2009). *IGLANCE: Transmission to medical high definition autostereoscopic displays.* In 3DTV Conference: The True Vision - Capture, Transmission and Display of 3D Video. Potsdam, Germany.

Smolic, A. (2011). 3D video and free viewpoint video – From capture to display. *Pattern Recognition, 44*(9), 1958–1968. doi:10.1016/j.patcog.2010.09.005

Smolic, A., Mueller, K., Stefanovski, N., Ostermann, J., Gotchev, A., & Akar, G. (2007). Coding algorithms for 3DTV – A survey. *IEEE Transactions on Circuits and Systems for Video Technology, 17*(11), 1606–1621. doi:10.1109/TCSVT.2007.909972

Telea, A. (2004). An image inpainting technique based on the fast marching method. *Journal of Graphics Tools, 9*(1), 23–34. doi:10.1080/10867651.2004.10487596

Vetro, A., Tourapis, A. M., Muller, K., & Chen, T. (2011). 3D-TV content storage and transmission. *IEEE Transactions on Broadcasting, 57*(2), 384–394. doi:10.1109/TBC.2010.2102950

Zinger, S., Do, L., & de With, P. H. N. (2010). Free-viewpoint depth image based rendering. *Journal of Visual Communication and Image Representation, 21*(5-6), 533–541. doi:10.1016/j.jvcir.2010.01.004

Zinger, S., Ruijters, D., & de With, P. H. N. (2009). *iGLANCE project: Free-viewpoint 3D video.* 17th International Conference on Computer Graphics, Visualization and Computer Vision (WSCG). Plzen, Czech Republic.

ADDITIONAL READING

Bruls, F., Zinger, S., & Do, L. (2011). Multi-view coding and view synthesis for 3DTV. *IEEE International Conference on Consumer Electronics (ICCE),* (pp. 698-699). Las Vegas, USA.

Do, L., Zinger, S., & de With, P. H. N. (2010). Objective quality analysis for free-viewpoint DIBR. *International Conference on Image Processing (ICIP),* (pp. 2629-2632). Hong Kong.

McMillan, L., Jr. (1997). *An image-based approach to three-dimensional computer graphics.* PhD thesis. Chapel Hill, NC: University of North Carolina at Chapel Hill.

Morvan, Y., Farin, D., & de With, P. H. N. (2007). *Joint depth/texture bit-allocation for multi-view video compression.* Picture Coding Symposium (PCS), Lisboa, Portugal.

Nguyen, T., & Do, M. N. (2009). Error analysis for image-based rendering with depth information. *IEEE Transactions on Image Processing, 18*(4), 703–716. doi:10.1109/TIP.2009.2012884

Oliveira, M. M. (2000). *Relief texture mapping.* PhD thesis, Chapel Hill, USA: University of North Carolina at Chapel Hill.

Pulli, K., Cohen, M., Duchamp, T., & Stuetzle, W. (1997). View-based rendering: Visualizing real objects from scanned range and color data. *Eurographics Rendering Workshop,* (pp. 23–34).

Smolic, A., & McCutchen, D. (2004). 3DAV exploration of video-based rendering technology in MPEG. *IEEE Transactions on Circuits and Systems for Video Technology, 14*(3), 348–356. doi:10.1109/TCSVT.2004.823395

Smolic, A., Muller, K., Dix, K., Merkle, P., Kauff, P., & Wiegand, T. (2008). Intermediate view interpolation based on multiview video plus depth for advanced 3D video systems. *International Conference on Image Processing (ICIP)*, (pp. 2448–2451).

Vetro, A., Wiegand, T., & Sullivan, G. J. (2011). Overview of the stereo and multiview video coding extensions of the H.264/MPEG-4 AVC standard. *Proceedings of the IEEE, 99*, 1–17. doi:10.1109/JPROC.2010.2098830

Zitnick, C. L., Kang, S. B., Uyttendaele, M., Winder, S., & Szeliski, R. (2004). High-quality video view interpolation using a layered representation. *ACM SIGGRAPH 2004 Papers*, (pp. 600–608). New York, USA.

KEY TERMS AND DEFINITIONS

3D Video, 3DTV: Video format that allows 3D visualization, for example, stereo images or texture and depth pairs.

Depth Map: Distance from the camera plane to the object.

DIBR: Depth Image Based Rendering technique, used for performing free-viewpoint interpolation.

Free-Viewpoint Interpolation: Interpolation (rendering) for obtaining a video sequence between the viewpoints of physical (reference) cameras.

Inpainting: Creating a part of the image that is missing, for example, as a result of free-viewpoint interpolation.

Multi-View Video: Video sequences of the same scene acquired from different points of view.

Warping: Recomputation of one camera view into another perspective.

Chapter 10
Peer-to-Peer Video Streaming

Jânio M. Monteiro
*ISE, University of Algarve Portugal/INOV,
Lisbon, Portugal*

Rui S. Cruz
*Instituto Superior Técnico/INESC-ID/INOV,
Portugal*

Charalampos Z. Patrikakis
*Technological Education Institute of Piraeus,
Greece*

Nikolaos C. Papaoulakis
*National Technical University of Athens,
Greece*

Carlos T. Calafate
Universidad Politécnica de Valencia, Spain

Mário S. Nunes
*Instituto Superior Técnico/INESC-ID/INOV,
Portugal*

ABSTRACT

The Internet as a video distribution medium has seen a tremendous growth in recent years. Currently, the transmission of major live events and TV channels over the Internet can easily reach hundreds or millions of users trying to receive the same content using very distinct receiver terminals, placing both scalability and heterogeneity challenges to content and network providers. In private and well-managed Internet Protocol (IP) networks these types of distributions are supported by specially designed architectures, complemented with IP Multicast protocols and Quality of Service (QoS) solutions. However, the Best-Effort and Unicast nature of the Internet requires the introduction of a new set of protocols and related architectures to support the distribution of these contents. In the field of file and non-real time content distributions this has led to the creation and development of several Peer-to-Peer protocols that have experienced great success in recent years. This chapter presents the current research and developments in Peer-to-Peer video streaming over the Internet. A special focus is made on peer protocols, associated architectures and video coding techniques. The authors also review and describe current Peer-to-Peer streaming solutions.

INTRODUCTION

The Internet as a video distribution medium has seen a tremendous growth in recent years with the advent of new broadband access networks and an explosive growth of media terminals supporting video reception and storage. This growth in the popularity of Internet video transmission, which resulted from the advances in video encoding solutions and the increase in the bandwidth offered by Internet providers. Moreover, this progress has also placed new challenges in current developments of video standards due to the

DOI: 10.4018/978-1-4666-2660-7.ch010

heterogeneous characteristics of current terminals and the content distribution over wired and wireless networks. The widening of image definition options, followed by a rise in user expectations for High Definition (HD) content, has placed new concerns in the bandwidth and the scalability of distribution systems.

In this field, the absence of global IP Multicast protocols has led to the introduction of privately managed overlay network companies. These solutions typically implement application layer multicast tree distributions which are currently responsible for the content distribution of many content creators. With this approach, they avoid neighborhood congestion in the server's network.

With the introduction of faster access networks, together with higher processing power and storage capabilities at terminal equipments, another application layer solution has also gained popularity in recent years. This solution modifies the client-server paradigm of the initial Internet, to allow the exchange data and other resources in what is usually called a Peer-to-Peer (P2P) network. These systems constitute an overlay mesh network of peers, where each peer acts both as server (that provides service for others) and also as client (that consumes resources from other peers).

In the field of network file sharing, the first implementations of P2P systems such as Napster (Napster, 2009), Gnutella (Gnutella, 2001) and Emule (Emule, 2010) have achieved great success. In these solutions however, files were only exchanged when any of the peers had the entire file. This led to the utilization of only a small fraction of the total peer upload capacity, because most users leave the system when the file is completely downloaded.

Currently, the BitTorrent protocol (BitTorrent, 2010) is one of the most popular solutions. It was designed for large-scale file sharing over the Internet, supporting scalable P2P distributions. The data to be distributed is firstly partitioned into small pieces or chunks, which are afterwards delivered in a non-sequential manner. The BitTorrent

protocol considers two types of peers: seeds and leeches. Seeds are peers that have all the chunks, and leeches are peers that only have some or none of the chunks. The architecture also includes a centralized process called tracker that maintains the information about the peers that host each of the content. Therefore, each leech entering the P2P distribution requests a list of peers from the tracker, and randomly selects a subset of them to become its neighbors. It then exchanges chunks with each of these neighbors usually trying to download first the chunks that are less available, in what is known as a rarest-first policy. It also uploads content to those peers that contribute with more chunks, in what is known as a Tit-for-Tat (TFT) incentive policy.

Although the utilization of such content distribution systems has been dazed by illegal content sharing that violates author's copyrights, they are capable of supporting many benefits like load balancing, fault-tolerance, self-adaptation and self-organization.

Nowadays, the main solutions for P2P file sharing have evolved to embrace non-real-time content sharing. In fact, with adequate modifications, P2P solutions can change the way real-time video transmission will be distributed over the Internet. Notice that the absence of IP Multicast routing in the Internet is the main reason that has prevented the widespread transmission of good quality television channels worldwide until now.

In section 2 we briefly outline the background in terms of P2P concepts, content search mechanisms, topologies, the issues associated with mobile and wireless environments and standardization efforts. In Section 3 we present the main developments in video streaming over P2P networks, streaming modes, multicast mechanisms, NAT traversal techniques, security and digital rights management issues, business models, and layered video encoding. In Section 4 we briefly review the main research directions and finally, in Section 5, we conclude the chapter.

BACKGROUND

Systems behaving in a peer-to-peer fashion have existed since the very beginning of the Internet, but not connoted from what is currently called by P2P.

In terms of P2P, "The Internet started as a peer-to-peer system" (Taylor & Harrison, 2009) and in fact, the goal of the original ARPANET was to connect a set of distributed resources, not in a master-slave or client-server relationship, but rather as equal computing peers using different network connectivity within one common network architecture.

P2P Systems are a consequence of the development of the Internet. A P2P System is a distributed environment composed by an underlying communication substrate to allow exchange of information among peers, applications running on top of the distributed environment for network addressing, routing (overlay network) and services, and algorithms to locate resources.

The following can summarize the main characteristics of P2P System:

- Are composed of a very large number of hosts called peers;
- Must scale gracefully with increasing number of participants;
- Computing resources are provided by the users' machines (often unreliable);
- Any given host machine may fail or disconnect at any point in time;
- Bandwidth should be treated in general as a scarce resource;
- Most users can (and are normally willing to) cooperate making some of their resources available to the system (e.g., their upload bandwidth) in order to benefit from the system, while others may not collaborate at all.

The following sections outline the background in terms of P2P concepts, the issues associated with mobile and wireless environments, the evolution into P2P media streaming and the issues associated with network address translation (NAT) and fire- wall traversal.

A P2P overlay network is therefore characterized as being a logical association of nodes that can reach each other using the underlying IP network through proper addressing and using specific content management and content retrieval protocols. In the following we will address some of the main issues regarding peer-to-peer overlay networks.

Peer-to-Peer Topologies

Peer-to-Peer overlays can be classified according to the type of model they use, in "pure", "centralized" or "hybrid" P2P. In a pure or decentralized P2P model there is no central server to convey meta-information about whom in the overlay stores certain pieces of information, or to verify user credentials. In these systems all peers have to perform the same tasks and the same pointer to a specific content may be stored in more than one node. Examples of such overlays are Gnutella (Gnutella, 2001) and Freenet(Clarke, Sandberg, Wiley, & Hong, 2001).

In hybrid P2P networks there is a hierarchy of nodes, with different nodes having different tasks to perform. Super-peers or supernodes are in those cases used to discover resources on behalf of other peers, and to answer their queries. Examples of such overlays can be found in the FastTrack (Liang, Kumar, & Ross, 2006) protocol used in Kazaa (KaZaA, 2010) and in the eDonkey file-sharing network (Heckmann, Bock, Mauthe, & Steinmetz, 2004).

In centralized P2P overlays, a central server is employed and peers contact it before they directly contact other peers. The disadvantages of these solutions include the congestion of the server and its vulnerability to attacks. Examples of networks that construct such overlays are Napster and BitTorrent.

Resource Discovery and Indexing in Peer-to-Peer Overlays

Although content transmission and routing between peers of a P2P network is supported by the same mechanisms available for other types of content distribution, including IP layer routing and transfer protocols. On the other hand, different methods exist to identify where a certain searched content might be found within the overlay network.

In the P2P overlay field, two main types of overlay graphs have been considered and implemented: unstructured overlays and structured overlays. In unstructured overlays data is discovered based on a random topology that is built based on simple node neighboring knowledge. In this field, the most commonly used routing mechanisms are flooding and random walk. Although many applications rely on these types of random graph implementations, as they have also verified scalability problems when the number of peers significantly increases. In unstructured overlays, data is discovered based on a more accurate routing mechanism, which is maintained by peers. A key is assigned to each object identifier, derived from information about its title, author and format. The system then routes each of these keys along the overlay network and stores it in a certain node, according to peer address identifiers, which will be responsible for answering queries for similar content searches. While these solutions have shown to be scalable, they are more prone to problems when nodes join and leave the overlay.

Unstructured Overlays

In unstructured overlays, a peer that wants to find a specific content in the network sends a query that is flooded through all or part of the network nodes. Those queries will hopefully find one or more peers that share the data. However, these types of methods either generate a significant amount of signaling traffic, or are prone to fail when searching for rare data.

Two main methods are used for query forwarding in Unstructured Overlays. In flooding, each search originator sends its query to all overlay neighboring nodes. Each of these neighbors either responds to the query, in case it has the object, or retransmits it to its other neighbors. In order to avoid loops, all nodes maintain a list of previously received queries, comparing each recently received query with the previous ones before processing or forwarding it. Additionally, scoping may be implemented using a Time-To-Live (TTL) field in query messages. In this case, each search originator sets the TTL value, which is afterwards decremented at each intermediate node. When a forwarding node verifies that the TTL of the query has reached zero, it silently discards it. A variation of flooding called expanding ring can also be used, where the requesting node starts by setting a low TTL, and then gradually increases it whenever it fails the attempt to locate the content. Figure 1 shows an example of the flooding of a query message.

In densely connected graphs, like the one shown in Figure 1, the flooding mechanism shown previously presents a high cost due to the fact that, within the maximum defined hop count, the query is transmitted to all the connected peers. To avoid that cost, another solution can be used called random walk.

In random walk, each node performs a random selection of the next hop, which also includes the starting node. This solution reduces the overhead imposed by the flooding process, but increases the probability of not covering part of the nodes in the overlay and, therefore, can fail in finding less common resources. A variant of random walk is shown in Figure 2. In this solution, the several parallel random walk query packets are launched at the same time by the source node.

Implementations of unstructured overlays can be found in several P2P applications such as Gnutella, Freenet and FastTrack. Gnutella was the first file sharing implementation to include a decentralized architecture that, in its initial versions, used flooding to find content. However, the increasing popularity achieved has more recently led to the implementation (in version 0.6) of a hierarchical architecture with two types of nodes, namely leaf and ultrapeers. In this solution flooding was restrained to ultrapeers, and the maximum hop count was reduced from 7 to 4.

Freenet is an open source software not limited to file sharing, but providing several tools and placing a strong emphasis on anonymity. In Freenet, the content is partitioned into encrypted blocks that are anonymously distributed among peers in the network. Therefore, after entering the network, the content does not stay in the original node, but is redundantly spread across the network. Among the several functions available, Freenet also includes a specially developed browser called FProxy, which permits the visualization of web sites stored within the overlay and message boards to announce new files and new Freenet websites (called freesites).

In terms of content search, although it is an unstructured overlay type of network, it implements a specific algorithm for content searching and retrieval. Each peer that receives a query for a file checks whether it has any part of it. In case it does, it responds to the query by sending the file through the overlay nodes. If not, it searches among the peers in its routing table for the one with the closest key and forwards the request to

it. A request failure is send backwards, pruning those paths that do not show any content storage.

FastTrack also builds an unstructured overlay, which is the core of several applications including KaZaA, iMesh (iMesh, 2010), Grokster (Grokster, 2005) and Morpheus (Streamcast Networks, 2008). It also uses a hierarchical structure with two distinct types of peers: nodes and supernodes. However, part of the protocol is unknown since its code is not open-source.

The simplicity of routing mechanisms in unstructured overlays leads to scalability problems that either result from a significant overhead in the number of transmitted plus forwarded query messages, or in an increased probability of not locating content that is available in the overlay. To solve these problems, almost all P2P architectures, which typically have started with pure unstructured overlays, have later on been complemented with improved scalability mechanisms.

Structured Overlays

In structured overlays a routing mechanism is created to more easily locate object information that is orderly distributed among the several peers in the architecture. Similar routing mechanisms are used both to route queries and define where objects should be stored among the peers. By partitioning the information about the available

Figure 1. Unstructured overlay showing the flooding of a query starting at node R, with a TTL of three

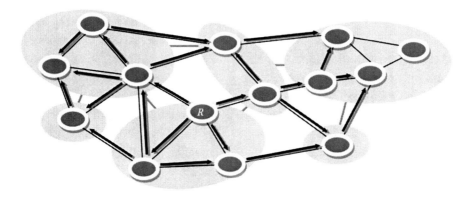

Figure 2. Unstructured overlay representing four parallel random walks starting at node R, with a TTL of three

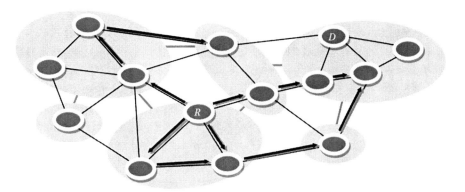

content among peers, a distributed database is built that works by mapping content identifiers to peer addresses, using Distributed Hash Tables (DHTs) for that purpose. Afterwards, a Key-Based Routing (KBR) mechanism is used that routes queries over the overlay according to the generated key, towards the node that was defined as responsible for that key.

Globally structured overlays can be based in constant degree or logarithmic degree graphs. In constant degree graphs, the maximum number of peer connections does not change according to the number of peers in the overlay. In these systems the advantage of setting a maximum routing table size is however negatively compensated by an increased complexity in the implementation of routing mechanisms when facing sparser graphs. In logarithmic degree graphs the number of peer interconnections grows logarithmically according to the maximum number of peers in the overlay, constituting the base of many implementations like Chimera(CURRENT Lab UCSB, 2010), Chord (Stoica et al., 2003), KAD (Steiner, 2007) and FreePastry, an open-source implementation of Pastry (Rowstron & Druschel, 2001). According to their structure, logarithmic degree graphs are still categorized in three groups: prefix based routing, ring based routing or specialized distance metric routing.

In prefix based logarithmic degree graphs, which were initially defined in (Plaxton, Rajararnan, & Richa, 1997), each of the symbols belonging to the computed key is used to decide, at each routing hop, where the message should be sent to, starting at the most and ending at the less significant digit of the key. For instance, if a query for a computed key 536A is sent, the first routing node forwards the message to the neighbor that has a NodeId starting with 5. NodeIds are randomly and uniquely distributed over the overlay. The second node receiving the query checks which of its neighbors has a NodeId starting with a 53. This process continues until a node is found that holds the information about where the content is stored in the overlay. Protocol specifications of prefix based logarithmic degree overlays such as Pastry (Rowstron & Druschel, 2001) and Tapestry (Zhao, Huang, Stribling, Rhea, & Kubiatowicz, 2004) have introduced some variations to this basic algorithm.

Tapestry has adapted the prefix based logarithmic degree graph to include peer join and leave procedures. In Tapestry the Secure Hash Algorithm 1 (SHA-1) algorithm is used to generate a 40 digit hexadecimal key. A Tapestry based content publish mechanism is represented in the left side of Figure 3, where a new object with a key 122B is published in the overlay. Each node along the path to the nearest NodeId stores the information about who is publishing the content. This guarantees a high level of redundancy. When a query about this content is generated, as shown in the right side of Figure 3, it is routed over the overlay until it finds a node that has a reference to the source of the searched key. When that happens, the query is forwarded to the peer that holds the content.

The Tapestry protocol has been implemented in several applications, including Oceanstore (OceanStore, 2010) and Bayeaux (Zhuang, Zhao, Joseph, Katz, & Kubiatowicz, 2001).

Along with Tapestry, other prefix based logarithmic degree protocols like Pastry were also introduced. In Pastry each node is identified with a circular 32 digit hexadecimal key. Peers start by discovering and exchanging information with their L neighbor closest peers, consisting of L/2 nodes in each direction, which is called the leaf set. Within the leaf set they keep track of new peers, peer failures and recoveries. When routing a packet two stages may be required if the destination does not belong to the leaf set of the node that initiated the search. In that case, a prefix based logarithmic degree mechanism firstly routes packets to a closer peer and, in the last stage, the packet is sent to a node belonging to its leaf set.

The Pastry protocol has been implemented in the PAST (Druschel & Rowstron, 2001) application, building a distributed file system, and in

Scribe (Castro, Druschel, Kermarrec, & Rowstron, 2002), which is used as a decentralized publishing network.

Other P2P protocols like P-Grid (Aberer et al., 2003), Bamboo (Liben-Nowell, Balakrishnan, & Karger, 2002) and Z-Ring (Lian, Chen, Zhang, Wu, & Zhao, 2005) have also been based in prefix based logarithmic degree mechanism.

Chord (Stoica et al., 2003) constitutes an example of a ring based logarithmic degree graph. Node keys are 40 hexadecimal digits long and are arranged in a logical circle with keys ranging between 0 and 2^m-1, for a maximum of m peers. The key address space is partitioned in m intervals, with each peer being responsible of an average of nearly K/m keys. When searching for a key, the starting node verifies if the destination key is between its own key and its successor's key. In that case the successor's id is returned. If not, the query is forwarded to the largest node key in its routing table (called finger table) that precedes the searched key. This procedure is repeated until the destination node, which holds the key information, is finally reached.

The Chord protocol has been implemented in DHash and CFS (Dabek, Kaashoek, Karger, Morris, & Stoica, 2001). Other P2P protocols like DKS (Alimal, El-Ansary, Brand, & Haridi, 2003) and Chord# (Schütt, Schintke, & Reinefeld, 2006) have also constructed ring based logarithmic degree graphs.

Figure 3. Example showing a tapestry publishing of a key 122Bh from node A40Ch (left side) and the routing of a query for the 122Bh content issued by node 1553h (right side)

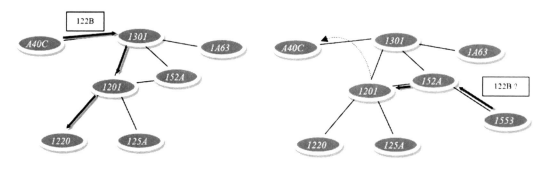

Kademlia (Maymounkov & Mazières, 2002) is an example of a specialized distance metric graph, which uses the bitwise exclusive-or (XOR) function as metric. As in Chord and Tapestry, Kademlia uses 40 hexadecimal digits to identify nodes. Every node keeps a list of typically 20 buckets, each one storing a list of nodes that have different distances from it, with each register of the list holding three IDs (IP address, UDP port and Node ID). For node replacement reasons, each of these lists is also sorted according to the last time the node has been in contact with each registered peer. Node lookups are done in a recursive and parallel way, with each node performing the XOR between its own address and the destination's address. The result of the XOR operation is used to index the routing table and several (typically three) parallel requests are then issued. This process is repeated for each of the nodes that receive this same node lookup. Kademlia protocol has been implemented in many applications, including the KAD network used in file sharing. An example of another P2P protocol that also uses a specialized distance metric is Content Addressable Network (CAN) (Ratnasamy, Francis, Handley, Karp, & Shenker, 2001).

Peer-to-Peer Operation

P2P technologies are most useful for the distribution across the Internet of the same content to a large number of users at the same time. With the P2P method the same content is stored on a large number of peer devices and shared mutually between them.

The operation of a P2P network can, in general, be described as follows, from the point of view of the user and from the point of view of the overlay network.

- **The User View:** A user downloads P2P application software from a Website on the Internet and installs it on his personal computer that is connected via a broadband connection (typically). After the P2P application is launched, it attempts to connect to certain hosts on the Internet (usually pre-configured in the application) for the so-called bootstrapping. The P2P application uses these hosts to find other peers to connect to (join the overlay).
- **The Overlay View:** For any type of overlay network, initially there may exist just a few computing devices in the Internet available to form the P2P network. These devices need some way to discover each other and form the initial overlay, i.e., bootstrap the overlay.

The bootstrap mechanism allows a newly joining peer to identify a peer already in the overlay in order to issue a join request. Since the new peer it is not yet part of the overlay, it cannot use search mechanisms of the overlay itself to locate a peer with which to connect. The possible ways to bootstrap include:

- **A Bootstrap Server:** One or more servers with well-known addresses configured to provide a list of rendezvous peers.
- **A Broadcast or Multicast Discovery Mechanism:** Rendezvous peers listen on a well-known broadcast or multicast address and respond by sending the necessary information for the connection to the rendezvous peer.
- **Cached Entries from Previous Sessions:** Peers can cache a list of rendezvous peers from previous sessions in the overlay.
- **A Bootstrap Overlay:** A universal overlay in which peers in every other overlay would be members.

For the bootstrapping process, most current P2P solutions are able to distinguish devices in private environments, i.e., when their IP addresses are not visible outside their own LANs, from devices in public environments, i.e., when their IP addresses are visible in the Internet. If some peers have the same IP address, they are typically behind a Network Address Translation (NAT) device. By checking the device capacity to establish TCP connections a peer can be further categorized as (Xie, Li, Keung, & Zhang, 2007):

- **Direct-Connect:** Peer with public address, that can establish partnerships to and from other peers;
- **Universal Plug and Play (UPnP):** Peer with private address, that can establish partnerships with other peers and the other peers can establish partnerships with it;
- **NAT:** Peer with private address, that the other peers cannot establish partnership with;
- **Firewall:** Peer with public address that the other peers cannot establish partnership with.

The majority of current P2P applications use sophisticated mechanisms to automatically deal with these connectivity issues, as will be described in section 3.4.

Peer-to-Peer Protocols

P2P network protocols are sets of rules (and communication messages) that every peer entity must interpret and follow in order to be a member of the corresponding overlay network and gain end-to-end communication with any other member of the P2P network. This means that the P2P protocols govern the network.

The main features of a P2P protocol are the following:

- Decide how membership of the network is achieved and maintained;
- Protect the network from external threats;

- Acquire and manage network assets and resources;
- Aid individuals or projects in the network;
- Define how the protocol is managed.

The most well known P2P protocols (as utilized by their homonymous applications) are:

- BitTorrent (Azureus, BitComet, BitSpirit, BitTornado, BitTorrent.Net, G3 Torrent, mlMac, MLdonkey, QTorrent, Shareaza, μTorrent);
- Ares (Ares Galaxy, Warez P2P);
- Direct Connect (BCDC++, DC++, NeoModus Direct Connect, etc.);
- Fasttrack (Grokster, iMesh, Kazaa, Morpheus, etc.);
- eDonkey (eMule, Overnet, etc.);
- Gnutella (BearShare, iMesh, Gnotella, Gnucleus, GTK-gnutella, LimeWire, Mactella, Shareaza, etc.);
- MANOLITO/MP2PN (Blubster, Piolet, RocketItNet);
- OpenNAP (Napigator, WinMX).

BitTorrent is the most popular P2P protocol in use today. The major usage of it, is for P2P file sharing and distribution of large amounts of data. It has been estimated that BitTorrent accounts for roughly 27% to 55% of all Internet traffic. In Bit-Torrent the peer distributing a data file treats the file as a set of identically sized pieces. Usually, the file size is counted of a power of 2, typically between 32 kB and 16 MB each. The peer creates a hash for each piece, using the SHA-1 hash function, and indexes them in a metainfo file (the .torrent file). Pieces with sizes greater than 512 kB can reduce the size of a .torrent file (easier to store or transmit), but claimed to reduce the efficiency of the protocol. When a peer receives a particular piece, the hash of the piece is compared to the recorded hash to test its integrity and that the received piece is error-free. Peers that provide a complete content are called seeders, and the peer providing the initial copy is called the initial seeder.

Peer-to-Peer in Mobile and Wireless Environments

The huge growth in Internet capable wireless and mobile devices is paving the way for P2P applications and more specifically for those supporting adaptive video streaming.

Five important characteristics differentiate mobile and wireless devices from desktop computers that affect their interaction with P2P overlays:

- **Node Heterogeneity:** Variation in network capacity and computing resources across the set of nodes in the overlay;
- **Energy Limitations:** Battery autonomy requires sophisticated power management mechanisms to reduce power consumption (as power-saving modes may be interpreted as nodes that left the overlay);
- **Multihomed Nodes:** Devices support multiple network interfaces (IEEE 802.11, 3G, Bluetooth);
- **Handovers:** Transitions between Base-Stations may be interpreted as node churn;
- **Roaming:** IP address changes in roaming transitions interpreted as node churn.

Routing indirection (that includes use of Mobile IP) is one of the mechanisms used to mitigate mobility churn caused by mobile nodes. Using managed stationary peers to proxy routing for mobile peers in the overlay is another method. The IETF Host Identity Protocol (HIP) (IETF HIP Working Group, 2010) considers HIP-Bone, an overlay using HIP addressing that includes mobility transparency.

P2P applications for mobile devices can be developed nowadays, although not using a pure P2P model as they require the support of the 3G network infrastructure to perform user and

resource location. The sharing of resources by such P2P applications is done however in a purely P2P manner.

Combining P2P and ad-hoc approaches for the delivery of multimedia streams to mobile users has already been addressed in many contributions. For instance, in (Do, Hua1, Jiang, & Liu, 2009) the authors propose the re-distribution of the video streaming between peersthat are using cellular access networks, instead of letting each peer download the video by itself. In MOVi (Yoon, Kim, Tan, & Hsieh, 2008), the issue of limited capacity in the wireless network is addressed by exploiting the opportunistic mix use of downlink and direct peer-to-peer communication. In CUBS (Tan, Guo, Chen, & Zhang, 2001) a combination of several fixed-line links are used to increase the upload bandwidth by coordination of the upload bandwidth sharing among neighboring residential users.

In (Yao, Duan, & Pan, 2006) the authors use multiple access links implementing an agent for mobile communications that aggregates bandwidth and the overall service availability on a mobile network. In (Stiemerling & Kiesel, 2010) the authors address the volatile nature of cellular links when moving at much higher speeds than walking, also evaluating the resulting requirements for chunk scheduling.

Implementing P2P overlays in Mobile Ad hoc Networks (MANETs) also requires the use of special routing algorithms such as Dynamic Source Routing (DSR) (Johnson, Hu, & Maltz, 2007) or Optimized Link State Routing (OLSR) (Clausen & Jacquet, 2003).

PEER-TO-PEER VIDEO STREAMING

Television (TV) has had a major impact on our daily lives for the last 50 years. However, the conventional one-to-many scheduled broadcasting TV model is being nowadays transformed into a many-to-many, user-centered, personalized paradigm with accessibility to an infinite pool of live TV programs, on-demand video and rich-media, through any capable video terminal, irrespective of the screen size, processing power, or type of network connection.

The huge growth in IP traffic in recent years, mainly due to the growth of video type of services and content, is challenging operators to take advantage of new technologies and efficiently shape their network to ensure quality on the services provided to end users. And the delivery of rich content, in particular video and TV services, is a huge opportunity for all players including broadcasters, content providers, Internet service providers (ISP) and telecommunications operators (Telco), as end users are spending more time in their social networks and surfing the Internet than watching TV. The broadcasting industry already understood this trend and is starting to distribute their contents over the Internet.

It is in this shift from classical "monopolist" linear TV distribution towards non-linear, on-demand, anytime, anywhere, cross device audio-visual consumption, that P2P technologies may become an important ingredient of both the digital convergence process and the entertainment industry, rather than its major enemy.

After introducing the current classification of TV services over IP networks, the next sections start by giving an overview of the evolution into P2P media streaming, its challenges and architectures. It will continue by introducing the main expected multimedia services, by comparing the Application Layer Multicast with the IP Multicast multipoint distributions and by describing the main mechanism to perform NAT traversal. It will also describe the state-of-the-art in appropriate video coding techniques for P2P streaming, by describing the business models for P2P Media Streaming, finishing with an overview of current P2P video distribution systems.

The Evolution into Peer-to-Peer Video Streaming

Although Internet and TV are nowadays integrated in several different platforms, each one of these technologies evolved as separate telecommunications infrastructures. Before the development of the Internet, TV was just a broadcast medium without bidirectional communication offering little freedom of choice and control (Thompson & Chen, 2009).

The expansion of the Internet Protocol (IP) technology and its integration in many access technologies has allowed a convergence of data services on all fronts. Due to IP technology, network operators started offering Triple-Play services: a bundle of voice (telephony), video, TV and data services along with some value added services, using one common technology. Internet Protocol Television (IPTV) provides real-time digital video streaming and television services over private and managed IP core and access networks. Different from the global Internet, in these networks Quality of Service and IP Multicast services are implemented.

WebTV has addressed similar objectives but over the global Internet and involving Web technologies, as is the case of Hypertext Transfer Protocol Adaptive Streaming (Cruz, Domingues, Menezes, & Nunes, 2010). WebTV tend to follow a channel organization with contents organized in directories of programs and movies, and providing a real-time stream transfer rate to each peer.

Nowadays, video streaming and Peer-to-Peer transferred data, are among the highest growing traffics on the Internet (Cisco, 2010). The growth of Internet video streaming have shown that in the years to come, it will surpass the amount of traffic of Peer-to-Peer file sharing. In fact, currently while Peer-to-Peer systems are extensively used for file sharing applications, most of the traffic exchanged in P2P overlays is already composed by audio and video content, including music and movies.

As representatives of decentralized, distributed network architectures, P2P applications are attractive solutions for carrying media across the Internet due essentially to the following:

- Are "overlays" to the existing broadband network, and do not require any type of change to the existing network infrastructure;
- Have a relatively low service cost (per GB delivered) compared to Content Delivery Networks (CDN);
- Have low investment and maintenance costs (low CAPEX, OPEX);
- Are scalable to millions of concurrent users; each additional peer adds capacity to the overall resources;
- No single points of failure;
- Are resilient to node and network infrastructures failures;
- Introduce a lower network load when compared to unicast for the same purpose;
- Can use multicast techniques (Application Layer Multicast) to improve the efficiency of delivery.

As happened some years ago in the beginning of video transmission over IP, the download-and-play solution preceded the video-on-demand, the real-time encoding capability and finally the video streaming solutions. The same happened with P2P, where the huge success of file sharing peer-to-peer systems motivated the use of P2P for streaming contents (Buford, Yu, & Lua, 2008) turning into reality the so-called "peercasting" services, e.g., P2P-based Internet TV (P2PTV), P2P Internet Radio and P2P music streaming, seen as content-delivering applications that run Over The Top (OTT) of an operator network. However in order to make the evolution into a fully developed P2P streaming some challenges must be met which include:

- **Video Content Unambiguous Identification and Location:** Different from the file based solution, in P2P streaming only one Peer acts as video source;
- **Peer Selection and Query:** Selection of the optimal peers for streaming is a difficult task due to the heterogeneity and asymmetry of the peers network conditions: upstream transmission rates vary from peer to peer, as well as the Round Trip Times (RTT);
- **Peer Churn:** The volatility of peers can cause gaps in the stream playback if the peer that would be the source of the next video segment suddenly leaves the P2P system;
- **Time-Varying Network Conditions:** Packet loss rates and upstream capacities vary due to external traffic and/or peer churn;
- **Packet Drop/Losses:** Packets may be lost, delayed or dropped due to peer churn, competing traffic, and network congestion and network failures;
- Constrained end-to-end delays and low startup latencies;
- **Scheduling of Data:** To minimize delays (i.e., sequential in-time arrival) and increase resilience to peer churn (i.e., to increase/decrease the number of peers) when handling video, versus efficient techniques when sharing files (i.e., indexing and searching objects);
- **Heterogeneous Receivers:** The support for different video qualities and definitions by an adaptive video encoding method.

The solving of these challenges must also be made by the standardization of proper P2P protocols, by the design of adequate architectures and by the definition of user-centric quality evaluation mechanisms.

The contribution of video coding is to implement an encoding method that, at the same time meets the variety of terminals' requirements and network conditions that currently exists, with the increasing expectations of users. In fact as terminal capabilities increase, in terms of display definitions, processing power and communication rate, users tend to require higher qualities from the received video stream. This imposes an adaptation of the content transmitted according to the receiving terminal. To meet these developments, in January 2005, the Joint Video Team (JVT) from ISO/IEC MPEG and the ITU-T VCEG started developing a scalable video coding extension for the H.264/AVC (ISO/IEC, 2005) standard, known as H.264 Scalable Video Coding. Standardized in 2007 as annex G of the H.264 standard (ISO/IEC, 2007; ITU-T, 2010), H.264 SVC augments the original encoder's functionality to generate several layers of quality. Enhancement layers may enhance the content represented by lower layers in terms of temporal resolution (i.e. the frame rate), spatial resolution (i.e. image size), or signal-to-noise ratio resolution (i.e. SNR).

In terms of architecture definitions, two main architectures have been used (Liu, Guo, & Liang, 2008), namely:

- Mesh-based approaches;
- Tree-based approaches.

In Mesh-based approaches, which derive from file sharing applications, peers organize themselves into a mesh, independently requesting pieces, or chunks, of the video content from neighbors, without any regard for the structure of the distribution path (Zhang, Liu, Li, & Yum, 2005); Zhang, Luo, Zhao, & Yang, 2005; Zhang, Zhao, Tang, Luo, & Yang, 2005). While these solutions are capable of providing good resilience to peer churn and a high network utilization performance, they usually lead to high end-to-end delays. This is due to the push-pull solutions implemented for the dissemination of the video pieces that do not require coordination between peers when downloading chunks. An example of such distribution is shown in Figure 4, where one video Source S distributes its content to the Mesh-based P2P overlay.

In order to minimize the delay spread in Mesh-based architectures, in (Nunes, R., Cruz, R. S., & Nunes, M. S. (2010)) the authors have defined and implementation a P2P Player prototype that uses a novel adaptive scheduling algorithm, the Prioritized Sliding Window. This mechanism was designed to improve a Scalable Video Coding distribution, reducing the startup latencies when using multiple layers. The evaluation of the prototype have shown that it achieves a robust real-time streaming service, supports several terminal setups, adapts bandwidth to various access networks and discourages free-riders in the network.

Different from these, in Tree-based approaches video packets are simply forwarded along a pre-defined route which links peers, forming of one (Chu, Gao, & Zhang, 2000) or more (Castro, et al. 2003; Padmanabhan, Wang, Chou, & Sripanidkulchai, 2002) multicast trees, rooted at the video source. The advantage of combining more than one multicast trees is that the resulting robustness of the system is increased, due to path diversity.

When compared with the Mesh-based approach, this solution usually supports a lower end-to-end delay in video streaming. However it still constitutes a more sensitive solution to uplink rate variations, potentially introducing severe quality degradations on the descendents of the same tree.

If properly considered these uplink rate variations can be compensated using the scalability properties offered by H.264/SVC, as shown in Figure 5, where two layers are distributed over a Tree-based P2P overlay. In (Baccichet, Schierl, Wiegand, & Girod, 2010) the authors implement the transmission of SVC layers on top of the Stanford Peer-to-Peer Multicast (SPPM) protocol,

Figure 4. Example of a P2P tree-based approach for video distribution

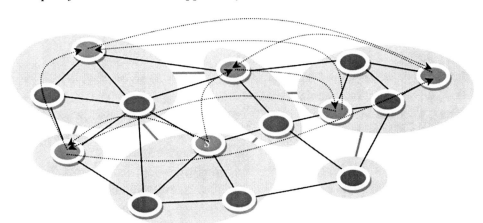

combined with a prioritization mechanism to react to network congestion.

Alternatively, some systems consider Hybrid solution. Some of these systems combine a P2P mesh-based downloading, for the majority of the video content, with a conventional client-server methodology. Examples of such systems can be found in (Xu et al. 2003) and (Hefeeda et al. 2003). In (Xu et al. 2003) the authors propose and analyze a hybrid architecture that integrates both CDN and P2P based streaming media distribution, which is capable of significantly reducing the cost of CDN capacity reservation. Additionally in (Tu et al., 2005) the authors present an analytical framework to quantitatively evaluate the dynamics of hybrid P2P streaming systems and the impact of various factors on its behavior.

By alleviating servers from the weight of all data transmission, they can be used for the transmission of more critical data, as for instance happens with missing pieces when a peer is reaching the playback time, or dealing with peer churn. When compared with pure P2P architectures, these hybrid streaming systems can support a faster distribution of media content, higher robustness to churn, quicker response to peer requests and better efficiency in terms of traffic overhead.

In terms of CDNs, such hybrid solutions present the advantage of distributing the costs by all participating peers reducing the required number of servers. This makes them suitable for IPTV distributions over the Internet.

Peer Selection in P2P Streaming

As in file based P2P systems, the selection of peers in P2P video streaming typically takes into account neighbor's available bandwidth, IP level hop distance and the content they store. The concept of content availability however changes in live and video-on-demand transmissions over P2P, since different peers might be playing and therefore storing different parts of the media. In these cases special purpose search mechanisms are required to indentify which neighboring peers store the content required for a certain playing index. The complexity of such peer and content selection mechanism grows as the number of peers increases, and as their storing capacity is considerable lower than the dispersion of user's playing times. This may typically happen in large scale Media-on-Demand Streaming Services, requiring special purpose solutions to both peer selection (Chi & Zhang, 2006; Cui, Li& Nahrstedt, 2004;Do,Hua & Tantaoui 2004;Hefeeda, Bhargava, & Yau,2004) and content search (Kostic,Rodriguez, Albrecht& Vahdat, 2003; Wang & Liu, 2006; Yiu, Chan, Xiong & Zhang, 2005; Wang & Liu, 2006).

Scheduling Mechanisms and Chunk Selection in P2P Streaming

In P2P streaming the aim of scheduling mechanisms is to define when pieces should be transmitted and how different pieces should have different priorities. Live and Media-on-Demand transmission over P2P requires appropriate types of scheduling mechanisms when compared with conventional P2P overlays. For instance, the rarest-first piece selection method used by the BitTorrent protocol is not suited for real-time applications in general, because the order of arrival of the downloaded pieces doesn't respect the chronological order of the events in the bit stream. One of the first attempts to consider this problem was (Vlavianos, Iliofotou & Faloutsos, 2006), defining a two levels priority system where higher priority is given to those blocks that are closer to the playing index. In (Nunes, R., Cruz, R. S., & Nunes, M. S. (2010))the authors define a sliding window mechanism for Scalable Video Coding transmission based in BitTorrent that gives higher priority to lower layers according to the upload capacity os each peer. As the chunk download window slides, different prioritization levels are given to higher enhancement layers if conditions are favorable.

Overlay Construction

As new nodes join to a P2P network there are several ways of connecting them to the existing P2P tree or mesh overlay. In P2P live streaming these solutions should consider both, the maximum stretch delay, computed between the streaming source and playback, and the average upload bandwidth of peers when compared with the video bandwidth. In order to reduce the streaming delay, a lower number of hops should be used, with each peer distributing its content to a high number of receiving peers. However a higher number of receivers per peer typically require a higher upload capacity, which is an important limitation of P2P networks.

Besides the overlay architecture construction the system should also should also consider its maintenance and particularly the problems associated with peer churn. The churn rate depends on the type of content distribution being made, but is typically higher and more critical when users watch a live streaming session when compared with a Video-on-Demand distribution. Since any peer may leave the distribution at any time, all its descendants will become at least temporarily disconnected from the overlay without being capable of receiving video. This requires a quick

Figure 5. Example of a P2P tree-based approach for video distribution of two transmission layers (L0 and L1) of scalable video coding

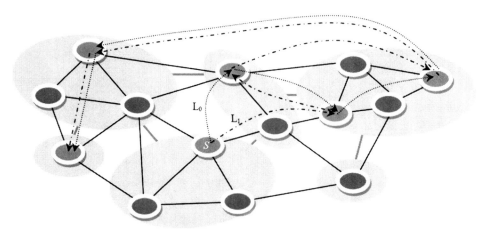

mechanism of re-establishing the connection of the affected peers to other unaffected ones.

The method used by peers to join and leave an existing overlay, depends on the implementation. It can either be made using a centralized solution or a distributed one. In a centralized solution, as each new peer joins the overlay it first contacts a central server, also called directory server, which according to peer's location and/or the existing topology decides which peer it should connects to. The central server also monitors the distribution to detect peers leaving the overlay. In this case it should review the topology instructing affected and remaining peers to form a new distribution. In such a solution however, the coordination server might become a point of failure or even a bottleneck when the number of peers increases.

To avoid the problems associated with a central server, several distributed algorithms, like (Tran, Hua & Do, 2003; Banerjee, Bhattacharjee & Kommareddy, 2002), were defined that do not use a central server to maintain the topology. In these cases an hierarchical organized overlay might be used, in which new clients follow down the hierarchy of peers, usually starting at the data source. Each level of the hierarchy decides whether the peer may join to an associated node, or continue following down the hierarchy. Such solutions however add complexity to the content search mechanism being more appropriate for live streaming than to Media-on-Demand (Ken, Jin & Chan, 2007).

In terms of architecture, P2P streaming systems are basically of three kinds, pull-based, push-based, and hybrid push-pull. In pull-based systems (as exemplified in Figure 6), a logical tracker (realized by geographically distributed tracker nodes or multiple server nodes in a data center) maintains the lists of active peers in swarms (groups of peers storing and exchanging media contents) to help in the selection of appropriate candidate peers (peer-list) for a requesting peer. Complete media content sources can be central-

ized (content provider in-network peers, called super-nodes, with better stability and higher storage and bandwidth) or distributed among peers (peer seeders).

In Hybrid pull-push streaming systems (Figure 7) the peers join the system in the same way as in push-based mode, but also exchange content availability with their siblings enabling them to retrieve media data, just like in pull-based mode. Each head peer retrieves media content from a parent node and maintains a certain number of connected sibling nodes.

For content providers a cooperative mode using Content Distribution Networks (CDN) is also common. This scenario uses intermediate peers that are in fact CDN surrogate nodes. These surrogate nodes provide higher QoS services for end users than services using only ordinary peers. The CDN surrogate nodes exchange signaling with trackers and peers, as illustrated in Figure 8, but may also communicate with end users using HTTP for non P2P enabled clients to distribute the same content.

Quality Assurance Solutions in Media Streaming

In terms of resilience and loss recovery, two major solutions can be considered: Automatic Repeat Request (ARQ) and Forward Error Correction (FEC), using network coding. ARQ is a technique that requires the retransmission of lost data packets. At the transport layer, ARQ is typically done authomatically by the TCP protocol. However it can also be implemented on top of non-reliable protocols like UDP or DCCP (Kohler, Handley, & Floyd, 2006). In these cases, ARQ can be combined with a selective retransmission mechanism, implementing an Unequal Loss Protection, which only retransmits packets with a higher priority in response to playback time or quality. In fact, this solution can be used in P2P distributions of both, Multimedia-on-Demand and Live Video.

Figure 6. A typical pull-based P2P streaming system, illustrating the signaling sequence for swarm creation and media flow among peers with different capabilities

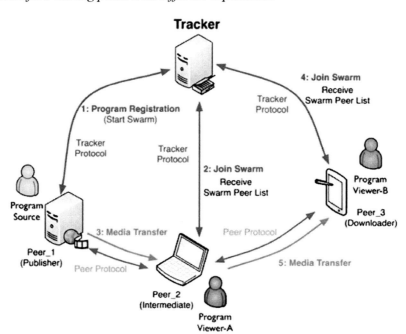

The aim of Forward Error Correction is to support the recovery of lost or erroneous data using redundancy. Different solutions for FEC can be used depending on the type of channel being considered. In binary erasure channels (BEC), like the Internet, packets either arrive or are discarded. Such types of losses are different from binary symmetric channels (BSC), typically found in lower layers, where bits are either decoded correctly or with an error. While in P2P networks we can find both types of effects, the mechanisms used for each one, are typically different.

In terms of BSC, the main solutions considered for FEC are the Reed-Solomon Codes (Reed, & Solomon, 1960), convolutional codes (Johannesson & Zigangirov, 1999) and LDPC codes (Gallager, 1962), while in terms of BEC we can find many solutions like for instance LT codes (Luby, 2002) and Raptor codes (Shokrollahi, 2006).

Network coding can be seen as a solution for data distribution in P2P, which although being based in BEC type of FEC, goes beyond loss recovery. In fact, the concept behind network coding is that a receiver can reconstruct the original data after downloading a certain amount of independently encoded symbols, either generated at the source or at intermediate peers. This enables not only the recovery from packet losses using other received blocks, but also the reception of data from different peers with a low probability of getting repeated symbols. Although the implementation of such solutions of network coding in video streaming over P2P is commonly associated with Multimedia-on-Demand distributions (Wang & Li,2007), where the same content is available in different sources, it can also be implemented in live distributions as proposed in (Wang & Li, 2007).

Multimedia Services and Delivery

Audiovisual services delivered over P2P networks can carry a variety of different types of service, and contents (audio, video, data or any combination of these) (EBU TECHNICAL, 2010). The most popular services are the following:

Figure 7. A typical push-based P2P streaming system, illustrating the signaling and media flow push to peers

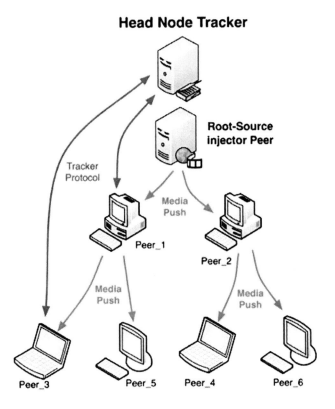

- Linear and on-demand radio over the Internet;
- Linear and on-demand television over the Internet;
- Interactive and personalized applications;
- Music downloads;
- Movie downloads;
- Media podcasting.

An important distinction must be made between the so-called non-linear services, like Video on Demand (VoD), and linear services. Linear services include all transmissions which are not triggered by the consumer himself, thereby remaining a broadcasting act, whether the technology used for the act is based on P2P delivery, via the Internet or mobile phones, via point-to-multipoint or otherwise. The rules applicable to linear services apply in a horizontal manner, independently of the

technical modes of signal delivery (over-the-air, by satellite, cable, broadband, microwave, telephone line, format, resolution, screen-size, protocol, etc.) (EBU TECHNICAL, 2010).

P2P technologies are able to utilize every peer joined in an overlay network as both a client and a server (a so-called prosumer, i.e., both producer and consumer). There are two typical application scenarios for Mesh-based P2P streaming:

- **Live Scenario:** When peers join the network, they can only apply for part of the programme being distributed, corresponding to the current future timeline. The content available to request depends on the moment the peers join the network.
- **Video on Demand (VoD) Scenario:** Peers can apply to full contents available when they join the network and additionally,

may have interactive operations with the contents (Fast Forward, Rewind, Pause, etc.).

In the Tree-based P2P streaming only the Live scenario applies. For IPTV services VoD has been considered the key feature to attract consumers as it allows users the flexibility and convenience of watching any point of a video at any time. However, P2P VoD is more challenging to design than the P2P Live streaming service. While in a Live scenario a very large number of users are watching the same stream in a "synchronous" fashion, in VoD users may be watching the same video but asynchronous to each other, i.e., watching different points of the same video at any given moment (Shen, Yu, Buford, & Akon, 2009).

A common assumption that needs to be made for these P2P systems is that all the peers can (and are willing to) cooperate to the replication of the streams, making some of their resources available to the system (e.g., their upload bandwidth) in order to pass the stream data they already own to other peers.

Another assumption is that each stream corresponds to continuous flows of media data encoded at the streaming source. The source splits the encoded stream into a series of chunks, typically containing a few seconds of video data, and these chunks correspond to the stream units that will be spread and available at the peers for the stream replication.

Application Layer Multicast vs. IP Multicast

The basic architecture for delivering multimedia streaming traffic over IP networks (and the Internet) is the client-server architecture. In this model a client connects with a server and the media is

Figure 8. A typical cooperative CDN - P2P streaming system, illustrating the signaling and media flow among peers and trackers

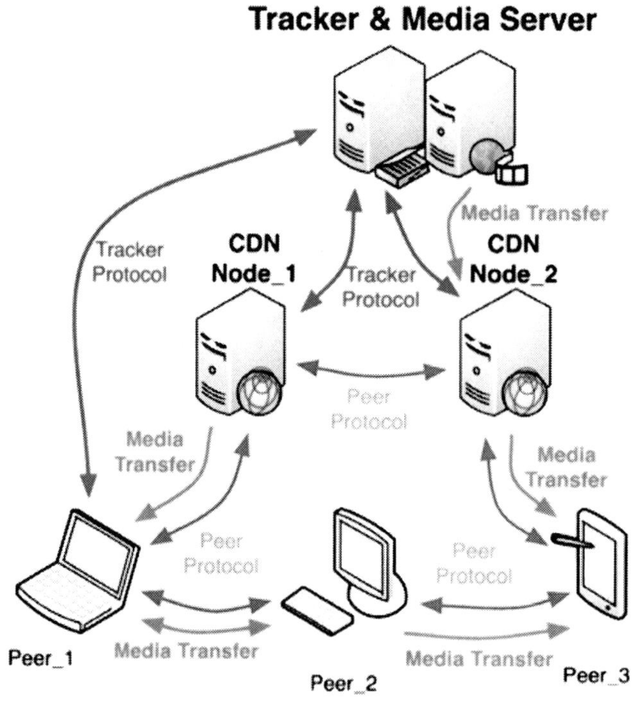

streamed to the client from that server. The access bandwidth at the server is the most limiting factor in terms of system scalability.

Another architecture that can be used for the same purpose is the peer-to-peer architecture, being scalability its main advantage when compared to the client-server model.

For both architectures, whenever there are multiple clients simultaneously requesting/receiving the same media stream from servers, a Multicast protocol can be implemented, i.e., a method to transmit IP datagrams from a data source to a group of receivers, avoiding unicast replication at the source.

Multicast is a special type of protocol that can be deployed at different network layers, and it is designed to simultaneously deliver each packet to a group of destinations using efficient strategies.

The most common approaches are IP Multicast, implemented at the IP routing level in routers, and the Application Layer Multicast (ALM), also known by P2P overlay multicast (OM), implemented at the host level. In the following we will briefly compare both solutions.

IP Multicast

IP Multicast is based on a group communication model in which hosts are aggregated into groups with a single IP address per group. Hosts can send datagrams to the group by setting the destination to the group's IP address. Data replication is performed within the router's infrastructure, which is in turn responsible for managing the group communication.

While a host or node on the Internet has typically only one unicast address, it can simultaneously be a member of several multicast groups.

In IPv4 multicast support is optional and the address space is defined in a global D "class" from 224.0.0.0 to 239.255.255.255 (dot decimal notation). In IPv6 multicast support is mandatory and the address space is reserved with the prefix 0xFF (hexadecimal). For the adequate management of the address space it was divided by zones, and sets of intervals were reserved for each Autonomous

System (AS) number of an Internet Service Provider (ISP) with correspondence to its AS prefix.

The most notable intra-AS multicast protocols include the Protocol Independent Multicast (PIM) (Estrin et al., 1998) the Distance Vector Multicast Routing Protocol (DVMRP) (Waitzman, Partridge, & Deering, 1988), and the Core Based Tree (CBT) (Ballardie, 1997). These protocols create a group address per multicast tree, and each router stores the state of each active group address, meaning that the state in the router grows with the number of simultaneous active groups.

For inter-domain multicast routing MBGP (Bates, Chandra, Katz, & Rekhter, 1988), a set of multiprotocol extensions to the Border Gateway Protocol (BGP) (Rekhter, Li, & Hares, 2006), has been adopted, as well as the intra-AS multicast protocols from the PIM family, the PIM-SM (Sparse Mode) and its variant PIM-SSM (Source Specific Multicast functionality) (Holbrook & Cain, 2006).

The support for IP multicast in its current model and implementations is difficult due essentially to the following:

- The group model address allocation is of a world-wide unique multicast address per application in order to avoid extraneous inter-domain cross traffic;
- Current implementations do not provide a means to restrict the allowed senders, i.e., any host can send to any IP multicast address, and preventing denial of service or intrusion is quite hard;
- Current implementations do not provide indication of group size (infeasible for an ISP to charge based on this metric);
- There is no unique solution to IP Multicast transport QoS assurance in the current model;
- The delivery cost of a large-scale multicast stream is much higher than that of a unicast stream of the same rate, due to the much higher operational costs that IP Multicast requires;

- Inter-accounting (inter-domain) cost model and billing is not a clear subject.

These constraints have prevented the wide implementation of IP Multicast globally in Internet, and their support by ISPs.

Application Layer Multicast

Application Layer Multicast (ALM) does not rely on router deployment and is built on top of the available network services. With ALM, peers self-organize into distributed networks that are overlaid on top of the IP networks. Data replication is performed at the end hosts that are interconnected by unicast connections. The end hosts are the only responsible entities for managing the group communication.

Multicast functions (e.g., group management, data replication and multicast routing) are performed at the overlay network level by forming unicast trees or meshes at the application layer. It is at the overlay network level that some basic communication functionalities between peers are provided, e.g., overlay maintenance and security, peer discovery, object search, message routing and multicast services (achieved through message forwarding among the multicast group members). All messages between peers are in fact transported via unicast connections across the underlying network infrastructure.

Application Layer Multicast meshing can be categorized in the following approaches (Banerjee, Bhattacharjee, & Kommareddy, 2002):

- **Mesh-First:** A mesh topology logic network (connection graph) between peers is established first, followed by a reverse-path forwarding (RPF) construction of multicast data topology tree (logic nodes);
- **Tree-First:** A logic data topology tree is constructed first, followed by control connections between logic nodes in the tree;
- **Implicit or Geographic:** The logic nodes and the logic network (control and data paths) are defined simultaneously, typically associated with the underlying overlay network structure;
- **Random:** The selection of logic nodes is done by means of gossip-based (epidemic) protocols.

The Mesh-first types are efficient for small groups. The Tree-first types are better suited to applications that require high-bandwidth transfers. The Implicit/geographic types support very large group sizes as well as latency-sensitive and high-bandwidth applications. The Random types are characteristic of unstructured overlay constructions due to the fast and reliable message diffusion process used (gossip-based) (Buford, Yu, & Lua, 2008).

The logic structure of the overlay network upon which the multicast application layer is built may be of type Structured or Unstructured, as previously described in section 2. Therefore, ALMs are established on top of either a Structured or an Unstructured overlay network layer that was constructed on top of the IP network infrastructure. The Multicast groups are formed among the peer nodes in the overlay network.

ALM approaches with topologies established close to the underlying overlay topologies, in themselves also built close to the underlying IP network, are typically very efficient. This is common with ALMs built over unstructured overlays, but more difficult with structured overlay approaches as these impose a predefined overlay topology (peers with close logical IDs may be far in terms of geographic proximity).

The Performance of ALM approaches is typically evaluated with the following fundamental metrics (Buford, Yu, & Lua, 2008; Shen, Yu, Buford, & Akon, 2009):

- **Stretch (delay penalty):** Ratio of a one-way overlay delay between a pair of nodes over the delay between the equivalent underlay nodes (ratio of delay between a packet sent over the overlay to a packet directly sent over the unicast path);

- **Stress:** Number of times a packet traverses an underlay link;
- **Control Overhead:** Number of control messages introduced by the ALM approach (and bandwidth overhead).

Other important metrics can also been used (Buford, Yu, & Lua, 2008):

- **Start-up Latency:** Time to start playback of a media stream from time of the join request;
- **Join Latency:** Time to receive the first multicast packet from the time of join request;
- **Error recovery Latency at Packet Loss:** Time to recover the erroneous packet from the time of error discovery;
- **Reconnection latency at node failure:** Time to be connected to a new parent node from the time of node failure detection;
- **Average loss rate per node:** The ratio of the number of packets lost (received) per session to the number of packets that should be have been received per session;
- **Maximum number of multicast groups:** Maximum number of multicast groups running simultaneously;
- **Multicast group scalability:** Capability to scale to a group size of N.

One of the first ALM protocols was NARADA (Banerjee, Bhattacharjee, & Kommareddy, 2002), a Mesh-first protocol that defined the Rendezvous Point (RP) as the root node. HMTP (Host Multicast Tree Protocol) (Zhang, Jamin, & Zhang, 2002) is an example of ALM Tree-first approach. CAN (Ratnasamy, Handley, Karp, & Shenker, 2001), Scribe (Castro, Druschel, Kermarrec, & Rowstron, 2002) and Bayeux (Zhuang, Zhao, Joseph, Katz, & Kubiatowicz, 2001) are examples of implicit ALMs implemented on top of Structured overlays.

ALM is the current best solution to eliminate the dependency on the lack of deployment of global multicast applications. However, ALM is not as efficient as IP Multicast as it typically requires a higher control overhead to maintain group membership and to monitor network conditions (probing messages), causing delay and consuming bandwidth. Another issue is related to the stability of the multicast trees when groups are large due to the high overhead in maintenance.

Incentives, Trading, and Reputation in Peer-to-Peer

The feasibility of P2P systems is based on the premise of cooperative behavior, i.e., the expected joint exploitation of the local resources of each participant, in benefit of the increase in capacity of the whole system, provides a better result than the simple sum of individual utilizations. A cooperative behavior incurs in "costs", as resources are consumed (bandwidth, processing power, storage, etc.), and theses costs may be of particular significance, for example in mobile devices.

A cooperative transaction consists of a negotiation phase, where the "provider" and the "consumer" reach agreement on the services and respective remunerations, and a processing phase, where the cooperation transaction is realized and a remuneration returned.

The basic mechanism to achieve cooperation among participants is based on Trust, and Reputation based on the history of past transactions and feedback for other participants, is the main ingredient to build Trust.

However, participant peers cannot be assumed permanently altruistic or obedient, as their behavior is self-interesting and autonomous, strategizing to maximize their own utility. The rationality of the peer may lead to some irrational results for a P2P system as a whole (Shneidman & Parkes, 2003). Misbehaved peers may forge their transaction history in order to manipulate their reputation (Tang, Wang, & Dou, 2004):

- **Collude Inflating:** A set of peers rate one another with fake (or not existing) transactions in order to increase their reputation values.
- **Deflating:** A set of peers rate other peer with fake (or not existing) transactions in order to decrease its reputation value.
- **Faker:** A peer of low reputation fakes itself as a peer with high reputation in order to get more profit.

The decision to cooperate, or not, has its rational on some kind of "incentive" or remuneration, i.e., without incentive the provider may refuse to cooperate.

Incentive Patterns

Incentive mechanisms for cooperation take into consideration the heterogeneous nature of participants and the circumstances when cooperation may not be possible, either due to a static reason, e.g., limited capacity, or to a dynamic reason, e.g, network congestion (Shen, Yu, Buford, & Akon, 2009). The set of abstract mechanisms that incentive schemes may apply for stimulating cooperation exhibit certain patterns. A taxonomy of these incentive patters, considering trust or trade mechanisms, as proposed in (Obreiter & Nimis 2005) and thoroughly described in (Shen, Yu, Buford, & Akon, 2009), is illustrated in Figure 9 (Obreiter & Nimis 2003).

In trust-based patterns, providers cooperate with consumers because they trust them. This trust may be static or dynamic, and does not imply any type of explicit remuneration:

- In the collective pattern, participants mutually help one another and do not have individual interests. This pattern exhibits a static trust, i.e., the reputation of participants does not vary over time as a result of their behavior, and dispenses remuneration

mechanisms. In this pattern, participants need to identify themselves to prove that they are trustworthy, turning impossible anonymity.

- In the community pattern, participants cooperate with one another based on individual interests, and in cooperating they build their reputation, necessary to enjoy later cooperation from other participants. In this pattern trustworthiness is dynamic, varying over time as a result of the participants behaviors. The remuneration in this pattern is the reputation, as it reflects the historical behavior of the participant. This pattern may however suffer from misbehavior, in terms of occurrences of defamation of good cooperators or in false praise for those who do not cooperate. In this pattern, participants also need to identify themselves to prove that they are trustworthy, turning impossible anonymity.

In trade-based patterns, providers obtain explicit remunerations from consumers for their cooperation. The remuneration consists of a return of cooperation, which may be immediate (occurs during the cooperation transaction), or deferred, by means of a promise. This promise can be honored by the consumer itself or by a third-party in its favor:

- In the barter trade pattern, the participants assume symmetrical roles, cooperating to complete a direct exchange of favors, which occurs simultaneously, and do not leave any obligations pending after termination of the cooperation transaction. Participants that refuse to cooperate obtain nothing from the other participants. In this pattern, participants can remain anonymous.
- In the bond-based pattern, participants cooperate to obtain explicit remuneration in

exchange but with a temporal de-linkage between cooperation and remuneration. The remuneration can take the form of promissory instruments, i.e., bearer notes, bearer bills, bank checks or banknotes. The motivation for participants to cooperate as providers is to obtain promissory instruments, making them creditors in the group in order to enjoy cooperation in the future.

- In the bearer notes pattern, it is the consumer issuing the promissory note that must honor it later. Both issuers and debtors of the bearer notes need to identify themselves to prove their trustworthiness.
- In the bearer bill pattern, it is a different participant, on an order from the consumer participant that must honor the bill in the future. Both issuers and debtors of the bearer bills need to identify themselves to prove their trustworthiness.
- In the banking pattern the remuneration takes the form of bank checks and each participant has a "bank account" (virtual). The bearer of a check presents it to his "bank" to have his account credited. Both the issuing entities of the checks and the debtors of the checks need to identify themselves to prove their trustworthiness.
- In the banknotes pattern the remuneration takes the form of banknotes pre-issued by a central authority. Anonymity of the consumer participant is guaranteed.

Incentive Schemes for Peer-to-Peer Streaming

In P2P streaming systems, cooperation among peers brings the following benefits:

- Peers may decide to cooperate even when they are "offline", i.e., not using the service (not enjoying a stream), seeking just to accumulate a balance;

- Peers with limited capacity may use their balances to obtain a better incoming streaming quality, harder to obtain if they would be accounted just for their limited outgoing bandwidth (due to the asymmetry of the access network technology);
- Peers may opt not to cooperate for a certain period provided they have accumulated a balance to pay for their future consumption;
- The system enjoys a larger streaming capacity, is more resilient to churn (peer departures) and peer failures, it is scalable and more economical in terms of infrastructure (system resources are distributed among participant peers).

It is important to consider that the decision to cooperate, or not, without any type of "incentive" may put at risk the efficiency of the system and its feasibility.

Incentive schemes typically combine different incentive patterns in order to bring together their advantages, offset their shortcomings and strengthen their effectiveness, especially when systems are subject to malicious behaviors (attacks), uncooperative behaviors like free-riding (peer uses services but does not contribute), tragedy of the commons (available resources are consumed without limit) or interferences like Sybil attacks (peers that forge identities) and white-washing, i.e., peers that leave and re-join using a different identity(Shen, Yu, Buford, & Akon, 2009).

A well-known incentive scheme, the Tit-for-Tat Protocol (TFT) used in the BitTorrent system, is a direct application of the barter trade incentive pattern.

Various incentive schemes have been proposed to mitigate free-riding or tragedy of the commons problems in P2P systems (Tang, Wang, & Dou, 2004; Park & Schaar, 2010):

Figure 9. Taxonomy of incentive patterns

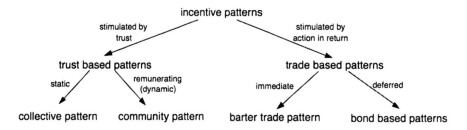

- **Cooperative schemes:** Utilize helpers that download files on behalf of a peer;
- **Pricing schemes:** Use virtual currency or micropayment to reward uploads and charge downloads;
- **Differential service schemes:** Treat peers differentially depending on ratings.

In P2P streaming systems the free-riding problem may have a huge impact on the efficacy and performance of the system, leading to scalability issues and service degradation. Various incentive schemes can be designed to fight free-riding and other forms of interference (Su & Dhaliwal, 2010), but, specifically for P2P streaming systems, the more appropriate incentive schemes can be categorized as reciprocal, reputation-based, game-theoretic, and taxation.

- **Reciprocal:** This incentive scheme maintains a private history of transaction characteristics (e.g., download rates) and rewards peers accordingly;
- **Reputation-Based:** This incentive scheme uses a global rank of peers to decide the priorities in the selection of peers and the desirable media segments;
- **Game-Theoretic:** This incentive scheme derives the peer strategy through game-theoretic modeling and analysis, turning it resistant to collusion attacks;
- **Taxation:** This incentive scheme motivates peers to contribute as much as they can to the system to improve the system's

social welfare (the overall streaming quality perceived by all users).

Peers are rational, having for goal the maximization of their own utilities. As such, if zero-contribution induces harm (e.g., punishments), they will choose to contribute. Therefore, in P2P streaming systems, effective incentives are indispensable in order to encourage selfish peers to contribute. The following key issues should be carefully addressed in the design of incentive schemes for these systems (Xiao, Zhang, Shi, & Gao, 2011):

- **Asymmetry:** Media data is transmitted in linear order causing asymmetry among peers (i.e., a peer is often unable to contribute anything in return);
- **Guarantee honest fulfillment of the incentives:** There should be effective methods to prevent peers from cheating (e.g. magnifying their own contribution);
- **Incentives should be easy to implement:** If an incentive mechanism is of high complexity, it will be difficult to deploy and will potentially bear defects;
- **Incentives should emphasize peers' instant contributions:** Due to the real-time requirement in streaming, peers are more strictly required to contribute and their current contribution should be emphasized more than their historical contribution, encouraging them to contribute during all the time;

- **Game-Based Model for Peer Behaviors:** In order to reflect more precisely peers' behaviors, the strategies to adopt should not be just "share" or "not share" but rather "how much to share".

Bandwidth Trading as Incentive

Bandwidth trading mechanisms provide peers with incentives in order to offer upload bandwidth to other peers in a P2P network. As a result, a bandwidth-trading scheme tries to minimize the free-riding problem where peers in a P2P network consume resources without contributing anything to the network (Eger & Killat, 2006).

The Tit-For-Tat strategy, also known as the choking algorithm, is a well-known example used in the BitTorrent protocol that allows a peer to control to which other peers to upload content. This peer selection strategy encourages peers to contribute data, hence, improving the BitTorrent's performance. Specifically, the Tit-For-Tat protocol achieves high performance in the distribution process by enabling a peer to upload more to those peers who upload data at high rates. Thus, fair-trading is encouraged. However, newly joined peers are unable to receive any content because they do not have any pieces yet to share, even though they are willing to be good contributors. This can be solved using the "optimistic unchoke" mechanism provided by the BitTorrent client. The mechanism allows a peer to send pieces to randomly selected peers trying to discover in this way even better peers to trade bandwidth. In addition, it ensures that newly joined peers will participate in the swarm (Eger & Killat, 2006; Cohen, 2003; Sirivianos, Han, Rex, & Yang, 2007; Legout, Liogkas, Kohler, & Zhang, 2007).

2Fast is a system that solves the problem of peer's not contributing bandwidth by preserving the fairness of bandwidth sharing. 2Fast forms groups of peers who collaborate in the file download process on behalf of a single group member who can use its full download bandwidth. A peer in 2Fast can use its idle bandwidth to help other peers with their downloading process and in return get help during their download.

2Fast introduces based bandwidth trading incentive whilst the existing P2P data distribution systems base their incentives on content trading. The 2Fast bandwidth trading incentive model enables any peer to act as a helper to any other peer by investing its unused bandwidth and getting this bandwidth in return in the future, therefore, no mutual interest between the peers is required. This approach eliminates the bottleneck of the upload capacity and limits the download speed of peers with asymmetric links in other P2P download protocols (Garbacki, Iosup, Epema, &van Steen, 2006).

In (Liu, Shen, Panwar, Ross, & Wang, 2007) a distributed protocol is proposed in which peers are encouraged to contribute more in a data-driven P2P live streaming network where multiple description coding (MDC) techniques are applied. With MDC, the video quality is dependent on the received number of descriptions, therefore, the more descriptions a peer receives the better the video quality is. The proposed protocol ensures that peers with high upload data rates receive more descriptions and therefore a better video quality.

Incentives for End-Users

In recent years P2P systems have grown rapidly, and many of them have large population bases, e.g., file sharing systems like BitTorrent and VoD systems like PPLive and PPStream (PPStream, 2011). Their architecture offers the benefit of utilizing the distributed resources at the peers, making the system more scalable and fault-tolerant than traditional client-server architectures. When an online content provider uses a P2P protocol, it faces an incentive issue: how to motivate clients that possess content to upload to others. This issue is of great importance because the performance of a P2P network is highly dependent on the users' willingness to contribute their uplink bandwidth.

However, selfish users tend not to share their bandwidth without external incentives (Gupta, Judge, & Ammar, 2003).

Generally, in P2P systems, cooperation may incur in significant communication and computation costs, and rational users may refuse to contribute their fair share of resources. Individual rationality is then in conflict with social welfare. Users who attempt to benefit from the resources of others without offering their own resources in exchange are termed "free-riders". This free-riding behavior is actually the result of a social dilemma that all users of such systems confront, even though they may not be aware of its existence. In a general social dilemma, a group of people attempts to utilize a common good in the absence of central authority. In the case of a P2P system one common good is the provision of a very large library of contents to the user community. Another might be the shared bandwidth in the system. The dilemma for each individual is then to either contribute to the common good, or to free-ride on the work of others. Since contents on the system can be treated like a public good and the users are not "charged" in proportion to their use, it appears rational for people to obtain contents without contributing by making their own contents accessible to other users. Because every individual can reason this way and free-ride on the efforts of others, the whole system's performance can degrade considerably. Another problem caused by free-riding is related to vulnerabilities created in a system giving origin to risks to individuals. If only a few individuals contribute to the public good, these few peers effectively act as centralized serving entities. Users in such an environment become vulnerable to lawsuits, denial of service attacks, and potential loss of privacy. A distinction needs to be made between lazy free-riders, that do not share content after they have finished obtaining it, versus die-hard free-riders, that create or obtain cheating clients to prevent uploading to the system.

A provider can address this problem by means of incentive schemes in order to cope or prevent free-riding. Especially in P2P VoD applications, content providers need to incentivize the peers to dedicate bandwidth and upload data to one another so as to alleviate the upload workload of their content servers. Compared to file sharing, VoD applications need to satisfy more stringent temporal and spatial constraints for data delivery-asmedia segments have to be received by the user within a short period and in adequate sequence. Even worse, predicting the data demand is difficult because users might fast-forward and/or rewind among the video segments.

A content provider with paying customers needs to offer better quality of service guarantees than the ones offered by existing P2P content distribution systems. If the content provider uses a protocol that offers strong incentives for cooperation, clients with abundant bandwidth may become reliable contributors, enabling the content provider to save both its bandwidth and costs and to offer speedy streaming services to its customers.

Reward-Based Incentive Scheme

This incentive category is based on credits, where clients earn credits by contributing with their resources. The rewarding methods for honest-contributorsusually have two expressions. First, if the peers are unable to return the favour, the content provider rewards the client's service with a credit, which can be redeemed for discounts on paid content or other type of rewards. Second, if the client's peers possess content of interest and have appropriate uplink capacity, the client is rewarded with reciprocal uploads from its peers. The content provider can use incentive mechanisms that reward the peers based on the amount of upload capacity they contribute.

The reward can have various forms, e.g., real money value rebate for the service fee or virtual credits or reputation records for advanced services. Any reward scheme can be represented by the currency flow from the content provider to the peers. Even for rewards in virtual currency or reputation imply that the P2P-VoD operator needs to invest money for developing advanced/prioritized services for users.

Punishment Based Incentive Mechanisms

This category attempts to identify misbehaving peersto isolate them from the network. These mechanisms usually assume a set of trusted nodes that detect and verify misbehavior from selfish peers, that are subsequently denied participation in the network. The fear of detection and punishment motivates peers to cooperate. One such mechanism is the Barter Trade pattern Tit-for-Tat (TFT), employed by BitTorrent, particularly successful in combating selfish free-riding behavior in P2P file sharing systems. TFT is used to ensure that only peers who actively contribute are the ones allowed downloading files from other peers, i.e.,incentive the peer cooperation via the fear of being punished.

This mechanism mitigates free-riding but does not provide explicit incentives for seeding. Although several BitTorrent deployments rely on clients to honestly report their uploading history (Andrade, Mowbary, Lima, Wagner, & Ripeanu, 2005), and use this history to decide which clients can join a swarm, practice has shown that clients can fake their upload history reports or collude (Lian, Zhang, Yang, Zhao, Dai, & Li, 2007). Seeders improve download completion times, because they increase the content availability and the aggregate upload bandwidth. Nonetheless, this mechanism bears two weaknesses. First, it does not encourage clients to seed, i.e., to upload to other peers after completing the file download. Second, it is vulnerable to manipulation (Sirivianos, Han, Rex, &Yang, 2007; Legout, Liogkas, Kohler, & Zhang, 2007; Shneidman, Parkes, & Massoulié, 2004; Jun & Ahamad, 2005; Locher,

Moor, Schmid, & Wattenhoffer, 2006), allowing modified clients to free-ride and still achieve download rates equal to or higher to the ones of cooperative clients. The TFT scheme does not work for VoD or real-time streaming applications, because the data demand and supply among the peers are highly volatile.

Instead of using a punishment-based scheme like TFT, providers could use a reward-based scheme that incentivizes peers to contribute upload capacity for VoD or real-time streaming systems.

Hybrid Incentive Mechanisms

Dandelion (Sirivianos, Park, Yang, & Jarecki, 2007), a novel hybrid incentive scheme, is suitable for P2P paid content distribution.

In case a client has content that interests a peer, but that peer does not have content that interests the client, or the peer is unable to reciprocate at the same rate that the client uploads to it, the system entices the selfish client to upload by explicitly rewarding the client with virtual credit. The server maintains a virtual economy and associates each client with its credit balance, which is used to track the bandwidth that the client has contributed to the network.

Security and Digital Rights Management in Peer-to-Peer Streaming

P2P streaming is susceptible to several security and privacy issues. Attacks can cause a loss of quality or even the complete unavailability of the content in some parts of the distribution (Gheorghe, Lo, Cigno& Montresor, 2011). Given the application and transport layer nature of such overlays there are several possible security concerns.

One of the problems that can occur is that malicious peers can alter the P2P protocol, for instance by generating false messages announcing content they don not have. They can also delay or not answer request messages from other peers intentionally presenting a random behaviour. In terms of media transmission, some peers can delay the forwarding of data or deliberately discard pieces, which combined with the time-sensitive and interdependent nature of video streaming can cause a severe degradation of QoS and consequently user Quality of Experience.

Another relevant concern in terms of P2P streaming is overlay routing. In fact, in solutions such as (Baccichet, Schierl, Wiegand, & Girod, 2010) the routing protocol specification should consider the possibility of some peers announcing a false available uplink throughput, or false hop distance and delay to the source. In these cases, some nodes can potentially compromise the reception of data by many peers that by that method would rely on them. This problem can partially be solved by limiting the number of peers that receive and send information to a certain node (Singh, Castro, Druschel, & Rowstron, 2004). In this field in (Conner, Nahrstedt, & Gupta, 2006) the authors present a framework that prevents selfish or malicious nodes from downloading an overwhelming amount of P2P media streaming data. Overlay routing should also consider the possibility of some malicious peers sending messages on behalf of other peers, which imposes the implementation of a method for secure transmission of messages (Wallach, 2003).

In P2P streaming architectures that include Supernodes, a special attention should be made to the monitoring of their behaviour. In fact their higher responsibility associated with an incorrect behaviour can potentially cause more damages to the data distribution.

Other security concerns involve the P2P application code, including the unauthorized access to user information or even access to the content being transferred by a certain node. In fact P2P applications have access to both, network connection and file systems (Wallach, 2003) and by that way can be misused to obtain user information. This requires restricting the application privileges

in terms of file system access and blocking operations that are not directly related with its purposes.

P2P applications for content and network resources sharing bring up potential security issues if special measures to prevent them are not carefully considered. More specifically, sharing resources on a computer with anonymous and unknown users over the public Internet goes against many of the basic network and computer security principles.

In enterprise environments, network security guidelines recommended the usage of a firewall, either built into the router accessing the Internet. Even in personal environments, personal firewall software is used in order to isolate and protect the networked computer from potential intruders. However, in order to share resources on a computer, or to access resources in other computers within a P2P overlay network, specific TCP ports must be opened through the firewall for the P2P protocols and for data exchange in the P2P overlay. Once these ports are opened the computer may no longer be protected from malicious traffic coming through them.

To avoid malicious situations a user should obtain the P2P application from trusted sources, and the install package file should be provided from the official website of the P2P platform or, if downloaded from mirror sites, to have integrity verification mechanisms (MD5, for example).

The basic security goals of any P2P application and protocol should aim for the following:

1. The P2P protocol has to provide maximum resistance against all kinds of Denial of Service (DoS) attacks;
2. The P2P platform has to provide theoretically secure anonymization;
3. The P2P application or transfer protocol has to provide secure end-to-end transport encryption, integrity verification mechanisms and anonymization on the context;
4. The P2P protocol has to provide (virtually) isolation from the "normal" Internet, in order to avoid or prevent illegal or criminal actions

to be perpetrated from the user IP address without his/her knowledge;

5. The P2P protocol should be designed with maximum protection against identification of protocol usage via simple traffic analysis;

6. The P2P application should be capable of handling larger volumes of data, with acceptable throughput;

7. The P2P protocol should be generic, with a well-abstracted design, compatible with all new and existing network enabled applications.

P2P overlays are typically viewed as a threat to digital Digital Rights Management (DRM). Currently most of the P2P based IPTV systems do not consider digital content management. In fact video and audio content can be unrestrictedly stored, copied or redistributed without any restriction. However, to be fully implemented in IPTV, content management is required and therefore P2P streaming development should include it. In this field Digital Rights Management (DRM) solutions can be used to control the storage and redistribution of the multimedia content, supporting data encryption and other technologies.

In (Androutsellis-Theotokis & Spinellis, 2004) an overview of the P2P content distribution technologies is given, together with the security issues characteristic of P2P content distribution systems. The analysis includes secure storage and routing, authentication, access control, and identity management.

In terms of multimedia distribution over P2P networks, the authors in (Chu, et al. 2006) propose a mobile DRM system that combines a client application with a tamper-resistant hardware to assure digital rights, requiring peer side hardware authentication. In (Zhang, Chen, & Sandhu, 2005) and (Balfe, Lakhani, & Paterson, 2005) the authors consider cryptography to provide or enhance the security for P2P systems. They enforce that only authorized code is executed on a system, based on Trusted Computing (TC) technologies. These solutions, while being effective methods to provide security in P2P systems, require dedicated hardware which typically is not available on the client side of most IPTV systems.

In (Balfe, Lakhani, & Paterson, 2005) the authors classify existing DRM architecture approaches in three types: conventional Server-Client based, distributed P2P based and semi-distributed P2P.

In (Liu, Huang, Huo, & Mou, 2007) the authors developed a Multimedia-on-demand P2P streaming with digital rights management. The architecture employs a central server that distributes a secret key that is used to both encrypt and decrypt a block using Windows Media DRM. The system is receiver-driven streaming and the peers do not collaborate during the streaming service.

In (Lan, Xue, Tian, Hu, Xu, & Zheng, 2009) the authors define a manageable peer-to-peer architecture for live media streaming with DRM that extends the Video-on-Demand P2P architecture of (Lan, Zheng, Xue, Chen, Wang, & Ma, 2008). They combine the advantages of a central-distributed peer-to-peer structure with a data-driven structure. The resulting architecture consists of register and index servers, supernodes and peers. After registration, peers receive a key and index server list. Afterwards, the index server periodically receives data availability information from peers. Supernodes are used to store more data for the support of live streaming.

While the topic of DRM topic has gained popularity in other fields of communications, its application to P2P technologies is still a field of research with many researches working in this area.

NAT Traversal Mechanisms

In overlay networks peers are typically spread over many private networks connected to the Internet through routers or gateways that perform Network

Address Translation (NAT) and may also have firewalls configured.

This situation affects P2P operation because peers must support both inbound and outbound connections with other peers and both NAT and firewall functions interfere with the ability of external peers to reach those with translated addresses or filtered packets.

The NAT is the mechanism that remaps the Network Address information of an IP packet header into another, and takes place when the packet passes through a routing device that supports this mechanism. Through the use of NAT it is then possible to provide Internet access to several nodes within a local access network via a single public IP address. This is possible since all the nodes behind the NAT device are able to have their own unique private IP address, while using the NAT device as a Gateway to the public Internet.

The NAT protocol alleviates the exhaustion of the IPv4 address space by allowing the use of private IP addresses at home or in corporate networks (intranets) behind residential gateways or routers, respectively, that share a single or a limited number of public IP addresses. Initially, this technique was called IP masquerading (Rekhter, Moskowitz, Karrenberg, de Groot, & Lear, 1996), and now it is used commonly with NAT as it hides an entire IP subnet behind a public IP address. More specifically, NAT operates at two levels:

- The Basic NAT, that handles the IP address translation: this level is responsible for managing the mapping of the unique IP address of the NAT device (visible to the Internet) to the local IP addresses behind the NAT;
- The Port Address Translation (PAT), that handles the translation of port numbers. This is necessary in order to be able to offer the full range of Internet services, as the combination of IP/port is necessary in order to support end-to-end communication over the Internet.

There are several types of NAT implementations:

- Full-cone NAT, known also as one-to-one NAT;
- Address restricted cone NAT;
- Port-restricted cone NAT;
- Symmetric NAT.

The internal network devices are able to communicate with hosts on the external network through the change of the source address of outgoing requests to the external IP address of the NAT device, and they relaying replies back to the originating device. This methodology keeps the internal network isolated from external IP packets (except for the packets belonging to TCP sessions that haves been initiated from inside hosts), as the NAT device has no automatic method of determining the internal host for which incoming packets are destined.

Generally, the NAT mechanism is implemented with the use of stateful translation tables that map the "hidden" addresses and utilized ports and the type of layer 4 protocol, into a single IP address and readdress the outgoing IP packets. In the reverse communication path, responses are mapped back to the originating IP address using the information stored in the translation maps, which are flushed after a short period unless new traffic refreshes their state.

As stated above, NAT became one of the solutions able to solve the problem of the limited number of IPv4 addresses, particularly after the introduction of the multihosting feature of Apache servers (Apache, 2010).

Problems Introduced by NAT

The NAT has a lot of advantages as it provides a solution on the limited number of IPv4 addresses and the increased network security for the nodes that are "behind" the NAT router. On the other hand there are a lot of limitations depending on the utilized transfer protocol (layer 4) and the network use case scenario. More specifically, there are protocols and applications that make use of the UDP transfer protocol, like the RTP that is commonly used on VoIP and video streaming applications. In this case, if a node behind the NAT tries to have a bidirectional communication with another external node having a public Internet IP address, this cannot be achieved, as the conventional NAT is able to provide a unidirectional communication from the node behind the NAT to the public node, but not vice versa. This is due to the connectionless type of the UDP protocol as the NAT mechanism could not "store" this information of a non-existing connection and maintain only the unidirectional communication, as the packets from the public node could not be "forwarded" inside the NAT router. Also, it is obvious that only the internal NAT node could call the external node with the public IP. This problem doesn't occur in applications and protocols that make use of the TCP transfer protocol, as in this case the NAT table temporarily stores the TCP connection characteristics (socket), but again this is valid only when the internal user initiates the TCP connection.

Similar is the case of a WWW server behind the NAT, as it is not possible to access this Web server from the public IP network without a manually and statically configured port forward rule that maps any TCP request for connection on the port 80 to the internal IP address of the WWW server.

Additionally, there are other complex scenarios like the use of the FTP protocol, which sends explicit network addresses within the application data (TCP port 20), as in active mode, but uses different connections for command line interface (TCP port 21) and for data traffic. This means that, when an internal NAT node is requesting a file transfer, the host making the request identifies the corresponding data connection through its network layer and transport layer addresses. Thus, if the host starting the connection is located behind a NAT router, the translation of the IP address and TCP port number makes the information received by the server invalid as it contains internal private addresses.

Finally, the biggest problem occurs in P2P applications and networks, as it is not possible to have communication between peer nodes that are located behind NAT routers. Notice that, when nodes operate in P2P networks, they are acting both as clients and servers. In the context of NATs, the latter operation is the most problematic and requires specific solutions to address this problem.

NAT Traversal Techniques

NAT traversal techniques manage to establish and maintain IP network connections, required for client-to-server or client-to-client network applications that traverse NAT gateways. There are a lot of mechanisms, but no single technique is able to support all use case scenarios.

The NAT traversal techniques could be distinguished in two categories:

- The proxy or tunneling techniques;
- The port forwarding techniques.

The proxy or tunneling techniques require assistance from a node-server on the external side of the NAT with a public IP address. Also, these methods could be categorized in two sub categories: methods which use the server only when establishing the connection, such as STUN (Rosenberg, Weinberger, Huitema, & Mahy, 2003), and others based on relaying all data through it (such as TURN (Mahy, Matthews, & Rosenberg, 2010)). The last technique could cover most of the NAT traversal cases but, on the other hand, adds overhead on the bandwidth and increases latency due to triangulations of the IP packets, something that does not fulfill the requirements for real-time applications like voice and video communications.

The other type of NAT traversal techniques are based on the idea of dynamically "informing" the NAT gateway in order to make the appropriate port forwards from the outside public IP of the NAT router to the inside private address. The conventional method performs this manually, something that of course requires access privilege to the NAT gateway (such as port forwarding) and network expertise. The new methods have as a goal to do this automatically, by enabling the inside nodes to make the corresponding port forwards to the NAT gateway without any human intervention (such as UPnP and NAT-PMP).

Simple Traversal of User Datagram Protocol through Network Address Translators (STUN)

STUN acronym stands for Simple Traversal of User Datagram Protocol (UDP) through Network Address Translators (NATs), and it is described in RFC 3489 (Rosenberg, Weinberger, Huitema & Mahy, 2003). The STUN protocol allows nodes utilizing applications over the UDP protocol and communicating via NAT gateways to discover the presence of a network address translator and to obtain the public IP address (NAT address) and port number of the application starting UDP connections to remote hosts. The protocol requires the intervention of a 3rd-party STUN server with a public IP address.

The STUN is a client-server protocol based on a simple query and response over UDP protocol. More specifically, the node inside the NAT-masqueraded router initiates a short sequence of requests to the STUN server listening at two IP addresses in the network on the public side of the NAT, traversing the NAT. The server responds with the results, which are the public IP address

and port on the "outside" of the NAT for each request. From the results of several different types of requests, the client application can learn the operating method of the network address translator according to a NAT characterization algorithm, including the lifetime of the NAT's port bindings.

When a client has discovered its NAT gateway IP address, it is able to initiate the communication with other peers by advertising its global IP NAT address to its peers, rather than the masqueraded internal address that is not reachable for its peers on the public network. The STUN protocol is utilized commonly for VoIP applications over protocols like the Real-time Transport Protocol (RTP) and the Session Initiation Protocol (SIP) that rely on UDP packets for the transfer of media and signaling traffic over the Internet

STUN can cooperate with all the aforementioned types of NAT, like full cone NAT, restricted cone NAT and port restricted cone NAT, with the exception of symmetric NAT.

Traversal Using Relay NAT (TURN)

TURN, that stands for Traversal Using Relay NAT, is a protocol, described in RFC 5766 (Mahy, Matthews & Rosenberg, 2010), which permits to a node behind a NAT router to communicate with other nodes on the external part of the router by receiving incoming packets over TCP or UDP transfer protocols. TURN is one of the mechanisms that could work in all types of NAT and firewalls, even behind a symmetrical NAT.

Similarly to STUN, TURN requires a 3rd party server with a public IP that manages data relaying towards nodes behind the NAT. The main disadvantages of TURN are the big delays associated with triangulations and the communications overhead due to the packet encapsulation process.

Teredo

Teredo (Huitema, 2006) is a tunneling protocol for providing IPv6 connectivity to nodes that are located behind IPv6-unaware NAT gateways. The functionality of Teredo is based on the encapsulation of IPv6 packets within IPv4 UDP datagrams that can be routed through NAT devices and over the conventional IPv4 Internet.

Teredo supports 3 types of nodes:

- Teredo client, which is the node that has IPv4 connectivity via a NAT gateway. Within Teredo this client could traverse the NAT functionality and additionally have access to the IPv6 network islands;
- Teredo server, used for the initial configuration of a Teredo tunnel; it never forwards any traffic for the client (apart from IPv6 pings);
- Teredo relay, which is a server that terminates the client tunnel and has a public IPv4 address, while simultaneously having access to an IPv6 network (e.g. a single campus/company, an ISP or a whole operator network, or even the whole IPv6 Internet). Therefore, a relay requires a lot of bandwidth and can only support a limited number of simultaneous clients. Each Teredo relay serves a range of IPv6 hosts (e.g. a single campus/company); it forwards traffic between any Teredo clients and any host within such range.

Universal Plug and Play (UPnP)

UPnP is a set of networking rules that are supported in residential gateways and networking nodes such as personal computers, printers, surveillance cameras and mobile devices, to seamlessly discover each other's presence on the network and establish functional network services for communications. One of these features is the automatic port forwarding in order for the internal device (behind NAT) to communicate with the other nodes on the external network.

Particularly, UPnP provides NAT traversal via the implementation of the Internet Gateway Device (IGD) Protocol. Many residential gateways routers allow any local UPnP controller to perform a variety of actions, including retrieving the external IP address of the device, enumerating existing port mappings, and adding and removing port forwards and mappings. By adding a port mapping, an UPnP compatible node behind the IGD can enable traversal of the IGD from an external address to an internal client.

The UPnP architecture supports zero-configuration networking so that UPnP compatible devices from any vendor can dynamically cooperate with other nodes within the local network. It is the UPnP Forum that promulgates the UPnP technology.

NAT Port Mapping Protocol (NAT-PMP)

Another NAT traversal technique based on port forwarding is the NAT Port Mapping Protocol (NAT-PMP). This technique is based on the idea that the internal device "indicates" to the NAT router, which ports it has available to map to its internal IP address, so that a packet destined to the external IP of the NAT gateway and to the port associated with the internal device can be forwarded to the correct internal IP. The NAT-PMP applies to those dedicated and static forwarding rules in the NAT table of the gateway without any human intervention.

The NAT-PMP has a lot of similarities with the UPnP protocol, but it is more focused on the NAT traversal and is much more elegant than UPnP. UPnP, on the other hand, has a large standards committee (the reference and standards documents reach up to 25 Megabytes). In comparison, NAT-PMP is summed up in one 1600 line RFC, something that it is very important as it provides much simpler implementation in routers that doesn't support it via a simple firmware update.

Adaptive and Layered Video Streaming

The environment in which most Peer-to-Peer Video Streaming applications operate is characterized by the asymmetric properties of the access networks at individual peers (i.e., the bandwidth for the downlink is higher than for the uplink), being the uplink capacity at each peer the limiting factor for sending data to other peers. For file transfers, this limitation only affects the duration of the transmission but for streaming it has a significant impact in the quality and the format of the video and audio streams.

In these packet-erasure networks, packets losses typically happen due to router congestion, transmission errors on the physical link (namely in wireless and mobile networks), node departure from the Peer-to-Peer overlay or even strict timing out due to real time visualization.

For real-time streaming applications over these heterogeneous networks, video encoding schemes (media-processing techniques) play a vital role for an efficient distribution of video data from one sender to a population of interested receivers. These media processing techniques are related to source compression, to packetization and to channel coding of the media, vital to overcome the constraints of the access networks asymmetry and vulnerability to errors, as well as to the available computational resources at individual peers.

The most relevant video encoding schemes are based on the concepts of Layered Coding and Multiple Description Coding. In Layered Coding, different levels (layers) can be recovered from a scalable video stream, provided that some basic information (the so-called base layer) is received. In Multiple Description Coding (MDC), two or more representations of the same data (descriptions) are generated (that can be independently decoded) so that the quality of the recovered video is only a function of the number of descriptions received.

The video coding standard H.264, also called MPEG-4 Advanced Video Coding or H.264/AVC (ISO/IEC, 2007; ITU-T, 2010) is currently the preferred scheme for video services in fixed, wireless and mobile IP networks as well as in Digital Video Broadcasting (DVB) -- Terrestrial (DVB-T), Cable

(DVB-S), Satellite (DVB-S) or mobile Handheld devices (DVB-H) (Reimers, 2004).

The widespread adoption of H.264/AVC has led to the definition of a scalable extension (based on layered coding) of this encoding method in the standard (Annex G) -- the Scalable Video Coding (SVC) -- that aims to efficiently support the transmission of several layers of video quality, providing several rate adaptation points for both point-to-point and point-to-multipoint distribution scenarios (Monteiro, 2010; Schwarz, Marpe & Wiegand, 2007).

MPEG-4 Advanced Video Coding (H.264/AVC)

The MPEG-4 H.264/AVC is a hybrid codec which combines block-wise transform coding and motion-compensated predictive coding in order to reduce the redundancy of a video signal (Ostermann et al., 2004; Wenger, 2003).

The H.264/AVC design divides the encoding process into two structural layers, a Video Coding Layer (VCL), which is responsible for creating a coded representation of the source content, and a Network Abstraction Layer (NAL), which encapsulates all bit stream components in a way that enables the mapping of the VCL data to a variety of transport systems, from file formats to different network protocols (see Figure 10).

The H.264/AVC NAL units are packets that start with a one-byte header and have an integer number of bytes. The last 5 bits of the header contain a NAL unit type field, which defines the type of content carried. Broadly, it can be classified as either a VCL or a non-VCL payload. VCL NAL units contain a complete or partitioned coded slice, while non-VCL NAL units contain auxiliary data that can either be necessary for the decoding process or, as in the case of Supplemental Enhancement Information (SEI) messages, just to help in the decoding process (not being essential, though) (Monteiro, 2010).

Similarly to other prior video coding standards, the VCL uses a block-based hybrid video coding. Pictures are partitioned into macro-blocks, which in turn are organized in slices. Macro-blocks typically include a rectangular picture area of 16x16 samples of the luma component and 8x8 samples of each of the two chroma components.

In H.264/AVC the input video signal is predicted from previously transmitted information available both at the encoder and the decoder, and the prediction error is compressed, typically with a transform coder operating on a block-by-block basis. The prediction can be based on information in other frames ("motion-compensated predictor") or in the same frame ("intra predictor"). Intra-prediction exploits correlation among adjacent pixels in the image. Motion-compensated prediction uses one or several previously encoded frames as references to predict the current frame.

Three slice coding types were considered: I, P and B slices:

- I-slices use spatial intra-picture predictive coding;
- P-slices may use both intra-picture and inter-picture predictive coding;
- B-slices may use intra-picture, inter-picture predictive coding or inter-picture bi-predictive coding.

After compression, VCL data is encapsulated in NAL units, which are organized as Access Units (AUs), when they refer to a certain temporal sampling instance. A coded video sequence is composed of several consecutive AUs, starting with an Instantaneous Decoding Refresh (IDR) AU, which employs intra-picture predictive coding only (I-slice). The first picture of a video sequence is always an IDR picture, making the decoding of the sequence independent from any other sequences.

A content encoded with this H.264/AVC standard has the following typical structure (see Figure 11):

- **Video Sequence:** A video is composed by a Group of Pictures (GOP);
- **GOP:** Each GOP is composed by pictures;
- **Picture:** Each picture is composed by groups of slices;
- **Slice:** Each slice is composed by macro-blocks;
- **Macro-block:** Each macro-block is composed by groups of 4 blocks (16x16 pixels).

The H.264/AVC standard specifies three major profiles: the Baseline profile, the Main profile, designed to take full advantage of the coding efficiency of H.264, and the Extended profile, which includes enhancements for streaming applications (Sullivan, & Wiegand, 2005).

Layered Coding (Scalable Video Coding)

In the context of video the term "scalable" stands for the process of coding an image sequence in a progressive manner (i.e., scalable). The internal structure of a scalable coded video allows for a trade-off between bitrate and subjective quality, whereby parts of the video bit stream can be discarded with the final result still representing a valid video sequence.

The scalable coding requires a layered structure within the coded video that distinguishes basic information (Base Layer) from parts that represent only details or refinements of the base layer quality (Enhancement Layers) and is capable of producing highly compressed bit-streams with a wide variety of bitrates, decodable and presentable with adaptive quality, video resolutions, and frame rates, i.e., coded in SNR (signal to noise ratio), spatial, and temporal dimensions, adequate for the capabilities of the end user device and the variations of network conditions.

The scalable extension (Annex G - Scalable Video Coding) of H.264/AVC, denoted as H.264/SVC, includes several layers of quality. The scalability property of SVC supports the partitioning

Figure 10. Data structures of H.264/AVC video encoder

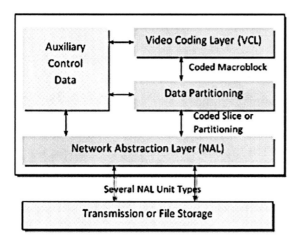

of a valid bit stream into several other valid substreams by simply cuttingparts of its data. This is especially important for rate adaptation purposes because, due to its simplicity, it may be performed in intermediate network elements without requiring computationally intensive mechanisms, like video transcoding does. Additionally, the base layer of an encoded H.264/SVC bit stream is by definition compatible with H.264/AVC, enabling backward compatibility with legacy equipments.

The scalable dimensions offered by SVC are the spatial (i.e., number of encoded pixels per image), the temporal (i.e., pictures per second) and the quality (or Signal-to-Noise Ratio) dimensions. In a bit stream, each NAL unit is associated with a given level of spatial, temporal and quality fidelities.

Temporal Scalability

Temporal scalability allows the support of multiple frame rates through the partitioning of the set of Access Units into several layers of quality that can be discarded after a certain point. Although the main concepts of temporal scalability were already included in H.264/AVC, in SVC, tempo-ral scalability is usually implemented by using hierarchical B-pictures.

Figure 12 exemplifies such an encoding structure partitioned into several temporal layers (from T_0 to T_4). Considering that the decoding of all temporal layers (from T_0 to T_4) results in a 30 fps sequence, and that the hierarchical encoding structure is the same as represented in Figure 6, the decoding of the base layer (T_0) would lead to a 1.875 fps decoded video sequence; the combined decoding of T_0 and T_1 originate a 3.75 fps sequence; T_0, T_1 and T_2 originate a 7.5 fps frame rate; and so forth. In this same figure, frames f_0 and f_{16}, are usually called key pictures. They can be either intra-coded or inter-coded by using motion-compensated prediction from previous key pictures.

The resulting number of temporal scalability levels depends on the specified Group of Pictures (GOP) size, which in turn may be equal to, or a ratio of, the period between intra-coded pictures. For instance, for a GOP size of 4 and a maximum frame rate of 30 fps, only three temporal scalability points are encoded (7.5, 15 and 30 fps).

Spatial Scalability

Spatial scalability provides support for several display resolutions with arbitrary ratios. Figure 13 illustrates an example of an encoding structure that uses a dyadic spatial scalability, where the spatial Base Layer (or reference layer) is represented by a Quarter Common Intermediate Format (QCIF) sequence and the Enhancement Layer by a Common Intermediate Format (CIF) sequence. Although in that figure there are only presented two spatial layers, the encoder supports multiple spatial scalability layers combined with temporal and/or quality layers.

NAL units of the different spatial resolutions of a certain time instant have to be transmitted by the decoding order. However, as illustrated in Figure 13, different frame rates can be used in each of the spatial layers and therefore, in those cases, some images have to be decoded using temporal scalability alone. In this case, different GOP sizes also exist for each of the scalable layers, where the GOP size of the lower layer is of 8 pictures, whereas the upper layer has a GOP size of 16 pictures.

Quality (or SNR) Scalability

Quality (or Signal-to-Noise Ratio) scalability reuses some of the concepts defined for spatial scalability, equally setting the picture sizes between base and enhancement layers. It relies on both Coarse-Grain quality Scalable (CGS) and Medium-Grain quality Scalable (MGS) coding.

CGS encodes the transform coefficients in a non-scalable way, which may only be decoded as a whole. In MGS, which is a variation of CGS, fragments of transform coefficients are split into several NAL units, enabling a definition of up to 16 MGS layers, and increasing the rate granularity for adaption purposes.

MGS defines pictures from the temporal base layer (or T0) as key pictures, for which SVC sets the motion parameters equal between the base and enhancement layers. This solution enables a single-loop decoding of these pictures, similar to the one used in spatial scalability. Regarding the remaining pictures, it is up to the encoder to decide whether to use the reconstructed base layer or the enhancement layer to compute the motion parameters. However, it usually uses the highest available quality for motion estimation and compensation. In such a case, the loss of MGS layers causes a drift error that will only be limited by the GOP size, or by the number of MGS layers available.

Combined Scalability Structure

All of the three scalability dimensions can be combined with each other within one bit stream and is called Combined Scalability. The general schematic structure of a global bit stream from the high level point of view is illustrated in Figure 14.

The combined scalable bit stream allows for extraction of different operation points of the video bit stream, where each point is characterized by a certain level of spatial, temporal and SNR quality definitions.

The loss of a NAL unit of a certain layer may not only cause a reduction of quality within that same scalability, but also cause a reduction on the quality of other layers or even prevent their correct decoding.

Since the decoder only enables switching between spatial layers at some points in the bit stream, changes in the definition of the decoded images can only be made accordingly. Switching between temporal and quality definitions can be made in any access unit and typically will affect other access units within the remaining of the same GOP. SEI messages are included in the encoded bit stream that assists the rate adaptation process, conveying information like the bitrate of each layer or their spatial resolution.

Multiple Description Coding

Multiple Description Coding (MDC) (Goyal, 2001) was developed at Bell Laboratories with the objective of transmitting data over multiple (telephone) lines by a method called "channel splitting". With this method, a source bit stream is partitioned into different descriptions that allow the reconstruction of the source at the receiver to a certain quality level as a function of the number of descriptions used.

MDC allows for a graceful degradation, i.e., a basic quality level is obtained from a single description but decoding of any further descriptions enhances the quality.

MDC uses Forward Error Concealment methods to deal with errors in the coding process by inserting redundancy among the descriptions. The redundant information is encoded with each descriptor making possible to decode each of the descriptions separately.

Figure 11. H.264 video structure

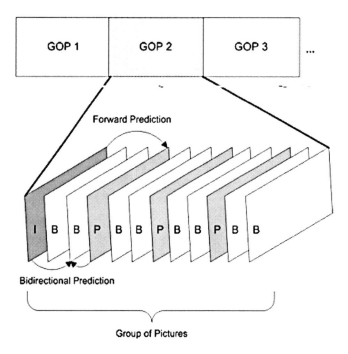

This redundancy is measured in terms of the extra rate required by the MDC scheme when compared to a single description reference system achieving the same performance level. The descriptions are somewhat correlated to each other, so that missing descriptions can be estimated from the received descriptions.

But the benefits of MDC features are paid for in terms of some impairment of the compression efficiency due to the inserted redundancy among the descriptions (a significant amount of basic information needs to be encoded redundantly with each description).

The tools and features provided in H.264/AVC can be used to form Multiple Description Encoding schemes exploring the temporal and spatial correlations between macro-blocks or the redundancy in the slices (Vermeirsch, Dhondt, Mys, & de Walle, 2007).

SVC and MDC in Peer-to-Peer Streaming

Both SVC and MDC are viable alternatives for P2P based video streaming. For both encoding techniques the video object does not necessarily have to be stored completely at one peer but single descriptions (MDC) or layers (SVC) of the video object may be stored at different peers. This feature alone makes both encoding techniques suited for P2P streaming (Zink & Mauthe, 2004). This means for MDC that no matter which descriptions are available they can always be combined to form a valid video stream. This is not possible with SVC layers, if one layer underneath is missing.

A platform that attempts to merge streaming of scalable coded media and streaming of multimedia using novel P2P techniques at the transport and application layers is being developed in the context of the European FP7 research project SARACEN (SARACEN Consortium, 2010).

The crucial difference between MDC and SVC is related to prioritization of the different parts of the video object. While in SVC the layers bear a

Figure 12. A SVC temporal layer encoding structure using a hierarchical prediction structure

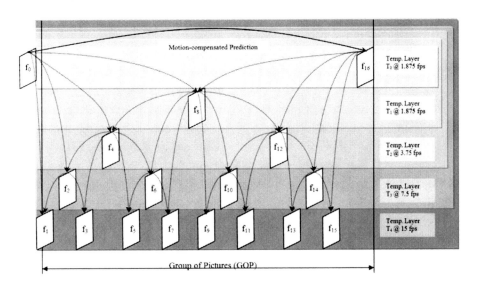

clear hierarchy (dependency from the base layer to the last enhancement layer) in MDC, all parts (or descriptions) are equally important and contribute in the same amount to the final quality.

One of the objections to the use of MDC in P2P streaming is that peers receiving a subset of the descriptions generally recover only an estimated version of the missing ones. Another concern is that MDC depends on the trade-off between the number of descriptions and the achievable qualities, as with large number of descriptions

the overhead introduced (due to redundancy) is quite significant.

For P2P streaming, SVC is a very promising encoding technique given that it creates the possibility to guarantee the correct and timely delivery of the base layer (through centralized servers/ super-peers or a reliable network infrastructure) while the peers improve the visual quality of the video by decoding enhancement layers received from other peers. Additionally, SVC can be used to serve peers with different requirements (e.g.,

Figure 13. A SVC combined temporal and spatial scalable coding considering two different frame rates at lower and higher layers

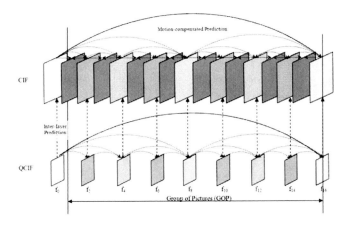

low quality and low bandwidth, high quality and high bandwidth).

There are still challenges in the use of these encoding techniques in a P2P environment (Zink & Mauthe, 2004):

- For MDC, the assignment and selection of the right sender for each description;
- For SVC, given two resolution layers (i.e., QCIF and CIF) how to distribute rate among these layers;
- For both MDC and SVC, how to handle transport and signaling issues.

Business Models for Peer-to-Peer Media Streaming

Most network operators consider P2P and other similar bandwidth-hungry applications as threats to their networks (ETSI-TISPAN, 2010). The main claimed reason is that P2P traffic may be pushing aside other traffic, deteriorating the Quality of Experience (QoE) for those other services. The typical counter-measure is throttling those bandwidth-hungry applications through Deep Packet Inspection.

From a different point of view, end users of those network operators may be willing to reserve (and pay for) bandwidth guarantees for those specific applications in order to enhance their own QoE, as the P2P delivery mechanisms are becoming important ingredients of the digital convergence processes which are about to drastically change the audio-visual media landscape.

The recent evolution of the telecommunications market is making evidence of such opposite trends, i.e., the technology and the end users are pushing for powerful multipurpose devices and cheaper broadband global data communications, available anytime, anywhere, but facing the "old time" marketers and technologists, still applying counter-measures instead of innovative solutions and business models.

Both backbone Internet connections and access links to the user's home are getting faster and faster, with deployment of broadband accesses rapidly expanding worldwide providing reliable and low latency networks with decreasing transmission costs.

Naturally, there are exceptions, and the mentioned threats may also be considered as business opportunities to some network operators, by getting involved in the actual content delivery by the P2P (over-the-top) applications, e.g., by placing caches and stream replicators in their own networks.

One such initiative is the Proactive network Provider Participation for P2P (P4P) (Alimi, Penno, & Yang, 2010) that provides network operators with additional degrees of freedom in terms of investment, which can be in transport capacity but for content delivery technologies (ETSI-TISPAN, 2010). P4P allows P2P networks to optimize traffic within each ISP, not only reducing the volume of data traversing the ISP infrastructure, but also creating a more manageable flow of data by providing additional information regarding network topology that P2P networks may choose to utilize to optimize network data delivery.

The use of Audiovisual Media is moving from a collective and passive approach to a personal active approach, at home and in mobility situations outside the home. At the same time, the usage patterns are shifting towards non-linear usages and away from the classic models of linear broadcast TV, in a process that can be regarded as a natural technological migration, where IP technologies add flexibility and interactivity (Sentinelli, Celetto, Lefol, Palazzi, & Pau, 2008).

The TV set has no longer the monopoly of delivery of audiovisual content as the PC and related media centers, mobile phones, and new devices such as smartphones, game consoles, notebooks, tablets, e-book readers, are all becoming increasingly important with their capability to stream and consume high-quality videos from operators or Internet services (e.g., YouTube).

Figure 14. SVC in combined scalability: high level view (S-Spatial, T-Temporal, Q-Quality)

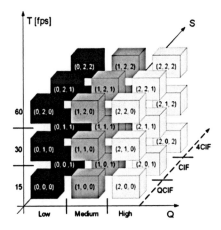

Broadcasters may start wishing to use P2P because it scales well when providing services to large number of concurrent peers.

The investments in servers and respective maintenance costs, as well as the bandwidth required by such servers, are much lower with P2P than with other content distribution mechanisms. Consequently, P2P may be more affordable and cost-effective than alternative content distribution systems. Also, since P2P systems are generally geographically distributed across the Internet, there are no single points of service failure.

With this trend, new emerging business models are seeing the light of day. Some of the identified models are (EBU TECHNICAL, 2010):

- **Free Content Distribution:** With the aim of attracting attention and interest for other revenue streams;
- **Advertisements Supported Distribution:** e.g., Advertising prior to receiving content, Sponsoring models;
- Pay-Per-View Distribution;
- Subscription Based Distribution;
- **Circular Content:** Super-distribution (Mori & Kawahara, 1990) of contents or recommendations.

Content Delivery Networks (CDNs) companies are also interested in P2P streaming implementations. CDNs build an overlay of network servers distributed along the world which continuously replicate the content among them. In the process of load balancing between servers, users are automatically and transparently redirected to the closest available server so the network can be changed dynamically without being noticed by final users.

A combined CDN plus P2P delivery can be an optimal solution for delivery, gaining the advantages for both overlays. In this solution, the CDN is seen as a default peer, always having all pieces available, so when a piece cannot be retrieved in time from the P2P network, it can be retrieved from the quicker but more costly CDN network.

Some successful services like Abacast (Abacast, 2010) are using this kind of transmission, because it offers the delivery availability and reliability of CDN networks, while reducing the cost of delivery for top demanded contents using P2P.

Overview of Current Peer-to-Peer Video Distribution Systems

The solutions, systems and developments for P2P Video Streaming are spread among commercial networks and delivery platforms, video and TV delivery services (mostly with free access) and end user applications.

In terms of networks and systems, they operate as mesh-based or tree-based distribution models and can deliver video services in Live Streaming or On-Demand Streaming modes. There are also a few European Union Seventh Framework Programme (FP7) research projects involved in the development of P2P multimedia content distribution and streaming solutions.

In the following sections the current most prominent examples of such solutions or initiatives are briefly described.

Commercial Mesh-Based Networks for Live video Distribution

The most successful mesh-based networks are PPlive (PPLive, 2010), SopCast (SopCast, 2010), CoolStreaming (CoolStreaming, 2010), UUSee (UUSee, 2010) and TVUnetwork (TVU networks, 2010).

PPLive (www.pptv.com) is the largest P2P streaming video network worldwide maintaining roughly 600 public live channels daily. The platform can stream Live and On-demand video. It uses a proprietary protocol with a mesh-based approach and with a distribution engine similar to the Bittorrent protocol. Channel selection is bootstrapped from a Web tracker (coordinator that provides rendezvous point functions), broadcast servers that source all content and the peers download/upload videos in chunks. The Trackers are used for maintaining state information in terms of peers in each channel, properties of peers (e.g., bandwidth capacity and NAT status), and the overall health of the channels. Peers use the broadcast servers source as a peer of last resort. PPLive traffic relies on TCP.

SopCast (www.sopcast.org) is a P2P streaming solution providing both VoD and Live services. SoP is the abbreviation for Streaming over P2P. SopCast uses a mesh-based approach, with a closed source proprietary protocol similar to the PPLive protocol, also chunk-driven. A performance study of SopCast is available in (Sentinelli, Marfia, Gerla, Kleinrock, & Tewari, 2007). SOPCast traffic relies mostly on UDP.

CoolStreaming (www.coolstreaming.us) is a Data-driven Overlay Network (called DONet, one of the first pull-based P2P streaming systems) for Live streaming (Zhang, Liu, Li, & Yum, 2005). The design of DONet includes a smart scheduling algorithm to deal with the bandwidth differences among peers, a membership manager to help peers maintain a partial view of other nodes, and a partnership manager for the peers. The protocol is chunk-driven (equal size chunks) a uses locality-aware strategy for the peering selection. Cool-Streaming traffic relies on TCP. Two interesting analysis of the CoolStreaming/DONet architecture are available in (Xie, Li, Keung, & Zhang, 2007; Zhang, Liu, Li, & Yum, 2005). CoolStreaming is the base technology for Roxbeam (Roxbeam, 2010). Currently CoolStreaming is evolving the architecture for Live broadcasting naming it CSLive.tv (Cslive.tv, 2010).

UUSee (www.uusee.com) is one of the largest P2P streaming video providers in China simultaneously sustaining over 800 media channels. The platform can stream Live and On-demand video. It uses a proprietary protocol with a mesh-based approach and with a distribution engine similar to the Bittorrent protocol. The streaming framework consists of media encoding servers, a large set of dedicated streaming servers, tracking servers and supernode peers. The streaming protocol allows peers to serve each other by exchanging the blocks of data that are received and cached in their local playback buffers. Buffer availability bitmaps are exchanged periodically between peers connected via TCP. A performance study of UUSee is available in (Wu, Li, & Zhao, 2008).

TVU Networks (www.tvunetworks.com) is a Live broadcast service for home users and companies based on a P2P proprietary Real-time Packet Replication (RPR) protocol. TVU networks offers free of charge stream broadcasting and viewing software for amateurs, but hardware and services for professional broadcasters.

Commercial Mesh-Based Infrastructure Content Providers for Live Video Delivery Services

The most relevant mesh-based infrastructure content providers are Abacast (Abacast, 2010), Rawflow (RawFlow, 2010), Octoshape (Octoshape, 2010) and BitTorrent DNA (BitTorrent, 2010).

Abacast (www.abacast.com) is a commercial Hybrid Content Distribution Network (CDN) offering the ability to distribute Live video, VoD and online radio broadcasts, as well as games and software to the Content industry. The delivery options include Unicast, P2P or a Hybrid combination of both. For linear Internet TV, Abacast provides complete end-to-end solutions for live broadcasting and VoD, with advertisement integration.

RawFlow (www.rawflow.com) is a provider of live P2P streaming technology that enables Internet broadcasting of audio and video. The architecture includes Intelligent Content Distribution (ICD) servers as the first contact point for clients in the network. The bandwidth required for broadcast is intelligently distributed over the entire network of participants, instead of being centralized at the broadcast's origin. RawFlow offers a media platform for user-generated broadcast (UGB) technology which enables individuals and communities to produce live and on-demand digital broadcasts.

Octoshape (www.octoshape.com) is a provider of live P2P streaming technology to deliver video and audio content. Their grid-cast technology, named Octoshape Infinite Edge Technology, can scale to accommodate millions of concurrent users and enables HD quality video streaming over the Internet. By relying on dynamic bitrate adaption, the Octoshape technology allows a publisher to stream content in multiple quality levels that are automatically selected at the end user for an optimal video quality experience.

BitTorrent DNA (www.bittorrent.com/dna) is a content delivery service that uses a secure, private, managed P2P network to deliver rich contents. BitTorrent DNA works with existing CDNs or origin servers, seamlessly accelerating downloads or Hypertext Transfer Protocol (HTTP) (Fielding et al., 1999) media streams. The technology carefully balances the use of P2P, CDN or server resources by downloading from all in parallel in order to meet per-object or streaming media QoS requirements.

Known Tree-Based Multicast Overlay Technologies for Live Video Delivery Services

The known tree-based multicast overlay technologies worth mentioning are Allcast (AllCast, 2010) and PeerCast (PeerCast.org, 2010), although both seem somewhat inactive.

AllCast (www.allcast.com) provides peer-to-multipeer content distribution. The network distribution model is based on a patented "cascading" peer-to-peer networking technology to ensure that there are no bandwidth or server bottlenecks regardless of the size of the stream or audience.

PeerCast (www.peercast.org) is an open-source project that uses tree-based multicast P2P technology to let anyone become a broadcaster of radio and video on the Internet.

Streaming Solutions for Peer-to-Peer Video-on-Demand (VoD) Content Distribution

The most relevant VoD content distribution solutions are Joost (Joost, 2010) and Babelgum (Babelgum, 2010), both conceived in Europe.

Joost (www.joost.com) is a hybrid mesh-based P2P streaming overlay system for distributing VoD TV contents. Joost employs UDP as transport protocol and TCP for control messages and includes a NAT detection mechanism in order to improve system performance. The Joost Content Network lets content partners to distribute their videos via the Apple iOS (iPhone/iPad), although without the rights to distribute videos over mobile (3G) networks. As a curiosity, Joost was created in 2006 by Niklas Zennstroem and Janus Friis, the Skype founders.

Babelgum (www.babelgum.com) is a hybrid VoD P2P streaming system with an architecture that includes some streaming servers located around the world to distribute the video contents. It uses TCP for both control and data packets distribution. Babelgum is an Internet and Mobile TV platform supported by advertising, having recently launched an original mobile application that brings web-tailored content to smart phones via 3G and Wi-Fi, namely for iOS (iPhone/iPad) and Android based devices.

Open-Source Advanced Architectures for P2P Streaming Services

The most relevant Open-source advanced architectures are Goalbit (GoalBit, 2010) and Tribler (TU Delft - Tribler, 2010).

GoalBit (goalbit-solutions.com) is an open source peer-to-peer platform for real-time video streaming in the Internet. The P2P system architecture is hybrid, with central control and distributed delivery components (broadcaster, super-peers and tracker). The central control maintains a simple tree-based structured P2P overlay network, while a multi–source streaming technique for P2P delivery. Streaming encapsulation is done by a so-called GoalBit Packetized Stream (GBPS) that takes the multiplexed stream and generates fixed size chunks, which are distributed using the GoalBit Transport Protocol (GBTP) a BitTorrent-like protocol (Bertinat et al., 2009).

Tribler (tribler.org) is a social open source, fully decentralized P2P application that enables users to find, enjoy and share video, audio, pictures, and other media. Tribler supports UPnP to open a listening port on the firewall automatically. The P2P video player the so-called SwarmPlayer is a web plug-in (installable in different browsers and computer platforms). The application runs a modified BitTorrent implementation that incorporates several extensions for social networking, peer selection and video streaming (Mol, Bakker, Pouwelse, Epema, & Sips, 2009; Pouwelse et al., 2008).

RESEARCH CHALLENGES, STANDARDIZATION EFFORTS AND RELEVANT PROJECTS ON P2P VIDEO STREAMING

The challenges faced by P2P video streaming are still far from being fulfilled. Current P2P overlays, which were designed for bulk transfer of files, are not capable of dealing properly with the different challenges associated with real-time video delivery.

In the field of standardization there is currently an ongoing effort to define several new protocols. This includes several fields of application, like the integration of the Voice over IP signaling protocol (SIP) and P2P mechanisms, the definition of new congestion control algorithms for P2P networks, and the exchange of network topology information between network operators and Internet service providers with P2P applications.

With regard to current research activity in this area, the European Union supports the efforts on P2P video streaming through different consortiums of very high relevance.

Below we provide more details about each these items.

Research Challenges

Despite recent advances, peer-to-peer video streaming remains a challenging topic with several open issues which should be tackled by the research community. The most relevant ones are:

1. **Peer dynamics, mobility and heterogeneity:** Since the percentage of mobile terminals in the Internet is experiencing a steady increase, P2P video streaming solutions should be able to handle not only traditional issues, such as having peers joining and leaving the network dynamically, but should also consider that mobile terminals while often experience temporary disconnections due to

roaming, and that the networks visited by the terminals will possible have quite different characteristics in terms capacity, delay, QoS, saturation conditions, etc. Additionally, the capabilities of some mobile terminals can be significantly worse than those of laptops and desktop PCs, which, together with the battery limitations of the former ones, evidence the need for introducing different terminal profiles in the P2P selection process.

2. **Overlay network construction and monitoring of network conditions:** Creating and maintaining an optimal overlay network efficiently and with a low overhead is an important goal. In particular, the different peers should be organized into a logical topology that is intimately related to the underlying physical topology to maximize performance. In addition, the overlay network created should be constantly monitored not only to detect topology changes, but also to maximize the utilization of available resources, as well as to minimize the packet drop ratios at certain links.

3. **Completing Decentralization - Trackless topologies:** Since trackers are servers that requires operational and maintenance resources, the future P2P protocols and architectures has to be functional without the existence of trackers. This could be achieved practically if every client acts as a lightweight tracker.

4. **Peer selection and incentives:** Since end-to-end delay is a critical issue, especially in live video streaming, peer selection should seek to optimize delays by selecting the most appropriate video sources, and also by reducing the number of intermediate peers to a minimum. Also, an incentive strategy should be adopted to avoid that some of the peers behave merely as clients, which could have an impact on performance if the ratio of such egoistic peers is high.

5. **Video encoding:** Although the major encoders support the encoding of different video qualities, it is not clear how these qualities might be efficiently delivered to a very broad range of heterogeneous IP terminals. This effort has led to the creation of an IETF working group that is currently dealing with this issue.

6. **Digital rights management:** The issue of enforcing digital rights in the traditional server-client based communications is a complex issue that is recently receiving much attention by digital rights societies, governments, Internet providers and users, usually with conflictive goals. In the scope of P2P video streaming, enforcing digital rights in a distributed fashion while avoiding introducing significant additional delays is certainly a complex and challenging goal that is currently lacking a definitive solution.

Standardization Efforts

As many other solutions, P2P networks have started to be deployed using proprietary solutions, each one using very distinct protocols and architectures. Currently there is a significant effort in making P2P protocols standard, with several IETF working groups (WGs) dealing with P2P technologies. Part of this interest results from the fact that content providers and network operators are starting to face these architectures as a solution for the quick deployment of their content, requiring standard procedures for different implementations to interact.

In this field, and in terms of Voice over IP, the P2PSIP (IETF P2PSIP Working Group, 2010) is working on a protocol for a distributed overlay to provide Session Initiation Protocol (SIP) registration and routing functionality. Also, the Host Identity Protocol (HIP) (IETF HIP Working Group, 2010) is defining a HIP-Based Overlay Networking Environment (HIP BONE) specification for

REsource LOcation And Discovery (RELOAD) in peer-to-peer networks.

An issue of concern about traffic generated by P2P file sharing applications is that it normally causes intolerable delays in multimedia applications, leading to a significant decrease in user quality of experience. This problem is being addressed by the Low Extra Delay Background Transport (LEDBAT) (IETF LEDBAT Working Group, 2010), defining a new congestion control algorithm for those types of applications that substitutes TCP as one of the main used protocols. Currently, significant developments have been made in this field that resulted from extensive research and with an implementation in the Bit-Torrent client.

Since many P2P applications form overlays on top of the Internet without any or with reduced knowledge of the network topology, peers typically make non-optimal or even purely random selection of the other peers, many times from far network and geographical locations. In this field, the Application-Layer Traffic Optimization (ALTO) (IETF ALTO Working Group, 2010) is chartered to define a protocol that enables the exchange of network topology information between network operators and Internet service providers with P2P applications. The aim of these mechanisms is to enable P2P applications in improving the peer selection process, leading to a more rational utilization of network resources. This issue is particularly relevant for media streaming applications due to their delay constraints.

In terms of media streaming, the Peer-to-Peer Streaming Protocol (PPSP) working group (IETF PPSP Working Group, 2010) was recently formed to define protocols and architectures for real-time content distribution. The main objective of this group is to specify how media chunks of both live and time-shifted content may be timely and efficiently distributed over a P2P overlay. To this aim, the associated architecture is considering two types of nodes: peers and trackers. Trackers maintain and distribute information about what content is shared by each peer, and peers, besides storing the content, are responsible for finding the location of the content they want, with the support of trackers, and for exchanging the content with the resulting peers. The group intends to use existing protocols like the Real-time Transport Protocol (RTP) (Schulzrinne, Casner, Frederick, & Jacobson, 2003) or the Hypertext Transfer Protocol (Fielding et al., 1999) for media transmission between peers.

The Decoupled Application Data Enroute (DECADE) (IETF DECADE Working Group, 2010) is defining a mechanism for users to store their content in the Internet service provider's network, ahead of the access and home bottleneck. It will try to specify a protocol for the management of files in that network storage, which can in the future become integrated in P2P applications.

European Union FP7 Research Projects Involving Peer-to-Peer Technologies for Media Streaming

The EU FP7 projects involving P2P technologies for media streaming are the following:

SEA - SEAmless Content Delivery (SEA Consortium, 2010) is a context-aware networking delivery platform that places the user acting as content consumer, content mediator and content producer. The architecture creates a tree-based overlay for video streaming with an innovative multi-source P2P IPTV-like application capable of streaming hybrid SVC/MDC videos via a SEACast protocol, a BitTorrent-like protocol.

NAPA-WINE - Network-Aware P2P-TV Application over Wise Networks (NAPA-WINE Consortium, 2010) goal is the study of a future system suitable for HQTV Live streaming based on P2P technology. This is achieved by the development of a core set of design patterns, communications and programming primitives and practices for a new class of P2P network-aware multimedia content streaming systems. The project demonstrates the results with a network-aware P2PTV application, called PULSE++, that integrates the GRAPES (Generic Resource-Aware P2P Environment for Streaming) libraries developed.

P2P-NEXT - Next generation Peer-to-Peer content delivery platform (P2P-NEXT Consortium, 2010) goal is to build an open-source, efficient, trusted, personalized, user-centric, and participatory television and media delivery system with social and collaborative connotation. The project is associated with the development efforts of Tribler (TU Delft - Tribler, 2010) and produces the so-called NextShare SwarmPlayer, a web plug-in (installable in different browsers and computer platforms), a modified BitTorrent implementation that incorporates several extensions for social networking, peer selection and video streaming supporting SVC videos.

SARACEN - Socially Aware, collaboRative, scAlable Coding mEdia distributioN (SARACEN Consortium, 2010) goal is to design and implement a prototype platform for offering QoE in personalized media streaming through the integration of SVC techniques, advanced media transport protocols, and P2P technologies with respect to user privacy.

CONCLUSION

This chapter provided an overview of the different challenges faced up when attempting to successfully delivery video contents over the Internet while adopting a peer-to-peer content delivery paradigm.

Throughout the chapter the different technologies and standards involved where described, evidencing the complexity of achieving a robust and reliable system that is able to integrate the various elements required to assure success in such endeavour. In particular, we first discussed more general concepts such as the different P2P overlay mechanisms and P2P topologies, where the differences between Pure, Centralized and Hybrid P2P networks where emphasized. Other

related topics such as bootstrapping mechanisms, specific issues over wireless and mobile networks and standardization efforts were also addressed.

The core of the chapter discussed P2P video streaming in detail, evidencing the different concepts involved. It first introduced the different Internet TV technologies currently available, along with the different business models for P2P media streaming, emphasizing on emerging P2P business models. An overview of the different Multimedia streaming modes is then presented to contextualize the different delivery solutions. From a network perspective, IP multicast and application-layer multicast streaming are then presented, and the pros and cons of such solutions at supporting efficient P2P video streaming solutions is discussed. Another related topic is concerned to traversal mechanisms when peers are hidden behind NATs, a topic described in depth and including the possible techniques that can be used. Follows a part dedicated to Adaptive and Layered Video Streaming, which first describes the H.264/AVC video coding standard, highlighting the properties that make it especially useful in the context of P2P video delivery. Afterwards, two enhancements to H.264/AVC, known as Scalable Video Coding (SVC) and Multiple Description Coding (MDC), are presented with a detailed discussion about their adequacy in P2P environments, evidencing the pros and cons of each solution. The last part gives an overview of current P2P video streaming solutions, from commercial networks and providers to open-source solutions, finishing with a brief description of current EU projects in the area.

Overall, this chapter attempts to provide researchers with some basic knowledge on this topic by providing a holistic perspective of the different technologies involved, thus allowing future research efforts to follow the right direction, and also prompting the research community to address some critical issues that remain untackled.

REFERENCES

P2P-NEXT Consortium. (2010). *Next generation peer-to-peer content delivery platform project home page*. Retrieved from http://p2p-next.org/

Abacast. (2010). *Abacast home page*. Retrieved from http://www.abacast.com/

Aberer, K., Cudré-Mauroux, P., Datta, A., Despotovic, Z., Hauswirth, M., Punceva, M., et al. (2003). Advanced peer-to-peer networking: The P-Grid system and its applications. *PIK - Praxis der Informationsverarbeitung und Kommunikation, Special Issue on P2P Systems, 26*(3), 86-89.

Alimal, L. O., El-Ansary, S., Brand, P., & Haridi, S. (2003). DKS(N, k, f): A family of low communication, scalable and fault-tolerant infrastructures for P2P applications. In *Proceedings 3rd IEEE/ACM International Symposium on Cluster Computing and the Grid, CCGrid 2003* (pp. 344-350). doi: 10.1109/CCGRID.2003.1199386

Alimi, R., Penno, R., & Yang, Y. (2010). *ALTO protocol*. Retrieved from http://www.ietf.org/internet-drafts/draft-ietf-alto-protocol-03.txt

AllCast. (2010). *AllCast home page*. Retrieved from http://www.allcast.com/

Andrade, N., Mowbray, M., Lima, A., Wagner, G., & Ripeanu, M. (2005). Influences on cooperation in BitTorrent communities. *Proceedings of the 2005 ACM SIGCOMM Workshop on Economics of Peer-to-Peer Systems* (pp. 111-115). New York, NY: ACM. doi: http://doi.acm.org/10.1145/1080192.1080198

Androutsellis-Theotokis, S., & Spinellis, D. (2004). A survey of peer-to-peer content distribution technologies. *ACM Computing Surveys, 36*(4), 335–371. doi:10.1145/1041680.1041681

Apache. (2010). *The Apache Software Foundation home page*. Retrieved from http://www.apache.org/foundation/

Babelgum. (2010). *Babelgum home page*. Retrieved from http://www.babelgum.com/

Baccichet, P., Schierl, T., Wiegand, T., & Girod, B. (2007). Low-delay peer-to-peer streaming using scalable video coding. In *Packet Video 2007* (pp. 173-181). doi: doi:10.1109/PACKET.2007.4397039

Balfe, S., Lakhani, A. D., & Paterson, K. G. (2005). DRM Enabled P2P Architecture. In *Fifth IEEE International Conference on Peer-to-Peer Computing*, Aug-Sept. 2005, (pp. 117 -124).

Balfe, S., Lakhani, A. D., & Paterson, K. G. (2005). Trusted computing: Providing security for peer-to-peer networks. In *Fifth IEEE International Conference on Peer-to-Peer Computing (P2P '05)*, 2005, (pp. 117-124).

Ballardie, A. (1997). *Core based trees (CBT version 2) multicast routing -- Protocol specification*. Request for Comments, IETF. Retrieved from http://www.ietf.org/rfc/rfc2189.txt

Banerjee, S., Bhattacharjee, B., & Kommareddy, C. (2002). Scalable application layer multicast. In *Proceedings of the 2002 Conference on Applications, Technologies, Architectures, and Protocols for Computer Communications, SIGCOMM '02* (pp. 205-217). New York, NY: ACM. doi: http://doi.acm.org/10.1145/633025.633045

Bates, T., Chandra, R., Katz, D., & Rekhter, Y. (1988). *Multiprotocol extensions for BGP-4*. Request for Comments. IETF. Retrieved from http://www.ietf.org/rfc/rfc2283.txt

Bertinat, M. E., Vera, D. D., Padula, D., Robledo, F., Rodríguez-Bocca, P., Romero, P., et al. (2009). GoalBit: The first free and open source peer-to-peer streaming network. In *Proceedings of the 5th International IFIP/ACM Latin American Conference on Networking, LANC '09*. New York, NY: ACM.

BitTorrent. (2010). *BitTorrent home page*. Retrieved from http://www.bittorrent.com/

Buford, J., Yu, H., & Lua, E. K. (2008). *P2P networking and applications*. San Francisco, CA: Morgan Kaufmann Publishers Inc.

Castro, M., Druschel, P., Kermarrec, A.-M., Nandi, A., Rowstron, A., & Singh, A. (2003). SplitStream: High-bandwidth content distribution in a cooperative environment. In *Proceedings of IPTPS '03*.

Castro, M., Druschel, P., Kermarrec, A.-M., & Rowstron, A. (2002). SCRIBE: A large-scale and decentralized application-level multicast infrastructure. *IEEE Journal on Selected Areas in Communications. Special Issue on Network Support for Group Communication, 20*(8), 1489–1499. doi:doi:10.1109/JSAC.2002.803069

Chi, H., & Zhang, Q. (2006). *Efficient search in P2P-based video-on-demand streaming service.* IEEE International Conference on Multimedia & Expo.

Chi, H., Zhang, Q., Jia, J., & Shen, X. (2007). Efficient search and scheduling in P2P-based media-on-demand streaming service. *IEEE Journal on Selected Areas in Communications, 25*(1).

Chu, C. C., Su, X., Prabhu, B. S., Gadh, R., Kurup, S., Sridhar, G., & Sridhar, V. (2006). Mobile DRM for multimedia content commerce in P2P networks. Consumer Communications and Networking Conference, 8-10 Jan. 2006, (pp. 1119–1123).

Chu, Y., Gao, S., & Zhang, H. (2000). A case for end system multicast. In *Proceedings ACM Sigmetrics*.

Cisco. (2010). *Cisco visual networking index: Forecast and methodology, 2009–2014.* Retrieved from http://www.cisco.com/en/US/solutions/collateral/ns341/ns525/ns537/ns705/ns827/white_paper_c11-481360.pdf

Clarke, I., Sandberg, O., Wiley, B., & Hong, T. W. (2001). Freenet: A distributed anonymous information storage and retrieval system. In *Proceedings of the International Workshop on Designing Privacy Enhancing Technologies* (pp. 46-66). New York, NY: Springer-Verlag New York, Inc.

Clausen, T., & Jacquet, P. (2003). *Optimized link state routing protocol (OLSR).* Retrieved from http://www.rfc-editor.org/rfc/rfc3626.txt

Cohen, B. (2003). Incentives build robustness in BitTorrent. *Proceedings of the 1st Workshop on Economics of Peer-to-Peer Systems.* Retrieved from http://www.sims.berkeley.edu/p2pecon/

Conner, W., Nahrstedt, K., & Gupta, I. (2006). Preventing DoS attacks in peer-to-peer media streaming systems. In *Proceedings 13th Annual Conference on Multimedia Computing and Networking, 2006.*

Consortium, S. E. A. (2010). *Seamless content delivery project home page.* Retrieved from http://www.ist-sea.eu/

CoolStreaming. (2010). *CoolStreaming US home page.* Retrieved from http://www.coolstreaming.us/hp.php?lang=en

Cruz, R. S., Domingues, J., Menezes, L., & Nunes, M. S. (2010). IPTV architecture for an IMS environment with dynamic QoS adaptation. *Multimedia Tools and Applications,* (pp. 1-33). Springer Netherlands. doi: http://dx.doi.org/10.1007/s11042-010-0537-8

Cslive.tv. (2010). *CSLive home page.* Retrieved from http://www.cslive.tv.

Cui, Y., Li, B., & Nahrstedt, K. (2004). oStream: Asynchronous streaming multicast. *IEEE Journal on Selected Areas in Communications, 22*(1).

Dabek, F., Kaashoek, M. F., Karger, D., Morris, R., & Stoica, I. (2001). Wide-area cooperative storage with CFS. In *Proceedings of the Eighteenth ACM Symposium on Operating Systems Principles, SOSP '01* (pp. 202-215). New York, NY: ACM. doi: http://doi.acm.org/10.1145/502034.502054

Do, T., Hua, K. A., Jiang, N., & Liu, F. (2009). PatchPeer: A scalable video-on-demand streaming system in hybrid wireless mobile peer-to-peer networks. *Peer-to-Peer Networking and Applications Journal, 2*(3), 182–201. doi:10.1007/s12083-008-0027-1

Do, T., Hua, K. A., & Tantaoui, M. (2004). P2VoD: Providing fault tolerant video-on-demand streaming in peer-to-peer environment. *Proceedings of IEEE ICC'04,* Paris, June 2004.

Druschel, P., & Rowstron, A. (2001). PAST: a large-scale, persistent peer-to-peer storage utility. In *Proceedings of the Eighth Workshop on Hot Topics in Operating Systems, 2001* (pp. 75-80).

Eger, K., & Killat, U. (2006). Bandwidth trading in unstructured P2P content distribution networks. *Proceedings of the Sixth IEEE International Conference on Peer-to-Peer Computing, P2P'06* (pp. 39-48). doi:10.1109/P2P.2006.6

Emule. (2010). *The Emule project home page.* Retrieved from http://www.emule-project.net/

Estrin, D., Farinacci, D., Helmy, A., Thaler, D., Deering, S., Handley, M., et al. (1998). *Protocol independent multicast-sparse mode (PIM-SM): Protocol specification.* Request for Comments. IETF. Retrieved from http://www.ietf.org/rfc/rfc2362.txt

ETSI-TISPAN. (2010). *Peer-to-peer for content delivery for IPTV services: Analysis of mechanisms and NGN impacts.*

Fielding, R., Gettys, J., Mogul, J., Frystyk, H., Masinter, L., Leach, P., et al. (1999). *Hypertext transfer protocol -- HTTP/1.1.* Request for Comments IETF. Retrieved from http://www.ietf.org/rfc/rfc2616.txt

Gallager, R. G. (1962). Low-density parity-check codes. *I.R.E. Transactions on Information Theory, 8*(1), 21–28. doi:10.1109/TIT.1962.1057683

Garbacki, P., Iosup, A., Epema, D., & van Steen, M. (2006). 2Fast : Collaborative downloads in P2P networks. *Proceedings of the Sixth IEEE International Conference on Peer-to-Peer Computing, P2P'06* (pp. 23-30). doi:10.1109/P2P.2006.1

Gheorghe, G., Lo Cigno, R., & Montresor, A. (2011). Security and privacy issues in P2P streaming systems: A Survey. *Peer-to-Peer Networking and Applications, 4.*

Gnutella. (2001). *The Gnutella protocol specification.* Retrieved from http://wiki.limewire.org/index.php?

GoalBit. (2010). *Goalbit-Solutions home page.* Retrieved from http://goalbit-solutions.com/

Goyal, V. K. (2001). Multiple description coding: Compression meets the network. *IEEE Signal Processing Magazine, 18*(5), 74–93. doi:10.1109/79.952806

Grokster. (2005). Grokster home page (Web archive). Retrieved from http://web.archive.org/web/*/grokster.com

Gupta, M., Judge, P., & Ammar, M. (2003). A reputation system for peer-to-peer networks. *Proceedings of the 13th International Workshop on Network and Operating Systems Support for Digital Audio and Video* (pp. 144-152). New York, NY: ACM. doi:http://doi.acm.org/10.1145/776322.776346

Heckmann, O., Bock, A., Mauthe, A., & Steinmetz, R. (2004). The eDonkey file-sharing network. *Proceedings of the Workshop on Algorithms and Protocols for Efficient Peer-to-Peer Applications, Informatik'04.*

Hefeeda, M., Bhargava, B., & Yau, D. (2004). A hybrid architecture for cost effective on demand media streaming. *Journal of Computer Networks, 44*(3), 353–382. doi:10.1016/j.comnet.2003.10.002

Hefeeda, M., Habib, A., Botev, B., Xu, D., & Bhargava, B. (2003). Promise: Peer-to-peer media streaming using collectcast. In *Proceedings of ACM Multimedia* (pp. 45-54).

Holbrook, H., & Cain, B. (2006). *Source-specific multicast for IP*. Request for Comments. IETF. Retrieved from http://www.ietf.org/rfc/rfc4607.txt

Hosseini, M., Ahmed, D. T., Shirmohammadi, S., & Georganas, N. D. (2007). A survey of application-layer multicast protocols. *IEEE Communications Surveys Tutorials*, *9*(3), 58–74. doi:10.1109/COMST.2007.4317616

Huitema, C. (2006). *Teredo: Tunneling IPv6 over UDP through network address translations (NATs)*. Retrieved from http://www.rfc-editor.org/rfc/rfc4380.txt

IETF P2PSIP Working Group. (2010). *Peer-to-peer session initiation protocol (P2PSIP)*. Retrieved from http://datatracker.ietf.org/wg/p2psip/charter

IETF ALTO Working Group. (2010). *Application-layer traffic optimization (ALTO)*. Retrieved from http://datatracker.ietf.org/wg/alto/charter/

IETF DECADE Working Group. (2010). *Decoupled application data enroute (DECADE)*. Retrieved from http://datatracker.ietf.org/wg/decade/charter/

IETF HIP Working Group. (2010). *Host identity protocol (HIP)*. Retrieved from http://datatracker.ietf.org/wg/hip/charter/

IETF LEDBAT Working Group. (2010). *Low extra delay background transport (LEDBAT)*. Retrieved from http://datatracker.ietf.org/wg/ledbat/charter/

IETF PPSP Working Group. (2010)*Peer to peer streaming protocol (PPSP)*. Retrieved from http://tools.ietf.org/wg/ppsp/

iMesh. (2010). *iMesh: The world's best P2P file sharing community! Home page*. iMesh Inc. Retrieved from http://www.imesh.com

ISO/IEC. (2007). *Information technology -- Coding of audio-visual objects -- Part 10: Advanced video coding*. International Organization for Standardization/ International Electrotechnical Commission.

ITU-T. (2010). *Advanced video coding for generic audiovisual services*. International Telecommunication Union, Telecommunication Standardization Sector.

Iwata, T., Abe, T., Ueda, K., et al. (2003). A DRM system suitable for P2P content delivery and the study on its implementation. *The 9th Asia-Pacific Conference on Communications*, 2003, (pp. 806-811).

Johannesson, R., & Zigangirov, K. S. (1999). *Fundamentals of convolutional coding*. IEEE Series on Digital and Mobile Communication. doi:10.1109/9780470544693

Johnson, D., Hu, Y., & Maltz, D. (2007). *The dynamic source routing protocol (DSR) for mobile ad hoc networks for IPv4*. Retrieved from http://www.rfc-editor.org/rfc/rfc4728.txt

Joost. (2010). *Joost home page*. Retrieved from http://www.joost.com/.

Jun, S., & Ahamad, M. (2005). Incentives in BitTorrent induce free riding. *Proceedings of the 2005 ACM SIGCOMM Workshop on Economics of Peer-to-Peer Systems* (pp. 116-121). New York, NY: ACM. doi:http://doi.acm.org/10.1145/1080192.1080199

KaZaA. (2010). *KaZaA home page*. Retrieved from http://www.kazaa.com/#/about

Ken, W.-P., Jin, X., & Chan, S.-H. (2007). Challenges and approaches in large-scale P2P media streaming. *IEEE MultiMedia*, *14*(2), 50–59. doi:10.1109/MMUL.2007.30

Kohler, E., Handley, M., & Floyd, S., (2006). *Datagram congestion control protocol* (DCCP). IETF RFC 4340, March 2006.

Kostic, D., Rodriguez, A., Albrecht, J., & Vahdat, A. (2003). Bullet: High bandwidth data dissemination using an overlay mesh. In *Proceedings of the 19th ACM Symposium on Operating Systems Principles, 2003.*

Lan, X., Xue, J., Tian, T., Hu, W., Xu, T., & Zheng, N. (2009). A peer-to-peer architecture for live streaming with DRM. *6th IEEE Consumer Communications and Networking Conference,* (pp. 1-5).

Lan, X., Zheng, N., Xue, J., Chen, W., Wang, B., & Ma, W. (2008). Manageable peer-to-peer architecture for video-on-demand. *Proceedings 22nd IEEE International Parallel and Distributed Processing Symposium (IPDPS2008)-10th Workshop of APDCM,* April 14-18, 2008, Miami, Florida USA.

Legout, A., Liogkas, N., Kohler, E., & Zhang, L. (2007). Clustering and sharing incentives in BitTorrent systems. *Proceedings of the 2007 ACM SIGMETRICS International Conference on Measurement and Modeling of Computer Systems* (pp. 301-312). New York, NY: ACM. doi: http://doi.acm.org/10.1145/1254882.1254919

Lian, Q., Chen, W., Zhang, Z., Wu, S., & Zhao, B. Y. (2005). Z-ring: fast prefix routing via a low maintenance membership protocol. In *13th IEEE International Conference on Network Protocols, ICNP 2005* (p. 12). doi: 10.1109/ICNP.2005.45

Lian, Q., Zhang, Z., Yang, M., Zhao, B. Y., Dai, Y., & Li, X. (2007). An empirical study of collusion behavior in the Maze P2P file-sharing system. *Proceedings of the 27th International Conference on Distributed Computing Systems, ICDCS'07* (p. 56). doi:10.1109/ICDCS.2007.84

Liang, J., Kumar, R., & Ross, K. W. (2006). The FastTrack overlay: A measurement study. *Computer Networks, 50*(6), 842–858. doi:10.1016/j.comnet.2005.07.014

Liben-Nowell, D., Balakrishnan, H., & Karger, D. (2002). Analysis of the evolution of peer-to-peer systems. In *Proceedings of the Twenty-First Annual Symposium on Principles of Distributed Computing, PODC'02* (pp. 233-242). New York, NY: ACM. doi: http://doi.acm.org/10.1145/571825.571863

Liu, X., Huang, T., Huo, L., & Mou, L. (2007). A DRM architecture for manageable P2P based IPTV system. *2007 IEEE International Conference on Multimedia and Expo,* (pp. 899-902). 2-5 July 2007.

Liu, Y., Guo, Y., & Liang, C. (2008). A survey on peer-to-peer video streaming systems. *Peer-to-Peer Networking and Applications, 1*(1), 18–28. doi:10.1007/s12083-007-0006-y

Liu, Z., Shen, Y., Panwar, S. S., Ross, K. W., & Wang, Y. (2007). P2P video live streaming with MDC: Providing incentives for redistribution. *Proceedings of the IEEE International Conference on Multimedia and Expo 2007* (pp. 48-51). doi:10.1109/ICME.2007.4284583

Locher, T., Moor, P., Schmid, S., & Wattenhofer, R. (2006). Free riding in BitTorrent is cheap. *Proceedings of the 5th Workshop on Hot Topics in Networks (HotNets).*

Luby, M. (2002). LT-codes. In Proceedings *43rd Annual IEEE Symposium on Foundations of Computer Science* (FOCS), Vancouver, Canada, Nov. 2002, (pp. 271–280).

Mahy, R., Matthews, P., & Rosenberg, J. (2010). *Traversal using relays around NAT (TURN): Relay extensions to session traversal utilities for NAT (STUN).* Retrieved from http://www.rfc-editor.org/rfc/rfc5766.txt

Maymounkov, P., & Mazières, D. (2002). *Kademlia: A peer-to-peer information system based on the XOR metric.* In International Workshop on Peer-To-Peer Systems.

Mol, J. J., Bakker, A., Pouwelse, J., Epema, D. H., & Sips, H. J. (2009). *The design and deployment of a BitTorrent live video streaming solution.* In ISM 2009. IEEE Computer Society. Retrieved from http://pds.twi.tudelft.nl/pubs/papers/ism2009.pdf

Monteiro, J. F. (2010). *Quality assurance solutions for multipoint scalable video distribution over wireless IP networks.* PhD Thesis, Instituto Superior Técnico, Technical University of Lisbon, Portugal.

Mori, R., & Kawahara, M. (1990). Superdistribution: The concept and the architecture. *Transactions of the IEICE, E73*(7), 1133-1146. Retrieved from http://www.virtualschool.edu/mon/ElectronicProperty/MoriSuperdist.html

NAPA-WINE Consortium. (2010). *Network-aware P2P-TV application over wise networks project home page.* Retrieved from http://www.napa-wine.eu/cgi-bin/twiki/view/Public

Napster. (2009). *Napster home page* (Web Archive). Retrieved from http://web.archive.org/web/*/http://www.napster.com/

Nunes, R., Cruz, R. S., & Nunes, M. S. (2010). Scalable video distribution in peer-to-peer architecture. In *Proceedings 10th National Networking Conference - CRC 2010*, Braga, Portugal.

Obreiter, P., & Nimis, J. (2003). *A taxonomy of incentive patterns -- The design space of incentives for cooperation.*

Obreiter, P., & Nimis, J. (2005). *A taxonomy of incentive patterns. Agents and Peer-to-Peer Computing* (*Vol. 2872*, pp. 89–100). Berlin, Germany: Springer.

OceanStore. (2010). *The OceanStore project home page.* Retrieved from http://www.oceanstore.org/.

Octoshape. (2010). *Octoshape home page.* Retrieved from http://www.octoshape.com/.

Ostermann, J., Bormans, J., List, P., Marpe, D., Narroschke, M., & Pereira, F. (2004). Video coding with H.264/AVC: Tools, performance, and complexity. *IEEE Circuits and Systems Magazine, 4*(1), 7–28. doi:10.1109/MCAS.2004.1286980

Padmanabhan, V. N., Wang, H. J., Chou, P. A., & Sripanidkulchai, K. (2002). Distributing streaming media content using cooperative networking. In *Proceedings of ACM NOSSDAV*.

Park, J., & van der Schaar, M. (2010). A game theoretic analysis of incentives in content production and sharing over peer-to-peer networks. *IEEE Journal of Selected Topics in Signal Processing, 4*(4), 704–717. doi:10.1109/JSTSP.2010.2048609

PeerCast.org. (2010). *PeerCast home page.* Retrieved from http://www.peercast.org/

Plaxton, C. G., Rajararnan, R., & Richa, A. W. (1997). Accessing nearby copies of replicated objects in a distributed environment. In *Proceedings of the Ninth Annual ACM Symposium on Parallel Algorithms and Architectures, SPAA '97* (pp. 311-320). New York, NY: ACM. doi: http://doi.acm.org/10.1145/258492.258523

Pouwelse, J. A., Garbacki, P., Wang, J., Bakker, A., Yang, J., & Iosup, A. (2008). TRIBLER: A social-based peer-to-peer system. *Concurrency and Computation, 20*(2), 127–138. doi:10.1002/cpe.1189

PPLive. (2010). *PPTV home page.* Retrieved from http://www.pptv.com/.

PPStream. (2011). *PPS Net TV home page.* Retrieved from http://www.pps.tv/en/

Ratnasamy, S., Francis, P., Handley, M., Karp, R., & Shenker, S. (2001). A scalable content-addressable network. In *Proceedings of the 2001 Conference on Applications, Technologies, Architectures, and Protocols for Computer Communications, SIGCOMM'01* (pp. 161-172). New York, NY: ACM. doi: http://doi.acm.org/10.1145/383059.383072

Ratnasamy, S., Handley, M., Karp, R., & Shenker, S. (2001). Application-level multicast using content-addressable networks. In *Proceedings of the Third International COST264 Workshop on Networked Group Communication, NGC '01* (pp. 14-29). London, UK: Springer-Verlag.

RawFlow. (2010). *RawFlow home page*. Retrieved from http://www.rawflow.com/.

Reed, I. S., & Solomon, G. (1960). Polynomial codes over certain finite fields. *Journal of the Society for Industrial and Applied Mathematics, 8*, 300–304. doi:10.1137/0108018

Reimers, U. (2004). *DVB* (2nd ed.). Springer Publishing Company, Incorporated.

Rekhter, Y., Li, T., & Hares, S. (2006). *A border gateway protocol 4 (BGP-4)*. Request for Comments IETF. Retrieved from http://www.ietf.org/rfc/rfc4271.txt

Rekhter, Y., Moskowitz, B., Karrenberg, D., de Groot, G. J., & Lear, E. (1996). *Address allocation for private internets*. Retrieved from http://www.rfc-editor.org/rfc/rfc1918.txt

Rosenberg, J., Weinberger, J., Huitema, C., & Mahy, R. (2003). *STUN - Simple traversal of user datagram protocol (UDP) through network address translators (NATs)*. Retrieved from http://www.rfc-editor.org/rfc/rfc3489.txt

Rowstron, A., & Druschel, P. (2001). Pastry: Scalable, decentralized object location, and routing for large-scale peer-to-peer systems. In *Proceedings of the IFIP/ACM International Conference on Distributed Systems Platforms, Middleware '01* (pp. 329-350). London, UK: Springer-Verlag.

Roxbeam. (2010). *Roxbeam home page*. Retrieved from http://www.roxbeam.com/english/index.html

SARACEN Consortium. (2010). *Socially aware, collaborative, scalable coding media distribution project home page*. Retrieved from http://www.saracen-p2p.eu/

Schulzrinne, H., Casner, S., Frederick, R., & Jacobson, V. (2003). *RTP: A transport protocol for real-time applications*. Retrieved from http://www.rfc-editor.org/rfc/rfc3550.txt

Schütt, T., Schintke, F., & Reinefeld, A. (2006). Structured overlay without consistent hashing: Empirical results. In *Sixth IEEE International Symposium on Cluster Computing and the Grid Workshops, 2006* (Vol. 2, p. 8). doi: 10.1109/CCGRID.2006.1630903

Schwarz, H., Marpe, D., & Wiegand, T. (2007). Overview of the scalable video coding extension of the H.264/AVC standard. *IEEE Transactions on Circuits and Systems for Video Technology, 17*(9), 1103–1120. doi:10.1109/TCSVT.2007.905532

Sentinelli, A., Celetto, L., Lefol, D., Palazzi, C., & Pau, G. (2008). A survey on P2P streaming clients: Looking at the end-user. In *Proceedings of the 4th Annual International Conference on Wireless Internet, WICON '08* (pp. 1-4). Brussels, Belgium: ICST (Institute for Computer Sciences, Social-Informatics and Telecommunications Engineering). doi: 10.4108/ICST.WICON2008.4994

Sentinelli, A., Marfia, G., Gerla, M., Kleinrock, L., & Tewari, S. (2007). Will IPTV ride the peer-to-peer stream? [Peer-to-Peer Multimedia Streaming]. *IEEE Communications Magazine, 45*(6), 86–92. doi:10.1109/MCOM.2007.374424

Shen, X., Yu, H., Buford, J., & Akon, M. (2009). *Handbook of peer-to-peer networking* (1st ed.). Springer Publishing Company, Incorporated.

Shneidman, J., & Parkes, D. (2003). Rationality and self-interest in peer to peer networks. In Kaashoek, M., & Stoica, I. (Eds.), *Peer-to-Peer Systems II* (*Vol. 2735*, pp. 139–148). Berlin, Germany: Springer. doi:10.1007/978-3-540-45172-3_13

Shneidman, J., Parkes, D. C., & Massoulié, L. (2004). Faithfulness in internet algorithms. *Proceedings of the ACM SIGCOMM Workshop on Practice and Theory of Incentives in Networked Systems* (pp. 220-227). New York, NY: ACM. doi:http://doi.acm.org/10.1145/1016527.1016537

Shokrollahi, A. (2006). Raptor codes. *IEEE Transactions on Information Theory, 52*(6), 2551–2567. doi:10.1109/TIT.2006.874390

Singh, A., Castro, M., Druschel, P., & Rowstron, A. (2004) Defending against eclipse attacks on overlay networks. *Proceedings of the 11th Workshop on ACM SIGOPS European Workshop*, (p. 21).

Sirivianos, M., Han, J., Rex, P., & Yang, C. X. (2007). Free-riding in BitTorrent networks with the large view exploit. *Proceedings of the 6th International Workshop on Peer-to-Peer Systems, IPTPS'07*. Retrieved from http://research.microsoft.com/en-us/um/redmond/events/iptps2007/

Sirivianos, M., Park, J. H., Yang, X., & Jarecki, S. (2007). Dandelion: Cooperative content distribution with robust incentives. *Proceedings of the USENIX Annual Technical Conference 2007* (p. 12:1-12:14). Berkeley, CA: USENIX Association. Retrieved from http://dl.acm.org/citation.cfm?id=1364385.1364397

SopCast. (2010). *SopCast home page*. Retrieved from http://www.sopcast.org/

Steiner, M., En-Najjary, T., & Biersack, E. W. (2007). A global view of Kad. In *Proceedings of 7th ACM SIGCOMM Conference on Internet Measurement IMC'07*. San Diego, CA, USA.

Stiemerling, M., & Kiesel, S. (2010). Cooperative P2P video streaming for mobile peers. *2010 Proceedings of 19th International Conference on Computer Communications and Networks* (ICCCN), (pp. 1-7).

Stoica, I., Morris, R., Liben-Nowell, D., Karger, D. R., Kaashoek, M. F., & Dabek, F. (2003). Chord: A scalable peer-to-peer lookup protocol for Internet applications. *IEEE/ACM Transactions on Networking, 11*(1), 17–32. doi:10.1109/TNET.2002.808407

Streamcast Networks. (2008). *Morpheus home page* (Web archive). Retrieved from http://web.archive.org/web/*/http://morpheus.com

Su, X., & Dhaliwal, S. K. (2010). Incentive mechanisms in P2P media streaming systems. *IEEE Internet Computing, 14*(5), 74–81. doi:10.1109/MIC.2010.119

Sullivan, G. J., & Wiegand, T. (2005). Video compression - From concepts to the H.264/AVC standard. *Proceedings of the IEEE, 93*(1), 18–31. doi:10.1109/JPROC.2004.839617

Tan, E., Guo, L., Chen, S., & Zhang, X. (2001). CUBS: Coordinated upload bandwidth sharing in residential networks. In *Proceedings of the 17th IEEE International Conference on Network Protocols* (ICNP'09). IEEE, Oct. 2009, (pp. 193-2002).

Tang, Y., Wang, H., & Dou, W. (2004). Trust based incentive in P2P network. *Proceedings of the IEEE International Conference on E-Commerce Technology for Dynamic E-Business* (pp. 302-305). doi:10.1109/CEC-EAST.2004.71

Taylor, I. J., & Harrison, A. (2009). *From P2P and grids to services on the web: Evolving distributed communities* (2nd ed.). Springer Publishing Company, Incorporated.

Technical, E. B. U. (2010). *Peer-to-peer (P2P) technologies and services*. Geneva, Switzerland: Author.

Thompson, G., & Chen, Y. R. (2009). IPTV: Reinventing television in the internet age. *IEEE Internet Computing, 13*(3), 11–14. doi:10.1109/MIC.2009.63

Tran, D. A., Hua, K., & Do, T. (2003). ZIGZAG: An efficient peer-to-peer scheme for media streaming. In *Proceedings of IEEE INFOCOM.*

Tu, Y.-C., Sun, J., Hefeeda, M., & Prabhakar, S. (2005). An analytical study of peer-to-peer media streaming systems. *ACM Transactions on Multimedia Computing. Communications and Applications, 1*(4), 354–376.

TU Delft - Tribler. (2010). *Tribler project home page.* Retrieved from http://tribler.org/trac/wiki

TVU networks. (2010). *TVU networks home page.* Retrieved from http://www.tvunetworks.com/

UUSee. (2010). *UUSee home page.* Retrieved from http://www.uusee.com/

Vermeirsch, K., Dhondt, Y., Mys, S., & de Walle, R. V. (2007). Low complexity multiple description coding for H.264/AVC. In *Eighth International Workshop on Image Analysis for Multimedia Interactive Services, WIAMIS '07* (p. 61). doi: 10.1109/WIAMIS.2007.55

Vlavianos, A., Iliofotou, M., & Faloutsos, M. (2006). BiTos: Enhancing bittorrent for supporting streaming applications. In *Proceedings of the 9th IEEE Global Internet Symposium*, Apr. 2006.

Waitzman, D., Partridge, C., & Deering, S. E. (1988). *Distance vector multicast routing protocol.* Request for Comments IETF. Retrieved from http://www.ietf.org/rfc/rfc1075.txt

Wallach, D. S. (2003). A survey of peer-to-peer security issues. In *Proceedings of the Mext-NSF-JSPS International Symposium on Software Security – Theories and Systems (ISSS '02), LNCS 2609,* (pp. 42–57). Tokyo, Japan, Nov. 2003. Springer.

Wang, D., & Liu, J. (2006). *A dynamic skip list based overlay network for on-demand media streaming with VCR interactions.* IEEE International Conference on Multimedia & Expo (ICME), Toronto, ON, Canada, July 9-12, 2006.

Wang, M., & Li, B. (2007). R^2: Random rush with random network coding in live peer-to-peer streaming. *IEEE Journal on Selected Areas in Communications, 25*(9), 1655–1666. doi:10.1109/JSAC.2007.071205

Wang, M., & Li, B. (2007). *Lava: A reality check of network coding in peer-to-peer live streaming.* In IEEE INFOCO, Anchorage, Alaska, May 2007.

Wenger, S. (2003). H.264/AVC over IP. *IEEE Transactions on Circuits and Systems for Video Technology, 13*(7), 645–656. doi:10.1109/TC-SVT.2003.814966

Wu, C., Li, B., & Zhao, S. (2008). Exploring large-scale peer-to-peer live streaming topologies. *ACM Transactions on Multimedia Computing Communivations and Applications, 4*(3), 1-23. New York, NY: ACM. doi: http://doi.acm.org/10.1145/1386109.1386112

Xiao, X., Zhang, Q., Shi, Y., & Gao, Y. (2011). How much to share: A repeated game model for peer-to-peer streaming under service differentiation incentives. *IEEE Transactions on Parallel and Distributed Systems, 99,* 1. doi:doi:10.1109/TPDS.2011.167

Xie, S., Li, B., Keung, G. Y., & Zhang, X. (2007). Coolstreaming: Design, theory, and practice. *IEEE Transactions on Multimedia, 9*(8), 1661–1671. doi:10.1109/TMM.2007.907469

Xu, D., Chai, H.-K., Rosenberg, C., & Kulkarni, S. (2003). Analysis of a hybrid architecture for cost-effective streaming media distribution. In *Proceedings of SPIE/ACM MMCN.*

Yao, J., Duan, Y., & Pan, J. (2006). Implementation of a Multihoming Agent for Mobile On-board Communication. In *Proceedings of VTC, 2006.*

Yiu, W., Chan, S. Xiong, Y., & Zhang, Q. (2005). *Supporting interactive media on-demand in peer-to-peer networks.* Technical report, 2005.

Yoon, H., Kim, J., Tan, F., & Hsieh, R. (2008). On-demand video streaming in mobile opportunistic networks. [Washington, DC: IEEE Computer Society.]. *Proceedings of PERCOM, 08,* 80–89.

Zhang, B., Jamin, S., & Zhang, L. (2002). Host multicast: A framework for delivering multicast to end users. In *Proceedings Twenty-First Annual Joint Conference of the IEEE Computer and Communications Societies INFOCOM 2002 IEEE* (Vol. 3, pp. 1366-1375). doi: 10.1109/INFCOM.2002.1019387

Zhang, M., Luo, J.-G., Zhao, L., & Yang, S.-Q. (2005). A peer-to-peer network for live media streaming using a push-pull approach. In *Proceedings of ACM International Conference on Multimedia.*

Zhang, M., Zhao, L., Tang, Y., Luo, J.-G., & Yang, S.-Q. (2005). Large-scale live media streaming over peer-to-peer networks through global internet. In *Proceedings ACM Internaitonal Conference on Multimedia, P2PMMS Workshop.*

Zhang, X., Chen, S., & Sandhu, R. (2005). Enhancing data authenticity and integrity in P2P systems. *IEEE Internet Computing, 9*(6), 42–49. doi:10.1109/MIC.2005.124

Zhang, X., Liu, J., Li, B., & Yum, T. P. (2005). CoolStreaming/DONet: A data-driven overlay network for peer-to-peer live media streaming. In *Proceedings of the 24th Annual Joint Conference of the IEEE Computer and Communications Societies, INFOCOM '05* (Vol. 3, pp. 2102-2111 vol. 3). doi: 10.1109/INFCOM.2005.1498486

Zhao, B. Y., Huang, L., Stribling, J., Rhea, S. C., & Kubiatowicz, A. D. (2004). Tapestry: A resilient global-scale overlay for service deployment. *IEEE Journal on Selected Areas in Communications, 22*(1), 41–53. doi:10.1109/JSAC.2003.818784

Zhuang, S. Q., Zhao, B. Y., Joseph, A. D., Katz, R. H., & Kubiatowicz, J. D. (2001). Bayeux: An architecture for scalable and fault-tolerant wide-area data dissemination. In *Proceedings of the 11th International Workshop on Network and Operating Systems Support for Digital Audio and Video, NOSSDAV '01* (pp. 11-20). New York, NY: ACM. doi: http://doi.acm.org/10.1145/378344.378347

Zink, M., & Mauthe, A. (2004). P2P streaming using multiple description coded video. *Proceedings 30th Euromicro Conference, 2004* (pp. 240-247). doi: 10.1109/EURMIC.2004.1333377

ADDITIONAL READING

Abbas, S. M., Pouwelse, J. A., Epema, D. H., & Sips, H. J. (2009). A gossip-based distributed social networking system. In *Proceedings of the 18th IEEE International Workshops on Enabling Technologies: Infrastructures for Collaborative Enterprises, WETICE '09* (pp. 93-98). doi: 10.1109/WETICE.2009.30

Agarwal, S., Singh, J. P., Mavlankar, A., Bacchichet, P., & Girod, B. (2008). Performance of P2P live video streaming systems on a controlled test-bed. In *Proceedings of the 4th International Conference on Testbeds and Research Infrastructures for the Development of Networks & Communities, TridentCom '08* (pp. 1-10). Brussels, Belgium: ICST (Institute for Computer Sciences, Social-Informatics and Telecommunications Engineering).

Asís López-Fuentes, F. (2010). Adaptive mechanism for P2P video streaming using SVC and MDC. In *2010 International Conference on Complex, Intelligent and Software Intensive Systems* (CISIS), (pp. 457-462). doi: 10.1109/CISIS.2010.111

Camarillo, G., & IAB. (2009). *Peer-to-peer (P2P) architecture: Definition, taxonomies, examples, and applicability.* Request for Comments. IETF. Retrieved from http://www.ietf.org/rfc/rfc5694.txt

Cha, M., Kwak, H., & Rodriguez, P. Yong-YeolAhn, & Moon, S. (2007). I tube, you tube, everybody tubes: Analyzing the world's largest user generated content video system. In *Proceedings of the 7th ACM SIGCOMM Conference on Internet Measurement, IMC '07* (pp. 1-14). New York, NY, USA: ACM. doi: http://doi.acm.org/10.1145/1298306.1298309

Chen, Z., Li, B., Keung, G., Yin, H., Lin, C., Wang, Y., et al. (2009). How scalable could P2P live media streaming system be with the stringent time constraint? In *Proceedings of the IEEE International Conference on Communications, ICC '09* (pp. 1-5). doi: 10.1109/ICC.2009.5199057

Ciullo, D., Garcia, M. A., Horvath, A., Leonardi, E., Mellia, M., & Rossi, D. (2010). Network awareness of P2P live streaming applications: A measurement study. *IEEE Transactions on Multimedia*, *12*(1), 54–63. doi:10.1109/TMM.2009.2036231

CURRENT Lab UCSB. (2010). *Chimera, a lightweight & efficient implementation of a structured peer-to-peer overlay network - Home page.* Retrieved from http://current.cs.ucsb.edu/projects/chimera/index.html

Deguo, Y., Lianqiang, N., & Xincun, W. (2009). A P2P-SIP architecture for real time stream media communication. In *Proceedings of the 9th International Conference on Hybrid Intelligent Systems, HIS '09* (Vol. 3, pp. 24-28). doi: 10.1109/HIS.2009.218

3GPP. (2010). *Transparent end-to-end packet-switched streaming service (PSS); Protocols and codecs.* Retrieved from http://www.3gpp.org/ftp/Specs/html-info/26234.htm

Huang, C., Lin, C., & Yang, C. (2010). Mobility management for video streaming on heterogeneous networks. *IEEE MultiMedia*, *17*(1), 35. doi:10.1109/MMUL.2010.17

Li, B., & Yin, H. (2007). Peer-to-peer live video streaming on the internet: Issues, existing approaches, and challenges [Peer-to-Peer Multimedia Streaming]. *IEEE Communications Magazine*, *45*(6), 94–99. doi:10.1109/MCOM.2007.374425

Liu, Z., Shen, Y., Ross, K. W., Panwar, S. S., & Wang, Y. (2009). LayerP2P: Using layered video chunks in P2P live streaming. *IEEE Transactions on Multimedia*, *11*(7), 1340–1352. doi:10.1109/TMM.2009.2030656

Lu, G., Zuniga, J., & Rahman, A. (2010). *P2P streaming for mobile nodes: Scenarios and related issues.* Retrieved from http://www.ietf.org/internet-drafts/draft-lu-ppsp-mobile-00.txt

Mirshokraie, S., & Hefeeda, M. (2010). Live peer-to-peer streaming with scalable video coding and networking coding. In *Proceedings of the First Annual ACM SIGMM Conference on Multimedia Systems, MMSys '10* (pp. 123-132). New York, NY: ACM. doi: http://doi.acm.org/10.1145/1730836.1730852

Niraula, N. B., Kanchanasut, K., & Laouiti, A. (2009). Peer-to-peer live video streaming over mobile ad hoc network. In *Proceedings of the International Conference on Wireless Communications and Mobile Computing, IWCMC '09* (pp. 1045-1050). New York, NY: ACM. doi: http://doi.acm.org/10.1145/1582379.1582609

Peltotalo, J., Harju, J., Jantunen, A., Saukko, M., & Väätämöinen, L. (2008). Peer-to-peer streaming technology survey. In *Seventh International Conference on Networking, ICN 2008* (pp. 342-350). doi: 10.1109/ICN.2008.86

Piatek, M., Madhyastha, H. V., John, J. P., Krishnamurthy, A., & Anderson, T. (2009). *Pitfalls for ISP-friendly P2P design*. In Eighth ACM Workshop on Hot Topics in Networks, HotNets-VIII. Retrieved from http://conferences.sigcomm.org/hotnets/2009/program.html

Picconi, F., & Massoulie, L. (2009). ISP friend or foe? Making P2P live streaming ISP-aware. In *Proceedings of the 29th IEEE International Conference on Distributed Computing Systems, ICDCS '09* (pp. 413-422). doi: 10.1109/ICDCS.2009.37

Sentinelli, A., Celetto, L., Lefol, D., Palazzi, C., & Pau, G. (2008). A survey on P2P streaming clients: Looking at the end-user. In *Proceedings of the 4th Annual International Conference on Wireless Internet, WICON'08* (pp. 1-4). Brussels, Belgium: ICST (Institute for Computer Sciences, Social-Informatics and Telecommunications Engineering). doi: 10.4108/ICST.WICON2008.4994

Sentinelli, A., Marfia, G., Gerla, M., Kleinrock, L., & Tewari, S. (2007). Will IPTV ride the peer-to-peer stream? [Peer-to-Peer Multimedia Streaming]. *IEEE Communications Magazine, 45*(6), 86–92. doi:10.1109/MCOM.2007.374424

Shen, X., Yu, H., Buford, J., & Akon, M. (2009). *Handbook of peer-to-peer networking* (1st ed.). Springer Publishing Company, Incorporated.

Silverston, T., & Fourmaux, O. (2007). Measuring P2P IPTV systems. In *Proceedings of the 17th International Workshop on Network and Operating Systems Support for Digital Audio & Video, NOSSDAV'07*. Retrieved from http://www.nossdav.org/2007/program.html

Technical, E. B. U. (2010). *Peer-to-peer (P2P) technologies and services*. Geneva, Switzerland: Author.

Thompson, G., & Chen, Y. R. (2009). IPTV: Reinventing television in the internet age. *IEEE Internet Computing, 13*(3), 11–14. doi:10.1109/MIC.2009.63

Vénot, S., & Yan, L. (2007). Peer-to-peer media streaming application survey. In *International Conference on Mobile Ubiquitous Computing, Systems, Services and Technologies, UBICOMM '07* (pp. 139-148). doi: 10.1109/UBICOMM.2007.18

Wu, K., Lei, Z., & Chiu, D. (2010). *P2P layered streaming for heterogeneous networks in PPSP*. Retrieved from http://www.ietf.org/internet-drafts/draft-wu-ppsp-p2p-layered-streaming-00.txt

Section 3
Multimedia Applications

Chapter 11
Improved Subject Identification in Surveillance Video Using Super-Resolution

Simon Denman
Queensland University of Technology, Australia

Vinod Chandran
Queensland University of Technology, Australia

Frank Lin
Queensland University of Technology, Australia

Sridha Sridharan
Queensland University of Technology, Australia

Clinton Fookes
Queensland University of Technology, Australia

ABSTRACT

The time consuming and labour intensive task of identifying individuals in surveillance video is often challenged by poor resolution and the sheer volume of stored video. Faces or identifying marks such as tattoos are often too coarse for direct matching by machine or human vision. Object tracking and super-resolution can then be combined to facilitate the automated detection and enhancement of areas of interest. The object tracking process enables the automatic detection of people of interest, greatly reducing the amount of data for super-resolution. Smaller regions such as faces can also be tracked. A number of instances of such regions can then be utilized to obtain a super-resolved version for matching. Performance improvement from super-resolution is demonstrated using a face verification task. It is shown that there is a consistent improvement of approximately 7% in verification accuracy, using both Eigenface and Elastic Bunch Graph Matching approaches for automatic face verification, starting from faces with an eye to eye distance of 14 pixels. Visual improvement in image fidelity from super-resolved images over low-resolution and interpolated images is demonstrated on a small database. Current research and future directions in this area are also summarized.

DOI: 10.4018/978-1-4666-2660-7.ch011

INTRODUCTION

Forensic use of surveillance video is limited by the low resolution of the frames and the human effort required for extracting useful footage from recordings. Good quality images provide sharp and clear facial, clothing, tattooed skin and other areas of interest and are essential for the surveillance footage to be useful. However, surveillance videos are low resolution due to two main factors.

Storage requirements make high resolution video prohibitive for use in a surveillance system. The video is often compressed using standards proposed by the Motion Pictures Expert Group (MPEG) to reduce file size. In a best case scenario, a DVD quality video could be encoded in the state of the art MPEG4 format at around 100KB/s. This still translates to 8.2GB of data for one camera per day. The total storage requirements become prohibitive very quickly as the number of cameras is increased or if the period of retention is lengthened.

Further, in order to reduce the number of cameras required to cover an area, wide angle lenses are fitted to cameras to increase their field of view (FOV). As a consequence subjects of interest occupy only small portions of the entire scene. Figure 1 contains a sample frame from the i-LIDS (i-LIDS Team, 2006) dataset which consists of surveillance footage for evaluating tracking algorithms. Although the video was captured at DVD resolution, the subjects' faces were less than 30 pixels (px) wide. It becomes progressively harder to distinguish the two faces once the width of the face drops below 32px, as can be seen from Figure2. Interpolation or "digital zoom" does not help because although these procedures add extra samples, they do not add extra information at high spatial frequencies.

Super-resolution is a signal-processing method that can be applied to enhance the resolution of the surveillance video by fusing complementary information contained in successive frames of the video. As super-resolution is a computationally intensive process, applying it to an entire sequence without any guidance is undesirable. A tracking system enables subjects of interest to be detected, tracked and super-resolved; resulting in a more computationally efficient and useful system. The tracking system also discards frames of the sequence that do not contain moving subjects, reducing the manual effort required in extracting useful frames.

In this chapter, we present an end-to-end system for detecting and tracking people, extracting sequences of faces for each subject and using super-resolution to improve the image quality prior to a face verification process. This process is illustrated in Figure 3. The proposed super-resolution approach uses a robust optical flow technique to guide the registration of a set of facial images, allowing for non-rigid deformations to be incorporated into the registration and super-resolution. This novel super-resolution approach is combined with an object tracking technique, resulting in a novel end-to-end system for automatically extracting, enhancing and recognizing facial images from surveillance footage.

The remainder of this chapter is organized as follows. An overview of super resolution and object tracking techniques is presented in Sections 2 (Super Resolution) and 3 (Person Tracking). An integrated system that performs super-resolution on areas identified by the tracking process is described in Section 4 (Integrated System). Current research trends and future directions are summarized in Section 5 (Future Research Directions). Concluding remarks are provided in Section 6 (Conclusion).

Super Resolution

Super-resolution image reconstruction is the process of combining multiple low-resolution (LR) images into one image with higher resolution. These low-resolution images may be aliased and related to each other through sub-pixel shifts -- essentially representing different "snapshots" of the same scene, each carrying some complementary information. Super-resolution techniques have

Figure 1. Typical image captured by a surveillance camera. The whole frame is 720 by 576px. The faces only occupy a small area compared to the frame. Widths of the highlighted faces are: a) 17px, b) 14px, c) 12px and d) 27px.

been applied to many areas including medical imaging, satellite imagery and some pattern recognition applications (Park et al, 2003).

The majority of super-resolution techniques are reconstruction-based, dating back to the work by Tsai and Huang on satellite images in 1984 (Tsai, 1984). These methods are versatile, in that they can super-resolve any image sequence (provided the motion between observations can be modelled) as they work directly with the image pixel intensities, and methods that work both in the frequency domain (Borman, 1999; Park, 2003; Tsai, 1984) and pixel domain (Goldberg, 2003; Patti, 2001; Schultz, 1996) have been proposed.

The more recent learning-based approaches enhance the images by using *a priori* information about the scene and synthesize the output (Baker, 2002; Freeman, 2002; Wang, 2004; Zitov, 2003). The term "hallucination" was proposed by Baker (2002), and has been widely adopted to describe the process. Such systems are trained with high and low resolution image pairs to learn the relationship between the high-resolution and corresponding low-resolution image patches. Various "hallucination" approaches have been proposed, including identifying common local patches, and storing the low and high resolution representation of the patches to allow the algorithm to super-resolve an image (Freeman, 2002); using Gaussian and Laplacian derivatives at each pixel to match between the input LR features and the learned HR features (Baker, 2002); and using Principal Component Analysis (PCA) trained on sets of high and low resolution images, determining how a low resolution input can best be represented from the low resolution training set, and applying the same transform to the high resolution set to obtain the super-resolved image (Wang, 2004).

Such systems require training to learn the relationship between the high and low resolution images, but higher magnification ratios can be obtained if low-resolution images are similar to the training images, e.g., frontal faces. Furthermore, such techniques can perform super-resolution from a single image, rather than a sequence of images. However, the techniques can introduce erroneous high frequency information, which becomes more apparent when there is mismatch between the training and test data. When the output of the super-resolution process is to be used in recognition (i.e. face recognition), such false high frequency data can lead to degradation in performance.

Reconstruction and learning based techniques have both been developed with the primary focus being image enhancement for viewing by a person. However in situations where super-resolution is being used to improve biometric performance, the primary aim is to improve recognition performance, rather than the perceptible image quality. With this in mind, feature domain super-resolution approaches have been proposed for biometrics such as face (Gunturk, 2003) and iris (Nguyen, 2011), where the aim is to enhance the feature vector that is extracted for recognition, rather than the initial image.

Despite the advantages of learning-based and feature domain techniques, for an unconstrained surveillance application the more traditional reconstruction based approaches are most appropriate. In a surveillance environment, viewpoints cannot be guaranteed as required by learning-based approaches, and the desired target for super-resolution may not always be a face or biometric trait suitable for automated recognition. With this in mind, a flexible approach that can be used to enhance a variety of features is desirable.

Many reconstruction-based super-resolution methods have been proposed, and systems typically have common steps such as registration, interpolation and restoration, The manner in which these steps are performed vary according to the method, and are outlined in the following subsections.

Sampling and Aliasing

To appreciate why super-resolution is required for resolution enhancement, we must understand the sampling process and the conditions that lead to aliasing. Recording a signal involves sampling its value or intensity at regular intervals. According to the Nyquist sampling theorem, the sampling rate f_s must be at least twice the highest frequency contained in the waveform f_{max} in order to capture all frequency components of a signal, $f_s = 2f_{max}$.

Figure 4 presents a sine wave with a frequency of 0.05 cycles/mm illustrated by the solid line. The minimum sampling rate required is therefore 0.1 cycles per mm, corresponding to a sampling interval 10mm). When sampled at 0.067 cycles/mm (sampling interval 15mm), the resulting sine wave shown in dashed lines aliases to a lower frequency. Even if the resulting signal was interpolated, it would not be possible to recover the original sine wave. Super-resolution attempts to reverse the effect of aliasing by using more than one set of samples shifted relative to each other.

Observation Model

One of the first steps in the super-resolution reconstruction problem is the formulation of an observation model. That is, to develop a model that relates the original HR image to the observed LR images. Several observation models have been proposed but generally the observation model can be expressed as,

$$y_k = DB_k M_k x + n_k \qquad (1)$$

where y_k denotes the $k = 1...p$ LR images, D is a sub-sampling matrix, B_k is the blur matrix, M_k is the warp matrix, x is the original HR image of the scene which we are trying to recover, and n_k is the additive noise that corrupts the image (Park et al, 2003). D and B_k simulate the blurring averaging process performed by the camera's optics and CCD sensor while M_k can be modelled by anything from simple parametric transformation to pixel-by-pixel flow fields. Figure 5 shows a graphical representation of the observation model.

As seen from Equation 1, the SR reconstruction problem essentially is an inversion problem as the process lies in the determination of the HR image x from multiple LR observations y_k. This scenario is an ill-posed inverse problem as a multiplicity of solutions exists for a given set of observation images (Borman, 1999). This is often managed by constraining the space of possible solutions according to *a priori* knowledge of the form of the end solution. Typical constraints include image properties such as smoothness and positivity.

Figure 2. Two progressively down-sampled faces (left to right). Widths of the faces are: a) 64px, b) 32px, and c) 16px. It becomes progressively harder to distinguish the two faces and extremely difficult to do so once the width of the face drops below 32px.

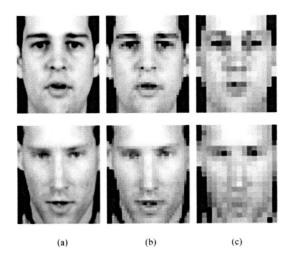

(a)   (b)   (c)

Registration and Transformation Models

Image registration, a form of the correspondence problem, is the process of matching two or more images (reference and sensed images) of the same scene, generally taken with different sensors or viewpoints (Brown, 1992). Accurate registration with sub-pixel precision is crucial to the success of any super-resolution algorithm (Capel, 2003). Generally, the registration process is divided into three steps: feature detection and matching, transform parameter estimation and warping. A description of these steps is given here. Interested readers are referred to (Zitov, 2003; Brown, 1992) for more in-depth information.

Feature Detection and Matching

To estimate the transformation parameters between two images, we must first detect and establish correspondence between groups of pixels that appear in both images. This can be done through feature-based or area-based matching. Feature-based methods are suitable for images with bland regions and clearly defined edges and corners while area-based approaches are useful for highly textured images (Banks, 1997).

Feature-Based Matching

These methods work with feature points such as corners and edges of the images only. The matching process begins by first identifying points of interest with automated methods like the Harris corner detector (Harris, 1998). It is essential that the features be present even in low resolution or coarse versions of the image. Correspondences between points are then computed by searching in a window around each feature point. Images that contain distinct edges and corners perform best with these methods.

Other notable methods that can be utilized for facial feature detection, tracking and registration are holistic-based and local-based feature methods such as the Active Shape Model (ASM) and the Active Appearance Model (AAM). These methods use models for the face and can track changes in the face from one frame to another through adaptation of the model parameters. An ASM (Cootes et al 1995) uses coordinates of facial landmarks, which are points on facial features such as eyebrows, eyes, nose, lips, etc. These coordinates can be represented in a vector space and the the model is deformable through translation, scale and rotation transformations. The shape parameters of the model are a lower dimensional set of weights obtained using principal component analysis on a training set of images. Given a set of coordinates in a new image, the best shape parameters are found by iterative energy minimization and the coordinates are adapted by inverse projection using eigenvectors corresponding to the shape parameters. ASMs work well with near frontal and non-occluded faces. AAMs take both shape and texture into representation and are more general.

The AAM approaches were popularized by Cootes and Edwards (2001). This work was heavily motivated by eigenspace representations (Turk and Pentland, 1991) where the whole face appearance is used during the registration process. The benefit of employing an eigenspace representation is they can provide a compact approximate encoding of a large set of images with a small set of orthogonal basis images. In general, AAM approaches estimate a parametric non-rigid warping vector p of the image I and an appearance vector λ of the eigenspace appearance model A that minimizes the expression,

$$\arg\min_{p,\lambda} \left\| l(p) - A(\lambda) \right\|^{2}. \qquad (2)$$

Initially, these types of approaches were limited to rigid 2D parametric warping functions and more complicated warps p, such as those describing non-rigid deformations, could not be solved due to the computational explosion of the warp parameter

Figure 3. Outline of the proposed system. Video footage from a CCTV network is analyzed by a person tracking routine that extracts sequences of faces images for each person observed in the network. These sequences are registered and super-resolution is used to obtain a high quality images for each subject. The resultant high resolution face images are compared to a database of biometric credentials to determine the subject identity.

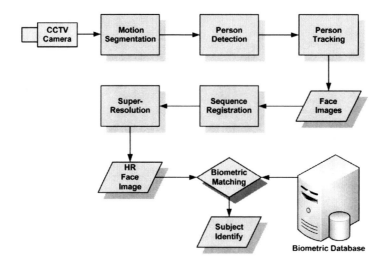

Figure 4. A sine wave with $f = 0.05$ cycles/mm (solid line) is sampled at less than Nyquist frequency. The resulting signal sampled at $f_s = 0.067$ cycles/mm (dashed line) has been aliased to a lower frequency.

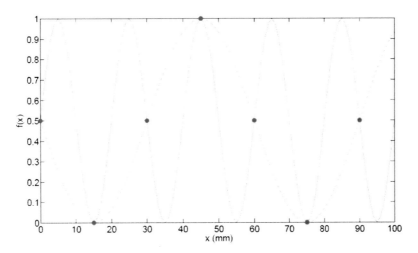

search space. However, Black and Jepson (1998) proposed the eigenspace model could be incorporated into the classical Lucas-Kanade algorithm to form a non-rigid registration framework (i.e. a non-linear optimization of the joint warp and appearance parameters via Gauss-Newton).

It became apparent eigenspace variants suffer from two inherent problems. First, the linear assumption in the appearance model $A(\lambda)$ starts to fail when attempting to model large amounts of object appearance due to overfitting, despite limiting its impact through regularization, mixtures of linear models or kernel techniques (Moghaddam & Pentland, 1997). Second, it is now well understood in machine learning and pattern recognition literature (Bishop, 2006) that least-squares cost criteria are extremely sensitive to outliers or noise (e.g., occlusion, codec artifacts, illumination, etc.).

Local methods attempt to abandon the direct link made between non-rigid face synthesis and registration in holistic methods like AAMs. The approach attempts to register a non-rigid face through the application of an ensemble of local experts to their respective local search regions within the source image being registered. Given

an appropriate non-rigid shape prior for the object, the response surfaces from these local regions are then employed within a joint optimization process to estimate the global non-rigid shape of the face. That is,

$$\arg \min_{p} \sum_{k=1}^{N} f_k \left\{ I, x_k(p) \right\} \qquad (3)$$

where N is the number of fiducial landmarks in the non-rigid shape model and $f_k \left\{ I, x_k(p) \right\}$ is the response of the kth local expert in source image I at local position x_k. The local expert's coordinates x_1 are dependent on the non-rigid warp parameter vector p affecting the whole face shape. The best known local method is the Active Shape Model (ASM) (Cootes et al, 1995) with successful extensions including the Bayesian Tangent Shape Model (BTSM) (Zhou et al, 2003), Pictorial Structure Matching (PSM) (Felzenszwalb and Huttenlocher, 2000) and Constrained Local Models (CLM) (Wang and Lucey 2008). It is clear that local methods have a number of advantages over holistic methods. Firstly, the search space has

Figure 5. Observation model. The low resolution images can be considered to be ideal images that have been degraded by warping, blurring and down-sampling, and having noise added to them.

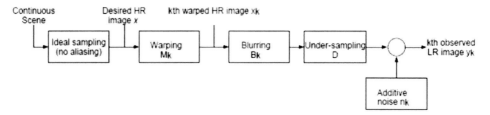

been considerably reduced as we are now only seeking the warp parameter vector p rather than both the warp p and appearance λ parameter vectors. Secondly, they offer local invariance to global illumination variation and occlusion. Thirdly, they model the non-rigid object as an ensemble of low dimensional independent local-experts. Finally, they do not employ complicated piece-wise affine texture warp operations that might introduce unwanted noise.

Thus, techniques such as AAMs and ASMs can be utilized to track features in video. They are particularly suitable for tracking of facial features where there is a specified feature-set and structure within this feature-set. However, these approaches are more problematic for application to whole-body tracking in surveillance video where the pre-determined structure of the feature-set is significantly more fluid and unconstrained. In this chapter, the approach is focused on the use of an optical-flow based technique which can cope with these non-rigid variabilities in a simpler and computationally more efficient manner.

Area-Based Matching

For area-based detection, small groups of pixels in the reference image are compared with pixel groups in the sensed image. A small search window is formed around each pixel group to be matched, where a matching metric such as correlation is used to provide a similarity measure (Banks et al, 1997; Fookes et al 2002). These matchers work on either the absolute or relative intensities of the images. This is computationally expensive, as an exhaustive search in the search window is performed for each pixel group in the image. Area-based approaches work best when the images contain texture information that helps distinguish pixel groups from each other.

Transform Parameter Estimation

A transformation or motion model determines how the sensed images are mapped onto the reference image grid during the process of estimating motion between the images. There are two classes of transformations that are commonly modeled: global and local.

Global Methods

Most common techniques assume global motion or rigid transformations whereby a single equation issued to transform all points from one image to the other. Translational, rotational, affine, perspective and projective motion all fall under this category and are simple to compute. These transformations are useful when the scene is relatively static such as satellite imagery, still scenes containing only camera motion, or where the type of motion is known *a priori*.

Matches from the previous stage will usually contain mismatches or outliers that need to be corrected in this stage. Once the model is chosen (rigid body, affine or projective), methods like the Random Sample Consensus (RANSAC) (Fischler, 1981) can be used to robustly estimate the model parameters. Instead of estimating the model using all available matches which include inliers and outlier data, RANSAC repeatedly estimates the model using random small subsets of the data to attempt to exclude outliers.

Local Methods

The performance of global methods suffers when applied to surveillance videos where motion consists of multiple independently moving subjects. Local methods like optical flow, however, can account for independent motion within the scene, making it ideal for surveillance type imagery. They are also needed when objects in the scene change appearance independently. These methods are able to model much more complex distortions because they can compute local area motion independently. There are three main techniques presented in literature: piecewise interpolation, elastic model-based matching and optical flow. The drawback of catering for local motion is the additional processing time needed and the difficulty of constraining the solution.

If accurate feature matching is possible, piecewise interpolation can be applied. Elastic model-based matching methods model the distortion in the image as deformations of an elastic material. Optical flow methods model the motion as a pixel flow field: a pixel-to-pixel mapping between the images. Popular optical methods include Lucas and Kanade (1981), Horn and Schunck (1981), and Black and Anandan (1993). Optical flow will be explained in more detail in this chapter since it has most relevance to enhancing face images. It also addresses some of the drawbacks of previous super resolution techniques when the main motivation is application to the human face. This is described further in the following section.

Face-Specific Motivation for Local Methods

Super-resolution techniques have been successfully used in a wide variety of applications including medical imaging, satellite imagery, and some pattern recognition applications (Park et al, 2003).

However, many of these proposed techniques have been developed on the assumption that the system operates in a constrained environment, for example: only rigid objects assumed in the scene or only simple transformations are employed. Consequently, many of these proposed techniques are not applicable to images involving the human face due to the inherent difficulties that exist in this domain. Some of challenges faced with processing the human face include (Fookes et al, 2004; Baker and Kanade, 1999),

1. **Non-Planarity:** A large majority of super-resolution systems employ simple parametric transformations in the registration stages, including translations, affine or projective transformations. These types of mappings, however, operate on the assumption that the environment is made up of planar objects. When such approaches are applied to images involving the human face, results are severely degraded as the human face is far from planar.

2. **Non-Rigidity:** To further compound this problem of non-planarity, the human face is also inherently non-rigid. Local deformations occur frequently as facial expressions transition from state to state as well as parts such as the eyes, nose, mouth and jaw that move independently from other parts of the face. Most super-resolution approaches fail on non-rigid scenes. Some are capable of handling independently moving objects; however, each object is assumed rigid (Schultz and Stevenson, 1996).

3. **Occlusions:** Movement of the human face will result in many occlusions as some parts of the face will block the viewing angle to other parts of the face. Faces can also be temporarily occluded by hands. These occlusions can be a large source of error for many super-resolution techniques.

4. **Illumination and Reflectance Variation:** Faces are subject to specular reflections,

particularly off certain parts, e.g.: the cheeks and forehead. These reflections introduce further difficulties into the registration process as well as introduce outliers into the fusion stage.

To overcome some of these problems, particularly the non-planarity and non-rigidity of the face, it is possible to use optical flow techniques to recover a dense flow field that describes a deformation or mapping for every pixel in the scene. By determining these local flows, it is possible to track the motion of a complicated non-planar and non-rigid object such as the human face. The remaining two problems of occlusions and illumination variation can be addressed through robust estimation methods. This will be described further in the following section.

Robust Optical Flow

Optical flow techniques relate the 2D projection of the physical movement of points in a scene relative to an observer to 2D displacement of pixels on the image plane. These techniques operate on the concept that an object or point in an image will be observed with intensity $I(t)$ at a certain time. Although the physical location of this point may change over time, it will always be observed with the same intensity. This is known as the *data conservation* constraint (Black, 1993) and can be expressed as,

$$I(x, y, t) = I(x + u\delta t, y + v\delta t, t + \delta t) \qquad (4)$$

where (u, v) are the horizontal and vertical velocities (or flow fields) of a point (x, y), and the change in time δt is assumed to be small.

The data conservation constraint alone is not enough to recover a unique flow estimate due to the aperture problem, where the motion is ambiguous when observed through a small window. Hence a spatial coherence constraint is needed to pool information from the surrounding neighbourhood.

Surfaces have extent and consequently neighbouring pixels in an image are likely to belong to the same surface. This assumption equates to a smoothness constraint which is imposed on the algorithm to ensure that the motion of neighbouring pixels varies smoothly.

Most optical flow algorithms break down when these above two constraints are not satisfied in practice. This occurs regularly, especially when motion boundaries, shadows and specular reflections are present. To overcome these problems a robust optical flow algorithm was proposed by Black et al. (Black, 1993). This method is based on a robust estimation framework using a Lorentzian estimator and overcomes significant flaws inherent in many optical flow algorithms by addressing these two key assumptions: the data conservation and spatial coherence assumptions.

The main goals of robust statistics are to identify outlier data points and to describe the structure that best fits the bulk of the data (Black, 1993). Figure 6 shows two clusters of data points -- the majority of the data (black) and the outliers (gray). A standard least-squares fit is heavily influenced by the outliers while the robust fit is not. As the solution to the robust formulation is not guaranteed to be convex, a graduated non-convexity algorithm is used to recover the optical flow and motion discontinuities. Interested readers are referred to (Black, 1993) for more details on the optical flow implementation.

Taking the flow vectors from a neighbourhood as an example (see Figure 7), a least-squares approach would tend to average all the flow vectors in the neighbourhood. By contrast, a robust estimator would identify the flow vectors in the rightmost column as outliers and remove them from the estimation process.

Sample results of the optical flow algorithm are given in Figure 8. This figure shows an image pair with the subject moving horizontally between the two frames (a) and (d). The calculated optical flow fields, u and v, for the horizontal and vertical directions are shown in (b) and (e) respectively. The optical flow algorithm also detects data and spatial discontinuities, i.e. pixels that do not satisfy the two assumptions described above. It's easy to see the subject moving horizontally from the outline of the head in (b). The head is also clearly visible in (f) from the spatial discontinuity plot. The sharp optical flow transition between the head and background prevents generation of ringing artifacts around the head that will otherwise be present due to motion vectors being smoothed around motion boundaries. Unfortunately the subject's left shoulder appears stationary due to the white shirt being saturated and blending into the background. This however is unavoidable as it's impossible to separate the shirt from the background from the pixel values in some regions.

Robust Optical Flow Super-Resolution

The super-resolution system described in this section takes an image sequence as input and outputs the super-resolution image sequence along with the optical flow between successive frames. This procedure is illustrated in Figure 9 which shows the super-resolution system flow diagram (Lin et al 2007b).

The individual steps of the algorithm are described as follows and are repeated for all images in the input sequence,

1. Interpolate each original image from the image sequence to twice the input resolution using bilinear interpolation.
2. For $N = No.$ of frames used in the reconstruction (where N is odd), compute the optical flow between the current reference image and the $(N - 1) / 2$ previous images and the $(N - 1) / 2$ following images. (see Section 2.4)
3. Register the $(N - 1) / 2$ previous and $(N - 1) / 2$ following images to the reference image using the displacements estimated from the optical flow stage. (see Section 2.3)

4. Estimate the super-resolution image using a fusion technique (robust mean or median) computed across the reference image and the $(N - 1)$ registered images.
5. Restore the final super-resolved image by applying a deblurring deconvolution filter.

Within the super-resolution process, it is assumed that there are no large changes in target size or pose in the set of frames to be super-resolved. As the optical flow and registration process are 2D, it is possible for the subject to move in such a way that the images will be unable to be registered (i.e. out of plane rotations). Ideally, super-resolution is intended to operate at very high frame rates which greatly restrict the amount of movement that can occur between frames. However, in the proposed system video captured at 25 frames per second is used, and at such a frame rate it is possible to observe out of plane deformations. The tracking system (see Section 3) assumes responsibility for ensuring that only suitable sequences of images are selected for super-resolution. This is achieved by monitoring the following:

1. The size of the detected faces.
2. The overlap between subsequent detected faces.
3. The speed at which the target object is moving.

Only if all detected faces are of similar size, have a sufficiently high overlap in image coordinates, and the target object is moving at a speed below a set threshold are the images accepted for super-resolution.

PERSON TRACKING

Subject identification from surveillance video requires the detection and analysis of facial images, or images showing other identifying features such as tattoos, scars or clothing. In a surveillance environment (where video quality is poor), it is

Figure 6. Fitting a straight line to the data. (a) The least-squares fit is heavily influenced by outliers (gray). (b) The robust fit using the Lorentzian estimator correctly fits to the bulk of the data (black).

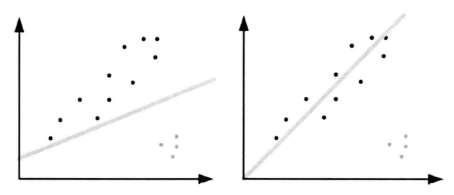

often beneficial to extract multiple images of these features; to locate an image of sufficient quality, or to obtain an enhanced image using super-resolution. It may also be beneficial to extract the path taken by an individual when moving through an area. Person tracking techniques can be used to update a person position from frame to frame accurately, as they move about an environment. By applying these techniques to surveillance video, it is possible to determine a person's trajectory, and extract a sequence of images that can be used to identify the person.

Tracking systems must cope with challenges such as changes in the background, caused by illumination changes or weather changes in outdoor scenes; and be able to effectively handle occlusions (the tracked target being temporarily obscured). It is also desirable for the tracking system to be able to operate in real-time. Tracking systems have a common structure consisting of a foreground segmentation step, a detection step and a tracking step. Foreground segmentation and object detection is commonly achieved by applying motion detection followed by object detection using the resultant motion image. Using model-based object detection techniques can allow these steps to be merged. In this section, we will address the three main processes involved with person tracking; motion detection techniques (see

Section 3.1); person detection and face detection techniques (see Section 3.2); and feature matching and tracking (see Section 3.3).

Motion Detection

Background Modeling

To track people, we need to be able to separate them from the background. Motion detection techniques compare incoming images to a learned

Figure 7. Flow vectors at a motion boundary. Two distinct types of motion are observed in the region, it is important that these regions of motion are recognized as distinct, and that the regions are not averaged.

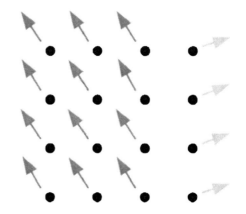

Figure 8. Optical flow results on 2 sample images: (a,d) face image pair; (b,e) horizontal and vertical flow fields scaled to the gray scale range; (c,f) data and spatial discontinuities represented as binary images where the detected points are black. From the flow fields, it can be seen that the subject is predominately moving horizontally (see b). Spatial discontinuities are predominately detected around the edge of the moving subject, while other discontinuities caused by factors such as lighting variations are scattered about the image.

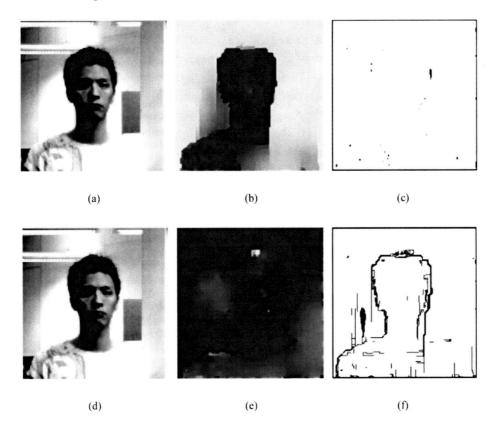

$\quad$(a)$\qquad\qquad\qquad\qquad$(b)$\qquad\qquad\qquad\qquad$(c)

$\quad$(d)$\qquad\qquad\qquad\qquad$(e)$\qquad\qquad\qquad\qquad$(f)

background and locate the moving objects in a scene (see Figure 10).

There are two main approaches: background subtraction and background modeling. In the case of background subtraction, single mode models of the background are used. An image subtraction followed by application of a threshold is used to determine foreground pixels,

$$I_{motion} = | I_{input} - I_{background} | > T \qquad (5)$$

where I_{motion} is the output motion image, I_{input} is the input image, $I_{background}$ is the background image

and T is the motion threshold. Depending on the implementation, $I_{background}$ may be a fixed image initialized at start up, or may adapt to changes in the scene (i.e. lighting fluctuations) using a moving average. The images (I_{input} and $I_{background}$) may contain multiple channels (i.e. red, green and blue).

Background modeling techniques use a multimodal approach. Each mode represents a specific colour and likelihood of occurrence, and multiple modes can be stored for each pixel to describe all the possible background modes and recently observed foreground modes. The background pixels do not undergo motion but do change with changed illumination. Background pixels may tend to take on one of a small number of colour values or regions in colour space. For example a wall might be blue and take on different shades depending on the illumination; a cabinet might be brown. If these colour regions are represented by their centroid and variance (as in a Gaussian), we can represent a background pixel as taking on a colour value with a probability given by a Gaussian mixture model. A pixel in a given frame can then be compared to such a multi-modal background model to decide whether it belongs to the background or not. In this manner, objects or groups of pixels that are undergoing motion (or are in the foreground) can be identified. The background model itself can be adapted in time to keep up with changes such as varying illumination, or new objects being added to the scene. The background model

$$I(x, y)_{background} = \{c, w, n\}; n = [1..N] \qquad (6)$$

where (x, y) is a pixel in the background model; $\{c, w, n\}$ is a single mode of background with c equal to the colour (this may be multiple values, such as red, green and blue), w is the weight and n is the index of the mode. N is the number of modes in the background model.

When using background modeling, incoming images must be compared to all possible background modes until a match is found, to determine if the pixel is foreground or not. An image is compared to each mode in descending order of the mode weight. This helps improve system efficiency as the highest weighted mode is the most likely match,

$$| I(x, y, n)_{background} - I(x, y)_{input} |$$
$$< T; where \; n = [1..N] \qquad (7)$$

where (x, y) is the coordinate of the pixel being tested, n is the background mode being compared

to. Once a match is found, the weight of the match is used in determining if the pixel is foreground. If there is no match, then the pixel must be foreground. Background segmentation routines update themselves over time, replacing modes that have low probabilities with new modes that appear, and gradually adjusting other modes as the scene gradually changes (i.e. lighting changes due to the time of day).

Background subtraction, being a simpler approach results in faster execution times, but it is less robust when applied to complex scenes containing environmental effects such as lighting fluctuations, or trees moving in the wind.

Stauffer and Grimson (Stauffer, 1999) proposed a multi-modal background model using a GMM to model each pixel. This allowed multimodal backgrounds to be effectively modeled, and for the model to learn and adapt to changes in the background. This mixture of Gaussians (MOGs) approach has become popular and several improvements and variations have been proposed since (see Harville, 2001; Bowden, 2001; Harville, 2002; Wang, 2005; Hayman, 2003; Javed, 2002; Zang, 2004).

Modeling each pixel with a set of GMMs is very processor intensive however, and not ideal when foreground segmentation is only the first step in a multi-step process (i.e. surveillance). A more computationally efficient multi-modal background segmentation technique has been proposed in (Butler, 2003), which uses an approximation to a MOGs approach. Butler et al. (Butler, 2003) proposed an adaptive background segmentation algorithm where the set of pixels in an image is modeled as a group of clusters. A cluster consists of a centroid, describing the pixel colour; and a weight, denoting the frequency of occurrence. Pixels are grouped into foreground and background based on cluster distance and weight. Higher weights indicate a greater likelihood of belonging to a background cluster. The cluster based approach has a computational advantage in updating over the MOGs approach arising from the elimination of the need to keep track of covariance. It also lends itself to some fast implementation techniques. The method described here is similar to the approach by Bulter and uses pairs of pixels instead of individual pixels.

The motion detection system described here uses colour images in Y'CbCr 4:2:2 format as input. Adjacent horizontal pixels are paired to create a cluster which consists of two luminance values (Y_1 and Y_2), a blue chrominance value (Cb), and red chrominance value (Cr) to describe the colour; and a weight, w. Each pixel is only paired once (which has the effect of halving the width of the image, increasing the speed of the algorithm at the cost of being unable to detect fine details). For each pixel pair, a set of K clus-

ters, $C(x, y, t, 1..K) = (Y_1, Y_2, Cb, Cr, w)$ is stored, which represents the multi-modal PDF.

Clusters are ordered from highest to lowest weight; and the current matching cluster, $C(x, y, t, m)$ (where m is the index of the matching cluster in the range $1..K$), can be used to provide an approximation of the image. This ordering allows speed improvements when searching for the matching cluster (the higher weighted clusters are more likely to match, so they should be compared first); and determining the likelihood of a pixel being foreground (by computing a summation of the cluster weights of all clusters with a higher weight than the matching cluster).

For each (x, y, t) the algorithm makes a decision assigning it to either foreground or back-

Figure 9. Super-resolution system flow diagram. Low resolution input images are interpolated to the desired resolution and the optical flow is calculated between pairs of consecutive images. The optical flow is used to warp and register the images, at which point they are fused and de-blurred to obtain a super-resolved image.

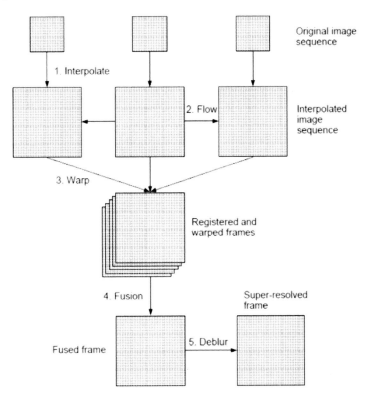

Figure 10. Example of motion detection: (a) shows the input image, (b) shows the resultant motion mask, with areas of motion shown as white. Note that the person is clearly separated from the background, however small regions of noise are also detected.

(a) Input Image   (b) Motion Mask

ground by matching $P(x,y,t)$ to $C(x,y,t,k)$, where k is an index in the range $1..K$. Clusters are compared to incoming pixels by computing the Manhattan distance, and are matched by finding the highest weighted cluster which satisfies,

$$|Y_1 - C(k)_{Y_1}| + |Y_2 - C(k)_{Y_2}| < T_{Lum} \qquad (8)$$

$$|Cb - C(k)_{Cb}| + |Cr - C(k)_{Cr}| < T_{Chr} \qquad (9)$$

where Y_1 and Cb are the luminance and chrominance values for the image pixel $p(x \times 2, y)$, Y_2 and Cr are the luminance and chrominance values for the image pixel $p(x \times 2 + 1, y)$, $C(k) = C(x, y, t, k)$; and T_{Lum} and T_{Chr} are fixed thresholds for evaluating matches. If both thresholds (T_{Lum} and T_{Chr}) are satisfied, then the pixel is suitably close to the cluster to be a match (see Figure 11). By separating luminance and chrominance a certain amount of tolerance to shadows is inbuilt. Thresholds are fixed, and should be set according to the expected noise in the scene. Values of $T_{Lum} = 80$ and $T_{Chr} = 50$ are generally good starting points. Scenes with more noise should use higher thresholds and those with less

should use lower thresholds. For a live system, thresholds should be adapted and tuned on sample data that has been captured. Given a segment or tape of such video and after preliminary manual screening segments that contain subjects of interest are identified. We can use a portion (or portions) of such video that show the different backgrounds possible to train the parameters of the background adaptation system. The entire video is then processed with these parameters to eliminate the background and track persons of interest.

The centroid of the matching cluster is adapted to reflect the current pixel colour,

$$C'(x, y, t, m) = C(x, y, t, m) + \frac{1}{L}|C(x, y, t, m) - P(x, y, t)| \qquad (10)$$

where $C(x, y, t, m)$ is the matching cluster, L is the inverse of the traditional learning rate and $P(x, y, t)$ is the input pixel. The weights of all clusters in the pixels group are adapted to reflect the new state,

$$w'_k = w_k + \frac{1}{L}|M_K - w_k| \qquad (11)$$

where w_k is the weight of the cluster being adapted; and M_k is 1 for the matching cluster and 0 for all others. If there is no match, then the lowest weighted cluster is replaced with a new cluster representing the incoming pixels.

The weights of all clusters with a higher weight than the matching cluster are summed to give the probability of the pixel being foreground,

$$p(x,y,t)_{fgnd} = \sum_{i=1}^{m-1} C(x,y,t,i)_w \qquad (12)$$

Based on the accumulated pixel information, the frame can be segmented into foreground,

$$\begin{aligned} fgnd &= \forall (x,y,t) \\ where\ &p(x,y,t)_{fgnd} > T(x,y,t) \end{aligned} \qquad (13)$$

where $T(x,y,t)$ is the foreground/background threshold, and background. $T(x,y,t)$ is fixed in the range $[0...1]$. Selecting higher values of $T(x,y,t)$ will result in less motion being detected, as objects that have been present for some time will not be detected as their weight will have increased to the point where they are outside the threshold. Lower values may result in some additional (non-primary) background modes being detected as foreground. Like the thresholds for cluster matching, the threshold should be tuned on sample data.

The clusters and weights are gradually adapted over time as more frames are processed, allowing the system to adapt to changes in the background model. New objects can thus be added to the scene (i.e. a box may be placed on the floor), and over time these objects will be incorporated into the background model. This approach can also be extended to include variable thresholds for the cluster matching (Denman et al, 2007b), to calculate optical flow simultaneously (Denman et al, 2007a) and to differentiate between temporarily stopped and moving objects (Denman et al, 2007b).

Shadow Detection and Lighting Changes

In scenes where there is strong or variable lighting (such as sunlight), additional routines to detect shadows and adjust to changing light conditions are required. The simplest approach to dealing with shadows and lighting changes is to use thresholds that are relaxed enough to accommodate changes caused by shadows. However, this approach is also likely to result in a large increase in the rate of false negatives (pixels that are incorrectly detected as background) from the motion detection, unless the shadows are very faint. Shadow regions appear as scaled down (darker) versions of the same region that is in the background model (Grest, 2003). When using a colour space that separates intensity and colour components (HSV or Y'CbCr), shadows across a region have the following properties when compared to the background model:

1. The luminance of a cast shadow is lower than that of the background,
2. The chrominance of the cast shadow is approximately equal to that of the background.

From Figure 12, it can be seen the chrominance of a region in shadow is approximately unchanged, while a significant drop in the luminance is observed. Provided the light source within a scene is emitting white light, these shadow conditions will hold, regardless of the environment (i.e. indoor, outdoor).

Using these properties, the following additional constraints can be added to the matching process in the motion detection algorithm described,

$$0 < (C(k)_{Y_1} - Y_1) + (C(k)_{Y_2} - Y_2) < T_{shadow} \qquad (14)$$

$$| Cb - C(k)_{Cb} | + | Cr - C(k)_{Cb} | < \frac{T_{Chr}}{S} \qquad (15)$$

If there is a positive difference in the luminance, less than the prescribed shadow threshold, T_{shadow}, and only a small difference in the chrominance (determined by dividing the chrominance threshold, T_{chr}, by an integer S) we have a shadow and motion is not detected at P.

Other approaches to shadows detection include using normalized cross correlation (Grest, 2003; Jacques, 2005), edge detection (Xu, 2004), edge analysis (Zhang, 2006) as well as adaptations to the mixture of Gaussiians (MOGs) foreground segmentation process (Martel-Brisson, 2005). Shadow detection is of most use in outdoor application, or indoor environments where there is strong lighting.

Fluctuations in the level of light in a scene can pose further challenges in a surveillance application as changing lighting can result in large amounts of erroneous motion. A simple adjustment can be added to the luminance threshold, T_{Lum}, to compensate for lighting changes. Lighting changes, such as those caused by the sun moving behind clouds, can be expected to cause uniform changes across all (or at least large parts of) a scene. For each frame, we calculate the weighted average of luminance changes,

$$Lum_{offset}(t) = \frac{\sum Lum_{Diff}(x,y,t) \times C(x,y,t,m)(w)}{\Sigma C(x,y,t,m)(w)} \qquad (16)$$

The use of weighted sum allows pixels that are only recently created, and so potentially created partially under the present lighting conditions to be weighted less highly. Provided this value is within a percentage threshold of the previous luminance offset, it is accepted and used for the next frame,

$$\alpha \leq \frac{Lum_{offset}(t)}{Lum_{offset}(t-1)} \leq \frac{1}{\alpha} \qquad (17)$$

where α is the change threshold for the luminance offset and is in the range $[0..1]$. α is used to try and detect rapid changes that have occurred (due to large objects moving through the scene, or dropped frames) which can result in large threshold changes that corrupt the motion detection results. Typically, a value of 0.2 is suitable. Setting

Figure 11. Incoming pixels are compared to each cluster in the background model, and the first cluster (searching from highest weight) to satisfy the constraints is accepted as a match

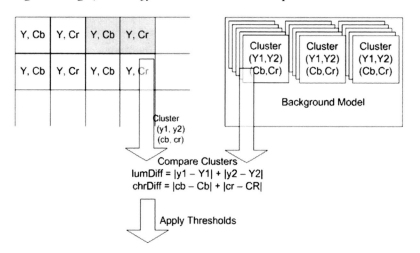

the value too high (above 0.5) can result in valid changes (i.e. from 1 to 2) being denied. If the change in the luminance threshold is outside of this limit, it indicates a very rapid lighting change has occurred, or a large object has entered the area. In this situation, the weighted standard deviation of the luminance offset is calculated, and if this is beneath a threshold, the lighting change is accepted. If it is outside the threshold, we do not. The luminance offset is incorporated into the match equation by adding the offset to the existing luminance threshold. The matching equations for incoming luminance pixels to a cluster then become,

$$(-T_{Lum} + Lum_{offset}) < (P(Y_1) - C(k)(Y_1)) + (P(Y_2) - C(k)(Y_2) < (T_{Lum} + Lum_{offset})$$

$$(18)$$

where P is the pixel and $C(k)$ is the cluster that is being matched.

To improve performance, this process can be applied on a region level. The image can be broken into a grid and the lighting variation at each grid square is considered separately. This allows different materials and their reflective properties, or regions that cast self shadows to be taken into consideration separately. In situations where colour lighting is present, the same approach could be applied to the chrominance threshold to compensate.

Person and Face Detection

Person Detection

Once a motion image has been obtained, it must be analyzed to determine the locations of people present. Motion images can contain significant errors, either as motion being detected where there is none, or motion not being detected where it should be. Any detection techniques should be robust to these false positive and false negative

errors. As we are using motion to detect, we do not have any texture information, only information relating to size and silhouette. To extract people from a motion image, the following process is used (Haritaoglu, 2000; Zhao, 2004),

1. Locate areas of the image which contain significant motion and are likely to contain people,
2. Locate the heads of people within those regions using vertical histograms and the top contour of the motion region,
3. Fit ellipses at the head locations to determine if there is sufficient motion to constitute a person.

This process requires that people appear vertical in the image (i.e. parallel to the left and right image bounds). It is still able to detect people that are stationary, as long as they have not become incorporated into the background.

Motion images are analyzed and broken into smaller segments containing patches of motion to correctly detect people who are vertically aligned. They occupy a similar set of columns at different heights in the image. The use of vertical histograms and the top contour means that only one head can exist in any given column. These regions are processed separately, so if there is spatial separation between two vertically aligned people, their motion regions will be analyzed separately and each person can be detected. During this same process, we can remove small, unconnected regions of motion which may lead to other inaccuracies. These are likely to be errors, or motion caused by objects too small to track (i.e. a piece of rubbish being blown across the floor by the wind). The remaining regions can be grouped into spatial groups, and analyzed individually.

A person's head in a silhouette image typically has the following properties:

1. It is the highest point on the person's silhouette,

Figure 12. Luminance and chrominance change under shadow. Without shadow, the mean luminance, blue chrominance and red chrominance of the area is 203, 125 and 128 respectively. Under shadow, the same region has the mean values of 88, 129 and 125. The luminance has dropped dramatically while the other values record little change, illustrating that shadows can be identified by locating regions recording a drop in luminance with relatively unchanged chrominance.

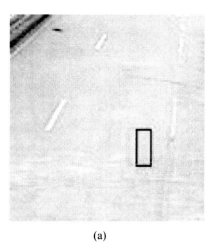 

(a)　　　　　　　　　　　　　　　　　　　(b)

2. The surrounding area is roughly curved and symmetrical.

The second condition may not hold if the person is wearing a hat, or an unusual hairstyle. As such, we will use the first property as the basis for detection.

To determine the height of a pixel in an image, two approaches can be used:

1. **Vertical Projection:** $v_{proj}(i) = \sum_{j=0}^{j=N-1} M(i,j)$,

   where $v_{proj}(i)$ is the vertical projection at column i, j is the row index and N is the number of rows (height) of the mask image, M.

2. **Top Contour:**

   $v_{contour}(i) = N -$
   $(\min j\ for\ which\ M(i,j) > 0)$,

   where $v_{contour}$ is the top contour. It is assumed that for the mask image (M) it is zero indexed and the top left corner is at the coordinate $(0,0)$.

The vertical projection counts the number of motion pixels in each column, so a region such as the head, which should have motion all the way below to the feet, should lie at a global maximum. However, if the motion image contains errors such as missing regions (i.e. a large portion of the person's shirt is not detected as motion), the vertical projection may not contain the head at a maxima. The top contour is simply the set of top most pixels from each column that is in motion; this accuracy of this, however, depends on the accuracy of the motion detection around the edge of the person. Either one of these, or a combination of both, can be used to detect the head of a person. Using both in combination can help overcome the individual weaknesses of each modality and improve detection results,

$$v_{HeightMap} = \alpha v_{proj} = \beta v_{contour} \qquad (19)$$

where $v_{HeightMap}$ is the combined height map, α is the weight of the vertical projection, and β is the weight of the top contour. An average filter can be applied to the height map to reduce noise and remove small local maxima. This height map can then be searched for maxima, which are the likely location of heads. The global maxima will provide a good estimate of the head of one person. If multiple people are present in the area being analyzed, then some local maxima will represent their heads. Analysis of the maxima (looking at their prominence and proximity to other maxima) can be used to determine which of these are likely to represent the heads of other people.

Once the heads have been located, ellipses are fitted at the heads. We orient the ellipse such that the major axis is vertical, and the length of the major axis of the ellipse is set to the height of the head as detected by the head detector. The dimensions of the ellipse are chosen by performing further analysis of the height map. The area surrounding the height map is searched to find the position either side where the height drops to below a predefined ratio of the total height (50%), or the minima in between two maxima. The maximum of the left and right distance is used as the width of the minor axis. The length of the major axis is determined using the height of the object.

After the ellipse dimensions are determined, a filled ellipse can be drawn overlaying the detected person, and the amount of motion within can be calculated such that,

$$O_{person} = \frac{\sum M(i,j) \,\&\, E(i,j)}{\sum E(i,j)} \qquad (20)$$

where O_{person} is the percentage of the ellipse that contains motion, i and j are the image coordinates, M is the motion image and E is the ellipse mask (M and E are binary images). If O_{person} is above a threshold, then the person is accepted as a valid detection. The motion for that person can now be removed from the motion image, to ensure that it is not used to detect a second person later.

This approach is invariant to small errors in the motion segmentation, such as holes appearing in people's torsos, or small segmentation errors around the silhouette. However, severe failure of the motion segmentation will result in the system either failing to detect people, or the detection of people who are not actually present.

Using Optical Flow and Colour

Optical flow allows us to detect a target person using their expected velocity. If we have a reasonable estimate of the velocity of the tracked object, we can use this and the optical flow for the present frame to extract the possible region for that object by finding all pixels that are within an acceptable distance of the expected velocity,

$$\begin{aligned} |\,h(x,y) - vx_n\,| &< T_{x-vel} \\ |\,v(x,y) - vy_n\,| &< T_{y-vel} \end{aligned} \qquad (21)$$

where h and v are the horizontal and vertical flow images, vx_n and vy_n are the x and y velocities of the target track, n; and T_{x-vel} and T_{y-vel} are the thresholds for matching velocities. Figure 13 illustrates an object being extracted from video using optical flow. If a colour histogram (see Section 3.2) has been created for the target object, then an additional constraint that the colour at a pixel must be present in the histogram can be added to further improve the detection results.

Any resulting mask image obtained by applying optical flow and/or colour constraints may be used for person detection, either by

1. Applying the previously described person detection technique to the mask,
2. Accepting any resulting regions as being the person and using these.

The second approach should be avoided in situations where ambiguities may arise (i.e. in the presence of occlusions).

Skin has a distinctive colour that can be modeled, and this model may be used to find all pixels that are skin colour. Skin colour may be modeled using mean and variance measures, or more complex models such as histograms or GMMs. A survey of techniques can be found in (Zhanwu, 2006). A wide variety of colour spaces are able to be used and ideally, the colour space chosen should be the same as that used elsewhere in a given system, or one that is quickly and easily converted to. Typically, more complex colour models require more training data (and thus more time to train).

A simple skin colour detection routine based on the mean and variance of skin colour values can be developed using normalised RG colour space. Normalized RG colour space is computed from RGB colour space using the following equations,

$$R(i, j)_{norm} = \frac{R(i, j)}{R(i, j) + G(i, j) + B(i, j)}$$
$$G(i, j)_{norm} = \frac{G(i, j)}{R(i, j) + G(i, j) + B(i, j)} \quad (22)$$

where i and j are the image coordinates.

To build the model, several skin points known to contain skin colour are selected, and the mean and standard deviation are calculated using,

$$\mu_R = \frac{1}{S} \sum R(i, j)_{norm}$$
$$\mu_G = \frac{1}{S} \sum G(i, j)_{norm}$$
$$\sigma_R = \sqrt{\frac{1}{S} \sum (\mu_R - R(i, j)_{norm})^2} \quad (23)$$
$$\sigma_G = \sqrt{\frac{1}{S} \sum (\mu_G - G(i, j)_{norm})^2}$$

where S is the total number of pixels in the image. These statistics are then used to determine if a pixel is skin colour by testing if the following two conditions are satisfied,

$$| R(i, j)_{norm} - \mu_R | < n\sigma_R$$
$$| G(i, j)_{norm} - \mu_G | < n\sigma_G \quad (24)$$

where n is the number of standard deviations tolerance when testing colours (assuming a Gaussian distribution, 2 standard deviations will result in detecting approximately 95% of skin colour).

After applying skin detection, morphological operations can be used to clean the image and large connected components can be located, and optionally filtered to find those that have a circular (or elliptical) shape. These are likely to represent regions of exposed skin such as arms or the face. By using the information provided by a person detection routine, the skin regions that lie closest to the heads, and thus are likely to represent the face, can be obtained.

Model Based Detection Processes

Other detection processes that use learned models can be used to detect people, faces, or other areas of interest. These approaches require models to be trained using a database of positive and negative examples of the desired object. The Viola-Jones object detection technique (Viola, 2001) has proved popular in tracking systems (Okuma, 2004; Seitner, 2005) and other areas where object detection is required (i.e. face recognition systems), however it is less suited when detecting small objects in a scene (i.e. less than 30 pixels square).

This approach works by using a cascade of simple classifiers to iteratively classify a scene (boosting). The classifiers are selected using a weighted error criterion where weights are assigned to images in the training set and adapted with each training iteration. Inputs that are correctly classified get lower weights for the next iteration and those that are misclassified are higher weighted. A simple classifier is added to the cascade at each iteration. This results in a very fast detection system, which can be used in conjunction with motion detection techniques to restrict the search area (to regions which only contain some motion) and to remove some false positives (due to a lack of motion at the detected area). An implementation of the Viola-Jones object detection routine (as well as code to train models) can be found in the OpenCV image processing libraries.

Detection approaches using models are very accurate when the training data used to build the models matches well to the target data (see Figure 14). To achieve this however, it is likely that a model will need to be built for each scenario, and for each different view of a person (i.e. front, back, side). As such, for situations where one-off analysis of a unique scene is required (rather than a permanent surveillance system), a model based approach may require too much effort to set up, as opposed to motion based approaches (see Section 3.2) which can be reconfigured for a new environment by changing a small number of parameters.

Other modeling techniques, such as those based on a histogram of orientated Gaussians (Dalal, 2005; Zhu, 2006), as well as those derived from the Hough transform (Liebe, 2008) have also been proposed and been shown to be suitable for detecting both people and faces in video footage.

Feature Matching and Tracking

Tracking Features

To track an object, features must be extracted to allow for comparison and matching in future frames. There are a wide variety of features that can be used:

1. **Position and Velocity:** A simple and easily extracted feature, which can use either the centroid or median pixel of the targets silhouette. Velocity can be determined either as a derivative of the position, or by using optical flow.

2. **Shape and/or Size:** The targets aspect ratio, or bounding box dimensions offer a simple method to compare the shape/size of an object. More complex approaches can compare silhouettes to determine the likelihood of a match.

3. **Colour:** In many situations colour can provide a reasonably unique feature for the tracked objects in a scene. This can be used as a feature either through a histogram, or simply by extracting the most common n colours.

4. **Appearance:** Takes into account the colours present in the object and their geographical distribution. As such, appearance models are much more discriminative, but also more computationally demanding (Haritaoglu, 2000).

The colour histogram is unaffected by pose change or motion, and so is a reliable metric for matching after occlusion. It is computed by quantizing the image into N bins, and maintaining a count indicating the number of pixels that belong in each bin. Histograms are matched by calculating the histogram intersection. The Bhattacharya coefficient,

$$B = \sum_{i=1}^{N} \sqrt{h_{source}(i) h_{target}(i)} \qquad (25)$$

compares corresponding bins in the source and target histograms (h_{source} and h_{target}), and is an effective measure for calculating the overlap between two statistical distributions. When calculating the histogram for use as a tracking feature, it is advisable to use the motion detection image to ensure that only pixels belonging to the object in motion are used to construct the histogram. This ensures that the histogram does not also

Figure 13. Extracting an object using optical flow. Images from left to right are the input image, motion detection image, vertical flow, horizontal flow, and the extracted object using $vx_n = 2$, and $vy_n = 1.5$ where vx_n and vy_n are determined from the object's movements in the previous 5 frames.

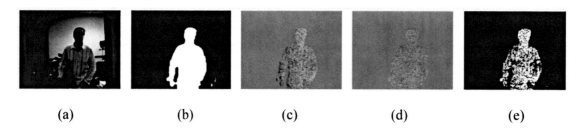

(a)   (b)   (c)   (d)   (e)

model the background. A similar approach is to use the histogram intersection,

$$I = \sum_{i=1}^{N} \min(h_{source}(i)h_{t\,\arg et}(i)) \qquad (26)$$

where the similarity, I, is determined by measuring the overlap between the two histograms.

Histograms can also be susceptible to problems caused by variable lighting, such as the sun moving behind clouds, or shadows as a person moves through the scene. To overcome this, histograms can be constructed to separate the colour and intensity components when constructing the colour model. Separate models can be built for the chrominance component (Cb and Cr components in the case of YCbCr) and for the luminance component (Y for YCbCr), so that the colour model is not invalidated by the tracked person moving into a shadowed region. To overcome the lack of position information in the histogram, multiple histograms can be extracted for a tracked object to represent different areas of the tracked object (Hu, 2004), or a colour correlogram (Rao, 2000; Zhao, 2005) - a variant of the histogram which encodes geometric information within the model which can be used.

A large number of additional techniques have been proposed to describe a person, such as the use of features derived from symmetry, the spatial arrangement of colour regions as well as recurrent textures (Farenzena, 2010); extracting individual features from each body part (i.e. arms, legs, torso, etc) (Bak, 2010); and a combination of colour and edge information extracted over person regions (Gheissari, 2006). For techniques such as these that generate complex feature vectors, matching techniques such as the Bhattacharya coefficient or the histogram intersection are not appropriate, and alternate matching schemes specific to the extracted features are required.

Predictors

Motion models are a simple type of predictor and are quite common among simple systems. Motion models aim to predict the next position based off a number of past observations. They may or may not make use of acceleration,

$$p(t+1) = p(t) + v(t) \qquad (27)$$

where $p(t+1)$ is the expected position at the next time step, $p(t)$ is the position at the current time step, and $v(t)$ is the velocity at the current time step.

For the simplest implementation,

$$v(t) = p(t) - p(t-1). \qquad (28)$$

Other implementations use the history of the object to determine its velocity, such that,

$$v(t) = \frac{p(t) - p(t-N)}{N} \qquad (29)$$

where N is the size of the history being used. Using a smaller history (or none) means that the model can react faster to changes in direction by the tracked object. However, it also makes the model more sensitive to errors in the object's position (caused by segmentation or detection faults) which can result in the poor prediction of future positions.

Kalman filters (Welch, 1995) are a linear predictive filter, and can be used to predict the state of a system in the presence of noise and track the state in a non-stationary environment. The filter estimates the process state at the next time step, and uses the measurement at that time step as feedback. A detailed explanation of the equations and the tuning of parameters is provided in (Welch, 1995). Extensions have been proposed such as the Extended Kalman Filter (EKF) (see (Welch, 1995)) and the Unscented Kalman Filter (UKF) (Julier, 1997) to try and overcome the limitations of the Kalman filter, such as the assumption of a Guassian distribution and linear relationships between the estimated process and the measurements.

Particle filters (Maskell, 2001) are a sequential, Monte Carlo method based on particle representation of probability densities. Particle filters have an advantage over Kalman filters in that they can model any multi-modal distribution, where as Kalman filters are constrained by the assumptions that state and sensory models are linear, and that noise and posterior distributions are Gaussian. Particle filters use a set of samples (particles) to approximate the posterior probability density function (PDF). Like a Kalman filter, the process contains two major steps each time step: prediction and update.

The state of the filter at time t, is represented by x_t, and its history is $X_t = (x_1, x_2, ..., x_t)$. The observation at time t is z_t, and its history is

$Z_t = (z_1, z_2, ..., z_t)$. It is assumed that the object dynamics form a temporal Markov chain so that the probability of a state depends only on the previous state (as opposed to more history),

$$p(x_t \mid X_{t-1}) = p(x_t \mid x_{t-1}) \qquad (30)$$

In the context of a person tracking system, the state is the position of the tracked object (represented by the centre, x and y, and the width and height, w and h, of its bounding box). The observation is determined by the result of the feature matching across the particle set, although the results from object detection can be incorporated into the distribution as in approaches such as (Okuma, 2004).

Observations are considered to be statistically independent (mutually and with respect to the process). The observation process is defined by specifying the conditional density, $p(z_t \mid x_t)$ at each time, t,

$$p(Z_t \mid \chi_t) = \prod_{t=1}^{t} p(x_i \mid t_i) \qquad (31)$$

The conditional state density at time t is defined as,

$$p_t(x_t) = p(x_t \mid Z_t) \qquad (32)$$

State density is propagated over time according to the rule,

$$p(x_t \mid Z_t) = k_t p(z_t \mid x_t) p(x_t \mid Z_{t-1}) \qquad (33)$$

where

$$p(x_t \mid Z_{t-1}) = \int_{x_{t-1}} p(x \mid x_{t-1})(x_{t-1} \mid z_{t-1}) \qquad (34)$$

Figure 14. Example of tracking system output with face detection. The red box indicates the location of the tracked person and the green box indicates the location of the detected face. In this example, the person is detected using motion information, and the face is detected using a trained model.

and k_t is a normalisation constant that does not depend on x_t.

In a computational environment, we approximate the posterior, $p(x_t \mid Z_t)$, as a set of N samples, $\{x_t^i\}_{i=1..N}$, where each sample has an importance weight, w_t^i. When the filter is initialized, this distribution is drawn from the prior density, $p(x)$. At each time step, the distribution is re-sampled to generate a uniformly weighted particle set. Re-sampling is done according to the importance weights. The generic particle filter algorithm is outlined below, and illustrated in Figure 15:

Initialization: At $t = 0$

1. For $i = 1..N$, select samples s_0^i from the prior distribution $p(x_0)$

Iterate: For $t = 1, 2...$

1. Importance Sampling
    a. Predict the samples next position,
    $$s_t^n = p(x_t \mid x_{t-1} = s_{t-1}^n).$$

    This prediction process is governed by the needs of the individual system, but typically involves adjusting the position according to predefined system dynamics and adding noise.

    b. Evaluate the importance weights based on the measured features, z_t,
    $$w_t^i = p(z_t \mid x_t = s_t^n).$$

    c. Normalize the importance weights,
    $$w_\times^i = \frac{w_t^i}{\sum_j^N w_t^j}.$$

2. Re-sampling
    a. Resample from x_t^i so that samples with a high weight, w_t^i are emphasized (sampled multiple times) and samples with a low weight are suppressed (re-sampled few times, if at all).

    b. Set w_t^i to $\frac{1}{N}$ for $i = 1..N$.

    c. The resultant sample set can be used to approximate the posterior distribution.

The re-sampling step (2(a)) is required to avoid degeneracy in the algorithm (see Kong et al (1994) for more details), by ensuring that one particle does not come to dominate the distribution. Sequential Importance Re-sampling (SIR) is a commonly used re-sampling scheme that uses the following process to select a new sample. The process is applied for $n = 1..N$:

1. Generate a random number, $r \in [0..1]$,
2. Find the smallest j which satisfies
    $$\sum_j^I w_t^j \geq r; j \in [1..N],$$

3. Set $x_t^n = x_{t-1}^j$.

The sequential importance re-sampling process is illustrated in Figure 16. Note that SIR uses the cumulative probability to select particles to resample. This means particles with a higher weight are more likely to be sampled, resulting in higher weighted samples being given greater emphasis in the next time step. Various implementations (Doucet, 1998; Pitt, 1999) have shown that this algorithm can be implemented with $O(N)$ complexity. Other re-sampling schemes, such as residual re-sampling and minimum variance sampling, have been proposed in (Liu, 1998; Higuchi, 1997) and (Kitagawa, 1996) respectively.

The condensation algorithm proposed by Isard (1998), is a specific implementation of particle filtering proposed to track curves in images. Like particle filtering, it is an iterative process where the sample set for time t is generated by re-sampling from the sample set for time $t-1$. It differs from the particle filter described above in

that the re-sampling step is done first. Thus the output at the end of the time step, is a weighted particle set rather than a uniformly weighted particle set.

There are two key challenges when using particle filters:

1. Tracking multiple objects within the one filter,
2. Using as few particles as possible to improve computational efficiency.

Tracking multiple objects within a single filter can pose problems because tracked objects that yield particles with higher probabilities than other tracks, can have their particles overwrite those particles belonging to other tracks using the SIR process. This has been addressed by approaches

Figure 15. Condensation filter process: the circles represent the particles, and their size indicates their weight. The weighted particle set from time $t-1$ is resampled, and the new particles are offset according to a motion model and random noise. Weights for the new particle set are calculated based on the frame at time t.

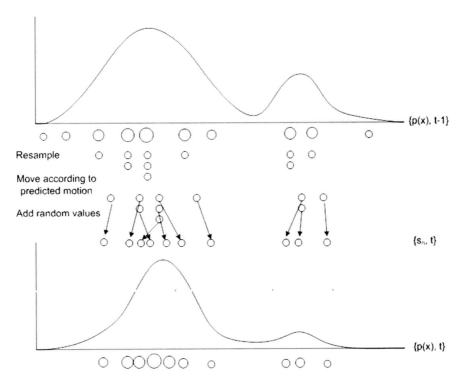

Figure 16. Sequential importance resampling. Random values in the range [0..1] are selected and used to sample particles based on the cumulative probability using the cumulative probability ensures that particles with a higher weight are more likely to be selected.

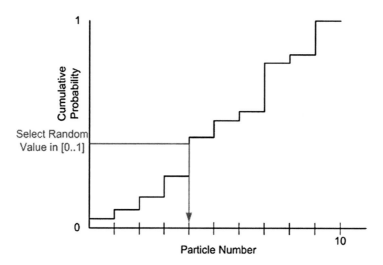

such as (Vermaak, 2003) and (Okuma, 2004). In these systems, each mode (target) is modeled by its own particle filter, which forms part of the overall mixture, and the individual filters only interact through the computation of the weights. This overcomes problems associated with previous multi-target trackers where the samples for a given target could become deleted and the target lost. However, the system still maintains just a single particle filter for the whole system, rather than one for each tracked object.

To use a condensation filter within a tracking system, particles are created that represent the bounding box of an object so that $s_i^n(t) = \{x, y, w, h\}$. When evaluating features for a match, the region within the bounding box described by the particle is analyzed and compared to the feature. In the case of a histogram feature,

Figure 17. Integrated system diagram. People are detected and tracked using object tracking. Faces are for the tracked subjects and sequences of faces are extracted for super-resolution. The resultant super-resolved faces can be then be used for tasks such as person recognition.

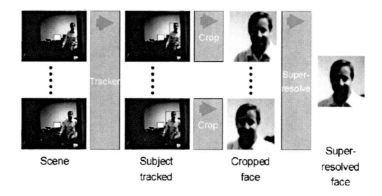

Figure 18. Example images and tracking output from the 'tattoo' sequence: (a) shows a frame from the input sequence with a frontal view of the subject; (b) shows five consecutive frames showing a side view and the tattoos on his left arm. The frames extracted by person tracking can be subject to further segmentation, manual or automated, to extract the tattoo region. The tattoo region segments can then be input to the super-resolution block. The text on the door visible in the frontal view could also be of interest in a forensic investigation.

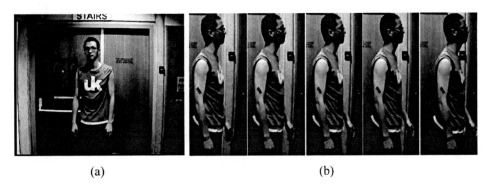

(a)   (b)

the histogram for the region $\{x, y, w, h\}$ is computed, and its intersection with the histogram feature is calculated to determine the match.

INTEGRATED SYSTEMS

The integrated system (Lin, 2007) combines the super-resolution and tracking systems to automatically track and super-resolve a subject's face from surveillance video. The person tracker detailed in Section 3 scans through the videos and identifies frames containing visible faces. The detected faces weren't necessarily full frontal as it is unrealistic to expect to always capture full frontal faces from surveillance footage. The tracker's output was used to crop the frames around the face for super-resolution. The cropped frames were converted to grayscale before super-resolving. The process is shown graphically in Figure 17.

Test Results

Three sets of experiments are conducted to evaluate the proposed system:

1.   Evaluate the proposed combined system for general purpose scene enhancement using surveillance data, and investigate the performance of super-resolution over the entire person region (Section 4.1.1).
2.   Evaluate the proposed system for facial image enhancement from surveillance video, using the Terrascope database to detect and track people, and extract and super-resolve their faces (Section 4.1.2).
3.   Evaluate the performance increase achieved through super-resolution when super-resolving faces, on the XM2VTS database (Section 4.1.3).

For all evaluations, the super-resolution algorithm was applied to a moving group of five frames, with the third frame being the reference. Five frames were chosen because it was a good trade-off between reconstruction quality and computation time (Lin, 2005b).

For evaluations 1 and 3, we compare the performance of the super-resolution algorithm with interpolation methods. Up-sampled images were generated for the reference frame of each 5-frame sequence using bilinear and cubic spline interpolation. In evaluation 2, we compare the performance of the proposed super-resolution system to reconstruction based technique of Schultz and Stevenson (1996), and the learning

Figure 19. Comparison between a sample low-resolution and enhanced images from the tattoo sequence: (a) low-resolution, (b) bilinear interpolation, (c) cubic spline interpolation, (d) super-resolution. The advantage of super-resolution over other enhancement methods is not very clear in these images. Visible differences in detail also depend on the display format.

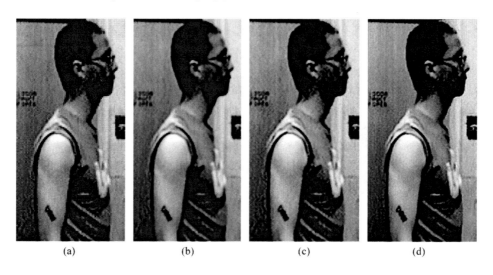

(a)   (b)   (c)   (d)

Figure 20. Close-up of the tattoo (first row) and the text on the door (second row), (a) low-resolution, (b) bilinear interpolation, (c) cubic spline interpolation, (d) super-resolution. The advantage of super-resolution over other enhancement methods can be better appreciated in these images, although the improvement of detail is still marginal. Even marginal improvements can be of use for follow up using human intelligence in interpretation.

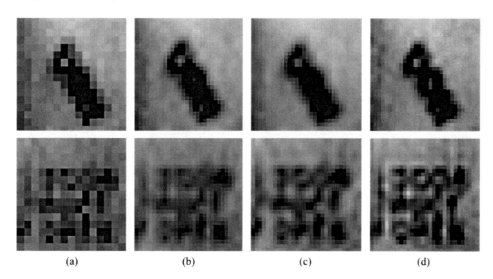

(a)   (b)   (c)   (d)

based technique of Baker and Kanade (2002). In evaluations 1 and 2, the super-resolution is driven by the tracking system.

Tattoo Sequence

The tattoo sequence captured in-house contains a subject wandering in the scene with the letters *DOH* drawn on his arm simulating a tattoo. The video was acquired in colour at 352×288px at 20 frames per second (fps) with a 1/90s exposure. The sequence is quite noisy due to the short exposure and high camera gain necessary due to the low ambient light level. The sequence was converted to grayscale before super-resolving. An example frame from the input video, as well as example output from the object tracker is shown in Figure 18.

Results for the super-resolution on the tattoo sequence are shown in Figures 19 and 20. The letters on the subject's arm in the low-resolution image are completely illegible. Bilinear interpolation improves upon this, separating the letter *D* from the rest. Cubic spline interpolation results in sharper letters again, although at the expense of noise. At this stage the tattoo is probably made up of three letters with the first letter being *D*. Finally the super-resolved image reveals that the second letter is an *O*, followed by either a capital *H* or two lowercase *l*'s. Also, the word *DOOR* from the top row on the door becomes partially legible. The two *O*'s are clear although the letters *D* and *R* are not. Notice how the super-resolved image is only slightly noisier than bilinear interpolation whilst recovering significant high frequency detail. This is due to the super-resolution process which makes use of multiple frames to reduce noise

Figure 21. Example input frames from the Terrascope database. Frames are 640x480 pixels in size, and faces appear at a variety of resolutions within the images. The images serve to illustrate the challenge in face recognition from the database used and the need for the proposed system.

Figure 22. Comparison between difference enhancement techniques on the Terrascope database: (a) bilinear interpolation, (b) Schultz and Stevenson (1996), (c) Baker and Kanade (2002), (d) proposed optical flow super-resolution technique. Enhanced quality obtained using the proposed super-resolution techniques is visible from the frames illustrated in (d) in comparison to others.

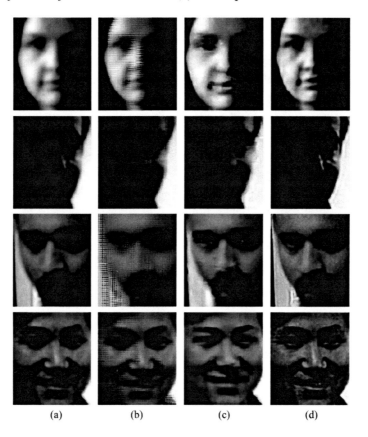

(a)   (b)   (c)   (d)

during frame fusion. Figure 19 shows a close-up of the regions of interest (the tattoo and the text on the door), to better demonstrate the enhanced resolution.

Terrascope Database

Videos from the Terrascope database (Jaynes, 2005) were used to investigate how the proposed super-resolution method performed with surveillance footage for enhancing faces. The database consists of videos captured by surveillance cameras placed in an office environment. The Terrascope video sequences were captured in colour at a resolution of 640×480px at 30fps.

The sequence was also converted to grayscale before super-resolving. Example images from the database are shown in Figure 21.

As well as comparing to bilinear interpolation, we compare to two additional super-resolution techniques: Schultz and Stevenson (1996), and Baker and Kanade (2002). Schultz and Stevenson (1996) proposed a reconstruction-based method that uses Bayesian maximum a posteriori (MAP) estimation for regularisation. Although only translational motions are modelled, independently moving objects are allowed. Baker and Kanade (2002) propose a learning-based technique, and the system was trained using manually aligned frontal faces from the FERET database (Phillips,

2000). As the Terrascope database contains only 12 subjects, we simply perform a visual evaluation of the proposed technique, as there are not enough subjects for a meaningful face verification evaluation.

Figure 22 shows interpolated and super-resolved faces from the Terrascope database. While all super-resolution algorithms produced sharper images than interpolation, we observe that Schultz and Stevenson's assumption of rigid objects has resulted in a grid-like noise pattern. The hallucinated face of (Baker, 2002) appears reasonably sharp and clean but the subjects take on a different appearance, and there are also many artefacts present near facial features such as the eyes and mouth. The robust optical flow-based super-resolution results in a visibly enhanced face, without the artefacts of the other super-resolution techniques.

XM2VTS Database

Because there are only 12 subjects in the Terrascope data base, sequences from the XM2VTS database were used for the face recognition experiments to obtain more statistically significant

Figure 23. Comparison between cropped sample enhanced images from the XM2VTS database. Face widths: first row 14px (ground truth 27px), second row 19px (37px), third row 27px (55px). (a) Bilinear interpolation, (b) cubic spline interpolation, (c) super-resolved, (d) ground truth. Enhanced quality of the proposed super-resolution system is visible in (c) compared to interpolation techniques in (a) and (b). A true resolution image of the same number of pixels shown in (d) serves as the target to check the extent of improvement in quality. In practice, the super-resolved face will be compared to a database of such exemplar faces.

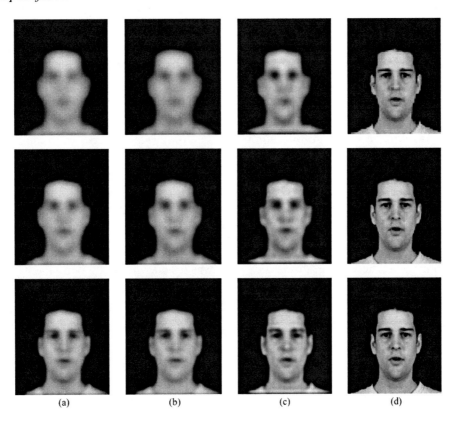

(a)   (b)   (c)   (d)

Figure 24. Face recognition accuracy with 14px face images from the XM2VTS database. The super-resolved images perform consistently better than interpolated images.

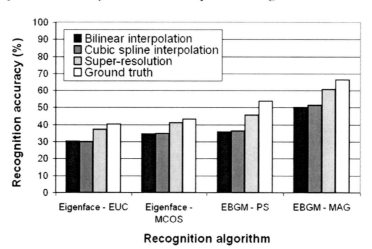

results. The XM2VTS database is a multi-modal (speech and video) database created to facilitate testing of multi-modal speech recognition systems. It contains 295 subjects recorded over four sessions in four months. The speech sequences contain only frontal faces and can represent the situation where a face detector has found a frontal face suitable for recognition whilst scanning through surveillance footage. The speech sequences were used in this evaluation. The original XM2VTS videos were captured in colour at a resolution of 720×576px at 25fps with the subject sitting close to and facing the camera, resulting in very high-resolution faces (approximately 220px wide). Hence these frames needed to be down-sampled first to simulate face sizes encountered under surveillance conditions. The images were downsized by factors of four (55px wide faces), six (37px) and eight (27px) respectively and converted to grayscale as ground truth images. These images were then down-sampled by a factor of two through blurring and decimation to simulate the low-resolution images which were then used as the input for the super-resolution and interpolation stages. The low-resolution faces were 28px, 19px and 14px wide respectively.

For the face recognition experiment, an object detector (Viola, 2001), trained using frontal faces,

and was applied to each of the enhanced images individually. Each image was then segmented and normalized. The CSU Face Identification Evaluation System (Bolme, 2003), specifically designed to compare face recognition algorithms, was then used to evaluate recognition performance of the super-resolved, interpolated and ground truth images. Low-resolution images were not tested since they would be interpolated in the segmentation and normalization stage. One image from each of the four sessions for the 295 subjects was used for testing.

Frontal face images from the Face Recognition Grand Challenge (FRGC) (Phillips, 2005) Fall2003 and Spring2004 datasets were used to train the facespace for the Eigenface system. The FRGC is a competition designed to promote and advance face recognition technology. A range (10-500) of values for the Eigenvectors retained was tested, with 250 giving the best overall performance. Hence the Eigenface system results given will be for 250 retained Eigenvectors. The normalized images from the XM2VTS database were then projected into the facespace and the distance to the enrolment images computed. Both Euclidean (EUC) and Mahalanobis Cosine (MCOS) distance metrics were tested. For the EBGM system, the Gabor jets used to detect the

Figure 25. Face recognition accuracy with 19px face images from the XM2VTS database. The gap between the super-resolved and interpolated images reduces. Super-resolution outperforms ground truth images for the MCOS metric due to eigenface being robust to down- sampling.

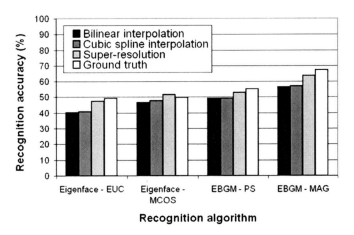

facial features were trained using 70 hand marked images from the FERET database (Phillips, 2000). The predictive step (PS) and magnitude (MAG) distance metrics were tested.

Figure 23 shows cropped sample super-resolved, interpolated and ground truth images from the XM2VTS database at the three resolutions tested. Although visual improvement at the lowest image size is limited, recognition accuracy noticeably improves as illustrated by Figure 24.

The super-resolved images performed consistently better than interpolated images across the face recognition algorithms and distance metrics tested, with the performance gap around 6-9%. For the two higher resolutions (see Figures 25 and 26), the ground truth images actually lose the lead to super-resolved and interpolated ones for the Eigenface method. This can be attributed to Eigenface being quite robust to downsampling and that the downsampling process actually smoothes

Figure 26. Face recognition accuracy with 27px face images from the XM2VTS database. The gap between the super-resolved and interpolated images diminishes further. Ground truth images lose the lead for both eigenface distance metrics due to eigenface being robust to down-sampling.

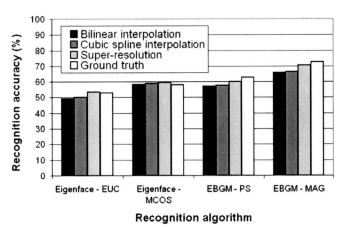

out some illumination variations and noise. The authors obtained similar results, where performance improved by smoothing the images when the resolution was sufficient (Lin, 2005a). This suggests that higher resolution isn't necessarily better beyond a certain limit and can actually introduce unwanted noise depending on the face recognition algorithm used. These results suggest that super-resolving low-resolution images will give worthwhile returns. The benefits of super-resolution diminish as resolution increases.

FUTURE RESEARCH DIRECTIONS

Tracking people in crowded environments is a growing area of interest. Algorithms have focused on two main tasks, trying to track everyone in the scene, regardless of how crowded it is; and trying to track only persons of interest. Breitenstein (2010) has proposed using particle filters that incorporate a person detection framework to track people through crowded scenes without the need for motion segmentation, or a stationary camera. Other recent work has focused on handing groups of people – either by treating the group as its own entity and tracking it, ignoring the configuration of people within the group (Galoogahi, 2010), or by trying to segment the group into its constituent objects (Denman, 2010). Tracking by detection approaches such as that of (Breitenstein, 2010) offer several advantages as they utilize learned models for detection, and thus avoid the problems associated with motion segmentation derived approaches such as changing lighting conditions, although efforts are being made to improve performance of motion segmentation in the presence of variable lighting conditions (Vijverberg, 2009), or shadows (Grest, 2003; Guan, 2010; Javed, 2002).

Within constrained environments, such as a highway, there are also additional approaches that can be used to improve object tracking. In such situations there is a structure to the scene (i.e. lanes of traffic, directions of travel) that can be used to improve the object tracking in a vehicle environment (Brulin, 2010). Such a tracking approach could be combined with a super-resolution approach such as that proposed in (Suresh, 2007), which has demonstrated super-resolution for license plate images, resulting in a similar system to that proposed here for vehicles.

With regards to super resolution approaches as part of a recognition process, one of the most promising avenues is feature-based super resolution techniques which adopt a different philosophy from traditional intensity-domain super resolution. The traditional approach is to super-resolve all intensities of an image before selecting a limited feature-set to utilize in a recognition application. However, feature-based super-resolution attempts to circumvent the superfluous intermediary step by directly super-resolving the feature-set only which is subsequently required for recognition. This approach has been applied successfully to face recognition (Gunturk et al, 2003), and iris recognition (Nguyen, 2011) for an eigenspace representation. Super resolution generally is also becoming more common-place in integrated model-based tracking systems that also aim to achieve resolution enhancement (Kuhl et al, 2008).

Soft biometrics (Denman, 2009) and person re-detection techniques (Bak, 2010; Farenzena, 2010; Gheissari, 2006) also offers a way to identify people from surveillance imagery and track people through complex, disjoint camera networks. Whilst these do not provide the same level of recognition as techniques such as face recognition, they have been shown to be suitable for short term recognition tasks in a surveillance situation. This makes them appealing for use when tracking in disjoint camera networks, or in the presence of crowds and frequent and/or prolonged occlusions.

In situations where tracking is not possible (either due to crowding, resolution, or other scene characteristics), persons of interest could be located using event recognition, and, if desired, the regions containing the detected events could be super-resolved. Various techniques for event recognition exist, however, those focused around machine learning techniques such as LDA (Blei, 2003) and HDP (Teh, 2006) are growing in popularity due to their ability to model the interactions between objects. Other techniques based around anomaly detection (Mahadevan, 2010; Ryan 2011) also offer a means to automatically detect abnormal events within surveillance footage, which could then be super-resolved.

CONCLUSION

Although surveillance cameras are ubiquitous in present society, their usefulness as providers of forensic evidence is hampered by the low quality of the images captured and the labour-intensive search process. This paper has presented a person tracking, super-resolution and recognition system to help overcome the aforementioned issues. Footage acquired in-house and from surveillance video database has been super-resolved to demonstrate the improvement in image fidelity over the low-resolution and interpolated images. In the case of the tattoo sequence, super-resolution dramatically increases the chances of the subject being identified by improving the legibility of the markings on the subject's arm. Face identification tests from a multi-modal video database have also been conducted to demonstrate the marginal but nonetheless useful improvement in automatic face recognition performance. When used offline, this system can reduce the time and effort in searching surveillance video for footage of value to forensic investigation. If a surveillance video camera network is used to check for persons of interest from a watch list such a system can also be useful on-line.

REFERENCES

Bak, S., Corvee, E., Bremond, F., & Thonnat, M. (2010, August 29 2010-September 1). Person re-identification using spatial covariance regions of human body parts. In the *Proceedings of the Seventh IEEE International Conference on Advanced Video and Signal Based Surveillance* (AVSS).

Baker, S., & Kanade, T. (1999). *Super-resolution optical flow*. Technical Report CMU-RI-TR-99-36, Robotics Institute, Carnegie Mellon University, October.

Banks, J., Bennamoun, M., & Corke, P. (1997). Fast and robust stereo matching algorithms for mining automation. In the *Proceedings of the International Workshop on Image Analysis and Information Fusion*, (pp. 139-149).

Bishop, C. M. (2006). *Pattern recognition and machine learning*. Springer.

Black, M., & Anandan, P. (1993). A framework for the robust estimation of optical flow. In the *Proceedings of the International Conference on Computer Vision* (ICCV), (pp. 231-236).

Black, M., & Jepson, A. (1998). Eigen-tracking: Robust matching and tracking of articulated objects using a view-based representation. *International Journal of Computer Vision, 36*(2), 101–130.

Blei, D. M., Ng, A. Y., & Jordan, M. I. (2003). Latent dirichlet allocation. *Journal of Machine Learning Research, 3*(4-5), 993–1022.

Bolme, D., Beveridge, R., Teixeira, M., & Draper, B. (2003). The CSU face identification evaluation system: Its purpose, features and structure. In the *Proceedings of International Conference on Vision Systems*, (pp. 304-311).

Borman, S., & Stevenson, R. (1999). Super-resolution from image sequences - A review. In the *Proceedings of 1998 Midwest Symposium on Circuits and Systems*, (pp. 374-378).

Bowden, R., & KaewTraKulPong, P. (2001). An improved adaptive background mixture model for real-time tracking with shadow detection. In *the Proceedings of the 2nd European Workshop on Advanced Video Based Surveillance Systems.*

Breitenstein, M. D., Reichlin, F., Leibe, B., Koller-Meier, E., & Gool, L. V. (2010). Online Multi-Person Tracking-by-Detection from a Single, Uncalibrated Camera. *IEEE Transactions on Pattern Analysis and Machine Intelligence, 33*(9), 1820–1833. doi:10.1109/TPAMI.2010.232

Brown, L. (1992). A survey of image registration techniques. *ACM Computing Surveys, 24*(4), 325–376. doi:10.1145/146370.146374

Brulin, M., Nicolas, H., & Maillet, C. (2010, 14-17 November 2010). Video surveillance traffic analysis using scene geometry. In the *Proceedings of the Fourth Pacific-Rim Symposium on Image and Video Technology* (PSIVT).

Butler, D., Sridharan, S., & Bove, V. M., Jr. (2003). Real-time adaptive background segmentation. In the *Proceedings of the International Conference on Acoustics, Speech, and Signal Processing* (ICASSP).

Capel, D., & Zisserman, A. (2003). Computer vision applied to super resolution. *IEEE Signal Processing Magazine, 25*(9), 75–86. doi:10.1109/MSP.2003.1203211

Cootes, T., & Cooper, D. (1995). Active shape models - Their training and application. *Computer Vision and Image Understanding, 61*(1), 38–59. doi:10.1006/cviu.1995.1004

Cootes, T. F., & Edwards, G. J. (2001). Active appearance models (AAMs). *IEEE Transactions on Pattern Analysis and Machine Intelligence, 23*(6), 681–685. doi:10.1109/34.927467

Dalal, N., & Triggs, B. (2005). Histograms of oriented gradients for human detection. In the *Proceedings of the IEEE Conference on Computer Vision and Pattern Recognition* (CVPR).

Denman, S., Chandran, V., & Sridharan, S. (2007a). An adaptive optical flow technique for person tracking systems. *Elsevier Pattern Recognition Letters, 28*(10), 1232–1239. doi:10.1016/j.patrec.2007.02.008

Denman, S., Chandran, V., & Sridharan, S. (2007b). Robust multi-layer foreground segmenation for surviellance applications. In the *Proceedings of the IAPR Conference on Machine Vision Applications,* The University of Tokyo, Japan.

Denman, S., Fookes, C., Bialkowski, A., & Sridharan, S. (2009, 1-3 December). *Soft-biometrics: Unconstrained authentication in a surveillance environment.* Paper presented at the Digital Image Computing: Techniques and Applications (DICTA), Melbourne, Australia.

Denman, S., Fookes, C., & Sridharan, S. (2010, 14-17 November). Group segmentation during object tracking using optical flow discontinuities. In the *Proceedings of the Fourth Pacific-Rim Symposium on Image and Video Technology* (PSIVT), 2010.

Doucet, A. (1998). *On sequential simulation-based methods for Bayesian filtering. Technical report cued/f-infeng/tr 310.* Department of Engineering, Cambridge University.

Farenzena, M., Bazzani, L., Perina, A., Murino, V., & Cristani, M. (2010, 13-18 June). Person re-identification by symmetry-driven accumulation of local features. In the *Proceedings of the IEEE Conference on Computer Vision and Pattern Recognition* (CVPR).

Felzenszwalb, P., & Huttenlocher, D. (2000). Efficient matching of pictorial structures. In the *Proceedings of the IEEE Conference on Computer Vision and Pattern Recognition.*

Fischler, M., & Bolles, R. (1981). Random sample consensus: A paradigm for model fitting with applications to image analysis and automated cartography. *Communications of the ACM, 24*(6), 381–395. doi:10.1145/358669.358692

Fookes, C. Lin, F. Chandran, V., & Sridharan, S. (2004, 20-22 December). Super-resolved face images using robust optical flow. In the *Proceedings of the Third Workshop on the Internet, Telecommunications and Signal Processing*, Adelaide.

Fookes, C., Bennamoun, M., & Lamanna, A. (2002). Improved stereo image matching using mutual information and hierarchical prior probabilities. In the *Proceedings of the International Conference on Pattern Recognition* (ICPR'02), Vol. 2, (pp. 937 – 940).

Freeman, W., Jones, T., & Pasztor, E. (2002). Example-based super-resolution. *IEEE Computer Graphics and Applications*, (March/April): 2002.

Galoogahi, H. K. (2010, 14-17 November). Tracking groups of people in presence of occlusion. In the *Proceedings of the Fourth Pacific-Rim Symposium on Image and Video Technology* (PSIVT).

Gheissari, N., Sebastian, T. B., & Hartley, R. (2006). Person reidentification using spatiotemporal appearance. In the *Proceedings of the IEEE Computer Society Conference on Computer Vision and Pattern Recognition.*

Goldberg, N., Feuer, A., & Goodwin, G. (2003). Super-resolution reconstruction using spatio-temporal filtering. *Journal of Visual Communication and Image Representation, 14*, 508–525. doi:10.1016/S1047-3203(03)00042-7

Grest, D., Frahm, J.-M., & Koch, R. (2003). A color similarity measure for robust shadow removal in real time. In the *Proceedings of the Vision, Modeling and Visualization Conference,* Munich, Germany.

Guan, Y. (2010). Spatio-temporal motion-based foreground segmentation and shadow suppression. *IET Computer Vision, 4*(1), 50–60. doi:10.1049/iet-cvi.2008.0016

Gunturk, B. K., Batur, A. U., Altunbasak, Y., Hayes, M. H. III, & Mersereau, R. M. (2003). Eigenface-domain super-resolution for face recognition. *IEEE Transactions on Image Processing, 12*(5), 597–606. doi:10.1109/TIP.2003.811513

Haritaoglu, I., Harwood, D., & Davis, L. (2000). An appearance-based body model for multiple people tracking. In the *Proceedings of the IEEE Conference on Pattern Recognition,* (pp. 184-187). Barcelona, Spain, 2000.

Harris, C., & Stephes, M. (1988). A combined corner and edge detector. In the *Proceedings of the 4th Alvey Vision Conference,* (pp. 147-151).

Harville, M. (2002). A framework for high-level feedback to adaptive, per-pixel, mixture-of-gaussian background models. In the *Proceedings of the 7th European Conference on Computer Vision,* Vol. 3, Copenhagen, Denmark.

Harville, M., Gordon, G. G., & Wood_ll, J. (2001). Foreground segmentation using adaptive mixture models in color and depth. In the *Proceedings of the IEEE Workshop on Detection and Recognition of Events in Video,* (pp. 3-11).

Hayman, E., & Eklundh, J. (2003). Statistical background subtraction for a mobile observer. In the *Proceedings of the International Conference on Computer Vision* (ICCV).

Higuchi, T. (1997). Monte Carlo filter using the genetic algorithm operators. *Journal of Statistical Computation and Simulation, 59*(1), 1–23. doi:10.1080/00949659708811843

Horn, B. K. P., & Schunck, B. G. (1981). Determining optical flow. *Artificial Intelligence, 17*, 185–203. doi:10.1016/0004-3702(81)90024-2

Hu, M., Hu, W., & Tan, T. (2004). Tracking people through occlusions. In the *Proceedings of the 17th International Conference on Pattern Recognition* (ICPR), (pp. 724-727).

Isard, M., & Blake, A. (1998). Condensation - Conditional density propagation for visual tracking. *International Journal of Computer Vision, 29,* 5–28. doi:10.1023/A:1008078328650

Jacques, J., Jung, C., & Musse, S. (2005). Background subtraction and shadow detection in grayscale video sequences. In the *Proceedings of the 18th Brazilian Symposium on Computer Graphics and Image Processing,* (SIBGRAPI), (pp. 189-196).

Javed, O., Shafique, K., & Shah, M. (2002). A hierarchical approach to robust background subtraction using color and gradient information. In the *Proceedings of the Workshop on Motion and Video Computing.*

Jaynes, C., Kale, A., Sanders, N., & Grossmann, E. (2005). The Terrascope dataset: Scripted multi-camera indoor video surveillance with ground-truth. In the *Proceedings of the IEEE International Workshop on Visual Surveillance and Performance Evaluation of Tracking and Surveillance,* (pp. 309-316).

Julier, S., & Uhlman, J. (1997). A consistent, debiased method for converting between polar and Cartesian coordinate systems. In the *Proceedings of the 11th International Symposium on Aerospace/Defence Sensing, Simulation and Controls, volume Multi Sensor Fusion, Tracking and Resource Management II,* Orlando, Florida

Kitagawa, G. (1996). Monte Carlo filter and smoother for non-Gaussian nonlinear state space models. *Journal of Computational and Graphical Statistics, 5*(1), 1–25.

Kong, A., Liu, J. S., & Wong, W. H. (1994). Sequential imputations and Bayesian missing data problems. *Journal of the American Statistical Association, 89*(425), 278–288. doi:10.1080/01621459.1994.10476469

Kuhl, A. Tan, T. Venkatesh, S. (2008, 8-11 December). Model-based combined tracking and resolution enhancement. In the *Proceedings of the International Conference on Pattern Recognition,* (pp. 1-4).

Leibe, B., Leonardis, A., & Schiele, B. (2008). Robust object detection with interleaved categorization and segmentation. *International Journal of Computer Vision, 77*(1-3), 259–289. doi:10.1007/s11263-007-0095-3

iLIDS Team. (2006). Imagery library for intelligent detection systems (i-lids); a standard for testing video based detection systems. In *the Proceedings of the 40th Annual IEEE International Carnahan Conferences Security Technology,* (pp. 75-80).

Lin, F., Cook, J., Chandran, V., & Sridharan, S. (2005a). Face recognition from super-resolved images. In the *Proceedings of International Conference on Information Science, Signal Processing and their Applications* (ISSPA), (pp. 667-670).

Lin, F., Denman, S., Chandran, V., & Sridharan, S. (2007). Automatic tracking and super-resolution of human faces from surveillance video. In the *Proceedings of the IAPR Conference on Machine Vision Applications* (MVA).

Lin, F., Fookes, C., Chandran, V., & Sridharan, S. (2005b). Investigation into optical flow super-resolution for surveillance applications. In the *Proceedings of the APRS Workshop on Digital Image Computing 2005,* (pp. 73-78).

Lin, F., Fookes, C., Chandran, V., & Sridharan, S. (2007b). Lecture Notes in Computer Science: *Vol. 4642. Super-resolved faces for improved face recognition from surveillance video* (pp. 1–10). Seoul, Korea: LNCS. doi:10.1007/978-3-540-74549-5_1

Liu, J. S., & Chen, R. (1998). Sequential Monte Carlo methods for dynamic systems. *Journal of the American Statistical Association, 93*(443), 1032–1044. doi:10.1080/01621459.1998.10473765

Lucas, B. D., & Kanade, T. (1981). An iterative image registration technique with an application to stereo vision. In the *Proceedings of the Imaging Understanding Workshop*, (pp. 121-130).

Mahadevan, V., Weixin, L., Bhalodia, V., & Vasconcelos, N. (2010, 13-18 June 2010). Anomaly detection in crowded scenes. In the *Proceedings of the IEEE Conference onComputer Vision and Pattern Recognition* (CVPR).

Martel-Brisson, N., & Zaccarin, A. (2005). Moving cast shadow detection from a Gaussian mixture shadow model. In the *Proceedings of the IEEE Conference on Computer Vision and Pattern Recognition* (CVPR) Vol. 2 (pp. 643-648).

Maskell, S., & Gordon, N. (2001). A tutorial on particle filters for on-line nonlinear/non-Gaussian Bayesian tracking. In *Target Tracking: Algorithms and Applications* (Ref. No. 2001/174), IEE Workshop, Vol. 2 (pp. 1-15).

Moghaddam, B., & Pentland, A. (1997). Probabilistic visual learning for object recognition. *IEEE Transactions on Pattern Analysis and Machine Intelligence, 19*(7), 696–710. doi:10.1109/34.598227

Nguyen Thanh, K., Fookes, C., Sridharan, S., & Denman, S. (2011). Feature-domain super-resolution for IRIS recognition. In the *Proceedings of the 18th IEEE International Conference on Image Processing* (ICIP 2011).

Okuma, K., Taleghani, A., Freitas, N. d., Little, J., & Lowe, D. (2004). A boosted particle filter: Multitarget detection and tracking. In the *Proceedings of the European Conference on Computer Vision*, (pp. 28-39).

Park, S., Park, M., & Kang, M. (2003). Super-resolution image reconstruction: A technical overview. *IEEE Signal Processing Magazine, 25*(9), 21–36. doi:10.1109/MSP.2003.1203207

Patti, A., & Altunbasak, Y. (2001). Artifact reduction for set theoretic super resolution image reconstruction with edge adaptive constraints and higher-order interpolants. [January.]. *IEEE Transactions on Image Processing, 10,* 179–186. doi:10.1109/83.892456

Phillips, P., Flynn, P., Scruggs, T., Bowyer, K., & Chang, J. Ho_man, K., Marques, J., Min, J., & Worek, W. (2005). Overview of the face recognition grand challenge. In the *Proceedings of the IEEE Conference on Computer Vision and Pattern Recognition* (CVPR), Vol. 1, (pp. 947-954).

Phillips, P., Moon, H., Rizvi, S., & Rauss, P. (2000). The feret evaluation methodology for face-recognition algorithms. *IEEE Transactions on Pattern Analysis and Machine Intelligence, 22,* 1090–1104. doi:10.1109/34.879790

Pitt, M. K., & Shephard, N. (1999). Filtering via simulation: Auxiliary particle filters. *Journal of the American Statistical Association, 94*(446), 590–599. doi:10.1080/01621459.1999.10474153

Rao, A., Srihari, R., & Zhang, Z. (2000). Geometric histogram: A distribution of geometric configurations of color subsets. *SPIE: Internet Imaging, 3964,* 91–101.

Ryan, D., Denman, S., Fookes, C., & Sridaharan, S. (2011). Textures of optical flow for real-time anomaly detection in crowds. *Proceedings of the 8th IEEE International Conference on Advanced Video and Signal Based Surveillance* (AVSS 2011), Klagenfurt University, Klagenfurt, Austria.

Schultz, R., & Stevenson, R. (1996). Extraction of high resolution frames from video sequences. *IEEE Transactions on Image Processing, 5*(6), 996–1011. doi:10.1109/83.503915

Seitner, F., & Lovell, B. C. (2005). Pedestrain tracking based on colour and spatial information. In the *Proceedings of the Digital Imaging Computer: Techniques and Applications* (DICTA 2005), (pp. 36-43). Cairns, Australia.

Stauffer, C., & Grimson, W. (1999). Adaptive background mixture models for real-time tracking. In the *Proceedings of the IEEE Conference on Computer Vision and Pattern Recognition* (CVPR), Vol. 2, (p. 252).

Suresh, K. V., Kumar, G. M., & Rajagopalan, A. N. (2007). Super-resolution of license plates in real traffic videos. *IEEE Transactions on Intelligent Transportation Systems, 8*(2), 321–331. doi:10.1109/TITS.2007.895291

Teh, Y. W., Jordan, M. I., Beal, M. J., & Blei, D. M. (2006). Hierarchical dirichlet processes. *Journal of the American Statistical Association, 101*(476), 1566–1581. doi:10.1198/016214506000000302

Tsai, R., & Huang, T. (1984). Multiframe image restoration and registration. *Advances in Computer Vision and image Processing, 1*, 317-339.

Turk, M. A., & Pentland, A. (1991). Face recognition using eigenfaces. In the *Proceedings of the IEEE Computer Vision and Pattern Recognition Conference* (CVPR), (pp. 586-591).

Vermaak, J., Doucet, A., & Perez, P. (2003). Maintaining multi-modality through mixture tracking. In the *Proceedings of the Ninth IEEE International Conference on Computer Vision* (ICCV'03), Nice, France.

Vijverberg, J., Loomans, M., Koeleman, C., & de-With, P. (2009). Global illumination compensation for background subtraction using Gaussian-based background difference modelling. In the *Proceedings of the Sixth IEEE International Conference on Advanced Video and Signal Based Surveillance* (AVSS) (pp. 448 –453).

Viola, P., & Jones, M. (2001a). Rapid object detection using a boosted cascade of simple features. In the *Proceedings of the IEEE Computer Vision and Pattern Recognition Conference* (CVPR).

Wang, H., & Suter, D. (2005). A re-evaluation of mixture-of-gaussian background modeling. In the *Proceedings of the IEEE International Conference on Acoustics, Speech, and Signal Processing*, (pp. 1017-1020). Philadelphia, PA, USA.

Wang, Y., & Lucey, S. (2008). Enforcing convexity for improved alignment with constrained local models. In the *Proceedings of the IEEE Computer Vision and Pattern Recognition Conference* (CVPR).

Welch, G., & Bishop, G. (1995). *An introduction to the Kalman filter. Technical report tr95-041.* University of North Carolina at Chapel Hill.

Xu, D., Liu, J., Liu, Z., & Tang, X. (2004). Indoor shadow detection for video segmentation. In the *Proceedings of the IEEE International Conference on Multimedia and Expo, 2004*, Vol. 1, (pp. 41-44).

Zang, Q., & Klette, R. (2004). Robust background subtraction and maintenance. In the *Proceedings of the 17th International Conference on Pattern Recognition*, (ICPR), Vol. 2, (pp. 90-93).

Zhang, W., Fang, X. Z., & Yang, X. (2006). Moving cast shadows detection based on ratio edge. In the *Proceedings of the 18th International Conference on Pattern Recognition* (ICPR), Vol. 4, (pp. 73-76).

Zhanwu, X., & Miaoliang, Z. (2006). Color-based skin detection: Survey and evaluation. In the *Proceedings of the 12th International Multi-Media Modelling Conference.*

Zhao, Q., & Tao, H. (2005). Object tracking using color correlogram. In the *Proceedings of the 2nd Joint IEEE International Workshop on Visual Surveillance and Performance Evaluation of Tracking and Surveillance*, (pp. 263-270).

Zhao, T., & Nevatia, R. (2004). Tracking multiple humans in complex situations. *IEEE Transactions on Pattern Analysis and Machine Intelligence, 26*(9), 1208–1221. doi:10.1109/TPAMI.2004.73

Zhou, Y., Gu, L., & Zhang, H. (2003). Bayesian tangent shape model: Estimating shape and pose parameters via Bayesian inference. In the *Proceedings of the IEEE Conference on Computer Vision and Pattern Recognition* (CVPR), (pp. 109-116).

Zhu, Q., Avidan, S., Yeh, M., & Cheng, K. (2006) Fast human detection using a cascade of histograms of oriented gradients. In the *Proceedings of the IEEE Conference on Computer Vision and Pattern Recognition* (CVPR).

Zitov, B., & Flusser, J. (2003). Image registration methods: A survey. *Image and Vision Computing, 21*(11), 977–1000. doi:10.1016/S0262-8856(03)00137-9

ADDITIONAL READING

Criminisi, A., Cross, G. B. A., & Kolmogorov, V. (2006, 17-22 June). Bilayer segmentation of live video. In the *Proceedings of the IEEE Computer Society Conference on Computer Vision and Pattern Recognition* (CVPR).

Dantcheva, A., Velardo, C., D'Angelo, A., & Dugelay, J.-L. (2011). Bag of soft biometrics for person identification: New trends and challenges. *Multimedia Tools and Applications, 51*(2), 739–777. doi:10.1007/s11042-010-0635-7

Dedeoglu, G., Kanade, T., & Baker, S. (2007). The asymmetry of image registration and its application to face tracking. *IEEE Transactions on Pattern Analysis and Machine Intelligence, 29*, 807–823. doi:10.1109/TPAMI.2007.1054

Dornaika, F., & Ahlberg, J. (2004). Fast and reliable active appearance model search for 3D face tracking. *IEEE Transactions on Systems, Man and Cybernetics. Part B, 34*, 1838–1853.

Fleuret, F., Berclaz, J., Lengagne, R., & Fua, P. A. F. P. (2008). Multicamera people tracking with a probabilistic occupancy map. *Transactions on Pattern Analysis and Machine Intelligence, 30*(2), 267–282. doi:10.1109/TPAMI.2007.1174

Haritaoglu, I., Harwood, D., & Davis, L. S. (2000). W4: Real-time surveillance of people and their activities. *IEEE Transactions on Pattern Analysis and Machine Intelligence, 22*(8), 809–830. doi:10.1109/34.868683

Hyung-Soo, L., & Daijin, K. (2009). Tensor-based AAM with continuous variation estimation: Application to variation-robust face recognition. *IEEE Transactions on Pattern Analysis and Machine Intelligence, 31*, 1102–1116. doi:10.1109/TPAMI.2008.286

Ince, S., & Konrad, J. (2008). Occlusion-aware optical flow estimation. *IEEE Transactions on Image Processing, 17*(8), 1443–1451. doi:10.1109/TIP.2008.925381

Patwardhan, K., Sapiro, G., & Morellas, V. (2008). Robust foreground detection in video using pixel layers. *IEEE Transactions on Pattern Analysis and Machine Intelligence, 30*(4), 746–751. doi:10.1109/TPAMI.2007.70843

Rodriguez, M., Ali, S., & Kanade, T. (2009, September 29 -October 2). Tracking in unstructured crowded scenes. In the *Proceedings of the IEEE 12th International Conference on Computer Vision* (CVPR).

Ryu, H., & Huber, M. (2007, October 29 - November 2). A particle filter approach for multi-target tracking. In the *Proceedings of the IEEE/RSJ International Conference on Intelligent Robots and Systems*, San Diego, CA, USA.

Sukno, F. M., Ordas, S., Butakoff, C., Cruz, S., & Frangi, A. F. (2007). Active shape models with invariant optimal features: Application to facial analysis. *IEEE Transactions on Pattern Analysis and Machine Intelligence, 29*, 1105–1117. doi:10.1109/TPAMI.2007.1041

Zach, C., Pock, T., & Bischof, H. (2007). A duality based approach for realtime TV-L1 optical flow. In the *Proceedings of the 29th DAGM Conference on Pattern Recognition.*

KEY TERMS AND DEFINITIONS

Aliasing: The degradation of a signal that occurs when the signal is sampled below the Nyquist rate.

Biometric: A physical characteristic that can be used identify a person.

Foreground Segmentation: The division of a scene into foreground and background regions through a modeling process, where foreground regions are those that consist of objects in motion of regions undergoing a change in appearance.

Identification: A one-to-many matching process, where an input token is matched to a database to determine the identity of the input token.

Interpolation: The process of estimating intermediate values within a signal, based on the surrounding values.

Object Tracking: The task of following one or more objects about a scene, from when they first appear to when the leave the scene, ensuring that the object is consistently labeled while it is being tracked.

Optical Flow: The motion of individual pixels between two images of the same scene.

Over-Fitting: A situation where a model is trained too closely on a training set, and comes to model the idiosyncrasies in the training set, rather than the underlying relationship. Over-fitting typically occurs when too few samples are used in training, or the model being trained is too complex (i.e. too many dimensions).

Particle Filter: An estimation technique where possible states of a system are represented by a distribution of particles, each of which represent a possible state of the system. At each time step the particles are evaluated using a feature that represents the system they are trying to model. Based on this evaluation the particle set is re-sampled in preparation for the next time step.

Pixel: A single element of an image.

Recognition: The process of matching an input token to a database. Recognition can be either a identification or a verification process.

Registration: The process of aligning a set of images from the same scene such that they share a common coordinate system.

Resolution: The number of pixels within an image.

Super-Resolution: The process of generating a high resolution image from one or more low resolution input images.

Verification: A one-to-one match, where the task is to match an input token to a claimed identity and determine if the claim is valid or not.

Chapter 12
Medical Quality of Service (m-QoS) and Quality of Experience (m-QoE) for 4G-Health Systems

Robert S. H. Istepanian
Medical Information and Network Technologies Research Centre, Kingston University, UK

Ali Alinejad
Medical Information and Network Technologies Research Centre, Kingston University, UK

Nada Y. Philip
Medical Information and Network Technologies Research Centre, Kingston University, UK

ABSTRACT

It is well known that the evolution of 4G-based mobile multimedia network systems will contribute significantly to future m-health applications that require high bandwidth, high data rates, and more critically better Quality of service and quality of experience. The key to the successful implementation of these emerging applications is the compatibility of emerging broadband wireless networks such as mobile WiMAX, HSUPA, and LTE networks with future m-health systems. Most recently, the concept of 4G-health is introduced. This is defined as the evolution of m-health towards targeted personalized medical systems with adaptable functionalities and compatibility with future 4G communications and network technologies. This new concept represents the evolution of m-health toward 4G mobility. It will have new challenges especially from the next generation of mobile communications and networks perspective and in particular from relevant quality of service and quality of experience issues. This chapter presents some of these challenges and illustrates the importance of the new concepts of medical Quality of Service (m-QoS) and medical Quality of Experience (m-QoE) for 4G-health systems. The chapter also presents a validation scenario of these concepts for medical video streaming application as a typical 4G-health scenario.

DOI: 10.4018/978-1-4666-2660-7.ch012

INTRODUCTION

The m-health concept is originally defined and introduced as 'emerging mobile computing, medical sensor, and communications technologies for healthcare'. This emerging concept represented the evolution of e-health systems from traditional desktop "telemedicine" platforms to wireless and mobile configurations (Istepanian, et al., 2004).

Since then and with the introduction of HSxPA and broadband wireless networks, numerous successful deployments of several m-health scenarios have been gained that support mobile real-time m-health applications. For example, with current wireless technologies, patient records, X-ray images, and CT scans can be accessed by healthcare professionals from any given location by connection to the specific medical center's information system using the 3G/3.5G/WiFi enabled iPhone or iPad terminals.

The increasing demand for high bandwidth applications with specific quality of service (QoS) and quality of experience (QoE) has been increasing sharply. More recently, the focus of different network service providers is switching from network quality of service to user quality of experience that describes the overall performance of network from the user's perspective.

This mechanism constitutes major challenges on future m-health systems in assuring both end-to-end QoE and QoS for next generation networks and to achieve high network QoS especially on the application layer.

In this chapter, we present the new concepts of medical quality of experience (m-QoE) and medical quality of service (m-QoS) and describe their perspective mapping issues for different m-health applications. We also validate these mapping issues in a typical video streaming application model.

4G-Health Systems

The last decade has witnessed major research progress on m-health systems using different wireless access technologies(Istepanian, et al., 2002; Istepanian, et al., 2000; Istepanian, 2000; Istepanian, 1999; Richards, 1999; Istepanian, 1999; Tachikawa, 2003). However, major limitations existed on earlier m-health network technologies based on 2.5G/3G networks that restricted their wider deployment. Some of these issues were summarized as follows (Istepanian, et al., 2004):

1. The lack of existing flexible and integrated "m-Health-on-demand" connectivity with different mobile telecommunication systems and standards for different healthcare services. This lack of compatibility exists due to the difficulty of achieving operational

Figure 1. Evolution timeline of beyond 3G (4G) networks (Berndt, 2008)

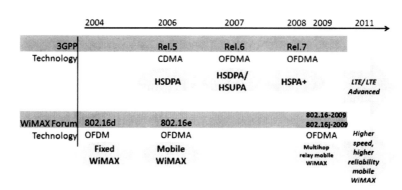

Table 1. Comparison of WiMAX and HSxPA systems (Goldsmith, 2005)

	Fixed WiMAX	Mobile WiMAX	HSxPA
Standards	IEEE 802.16_2004	IEEE 802.16e_2005	3GPP Release6
Bandwidth	3.5 MHz and 7 MHz in 3.5 GHz band; 10 MHz in 5.8 GHz band	5 -25 MHZ	5MHz
Peak downlink/ Uplink data rate	9.4Mbps/3.3 Mbps	46Mbps/7Mbps	14.4Mbps/ 1.4Mbps
Modulation	QPSK, 16QAM, 64 QAM	QPSK, 16QAM, 64QAM	QPSK, 16QAM
Coverage(typical)	3–5miles	< 2miles	1–3miles
Mobility	Not applicable	Mid	High

compatibility between the different mobile technologies, terminals and relevant protocols from the m-health perspective.

2. The limitation of existing practical wireless data rates combined with the non-availability of robust secure mobile internet connectivity and information access.

3. Health-care is a very complex industry that is difficult to change. Organizational changes are very often required for health-care institutions to benefit from e-health and m-health services.

4. The short-term and long-term economic consequences and working conditions for physicians and health-care experts using these technologies are not yet fully understood or properly investigated.

5. The methods of payment and reimbursement issues for e-Health and m-Health services are not yet fully developed and standardized.

6. There is a lack of integration between existing m-health services and other information systems, e.g., referral and ordering systems, medical records, etc.

Since then, some of these limitations especially on connectivity, data rate, and network compatibility levels have been alleviated by the introduction of 3.5G/WiMAX/LTE networks.

More recently, the concept of "4G-health" was introduced (Istepanian, 2012).This concept is defined as "the evolution of m-health towards targeted personalized medical systems with adaptable functionalities and compatibility with future 4G communications and network technologies".

The introduction of this concept provided other challenges that correspond to this evolution of m-health systems. In particular, there are two critical issues that are not yet finally addressed that constitute the main focus of this chapter (Philip, 2008):

1. Future 4G-health systems are required to provide effective and very accurate diagnosis and large data analysis requirements including bandwidth demanding services such as real-time tele-ultrasonography and other medical diagnostics applications.

2. The Quality of Service (QoS) and Quality of Experience (QoE) issues and their objective to provide robust 4G-health services with clinically acceptable diagnostic quality and services. These services must provide the end users (patients, specialists, and healthcare provider) with an acceptable m-QoS and m-QoE from the medical users' perspective.

From the network's perspective, Figure 1 illustrates the evolution toward 4G systems(Berndt,

Table 2. M-health QoS requirements (Komnakos, et al., 2008; Niyato, et al., 2007; Soomro, et al., 2007)

m-health service	Real-time application	Non real-time application	Data rate	QoS indices
Electrocardiography (ECG) monitoring	√		24 kb/s/12 channels	Delay
Blood pressure monitoring (Sphygmomanometer)	√		< 10 kb/s	Delay
Digital audio stethoscope (heart Sound)	√		~ 120kb/s	Packet loss, Delay
Region of Interest JPEG Image	√		15- 19 MBytes	PSNR, Frame size, Packet loss,
Radiology		√	~ 6 MBytes	PSNR, Frame size, Packet loss
Magnetic resonance imaging (*MRI*)		√	< 1MBytes	PSNR, Frame size, Packet loss
Ultrasound video streaming	√		250 kb/s – 1.2 Mb/s (WMV2)	PSNR, Frame Rate, Frame size, Packet loss, Delay
Wireless medical consultation (e.g. Accessing to patient records)		√	~ 10 Mb/s	Packet loss
Video/Audio conference	√		~ 1 Mb/s	Packet loss, Delay
Remote control applications (e.g. Robotic control)	√		~ 1 kb/s	Packet loss, Delay

2008).It is well known that 4G systems aims to provide high speed, high capacity, low cost, IP based connectivity services for nomadic and mobile wireless environment (Kaur, 2010).

In particular, HSxPA and WiMAX are the two significant broadband standards that were introduced by 3G partnership project (3GPP) and WiMAX forum respectively as initial targets of beyond 3G networks. The recent LTE system constitutes the first 4G network deployment pathway.

In the following section, we describe briefly the basics of the HSxPA and WiMAX technologies for completeness. For more comprehensive details, several references and texts can be cited (Komnakos, et al., 2008; ETSI TS 125 308 V5.4.0 (2003-03)).

HSxPA

The introduction of 3.5G or High Speed Downlink Packet Access (HSDPA) represented the enhancement of W-CDMA networks with higher data transfer speeds, improved spectral efficiency, and greater system capacity with a theoretical downlink peak of 14.4 Mbps (typically around 1.4 Mbps) and an uplink of 384 kbps(ETSI TS 125 308 V5.4.0 (2003-03)). Emerging m-health systems can benefit from these downlink data transfer speeds that were previously only feasible on wired communication networks. HSUPA is the 3GPP's release 6, introduced in 2006 to improve the uplink data rate of HSDPA, and offers an enhanced data rate, fast packet retransmission mechanisms, and reduced packet latencies with an uplink data rate up to a theoretical maximum of 5.6 Mb/s (typically around 1.5 Mbps).

WiMAX

The other 4G broadband technology candidate, WiMAX, is an emerging broadband wireless technology based on IEEE 802.16 standard (Vaughan-Nichols, 2004; Cherry, 2004). The main objective of the Mobile WiMAX standard is to cover the major weaknesses of Wireless LAN and 3G cellular systems such as data rate and coverage area. Because WLANhas shortrange coverage and 3G networks cannot supporthigh data rate despite of their long range coverage.To this aim,this standard deploys a specification that supports a mobile broadband access system and high data rate(Teo, Tao, & Zhang, 2007).

Mobile WiMAX is next release of fixed WiMAX introduced by WiMAX forum with optimization in communication technology to overcome the mobility and coverage issues.

WiMAX operates at radio frequencies between 2 GHz and 11 GHz for non-line-of-sight (N-LOS) operation and between 10 GHz and 66 GHz for line-of-sight (LOS) operation (Goldsmith, 2005).

Table 1 shows a comparison fixed/mobile WiMAX and HSxPA technologies in terms of coverage area, peak DL/UL data rate, supported modulation, and bandwidth.

The evolution of broadband wireless technologies such as LTE could be a major driving force for future development of 4G-health systems(Istepanian, et al., 2012). With the expected wider usage for 4G-health technologies, these technologies can substantially contribute to improve the limitations described earlier.

It is expected that the increased availability, miniaturization, performance, enhanced data rates, and the expected convergence of future wireless communication and network technologies around mobile health systems will accelerate the deployment of 4G-health systems and services within the next decade.

Quick delivery and reliable service are extremely important for m-health services (Zvikhachevskaya, et al., 2009). However, Different medical scenario and services require their specific quality of service parameters. Table 2 shows a summary of different m-health services and their corresponding data ratesand corresponding QoS requirements (Komnakos, et al., 2008; Niyato, et al., 2007; Soomro, et al., 2007). The table also

highlights some of the potential 4G-health applications that require higher data rates with critical QoS and QoE metrics. One such application is real-time medical video streaming and diagnostics (Istepanian, et al., 2009).

M-QoS and M-QoE for 4G-Health Systems

In this section, we describe briefly the concepts of m-QoS and m-QoE presented earlier. In m-health environments providing the necessary QoS and QoE in uncertain wireless environments is a challenging problem that requires further research and investigation. In particular, for real-time medical video streaming and diagnostics, three important user qualities can be identified. These are:

1. Image quality
2. Frame rate of the received images
3. End-to-end delay

As mentioned earlier, the QoS/QoE indices are dependent on lower network layersand their QoS requirements. In order to match the required resources with the available network conditions, there must be a tradeoff between these QoS requirements in order to satisfy the diagnostic (clinical) requirements and the required bounds

Figure 2. WiMAX QoS envelope model (IEEE 802.16e Standard, 2009)

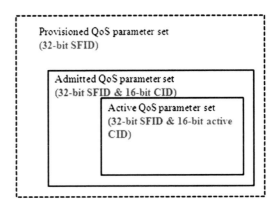

Table 3. Comparison of different WiMAX classes (Bachmutsky, 2009)

QoS	Pros	Cons	Possible Application
UGS	No overhead. Meet guaranteed latency for real-time service	Bandwidth may not be utilized fully since allocations are granted regardless of current need.	CBR Voice (no silence submission), circuit emulation
ertPS	Optimal latency and data overhead efficiency	Need to use the polling mechanism (to meet the delay guarantee) and a mechanism to let the BS know when the traffic starts during the silent period.	Voice with silence suppression
rtPS	Optimal data transport efficiency	Require the overhead of bandwidth request and the polling latency (to meet the delay guarantee)	MPEG Video
nrtPS	Provide efficient service for non-real-time traffic with minimum reserved rate	N/A	Data application with minimum rate requirements, e.g. FTP
BE	Provide efficient service for BE traffic	No service guarantee; some connections may starve for long period of time.	Data applications with no minimum rate requirements

of relevant QoS metrics. The concept of m-QoS was introduced as a sub category of QoS from the m-health perspective and defined as: ' An augmented requirements of critical mobile health care applications and the traditional wireless Quality of Service requirements'(Istepanian, et al., 2009; Philip, 2008).

Furthermore, theQoS can be defined as a set of specific requirements for a particular service provided by a network to its users. In general, QoS can be divided into two levels (Jamalipour, 2003):

1. **Network QoS:** The QoS that the network and technology can offer to the user, e.g. bandwidth, time delay andreliability.
2. **Application QoS:** The quality of the perceived services by the user; different users have different translation for QoS.

In recent years, different service provides are exploring the quality of experience issues. These constitute the ultimate measure of services tendered by a network and perceived as the overall acceptability of an application that is observed subjectively by the end-user.

From the m-health perspective, the medical quality of experience (m-QoE) can be defined 'as the overall acceptability of m-health application as perceived subjectively by the end users of these applications'. From the 4G-health perspective the m-QoE considers all the patients and stakeholders acting as healthcare providers (nurses, doctors) and their perception of the underlying next generation network services and their performance from the medical perspective. In general, QoE has many contributing factors, among which some are subjective and not controllable, while others are objective and can be controlled. For m-QoE scenario the specific subjective factors include factors such as healthcare provider/patient emotion, experience, and expectation. In this chapter, we propose the use of MOS (Mean opinion score) as a performance test parameter to map the relevant m-QoE evaluation indices.

In the following subsections, we will briefly discuss QoS indices for both mobile WiMAX and HSxPA followed by the correlation between m-QoS and m-QoE issues.

QoS in Mobile WiMAX

The IEEE.802.16/WiMAX standard does not specify any specific resource allocation algorithm for QoS purposes. The WiMAX equipment suppliers have their own mechanisms and relevant algorithms to adapt. These include Fair Schedul-

Figure 3. Model diagram of WiMAX BS and SS (Zhang & Chen, 2007; Zhang, 2009)

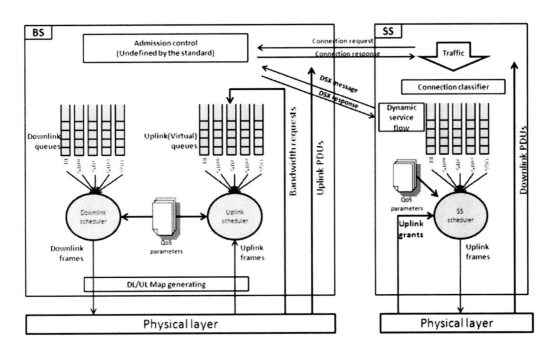

ing, Distributed Fair Scheduling, Max Min Fair Scheduling, Energy Efficient Scheduling, Feasible Earliest Due Date (FEDD), and Channel State Dependent Round Robin (CSD-RR) (So-In, et al., 2009).

WiMAX QoS mechanisms include scheduling, bandwidth request, admission control, and bandwidth control (Zhang, 2009). The WiMAX is designed to support QoS, however it is difficult to guarantee QoS in wireless networks. This is due to the variable and unpredictable characteristics of wireless networks(Zhang & Chen, 2007). To this aim, WiMAX standard specifies following QoS related concepts: service flow QoS scheduling, dynamic service establishing, and two-phase activation model.

A service flow provides unidirectional packet transport either in uplink or downlink that includes a set of QoS indices such as latency, jitter, minimum and maximum traffic, and traffic priority. A 32 bit SFID (service flow ID) and the flow direction are assigned to each service flow. The standard defines three types of service flows:

provisioned, admitted, and active service flow. The provisioned service flow is defined by, for example, network management system and the standard assigns a 32-bit SFID to it. In the admitted service flow, BS reserves the required resources and this type of service flow has a 32-bit SFID and a 16-bit CID. And finally, in the active service flow, the reserved resources are committed. This service flow also has both 32-bit SFID and 16-bit CID. Figure 2 illustrates above concept in envelope model. From this figure, it can be seen that 802.16e standard provides the management

Table 4. WiMAX QoS parameter (Bachmutsky, 2009)

	UGS	ertPS	rtPS	nrtPS	BE
Maximum sustained traffic rate	√	√	√	√	√
Minimum reserved traffic rate			√	√	
Maximum latency	√	√	√		
Tolerated jitter	√	√			

Table 5. UMTS QoS classes and requirements (Furht & Ahson, 2010)

QoS classes	Real-time application	Quality of service requirements		Sample application
		Delay	**Packet ordering**	
Conversational	Yes	Low	Strict	Voice
Streaming	Yes	Modest	Strict	Video
Interactive	No	Modest	Modest	Web browsing
Background	No	No	No	Data transfer

frames for creating, changing, or deleting service flow known as dynamic service activate (DSA), dynamic service change (DSC), and dynamic service delete (DSD) respectively(IEEE 802.16e Standard, 2009; Zhang & Chen, 2007).

In general, mobile WiMAX is a connection oriented system where the base station assigns a 16-bits connection identifier (CID) to each connection or subscriber which is usually shared for uplink and downlink connectivity (Kwang-Cheng & J.Roberto, 2008).

IEEE 802.16 has five QoS classes classified as follows (Bachmutsky, 2009; Zhang & Chen, 2007):

1. **UGS(Unsolicited Grant Scheme):** This service class supports constant-bit-rate in other words it has a fixed periodic bandwidth allocation whenever the connection is established. The requirement grant size is calculated by the BS without any further requests or polls. It is suitable for applica-

tions with fixed periodic packet size such as VOIP without silence suppression.

2. **rtPS (Real Time Polling Service):** This service class is for real time variable bit rate (VBR) traffic at periodic interval such as MPEG video. The bandwidth is allocated based on the required QoS parameters such as delay or traffic arrival rates. Since the traffic is variable; the BS needs to regularly poll each MS to determine what allocations need to be made.

3. **ertPS (Extended Real Time Polling Service):** This service class is based on UGS and rtPS, it is suitable for VOIP with silent period, unlike the UGS, BS should poll the MS during the silent periods to determine when the traffic will be started.

4. **nrtPS (Non Real Time Polling Service):** This service class is designed for non-real time variable bit rate traffic which the delay is not important however minimum band width is guaranteed. This class is usually used for FTP traffic.

Table 6. m-QoS for ultrasound video streaming (Garawi, et al., 2006; Garawi, et al., 2004; Canero, et al., 2005)

m-QoS index	Acceptable value
Ultrasound frame size	QCIF (176×144), CIF (352×288), 4CIF (704×576)
PSNR	>35 dB
SSIM	>0.959
MSE	<14.07
Frames per Second:	>5
End-to-end delay	<350ms

Table 7. m-QoE evaluation indices

m-QoE score	Overall conception	Subjective Quality indices
5	Excellent	Resolution: same as original, Smooth and no jitters
4	Good	Resolution: good, almost same as original, smooth. Very few jitters
3	Fair	Resolution: good but occasionally bad, Image jitters and breaks at periphery but is tolerable as long as region of interest (ROI) not affected, obvious flow discontinuity of video due to image obstruction
2	Poor	Resolution: poor, Image jitters throughout the clip. ROI was minimally affected
1	Bad	Resolution: bad, Image jitters and breaks for longer intervals in various areas affecting ROI: Not acceptable

5. **BE (Best Effort):** This service class is used for data stream with no support for delay or throughput; the Telnet and web browser data use this class.

Table 3 shows a comparison of the WiMAX QoS service classes and pros and cons of each class. In summary, UGS class has a static allocation and ertPS is a combination of UGS and rtPS. Both UGS and ertPS can reserve the bandwidth during setup. Unlike UGS, ertPS allows all kinds of bandwidth request including contention resolution. rtPS cannot participate in contention resolution. nrtPS and BE use several types of bandwidth requests such as piggybacking, bandwidth stealing, unicast polling and contention resolution.

Table 4 shows the mapping of QoS parameters for different WiMAX QoS classes. Similarly most of these classes can be mapped for different m-health applications.

Figure 3 illustrates a model diagram of BS and SS implementation in terms of data traffic and QoS classes. Each connection associated with a service flow which has its own QoS requirements.

In this model, the BS assigns up to three dedicated connection identifier (CID) to every MS in initializing phase, so they can belong to different quality of service and also allocates the band width according to MS requirements and its policy. And the MS uses the channel quality information channel (CQICH) to report the DL carrier-to-interference-plus-noise ratio (CINR),

in other words; CQICH is allocated to an MS for receiving CINR (Kwang-Cheng & J.Roberto, 2008; So-In, et al., 2009; Ghazal, et al., 2008). This model can be adapted easily to test the new m-QoS issues defined earlier.

QoS in HSxPA Network

In general, HSxPA technology is able to achieve increased individual wireless connection throughputs, increased total cell throughputs, and reduced round trip times that help to improve quality of service experienced by the end-user (Johnson, 2008).

The 3GPP defines four general QoS classes (Holma & Toskala, 2006; Etoh & Yoshimura, 2005): conversational, streaming, background, and interactive. The main QoS parameters that are considered in HSPA networks are GBR (Guaranteed Bit Rate), SPI (Scheduling Priority Indicator), and DT (Discard Timer). Call admission control (CAC) located inside the RNC to ensure the desired QoS for traffic classes. The CAC can decide accept or reject a new flow. Table 5 presents different QoS classes and the requirements according to UMTS standard that can be applied to HSxPA networks (Furht & Ahson, 2010).

In general, the streaming traffic class has a higher priority than the background and interactive classes; all streaming connections should be served prior to all interactive connections, and GBR can be set according to the required bit rate. DT is the

Figure 4. Medical QoS mapping for WiMAX and HSxPA networks

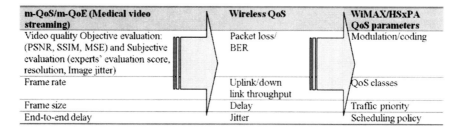

m-QoS/m-QoE (Medical video streaming)	Wireless QoS	WiMAX/HSxPA QoS parameters
Video quality Objective evaluation: (PSNR, SSIM, MSE) and Subjective evaluation (experts' evaluation score, resolution, Image jitter)	Packet loss/ BER	Modulation/coding
Frame rate	Uplink/down link throughput	QoS classes
Frame size	Delay	Traffic priority
End-to-end delay	Jitter	Scheduling policy

maximum delay time in Node-B and it is set based on the QoS requirements (Johnson, 2008; Etoh & Yoshimura, 2005).

Mapping of m-QoS and m-QoE

In general, the effective QoS mapping across different network layers is one of the key issues for QoS provisioning. More specifically, end-to-end QoS mapping considers QoS/QoE parameters at different layers and provides a correlation between these parameters. In this section, we hypothesize on the correlation between m-QoS and m-QoE for a specific 4G-health application, namely: ultrasound video streaming to satisfy the clinical and diagnostic requirements and illustrate the effectiveness of these concepts for future 4G-health applications.

We assume that the classification of this application can be categorized to three major traffic classes that are based on typical medical

Figure 5. Typical broadband m-health scenario model over mobile WiMAX network

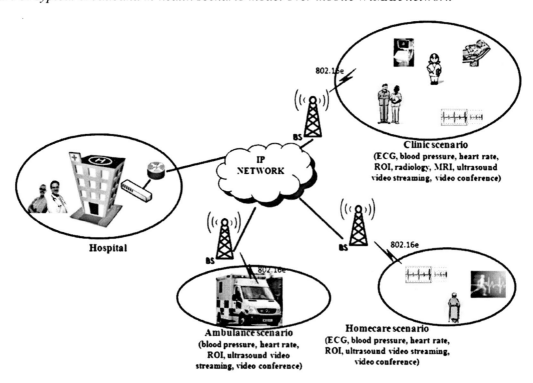

Figure 6. Performance of PSNR vs. packet loss probability (a) sample video 1 (b) sample video 2

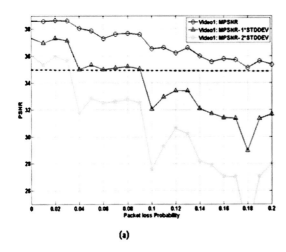

(a)

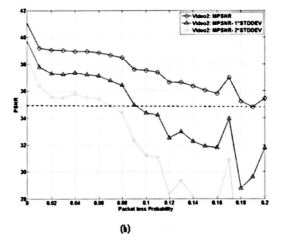

(b)

services required for such data traffic (Alinejad, et al., 2011):

1. Clinic care scenario
2. Accident/A&E care scenario
3. Home care scenario

It has to be noted that different m-health scenarios require different sets and levels of m-QoS requirements. Next, we define some of the relevant m-QoS requirements based on the general bandwidth, timeliness, and reliability issues. In particular for the bandwidth metric the generated data rate of the specific application is considered. For the timeliness metric, the delay element is considered. And finally for the reliability the packet loss element is chosen as the most common measurable element in network studies(Jha & Hassan, 2002). To prove such hypothesis, the relevant objective image quality assessment methods are selected next; these are defined as follows:

Peak signal-to-noise ratio (PSNR) index, which can be defined as following equation (Cosman, et al., 2002).

$$PSNR = 10.\log\left[\frac{255^2}{\frac{1}{NM}\sum_{i=0}^{N-1}\sum_{j=0}^{M-1}\left(x(i,j)-y(i,j)\right)^2}\right]$$

(1)

where $x(i, j)$ refers to the pixel (i, j) in the original image and $y(i, j)$ to the pixel (i, j) in the test image. Both images are size of N×M.

Structural SIMilarity (SSIM) index, which can be defined as in the following equation(Hands, et al., 2004):

$$SSIM(x,y) = \frac{2(\mu_x\mu_y + c1)(2\sigma_{xy} + c2)}{(\mu_x^2 + \mu_y^2 + c1)(\sigma_x^2 + \sigma_y^2 + c2)},$$
$$-1 < Q < 1$$

(2)

where

$$\mu_x = \frac{1}{L}\sum_{i=1}^{L} x_i, \ \mu_y = \frac{1}{L}\sum_{i=1}^{L} y_i,$$

$$\sigma_x^2 = \frac{1}{L-1}\sum_{i=1}^{L}(x_i - \mu_x)^2,$$

$$\sigma_y^2 = \frac{1}{L-1}\sum_{i=1}^{L}(y_i - \mu_y)^2,$$

Figure 7. Test ultrasound images with different packet losses: (a) and (c) Packet loss =0.00% Average PSNR=38.61dB Average SSIM=0.966 Average MSE =9.43; (b) Packet loss =0.10% Average PSNR=35.37dB Average SSIM = 0.944 Average MSE =20.00; (d) Packet loss =0.18% Average PSNR=34.97dB Average SSIM = 0.941 Average MSE =63.31

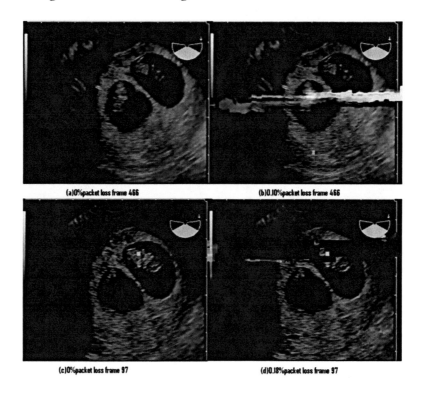

Figure 8. (a) SSIM vs. packet loss (b) MSE vs. packet loss

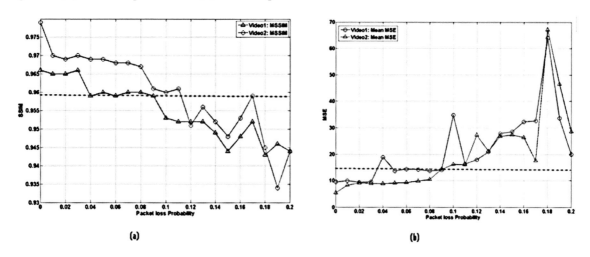

Table 8. Objective quality indices for the tested ultrasound video streaming samples

Packet loss	Sample video1 (PSNR 38.5 dB)				Sample video2 (PSNR 40 dB)			
	MPSNR	SSIM	MSE	MPSNR-δ	MPSNR	SSIM	MSE	MPSNR- δ
0.02	38.5	0.965	9.33	37.3	39.05	0.969	9.11	37.3
0.04	38.05	0.959	18.91	34.9	38.95	0.969	8.85	37.36
0.06	37.29	0.959	14.38	34.9	38.85	0.968	9.25	37.13
0.08	37.67	0.96	13.71	35.21	38.48	0.967	10.48	36.43
0.10	36.53	0.953	34.73	32.05	37.54	0.96	16.18	34.37
0.12	36.22	0.952	18	33.42	36.66	0.951	27.27	32.52
0.14	35.99	0.949	27.85	32.08	36.36	0.952	26.81	32.26
0.16	35.79	0.948	32.3	31.41	35.81	0.953	26.41	31.8
0.18	34.97	0.941	63.31	28.96	35.24	0.945	67.05	28.77
0.20	35.37	0.944	20	31.67	35.44	0.944	28.56	31.77

$$\sigma_{xy} = \frac{1}{L-1} \sum_{i=1}^{L} (x_i - \mu_x)(y_i - \mu_y),$$

x, y and *L* represent the original image, the test image and the number of pixels in the portion of the image under processing respectively.

The *c1* and *c2* are constant values used to calculate the SSIM metric which are equivalent to 6.5025 and 58.5225 respectively. The mean value of the proper number of image subwindows is then calculated (Istepanian et al., 2008). The dynamic range of SSIM is [-1, 1]. The best value 1 is achieved if and only if *x=y*.

Mean squared error (MSE) index, which can be defined as following equation:

$$MSE = \frac{1}{NM} \sum_{i=0}^{N-1} \sum_{j=0}^{M-1} \left(x(i,j) - y(i,j) \right)^2 \qquad (3)$$

where *x(i, j)* refers to the pixel *(i, j)* in the original image and y*(i, j)* to the pixel *(i, j)* in the test image. Both images are size of N×M.

m-QoE includes different subjective indices that are evaluated by the end users. These include indices such as: user perception, user emotional state, perception time, security issues, privacy issues, cost, and user environment (in the medical

case: ambulance, hospital, or home environments). This chapter considers the m-QoE in terms of the perceptional quality of ultrasound video streaming which is evaluated by the medical experts.

Tables6 and7 summarize the ultrasound video streaming m-QoS and m-QoE requirements respectively. The quality indices and functional bounds shown in the table 6 are specified by earlier clinical evaluation studies (Garawi, et al., 2006; Garawi, et al., 2004; Canero, et al., 2005).

The main quality of service metrics are summarized in terms of utilization, packet Loss, end-to-end delay and delay jitter. The m-QoS/m-QoE requirements need to be guaranteed by the network in order to provide a satisfactory video streaming service.

Hence, it can be concluded that the QoS issues of both targeted networks (mobile WiMAX and HSxPA) require different QoS indices that can be

Table 9 Proposed m-QoE stakeholders

QoE parameters	Medical example
Medical user group	Patients, radiologist, A&E specialist
Medical user environment	Ambulance, Homecare, Hospital units, Community care

Figure 9. Performance of MOS vs. packet loss for the tested ultrasound video streaming

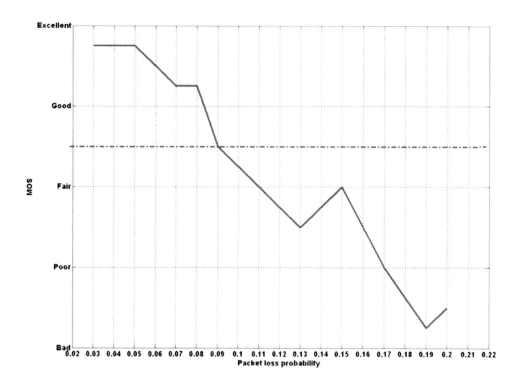

matched or cross-mapped with earlier m-QoSThis process is illustrated in Figure 4.

PERFORMANCE ANALYSIS AND RESULTS

Figure 5 shows typical m-health scenario model for medical video streaming over mobile WiMAX network. As explained earlier, this figure includes three main medical scenarios (Clinic, Accident/ A&E, and Home care). This model has been implemented using OPNET Modeler® to evaluate the performance issues outlined earlier.

To validate the earlier hypothesis, we tested this model using several medical video test streams evaluated by several medical experts in this area. The Figure 6 shows the results of the MPSNR (Mean PSNR), *MPSNR-1*stddev*(standard deviation) and *MPSNR - 2*stddev* for different packet loss values of the tested *video1* and *vid-*

*eo2*samples. From these figures the PSNR value is gradually reduced as the packet loss increases to a max reduction of 3.6 dB and 6.2 dB at 0.2% packet loss for video1 and video2 samples respectively. However, the results of the *MPSNR-1*stddev* and *MPSNR-2*stddev* show a more accurate picture. These results show that in some cases the PSNR is as low as 27 dB with 0.10 packet losses and 23dB with packet loss of 0.18. However, thesewere not clinically acceptable values as examined by the medical experts.

Video quality can be interpreted as the quality of the majority of frames. In the tested data streams, the majority of the frames(68.2% and 95.4% of frames) are within the one time standard deviations ($\mu \pm \sigma$) and two- times standard deviations ($\mu \pm 2\sigma$) respectively, where μ is average and σ is standard deviation. The visual evaluation shows if packet loss is less than 0.10%, the effected medical video stream is acceptable. The Video1: (*MPSNR- 1*STDDEV*) and Video2:

(*MPSNR- 1*STDDEV*) graphs shown in figure 6indicate more than half of the frames (68.2%) obtain PSNR values greater than the acceptable medical QoS bound (35 dB).

Figure 7 shows the comparative visual results for the tested ultrasound video frames. Images (a) and (c) are part of a video with MPSNR 38.61, Image (b) is part of a video sample with MPSNR 35.37 and Image (d) is part of a video sample with MPSNR 34.97.However, the PSNR of images (b) and (d) [22.94 dB and 22.34 dB respectively] are less than acceptable range for accurate clinical diagnostics. In other words the mean PSNR is not sufficient for evaluating the packet loss.

Figure 8 shows the mean SSIM and mean MSE as the packet loss evaluating parameters. From the clinical visual evaluation the video streaming with SSIM that is less than 0.959 and with MSE greater than 14.07 are found asclinically unacceptable. Table 8 summarizes the video1 performance and relevant analysis results; the highlighted part represents clinically the acceptable range.

Table 9 summarizes the proposed parameters that can be considered for the tested medical application. In this study the user groups considered are the physician and the selected environment is the hospital and the mobile terminal used is a mobile laptop with WiMAX and HSxPA connectivity.

The ultrasound video has been evaluated by 4 medical expert/observers that provided MOS score in range of 1 to 5 (equivalent from 'Bad' to 'Excellent' quality). Figure 9 shows the subjective evaluation results based on this scoring evaluation.

The result shows that the proper combination of objective quality metrics can provide precise evaluation of clinically acceptable medical video streaming. These results also indicate that the overall packet loss greater than 0.09% is not acceptable clinically for the WiMAX testbed ultrasound video streaming scenario described earlier.

CONCLUSION

The next four years will witness major increase in the use and volume of video data streaming over 4G/LTE mobile networks in application such as video movie, games streaming. However, few studies are addressing the expected challenges from the medical perspective. In this chapter, we presented the new concept of 4G-health introduced recently as the evolution of m-health system. Furthermore, the concepts of m-QoS and m-QoE are also introduced together with their mapping issues.

The correlation hypothesis of these concepts was validated using real-time ultrasound medical video streaming scenario as a typical 4G-health application over HSxPA and WiMAX networks.

The relevant subjective and objective image quality studies applied to samples of medical ultrasound images using simulated HSxPA and mobile WiMAX were also shown.

The preliminary results indicate the successful validation of the correlation hypothesis between m-QoS and m-QoE to provide accurate evaluation of clinically acceptable medical video streaming using both network connectivity options.

Further work in this area require with future 4G networks and services with relevant regulation issues from the m-health perspective. Further ongoing work is currently underway to validate the presented concepts using other medical applications.

ACKNOWLEDGMENT

The authors would like to acknowledge Dr. N. Amso from CardiffUniversityMedicalSchool and his team for their medical advice and for providing the relevant medical images and ultrasound video data.

REFERENCES

Alinejad, A., Philip, N., & Istepanian, R. S. (2011). Mapping of multiple parameter m-health scenarios to mobile WiMAX QoS variables. *33rd Annual International Conference of the IEEE EMB*, (pp. 1532-1535). Boston, MA: IEEE.

Bachmutsky, A. (2009). *WiMAX evolution: Emerging technologies and applications* (Katz, M., & Fitzek, F., Eds.). 1st ed.). Wiley.

Berndt, H. (2008). *Towards 4G technologies: Services with initiative* (1st ed.). Wiley. doi:10.1002/9780470010334

Canero, C., Thomos, N., Triantafyllidis, G., Litos, G., & Strintzis, M. (2005). Mobile tele-echography: user interface design. *IEEE Transactions on Information Technology in Biomedicine*, *9*(1), 44–49. doi:10.1109/TITB.2004.840064

Cherry, S. M. (2004). WiMax and Wi-Fi: Separate and unequal. *IEEE Spectrum*, *41*(3). doi:10.1109/MSPEC.2004.1270541

Cosman, P., Gray, R., & Olshen, R. (2002). Evaluating quality of compressed medical images: SNR, subjective rating, and diagnostic accuracy. *Proceedings of the IEEE*, (pp. 919-932).

Etoh, M., & Yoshimura, T. (2005). Advances in wireless video delivery. *Special Issue on Advances in Video Coding and Delivery*, *93*(1), 111–122.

ETSI TS 125 308 V5.4.0 (2003-03). (n.d.). *3GPP TS 25.308 version 5.4.0 release 5.*

Furht, B., & Ahson, S. A. (2010). *HSDPA/HSUPA handbook* (1st ed.). CRC Press. doi:10.1201/b10268

Garawi, S., Courreges, F., Istepanian, R., Zisimopoulos, H., & Gosset, P. (2004). Performance analysis of a compact robotic tele-echography E-health system over terrestrial and mobile communication links. *3G Mobile Communication Technologies*, (pp. 118-122).

Garawi, S., Istepanian, R., & Abu-Rgheff, M. (2006). 3G wireless communications for mobile robotic tele-ultrasonography systems. *IEEE Communications Magazine*, *44*(4), 91–96. doi:10.1109/MCOM.2006.1632654

Ghazal, S., Mokdad, L., & Ben-Othman, J. (2008). Performance analysis of UGS, rtPS, nrtPS admission control in WiMAX networks. *Proceedings of IEEE International Conference on Communications*, (pp. 2696-2701). Beijing, China: IEEE.

Goldsmith, A. (2005). *Wireless communications*. Cambridge, UK: Cambridge University Press.

Hands, D., Huynh-Thu, Q., Rix, A., Davis, A., & Voelcker, R. (2004). Objective perceptual quality measurement of 3G video services. *3G Mobile Communication Technologies*, (pp. 437-441).

Holma, H., & Toskala, A. (2006). *HSDPA/HSUPA for UMTS: High speed radio access for mobile communications*. Wiley-Blackwell.

Istepanaian, R. S. H., & Zhang, Y.-T. (2012). 4G health—The Long-term evolution of m-health. *IEEE Transactions on Information Technology in Biomedicine*, *16*(1), 1–5. doi:10.1109/TITB.2012.2183269

Istepanian, R., Jovanov, E., & Zhang, Y. (2004). Guest editorial introduction to the special section on m-health: Beyond seamless mobility and global wireless health-care connectivity. *IEEE Transactions on Information Technology in Biomedicine*, *8*(4), 405–414. doi:10.1109/TITB.2004.840019

Istepanian, R., & Petrosian, A. (2000). Optimal zonal wavelet-based ECG data compression for a mobile telecardiology system. *IEEE Transactions on Information Technology in Biomedicine*, *4*(3), 200–211. doi:10.1109/4233.870030

Istepanian, R., Philip, N., & Martini, M. (2009). Medical QoS provision based on reinforcement learning in ultrasound streaming over 3.5G wireless systems. *IEEE Journal on Selected Areas in Communications*, *27*(4), 566–574. doi:10.1109/JSAC.2009.090517

Istepanian, R. S. (1999). Telemedicine in the United Kingdom: Current status and future prospects. *IEEE Transactions on Information Technology in Biomedicine, 3*(2), 158–159. doi:10.1109/4233.767091

Istepanian, R. S. (1999). The comparative performance of mobile telemedical systems using the IS-54 and GSM cellular telephone standards. *Journal of Telemedicine and Telecare, 5*(2), 97–104. doi:10.1258/1357633991933396

Istepanian, R. S. (2000). Telemedicine in Armenia: A perception of telehealth services in the former Soviet Republics. *Journal of Telemedicine and Telecare, 6*, 268–272. doi:10.1258/1357633001935897

Istepanian, R. S., & Woodward, B. (2002). *Programmable underwater acoustic telemedicine system in Acoustica.*

Istepanian, R. S. H., Philip, N., Martini, M. G., Amso, N., & Shorvon, P. (2008). *Subjective and objective quality assessment in wireless teleultrasonography imaging* (pp. 5346–5349). Vancouver, BC: Engineering in Medicine and Biology Society. doi:10.1109/IEMBS.2008.4650422

Jamalipour, A. (2003). *The wireless mobile internet: Architectures, protocols and services* (1st ed.). Wiley.

Jha, S., & Hassan, M. (2002). *Engineering internet QoS.* Artech House.

Johnson, C. (2008). *Radio access networks for UMTS: Principles and practice.* Wiley-Blackwell.

Kaur, B. (2010). Factors influencing implementation of 4G with mobile ad-hoc networks in m-governance environment. *International Journal of Computers and Applications, 3.*

Komnakos, D., Vouyioukas, D., Maglogiannis, I., & Constantinou, P. (2008). Performance evaluation of an enhanced uplink 3.5G system for mobile healthcare applications. *International Journal of Telemedicine and Applications, 2008.* doi:10.1155/2008/417870

Kwang-Cheng, C., & Roberto, B. D. (2008). *Mobile WiMAX.* Wiley.

Niyato, D., Hossain, E., & Diamond, J. (2007). IEEE 802.16/WiMAX-based broadband wireless access and its application for telemedicine/e-health services. *IEEE Wireless Communications, 14*(1), 72–83. doi:10.1109/MWC.2007.314553

Philip, N. (2008). *Medical quality of service for optimized ultrasound streaming in wireless robotic tele-ultrasonography system.* PhD Thesis, Kingston University.

Richards, C. W. (1999). Exploiting mobile telephone technology for telemedicine applications. *Medical & Biological Engineering & Computing, 37*, 110–111.

So-In, C., Jain, R., & Tamimi, A.-K. (2009). Scheduling in IEEE 802.16e mobile WiMAX networks: Key issues and a survey. *IEEE Journal on Selected Areas in Communications, 27*(2), 156–171. doi:10.1109/JSAC.2009.090207

Soomro, A., & Cavalcanti, D. (2007). Opportunities and challenges in using WPAN and WLAN technologies in medical environments. *IEEE Communications Magazine, 45*(2), 114–122. doi:10.1109/MCOM.2007.313404

Standard, 8.-2.1. (2009). *802.16-2009 IEEE standard for local and metropolitan area networks part 16: Air interface for broadband wireless access systems.* IEEE.

Tachikawa, K. (2003). A perspective on the evolution of mobile communications. *IEEE Communications Magazine, 43*(10), 66–73. doi:10.1109/MCOM.2003.1235597

Teo, K. H., Tao, Z., & Zhang, J. (2007). The mobile broadband WiMAX standard. *IEEE Signal Processing Magazine, 24*(5), 144–148. doi:10.1109/MSP.2007.904740

Vaughan-Nichols, S. (2004). Achieving wireless broadband with WiMAX. *Computer, 37*(6), 10–13. doi:10.1109/MC.2004.1266286

Zhang, Y. (2009). *WiMAX network planning and optimization*. CRC Press. doi:10.1201/9781420066630

Zhang, Y., & Chen, H.-H. (2007). *Mobile WiMAX: Toward broadband wireless metropolitan area networks*. Auerbach Publications. doi:10.1201/9780849326400

Zvikhachevskaya, A., Markarian, G., & Mihaylova, L. (2009). Quality of service consideration for the wireless telemedicine and e-health services. *Wireless Communications and Networking Conference*, Budapest, Hungary, (pp. 1-6).

Chapter 13
Peer-to-Peer Network-Based Image Retrieval

Chun-Rong Su
National Taiwan University of Science and Technology, Taiwan

Jiann-Jone Chen
National Taiwan University of Science and Technology, Taiwan

ABSTRACT

Performing Content-Based Image Retrieval (CBIR) in Internet connected databases through Peer-to-Peer (P2P) network (P2P-CBIR) helps to effectively explore the large-scale image database distributed over connected peers. Decentralized unstructured P2P framework is adopted in our system to compromise with the structured one while still reserving flexible routing control when peers join/leave or network fails. The P2P-CBIR search engine is designed to provide multi-instance query with multi-feature types to effectively reduce network traffic while maintaining high retrieval accuracy. In addition, the proposed P2P-CBIR system is also designed in the way to provide scalable retrieval function, which can adaptively control the query scope and progressively refine the accuracy of retrieved results. To reflect the most updated local database characteristics for the P2P-CBIR users, reconfiguring system at each regular interval time can effectively reduce trivial peer routing and retrieval operations due to imprecise configuration. Experiments demonstrated that the average recall rate of the proposed P2P-CBIR with reconfiguration is higher than the one without about 20%, and the latter outperforms previous methods, i.e., firework query model (FQM) and breadth-first search (BFS) about 20% and 120%, respectively, under the same range of TTL values.

INTRODUCTION

Peer to Peer (P2P) networks have been proficiently developed to share files, transferring real-time video streams, and performing CBIR in recent decades. In P2P networks, each connected peer serves as a server/client simultaneously, which can effectively distribute computation (King et al., 2004) and network traffic among connected peers to provide efficient streaming and CBIR services. P2P networks could be categorized into three network models: centralized (C-P2P), decen-

DOI: 10.4018/978-1-4666-2660-7.ch013

tralized structured (DS-P2P), and decentralized unstructured (DU-P2P). In the C-P2P model as shown in Figure 1(a), such as Napster (Fanning 2007), the query peer must communicate with the central server to access files stored in other peers. It provides fast responses but suffers the single point failure, which can be eliminated by adopting the DS-P2P model, such as the distributed hash table (DHT) (Ratnasamy et al., 2002), which assigns one key for each file and provides strict rules for file placement and object discovery. In this model, each file is represented by one key, and each peer is responsible for some fixed keys. In general, it takes $\log(N_{peer})$ hops to reach the destination file. Figure 1(b) shows that the DU-P2P model, such as Gnutella (Gnutella 2004) and Freenet (Clarke et al., 2000), the location of each file is random, i.e., each peer operates independently to each other. The query message m^Q is propagated by blind flooding, such that it would consume excessive network resources and computation power. The DU-P2P acts as a contrary extreme case of the C-P2P and demonstrates much flexible control capabilities. The DS-P2P compromises between C-P2P and DU-P2P. By comparing the CBIR performances for DS-P2P and DU-P2P, the routing of the latter is much flexible but would suffer traffic flooding due to blind and potential duplicated query processing. However, it is inefficient for the former to update the system when peers join or leave resulted from PC failures or routing change as compared to the latter. Considering the probing diversity for queries and imposing scalable retrieval control on the P2P network, the DU-P2P is adopted since its generalized framework can provide regular operations for CBIR. To solve the potential flooding problem in DU-P2P, we proposed to perform peer clustering to compromise with DS-P2P.

In terms of system configuration, the P2P-CBIR system performs peer clustering to group peers with relevant contents to eliminate excessive routings for efficient retrieval. In general, k-means clustering is better than randomly selecting cluster centroids (Eisenhardt et al., 2006). Methods

which adopt this model include directory node (Inaba et al., 2006), R-tree (Liu et al., 2005), and table of interest (Yang et al., 2003), etc. The directory node manages the peer cluster information to help to propagate the m^Q to peers with relevant contents, denoted as P_d *(Q)* that stands for the destination peers of *Q*. The *R*-tree (Liu et al., 2005) performs image feature clustering and each cluster is managed by several super-peers. In (Yang et al., 2003), results of past queries are recorded to help propagating the m^Q to P_d *(Q)*. In (Li & Wu 2005), each peer stores information of neighbor peers, such as the number of images and connections to other peers, and before propagating a m^Q, it estimates the gain and cost (overlay hops) of all neighbor peers to determine which peer to propagate the message first.

In terms of information retrieval (IR), methods such as breadth-first search (BFS), intelligent search mechanism (ISM), and random-walker searches (RWS) have been developed based on the P2P network (Zeinalipour-Yazti et al., 2004). In

Figure 1. (a) Napster structure, (b) Gnutella structure

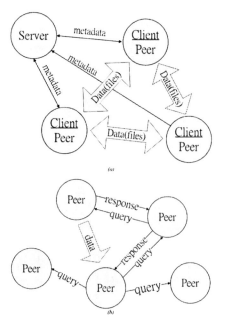

BFS, each peer propagates the m^Q to all neighbor peers such that the network traffic is increased due to trivial routings as shown in Figure 2(a). In ISM, retrieved results from destination peers of previous queries are recorded to help later queries to find the desired peers rapidly. In RWS as shown in Figure 2(b), each peer forwards the m^Q to one randomly selected peer, and then some peers are not visited in random walkers. It may lead that fewer relevant objects are searched while saving network traffic. As compared to RWS, BFS would yield better recall rate $R(Q)$, while it suffers heavy network traffic. The Gnutella-like efficient search system (GES) (Zhu et al.,2005) uses a biased walk at first and, after reaching relevant peers, it floods the m^Q to the all peers of this cluster. The biased walk probing saves bandwidth before the target peer/cluster being reached. Flooding the m^Q in the target peer cluster would increase the probability of m^Q to reach $P_d(Q)$. A hybrid search algorithm, similar to GES, is proposed to perform CBIR (Lin et al., 2004).

Concerning the P2P-CBIR, studies on the P2P information retrieval can be found by many (Liu et al., 2005; King et al., 2004; Eisenhardt et al., 2006; Zhanget al., 2004; Ardizzone et al., 2006). In general, image features are more complex than document information, especially in the P2P-CBIR system. A P2Padaptation R*-tree for indexing and querying multi-dimensional data is proposed (Liu et al., 2005) to reduce the query complexity. A mediator-free multi-agent P2P framework (Zhanget al., 2004) dynamically reorganizes the agent-view topology and deploys context-sensitive distributed search algorithm to improve the performance. An adaptive overlay routing algorithm (Ardizzone et al., 2006) adapts the network topology to peer interest to limit the network traffic cost and maximizes the usefulness of each activated peer. To reduce the network traffic of query passing, the firework query model(FQM) (King et al., 2004) utilizes random walk and flooding to forward the query message, in which

each peer records IDs (or attractive links) of relevant peers. When a query Q was received by one peer p, p computes the feature similarity between Q and the peer database I_p. When the similarity is higher than a predefined threshold T^I, a m^Q would be propagated by the flooding approach like an exploding firework. If not, the m^Q would be propagated by the random-walker approach. The time-to-live (TTL) is set to control the query depth for a Q.For more flexible query controls, when Q was propagated by attractive links, it also determines a probability of decreasing TTL, called chance-to-survive, to let a m^Q be propagated much deeper in the P2P overlay. These P2P-CBIR systems are designed to reduce the network traffic and to improve retrieval and mining performance from the viewpoint of forwarding query messages. However, controlling both retrieval and traffic on the backward routing path toward the query peer have not been well investigated. We propose to utilize forward and backward routing topology to progressively refine retrieval results and reduce the network traffic to improve the retrieval efficiency. The network traffic and query scope can be largely reduced as compared to previous researches, while still providing higher recall rate. Concerning the P2P-CBIRsystem performance, in addition to improving the precision $P(Q)$and recall rates $R(Q)$ of the single server retrieval, minimizing query scope $C(Q)$and maximizing efficiency $E(Q)$ are considered as control targets.

To perform CBIR based on server-client framework, the server has to record addresses and feature characteristics of all client peers. To respond a query, the server helps the query peer P_Q to forward the message m^Q to all peers with relevant contents. Relevant peers received m^Q would perform retrieval and transmit relevant images toward P_Q. This centralized approach suffers heavy network traffic in that unnecessary retrieval and transmission are involved. To eliminate the centralized traffic loading, we proposed

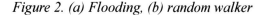

Figure 2. (a) Flooding, (b) random walker

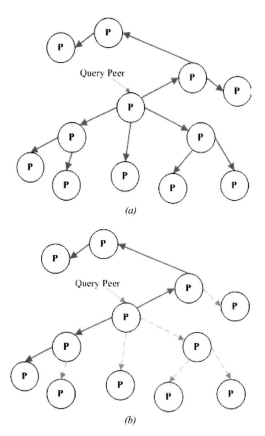

to perform CBIR based on the DU-P2P network framework. All activated peers perform retrieval and transmission concurrently and the retrieval accuracy are progressively refined through the level-by-level top-rank n_{top} image filtering.

Image Features and Retrieval

The MPEG-7 standard provides normative descriptors, such as color, texture, region, and shape descriptors, for effective visual data retrieval (Martinez, 2004; Bolettieri et al., 2009; Batko et al., 2010). These descriptors represent visual contents with numerical feature values from which the similarity could be measured quantitatively. They provide a numerical measurement space for image knowledge discovery and data mining (KDD). In general, one CBIR search engine provides the

relevance feedback function to recognize user's definition on image similarity. In addition, utilizing multiple feature types would help the search engine to increase the retrieval accuracy and reduce the network traffic in the P2P-CBIR system.

OVERVIEW OF CBIR AND MPEG-7

CBIR has been developed over the past decade since international image/video coding standards, such as JPEG, MPEG-1, -2, -4, have been widely used and distributed over Internet. People can easily find many relevant multimedia contents from Internet. However, with the growth of media contents and Internet, people can seek to find interest media contents through an effective CBIR multimedia search engine. Before developing the

CBIR search engine, text information is the only precise data for performing content similarity retrieval, i.e., filename, creator, and content descriptions. However, the text-based CBIR requires human annotation and content categorization, such that large scale retrieval is not feasible. In addition, the categorization and annotations would be different for different human, which would bias the retrieval results. The MPEG-7 was proposed to provide formal image descriptors for an objective CBIR platform, by which users need only to provide some query images for the search engine to perform CBIR from an large scale image database. The similarity between two media object is measured by computing the Euclidean distance between the two numerical feature descriptors. Notwithstanding, the algorithms used to extract meaningful features exactly from an image will dominate the CBIR performance. Since efficient retrieval algorithms alone cannot promise good CBIR performance based on biased/imprecise image descriptors. Previous works, such as IBM's Query by Image Content (QBIC) (Flickner et al., 1995), Blobworld (Carson et al., 2002), and VisualSEEk (Smith & Chang 1996), extract low-level features from locally segmented image regions. For the QBIC system, it manually identifies the objects or regions in images. The color, texture, and shape features could be extracted from the objects, regions, or the whole image. The Blobworld proposed to segment an image into a set of regions that are coherent in color and texture features. The similarity between the query image and the one in database is computed through the similarity regions matching. The VisualSEEk extracts the color and texture features from the salient regions segmented in the images, and further takes the geometric properties of regions (e.g., size, absolute and relative spatial locations) into considerations. PicToSeek (Gevers & Smeulders 2000) is an object based retrieval system. It considers the invariants of color and shape features for the object in each image based on the criteria:

illumination conditions, viewpoint invariance, and geometry properties of the object. However, how to justify image segmentation results become critical in terms of image segmentation techniques. In addition, the problem of computing a similar region pair set with the maximum covered area is NP-hard (Natsev, Rastogi & Shim, 1998). Some researches (Rahmani, et al., 2008; Chen et al., 2006; Zhang et al., 2005) applied the multi-instance learning measure to select the semantic regions from query images automatically. The selected regions of query images are labeled as common positive from users' relevance feedback. Instead of using supervised or semi-supervised image segmentation methods, we proposed to developed un-supervised segmentation method to extract low-level features, such as color, texture and shape, from the entire image without time-consuming pre-processing.

In recently years, several researches (Deselaers et al., 2008; Datta et al., 2008; Liu et al., 2011) proposed to extract global or local features from images to perform image classification and image/video retrieval. To extract the local features from images, Scale Invariant Feature Transform (SIFT) (Lowe 2004) is a widely used descriptor that extracts distinctive invariant keypoints from local patches in images. Based on the clustering procedure, each patch described by the feature keypoint is categorized into the set corresponding to specific words. Therefore, a bag-of-words (BOW) (Fei-Fei & Perona 2005; Quelhas & Odobez 2007) is built as the feature vector to describe the visual content of one image. Speeded Up Robust Features (SURF) (Bay et al., 2006) descriptor approximates the second order Gaussian derivatives in Hessian matrix, and exploits integral images to extract the local feature points. Principal Component Analysis (PCA)-SIFT (Ke & Sukthankar 2004) projects the normalized gradient image vector to a compact feature vector. As compared to the SIFT, it spends less time for matching between two images when using SURF and PCA-SIFT, since SURF and PCA-

SIFT descriptors demonstrate lower dimensional feature vectors (Juan & Gwun 2009). In contrast, global features can be extracted from images such as color correlogram and Tamura texture descriptors. The color correlogram (Huang et al., 1997) considers the spatial correlation between pairs of pixels' colors with distance. As compared to the color histogram, color correlogram is more robust to different image processing procedures (e.g., spatial translation, different view of the same scene, and large changes in appearance). For Tamura texture descriptor (Tamura et al., 1978), the authors propose six basic texture features corresponding to human visual perception: coarseness, contrast, directionality, line-likeness, regularity, and roughness. Experiments suggest that the first three texture features are useful for images classification and segmentation.

The MPEG-7 specifies the syntax for standard media description. The CBIR is usually developed based on the formal description platform. Figure 3 depicts a processing chain to explain the scope of the MPEG-7 standard. The MPEG-7 specifies many formal multimedia description methods, which include still pictures, graphic, audio, video, speech, 3D models, and composition information. Based on MPEG-7, formal image descriptors (e.g., color, region, contour, and texture) can be extracted and utilized for objective CBIR. In general, relevance feedback or multi-instance query mechanisms are provided for user to refine the query results. The retrieved images will be sorted according to their similarity to the query sample(s) and the N top-ranked images are displayed in the interface for advanced refine procedures.

Color Descriptors

Presenting images with an appropriate color space (e.g., RGB, HSV, CIE Lab or the Hue-Max-Min-Difference (HMMD)) (Manjunath et al., 2001; Coimbra et al., 2006) would help to represent color features with little data redundancy. One of MPEG-7 color descriptors (Martinez, 2004), dominant color descriptor (DCD) (Manjunath et al., 2001) is used to describe the representative colors in an image or an image region. Scalable color descriptor (SCD) (Manjunath et al., 2001) is derived from a color histogram in HSV color space, which is normalized as the input histogram through Haar transform. The high- and low-pass coefficients obtained from Haar transform are quantized to n-bins color histogram that represents the colors of an image. Color layout descriptor (CLD) (Manjunath et al., 2001) describes the spatial color distributions of an image. First, the image is divided into 8×8 blocks, and the average color of each block is computed as the representative corresponding color. Each block represents the corresponding color in the original image is regarded as a pixel to present a new 8×8 tiny image. Then, the tiny image by DCT transformation extracts the DC and AC coefficients in zigzag order that consist of the CLD. Color structure descriptor (CSD) (Manjunath et al., 2001) represents an image as a scalable quantized n-bins color histogram in the HMMD color space. CSD describes the color distribution and the color spatial structure in one image. In considering that HSV and HMMD color spaces resemble human color perception, they are used to perform im-

Figure 3. The scope of the MPEG-7 standard

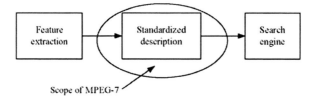

382

ages search and retrieval. Furthermore, considering the color distribution and spatial structure of the color in an image, we apply the CSD with three components, i.e., Hue $(H = [0°, 360°])$, colorfulness Diff (=[0, 255]) and brightness of color Sum (=[0, 255]), which are quantized to 128-bins color structure histogram of one image in the HMMD space. In addition, it is verified (Chatzichristofis & Boutalis, 2008; Shao et al., 2007) that the CSD would yield the best retrieval results as compared to the other three MPEG-7 color descriptors. The CSD histogram is invariant under shift, rotation, translation, and shape changed in one image. CSD is represented as: $f_{color}(I) = \{f_{colori}\}_{i=1,2,...,n^c} = \{h(1), h(2), ..., h(n^c)\}$, where n^c is the number of color bins that quantizes the color space and $h(\cdot)$ is the number of quantized colors for a specific bin appeared for the whole image. It uses the histogram intersection of two $f_{color}s$ to measure the similarity between two images, a and b, i.e.,

$$S(f_{color}(a), f_{color}(b)) = \frac{1}{l_t} \frac{\sum_{i=1}^{l_t} \min(f_{colori}^a, f_{colori}^b)}{\max(f_{colori}^a, f_{colori}^b)}, \quad (1)$$

where $l_t = |f_{color}|$ is the dimension of the feature vector f_{color}, and $0 \le S(\cdot) \le 1$. For clarity, the similarity between images a and b, in terms of color feature, is denoted as

$$S_{color}^I(a, b) = S(f_{color}(a), f_{color}(b)). \quad (2)$$

Texture Descriptors

The MPEG-7 specified texture descriptors, such as edge histogram descriptor (EHD) (Martinez, 2004), are adopted to describe natural images in large-scale P2P network databases. Specifically, dividing the image into 4×4 subimages, each subimage is described with the local-edge distri-

bution by five edge types: vertical, horizontal, 45° diagonal, 135° diagonal and nondirectional edges. Based on the histogram of the five edge types from all the 16 subimages (i.e., 16×5=80 histogram bins), a local EHD is presented to describe the local texture properties of an image. To provide robust image matching, the EHD also adopts both global and semi-global edge distribution with five edge types in an image. The other texture descriptors, such as the discrete wavelet transform (DWT) (Kokare et al., 2007), can also effectively extract the image texture characteristics. For the DWT, the 4-tap Daubechies (1992) filter is applied to decompose one image twice to yield 7 sub-bands *(SB)*. The Energy and Standard Deviation of each sub-band are computed and, as a result, the 7 sub-bands provide a texture vector (i.e., 14 histogram bins) to represent the image. The Energy μ_{SB_i} and Standard Deviation SD_{SB_i} for each sub-band SB_i are defined as follows:

$$\mu_{SB_i} = \frac{1}{M_i \times N_i} \sum_{x=1}^{M_i} \sum_{y=1}^{N_i} \left| SB_{xy}^i \right|, i = 0, 1, ..., 6, \quad and \quad (3)$$

$$SD_{SB_i} = \left[\frac{1}{M_i \times N_i} \sum_{x=1}^{M_i} \sum_{y=1}^{N_i} (SB_{xy}^i - \mu_{SB_i})^2 \right]^{\frac{1}{2}}, \quad i = 0, 1, ..., 6, \quad (4)$$

where SB_{xy}^i denotes the i-th wavelet coefficient to calculate the μ_{SB_i} and SD_{SB_i} in sub-band SB_i with size $M_i \times N_i$. The similarity in texture descriptor between images a and b is measured by

$$S_{texture}^I(a, b) = \left\| f_{texture}(a) - f_{texture}(b) \right\|^{-1}, \quad (5)$$

where $\|f\|$ denotes the Euclidean norm of the vector f.

Shape Descriptors

For 2-D binary images, the MPEG-7 region shape descriptors(Martinez, 2004),angular radial transform (ART) coefficients, are represented as $f_s(I) = \{F_{nm} / F_{00}\}$, where

$$F_{nm} = \int_{\theta=0}^{2\pi} \int_{\rho=0}^{1} V_{nm}^*(\rho,\theta). \ I(\rho,\theta)\rho d\rho d\theta, I(\rho,\theta)$$

is the image signal function in polar coordinates and $V_{nm}^*(\rho,\theta)s$ are the ART basis functions(Bober 2001) with different order m and repetition n along radial and angular directions, respectively. The region shape descriptor can describe various shapes composed of several sub-regions or disjoint regions. To automatically segment shapes from volume images, instead of utilizing heuristic methods with fine-tuned control parameters, it uses a general processing method to yield unwanted perturbations in the segmented result such as speckles and biased shapes. In terms of contour shaped escriptors (Biswas et al., 2010), our practical implementations for automatically segmenting shape contours are not easy to obtain semantically correct result. The histogram of edge directions (HED) (Chalechale et al., 2005) is used to represent the shape information of an image by Mohamed (2004), who utilizes Canny edge detector to extract the significant edges along horizontal, vertical and two diagonal directions. Another work (Yoo et al., 2002) also applies Canny edge detector on one image to extract the edges, which are quantized into 72 bins with edge orientations that are $5°$ apart. To support the scale invariant property, the quantized 72 bins vector is normalized by the total number of image-blocks. The similarity in the shape feature between images a and b is measured by

$$S_{shape}^I(a,b) = \left\| f_{shape}(a) - f_{shape}(b) \right\|^{-1}, \qquad (6)$$

where $\left\| f \right\|$ denotes the Euclidean norm of the shape feature vector f.

Similarity Measure between Peer Databases

To perform CBIR in P2P networks, it needs to configure the system based on image characteristics in peer databases. Each image in the database of p is described with four features including: (1) color structure descriptor (CSD);(2) one texture feature of edge histogram descriptor (EHD); (3) one texture feature of discrete wavelet transform (DWT); (4) shape descriptor for histogram of edge directions (HED). Let l_t and n_t^p denote the size of the feature vector f_t and the number of images in the database of peer p, respectively, and t is the feature vector type for $t \in \{Color, Texture1, Texture2, Shape\}$. Statistical behaviors, such as mean μ_t^p and standard deviation σ_t^p feature vectors, are computed for similarity measurement between peers, i.e.,

$$\mu_t^p = \left\{ \mu_{tj}^p \right\}_{j=1.2....l_t} =$$
$$\left\{ E_k \left[f_{tj}^k \right] = \frac{1}{n_t^p} \sum_{k=1}^{n_t^p} f_{tj}^k \right\}_{j=1.2....l_t}, \qquad (7)$$

and

$$\sigma_t^p = \left\{ \sigma_{tj}^p \right\}_{j=1.2....l_t} =$$
$$\left\{ \frac{1}{n_t^p} \sum_{k=1}^{n_t^p} (f_{tj}^k - \mu_{tj}^p)^2 \right\}_{j=1.2....l_t},$$

The similarity measurement, in terms of texture feature, between two peers' image databases, A and B, is computed as

$$S_{texture1}^p(A,B) = \left[\frac{\left\| \mu_{texture1}^A - \mu_{texture1}^B \right\| \times}{\sqrt{\sigma_{texture1}^A \cdot \sigma_{texture1}^B}} \right]^{-1}, \qquad (8)$$

where the "$\cdot$" symbol denotes inner product. Larger $S_{texture1}^p$ values mean that vectors $\mu_{texture1}^A$

and $\mu_{texture1}^{B}$ are close to each other and elements in vectors, $\sigma_{texture1}^{A}$ and $\sigma_{texture1}^{B}$, are small, i.e., the database images of A and B are with similar and homogeneous feature properties. The similarity measurements, in terms of texture2 and shape features, between two peers' image databases, *A* and *B*, are also computed following Equation (8). For color feature, the similarity measurement between image databases of peers A and B is computed as

$$S_{color}^{p}(A,B) = \frac{1}{l_t} \frac{\sum_{i=1}^{l_t} \min\left(\mu_{colori}^{A}, \mu_{colori}^{B}\right)}{\max\left(\mu_{colori}^{A}, \mu_{colori}^{B}\right)}.$$

(9)

Multi-Instance Query with Multiple Features

In CBIR applications, multi-instance query or relevance feedback interface are usually provided to enhance retrieval efficiency. In addition, more than one kind of feature can be extracted from one image. Performing multi-instance query with multi-feature types is assigned proper weighting factors to different feature types and ranks (Jin & French, 2005), which would help to yield relatively accurate and stable retrieval results. In general, the retrieval algorithm is designed based on pre-processing results. We proposed to perform multi-instance query with multi-feature types on the P2P paradigm to provide progressive and scalable retrieval functions. Above features are extracted from images to provide robust retrieval performance through multi-instance query. For the multi-instance query, denoted by $Q=\{q(1), q(2),...,q(n^Q)\}$, the search engine has to find the representative feature vector for a Q. Support Vector Machines (SVM) (Nello, 2000) and Adaboost (Freund, 1997) are widely used to find salient common features among query samples according to different feature types. For simple and regular operations, the mean feature

vector is adopted as the representative feature vector. The salient common feature, denoted by m^Q, is used as the representative feature vector for the multi-instance query. As several feature types are involved in the retrieval, each image in the database would present different ranks for different feature types.

Denote the database of a peer p as

$$I_p = \left\{I(k)\right\}_{k=1,2,...,n_I^p}.$$

Experiments show that the representative feature vector consists only 5% to 7% of the overall feature elements, while still providing high recall rates and retrieval accuracy. Due to different feature characteristics, it uses the mean feature vectors of color, texture1, texture2 and shape as the representative feature vectors for a Q, i.e., m_{color}^{Q}, $m_{texture1}^{Q}$, $m_{texture2}^{Q}$, and m_{shape}^{Q}, respectively. The similarity between m_t^Q and the image can be measured as $S_t^I(m_t^Q, f_t^{I(k)})$, where $t \in \left\{Color, Texture1, Texture2, Shape\right\}$ [cf. (2), (5) and (6)]. For feature type t, the rank $r_t^Q(I(k))$ reports how $I(k)$ resembles Q relatively. A small rank corresponds to high similarity. The set of ranked list for feature type t could be represented as

$$R_t^Q(I_p) = \left\{r_t^Q(I(k))\right\}_{k=1,2,...,n_I^p},$$

(10)

where

$$r_t^Q(I(a)) < r_t^Q(I(b))$$

if $S_t(m_t^Q, f_t^{I(a)}) > S_t(m_t^Q, f_t^{I(b)})$. To evaluate the similarity rank for one candidate image $I(k)$, the integrated rank is computed as (Jeong et al., 1999)

$$r^Q(I(k)) = \sum_t w_t \times r_t^Q(I(k)).$$

(11)

In general, the weights for feature type t, w_t, should be made larger to reflect the saliency of the feature type against other ones (Chang & Hang, 2006). The normalized correlation coefficient (NCC), which is computed for feature elements of the same type, is adopted to evaluate the feature saliency. The control steps to compute the weighting w_t for the integrated rank for a query Q are listed below.

1. Calculate the mean feature vector of feature type t off Q, similar to (7), i.e.,

$$\mu_t^Q = \left\{ \mu_{ti}^Q = E_k \left[m_{ti}^{q(k)} \right] \right\}_{i=1,2,\dots,l_t}, \quad (12)$$

where $E_k \left[m_{ti}^{q(k)} \right]$ is the average of $m_{ti}^{q(k)}$ with respect to index k.

2. Compute the NCC of type t in regard to the query image $q(k)$ and the mean feature vector μ_t^Q : Let

$$m_t^k = \left\{ m_{ti}^{q(k)} - E_i \left[m_{ti}^{q(k)} \right] \right\}_{i=1,2,\dots,l_t} \quad \text{and}$$

$$M_t^Q = \left\{ \mu_{ti}^Q - E_i \left[\mu_{ti}^Q \right] \right\}_{i=1,2,\dots,l_t}, \quad \text{the average}$$

of NCCs for the type t can be computed as

$$NCC(t) = \frac{1}{n^Q} \sum_{k=1}^{n^Q} \left[\frac{m_t^k}{\left\| m_t^k \right\|} \cdot \frac{M_t^Q}{\left\| M_t^Q \right\|} \right]. \quad (13)$$

3. The normalized weights for each feature type are computed as $w_t = NCC(t) / \sum_{i=1}^{n_t} NCC(i)$, for $t \in \left\{ Color, Texture1, Texture2, Shape \right\}$.

The similarity measure in (11) is imposed on every candidate image in I_p and another ranked list is obtained

$$\hat{I}_p = NCCA(I_p) = \left\{ \hat{I}(k) \right\}_{k=1,2,\dots,n_I^p} \quad (14)$$

where

$$r^Q(\hat{I}(k)) \le r^Q(\hat{I}(k+1))$$

THE P2P-CBIR SYSTEM

The peer clustering and update procedures are performed to configure the DU-P2PCBIR system to compromise well with DS-P2P while reserves flexible routing control properties. The peer clustering is performed based on the similarity between peer databases with specific image features, i.e., $S_t^p(\cdot)$ in (8) and (9), while using the represented feature vectors of peer p consist of μ_t^p and σ_t^p in (7) for $t \in \left\{ Color, Texture1, Texture2, Shape \right\}$ as p's four clustering centroids. After clustering, each peer would record IDs of peers with similar database features. To provide regular P2P operations, each peer records of the most relevant peers n_E in regard to similarity measurement of each feature type $t \in \left\{ Color, Texture1, Texture2, Shape \right\}$, respectively, as attractive links $\left\{ \vec{E}_k^t s \mid k = 1,2,\dots,n_E \right\}$ shown in Figure 4(a). In addition, for irrelevant peers n_R to propagate m^Q to potential target peers, random links $\left\{ \vec{R}_k s \mid k = 1,2,\dots,n_R \right\}$ are used. If m^Q was transferred to a peer p whose database bears little relevance to Q, then p propagated Q through $\vec{R}_k s$. The regular operations of one peer, i.e., receive and transmit the query message and relevant results, are shown in Figure4(b).If one peer received a m^Q, it can propagate the m^Q to other peers through $\vec{E}_k s$ or $\vec{R}_k s$. When one active p is performing retrieval, the broadcasting policy unit (BPU) computes the similarity between the m^Q and mean feature vector of images in I_p, i.e.,

$$S_t^p = S \left(m_t^Q, \mu_t^p \right) \quad (15)$$

for $t \in \left\{ Color, Texture1, Texture2, Shape \right\}$. If $S_t^p > T_t$ for p, which means that I_p contains relevant images of Q, the search engine finds out and transmits relevant images to the source peer p_s and then p propagates m^Q through $\vec{E}_k^t s$, else through $\vec{R}_k s$. By using attractive links, the retrieval accuracy can be improved while speeding up the retrieval process. In contrast, the random link is used to provide the random walk function to diverse the query when irrelevant peers are visited.

The internal architecture of peers in the proposed P2P-CBIR system is illustrated in Figure 4(c). The I/O units $(I/O_1 \ and \ I/O_2)$ not only deal with inputs and outputs from target and source peers, respectively, but also receive and analyze the m^Q and header information of m^Q, $h(m^Q)$. The operations and information processed by one peer p consists of: (1) the caller ID of $h(m^Q)$ for p to transmit relevant images to its source peer p_s and; (2) check against the local cache to avoid processing duplicated query messages; (3) analyze m^Q and determine the weights for different feature types; (4) $h(m^Q)$ records Time-To-Live (TTL) to control the query propagation depth; and (5) perform CBIR using feature vectors m_t^Q. The I/O_1 is responsible to transmit the retrieved results to the source peer specified by the caller ID, and receives m^Q from its source peer p_s. The I/O_2 propagates m^Q to peers through either $\vec{E}_k s$ or $\vec{R}_k s$, according to the decision of the BPU and receives the relevant results from its destination peers p_{d^s}. The received images from target peers will be stored in the image buffer I_p^{buf} during retrieval such that the properties of the local database I_p will not be influenced. The search engine performs similarity retrieval on the database union, i.e., $\hat{I}_p = NCCA(I_p \cup I_p^{buf})$.

Considering network traffics, only top-ranked n_{top} images would be transmitted at each processing stage. The re-indexing operation, $NCCA(I_p \cup I_p^{buf})$, would be performed when the source peer requests the active peer for relevant images. In transmitting relevant images, the threshold T_t^I is set to control the user requested image similarity. If link similarity measurements, S_{color}^p, $S_{texture1}^p$, $S_{texture2}^p$ and S_{shape}^p, are smaller than

the threshold, which means that the m^Q has not been forwarded to the expected peer, the query Q will be propagated through $\vec{R}_k s$. In this case, the TTL value will also be decreased by one. When *TTL* becomes 0, it would not propagate m^Q anymore.

In terms of performance evaluations, in addition to recall and precision, the query scope and query efficiency (King et al., 2004) are defined to evaluate objectively the P2P-CBIR performance: 1) the Recall $R(Q)$ reports the success rate of the desired results retrieved for the query, i.e., $R(Q) = \left(\left| I_R \wedge I_G \right| / I_G \right)$, where $I_R = I_R(Q)$ and $I_G = I_G(Q)$ denote the retrieved relevant images and the set of ground-truth images of Q in the P2P network, respectively, and $\left| I \right|$ denotes the number of images in the set I; (2) Query scope $C(Q)$ is the fraction of visited peers for a $Q : C(Q) = V(Q) / N_{peer}$, where $V(Q)$ is the number of peers that have been activated for the Q and N_{peer} is the total number of peers in the P2P network; (3) Query efficiency is defined as the ratio between $R(Q)$ and $C(Q) : E(Q) = R(Q) / C(Q)$. If the algorithm can retrieve more relevant images and visit fewer peers, the value of $E(Q)$ will be larger.

Scalable Retrieval

In general, one peer will start to transmit retrieved results when it completed the query of m_t^Q. Some peers have to wait for transmitting relevant images during the query such that the network bandwidth and allowed transmission time are not fully utilized. When the peer p receives a Q or m^Q, and completes the query, it starts to transmit retrieved images to p_s and at the same time, determines how to propagate the m^Q. If the number of relevant images in one peer p is smaller than n_{top}, all relevant images in p will be transmitted from p to p_s. However, it could save transfer time not used for other peers.

Figure 4. P2P configuration: (a) the system diagram of the P2P-CBIR system; and (b) the input and output of a peer; and (c) the internal structure of one peer

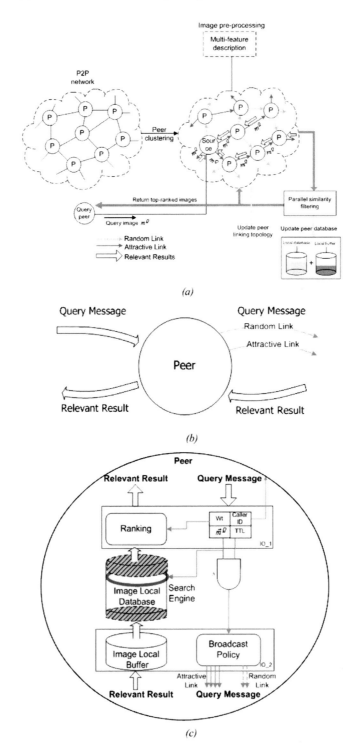

The process of scalable retrieval is described with the aid of Figure 5. The framed alphabets denote the peer IDs, whose retrieved results have been received by the query peer and the framed number indicates how many relevant images are retrieved in p. The timing analysis, provided later, indicates that the time to perform retrieval is much less than the time to transmit one image. To simplify the description for the scalable retrieval, the query peer is assumed to complete the retrieval right after receiving the query, as shown in Figure 5(a). At time $t=1$, the peer A propagates the query m^Q to B, C, and D, according to the BPU decision and the TTL values is decreased by one. The retrieval operations are assumed to be completed at the same time slot as shown in Figure 5(b). At time $t=2$, C propagates m^Q to E, and D propagates m^Q to F and G simultaneously, as shown in Figure 5(c). At the same time slot, the retrieval operations on E, F, and G are completed and B starts to transmit the retrieved relevant images, $\hat{I}_B(\cdot)$, to its source peer A. Considering practical computer gateways, peer A can only receive retrieved results from B at one link time, instead of B, C and D simultaneously. At time $t=3$, while B is still transmitting images, E begins to transmit retrieved images to C, and F to D [Figure 5(d)]. In Figure 5(e), when B completes its transmission after F, C begins to transmit the retrieved images at time $t=4$. At the same time, E keeps and G starts their transmissions. The peer E would complete its transmission before G, whose transmission was delayed due to F's, as shown in Figure 5(f). The peer C needs much time for transmission because it has more relevant images about Q [Figure 5(g)]. D starts to transmit images after C completing its transmission at time $t=8$, as shown in Figure 5(h).

When all relevant images of the activated peers, e.g., A, B,…,G have been received by the query peer A, it would send one signal to notify the user. Instead of waiting for the whole query process to be completed, users can decide to stop the query process at any time when satisfactory results have been presented by the query peer.

RECONFIGURABLE P2P-CBIR

For the P2P-CBIR to respond a query Q, each activated peer constantly performs similarity retrieval from its local database, and transmits n_{top} relevant images to its source peer until the process is completed. As the connected peers are ready for multi-purpose applications, the local image database characteristics would be time-varying. To reflect the most updated local database characteristics, reconfiguring the P2P-CBIR profile at each regular time interval is required. In addition, peer clustering information, i.e., attractive and random links, is also updated accordingly. This reconfiguration procedure requires little time-complexity and can be performed dynamically at suitable time according to peer computation loading and network connection conditions. This P2P-CBIR reconfiguration helps to accurately forward m^Q to target peers and effectively reduces trivial peer routing and retrieval operations due to imprecise configuration.

Timing Analysis

The network traffic versus peer transferring time during the query process is analyzed to observe the performance along the elapsing time. At first, the operation time for performing retrieval within one peer is analyzed. For one Pentium-4 2GCPU, one peer spends about 10^{-3} seconds in total to perform the retrieval, which includes: 1) 9.3×10^{-4}secs. in performing the NCCA similarity retrieval algorithm; 2) 4.2×10^{-4}secs. in sorting and providing ranks for each image in $(I_p \cup I_{buf})$; 3) 4×10^{-5}secs. to determine the broadcasting policy. If the available transmission rate is 100 kbps and one image size is about 10 kbytes, then it needs about $T_m = 10^{-1}$ seconds to transmit one image,

Figure 5. Scalable retrieval example, where the dashed circles denote peers which would be but have not been activated at that time

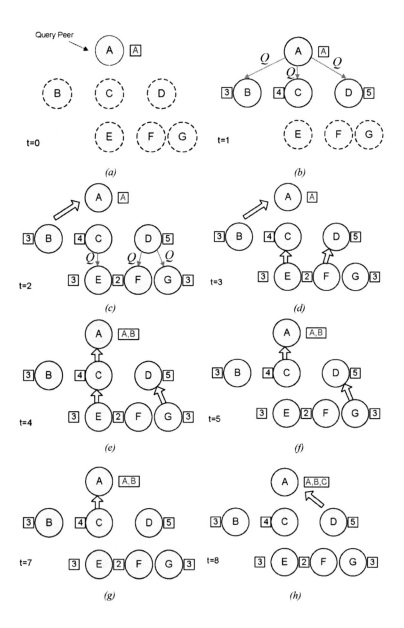

which is much longer than that of the retrieval operation time in one peer. In addition, the time needed to broadcast a m^Q is also small, as compared to T_m, since the size of the representative feature vector would be smaller than 100 bytes. The retrieval processing time and the broadcasting time can thus be ignored to simplify the timing analysis. The IDs of activated peers and the streaming between two peers are demonstrated in Figure 6(a). The three vertical lines represent three different hops (or query depths) in the P2P networks and the downward arrow denotes the direction of elapsing time. The peer IDs along the elapsing time denote peers whose relevant images have been received by the query peer at that time.

In practical retrieval and mining operations, the link time of two peers would be determined by how many relevant images are there in the destination peer, such that the number of images received by the query peer may not be the same as those shown in Figure 6(a). For example, the second "*D to A*" transmission would deliver the relevant images retrieved from peers {*F*, *G*} to *A*, since it begins after peers *F* and *G* having completed their transmissions.

After the query process being completed, the number of average active peers at time can be obtained by

$$n_{peer}(t) = \sum_{p \in P_{op}} (t \in T_p)?1:0, \tag{16}$$

where P_{op} records all the activated peers for one query Q and T_p records the active time periods $\left[t_p^1, t_p^2\right]$ of the peer p. Equation (16) is self-ex-

Figure 6. Timing analyses of the P2P-CBIR system: (a) timing diagram of the scalable retrieval, and (b) active periods of each peer along the elapsed time

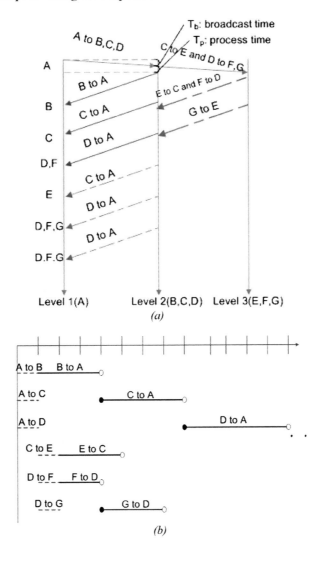

plained with the help of Figure6(b). The execution of the function $n_{peer}(t)$ is just computing the crossing points along the vertical direction for a certain time index t in Figure 6(b).

Bandwidth Loading

In the proposed P2P-CBIR system, the average bandwidth loading (Yang & Garcia-Molina, 2002) of each activated peer was estimated for evaluation. Initially, the m^Q was transferred from p_Q which acts as the source peer p_s. As shown in Figure 1(a), the source peer p_s transmits the m^Q to its three peers through attractive links when the similarity between m^Q and local database is

higher than a threshold. The initial Time-To-Live is set to $TTL=L$ to control the query scope. The activated peers further transmit m^Q with the same forwarding strategy to other relevant peers whose $TTL=L-1$. When the m^Q was transmitted to one peer with $TTL=0$, it will not be propagated anymore which means the m^Q has reached the boundary of the specified query scope. The total bandwidth loading for propagation m^Q in the P2P-CBIR process is calculated as

$$BW_{forward} = \left[\sum_{\ell=L}^{0} N_p^\ell(Q) \right] \times \left[m^Q + h(m^Q) \right],$$

(17)

Figure 7. Performance comparisons among FQM, BFS, P2P-CBIR with and without reconfigurations: (a) average efficiency at different TTLs; (b) recall rate at different TTLs; (c) network traffic loading along elapsed time during retrieval process; (d) recall rate along elapsed time during retrieval process

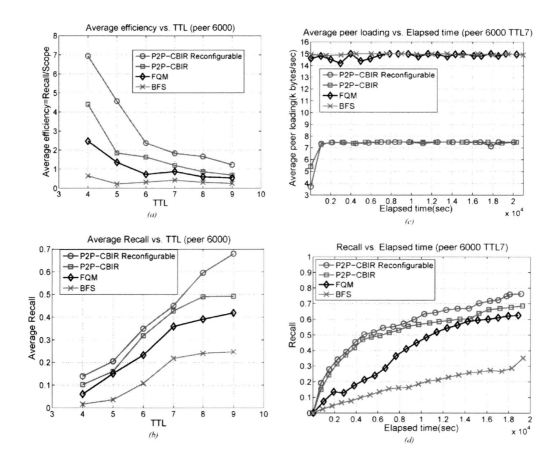

Figure 8. Subjective performance evaluations of the P2P-CBIR in progressive refinement and multi-instance query, with 1000 total peers and TTL = 7. One-instance query: (a) retrieved images with one-instance query at 20th sec; (b) retrieved images with one-instance query at 30th sec. Two-instance query: (c) retrieved images with two-instance query at 20th sec; (d) retrieved images with two-instance query at 30th sec.

(a) Retrieved images with one-instance query at 20th sec.

(b) Retrieved images with one-instance query at 30th sec.

(c) Retrieved images with two-instance query at 20th sec.

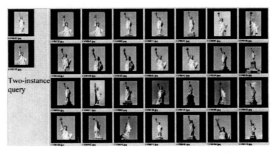

(d) Retrieved images with two-instance query at 30th sec.

where $Q, m^Q, h(m^Q)$ and $N_p^\ell(Q)$ denote the query instance(s), query message size, header information of m^Q and the number of operative peers at level ℓ, respectively. In our experiments, one query message m^Q contains four feature vectors, which can be packaged within 4k bytes. The other meta-data, such as query peer ID, current TTL, image format, and image resolution are stored in the header $h(m^Q)$, which required 80 bytes.

At the backward stage, all operative peers keep re-ranking and transmitting images at the same time and the whole system keep filtering top-ranked images progressively level-by-level toward p_Q. The average bandwidth loading of the retrieval backward stage can be represented by the following equation:

$$BW_{backward} = \sum_{t=0}^{T_A(Q)} \sum_{\ell=L}^{0} \sum_{i=1}^{N_p^\ell} \left[\begin{matrix} N_i^p(m^Q, \ell, t) \times \\ (|I_{th}| + |h(m^Q)|) \end{matrix} \right]_{-}^{-},$$

where the $|I_{th}|$ and $|h(m^Q)|$ denote the image (thumbnail) size and header size, $N_i^p(m^Q, \ell, t)$ denotes the number of descendant peers that would transmit retrieved top-ranked images to the ith peer at level $TTL = \ell$ at time t and $T_A(Q)$ is the total retrieval operation time for the query Q. The thumbnail image size is 10k bytes and the image header requires 80 bytes. The header $h(m^Q)$ consisted of the query peerID, current TTL, image format and image resolution etc. With above bandwidth analysis for forward and backward stages of retrieval represented in Equations (17)-(18), the average traffic loading for one peer can be estimated by

$$\bar{m}_{BW} = (BW_{forward} + BW_{backward}) / V(Q),$$
(19)

where $V(Q)$ is the number of peers that have been activated for query during the retrieval process, and the network traffic performance is evaluated based on $\bar{m}_{BW}$.

EXPERIMENTAL STUDY

The databases consist of 20000 images with 150 categories (ground-truth-set), some are collected from Corel image database and Caltech 101 (Fei-Fei et al., 2004), and the others are collected from professional image database websites. Each peer contains 15 images from the same category and 5 randomly selected images from different categories. For peer clustering, each peer records three random links and two attractive links for SCD, EHD, DWT and HED features, respectively. The retrieval efficiency, defined as recall-rate/query-scope, under different TTLs for different retrieval control strategy in 6000 peers. Figure 7(a) shows that the proposed reconfigurable P2P-CBIR demonstrates the highest retrieval efficiency for different TTLs. In addition, the efficiency is the highest for the smallest TTL, which means that the reconfigurable P2P-CBIR can retrieve relatively relevant images that producing better recall rate in a shorter period of time for different TTLs, as shown in Figure 7(b). The P2P-CBIR with and without reconfiguration both show better retrieval efficiency than the FQM and BFS, while activating fewer peers and consuming less bandwidth as compared to the latter. Figure 7(c) shows that the average per peer network traffic loading is 15 kbytes/sec in FQM and BFS CBIR, while the P2P-CBIR with and without reconfiguration consumes only 7.5 kbytes/sec along different elapsed time. For the recall rate at different elapsed time, Figure 7(d) shows that the proposed P2P-CBIR with and without reconfiguration could retrieve more relevant images and yield higher recall rate than that of the FQM and BFS. For FQM and BFS CBIR topologies, each active peer directly transmits the n_{top} relevant images to the

p_Q that yields heavy computations and bandwidth loading for p_Q, as compared to the P2P-CBIR with and without reconfiguration, which efficient distributes loadings to each peer. During the retrieval, the user can decide to stop the process when he is satisfied subjectively by the retrieved results, in which the whole active peers can be released instantly.

Subjective retrieval performance evaluation is provided in Figure 8. The progressive refinement capability can be verified by observing the accuracy of retrieved images. As shown, the most top 28 relevant images were retrieved along the elapsed time for given one- and two-instance query. As compared to that of one-instance query, the two-instance query yielded higher retrieval accuracy with the contribution of relevance feedback, cf. Figures 8(a)-(d). During the retrieval, the user can decide to stop the process when he is satisfied subjectively by the retrieved results, in which the whole active peers can be released instantly.

CONCLUSION

We proposed a P2P-CBIR system that can perform image retrieval in the Internet scale. A progressive and scalable retrieval algorithm was developed based on this P2P-CBIR system. Experiments demonstrated better retrieval performances than previous works, e.g., higher recall rate and shorter waiting time, which would effectively improve image knowledge discovery. Major contributions of the proposed P2P-CBIR system are: (1) Performing multi-instance retrieval with multiple features on Internet database effectively utilized the processing and transmission capability of P2P framework to provide efficient retrieval service; (2) Progressive refinement mechanism is developed based on the regular level-by-level retrieval and transmission operations; (3) Reconfiguration can be performed based on the P2P-CBIR framework to yield better retrieval performances,

e.g., higher retrieval accuracy and lower network traffic; (4) It effectively distributes the computation and bandwidth loadings into connected peers and demonstrates lower network traffic loading, as compared to the FQM and BFS frameworks.

For potential future researches, performing the P2P-CBIR on a larger network scale would reveal more practical message passing and transmission bottlenecks, which, when improved, would help the proposed P2P-CBIR to operate on a larger scale. In the P2P networks, peers are assumed to be logically connected. The timing analysis and performance evaluations were developed based on this assumption. For practical P2P network routing topology, it needs to investigate the physical linking properties and transmission delay to enhance the feasibility of our method. In addition, how to cluster peers according to different retrieval and mining targets under different conditions, e.g., retrieval frequencies, database properties and scales, to enhance the retrieval and mining efficiency with above mentioned works are considered as future researches.

REFERENCES

Ardizzone, E., Gatani, L., Cascia, M. L., Re, G. L., & Ortolani, M. (2006). Enhanced P2P services providing multimedia content. In *Proceedings of the IEEE International Symposium on Multimedia*, (pp. 637-646).

Batko, M. (2010). Building a web-scale image similarity search system. *Multimedia Tools and Applications*, *47*(3), 599–623. doi:10.1007/s11042-009-0339-z

Bay, H., Tuytelaars, T., & Gool, L. V. (2006). Surf: speeded up robust features. *In Computer Vision - ECCV*, Vol. 3951, (pp. 404-417).

Biswas, S., Aggarwal, G., & Chellappa, R. (2010). An efficient and robust algorithm for shape indexing and retrieval. *IEEE Transactions on Multimedia*, *12*(5). doi:10.1109/TMM.2010.2050735

Bober, M. (2001). MPEG-7 visual shape descriptors. *IEEE Transactions on Circuits and Systems for Video Technology, 11*(6), 716–719. doi:10.1109/76.927426

Bolettieri, P., Esuli, A., Falchi, F., Lucchese, C., Perego, R., Piccioli, T., & Rabitti, F. (2009). CoPhIR: A test collection for content-based image retrieval. *CoRR.*

Carson, C., Belongie, S., Greenspan, H., & Malik, J. (2002). Blobworld: Image segmentation using expectation-maximizations and it application to image querying. *IEEE Transactions on Pattern Analysis and Machine Intelligence, 24,* 1026V38.

Chalechale, A., Mertins, A., & Naghdy, G. (2004). Edge image description using angular radial partitioning. *IEE Proceedings. Vision Image and Signal Processing, 151,* 93–101. doi:10.1049/ip-vis:20040332

Chang, F.-C., & Hang, H.-M. (2006). A relevance feedback image retrieval scheme using multi-instance and pseudo image concepts. *The Institute of Electronics Information and Communication Engineers Transactions* on *Information* and *Systems, E89VD*(5).

Chatzichristofis, S. A., & Boutalis, Y. S. (2008). Cedd: Color and edge directivity descriptor. A compact descriptor for image indexing and retrieval. *International Conference on Computer Vision Systems,* (pp. 312-322). Santorini, Greece.

Chawathe, Y., Ratnasamy, S., Breslau, L., Lanham, N., & Shenker, S. (2003). Making Gnutella like P2P systems scalable. In *Proceedings of 2003 Conference Applications, Technologies, Architectures, and Protocols for Computer Communications,* (pp. 407-418).

Chen, J.-J., Liul, C.-Y., Huang, Y.-S., & Hsieh, J.-W. (2001). Similarity retrieval in image databases by boosted common shape features among query images. In *Proceedings of IEEE Pacific Rim Conference on Multimedia,* (pp. 285-292).

Chen, Y., Bi, J., & Wang, J. Z. (2006). MILES: Multiple-instance learning via embedded instance selection. *IEEE Transactions on Pattern Analysis and Machine Intelligence, 28,* 1931–1947. doi:10.1109/TPAMI.2006.248

Clarke, I., Sandberg, O., Wiley, B., Hong, W. T., et al. (2000). Freenet: A distributed anonymous information storage and retrieval system. In H. Federrath (Ed.), *Designing privacy enhancing tech,* (pp. 46-66). Berkeley, CA, USA, July.

Coimbra, M., & Silva Cunha, J. P. (2006). MPEG-7 visual descriptors – Contributions for automated feature extraction in capsule endoscopy. *IEEE Transactions on Circuits and Systems for Video Technology, 16*(5). doi:10.1109/TCSVT.2006.873158

Datta, R., Joshi, D., Li, J., & Wang, J. Z. (2008). Image retrieval: Ideas, influences, and trends of the new age. *ACM Computing Surveys, 40*(2), 1–60. doi:10.1145/1348246.1348248

Datta, S., Giannella, C. R., & Kargupta, H. (2009). Approximate distributed k-means clustering over a peer-to-peer network. *IEEE Transactions on Knowledge and Data Engineering, 21*(10), 1372–1388. doi:10.1109/TKDE.2008.222

Daubechies, I. (1992). *Ten lectures on wavelets.* Philadelphia, PA: SIAM. doi:10.1137/1.9781611970104

Deselaers, T., Keysers, D., & Ney, H. (2008). Features for image retrieval: An experimental comparison. *Information Retrieval, 11*(2), 77–107. doi:10.1007/s10791-007-9039-3

Dimitriadis, S., Marias, K., & Orphanoudakis, S. (2007). A multi-agent platform for content-based image retrieval. *Multimedia Tools and Applications, 33*(1), 57–72. doi:10.1007/s11042-006-0095-2

Dohnal, V., & Zezula, P. (2009). Similarity searching in structured and unstructured P2P networks. *Quality of Service in Heterogeneous Networks,* Lecture Notes of the Institute for Computer Sciences. *Social Informatics and Telecommunications Engineering, 22,* 400–416.

Eisenhardt, M., Muller, W., Henrich, A., Blank, D., & Allali, S. E. (2006). Clustering-based source selection for efficient image retrieval in peer-to-peer networks. In *Proceedings of IEEE International Symbolic Multimedia.*

Fanning, S. (2007). Napster. Retrieved from http://www.napster.com/

Fei-Fei, L., Fergus, R., & Perona, P. (2004). *Learning generative visual models from few training examples: An incremental Bayesian approach tested on 101 Object Categories.* In Workshop on Generative Model Based Vision.

Fei-Fei, L., & Perona, P. (2005). A Bayesian hierarchical model for learning natural scene categories. In *Proceedings of IEEE Conference in Computer Vision and Pattern Recognition,* San Diego.

Flickner, M., Sawhney, H., Niblack, W., Ashley, J., Huang, Q., & Dom, B. (1995). Query by image and video content: The QBIC system. *IEEE Computer, 28*(9), 23–32. doi:10.1109/2.410146

Freund, Y., & Schapire, R. E. (1997). A decision-theoretic generalization of on-line learning and an application to boosting. *Journal of Computer and System Sciences, 55*(1), 119–139. doi:10.1006/jcss.1997.1504

Gevers, T., & Smeulders, A. (2000). Pictoseek: Combining color and shape invariant features for image retrieval. *IEEE Transactions on Image Processing,* 102–119. doi:10.1109/83.817602

Gnutella. (2004). *The Gnutella protocol specification v0.41* Retrieved from http://www9.limewire.com/developer/gnutella protocol 0.4.pdf

Huang, J., Kumar, S., Mitra, M., Zhu, W.-J., & Zabih, R. (1997). Image indexing using color correlogram. In *Proceedings of IEEE Conf. on Computer Vision and Pattern Recognition.*

Inaba, T., Okawa, T., Murata, Y., Takizawa, H., & Kobayashi, H. (2006). Design and implementation of an efficient search mechanism based on the hybrid P2P model for ubiquitous computing systems. In *Proceedings International Symposium on Applications of the Internet,* (pp. 45-53).

Jeong, S., Kim, K., Chun, B., Lee, J., & Bae, Y. J. (1999). An effective method for combining multiple features of images retrieval. In *Proceedings of IEEE TENCON,* (pp. 982-985).

Jin, X., & French, J. C. (2005). Improving image retrieval effectiveness via multiple queries. *Multimedia Tools and Applications, 26*(2), 221–245. doi:10.1007/s11042-005-0453-5

Juan, L., & Gwun, O. (2009). A comparison of sift, PCA-sift and surf. *International Journal of Image Processing, 3,* 143–152.

Ke, Y., & Sukthankar, R. (2004). PCA-SIFT: A more distinctive representation for local image descriptors. In *Proceedings of the Conference on Computer Vision and Pattern Recognition,* (pp. 511-517).

King, I., Ng, C. H., & Sia, K. C. (2004). Distributed content-based visual information retrieval system on peer-to-peer networks. *ACM Transactions on Information Systems, 22,* 477–501. doi:10.1145/1010614.1010619

Kokare, M., Biswas, P. K., & Chatterji, B. N. (2007). Texture image retrieval using rotated wavelet filters. *Pattern Recognition Letters, 28,* 1240–1249. doi:10.1016/j.patrec.2007.02.006

Li, X., & Wu, J. (2005). A hybrid searching scheme in unstructured P2P networks. In *Proceedings of the International Conference on Parallel Processing,* (pp. 277-284).

Lin, T., Wang, H., & Wang, J. (2004). Search performance analysis and robust search algorithm in unstructured peer-to-peer networks. In *Proceedings of the IEEE/ACM International Symposium on Cluster Computing and the Grid*, (pp. 346-354).

Liu, B., Lee, W.-C., & Lee, D. L. (2005). Supporting complex multi-dimensional queries in P2P systems. In *Proceedings of the IEEE Conference on Distributed Computing Systems*, (pp. 155-164).

Liu, C., Yuen, J., & Torralba, A. (2011). Sift flow: Dense correspondence across scenes and its applications. *IEEE Transactions on Pattern Analysis and Machine Intelligence*, *33*(5), 978–994. doi:10.1109/TPAMI.2010.147

Liu, Y., Zhang, D., Lu, G., & Ma, W.-Y. (2007). A survey of content-based image retrieval with high-level semantics. *Pattern Recognition*, *40*(1), 262–282. doi:10.1016/j.patcog.2006.04.045

Lowe, D. (2004). Distinctive image features from scale-invariant keypoints. *International Journal of Computer Vision*, *60*(2), 91–110. doi:10.1023/B:VISI.0000029664.99615.94

Manjunath, B. S. (2001). Color and texture descriptors. *IEEE Transactions on Circuits and Systems for Video Technology*, *11*(6), 703–715. doi:10.1109/76.927424

Martinez, J. M. (2004). *MPEG-7 overview* (version 10). ISO/IEC JTC1/SC29/WG11N6828.

Mohamed, A.-M., & Krishnamachari, S. (2004). Multimedia descriptions based on MPEG-7 extraction and applications. *IEEE Transactions on Multimedia*, *6*(3), 459–468. doi:10.1109/TMM.2004.827500

Natsev, P., Rastogi, R., & Shim, K. (1998). *WALRUS: A similarity matching algorithm for image databases*. Technical report, Bell Laboratories, Murray Hill.

Nello, C., & John, S.-T. (2000). *An introduction to support vector machines and other kernel-based learning methods*. Cambridge University Press.

Novak, D., & Zezula, P. (2006). M-Chord: A scalable distributed similarity search structure. In *Proceedings of the 1st International Conference on Scalable Information Systems*, NY, USA.

Oliva, A., & Torralba, A. (2006). Building the gist of a scene: The role of global image features in recognition. In *Visual Perception* (*Vol. 155*). Progress in Brain Research. doi:10.1016/S0079-6123(06)55002-2

Ozdena, M., & Polat, E. (2007). A color image segmentation approach for content-based image retrieval. *Pattern Recognition*, *40*(4), 1318–1325. doi:10.1016/j.patcog.2006.08.013

Quelhas, P., & Odobez, J. M. (2007). Multi-level local descriptor quantization for Bag-of-Visterms image representation. In *Proceedings of the 6th ACM International Conference on Image and Video Retrieval*, (pp. 242-249).

Rahmani, R., Goldman, S., Zhang, H., Cholleti, S., & Fritts, J. (2008). Localized content based image retrieval. *IEEE Transactions on Pattern Analysis and Machine Intelligence*, *30*(11). doi:10.1109/TPAMI.2008.112

Ratnasamy, S., Stoica, I., & Shenker, S. (2002). Routing algorithm for DHTs: Some open question. In *Proceedings of the 1st International Peer-to-Peer Workshop*, (pp. 45-52).

Sedmidubsky, J., Barton, S., Dohnal, V., & Zezula, P. (2008). A self-organized system for content-based search in multimedia. In *Proceedings of IEEE International Symposium on Multimedia*, (pp. 322-327).

Shao, W., Naghdy, G., & Phung, S. L. (2007). Automatic image annotation for semantic image retrieval. *Lecture Notes in Computer Science*, *4781*, 369–378. doi:10.1007/978-3-540-76414-4_36

Smith, J. R., & Chang, S.-F. (1996). Visualseek: A fully automated content-based image query system. In *Proceedings of ACM Multimedia*.

Tamura, H., Mori, S., & Yamawaki, T. (1978). Textural features corresponding to visual perception. *IEEE Transactions on Systems, Man, and Cybernetics*, 8, 460–473. doi:10.1109/TSMC.1978.4309999

Yang, B., & Hector, G.-M. (2002). Efficient search in peer-to-peer networks. In *Proceedings of the 22-th IEEE International Conference on Distributed Computing Systems.*

Yang, J., Zhong, Y., & Zhang, S. (2003). An efficient interest-group based search mechanism in unstructured peer-to-peer networks. In *Proceedings of the International Conference on Computer Networks and Mobile Computing*, (pp. 247-252).

Yoo, H.-W. (2002). Visual information retrieval system via content-based approach. *Pattern Recognition*, 35(3), 749–769. doi:10.1016/S0031-3203(01)00072-3

Zeinalipour-Yazti, D., Kalogeraki, V., & Gunopulos, D. (2004). Information retrieval in peer-to-peer networks. *The IEEE CS and the AIP*, 6(4), 20–26.

Zhang, C., Chen, X., Chen, M., Chen, S.-C., & Shyu, M.-L. (2005). A multiple instance learning approach for content-based image retrieval using one-class support vector machine. *IEEE International Conference on Multimedia & Expo*, (pp. 1142-1145).

Zhang, D., Wang, F., Shi, Z., & Zhang, C. (2010). Interactive localized content based image retrieval with multiple-instance active learning. *Pattern Recognition*, 43(2), 478–484. doi:10.1016/j.patcog.2009.03.002

Zhang, H., Bruce, C., Brian, L., & Victor, L. (2004). A multi-agent approach for peer-to-peer-based information retrieval systems. In *Proceedings of the International Joint Conference on Autonomous Agents and Multiagent Systems*, (pp. 456-464).

Zhu, Y., Yang, X., & Hu, Y. (2005). Making search efficient on Gnutella-like P2P systems. In *Proceedings of the International Parallel Distributed Processing Symposium*, (p. 56a).

ADDITIONAL READING

Felzenszwalb, P. F., Girshick, R. B., McAllester, D. A., & Ramanan, D. (2010). Object detection with discriminatively trained part-based models. *IEEE Transactions on Pattern Analysis and Machine Intelligence*, 1627–1645. doi:10.1109/TPAMI.2009.167

Jain, A. K. (2010). Data clustering: 50 years beyond K-means. *Pattern Recognition Letters*, 31(8), 651–666. doi:10.1016/j.patrec.2009.09.011

Jégou, H., Douze, M., & Schmid, C. (2011). Product quantization for nearest neighbor search. *IEEE Transactions on Pattern Analysis and Machine Intelligence*, 33(1), 117–128. doi:10.1109/TPAMI.2010.57

Ke, Y., Sukthankar, R., & Huston, L. (2004). Efficient near-duplicate detection and sub-image retrieval. In A*CM International Conference on Multimedia*, (pp. 869-876).

Rui, Y., Huang, T. S., & Chang, S.-F. (1999). Image retrieval: Current techniques, promising directions, and open issues. *Journal of Visual Communication and Image Representation*, 10(1), 36–92. doi:10.1006/jvci.1999.0413

Smith, J. R., & Chang, S.-F. (1997). An image and video search engine for the World-Wide Web. *Proceedings of the SPIE Storage and Retrieval for Image and Video Databases*, (pp. 84-95).

Szeliski, R. (2010). *Computer vision: Algorithms and applications*. Springer.

van de Sande, K. E. A., Gevers, T., & Snoek, C. G. M. (2010). Evaluating color descriptors for object and scene recognition. *IEEE Transactions on Pattern Analysis and Machine Intelligence*, 23(9), 1582–1596. doi:10.1109/TPAMI.2009.154

Wang, J., Yang, J., Yu, K., Lv, F., Huang, T. S., & Gong, Y. (2010).Locality-constrained linear coding for image classification. In *Proceedings of IEEE Conference in Computer Vision and Pattern Recognition*, (pp. 3360-3367).

Compilation of References

Abacast. (2010). *Abacast home page*. Retrieved from http://www.abacast.com/

Abdullah-Al-Wadud, M., & Oksam, C. (2007). Region-of-Interest selection for skin detection based applications. *International Conference on Convergence Information Technology*, 2007, (pp. 1999-2004). 21-23 Nov. 2007.

Aberer, K., Cudré-Mauroux, P., Datta, A., Despotovic, Z., Hauswirth, M., Punceva, M., et al. (2003). Advanced peer-to-peer networking: The P-Grid system and its applications. *PIK - Praxis der Informationsverarbeitung und Kommunikation, Special Issue on P2P Systems, 26*(3), 86-89.

Abousleman, G. P. (2009). Target-tracking-based ultra-low-bit-rate video coding. *Military Communications Conference, MILCOM 2009*, IEEE, (pp. 1-6).

Aggarwal, A., Biswas, S., Singh, S., Sural, S., & Majumdar, A. K. (2006). *Object tracking using background subtraction and motion estimation in MPEG videos. ACCV 2006, LNCS* (Vol. 3852, pp. 121–130). Heidelberg, Germany: Springer.

Aggarwal, J. K., & Nandhakumar, N. (1988). On the computation of motion from sequences of images-A review. *Proceedings of the IEEE, 76*, 917–935. doi:10.1109/5.5965

Ahlswede, R., Cai, N., Li, S.-Y. R., & Yeung, R. W. (2000). Network information flow. *IEEE Transactions on Information Theory, 46*(4), 1204–1216. doi:10.1109/18.850663

Ahmad, S., Hamzaoui, R., & Al-Akaidi, M. (2007). Robust live unicast video streaming with rateless codes. In *Proceedings of the 16th International Packet Video Workshop*, (pp. 78–84).

Aign, S., & Fazel, K. (1995, June). Temporal and spatial error concealment techniques for hierarchical mpeg-2 video codec. *Proceedings of IEEE ICC, 3*, 1778–1783. doi:10.1109/ICC.1995.524505

Akyildiz, I. F., Melodia, T., & Chowdhury, K. R. (2007). A survey on wireless multimedia sensor networks. *Computer Networks, 51*, 921–960. doi:10.1016/j.comnet.2006.10.002

Albanese, A., Blömer, J., Edmonds, J., Luby, M., & Sudan, M. (1996). Priority encoding transmission. *IEEE Transactions on Information Theory, 42*(6), 1737–1744. doi:10.1109/18.556670

Ali, M., & Murshed, M. (2010). Motion compensation for block-based lossless video coding using lattice-based binning. In the *Proceedings of International Symposium on Circuits and Systems*, (pp. 2183-2186).

Alimal, L. O., El-Ansary, S., Brand, P., & Haridi, S. (2003). DKS(N, k, f): A family of low communication, scalable and fault-tolerant infrastructures for P2P applications. In *Proceedings 3rd IEEE/ACM International Symposium on Cluster Computing and the Grid, CCGrid 2003* (pp. 344-350). doi: 10.1109/CCGRID.2003.1199386

Alimi, R., Penno, R., & Yang, Y. (2010). *ALTO protocol*. Retrieved from http://www.ietf.org/internet-drafts/draft-ietf-alto-protocol-03.txt

Alinejad, A., Philip, N., & Istepanian, R. S. (2011). Mapping of multiple parameter m-health scenarios to mobile WiMAX QoS variables. *33rd Annual International Conference of the IEEE EMB*, (pp. 1532-1535). Boston, MA: IEEE.

AllCast. (2010). *AllCast home page*. Retrieved from http://www.allcast.com/

Altaf, M., Fleury, M., & Ghanbari, M. (2011). Error resilient video stream switching for mobile wireless channels. *International Journal of Mobile Multimedia, 7*(3), 216–235.

Andrade, N., Mowbray, M., Lima, A., Wagner, G., & Ripeanu, M. (2005). Influences on cooperation in Bit-Torrent communities. *Proceedings of the 2005 ACM SIGCOMM Workshop on Economics of Peer-to-Peer Systems* (pp. 111-115). New York, NY: ACM. doi: http://doi.acm.org/10.1145/1080192.1080198

Androutsellis-Theotokis, S., & Spinellis, D. (2004). A survey of peer-to-peer content distribution technologies. *ACM Computing Surveys, 36*(4), 335–371. doi:10.1145/1041680.1041681

Anselmo, T., & Alfonso, D. (2010). Constant quality variable bit-rate control for SVC. *2010 11th International Workshop on Image Analysis for Multimedia Interactive Services* (WIAMIS), (pp. 1-4).

Apache. (2010). *The Apache Software Foundation home page.* Retrieved from http://www.apache.org/foundation/

Apostolopoulos, J. G., Wong, T., Tan, W., & Wee, S. J. (2002, Nov.). On multiple description streaming with content delivery networks. *Proceedings - IEEE INFO-COM, 3*, 1736–1745.

Aravind, R., Civanlar, M. R., & Reibman, A. R. (1996, Oct.). Packet loss resilience of MPEG-2 scalable video coding algorithms. *IEEE Transactions on Circuits and Systems for Video Technology, 6*(5), 426–435. doi:10.1109/76.538925

Ardizzone, E., Gatani, L., Cascia, M. L., Re, G. L., & Ortolani, M. (2006). Enhanced P2P services providing multimedia content. In *Proceedings of the IEEE International Symposium on Multimedia*, (pp. 637-646).

Armanito, R., & Schafer, R. (1996). Motion vector estimation using spatio-temporal prediction and its application to video coding. In the *Proceedings of International Conference of SPIE- Digital Video Compression*, San Jose, CA, Vol. 2668, (pp. 290-301).

Babelgum. (2010). *Babelgum home page.* Retrieved from http://www.babelgum.com/

Babu, R. V., Ramakrishnan, K. R., & Srinivasan, S. H. (2004). Video object segmentation: A compressed domain approach. *IEEE Transactions on Circuits and Systems for Video Technology, 14*(4), 462–474.

Baccichet, P., Schierl, T., Wiegand, T., & Girod, B. (2007). Low-delay peer-to-peer streaming using scalable video coding. In *Packet Video 2007* (pp. 173-181). doi: doi:10.1109/PACKET.2007.4397039

Baccichet, P., Shantanu, R., & Girod, B. (2006). Systematic lossy error protection based on H. 264/AVC redundant slices and flexible macroblock ordering. *Springer Journal of Zhejiang University-Science A, 7*(5), 900–909. doi:10.1631/jzus.2006.A0900

Bachmutsky, A. (2009). *WiMAX evolution: Emerging technologies and applications* (Katz, M., & Fitzek, F., Eds.). 1st ed.). Wiley.

Bak, S., Corvee, E., Bremond, F., & Thonnat, M. (2010, August 29 2010-September 1). Person re-identification using spatial covariance regions of human body parts. In the *Proceedings of the Seventh IEEE International Conference on Advanced Video and Signal Based Surveillance* (AVSS).

Baker, S., & Kanade, T. (1999). *Super-resolution optical flow.* Technical Report CMU-RI-TR-99-36, Robotics Institute, Carnegie Mellon University, October.

Balfe, S., Lakhani, A. D., & Paterson, K. G. (2005). DRM Enabled P2P Architecture. In *Fifth IEEE International Conference on Peer-to-Peer Computing*, Aug-Sept. 2005, (pp. 117 -124).

Balfe, S., Lakhani, A. D., & Paterson, K. G. (2005). Trusted computing: Providing security for peer-to-peer networks. In *Fifth IEEE International Conference on Peer-to-Peer Computing (P2P'05)*, 2005, (pp. 117-124).

Ballardie, A. (1997). *Core based trees (CBT version 2) multicast routing -- Protocol specification.* Request for Comments, IETF. Retrieved from http://www.ietf.org/rfc/rfc2189.txt

Bandyopadhyay, S. K., Wu, Z., Pandit, P., & Boyce, J. M. (2006). An error concealment scheme for entire frame losses for H. 264/AVC. In *IEEE Sarnoff Symposium*, (pp. 1–4).

Banerjee, S., Bhattacharjee, B., & Kommareddy, C. (2002). Scalable application layer multicast. In *Proceedings of the 2002 Conference on Applications, Technologies, Architectures, and Protocols for Computer Communications, SIGCOMM '02* (pp. 205-217). New York, NY: ACM. doi: http://doi.acm.org/10.1145/633025.633045

Banks, J., Bennamoun, M., & Corke, P. (1997). Fast and robust stereo matching algorithms for mining automation. In the *Proceedings of the International Workshop on Image Analysis and Information Fusion*, (pp. 139-149).

Barmada, B., Ghandi, M. M., Jones, E. V., & Ghanbari, M. (2005). Prioritized transmission of data-partioned H. 264 video with hierarchical modulation. *IEEE Signal Processing Letters, 12*(8), 577–580. doi:10.1109/LSP.2005.851261

Barron, J. L., Fleet, D. J., & Beauchemin, S. S. (1994). Performance of optical flow techniques. *International Journal of Computer Vision, 12*, 43–77. doi:10.1007/BF01420984

Bartrina-Rapesta, J., Serra-Sagrista, J., & Auli-Llinas, F. (2009). JPEG2000 ROI coding with fine-grain accuracy through rate-distortion optimization techniques. *Signal Processing Letters, 16*(1), 45–48.

Bates, T., Chandra, R., Katz, D., & Rekhter, Y. (1988). *Multiprotocol extensions for BGP-4.* Request for Comments. IETF. Retrieved from http://www.ietf.org/rfc/rfc2283.txt

Batko, M. (2010). Building a web-scale image similarity search system. *Multimedia Tools and Applications, 47*(3), 599–623. doi:10.1007/s11042-009-0339-z

Bay, H., Tuytelaars, T., & Gool, L. V. (2006). Surf: speeded up robust features. *In Computer Vision - ECCV*, Vol. 3951, (pp. 404-417).

Belfiore, S., Grangetto, M., Magli, E., & Olmo, G. (2003). An error concealment algorithm for streaming video. *IEEE International Conference on Image Processing 2003* (ICIP 2003), Vol. 22, (pp. 649-652).

Ben-Ezra, M., & Nayar, S. K. (2004). Motion-based motion deblurring. *IEEE Transactions on Pattern Analysis and Machine Intelligence, 26*(6), 689–698. doi:10.1109/TPAMI.2004.1

Benoit, A., Le Callet, P., Campisi, P., & Cousseau, R. (2008). Quality assessment of stereoscopic images. *EURASIP Journal on Image and Video Processing, 2008*, 659024. doi:10.1155/2008/659024

Benzougar, A., Bouthemy, P., & Fablet, R. (2001). MRF-based moving object detection from MPEG coded video. In *Proceedings of the IEEE International Conference on Image Processing, 2001*, Vol. 3, (pp. 402-405).

Berndt, H. (2008). *Towards 4G technologies: Services with initiative* (1st ed.). Wiley. doi:10.1002/9780470010334

Bertalmio, M., Vese, L., Sapiro, G., & Osher, S. (2003). Simultaneous structure and texture image inpainting. *IEEE Transactions on Image Processing, 12*, 882–889. doi:10.1109/TIP.2003.815261

Bertinat, M. E., Vera, D. D., Padula, D., Robledo, F., Rodríguez-Bocca, P., Romero, P., et al. (2009). GoalBit: The first free and open source peer-to-peer streaming network. In *Proceedings of the 5th International IFIP/ACM Latin American Conference on Networking, LANC '09*. New York, NY: ACM.

Bhanu, B., Dudgeon, D. E., Zelnio, E. G., Rosenfeld, A., Casasent, D., & Reed, I. S. (1997). Guest editorial introduction to the special issue on automatic target detection and recognition. *IEEE Transactions on Image Processing, 6*(1), 1–6. doi:10.1109/TIP.1997.552076

Biemond, J., Lagendijk, R. L., & Mersereau, R. M. (1990). Iterative methods for image deblurring. *Proceedings of the IEEE, 78*(5), 856–883. doi:10.1109/5.53403

Bing, B. (2010). *3D and HD broadband video networking.* Norwood, MA: Artech House.

Bishop, C. M. (2006). *Pattern recognition and machine learning.* Springer.

Biswas, S., Aggarwal, G., & Chellappa, R. (2010). An efficient and robust algorithm for shape indexing and retrieval. *IEEE Transactions on Multimedia, 12*(5). doi:10.1109/TMM.2010.2050735

BitTorrent. (2010). *BitTorrent home page.* Retrieved from http://www.bittorrent.com/

Bjøntegaard, G. (2001, Apr.). *Calculation of average psnr differences between rd-curves.* ITU-T Q.6/SG16 VCEG, VCEG-M33.

Black, M., & Anandan, P. (1993). A framework for the robust estimation of optical flow. In the *Proceedings of the International Conference on Computer Vision* (ICCV), (pp. 231-236).

Black, M., & Jepson, A. (1998). Eigen-tracking: Robust matching and tracking of articulated objects using a view-based representation. *International Journal of Computer Vision, 36*(2), 101–130.

Blei, D. M., Ng, A. Y., & Jordan, M. I. (2003). Latent dirichlet allocation. *Journal of Machine Learning Research, 3*(4-5), 993–1022.

Bober, M. (2001). MPEG-7 visual shape descriptors. *IEEE Transactions on Circuits and Systems for Video Technology, 11*(6), 716–719. doi:10.1109/76.927426

Boev, A., Hollosi, D., & Gotchev, A. (2008). *Classification of stereoscopic artifacts*. Retrieved February 1, 2011, from http://sp.cs.tut.fi/mobile3dtv/results/tech/D5.1_Mobile3DTV_v1.0.pdf

Bolettieri, P., Esuli, A., Falchi, F., Lucchese, C., Perego, R., Piccioli, T., & Rabitti, F. (2009). CoPhIR: A test collection for content-based image retrieval. *CoRR.*

Bolme, D., Beveridge, R., Teixeira, M., & Draper, B. (2003). The CSU face identification evaluation system: Its purpose, features and structure. In the *Proceedings of International Conference on Vision Systems*, (pp. 304-311).

Borman, S., & Stevenson, R. (1999). Super-resolution from image sequences - A review. In the *Proceedings of 1998 Midwest Symposium on Circuits and Systems*, (pp. 374-378).

Boroczky, L. (1991). *Pel-recursive motion estimation for image coding*. Delft University of Technology.

Bourges-Sevenier, M., & Jang, E. (2004). An introduction to the MPEG-4 animation framework extension. *IEEE Transactions on Circuits and Systems for Video Technology, 14*, 928–936. doi:10.1109/TCSVT.2004.830662

Bowden, R., & KaewTraKulPong, P. (2001). An improved adaptive background mixture model for real-time tracking with shadow detection. In *the Proceedings of the 2nd European Workshop on Advanced Video Based Surveillance Systems.*

Boyce, J. (2004, May). Weighted prediction in the H.264/MPEG AVC video coding standard. In *Proceedings IEEE International Symposium on Circuits and Systems (ISCAS'04)* (Vol. 3, pp. 789-792). Nagoya, Japan.

Boykov, Y., Veksler, O., & Zabih, R. (2001). Fast approximate energy minimization via graph cuts. *IEEE Transactions on Pattern Analysis and Machine Intelligence, 23*, 1222–1239. doi:10.1109/34.969114

Bradley, A. P., & Stentiford, F. W. M. (2002). JPEG2000 and region of interest coding. *Digital Image Computing: Techniques and Applications* (DICTA'02), Melbourne, Australia, (pp. 303-308). Jan. 2002.

Breitenstein, M. D., Reichlin, F., Leibe, B., Koller-Meier, E., & Gool, L. V. (2010). Online Multi-Person Tracking-by-Detection from a Single, Uncalibrated Camera. *IEEE Transactions on Pattern Analysis and Machine Intelligence, 33*(9), 1820–1833. doi:10.1109/TPAMI.2010.232

Brown, L. (1992). A survey of image registration techniques. *ACM Computing Surveys, 24*(4), 325–376. doi:10.1145/146370.146374

Brulin, M., Nicolas, H., & Maillet, C. (2010, 14-17 November 2010). Video surveillance traffic analysis using scene geometry. In the *Proceedings of the Fourth Pacific-Rim Symposium on Image and Video Technology* (PSIVT).

Brunnström, K. (2009). VQEG validation and ITU standardization of objective perceptual video quality metrics. *IEEE Signal Processing Magazine, 96*. doi:10.1109/MSP.2009.932162

Buford, J., Yu, H., & Lua, E. K. (2008). *P2P networking and applications*. San Francisco, CA: Morgan Kaufmann Publishers Inc.

Butler, D., Sridharan, S., & Bove, V. M., Jr. (2003). Real-time adaptive background segmentation. In the *Proceedings of the International Conference on Acoustics, Speech, and Signal Processing* (ICASSP).

Buxton, W. (1995). Integrating the periphery and context: A new taxonomy of telematics. *Proceedings of Graphics Interface, 1995*, 239–246.

Canero, C., Thomos, N., Triantafyllidis, G., Litos, G., & Strintzis, M. (2005). Mobile tele-echography: user interface design. *IEEE Transactions on Information Technology in Biomedicine, 9*(1), 44–49. doi:10.1109/TITB.2004.840064

Cao, N., & Wei, B. W. Y. (1997). A 4:1 checker-board algorithm for motion estimation. In the *Proceedings of International Conference of SPIE- the International Society for Optical Engineering*, Vol. 2847, (pp. 408-412).

Capel, D., & Zisserman, A. (2003). Computer vision applied to super resolution. *IEEE Signal Processing Magazine, 25*(9), 75–86. doi:10.1109/MSP.2003.1203211

Carlbom, I., & Paciorek, J. (1978). Planar geometric projections and viewing transformations. *ACM Computing Surveys, 10*(4), 465–502. doi:10.1145/356744.356750

Carranza, J., Theobalt, C., Magnor, M., & Seidel, H. (2003). Free-viewpoint video of human actors. *ACM Transactions on Graphics, 22*(3), 569–577. doi:10.1145/882262.882309

Carson, C., Belongie, S., Greenspan, H., & Malik, J. (2002). Blobworld: Image segmentation using expectation-maximizations and it application to image querying. *IEEE Transactions on Pattern Analysis and Machine Intelligence, 24*, 1026V38.

Castro, M., Druschel, P., Kermarrec, A.-M., Nandi, A., Rowstron, A., & Singh, A. (2003). SplitStream: High-bandwidth content distribution in a cooperative environment. In *Proceedings of IPTPS'03*.

Castro, M., Druschel, P., Kermarrec, A.-M., & Rowstron, A. (2002). SCRIBE: A large-scale and decentralized application-level multicast infrastructure. *IEEE Journal on Selected Areas in Communications. Special Issue on Network Support for Group Communication, 20*(8), 1489–1499. doi:doi:10.1109/JSAC.2002.803069

Chalechale, A., Mertins, A., & Naghdy, G. (2004). Edge image description using angular radial partitioning. *IEE Proceedings. Vision Image and Signal Processing, 151*, 93–101. doi:10.1049/ip-vis:20040332

Chan, Y.-L., Hui, W.-L., & Siu, W.-C. (1997). A block motion vector estimation using pattern based pixel decimation. In the *Proceedings of IEEE International Symposium on Circuits and Systems*, Hong Kong, Vol. 2, (pp. 1153-1156).

Chang, F.-C., & Hang, H.-M. (2006). A relevance feedback image retrieval scheme using multi-instance and pseudo image concepts. *The Institute of Electronics Information and Communication Engineers Transactions on Information and Systems, E89VD*(5).

Chang, Y.-W., & Chen, Y.-Y. (2005). *Alleviating-ringing-artifact filter using voting scheme*. Paper presented at the ICGST International Conference on Graphics, Vision and Image Processing, Cairo, Egypt.

Chang, J. F., & Leou, J. J. (2006). A quadratic prediction basedfractional-pixel motion estimation algorithm for H.264. *Journal of Visual Communication and Image Representation, 17*, 1074–1089. doi:10.1016/j.jvcir.2006.01.001

Chang, P.-C., & Lee, T.-H. (2000, June). Precise and fast error tracking for error-resilient transmission of h.263 video. *IEEE Transactions on Circuits and Systems for Video Technology, 10*(4), 600–607. doi:10.1109/76.845005

Chao, P. A., & Miao, Z. (2006). Rate-distortion optimized streaming of packetized media. *IEEE Transactions on Multimedia, 8*(2), 390–404. doi:10.1109/TMM.2005.864313

Chatzichristofis, S. A., & Boutalis, Y. S. (2008). Cedd: Color and edge directivity descriptor. A compact descriptor for image indexing and retrieval. *International Conference on Computer Vision Systems*, (pp. 312-322). Santorini, Greece.

Chawathe, Y., Ratnasamy, S., Breslau, L., Lanham, N., & Shenker, S. (2003). Making Gnutella like P2P systems scalable. In *Proceedings of 2003 Conference Applications, Technologies, Architectures, and Protocols for Computer Communications*, (pp. 407-418).

Chen, C.-C., & Chen, O. T.-C. (2004). Region of interest determined by perceptual-quality and rate-distortion optimization in JPEG 2000. *Proceedings of the 2004 International Symposium on Circuits and Systems, ISCAS '04*, Vol. 3, (pp. III- 869-72).

Chen, H., Han, Z., Hu, R., & Ruan, R. (2008). Adaptive FMO selection strategy for error resilient H.264 coding. *International Conference on Audio, Language and Image Processing, ICALIP 2008*, July 7-9, (pp. 868-872). Shanghai, China.

Chen, J.-J., Liul, C.-Y., Huang, Y.-S., & Hsieh, J.-W. (2001). Similarity retrieval in image databases by boosted common shape features among query images. In *Proceedings of IEEE Pacific Rim Conference on Multimedia*, (pp. 285-292).

Chen, M.-J., Chi, M.-C., Hsu, C.-T., & Chen, J.-W. (2003). ROI video coding based on H.263+ with robust skin-color detection technique. *2003 IEEE International Conference on Consumer Electronics, ICCE 2003*, (pp. 44-45).

Chen, Q.-H., Xie, X.-F., Guo, T.-J., Shi, L., & Wang, X.-F. (2010). The study of ROI detection based on visual attention mechanism. *2010 6th International Conference on Wireless Communications Networking and Mobile Computing* (WiCOM), (pp. 1-4).

Chen, S., & Williams, L. (1993). View interpolation for image synthesis. *SIGGRAPH 93 Proceedings*, (pp. 279–288).

Chen, Y., Chen, J., & Cai, C. (2006). *Luminance and chrominance correction for multi-view video using simplified color error model.*

Cheng, W.-H., Chu, W.-T., Kuo, J.-H., & Wu, J.-L. (2005). Automatic video region-of-interest determination based on user attention model. In *Proceedings of IEEE International Symposium on Circuits and Systems* (ISCAS '05), (pp. 3219-3222).

Cheng, C., Li, C., & Chen, L. (2010). A 2D to 3D conversion scheme based on depth cues analysis for MPEG videos. *IEEE Transactions on Consumer Electronics*, *56*(3), 1739–1745. doi:10.1109/TCE.2010.5606320

Chen, O. T.-C., & Chen, C.-C. (2007). Automatically-determined region of interest in JPEG 2000. *IEEE Transactions on Multimedia*, *9*(7), 1333–1345. doi:10.1109/TMM.2007.906572

Chen, V. W., Hsiao, M. H., Chen, H. T., Liu, C. Y., & Lee, S. Y. (2008). Content-aware fast motion estimation algorithm. *Journal of Visual Communication and Image Representation*, *19*, 256–296. doi:10.1016/j.jvcir.2008.01.002

Chen, Y., Bi, J., & Wang, J. Z. (2006). MILES: Multiple-instance learning via embedded instance selection. *IEEE Transactions on Pattern Analysis and Machine Intelligence*, *28*, 1931–1947. doi:10.1109/TPAMI.2006.248

Chen, Z., & Wu, D. (2010, November). Prediction of transmission distortion for wireless video communication: Algorithm and application. *Journal of Visual Communication and Image Representation*, *21*, 948–964. doi:10.1016/j.jvcir.2010.09.004

Cherry, S. M. (2004). WiMax and Wi-Fi: Separate and unequal. *IEEE Spectrum*, *41*(3). doi:10.1109/MSPEC.2004.1270541

Cheung, C.-H., & Po, L.-M. (2001). A fast block motion estimation using progressive partial distortion search. In the *Proceedings of International Symposium on Intelligent Multimedia, Video and Speech Processing*, Hong Kong, (pp. 406-409).

Cheung, P. Y. S., Chung, H. Y., & Yung, N. H. C. (1998). Adaptive search center non-linear three step search. In the *Proceedings of International Conference on Image Processing (ICIP '98)*, (pp. 191-194).

Cheung, C.-K., & Po, L.-M. (2000). Normalized partial distortion search algorithm for block motion estimation. *IEEE Transactions on Circuits and Systems for Video Technology*, *10*, 417–422. doi:10.1109/76.836286

Chi, H., & Zhang, Q. (2006). *Efficient search in P2P-based video-on-demand streaming service.* IEEE International Conference on Multimedia & Expo.

Chi, H., Zhang, Q., Jia, J., & Shen, X. (2007). Efficient search and scheduling in P2P-based media-on-demand streaming service. *IEEE Journal on Selected Areas in Communications*, *25*(1).

Chi, M.-C., Chen, M.-J., Yeh, C.-H., & Jhu, J.-A. (2008). Region-of-interest video coding based on rate and distortion variations for H.263+. *Signal Processing Image Communication*, *23*(2), 127–142. doi:10.1016/j.image.2007.12.001

Chou, P. A., Wu, Y., & Jain, K. (2003). Practical network coding. In *Proceedings of Allerton Conference on Communication, Control and Computing.*

Chou, P. A., & Miao, Z. (2006, April). Rate-distortion optimized streaming of packetized media. *IEEE Transactions on Multimedia*, *8*(2), 390–404. doi:10.1109/TMM.2005.864313

Chou, P. A., Mohr, A. E., Wang, A., & Mehrotra, S. (2001, March). Error control for receiver-driven layered multicast of audio and video. *IEEE Transactions on Multimedia*, *3*(1), 108–122. doi:10.1109/6046.909598

Chu, C. C., Su, X., Prabhu, B. S., Gadh, R., Kurup, S., Sridhar, G., & Sridhar, V. (2006). Mobile DRM for multimedia content commerce in P2P networks. Consumer Communications and Networking Conference, 8-10 Jan. 2006, (pp. 1119–1123).

Chu, Y., Gao, S., & Zhang, H. (2000). A case for end system multicast. In *Proceedings ACM Sigmetrics*.

Chun, S. S., Kim, J. R., & Sull, S. (2006). Intra prediction mode selection for flicker reduction in H.264/AVC. *IEEE Transactions on Consumer Electronics*, *52*(4), 1303–1310. doi:10.1109/TCE.2006.273149

Cisco. (2010). *Cisco visual networking index: Forecast and methodology, 2009–2014*. Retrieved from http://www.cisco.com/en/US/solutions/collateral/ns341/ns525/ns537/ns705/ns827/white_paper_c11-481360.pdf

Clarke, I., Sandberg, O., Wiley, B., Hong, W. T., et al. (2000). Freenet: A distributed anonymous information storage and retrieval system. In H. Federrath (Ed.), *Designing privacy enhancing tech*, (pp. 46-66). Berkeley, CA, USA, July.

Clausen, T., & Jacquet, P. (2003). *Optimized link state routing protocol (OLSR)*. Retrieved from http://www.rfc-editor.org/rfc/rfc3626.txt

Coelho, A. M., & Estrela, V. V. (2012a). Data-driven motion estimation with spatial adaptation. *International Journal of Image Processing*, *6*(1), 53-67. Retrieved May 7, 2012, from http://www.cscjournals.org/csc/manuscript/Journals/IJIP/volume6/Issue1/IJIP-513.pdf

Coelho, A. M., & Estrela, V. V. (2012b). EM-based mixture models applied to video event detection. In P. Sanguansat (Ed.), *Principal component analysis - Engineering applications*, (pp. 102-124). Intech. Retrieved in May 7, 2012 from http://www.intechopen.com/books/principal-component-analysis-engineering-applications/em-based-mixture-models-applied-to-video-event-detection

Coelho, A., Estrela, V. V., & de Assis, J. (2009). *Error concealment by means of clustered blockwise PCA*. Picture Coding Symposium, Chicago, IL: IEEE.

Cohen, B. (2003). Incentives build robustness in BitTorrent. *Proceedings of the 1st Workshop on Economics of Peer-to-Peer Systems*. Retrieved from http://www.sims.berkeley.edu/p2pecon/

Coimbra, M., & Silva Cunha, J. P. (2006). MPEG-7 visual descriptors – Contributions for automated feature extraction in capsule endoscopy. *IEEE Transactions on Circuits and Systems for Video Technology*, *16*(5). doi:10.1109/TCSVT.2006.873158

Conklin, G., Greenbaum, G., Lillevold, K., Lippman, A., & Reznik, Y. (2001). Video coding for streaming media delivery over the Internet. *IEEE Transactions on Circuits and Systems for Video Technology*, *11*(3), 269–281. doi:10.1109/76.911155

Conner, W., Nahrstedt, K., & Gupta, I. (2006). Preventing DoS attacks in peer-to-peer media streaming systems. In *Proceedings 13th Annual Conference on Multimedia Computing and Networking*, 2006.

Consortium, S. E. A. (2010). *Seamless content delivery project home page*. Retrieved from http://www.ist-sea.eu/

CoolStreaming. (2010). *CoolStreaming US home page*. Retrieved from http://www.coolstreaming.us/hp.php?lang=en

Cootes, T. F., & Edwards, G. J. (2001). Active appearance models (AAMs). *IEEE Transactions on Pattern Analysis and Machine Intelligence*, *23*(6), 681–685. doi:10.1109/34.927467

Cootes, T., & Cooper, D. (1995). Active shape models - Their training and application. *Computer Vision and Image Understanding*, *61*(1), 38–59. doi:10.1006/cviu.1995.1004

Cosman, P., Gray, R., & Olshen, R. (2002). Evaluating quality of compressed medical images: SNR, subjective rating, and diagnostic accuracy. *Proceedings of the IEEE*, (pp. 919-932).

Cote, G., Kossentini, F., & Wenger, S. (2001). Error resiliency coding. In Sun, M.-T., & Reibmen, A. R. (Eds.), *Compressed video over networks*. New York, NY: Marcel Deck Inc.

Cote, G., Shirani, S., & Kossentini, F. (2000, Jun.). Optimal mode selection and synchronization for robust video communications over error-prone networks. *IEEE Journal on Selected Areas in Communications, 18*(6), 952–965. doi:10.1109/49.848249

Crop, J., Erwig, A., & Selvaraj, V. (2010). *Ogg video coding.* Retrieved September 21, 2011, from http://people.oregonstate.edu/~cropj/uploads/Classes/577finalreport.pdf

Cruz, R. S., Domingues, J., Menezes, L., & Nunes, M. S. (2010). IPTV architecture for an IMS environment with dynamic QoS adaptation. *Multimedia Tools and Applications,* (pp. 1-33). Springer Netherlands. doi: http://dx.doi.org/10.1007/s11042-010-0537-8

Cslive.tv. (2010). *CSLive home page.* Retrieved from http://www.cslive.tv.

Cui, Y., Li, B., & Nahrstedt, K. (2004). oStream: Asynchronous streaming multicast. *IEEE Journal on Selected Areas in Communications, 22*(1).

Dabek, F., Kaashoek, M. F., Karger, D., Morris, R., & Stoica, I. (2001). Wide-area cooperative storage with CFS. In *Proceedings of the Eighteenth ACM Symposium on Operating Systems Principles, SOSP '01* (pp. 202-215). New York, NY: ACM. doi: http://doi.acm.org/10.1145/502034.502054

Dalal, N., & Triggs, B. (2005). Histograms of oriented gradients for human detection. In the *Proceedings of the IEEE Conference on Computer Vision and Pattern Recognition* (CVPR).

Daribo, I., Miled, W., & Pesquet-Popescu, B. (2010). Joint depth-motion dense estimation for multiview video coding. *JVCI Special Issue on Multi-Camera Imaging, Coding and Innovative Display: Techniques and Systems.*

Datta, R., Joshi, D., Li, J., & Wang, J. Z. (2008). Image retrieval: Ideas, influences, and trends of the new age. *ACM Computing Surveys, 40*(2), 1–60. doi:10.1145/1348246.1348248

Datta, S., Giannella, C. R., & Kargupta, H. (2009). Approximate distributed k-means clustering over a peer-to-peer network. *IEEE Transactions on Knowledge and Data Engineering, 21*(10), 1372–1388. doi:10.1109/TKDE.2008.222

Daubechies, I. (1992). *Ten lectures on wavelets.* Philadelphia, PA: SIAM. doi:10.1137/1.9781611970104

Deng, X., Jiang, X., Liu, Q., & Wang, W. (2008). Automatic depth map estimation of monocular indoor environments. *2008 International Conference on Multimedia and Information Technology (MMIT 2008),* (pp. 646-649).

Denman, S., Chandran, V., & Sridharan, S. (2007b). Robust multi-layer foreground segmenation for surviellance applications. In the *Proceedings of the IAPR Conference on Machine Vision Applications,* The University of Tokyo, Japan.

Denman, S., Fookes, C., & Sridharan, S. (2010, 14-17 November). Group segmentation during object tracking using optical flow discontinuities. In the *Proceedings of the Fourth Pacific-Rim Symposium on Image and Video Technology* (PSIVT), 2010.

Denman, S., Fookes, C., Bialkowski, A., & Sridharan, S. (2009, 1-3 December). *Soft-biometrics: Unconstrained authentication in a surveillance environment.* Paper presented at the Digital Image Computing: Techniques and Applications (DICTA), Melbourne, Australia.

Denman, S., Chandran, V., & Sridharan, S. (2007a). An adaptive optical flow technique for person tracking systems. *Elsevier Pattern Recognition Letters, 28*(10), 1232–1239. doi:10.1016/j.patrec.2007.02.008

DERS. (n.d.). *Depth estimation reference software.* Retrieved from http://wg11.sc29.org/svn/repos/MPEG-4/test/trunk/3D/depth_estimation/DERS/DERS

Deselaers, T., Keysers, D., & Ney, H. (2008). Features for image retrieval: An experimental comparison. *Information Retrieval, 11*(2), 77–107. doi:10.1007/s10791-007-9039-3

Dhondt, Y., Mys, S., Vermeirsch, K., & Van de Walle, R. (2007). Constrained inter prediction: Removing dependencies between different data partitions. In *Advanced Concepts for Intelligent Visual Systems,* (pp. 720-731).

Dimitriadis, S., Marias, K., & Orphanoudakis, S. (2007). A multi-agent platform for content-based image retrieval. *Multimedia Tools and Applications, 33*(1), 57–72. doi:10.1007/s11042-006-0095-2

Do, L., Zinger, S., & de With, P. H. N. (2010a). Quality improving techniques for free-viewpoint DIBR. *IS&T / SPIE Electronic Imaging, Vol. 7524, SDA XXI*, San Jose, USA.

Do, L., Zinger, S., & de With, P. H. N. (2010b). Conversion of free-viewpoint 3D multi-view video for stereoscopic displays. *IEEE International Workshop on Hot Topics in 3D, in conjunction with International Conference on Multimedia & Expo (ICME)*, (pp. 1730-1734). Singapore.

Do, T., Hua, K. A., & Tantaoui, M. (2004). P2VoD: Providing fault tolerant video-on-demand streaming in peer-to-peer environment. *Proceedings of IEEE ICC '04*, Paris, June 2004.

Dohnal, V., & Zezula, P. (2009). Similarity searching in structured and unstructured P2P networks. *Quality of Service in Heterogeneous Networks*, Lecture Notes of the Institute for Computer Sciences. *Social Informatics and Telecommunications Engineering, 22*, 400–416.

Do, L., Zinger, S., & de With, P. H. N. (2011). *Warping error analysis and reduction for depth image based rendering in 3DTV*. San Francisco, USA: IS&T / SPIE Electronic Imaging, Stereoscopic Displays and Applications XXI. doi:10.1117/12.873384

Do, T., Hua, K. A., Jiang, N., & Liu, F. (2009). PatchPeer: A scalable video-on-demand streaming system in hybrid wireless mobile peer-to-peer networks. *Peer-to-Peer Networking and Applications Journal, 2*(3), 182–201. doi:10.1007/s12083-008-0027-1

Doucet, A. (1998). *On sequential simulation-based methods for Bayesian filtering. Technical report cued/f-infeng/tr 310*. Department of Engineering, Cambridge University.

Druschel, P., & Rowstron, A. (2001). PAST: a large-scale, persistent peer-to-peer storage utility. In *Proceedings of the Eighth Workshop on Hot Topics in Operating Systems, 2001* (pp. 75-80).

Duchowski, A. T. (2000). Acuity-matching resolution degradation through wavelet coefficient scaling. *IEEE Transactions on Image Processing, 9*(8), 1437–1440. doi:10.1109/83.855439

Dufaux, F., & Moscheni, F. (1995). Motion estimation techniques for digital TV: A review and a new contribution. *Proceedings of the IEEE, 83*, 858–876. doi:10.1109/5.387089

Duong, T. Q., & Zepernick, H.-J. (2008). On the performance of ROI-based image transmission using cooperative diversity. *IEEE International Symposium on Wireless Communication Systems, ISWCS '08*, (pp. 340-343).

Eger, K., & Killat, U. (2006). Bandwidth trading in unstructured P2P content distribution networks. *Proceedings of the Sixth IEEE International Conference on Peer-to-Peer Computing, P2P '06* (pp. 39-48). doi:10.1109/P2P.2006.6

Eisenhardt, M., Muller, W., Henrich, A., Blank, D., & Allali, S. E. (2006). Clustering-based source selection for efficient image retrieval in peer-to-peer networks. In *Proceedings of IEEE International Symbolic Multimedia.*

Emule. (2010). *The Emule project home page*. Retrieved from http://www.emule-project.net/

Engelke, U., Zepernick, H.-J., & Maeder, A. (2009). Visual attention modeling: Region-of-interest versus fixation patterns. *Picture Coding Symposium, PCS 2009*, (pp. 1-4).

Estrela, V. V., & Galatsanos, N. (2000). Spatially-adaptive regularized pel-recursive motion estimation based on the EM algorithm. *SPIE/IEEE Proceedings of the Electrical Imaging 2000 (EI00)*, (pp. 372-383). San Diego, CA, USA.

Estrin, D., Farinacci, D., Helmy, A., Thaler, D., Deering, S., Handley, M., et al. (1998). *Protocol independent multicast-sparse mode (PIM-SM): Protocol specification*. Request for Comments. IETF. Retrieved from http://www.ietf.org/rfc/rfc2362.txt

Etoh, M., & Yoshimura, T. (2005). Advances in wireless video delivery. *Special Issue on Advances in Video Coding and Delivery, 93*(1), 111–122.

ETSI TS 125 308 V5.4.0 (2003-03). (n.d.). *3GPP TS 25.308 version 5.4.0 release 5.*

ETSI-TISPAN. (2010). *Peer-to-peer for content delivery for IPTV services: Analysis of mechanisms and NGN impacts.*

Fanning, S. (2007). Napster. Retrieved from http://www.napster.com/

Farenzena, M., Bazzani, L., Perina, A., Murino, V., & Cristani, M. (2010, 13-18 June). Person re-identification by symmetry-driven accumulation of local features. In the *Proceedings of the IEEE Conference on Computer Vision and Pattern Recognition* (CVPR).

Farrugia, R., & Debono, C. (2010). Resilient digital video transmission over wireless channels using pixel-level artefact detection mechanisms. In De Rango, F. (Ed.), *Digital video* (pp. 71–96). Intech.

Fehn, C. (2004). Depth-image-based rendering (DIBR), compression and transmission for a new approach on 3D-TV. In *Stereoscopic Displays and Virtual Reality Systems XI*, (pp. 93-104).

Fehn, C., Kauff, P., De Beeck, M., & Ernst, F. Ijssel-Steijn, W., Pollefeys, M., et al. (2002). An evolutionary and optimised approach on 3D-TV. *Proceedings of International Broadcast Conference*, (pp. 357–365).

Fehn, C. (2006). *Depth-image-based rendering (dibr), compression, and transmission for a flexible approach on 3DTV. (B.M. Berlin, Germany: Technical University, Ed.*

Fehn, C., Kauff, P., De Beeck, M., Ernst, F., Ijssel-Steijn, W., & Javidi, B. (2002). *Three-dimensional television, video, and display technologies*. Springer-Verlag.

Fei-Fei, L., & Perona, P. (2005). A Bayesian hierarchical model for learning natural scene categories. In *Proceedings of IEEE Conference in Computer Vision and Pattern Recognition*, San Diego.

Fei-Fei, L., Fergus, R., & Perona, P. (2004). *Learning generative visual models from few training examples: An incremental Bayesian approach tested on 101 Object Categories*. In Workshop on Generative Model Based Vision.

Felzenszwalb, P., & Huttenlocher, D. (2000). Efficient matching of pictorial structures. In the *Proceedings of the IEEE Conference on Computer Vision and Pattern Recognition*.

Feng, J., Liu, T. Y., Lo, K. T., & Zhang, X. D. (2001). Adaptive motion tracking for fast block motion estimation. In the *Proceedings of IEEE International Symposium on Circuits and Systems*, Sydney, NSW, Australia, Vol. 5, (pp. 219-222).

Feng, J., Lo, K.-T., Mehrpour, H., & Karbowiak, A. E. (1998). Adaptive block matching algorithm for video compression. *IEE Proceedings. Vision Image and Signal Processing, 145*, 173–178. doi:10.1049/ip-vis:19981916

Fernandes, S. R., do Carmo, F., Estrela, V. V., & Assis, J. (2009). Using the SIFT (scale invariant feature transform) to determine pairs of image points for using in the SITH (3D hybrid imaging system). *Proceedings of the XII Workshop on Computer Modeling (XII EMC)*. Volta Redonda, RJ, Brazil.

Ferré, P., Agrafiotis, D., & Bull, D. (2010). A video error resilience redundant slices algorithm and its performance relative to other fixed redundancy schemes. *Image Communication, 25*(3), 163–178.

Fielding, R., Gettys, J., Mogul, J., Frystyk, H., Masinter, L., Leach, P., et al. (1999). *Hypertext transfer protocol -- HTTP/1.1*. Request for Comments IETF. Retrieved from http://www.ietf.org/rfc/rfc2616.txt

Fischler, M., & Bolles, R. (1981). Random sample consensus: A paradigm for model fitting with applications to image analysis and automated cartography. *Communications of the ACM, 24*(6), 381–395. doi:10.1145/358669.358692

Flickner, M., Sawhney, H., Niblack, W., Ashley, J., Huang, Q., & Dom, B. (1995). Query by image and video content: The QBIC system. *IEEE Computer, 28*(9), 23–32. doi:10.1109/2.410146

Flierl, M., Mavlankar, A., & Girod, B. (2006). Motion and disparity compensated coding for video camera arrays. *IEEE Proceedings of Picture Coding Symposium (PCS2006)*. Beijing, China.

Flierl, M., & Girod, B. (2003). Generalized B pictures and the draft H. 264/AVC video compression standard. *IEEE Transactions on Circuits and Systems for Video Technology, 13*(7), 587–597. doi:10.1109/TCSVT.2003.814963

Fookes, C. Lin, F. Chandran, V., & Sridharan, S. (2004, 20-22 December). Super-resolved face images using robust optical flow. In the *Proceedings of the Third Workshop on the Internet, Telecommunications and Signal Processing*, Adelaide.

Fookes, C., Bennamoun, M., & Lamanna, A. (2002). Improved stereo image matching using mutual information and hierarchical prior probabilities. In the *Proceedings of the International Conference on Pattern Recognition* (ICPR'02), Vol. 2, (pp. 937 – 940).

Fragouli, C., & Soljanin, C. (2007). Network coding fundamentals. *Foundations and Trends in Networking*, 2(1), 1–133. doi:10.1561/1300000003

Francois, E., & Vieron, J. (2006). Extended spatial scalability: a generalization of spatial scalability for non dyadic configurations. *2006 IEEE International Conference on Image Processing*, (pp. 169-172).

Freeman, W., Jones, T., & Pasztor, E. (2002). Example-based super-resolution. *IEEE Computer Graphics and Applications*, (March/April): 2002.

Freund, Y., & Schapire, R. E. (1997). A decision-theoretic generalization of on-line learning and an application to boosting. *Journal of Computer and System Sciences*, 55(1), 119–139. doi:10.1006/jcss.1997.1504

Fukuma, S., Ikuta, S., Ito, M., Nishimura, S., & Nawate, M. (2003). An ROI image coding based on switching wavelet transform. *Proceedings of the 2003 International Symposium on Circuits and Systems, ISCAS '03*, Vol. 2, (pp. II-420- II-423).

Furht, B. (2008). *Encyclopedia of multimedia*. Springer. doi:10.1007/978-0-387-78414-4

Furht, B., & Ahson, S. A. (2010). *HSDPA/HSUPA handbook* (1st ed.). CRC Press. doi:10.1201/b10268

Fusiello, A., Trucco, E., & Verri, A. (2000). Compact algorithm for rectification of stereo pairs. *Machine Vision and Applications, 12*, 16–22. doi:10.1007/s001380050120

Fu, X., Lei, J., & Shi, L. (2007). *An experimental analysis of Joost peer-to-peer VoD service. Technical Report*. Institute of Computer Science, University of Goettingen.

Gallager, R. G. (1962). Low-density parity-check codes. *I.R.E. Transactions on Information Theory, 8*(1), 21–28. doi:10.1109/TIT.1962.1057683

Galoogahi, H. K. (2010, 14-17 November). Tracking groups of people in presence of occlusion. In the *Proceedings of the Fourth Pacific-Rim Symposium on Image and Video Technology* (PSIVT).

Garawi, S., Courreges, F., Istepanian, R., Zisimopoulos, H., & Gosset, P. (2004). Performance analysis of a compact robotic tele-echography E-health system over terrestrial and mobile communication links. *3G Mobile Communication Technologies*, (pp. 118-122).

Garawi, S., Istepanian, R., & Abu-Rgheff, M. (2006). 3G wireless communications for mobile robotic tele-ultrasonography systems. *IEEE Communications Magazine, 44*(4), 91–96. doi:10.1109/MCOM.2006.1632654

Garbacki, P., Iosup, A., Epema, D., & van Steen, M. (2006). 2Fast : Collaborative downloads in P2P networks. *Proceedings of the Sixth IEEE International Conference on Peer-to-Peer Computing, P2P '06* (pp. 23-30). doi:10.1109/P2P.2006.1

Garbas, J., Fecker, U., Troger, T., & Kaup, A. (2006). 4D scalable multi-view video coding using disparity compensated view filtering and motion compensated temporal filtering. *Proceedings of the IEEE International Workshop on Multimedia Signal Processing 2006 (MMSP06)*. Victoria, Canada.

Gevers, T., & Smeulders, A. (2000). Pictoseek: Combining color and shape invariant features for image retrieval. *IEEE Transactions on Image Processing*, 102–119. doi:10.1109/83.817602

Ghanbari, M. (2003). *Standard codecs: Image compression to advanced video coding*. London, UK: Institution of Engineering and Technology.

Ghanbari, M. (1990). The cross-search algorithm for motion estimation (image coding). *IEEE Transactions on Communications, 38*(7), 950–953. doi:10.1109/26.57512

Ghandi, M., Barmada, B., Jones, E., & Ghanbari, M. (2006, May). Unequally error protected data partitioned video with combined hierarchical modulation and channel coding. *Proc. of ICASSP '06, 2*, (pp. 529-531).

Ghazal, S., Mokdad, L., & Ben-Othman, J. (2008). Performance analysis of UGS, rtPS, nrtPS admission control in WiMAX networks. *Proceedings of IEEE International Conference on Communications*, (pp. 2696-2701). Beijing, China: IEEE.

Gheissari, N., Sebastian, T. B., & Hartley, R. (2006). Person reidentification using spatiotemporal appearance. In the *Proceedings of the IEEE Computer Society Conference on Computer Vision and Pattern Recognition.*

Gheorghe, G., Lo Cigno, R., & Montresor, A. (2011). Security and privacy issues in P2P streaming systems: A Survey. *Peer-to-Peer Networking and Applications, 4.*

Girod, B. (2000, Feb.). Efficiency analysis of multihypothesis motion-compensated prediction for video coding. *IEEE Transactions on Image Processing, 9*(2), 173–183. doi:10.1109/83.821595

Girod, B., & Farber, N. (1999, Oct.). Feedback-based error control for mobile video transmission. *Proceedings of the IEEE, 87*(10), 1707–1723. doi:10.1109/5.790632

Gnutella. (2004). *The Gnutella protocol specification v0.41* Retrieved from http://www9.limewire.com/developer/gnutella protocol 0.4.pdf

GoalBit. (2010). *Goalbit-Solutions home page.* Retrieved from http://goalbit-solutions.com/

Gokturk, S., Yalcin, H., & Bamji, C. (2005). A time-of-flight depth sensor - System description, issues and solutions. *IEEE Computer Society Conference on Computer Vision and Pattern Recognition Workshops 2004* (pp. 35-45). IEEE.

Goldberg, N., Feuer, A., & Goodwin, G. (2003). Super-resolution reconstruction using spatio-temporal filtering. *Journal of Visual Communication and Image Representation, 14*, 508–525. doi:10.1016/S1047-3203(03)00042-7

Goldsmith, A. (2005). *Wireless communications.* Cambridge, UK: Cambridge University Press.

Goldstein, E. B. (2002). *Sensation and perception.* Pacific Grove, CA.

Gong, W., Rao, K. R., & Manry, M. T. (1993). Progressive image transmission. *IEEE Transactions on Circuits and Systems for Video Technology, 3*(5), 380–383. doi:10.1109/76.246089

Gopalan, R. (2009). *Exploiting region-of-interest for improved video coding.* Department of Electrical and Computer Engineering, Ohio State University, Thesis, 2009.

Goyal, V. K. (2001). Multiple description coding: Compression meets the network. *IEEE Signal Processing Magazine, 18*(5), 74–93. doi:10.1109/79.952806

Grest, D., Frahm, J.-M., & Koch, R. (2003). A color similarity measure for robust shadow removal in real time. In the *Proceedings of the Vision, Modeling and Visualization Conference,* Munich, Germany.

Grois, D., & Hadar, O. (2011a). Efficient adaptive bit-rate control for scalable video coding by using computational complexity-rate-distortion analysis. *2011 IEEE International Symposium on Broadband Multimedia Systems and Broadcasting* (BMSB), (pp. 1-6). Nuremberg, Germany, 8-10 Jun. 2011.

Grois, D., & Hadar, O. (2011c). Complexity-aware adaptive bit-rate control with dynamic ROI pre-processing for scalable video coding. *2011 IEEE International Conference on Multimedia and Expo* (ICME), (pp. 1-4). Barcelona, Spain, 11-15 Jul. 2011.

Grois, D., & Hadar, O. (2011d). *Complexity-aware adaptive spatial pre-processing for ROI scalable video coding with dynamic transition region.* International Conference on Image Processing (ICIP 2011), Brussels, Belgium, 11-14 Sep. 2011.

Grois, D., Kaminsky, E., & Hadar, O. (2009). Buffer control in H.264/AVC applications by implementing dynamic complexity-rate-distortion analysis. *IEEE International Symposium on Broadband Multimedia Systems and Broadcasting, BMSB '09*, (pp. 1-7).

Grois, D., Kaminsky, E., & Hadar, O. (2010a). ROI adaptive scalable video coding for limited bandwidth wireless networks. *2010 IFIP Wireless Days* (WD), (pp. 1-5).

Grois, D., Kaminsky, E., & Hadar, O. (2010b). Adaptive bit-rate control for region-of-interest scalable video coding. *2010 IEEE 26th Convention of Electrical and Electronics Engineers in Israel* (IEEEI), (pp. 761-765).

Grois, D., & Hadar, O. (2011b). Recent advances in region-of-interest coding. In Del Ser Lorente, J. (Ed.), *Recent advances on video coding* (pp. 49–76). Intech. doi:10.5772/17789

Grois, D., Kaminsky, E., & Hadar, O. (2010c). Optimization methods for H.264/AVC video coding. In Angelides, M. C., & Agius, H. (Eds.), *The handbook of MPEG applications: Standards in practice*. Chichester, UK: John Wiley & Sons, Ltd.doi:10.1002/9780470974582.ch7

Grokster. (2005). Grokster home page (Web archive). Retrieved from http://web.archive.org/web/*/grokster.com

Guan, Y. (2010). Spatio-temporal motion-based foreground segmentation and shadow suppression. *IET Computer Vision*, *4*(1), 50–60. doi:10.1049/iet-cvi.2008.0016

Gunawan, I. P., & Ghanbari, M. (2003). *Reduced-reference picture quality estimation by using local harmonic amplitude information*. London Communications Symposium 2003.

Gunturk, B. K., Batur, A. U., Altunbasak, Y., Hayes, M. H. III, & Mersereau, R. M. (2003). Eigenface-domain super-resolution for face recognition. *IEEE Transactions on Image Processing*, *12*(5), 597–606. doi:10.1109/TIP.2003.811513

Guo, X., Lu, Y., Wu, F., & Gao, W. (2006). Inter-view direct mode for multiview video coding. *IEEE Transactions on Circuits and Systems for Video Technology*, *16*(12), 1527–1532. doi:10.1109/TCSVT.2006.885724

Gupta, M., Judge, P., & Ammar, M. (2003). A reputation system for peer-to-peer networks. *Proceedings of the 13th International Workshop on Network and Operating Systems Support for Digital Audio and Video* (pp. 144-152). New York, NY: ACM. doi:http://doi.acm.org/10.1145/776322.776346

Hamzaoui, R., Stanković, V., & Xiong, Z. (2007). Forward error control for packet loss and corruption. In van der Schaar, M., & Chou, P. A. (Eds.), *Multimedia over IP and wireless networks* (pp. 271–292). Burlington, MA: Academic Press. doi:10.1016/B978-012088480-3/50010-2

Han, S., & Vasconcelos, N. (2008). Object-based regions of interest for image compression. *Data Compression Conference, DCC 2008*, (pp. 132-141).

Handley, M., Floyd, S., Padhye, J., & Widmer, J. (2003). *TCP friendly rate control (TFRC) protocol specification*. IETF, RFC 3448.

Hands, D., Huynh-Thu, Q., Rix, A., Davis, A., & Voelcker, R. (2004). Objective perceptual quality measurement of 3G video services. *3G Mobile Communication Technologies*, (pp. 437-441).

Hanfeng, C., Yiqiang, Z., & Feihu, Q. (2001). Rapid object tracking on compressed video. In *Proceeding of the 2nd IEEE Pacific Rim Conference on Multimedia*, Oct. 2001, (pp. 1066-1071).

Hannuksela, M. (2009). *Error-resilient communication using the h.264/avc video coding standard*. Unpublished doctoral dissertation, Tampere University of Technology, Tampere, Finland.

Hannuksela, M. M., Wang, Y.-K., & Gabboj, M. (2004). Isolated regions in video coding. *IEEE Transactions on Multimedia*, *6*(2), 259–267. doi:10.1109/TMM.2003.822784

Han, T.-H., & Hwang, S. H. (1998). A novel hierarchical-search block matchingalgorithm and VLSI architecture considering the spatial complexity of the macroblock. *IEEE Transactions on Consumer Electronics*, *44*, 337–342. doi:10.1109/30.681947

Haritaoglu, I., Harwood, D., & Davis, L. (2000). An appearance-based body model for multiple people tracking. In the *Proceedings of the IEEE Conference on Pattern Recognition*, (pp. 184-187). Barcelona, Spain, 2000.

Haritaoglu, I., Harwood, D., & Davis, L. S. (2000). W4: real-time surveillance of people and their activities. *IEEE Transactions on Pattern Analysis and Machine Intelligence*, *22*(8), 809–830. doi:10.1109/34.868683

Harmanci, O., & Tekalp, A. (2004, Oct.). Optimization of H.264 for low delay video communications over lossy channels. *Proceedings of ICIP '04*, Vol. 5, (pp. 3209-3212).

Harmanci, O., & Tekalp, A. M. (2007, March). A stochastic framework for rate-distortion optimized video coding over error-prone networks. *IEEE Transactions on Image Processing*, *16*(3), 684–697. doi:10.1109/TIP.2006.891047

Harris, C., & Stephes, M. (1988). A combined corner and edge detector. In the *Proceedings of the 4th Alvey Vision Conference*, (pp. 147-151).

Hartley, R., & Zisserman, A. (2003). *Multiple view geometry in computer vision*. Cambridge, UK: Cambridge University Press.

Harville, M. (2002). A framework for high-level feedback to adaptive, per-pixel, mixture-of-gaussian background models. In the *Proceedings of the 7th European Conference on Computer Vision*, Vol. 3, Copenhagen, Denmark.

Harville, M., Gordon, G. G., & Wood_ll, J. (2001). Foreground segmentation using adaptive mixture models in color and depth. In the *Proceedings of the IEEE Workshop on Detection and Recognition of Events in Video*, (pp. 3-11).

Hayman, E., & Eklundh, J. (2003). Statistical background subtraction for a mobile observer. In the *Proceedings of the International Conference on Computer Vision* (ICCV).

He, R., Yu, M., Yang, Y., & Jiang, G. (2008). Comparison of the depth quantification method in terms of coding and synthesizing capacity in 3DTV system. *Proceedings of the 9th International Conference on Signal Processing (ICSP) 2008*, (pp. 1279–1282). Leipzig, Germany.

Heckmann, O., Bock, A., Mauthe, A., & Steinmetz, R. (2004). The eDonkey file-sharing network. *Proceedings of the Workshop on Algorithms and Protocols for Efficient Peer-to-Peer Applications, Informatik '04*.

Hefeeda, M., Habib, A., Botev, B., Xu, D., & Bhargava, B. (2003). Promise: Peer-to-peer media streaming using collectcast. In *Proceedings of ACM Multimedia* (pp. 45-54).

Hefeeda, M., Bhargava, B., & Yau, D. (2004). A hybrid architecture for cost effective on demand media streaming. *Journal of Computer Networks*, *44*(3), 353–382. doi:10.1016/j.comnet.2003.10.002

Held, G., & Marshall, T. R. (1991). *Data compression*. Wiley. ISBN 0 471 92941 7

Hewage, C., Karim, H., Worrall, S., Dogan, S., & Kondoz, A. (2007). Comparison of stereo video coding support in MPEG-4 MAC, H.264/AVC and H.264/SVC. *Proceedings of IET Visual Information Engineering-VIE07*.

He, Z., & Xiong, H. (2006, Sept.). Transmission distortion analysis for real-time video encoding and streaming over wireless networks. *IEEE Transactions on Circuits and Systems for Video Technology*, *16*(9), 1051–1062. doi:10.1109/TCSVT.2006.881198

Higuchi, T. (1997). Monte Carlo filter using the genetic algorithm operators. *Journal of Statistical Computation and Simulation*, *59*(1), 1–23. doi:10.1080/00949659708811843

Hofbauer, H., & Uhl, A. (2010). *Visual quality indices and low quality images*. Paper presented at the IEEE 2nd European Workshop on Visual Information Processing, Paris, France.

Holbrook, H., & Cain, B. (2006). *Source-specific multicast for IP*. Request for Comments. IETF. Retrieved from http://www.ietf.org/rfc/rfc4607.txt

Holma, H., & Toskala, A. (2006). *HSDPA/HSUPA for UMTS: High speed radio access for mobile communications*. Wiley-Blackwell.

Horn, B. K. P., & Schunck, B. G. (1981). Determining optical flow. *Artificial Intelligence*, *17*, 185–203. doi:10.1016/0004-3702(81)90024-2

Hosseini, M., Ahmed, D. T., Shirmohammadi, S., & Georganas, N. D. (2007). A survey of application-layer multicast protocols. *IEEE Communications Surveys Tutorials*, *9*(3), 58–74. doi:10.1109/COMST.2007.4317616

Hossfeld, T., & Leibnitz, K. (2008). A qualitative measurement survey of popular Internet-based IPTV systems. *Second International Conference on Communications and Electronics*, (pp. 156-161).

Howard, I. P., & Rogers, B. J. (1996). *Binocular vision and stereopsis*. Oxford. doi:10.1093/acprof:oso/9780195084764.001.0001

Hsieh, C.-H., Lu, P., Shyn, J.-S., & Lu, E.-H. (1990). Motion estimation algorithm using interblock correlation. *Electronics Letters*, *26*, 276–277. doi:10.1049/el:19900183

Hu, M., Hu, W., & Tan, T. (2004). Tracking people through occlusions. In the *Proceedings of the 17th International Conference on Pattern Recognition* (ICPR), (pp. 724-727).

Huang, J., Kumar, S., Mitra, M., Zhu, W.-J., & Zabih, R. (1997). Image indexing using color correlogram. In *Proceedings of IEEE Conf. on Computer Vision and Pattern Recognition*.

Huang, H.-C., & Hung, Y.-P. (1997). Adaptive early jump-out technique for fast motion estimation in video coding. *Graphical Models & Image Processing*, *59*, 388–394. doi:10.1006/gmip.1997.0449

Huang, H., Wang, C., & Chiang, T. (2002, Jun.). A robust fine granularity scalability using trellis-based predictive leak. *IEEE Transactions on Circuits and Systems for Video Technology, 12*(6), 372–385. doi:10.1109/TCSVT.2002.800314

Huffman, D. (1952). A method for the construction of minimum redundancy codes. *Proceedings of the IRE, 40*, 1098–1101. doi:10.1109/JRPROC.1952.273898

Huitema, C. (2006). *Teredo: Tunneling IPv6 over UDP through network address translations (NATs)*. Retrieved from http://www.rfc-editor.org/rfc/rfc4380.txt

Hu, Y., Rajan, D., & Chia, L. (2008). Detection of visual attention regions in images using robust subspace analysis. *Journal of Visual Communication and Image Representation, 19*(3), 199–216. doi:10.1016/j.jvcir.2007.11.001

IETF ALTO Working Group. (2010). *Application-layer traffic optimization (ALTO)*. Retrieved from http://datatracker.ietf.org/wg/alto/charter/

IETF DECADE Working Group. (2010). *Decoupled application data enroute (DECADE)*. Retrieved from http://datatracker.ietf.org/wg/decade/charter/

IETF HIP Working Group. (2010). *Host identity protocol (HIP)*. Retrieved from http://datatracker.ietf.org/wg/hip/charter/

IETF LEDBAT Working Group. (2010). *Low extra delay background transport (LEDBAT)*. Retrieved from http://datatracker.ietf.org/wg/ledbat/charter/

IETF P2PSIP Working Group. (2010). *Peer-to-peer session initiation protocol (P2PSIP)*. Retrieved from http://datatracker.ietf.org/wg/p2psip/charter

IETF PPSP Working Group. (2010)*Peer to peer streaming protocol (PPSP)*. Retrieved from http://tools.ietf.org/wg/ppsp/

iLIDS Team. (2006). Imagery library for intelligent detection systems (i-lids); a standard for testing video based detection systems. In *the Proceedings of the 40th Annual IEEE International Carnahan Conferences Security Technology*, (pp. 75-80).

Ilie, A., & Welch, G. (2005). Ensuring color consistency across multiple cameras. *Proceedings of the IEEE International Conference on Computer Vision*, (pp. 1268-1275).

iMesh. (2010). *iMesh: The world's best P2P file sharing community! Home page*. iMesh Inc. Retrieved from http://www.imesh.com

Inaba, T., Okawa, T., Murata, Y., Takizawa, H., & Kobayashi, H. (2006). Design and implementation of an efficient search mechanism based on the hybrid P2P model for ubiquitous computing systems. In *Proceedings International Symposium on Applications of the Internet*, (pp. 45-53).

International Telecommunication Union. (2010). *Recommendation ITU-T H.264 – Advanced video coding for generic audiovisual services (03/2010)*. Geneva, Switzerland: International Telecommunication Union.

Isard, M., & Blake, A. (1998). Condensation - Conditional density propagation for visual tracking. *International Journal of Computer Vision, 29*, 5–28. doi:10.1023/A:1008078328650

Ishfaq, A., Weiguo, Z., Jiancong, L., & Ming, L. (2006). A fast adaptive motion estimation algorithm. *IEEE Transactions on Circuits and Systems for Video Technology, 16*(3), 420–438. doi:10.1109/TCSVT.2006.870022

ISO/IEC JTC1/SC29/WG11. (2003). *Report on 3DAV exploration*. MPEG output document N5878, July 2003.

ISO/IEC JTC1/SC29/WG11. (2008). Call for contributions on 3D video test material (update). MPEG output document N9595, Jan. 2008.

ISO/IEC JTC1/SC29/WG11. (2008). *Multiview video test sequence and camera parameters*. MPEG intput document m15419, April 2008.

ISO/IEC JTC1/SC29/WG11. (2009). *View synthesis method without blending*. MPEG input document M16091, Feb. 2009.

ISO/IEC JTC1/SC29/WG11. (2009). *Vision on 3D video*. MPEG output document N10357, Jan. 2009.

ISO/IEC JTC1/SC29/WG11. (2010). *Report on experimental framework for 3D video coding*. MPEG output document N11631, Oct. 2010.

ISO/IEC JTC1/SC29/WG11. (2011). *Applications and requirements on 3D video coding*. MPEG output document N11829, Jan. 2011.

ISO/IEC JTC1/SC29/WG11. (2011). *Call for proposals on 3D video coding technology*. MPEG output document N12036, March 2011.

ISO/IEC JTC1/SC29/WG11. (2011). *Description of AVC compatible 3D video coding technology by Samsung*. MPEG input document M22632, Nov. 2011.

ISO/IEC JTC1/SC29/WG11. (2011). *Descriptions of 3D video coding proposal* (HEVC-compatible category). MPEG input document M22566, Nov. 2011.

ISO/IEC JTC1/SC29/WG11. (2012). *3D-AVC-CE06 results on in-loop depth resampling by Mitsubishi*. MPEG input document M23774, Feb. 2012.

ISO/IEC JTC1/SC29/WG11. (2012). *3D-AVC-CE7 results on: Joint RDO for depth coding of 3D video by ZJU*. MPEG input document M23627, Feb. 2012.

ISO/IEC JTC1/SC29/WG11. (2012). *Description of core experiments in 3D video coding*. MPEG output document N12561, Feb. 2012.

ISO/IEC JTC1/SC29/WG11. (2012). *Overview of the coding performance of 3D video architectures*. MPEG input document M24968, April 2012.

ISO/IEC. (2007). *Information technology -- Coding of audio-visual objects -- Part 10: Advanced video coding*. International Organization for Standardization/ International Electrotechnical Commission.

Istepanaian, R. S. H., & Zhang, Y.-T. (2012). 4G health— The Long-term evolution of m-health. *IEEE Transactions on Information Technology in Biomedicine*, *16*(1), 1–5. doi:10.1109/TITB.2012.2183269

Istepanian, R. S., & Woodward, B. (2002). *Programmable underwater acoustic telemedicine system in Acoustica*.

Istepanian, R. S. (1999). Telemedicine in the United Kingdom: Current status and future prospects. *IEEE Transactions on Information Technology in Biomedicine*, *3*(2), 158–159. doi:10.1109/4233.767091

Istepanian, R. S. (1999). The comparative performance of mobile telemedical systems using the IS-54 and GSM cellular telephone standards. *Journal of Telemedicine and Telecare*, *5*(2), 97–104. doi:10.1258/1357633991933396

Istepanian, R. S. (2000). Telemedicine in Armenia: A perception of telehealth services in the former Soviet Republics. *Journal of Telemedicine and Telecare*, *6*, 268–272. doi:10.1258/1357633001935897

Istepanian, R. S. H., Philip, N., Martini, M. G., Amso, N., & Shorvon, P. (2008). *Subjective and objective quality assessment in wireless teleultrasonography imaging* (pp. 5346–5349). Vancouver, BC: Engineering in Medicine and Biology Society. doi:10.1109/IEMBS.2008.4650422

Istepanian, R., Jovanov, E., & Zhang, Y. (2004). Guest editorial introduction to the special section on m-health: Beyond seamless mobility and global wireless health-care connectivity. *IEEE Transactions on Information Technology in Biomedicine*, *8*(4), 405–414. doi:10.1109/TITB.2004.840019

Istepanian, R., & Petrosian, A. (2000). Optimal zonal wavelet-based ECG data compression for a mobile telecardiology system. *IEEE Transactions on Information Technology in Biomedicine*, *4*(3), 200–211. doi:10.1109/4233.870030

Istepanian, R., Philip, N., & Martini, M. (2009). Medical QoS provision based on reinforcement learning in ultrasound streaming over 3.5G wireless systems. *IEEE Journal on Selected Areas in Communications*, *27*(4), 566–574. doi:10.1109/JSAC.2009.090517

ITU-R (1993). *Recommendation H.261 (03/93): Video codec for audiovisual services at p x 64 kbit/s*.

ITU-R (2005). *Recommendation H.263 (01/05): Video coding for low bit rate communication*.

ITU-T. (2010). *Advanced video coding for generic audio-visual services*. International Telecommunication Union, Telecommunication Standardization Sector.

Iwata, T., Abe, T., Ueda, K., et al. (2003). A DRM system suitable for P2P content delivery and the study on its implementation. *The 9th Asia-Pacific Conference on Communications*, 2003, (pp. 806-811).

J. V. T. (2009, Apr.). *H.264/AVC reference software (ver JM 15.1)*. Retrieved from http://iphome.hhi.de/suehring/tml/

J. V. T. (2010, Jan.). *H.264/SVC reference software (jsvm 9.19) and manual*. Retrieved from garcon.ient. rwth-aachen.de

Jacques, J., Jung, C., & Musse, S. (2005). Background subtraction and shadow detection in grayscale video sequences. In the *Proceedings of the 18th Brazilian Symposium on Computer Graphics and Image Processing*, (SIBGRAPI), (pp. 189-196).

Jain, J. R., & Jain, A. K. (1984). Displacement measurement and its application in inter frame image coding. *IEEE Transactions on Communications, 29*, 1799–1808. doi:10.1109/TCOM.1981.1094950

Jamalipour, A. (2003). *The wireless mobile internet: Architectures, protocols and services* (1st ed.). Wiley.

Jamrozik, M. L., & Hayes, M. H. (2002). A compressed domain video object segmentation system. In *Proceedings of the IEEE International Conference on Image Processing, 2002*, Vol. 1, (pp. 113-116).

Javed, O., Shafique, K., & Shah, M. (2002). A hierarchical approach to robust background subtraction using color and gradient information. In the *Proceedings of the Workshop on Motion and Video Computing.*

Javidi, B., & Okano, F. (2002). *Three-dimensional television, video, and display technologies.* Springer-Verlag.

Jaynes, C., Kale, A., Sanders, N., & Grossmann, E. (2005). The Terrascope dataset: Scripted multi-camera indoor video surveillance with ground-truth. In the *Proceedings of the IEEE International Workshop on Visual Surveillance and Performance Evaluation of Tracking and Surveillance*, (pp. 309-316).

Jebara, T. A., & Pentland, A. (1999). 3-D structure from 2-D motion. *IEEE Signal Processing Magazine, 16*(3), 66–84. doi:10.1109/79.768574

Jeong, C. Y., Han, S. W., Choi, S. G., & Nam, T. Y. (2006). An objectionable image detection system based on region of interest. *2006 IEEE International Conference on Image Processing*, (pp.1477-1480).

Jeong, S., Kim, K., Chun, B., Lee, J., & Bae, Y. J. (1999). An effective method for combining multiple features of images retrieval. In *Proceedings of IEEE TENCON*, (pp. 982-985).

Jeong, W.-H., Yoon, Y.-S., & Ho, Y.-S. (2004). *Design of asymmetrical reversible variable-length codes and comparison of their robustness.* In European Signal Processing Conference.

Jerbi, A., Jian, W., & Shirani, S. (2004). Error-resilient ROI coding using pre- and post-processing for video sequences. *Proceedings of the 2004 International Symposium on Circuits and Systems, ISCAS '04*, Vol.3, (pp. 757-60).

Jerbi, A., Jian, W., & Shirani, S. (2005). Error-resilient region-of-interest video coding. *IEEE Transactions on Circuits and Systems for Video Technology, 15*(9), 1175–1181. doi:10.1109/TCSVT.2005.852619

Jha, S., & Hassan, M. (2002). *Engineering internet QoS.* Artech House.

Jia, J., Choi, H.-C., Kim, J.-G., Kim, H.-K., & Chang, Y. (2007). Improved redundant picture coding using polyphase downsampling. *ETRI Journal, 29*(1), 18–26. doi:10.4218/etrij.07.0106.0159

Jiang, G., Shao, F., Yu, M., Chen, K., & Chen, X. (2006). New color correction approach to multi-view images with region correspondence. *LNCS, 4113*, 1224–1228.

Jiang, W., Latecki, L. J., Liu, W., Liang, H., & Gorman, K. (2009). A video coding scheme based on joint spatiotemporal and adaptive prediction. *IEEE Transactions on Image Processing, 8*(5), 1025–1036. doi:10.1109/TIP.2009.2016140

Jin, X., & French, J. C. (2005). Improving image retrieval effectiveness via multiple queries. *Multimedia Tools and Applications, 26*(2), 221–245. doi:10.1007/s11042-005-0453-5

Ji, S., & Park, H. W. (2000). Moving object segmentation in DCT-based compressed video. *Electronics Letters, 36*(21). doi:10.1049/el:20001279

Johannesson, R., & Zigangirov, K. S. (1999). *Fundamentals of convolutional coding.* IEEE Series on Digital and Mobile Communication. doi:10.1109/9780470544693

Johnson, C. (2008). *Radio access networks for UMTS: Principles and practice.* Wiley-Blackwell.

Johnson, D., Hu, Y., & Maltz, D. (2007). *The dynamic source routing protocol (DSR) for mobile ad hoc networks for IPv4.* Retrieved from http://www.rfc-editor.org/rfc/rfc4728.txt

Joost. (2010). *Joost home page.* Retrieved from http://www.joost.com/.

JSVM. (2009). *JSVM software manual*, ver. JSVM 9.19 (CVS tag: JSVM_9_19), Nov. 2009.

Juan, L., & Gwun, O. (2009). A comparison of sift, PCA-sift and surf. *International Journal of Image Processing, 3*, 143–152.

Julier, S., & Uhlman, J. (1997). A consistent, debiased method for converting between polar and Cartesian coordinate systems. In the *Proceedings of the 11th International Symposium on Aerospace/Defence Sensing, Simulation and Controls, volume Multi Sensor Fusion, Tracking and Resource Management II*, Orlando, Florida

Jun, S., & Ahamad, M. (2005). Incentives in BitTorrent induce free riding. *Proceedings of the 2005 ACM SIG-COMM Workshop on Economics of Peer-to-Peer Systems* (pp. 116-121). New York, NY: ACM. doi:http://doi.acm.org/10.1145/1080192.1080199

Jung, J.-I., & Ho, Y. S. (2012). (in press). Color correction algorithm based on camera characteristics for multiview video coding. *Signal Image and Video Processing.* doi:10.1007/s11760-012-0341-1

Jurdak, R. (2007). *Wireless ad hoc and sensor networks: A cross-layer design perspective.* Berlin, Germany: Springer Verlag.

Jurkiewicz, A., et al. (2011). *X264 settings.* Retrieved February 1, 2011, from http://mewiki.project357.com/wiki/X264_Settings

Kaminsky, E., Grois, D., & Hadar, O. (2008). Dynamic computational complexity and bit allocation for optimizing H.264/AVC video compression. *Journal of Visual Communication and Image Research, 19*(1), 56–74. doi:10.1016/j.jvcir.2007.05.002

Kanatani, K. (1990). *Group-theoretical methods in image understanding (Vol. 20).* Springer Series in Information Sciences. doi:10.1007/978-3-642-61275-6

Karczewicz, M., & Kurceren, R. (n.d.). (J2003). The SP-and SI-frames design for H.264/AVC. *IEEE Transactions on Circuits and Systems for Video Technology, 13*(7), 637–644. doi:10.1109/TCSVT.2003.814969

Karlsson, L. S., & Sjostrom, M. (2005). Improved ROI video coding using variable Gaussian pre-filters and variance in intensity. *IEEE International Conference on Image Processing, ICIP 2005*, Vol. 2, (pp. 313-16).

Kas, C., & Nicolas, H. (2009). Compressed domain indexing of scalable H.264/SVC streams. *Signal Processing Image Communication (2009), Special Issue on Scalable Coded Media beyond Compression*, 484-498.

Katz, B., Greenberg, S., Yarkoni, N., Blaunstein, N., & Giladi, R. (2007). New error-resilient scheme based on FMO and dynamic redundant slices allocation for wireless video transmission. *IEEE Transactions on Broadcasting, 53*(1), 308–319. doi:10.1109/TBC.2006.889694

Kauff, P., Atzpadin, N., Fehn, C., Muller, M., Schreer, O., Smolic, A., et al. (2007). Depth map creation and image based rendering for advanced 3DTV services providing interoperability and scalability. *Signal Processing: Image Communication, Special Issue on 3DTV, 22*(2), 217-234.

Kaur, B. (2010). Factors influencing implementation of 4G with mobile ad-hoc networks in m-governance environment. *International Journal of Computers and Applications, 3.*

KaZaA. (2010). *KaZaA home page.* Retrieved from http://www.kazaa.com/#/about

Ke, C.-H., Chilamkurti, N., Dudeja, G., & Shieh, C.-K. (2006). *A new adaptive FEC algorithm for wireless LAN networks.* The IASTED International Conference on Networks and Communication Systems, March 29-31, 2006, Chiang Mai, Thailand.

Ke, Y., & Sukthankar, R. (2004). PCA-SIFT: A more distinctive representation for local image descriptors. In *Proceedings of the Conference on Computer Vision and Pattern Recognition*, (pp. 511-517).

Kearney, J. K., Thomson, W. B., & Boley, D. L. (1987). Optical flow estimation: An error analysis of gradient-based methods with local optimization. *IEEE Transactions on Pattern Analysis and Machine Intelligence, 9*, 229–244. doi:10.1109/TPAMI.1987.4767897

Ken, W.-P., Jin, X., & Chan, S.-H. (2007). Challenges and approaches in large-scale P2P media streaming. *IEEE MultiMedia, 14*(2), 50–59. doi:10.1109/MMUL.2007.30

Kerr, D. A. (2009). *Chrominance subsampling in digital images.* Retrieved February 1, 2011, from http://dougkerr.net/pumpkin/articles/Subsampling.pdf

Kienzle, W., Schölkopf, B., Wichmann, F., & Franz, M. (2007). How to find interesting locations in video: A spatiotemporal interest point detector learned from human eye movements. *Pattern Recognition (DAGM 2007)* (pp. 405-411). Darmstadt, Germany: Springer, LNCS.

Kim, D.-K., & Wang, Y.-F. (2009). Smoke detection in video. *2009 WRI World Congress on Computer Science and Information Engineering*, Vol. 5, (pp. 759-763).

Kim, S. Y., Lee, E. K., & Ho, Y. S. (2008). Generation of ROI enhanced depth maps using stereoscopic cameras and a depth camera. *IEEE Transactions on Broadcasting, 54*, 732–740. doi:10.1109/TBC.2008.2002338

King, I., Ng, C. H., & Sia, K. C. (2004). Distributed content-based visual information retrieval system on peer-to-peer networks. *ACM Transactions on Information Systems, 22*, 477–501. doi:10.1145/1010614.1010619

Kitagawa, G. (1996). Monte Carlo filter and smoother for non-Gaussian nonlinear state space models. *Journal of Computational and Graphical Statistics, 5*(1), 1–25.

Kodikara Arachchi, H., Fernando, W. A. C., Panchadcharam, S., & Weerakkody, W. A. R. J. (2006). Unequal error protection technique for ROI based H.264 video coding. *Canadian Conference on Electrical and Computer Engineering*, (pp. 2033-2036).

Koga, T., Iinuma, K., Hirano, A., Iijima, Y., & Ishiguro, T. (1981). Motion compensated inter frame coding for videoconferencing. In *Proceedings of the National Telecommunications Conference*, New Orleans, LA, December (pp. G5. 3.1–G5.3.5).

Kohler, E., Handley, M., & Floyd, S., (2006). *Datagram congestion control protocol* (DCCP). IETF RFC 4340, March 2006.

Kokare, M., Biswas, P. K., & Chatterji, B. N. (2007). Texture image retrieval using rotated wavelet filters. *Pattern Recognition Letters, 28*, 1240–1249. doi:10.1016/j.patrec.2007.02.006

Komnakos, D., Vouyioukas, D., Maglogiannis, I., & Constantinou, P. (2008). Performance evaluation of an enhanced uplink 3.5G system for mobile healthcare applications. *International Journal of Telemedicine and Applications, 2008*. doi:10.1155/2008/417870

Kong, H.-S., Vetro, A., Hata, T., & Kuwahara, N. (2005). Fast region-of-interest transcoding for JPEG 2000 images. *IEEE International Symposium on Circuits and Systems, ISCAS 2005*, Vol. 2 (pp. 952- 955).

Kong, A., Liu, J. S., & Wong, W. H. (1994). Sequential imputations and Bayesian missing data problems. *Journal of the American Statistical Association, 89*(425), 278–288. doi:10.1080/01621459.1994.10476469

Koo, H. S., Jeon, Y. J., & Jeon, B. M. (2007). *MVC motion skip mode*. JVT of ISO/IEC MPEG & ITU-T VCEG JVT-W081, April 2007.

Kostic, D., Rodriguez, A., Albrecht, J., & Vahdat, A. (2003). Bullet: High bandwidth data dissemination using an overlay mesh. In *Proceedings of the 19th ACM Symposium on Operating Systems Principles, 2003*.

Koumaras, H., Pallis, E., Xilouris, G., Kourtis, A., Martakos, D., & Lauterjung, J. (2004). *Pre-encoding PQoS assessment method for optimized resource utilization*. 2nd International Conference on Performance Modelling and Evaluation of Heterogeneous Networks, Het-NeTs04, Ilkley, United Kingdom, 2004.

Koumaras, H., Kourtis, A., Lin, C.-H., & Shieh, C.-K. (2009). A theoretical framework for end-to-end video quality prediction of MPEG-based sequences. *International Journal on Advances in Networks and Services, 1*(1).

Koumaras, H., Kourtis, A., & Martakos, D. (2005). Evaluation of video quality based on objectively estimated metric. *Journal of Communications and Networking, 7*(3).

Krylov, A., & Nasonov, A. (2008). Adaptive total variation deringing method for image interpolation. *Proceedings of the 15th IEEE International Conference on Image Processing 2008*, (pp. 2608–2611).

Kubota, A., Smolic, A., Magnor, M., Tanimoto, M., Chen, T., & Zhang, C. (2007). Multiview imaging and 3DTV. *IEEE Signal Processing Magazine, 24*(6), 10–21. doi:10.1109/MSP.2007.905873

Kuhl, A. Tan, T. Venkatesh, S. (2008, 8-11 December). Model-based combined tracking and resolution enhancement. In the *Proceedings of the International Conference on Pattern Recognition*, (pp. 1-4).

Kumar, S., Xu, L., Mandal, M. K., & Panchanathan, S. (2006, Apr.). Error resiliency schemes in H.264/AVC standard. *Journal of Visual Communication and Image Representation, 17*(2), 425–450. doi:10.1016/j.jvcir.2005.04.006

Kwang-Cheng, C., & Roberto, B. D. (2008). *Mobile WiMAX*. Wiley.

Kwon, H., Han, H., Lee, S., Choi, W., & Kang, B. (2010). New video enhancement preprocessor using the region-of-interest for the videoconferencing. *IEEE Transactions on Consumer Electronics, 56*(4), 2644–2651. doi:10.1109/TCE.2010.5681152

Lai, K. C., & Wong, S. C. (2002). A fast motion estimation using a three-dimensional reference motion vector. *International Conference on Acoustics, Speech, and Signal Processing (ICASSP 2002)*, Vol. 4, (pp. 3429-3432).

Lam, W. M., Reibman, A. R., & Liu, B. (1993). Recovery of lost or erroneously received motion vectors. In *IEEE International Conference on Acoustics, Speech, and Signal Processing* (pp. 417–420).

Lambert, P., de Neve, W., Dhondt, Y., & van de Walle, R. (2006). Flexible macroblock ordering in H. 264/AVC. *Journal of Visual Communication, 17*, 358–375.

Lambert, P., Schrijver, D. D., Van Deursen, D., De Neve, W., Dhondt, Y., & Van de Walle, R. (2006). *A real-time content adaptation framework for exploiting ROI scalability in H.264/AVC* (pp. 442–453). Advanced Concepts for Intelligent Vision Systems. doi:10.1007/11864349_40

Lam, W. M., Reibman, A. R., & Liu, B. (1993, Apr.). Recovery of lost or erroneously received motion vectors. *Proceedings of IEEE ICASSP, 5*, 417–420.

Lan, X., Xue, J., Tian, T., Hu, W., Xu, T., & Zheng, N. (2009). A peer-to-peer architecture for live streaming with DRM. *6th IEEE Consumer Communications and Networking Conference*, (pp. 1-5).

Lan, X., Zheng, N., Xue, J., Chen, W., Wang, B., & Ma, W. (2008). Manageable peer-to-peer architecture for video-on-demand. *Proceedings 22nd IEEE International Parallel and Distributed Processing Symposium (IPDPS2008)-10th Workshop of APDCM*, April 14-18, 2008, Miami, Florida USA.

Lang, M., Hornung, A., Wang, O., Poulakos, S., Smolic, A., & Gross, M. (2010). *Non-linear disparity mapping for stereoscopic 3D.* Presented at the ACM SIGGRAPH 2010, July 2010.

Lee, I. (2010). A scalable P2P video streaming framework. In A. -E. Hassanien, et al. (Eds.), *Pervasive computing: Innovations in intelligent multimedia and applications* (pp. 341-363), London, UK: Springer Verlag.

Lee, J.-B., & Kalva, H. (2008). *The VC-1 and H.264 video compression standards for broadband video services.* New York, NY: Springer Science+Business Media LLC.

Lee, Y. L., Hur, J. H., Lee, Y. K., Han, K. H., Cho, S. H., Hur, N. H … Gomila, C. (2006). *CE11: Illumination compensation.* JVT of ISO/IEC MPEG & ITU-T VCEG JVT-U052, Oct. 2006.

Lee, C., Choi, B. H., & Ho, Y. S. (2011). Efficient multiview depth video coding using depth synthesis prediction. *Optical Engineering (Redondo Beach, Calif.), 20*.

Legout, A., Liogkas, N., Kohler, E., & Zhang, L. (2007). Clustering and sharing incentives in BitTorrent systems. *Proceedings of the 2007 ACM SIGMETRICS International Conference on Measurement and Modeling of Computer Systems* (pp. 301-312). New York, NY: ACM. doi: http://doi.acm.org/10.1145/1254882.1254919

Leibe, B., Leonardis, A., & Schiele, B. (2008). Robust object detection with interleaved categorization and segmentation. *International Journal of Computer Vision, 77*(1-3), 259–289. doi:10.1007/s11263-007-0095-3

Leung, C., & Lovell, B. C. (2003). 3D reconstruction through segmentation of multi-view image sequences. *Workshop on Digital Image Computing*, Vol. 1, (pp. 87–92).

Li, B., Sullivan, G. J., & Xu, J. (2011). Comparison of compression performance of HEVC working draft 4 with AVC high profile. In *Proceedings of 7th Meeting of Joint Collaborative Team on Video Coding JCT-VC*, (document no JCTVC-G399-r2).

Li, F., & Gao, Y. (2011). ROI-based error resilient coding of H.264 for conversational video communication. *2011 7th International Wireless Communications and Mobile Computing Conference* (IWCMC), (pp. 1719-1723).

Li, X., & Wu, J. (2005). A hybrid searching scheme in unstructured P2P networks. In *Proceedings of the International Conference on Parallel Processing*, (pp. 277-284).

Li, Z. G., Yao, W., Rahardja, S., & Xie, S. (2007). New framework for encoder optimization of scalable video coding. *2007 IEEE Workshop on Signal Processing Systems*, (pp. 527-532).

Li, Z., Pan, F., Lim, K. P., Feng, G., Lin, X., & Rahardja, S. (2003). *Adaptive basic unit layer rate control for JVT*. In Joint Video Team (JVT) of ISO/IEC MPEG and ITU-T VCEG (ISO/IEC JTC1/SC29/WG11 and ITU-T SG16 Q.6), Doc. JVT-G012, Pattaya, Thailand, Mar. 2003.

Li, Z., Zhang, X., Zou, F., & Hu, D. (2010). Study of target detection based on top-down visual attention. *2010 3rd International Congress on Image and Signal Processing (CISP)*, Vol. 1, (pp.377-380).

Lian, Q., Chen, W., Zhang, Z., Wu, S., & Zhao, B. Y. (2005). Z-ring: fast prefix routing via a low maintenance membership protocol. In *13th IEEE International Conference on Network Protocols, ICNP 2005* (p. 12). doi: 10.1109/ICNP.2005.45

Lian, Q., Zhang, Z., Yang, M., Zhao, B. Y., Dai, Y., & Li, X. (2007). An empirical study of collusion behavior in the Maze P2P file-sharing system. *Proceedings of the 27th International Conference on Distributed Computing Systems, ICDCS'07* (p. 56). doi:10.1109/ICDCS.2007.84

Liang, J., Kumar, R., & Ross, K. W. (2006). The FastTrack overlay: A measurement study. *Computer Networks, 50*(6), 842–858. doi:10.1016/j.comnet.2005.07.014

Liben-Nowell, D., Balakrishnan, H., & Karger, D. (2002). Analysis of the evolution of peer-to-peer systems. In *Proceedings of the Twenty-First Annual Symposium on Principles of Distributed Computing, PODC'02* (pp. 233-242). New York, NY: ACM. doi: http://doi.acm.org/10.1145/571825.571863

Lim, D.-K., & Ho, Y.-S. (1998). A fast block matching motion estimation algorithm based on statistical properties of object displacement. In the *Proceedings of IEEE Region 10 International Conference on Global Connectivity in Energy, Computer, Communication and control,* Vol. 1, (pp. 138-141).

Lim, J.-H., & Choi, H.-W. (2001). Adaptive motion estimation algorithm using spatial and temporal correlation. In the *Proceedings of IEEE Pacific Rim Conference on Communications, Computers and Signal Processing,* Piscataway, NJ, USA, Vol. 2, (pp. 473-476).

Lim, K., & Ra, J. B. (1997). Improved hierarchical search block matching algorithm by using multiple motion vector candidates. *Electronics Letters, 33*, 1771–1772. doi:10.1049/el:19971222

Lim, N.-K., Kim, D.-Y., & Lee, H. (2010). Interactive progressive image transmission for realtime applications. *IEEE Transactions on Consumer Electronics, 56*(4), 2438–2444. doi:10.1109/TCE.2010.5681125

Lin, F., Cook, J., Chandran, V., & Sridharan, S. (2005a). Face recognition from super-resolved images. In the *Proceedings of International Conference on Information Science, Signal Processing and their Applications (ISSPA)*, (pp. 667-670).

Lin, F., Denman, S., Chandran, V., & Sridharan, S. (2007). Automatic tracking and super-resolution of human faces from surveillance video. In the *Proceedings of the IAPR Conference on Machine Vision Applications* (MVA).

Lin, F., Fookes, C., Chandran, V., & Sridharan, S. (2005b). Investigation into optical flow super-resolution for surveillance applications. In the *Proceedings of the APRS Workshop on Digital Image Computing 2005*, (pp. 73-78).

Lin, T., Wang, H., & Wang, J. (2004). Search performance analysis and robust search algorithm in unstructured peer-to-peer networks. In *Proceedings of the IEEE/ACM International Symposium on Cluster Computing and the Grid*, (pp. 346-354).

Lin, F., Fookes, C., Chandran, V., & Sridharan, S. (2007b). Lecture Notes in Computer Science: *Vol. 4642. Super-resolved faces for improved face recognition from surveillance video* (pp. 1–10). Seoul, Korea: LNCS. doi:10.1007/978-3-540-74549-5_1

Lin, S., & Costello, D. J. (2004). *Error control coding* (2nd ed.). Upper Saddle River, NJ: Prentice Hall.

Lin, W., Panusopone, K., Baylon, D. M., & Sun, M.-T. (2010). A computation control motion estimation method for complexity-scalable video coding. *IEEE Transactions on Circuits and Systems for Video Technology, 20*(11), 1533–1543. doi:10.1109/TCSVT.2010.2077773

Lin, Y., & Bhanu, B. (2005). Object detection via feature synthesis using MDL-based genetic programming. *IEEE Transactions on Systems, Man, and Cybernetics. Part B, Cybernetics, 35*(3), 538–547. doi:10.1109/TSMCB.2005.846656

Li, R., Zeng, B., & Liou, M. L. (1994). A new three-step search algorithm for block motion estimation. *IEEE Transactions on Circuits and Systems for Video Technology, 4*, 438–442. doi:10.1109/76.313138

Liu, B., Lee, W.-C., & Lee, D. L. (2005). Supporting complex multi-dimensional queries in P2P systems. In *Proceedings of the IEEE Conference on Distributed Computing Systems*, (pp. 155-164).

Liu, B., Sun, M., Liu, Q., Kassam, A., Li, C.-C., & Sclabassi, R. J. (2006). Automatic detection of region of interest based on object tracking in neurosurgical video. *27th Annual International Conference of the Engineering in Medicine and Biology Society, IEEE-EMBS 2005*, (pp. 6273-6276).

Liu, H., Klomp, N., & Heynderickx, I. (2010). *A no-reference metric for perceived ringing*. Paper presented at the Fourth International Workshop on Video Processing and Quality Metrics for Consumer Electronics, Scottsdale, Arizona.

Liu, L., Zhang, S., Ye, X., & Zhang, Y. (2005). Error resilience schemes of H.264/AVC for 3G conversational video services. *The Fifth International Conference on Computer and Information Technology*, (pp. 657- 661).

Liu, X., Huang, T., Huo, L., & Mou, L. (2007). A DRM architecture for manageable P2P based IPTV system. *2007 IEEE International Conference on Multimedia and Expo*, (pp. 899-902). 2-5 July 2007.

Liu, Y., Zhang, S., Xu, S., & Zhang, Y. (2009). H. 264/SVC error resilience strategies for 3G video service. In *International Conference on Image Analysis and Signal Processing*, (pp. 207-211).

Liu, Z., Chai, Z., & Xing, P. (2009). ROI auto-detecting and coding method for MRI images transmission. *ICME International Conference on Complex Medical Engineering*, (pp. 1-4).

Liu, Z., Shen, Y., Panwar, S. S., Ross, K. W., & Wang, Y. (2007). P2P video live streaming with MDC: Providing incentives for redistribution. *Proceedings of the IEEE International Conference on Multimedia and Expo 2007* (pp. 48-51). doi:10.1109/ICME.2007.4284583

Liu, Z., Wu, Z., Liu, H., & Stein, A. (2007). A layered hybrid-ARQ scheme for scalable video multicast over wireless networks. In *Proceedings of the Asilomar Conference on Signals, Systems and Computers*, (pp. 914-919).

Liu, B., & Zaccarin, A. (1993). New fast algorithms for the estimation of block motion vectors. *IEEE Transactions on Circuits and Systems for Video Technology, 3*, 148–157. doi:10.1109/76.212720

Liu, C., Yuen, J., & Torralba, A. (2011). Sift flow: Dense correspondence across scenes and its applications. *IEEE Transactions on Pattern Analysis and Machine Intelligence, 33*(5), 978–994. doi:10.1109/TPAMI.2010.147

Liu, J. S., & Chen, R. (1998). Sequential Monte Carlo methods for dynamic systems. *Journal of the American Statistical Association, 93*(443), 1032–1044. doi:10.1080/01621459.1998.10473765

Liu, L. K., & Feig, E. (1996). A block-based gradient descent search algorithm for block motion estimation in video coding. *IEEE Transactions on Circuits and Systems for Video Technology, 6*, 419–422. doi:10.1109/76.510936

Liu, L., & Fan, G. (2003). A new JPEG2000 region-of-interest image coding method: Partial significant bitplanes shift. *Signal Processing Letters, 10*(2), 35–38. doi:10.1109/LSP.2002.807867

Liu, Y., Guo, Y., & Liang, C. (2008). A survey on peer-to-peer video streaming systems. *Peer-to-Peer Networking and Applications, 1*(1), 18–28. doi:10.1007/s12083-007-0006-y

Liu, Y., Li, Z. G., & Soh, Y. C. (2008a). Rate control of H.264/AVC scalable extension. *IEEE Transactions on Circuits and Systems for Video Technology, 18*(1), 116–121. doi:10.1109/TCSVT.2007.903325

Liu, Y., Li, Z.-G., & Soh, Y.-C. (2008b). Region-of-Interest based resource allocation for conversational video communication of H.264/AVC. *IEEE Transactions on Circuits and Systems for Video Technology, 18*(1), 134–139. doi:10.1109/TCSVT.2007.913754

Liu, Y., Zhang, D., Lu, G., & Ma, W.-Y. (2007). A survey of content-based image retrieval with high-level semantics. *Pattern Recognition, 40*(1), 262–282. doi:10.1016/j.patcog.2006.04.045

Liu, Y., Zhang, S., Xu, S., & Zhang, Y. H. (2005). H. 264/AVC error resilience tools suitable for 3G mobile video services. *Journal of Zhejiang University, 6*(1), 41–46. doi:10.1631/jzus.2005.AS0041

Li, W., & Salari, E. (1995). Successive elimination algorithm for motion estimation. *IEEE Transactions on Image Processing, 4*(1), 105–107. doi:10.1109/83.350809

Locher, T., Moor, P., Schmid, S., & Wattenhofer, R. (2006). Free riding in BitTorrent is cheap. *Proceedings of the 5th Workshop on Hot Topics in Networks (HotNets)*.

Lowe, D. (2004). Distinctive image features from scale-invariant keypoints. *International Journal of Computer Vision, 60*(2), 91–110. doi:10.1023/B:VISI.0000029664.99615.94

Lu, J., Lieu, M. L., Letaief, K. B., & Chuang, J. I. (1998, June). Error resilient transmission of H.263 coded video over mobile networks. In *Proceedings of IEEE International Symposium on Circuits and Systems* (Vol. 4, p. 502-505).

Lu, L., Wang, Z., Bovik, A. C., & Kouloheris, J. (2002). *Full-reference video quality assessment considering structural distortion and no-reference quality evaluation of MPEG video*. IEEE International Conference on Multimedia.

Lu, Z., Lin, W., Li, Z., Pang Lim, K., Lin, X., Rahardja, S., et al. (2005b). *Perceptual region-of-interest (ROI) based scalable video coding*. JVT-O056, Busan, KR, 16-22 Apr., 2005.

Lu, Z., Peng, W.-H., Choi, H., Thang, T. C., & Shengmei, S. (2005a). *CE8: ROI-based scalable video coding*. JVT-O308, Busan, KR, 16-22 April, 2005.

Luby, M. (2002). LT-codes. In Proceedings *43rd Annual IEEE Symposium on Foundations of Computer Science* (FOCS), Vancouver, Canada, Nov. 2002, (pp. 271–280).

Lucas, B., & Kanade, T. (1981). An iterative image registration technique with an application to stereo vision. In the *Proceedings of DARPA Image Understanding Workshop*, (pp. 121-130).

Lucchese, L., Doretto, G., & Cortelazzo, G. M. (2002). A frequency domain technique for 3D view registration. *IEEE Transactions on Pattern Analysis and Machine Intelligence, 24*(11), 1468–1484. doi:10.1109/TPAMI.2002.1046160

Lu, J., & Liou, M. L. (1997). A simple and efficient search algorithm for block-matching motion estimation. *IEEE Transactions on Circuits and Systems for Video Technology, 7*, 429–433. doi:10.1109/76.564122

Luo, R., & Chen, B. (2008). A hierarchical scheme of flexible macroblock ordering for ROI based H.264/AVC video coding. *10th International Conference on Advanced Communication Technology, ICACT 2008*, Vol. 3, (pp. 1579-1582).

Luo, Z., Li, S., & Shibao, Z. (2009). Offset based leaky prediction for error resilient ROI coding. *IEEE International Conference on Multimedia and Expo, ICME 2009*, (pp. 145-148).

Luo, J., Ahmad, I., Liang, Y., & Swaminathan, V. (2008). Motion estimation for content adaptive video compression. *IEEE Transactions on Circuits and Systems for Video Technology, 18*(7), 900–909. doi:10.1109/TCSVT.2008.923423

Luo, L., Zou, C., Gao, X., & Zhenya, H. (1997). A new prediction search algorithm for block motion estimation in video coding. *IEEE Transactions on Consumer Electronics, 43*(1), 56–61. doi:10.1109/30.580385

MacKay, D. (2003). *Information theory, inference, and learning algorithms*. Cambridge, UK: Cambridge University Press.

Magnor, M., Ramanathan, P., & Girod, B. (2003). Multiview coding for image-based rendering using 3-D scene geometry. *IEEE Transactions on Circuits and Systems for Video Technology, 13*(11), 1092–1106. doi:10.1109/TCSVT.2003.817630

Mahadevan, V., Weixin, L., Bhalodia, V., & Vasconcelos, N. (2010, 13-18 June 2010). Anomaly detection in crowded scenes. In the *Proceedings of the IEEE Conference on Computer Vision and Pattern Recognition* (CVPR).

Mahy, R., Matthews, P., & Rosenberg, J. (2010). *Traversal using relays around NAT (TURN): Relay extensions to session traversal utilities for NAT (STUN)*. Retrieved from http://www.rfc-editor.org/rfc/rfc5766.txt

Mai, Z.-Y., Yang, C. L., & Xie, S. L. (2005). Improved best prediction mode(s) selection methods based on structural similarity in H.264 I-frame encoder. *IEEE International Conference on Systems, Man and Cybernetics*, Vol. 3, (pp. 2673–2678).

Maitre, M., Shinagawa, Y., & Do, M. N. (2008). Wavelet-based joint estimation and encoding of depth-image-based representations for free-viewpoint rendering. *IEEE Transactions on Image Processing, 17*, 946–957. doi:10.1109/TIP.2008.922425

Malvar, H. S., Hallapuro, A., & Karczewicz, M., & Louis Kerofsky. (2003). Low-complexity transform and quantization in H.264/AVC. *IEEE Transactions on Circuits and Systems for Video Technology, 13*(7), 598–603. doi:10.1109/TCSVT.2003.814964

Manerba, F., Benois-Pineau, J., Leonardi, R., & Mansencal, B. (2008). Multiple object extraction from compressed video. *EURASIP Journal on Advances in Signal Processing, 2008*, 231930. doi:10.1155/2008/231930

Manjunath, B. S. (2001). Color and texture descriptors. *IEEE Transactions on Circuits and Systems for Video Technology, 11*(6), 703–715. doi:10.1109/76.927424

Manjunath, B., Salembier, P., & Sikora, T. (2002). *Introduction to MPEG-7: Multimedia content description language*. John Wiley & Sons.

Martel-Brisson, N., & Zaccarin, A. (2005). Moving cast shadow detection from a Gaussian mixture shadow model. In the *Proceedings of the IEEE Conference on Computer Vision and Pattern Recognition* (CVPR) Vol. 2 (pp. 643-648).

Martinez, J. M. (2004). *MPEG-7 overview* (version 10). ISO/IEC JTC1/SC29/WG11N6828.

Martinian, E., Behrens, A., Xin, J., Vetro, A., & Sun, H. (2006). Extensions of H.264/AVC for multiview video compression. *Proceedings of IEEE International Conference on Image Processing (ICIP2006)*. Atlanta, GA, USA.

Maskell, S., & Gordon, N. (2001). A tutorial on particle filters for on-line nonlinear/non-Gaussian Bayesian tracking. In *Target Tracking: Algorithms and Applications* (Ref. No. 2001/174), IEE Workshop, Vol. 2 (pp. 1-15).

May, P. (2005). *A survey of 3D display technologies*. Retrieved February 1, 2011, from http://www.ocuity.co.uk/Ocuity_white_paper_Survey_of_3D_display_technologies.pdf

Maymounkov, P., & Mazières, D. (2002). *Kademlia: A peer-to-peer information system based on the XOR metric*. In International Workshop on Peer-To-Peer Systems.

McCann, K., Han, W.-J., & Kim, I. K. (2010). *Samsung's response to the call for proposals on video compression technology (JCTVC-A124)*. Retrieved February 1, 2011, from http://wftp3.itu.int/av-arch/jctvc-site/2010_04_A_Dresden/JCTVC-A124.zip

McMillan, L., & Pizer, R. S. (1997). *An image based approach to three-dimensional computer graphics*. Technical Report TR97-013, University of North Carolina at Chapel Hill.

Mehmood, M. O. (2009). Study and implementation of color-based object tracking in monocular image sequences. *2009 IEEE Student Conference on Research and Development* (SCOReD), (pp. 109-111).

Melodia, T., & Akyildiz, I. F. (2011). Research challenges for wireless multimedia sensor networks. In Bhahu, B. (Eds.), *Distributed Video Sensor Networks* (pp. 233–246). Berlin, Germany: Springer Verlag. doi:10.1007/978-0-85729-127-1_16

Merkle, P., Smolic, A., Mueller, K., & Wiegand, T. (2007). Experiments on coding of multi-view video plus depth. *Joint Video Team of ISO/IEC MPEG & ITU-T VCEG, Doc. JVT-X064*, Geneva, Switzerland.

Merkle, P., Morvan, Y., Smolic, A., Farin, D., Muller, K., de With, P. H. N., & Wiegand, T. (2009). The effects of multiview depth video compression on multiview rendering. *Signal Processing Image Communication, 24*(1-2), 73–88. doi:10.1016/j.image.2008.10.010

Miao, Z., & Ortega, A. (2002, Apr.). Expected run-time distortion based scheduling for delivery of scalable media. In *Proceedings of packet video workshop*.

Micallef, B. W., Debono, C., & Farrugia, R. (2010). Exploiting depth information for fast multi-view video coding. *IEEE Proceedings of International Picture Coding Symposium 2010 (PCS 2010)*. Nagoya, Japan.

Micallef, B., Debono, C., & Farrugia, R. (Sep. 2010). Error concealment techniques for H.264/MVC encoded sequences. *IEEE Proceedings of International Conference of Electrotechnical and Computer Science (ERK)*. Portoroz, Slovenia.

Micheloni, C., Salvador, E., Bigaran, F., & Foresti, G. L. (2005). An integrated surveillance system for outdoor security. *IEEE Conference on Advanced Video and Signal Based Surveillance, AVSS 2005* (pp. 480- 485).

Milani, S., Zanuttigh, P., Zamarin, M., & Forchhammer, S. (2011). *Efficient depth map compression exploiting segmented color D*. 2011.

Min, J.-H., Lee, S., Kim, I.-K., Han, W.-J., Lainema, J., & Ugur, K. (2010). *Unification of the directional intra prediction methods in TMuC (JCTVC-B100)*. Retrieved February 1, 2011, from http://wftp3.itu.int/av-arch/jctvc-site/2010_07_B_Geneva/JCTVC-B100.zip

Moghaddam, B., & Pentland, A. (1997). Probabilistic visual learning for object recognition. *IEEE Transactions on Pattern Analysis and Machine Intelligence, 19*(7), 696–710. doi:10.1109/34.598227

Mohamed, A.-M., & Krishnamachari, S. (2004). Multimedia descriptions based on MPEG-7 extraction and applications. *IEEE Transactions on Multimedia, 6*(3), 459–468. doi:10.1109/TMM.2004.827500

Mohr, A. E., Riskin, E. A., & Ladner, R. E. (2000). Unequal loss protection: Graceful degradation of image quality over packet erasure channels through forward error correction. *IEEE Journal on Selected Areas in Communications, 18*(6), 819–828. doi:10.1109/49.848236

Mol, J. J., Bakker, A., Pouwelse, J., Epema, D. H., & Sips, H. J. (2009). *The design and deployment of a Bit-Torrent live video streaming solution*. In ISM 2009. IEEE Computer Society. Retrieved from http://pds.twi.tudelft.nl/pubs/papers/ism2009.pdf

Monteiro, J. F. (2010). *Quality assurance solutions for multipoint scalable video distribution over wireless IP networks*. PhD Thesis, Instituto Superior Técnico, Technical University of Lisbon, Portugal.

Mori, R., & Kawahara, M. (1990). Superdistribution: The concept and the architecture. *Transactions of the IEICE, E73*(7), 1133-1146. Retrieved from http://www.virtualschool.edu/mon/ElectronicProperty/MoriSuperdist.html

Mori, Y., Fukushima, N., Yendo, T., Fujii, T., & Tanimoto, M. (2009). View generation with 3D warping using depth information for FTV. *Image Communication, 24*(1-2), 65–72.

Morvan, Y. (2009). *Acquisition, compression and rendering of depth and texture for multi-view video*. Ph.D. thesis, Eindhoven, the Netherlands: Eindhoven University of Technology.

Morvan, Y., Farin, D., & de With, Peter H. N. (2006). Design considerations for view interpolation in a 3D video coding framework. *27th Symposium on Information Theory in the Benelux*, Vol. 1, Noordwijk, The Netherlands.

Moschetti, F. (2001). *A statistical approach to motion estimation*. Ecole polytechnique Federale De Lausanne, PhD Thesis.

Moshnyaga, V. G. (2001). A new computationally adaptive formulation of block-matching motion estimation. *IEEE Transactions on Circuits and Systems for Video Technology, 11*, 118–124. doi:10.1109/76.894295

MPEG. (1998). *MPEG-1 ISO/IEC 11172-5:1998: Coding of moving pictures and associated audio for digital storage media at up to about 1,5 Mbit/s*.

MPEG. (2005). *MPEG-2 ISO/IEC 13818-5:2005: Generic coding of moving pictures and associated audio information*.

MPEG. (2005). *MPEG-4 ISO/IEC 14496-5:2001/Amd.6:2005, MPEG-4 coding of audio visual objects*.

Mullin, J., Smallwood, L., Watson, A., & Wilson, G. (2001). *New techniques for assessing audio and video quality in real-time interactive communications*. Third International Workshop on Human Computer Interaction with Mobile Devices, Lille, France, 2001.

Mustafah, Y. M., Bigdeli, A., Azman, A. W., & Lovell, B. C. (2009). Face detection system design for real time high resolution smart camera. *Third ACM/IEEE International Conference on Distributed Smart Cameras, ICDSC 2009* (pp. 1-6).

Nam, J.-Y., Seo, J.-S., Kwak, J.-S., Lee, M.-H., & Yeong, H. H. (2000). New fast-search algorithm for block matching motion estimation using temporal and spatial correlation of motion vector. *IEEE Transactions on Consumer Electronics, 46*, 934–942. doi:10.1109/30.920443

NAPA-WINE Consortium. (2010). *Network-aware P2P-TV application over wise networks project home page*. Retrieved from http://www.napa-wine.eu/cgi-bin/twiki/view/Public

Napster. (2009). *Napster home page* (Web Archive). Retrieved from http://web.archive.org/web/*/http://www.napster.com/

Natsev, P., Rastogi, R., & Shim, K. (1998). *WALRUS: A similarity matching algorithm for image databases*. Technical report, Bell Laboratories, Murray Hill.

Ndili, O., & Ogunfunmi, T. (2006). On the performance of a 3D flexible macroblock ordering for H.264/AVC. *Digest of Technical Papers International Conference on Consumer Electronics, 2006*, (pp. 37-38).

Nello, C., & John, S.-T. (2000). *An introduction to support vector machines and other kernel-based learning methods*. Cambridge University Press.

Ng, M. K., Chan, R. H., & Tang, W.-C. (1999). A fast algorithm for deblurring models with Neumann boundary conditions. *SIAM Journal on Scientific Computing, 21*(3), 851–866. doi:10.1137/S1064827598341384

Nguyen Thanh, K., Fookes, C., Sridharan, S., & Denman, S. (2011). Feature-domain super-resolution for IRIS recognition. In the *Proceedings of the 18th IEEE International Conference on Image Processing* (ICIP 2011).

Nguyen, T., & Zakhor, A. (2002, Jan.). Distributed video streaming over the internet. In *Proceedings of SPIE Conference on Multimedia Computing and Networking* (pp. 186-195).

Nguyen, A., Chandran, V., Sridharan, S., & Prandolini, R. (2003). Interpretability performance assessment of JPEG2000 and part 1 compliant region of interest coding. *IEEE Transactions on Consumer Electronics, 49*(4), 808–817. doi:10.1109/TCE.2003.1261159

Nguyen, K., Nguyen, T., & Cheung, S. (2010). Video streaming with network coding. *Journal of Signal Processing Systems for Signal, Image, and Video Technology, 57*(3), 319–333. doi:10.1007/s11265-009-0342-7

Nguyen, K., & Zakhor, A. (2004). Multiple sender distributed video streaming. *IEEE Transactions on Multimedia, 6*(2), 315–326. doi:10.1109/TMM.2003.822790

Nisar, H., & Choi, T.-S. (2000). An advanced center biased search algorithm for motion estimation. In the *Proceedings of International Conference on Image Processing (ICIP '00)*, Vol. 1, (pp. 832-835).

Nisar, H., & Choi, T. S. (2009). Multiple initial point prediction based search pattern selection for fast motion estimation. *Pattern Recognition, 42*, 475–48. doi:10.1016/j.patcog.2008.08.010

Niu, Y., Wu, X., & Shi, G. (2009). Edge-based dynamic ROI coding with standard compliance. *IEEE International Workshop on Multimedia Signal Processing, MMSP '09*, (pp. 1-6).

Niyato, D., Hossain, E., & Diamond, J. (2007). IEEE 802.16/WiMAX-based broadband wireless access and its application for telemedicine/e-health services. *IEEE Wireless Communications, 14*(1), 72–83. doi:10.1109/MWC.2007.314553

Novak, D., & Zezula, P. (2006). M-Chord: A scalable distributed similarity search structure. In *Proceedings of the 1st International Conference on Scalable Information Systems*, NY, USA.

Nunes, R., Cruz, R. S., & Nunes, M. S. (2010). Scalable video distribution in peer-to-peer architecture. In *Proceedings 10th National Networking Conference - CRC 2010*, Braga, Portugal.

Nyamweno, S., Satyan, R., & Labeau, F. (2009, July). Error resilient video coding via weighted distortion. *Proceedings of ICME, 09*, 734–737.

Nyamweno, S., Satyan, R., Solak, S., & Labeau, F. (2008, Oct.). Weighted distortion for robust video coding. *Proceedings of ASILOMAR, 08*, 1277–1281.

Obreiter, P., & Nimis, J. (2003). *A taxonomy of incentive patterns -- The design space of incentives for cooperation.*

Obreiter, P., & Nimis, J. (2005). *A taxonomy of incentive patterns. Agents and Peer-to-Peer Computing* (*Vol. 2872*, pp. 89–100). Berlin, Germany: Springer.

OceanStore. (2010). *The OceanStore project home page.* Retrieved from http://www.oceanstore.org/.

Octoshape. (2010). *Octoshape home page.* Retrieved from http://www.octoshape.com/.

Ogunfunmi, T., & Huang, W. (2005, May.). A flexible macroblock ordering with 3D MBA MAP for H.264/AVC. *IEEE International Symposium on Circuits and Systems, ISCAS 2005*, Vol. 4, (pp. 3475-3478).

Oh, K.-J., Sehoon, Y., & Ho, Y.-S. (2009). *Hole-filling method using depth based in-painting for view synthesis in free viewpoint television (FTV) and 3D video.* Picture Coding Symposium (PCS), Chicago, USA.

Ohm, J.-R. (2008). *Recent, current and future developments in video coding.* Retrieved February 1, 2011, from http://wiamis2008.itec.uni-klu.ac.at/keynotes/ohm.pdf

Okuma, K., Taleghani, A., Freitas, N. d., Little, J., & Lowe, D. (2004). A boosted particle filter: Multitarget detection and tracking. In the *Proceedings of the European Conference on Computer Vision*, (pp. 28-39).

Oliensis, J. (2000, Nov.). A critique of structure from motion algorithms. *Computer Vision and Image Understanding, 80*(2), 172–214. doi:10.1006/cviu.2000.0869

Oliva, A., & Torralba, A. (2006). Building the gist of a scene: The role of global image features in recognition. In *Visual Perception* (*Vol. 155*). Progress in Brain Research. doi:10.1016/S0079-6123(06)55002-2

Olson, J. (1994). In a framework about task-technology fit, what are the tasks features. *Proceedings of CSCW '94: Workshop on Video Mediated Communication: Testing, Evaluation & Design Implications*, 1994.

Onural, L. (2010). Signal processing and 3DTV. *IEEE Signal Processing Magazine, 27*, 144+141-142.

Oosa, K. (1998). *A new deblocking filter for digital image compression.* Retrieved February 1, 2011, from http://www.nsc.co.jp/en/tech/report/pdf/7716.pdf

Ostermann, J., Bormans, J., List, P., Marpe, D., Narroschke, M., & Pereira, F. (2004). Video coding with H.264/AVC: Tools, performance, and complexity. *IEEE Circuits and Systems Magazine, 4*(1), 7–28. doi:10.1109/MCAS.2004.1286980

Ozaktas, H., & Onural, L. (2008). *Three-dimensional television capture, transmission, display.* Springer-Verlag.

Ozdena, M., & Polat, E. (2007). A color image segmentation approach for content-based image retrieval. *Pattern Recognition, 40*(4), 1318–1325. doi:10.1016/j.patcog.2006.08.013

P2P-NEXT Consortium. (2010). *Next generation peer-to-peer content delivery platform project home page.* Retrieved from http://p2p-next.org/

Padmanabhan, V. N., Wang, H. J., Chou, P. A., & Sripanidkulchai, K. (2002). Distributing streaming media content using cooperative networking. In *Proceedings of ACM NOSSDAV*.

Padmanabhan, V., Wang, H., & Chou, P. (2003). Resilient peer-to-peer streaming. *Proceedings of 11th IEEE International Conference on Network Protocols*, (pp. 16- 27).

Pallis, G., & Vakali, A. (2006). Content delivery networks. *Communications of the ACM, 49*(1), 101–106. doi:10.1145/1107458.1107462

Park, G. H., Park, M. W., Lim, S. C., Shim, W. S., & Lee, Y. L. (2008). Deblocking filtering for illumination compensation in multiview video coding. *IEEE Transactions on Circuits and Systems for Video Technology, 18*(10), 1457–1461. doi:10.1109/TCSVT.2008.2002890

Park, H. W., & Lee, Y. L. (1999). A postprocessing method for reducing quantization effects in low bit-rate moving picture coding. *IEEE Transactions on Circuits and Systems for Video Technology, 9*(1), 161–171. doi:10.1109/76.744283

Park, J., & van der Schaar, M. (2010). A game theoretic analysis of incentives in content production and sharing over peer-to-peer networks. *IEEE Journal of Selected Topics in Signal Processing, 4*(4), 704–717. doi:10.1109/JSTSP.2010.2048609

Park, K.-H., & Park, H.-W. (2002). Region-of-interest coding based on set partitioning in hierarchical trees. *IEEE Transactions on Circuits and Systems for Video Technology, 12*(2), 106–113. doi:10.1109/76.988657

Park, S., & Jeong, S.-H. (2009). Mobile IPTV: Approaches, challenges, standards and QoS support. *IEEE Internet Computing, 13*(3), 23–31. doi:10.1109/MIC.2009.65

Park, S., Park, M., & Kang, M. (2003). Super-resolution image reconstruction: A technical overview. *IEEE Signal Processing Magazine, 25*(9), 21–36. doi:10.1109/MSP.2003.1203207

Patti, A., & Altunbasak, Y. (2001). Artifact reduction for set theoretic super resolution image reconstruction with edge adaptive constraints and higher-order interpolants. [January.]. *IEEE Transactions on Image Processing, 10*, 179–186. doi:10.1109/83.892456

PeerCast.org. (2010). *PeerCast home page*. Retrieved from http://www.peercast.org/

Pelletier, G., & Sandlund, K. (2008). *Robust header compression version 2 (ROHCv2): Profiles for RTP, UDP, IP, ESP and UDP-Lite*. Internet Engineering Task Force, RFC 5225.

Perkins, C. (2003). *RTP: Audio and video for the internet*. Boston, MA: Addison Wesley.

Pesquet-Popescu, B., Daribo, I., & Tillier, C. (2009). Motion vector sharing and bitrate allocation for 3D video-plus-depth coding. *EURASIP Journal on Advances in Signal Processing*.

Petrovic, G., Farin, D., & de With, P. H. N. (2008). Toward 3D-IPTV: Design and implementation of a stereoscopic and multiple-perspective video streaming system. *SPIE Stereoscopic Displays and Applications (SDA 2008)*, Vol. 6803 (pp. 505-512). San Jose, USA.

Phadikar, A., & Maity, S. P. (2009). ROI based error concealment of object based image using data hiding in JPEG 2000 coding pipeline. *2009 Annual IEEE India Conference* (INDICON), (pp. 1-4).

Phadikar, A., & Maity, S. P. (2010). ROI based error concealment of compressed object based image using QIM data hiding and wavelet transform. *IEEE Transactions on Consumer Electronics, 56*(2), 971–979. doi:10.1109/TCE.2010.5506028

Philip, N. (2008). *Medical quality of service for optimized ultrasound streaming in wireless robotic tele-ultrasonography system*. PhD Thesis, Kingston University.

Phillips, P., Flynn, P., Scruggs, T., Bowyer, K., & Chang, J. Ho_man, K., Marques, J., Min, J., & Worek, W. (2005). Overview of the face recognition grand challenge. In the *Proceedings of the IEEE Conference on Computer Vision and Pattern Recognition* (CVPR), Vol. 1, (pp. 947-954).

Phillips, P., Moon, H., Rizvi, S., & Rauss, P. (2000). The feret evaluation methodology for face-recognition algorithms. *IEEE Transactions on Pattern Analysis and Machine Intelligence, 22*, 1090–1104. doi:10.1109/34.879790

Pitt, M. K., & Shephard, N. (1999). Filtering via simulation: Auxiliary particle filters. *Journal of the American Statistical Association, 94*(446), 590–599. doi:10.1080/01621459.1999.10474153

Plaxton, C. G., Rajararnan, R., & Richa, A. W. (1997). Accessing nearby copies of replicated objects in a distributed environment. In *Proceedings of the Ninth Annual ACM Symposium on Parallel Algorithms and Architectures, SPAA '97* (pp. 311-320). New York, NY: ACM. doi: http://doi.acm.org/10.1145/258492.258523

Podolsky, M., McCanne, S., & Vetterli, M. (2001). Soft ARQ for layered streaming media. *Journal of VLSI Signal Processing Systems, 27*(1-2), 81–97.

Po, L.-M., & Ma, W.-C. (1996). Novel four-step search algorithm for fast block motion estimation. *IEEE Transactions on Circuits and Systems for Video Technology, 6*, 313–317. doi:10.1109/76.499840

Porikli, F., & Sun, H. (2005). *Compressed domain video object segmentation*. Technical Report TR2005-040, Mitsubishi Electric Research Lab, 2005.

Pourazad, M., Nasiopoulos, P., & Ward, R. (2009, May). An H.264-based scheme for 2D to 3D video conversion. *IEEE Transactions on Consumer Electronics, 55*(2), 742–748. doi:10.1109/TCE.2009.5174448

Pouwelse, J. A., Garbacki, P., Wang, J., Bakker, A., Yang, J., & Iosup, A. (2008). TRIBLER: A social-based peer-to-peer system. *Concurrency and Computation, 20*(2), 127–138. doi:10.1002/cpe.1189

PPLive. (2010). *PPTV home page*. Retrieved from http://www.pptv.com/.

PPStream. (2011). *PPS Net TV home page*. Retrieved from http://www.pps.tv/en/

Qadri, N., Fleury, M., Altaf, M., & Ghanbari, M. (2009). Emergency video multi-path transfer over ad hoc wireless networks. *The Journal of Communication, 4*(5), 324–338.

Qadri, N., Fleury, M., Rofoee, B., Altaf, M., & Ghanbari, M. (2012). Robust P2P multimedia exchange within a VANET. *Wireless Personal Communications, 63*, 561–577. doi:10.1007/s11277-010-0150-1

Qayyum, U., & Javed, M. Y. (2006). Real time notch based face detection, tracking and facial feature localization. *International Conference on Emerging Technologies, ICET '06*, (pp. 70-75).

Quast, K., & Kaup, A. (2008). Spatial scalable region of interest transcoding of JPEG2000 for video surveillance. *IEEE Fifth International Conference on Advanced Video and Signal Based Surveillance, AVSS '08*, (pp. 203-210).

Quelhas, P., & Odobez, J. M. (2007). Multi-level local descriptor quantization for Bag-of-Visterms image representation. In *Proceedings of the 6th ACM International Conference on Image and Video Retrieval*, (pp. 242-249).

Rahmani, R., Goldman, S., Zhang, H., Cholleti, S., & Fritts, J. (2008). Localized content based image retrieval. *IEEE Transactions on Pattern Analysis and Machine Intelligence, 30*(11). doi:10.1109/TPAMI.2008.112

Rahnavard, N., Vellambi, B. N., & Fekri, F. (2007). Efficient broadcasting via rateless coding in multihop wireless networks with local information. In *Proceedings of the International Wireless Communications and Mobile Computing Conference*, (pp. 85–95).

Raj, K. C. E., Venkataraman, S., & Varadan, G. (2008). A fuzzy approach to region of interest coding in JPEG 2000 for automatic target recognition applications from high-resolution satellite images. Sixth Indian Conference on Computer Vision, Graphics & Image Processing, ICVGIP '08, (pp. 193-200).

Ramos, M. G., & Hemami, S. S. (2001). Suprathreshold wavelet coefficient quantization in complex stimuli: Psychophysical evaluation and analysis. *Journal of the Optical Society of America. A, Optics, Image Science, and Vision, 18*(10), 2385–2397. doi:10.1364/JOSAA.18.002385

Rao, A., Srihari, R., & Zhang, Z. (2000). Geometric histogram: A distribution of geometric configurations of color subsets. *SPIE: Internet Imaging, 3964*, 91–101.

Rappaport, T. S. (2002). *Wireless communications: Principles and practice* (2nd ed.). Upper Saddle River, NJ: Prentice Hall.

Ratnasamy, S., Francis, P., Handley, M., Karp, R., & Shenker, S. (2001). A scalable content-addressable network. In *Proceedings of the 2001 Conference on Applications, Technologies, Architectures, and Protocols for Computer Communications, SIGCOMM'01* (pp. 161-172). New York, NY: ACM. doi: http://doi.acm.org/10.1145/383059.383072

Ratnasamy, S., Handley, M., Karp, R., & Shenker, S. (2001). Application-level multicast using content-addressable networks. In *Proceedings of the Third International COST264 Workshop on Networked Group Communication, NGC '01* (pp. 14-29). London, UK: Springer-Verlag.

Ratnasamy, S., Stoica, I., & Shenker, S. (2002). Routing algorithm for DHTs: Some open question. In *Proceedings of the 1st International Peer-to-Peer Workshop*, (pp. 45-52).

RawFlow. (2010). *RawFlow home page*. Retrieved from http://www.rawflow.com/.

Razavi, R., Fleury, M., & Ghanbari, M. (2008). Unequal protection of video streaming through adaptive modulation with a tri-zone buffer over Bluetooth Enhanced Data Rate. *EURASIP Journal on Wireless Communications and Networking*. Article ID 658794, 16 pages. doi:10.1155/2008/658794

Reed, I. S., & Solomon, G. (1960). Polynomial codes over certain finite fields. *Journal of the Society for Industrial and Applied Mathematics, 8*, 300–304. doi:10.1137/0108018

Reichel, J., & Nadenau, M. J. (2000). How to measure arithmetic complexity of compression algorithms: A simple solution. *2000 IEEE International Conference on Multimedia and Expo, ICME 2000*, Vol. 3, (pp. 1743-1746).

Reimers, U. (2004). *DVB* (2nd ed.). Springer Publishing Company, Incorporated.

Rejaie, R., Handley, M., & Estrin, D. (1999). RAP: An end-to-end rate-based congestion control mechanism for realtime streams in the Internet. In *Proceedings of the IEEE INFOCOM*, (pp. 1337–1345).

Rekhter, Y., Li, T., & Hares, S. (2006). *A border gateway protocol 4 (BGP-4)*. Request for Comments IETF. Retrieved from http://www.ietf.org/rfc/rfc4271.txt

Rekhter, Y., Moskowitz, B., Karrenberg, D., de Groot, G. J., & Lear, E. (1996). *Address allocation for private internets*. Retrieved from http://www.rfc-editor.org/rfc/rfc1918.txt

Reza, R. (2006). Anyone can broadcast video over the internet. *Communications of the ACM, 49*(11), 55–57. doi:10.1145/1167838.1167863

Rhee, I., Ozdemir, V., & Yi, T. (2000). *TEAR: TCP emulation at receivers*. Department of Computer Science, NCSU, Technical Report.

Richards, C. W. (1999). Exploiting mobile telephone technology for telemedicine applications. *Medical & Biological Engineering & Computing, 37*, 110–111.

Richardson, E. (2003). *H.264 and MPEG-4 video compression: Video coding for next-generation multimedia*. Chichester, UK: John Wiley & Sons Ltd. doi:10.1002/0470869615

Richardson, I. E. G. (2002). *Video codec design*. John Wiley & sons, ltd. doi:10.1002/0470847832

Richardson, I. E. G. (2010). *The H. 264 advanced video compression standard*. Chichester, UK: J. Wiley & Sons. doi:10.1002/9780470989418

Robbins, J. D., & Netravali, A. N. (1983). Recursive motion compensation: A review. In *Image sequence processing and dynamic sconce analysis* (pp. 76–103). Springer-Verlag. doi:10.1007/978-3-642-81935-3_3

Roodaki, H., Rabiee, H. R., & Ghanbari, M. (2010). Rate-distortion optimization of scalable video codecs. *Signal Processing Image Communication, 25*(4), 276–286. doi:10.1016/j.image.2010.01.004

Rosenberg, J., Weinberger, J., Huitema, C., & Mahy, R. (2003). *STUN - Simple traversal of user datagram protocol (UDP) through network address translators (NATs)*. Retrieved from http://www.rfc-editor.org/rfc/rfc3489.txt

Rowstron, A., & Druschel, P. (2001). Pastry: Scalable, decentralized object location, and routing for large-scale peer-to-peer systems. In *Proceedings of the IFIP/ACM International Conference on Distributed Systems Platforms, Middleware '01* (pp. 329-350). London, UK: Springer-Verlag.

Roxbeam. (2010). *Roxbeam home page*. Retrieved from http://www.roxbeam.com/english/index.html

Rubenstein, D., Kurose, J., & Towsley, D. (1998). *Real-time reliable multicast using proactive forward error correction*. Technical Report 98-19, Dept. of Computer Science, University of Massachusetts, Amherst, MA, 32 pages.

Ruijters, D., & Zinger, S. (2009). *IGLANCE: Transmission to medical high definition autostereoscopic displays*. In 3DTV Conference: The True Vision - Capture, Transmission and Display of 3D Video. Potsdam, Germany.

Ryan, D., Denman, S., Fookes, C., & Sridaharan, S. (2011). Textures of optical flow for real-time anomaly detection in crowds. *Proceedings of the 8th IEEE International Conference on Advanced Video and Signal Based Surveillance* (AVSS 2011), Klagenfurt University, Klagenfurt, Austria.

Sadka, A. (2002). *Compressed video communications*. Chichester, UK: J. Wiley & Sons. doi:10.1002/0470846712

Sadykhov, R. K., & Lamovsky, D. V. (2008). Algorithm for real time faces detection in 3D space. *International Multiconference on Computer Science and Information Technology, IMCSIT 2008*, (pp. 727-732).

Salama, F., Shroff, N. B., & Delp, E. J. (1998). Error concealment in encoded video. In *Image recovery techniques for image compression applications*. Norwell, MA: Kluwer.

Samek, H., Fleury, M., & Ghanbari, M. (2011). Robust video communication for ubiquitous network access. *Journal of Personal and Ubiquitous Computing, 15*(8), 811–820. doi:10.1007/s00779-011-0367-3

Sanchez, V., Basu, A., & Mandal, M. K. (2004). Prioritized region of interest coding in JPEG2000. *IEEE Transactions on Circuits and Systems for Video Technology, 14*(9), 1149–1155. doi:10.1109/TCSVT.2004.833168

SARACEN Consortium. (2010). *Socially aware, collaborative, scalable coding media distribution project home page.* Retrieved from http://www.saracen-p2p.eu/

Satyan, R., Nyamweno, S., & Labeau, F. (2010). Novel prediction schemes for error resilient video coding. *Signal Processing Image Communication, 25*(9), 648–659. doi:10.1016/j.image.2010.05.001

Scharstein, D., & Szeliski, R. (2002). A taxonomy and evaluation of dense two-frame stereo correspondence algorithms. *International Journal of Computer Vision, 47,* 7–42. doi:10.1023/A:1014573219977

Schierl, T., Hellge, C., Mirta, S., Gruneberg, K., & Wiegand, T. (2007). Using H.264/AVC-based scalable video coding (SVC) for real time streaming in wireless IP networks. *IEEE International Symposium on Circuits and Systems, ISCAS 2007,* (pp. 3455-3458).

Schmid, C., Mohr, R., & Bauckhage, C. (2000). Evaluation of interest point detectors. *International Journal of Computer Vision, 37*(2), 151–172. doi:10.1023/A:1008199403446

Schoepflin, T., Chalana, V., Haynor, D. R., & Kim, Y. (2001). Video object tracking with a sequential hierarchy of template deformations. *IEEE Transactions on Circuits and Systems for Video Technology, 11,* 1171–1182. doi:10.1109/76.964784

Schreier, R. M., & Rothermel, A. (2006). Motion adaptive intra refresh for low-delay video coding. In *International Conference on Consumer Electronics* (pp. 453-454).

Schultz, R., & Stevenson, R. (1996). Extraction of high resolution frames from video sequences. *IEEE Transactions on Image Processing, 5*(6), 996–1011. doi:10.1109/83.503915

Schulzrinne, H., Casner, S., Frederick, R., & Jacobson, V. (2003). *RTP: A transport protocol for real-time applications.* Retrieved from http://www.rfc-editor.org/rfc/rfc3550.txt

Schütt, T., Schintke, F., & Reinefeld, A. (2006). Structured overlay without consistent hashing: Empirical results. In *Sixth IEEE International Symposium on Cluster Computing and the Grid Workshops, 2006* (Vol. 2, p. 8). doi: 10.1109/CCGRID.2006.1630903

Schuur, K., Fehn, C., Kauff, P., & Smolic, A. (2002). *About the impact of disparity coding on novel view synthesis, MPEG02/M8676 doc.* Klagenfurt.

Schwarz, H., Marpe, D., & Wiegand, T. (2006). Analysis of hierarchical B pictures and MCTF. *Proceedings of IEEE International Conference on Multimedia and Expo (ICME 2006).* Toronto, Ontario, CA.

Schwarz, H., Marpe, D., & Wiegand, T. (2007). Overview of the scalable video coding extension of the H. 264/AVC standard. *IEEE Transactions in Circuits and Systems for Video Technology, 17*(9), 1103:1120.

Schwarz, H., Marpe, D., & Wiegand, T. (2007). Overview of the scalable video coding extension of the H.264/AVC standard. *IEEE Transactions on Circuits and Systems for Video Technology, 17*(9), 1103–1120. doi:10.1109/TCSVT.2007.905532

Sedmidubsky, J., Barton, S., Dohnal, V., & Zezula, P. (2008). A self-organized system for content-based search in multimedia. In *Proceedings of IEEE International Symposium on Multimedia,* (pp. 322-327).

Seeling, P., Reisslein, M., & Kulapala, B. (2004). Network performance evaluation using frame size and quality traces of single layer and two layer video: A tutorial. *IEEE Communications Surveys, 6*(3).

Seitner, F., & Lovell, B. C. (2005). Pedestrain tracking based on colour and spatial information. In the *Proceedings of the Digital Imaging Computer: Techniques and Applications* (DICTA 2005), (pp. 36-43). Cairns, Australia.

Sentinelli, A., Celetto, L., Lefol, D., Palazzi, C., & Pau, G. (2008). A survey on P2P streaming clients: Looking at the end-user. In *Proceedings of the 4th Annual International Conference on Wireless Internet, WICON'08* (pp. 1-4). Brussels, Belgium: ICST (Institute for Computer Sciences, Social-Informatics and Telecommunications Engineering). doi: 10.4108/ICST.WICON2008.4994

Sentinelli, A., Marfia, G., Gerla, M., Kleinrock, L., & Tewari, S. (2007). Will IPTV ride the peer-to-peer stream? *IEEE Communications Magazine, 45*(6), 86–92. doi:10.1109/MCOM.2007.374424

Setton, E., Yoo, T., Xhu, X., Goldsmith, A., & Girod, B. (2005). Cross-layer design of ad-hoc networks for realtime video streaming. *IEEE Wireless Communications Magazine, 12*(4), 59–65. doi:10.1109/MWC.2005.1497859

Shah, P., & Pâris, J. F. (2007). *Peer-to-peer multimedia streaming using BitTorrent* (pp. 340–347). IEEE International Performance, Computing, and Communications Conference.

Shanableh, T., May, T., & Ishtiaq, F. Applications of distributed source coding to error resiliency of pre-encoded video. *2008 IEEE International Conference on Multimedia and Expo*, (pp. 597-600).

Shao, W., Naghdy, G., & Phung, S. L. (2007). Automatic image annotation for semantic image retrieval. *Lecture Notes in Computer Science, 4781*, 369–378. doi:10.1007/978-3-540-76414-4_36

Sheikh, H. R., Sabir, M. F., & Bovik, A. C. (2006). A statistical evaluation of recent full reference image quality assessment algorithms. *IEEE Transactions on Image Processing, 15*(11), 3440–3451. doi:10.1109/TIP.2006.881959

Shen, M. Y., & Kuo, C.-C. J. (1998). Review of postprocessing techniques for compression artifact removal. *Journal of Visual Communication and Image Representation, 9*(1), 2–14. doi:10.1006/jvci.1997.0378

Shen, X., Yu, H., Buford, J., & Akon, M. (2009). *Handbook of peer-to-peer networking* (1st ed.). Springer Publishing Company, Incorporated.

Shi, Y. Q., & Sun, H. (2008). *Image and video compression for multimedia engineering: Fundamentals, algorithms, and standards* (2nd ed.). Boca Raton, Fl: CRC Press. doi:10.1201/9781420007268

Shneidman, J., Parkes, D. C., & Massoulié, L. (2004). Faithfulness in internet algorithms. *Proceedings of the ACM SIGCOMM Workshop on Practice and Theory of Incentives in Networked Systems* (pp. 220-227). New York, NY: ACM. doi:http://doi.acm.org/10.1145/1016527.1016537

Shneidman, J., & Parkes, D. (2003). Rationality and self-interest in peer to peer networks. In Kaashoek, M., & Stoica, I. (Eds.), *Peer-to-Peer Systems II* (Vol. 2735, pp. 139–148). Berlin, Germany: Springer. doi:10.1007/978-3-540-45172-3_13

Shoaib, M., & Anni, C. (2010). Efficient residual prediction with error concealment in extended spatial scalability. *Wireless Telecommunications Symposium* (WTS), 2010, (pp. 1-6).

Shokorallahi, A. (2006). Raptor codes. *IEEE Transactions on Information Theory, 52*(6), 2551–2567. doi:10.1109/TIT.2006.874390

Shokurov, A., Khropov, A., & Ivanov, D. (2003). Feature tracking in images and video. In *International Conference on Computer Graphics between Europe and Asia* (GraphiCon-2003), (pp. 177-179).

Signoroni, A., Lazzaroni, F., & Leonardi, R. (2003). Exploitation and extension of the region-of-interest coding functionalities in JPEG2000. *IEEE Transactions on Consumer Electronics, 49*(4), 818–823. doi:10.1109/TCE.2003.1261160

Sikora, T. (2001). The MPEG-7 visual standard for content description – an overview. *IEEE Transactions on Circuits and Systems for Video Technology, 11*(6), 696–702. doi:10.1109/76.927422

Singh, A., Castro, M., Druschel, P., & Rowstron, A. (2004) Defending against eclipse attacks on overlay networks. *Proceedings of the 11th Workshop on ACM SIGOPS European Workshop*, (p. 21).

Sirivianos, M., Han, J., Rex, P., & Yang, C. X. (2007). Free-riding in BitTorrent networks with the large view exploit. *Proceedings of the 6th International Workshop on Peer-to-Peer Systems, IPTPS'07*. Retrieved from http://research.microsoft.com/en-us/um/redmond/events/iptps2007/

Sirivianos, M., Park, J. H., Yang, X., & Jarecki, S. (2007). Dandelion: Cooperative content distribution with robust incentives. *Proceedings of the USENIX Annual Technical Conference 2007* (p. 12:1-12:14). Berkeley, CA: USENIX Association. Retrieved from http://dl.acm.org/citation.cfm?id=1364385.1364397

Sisalem, D., & Wolisz, A. (2000). LDA+ TCP-friendly adaptation: A measurement and comparison study. In *Proceedings of the 10th International Workshop on Network and Operating Systems Support for Digital Audio and Video*, (pp. 25-28).

Smith, J. R., & Chang, S.-F. (1996). Visualseek: A fully automated content-based image query system. In *Proceedings of ACM Multimedia*.

Smolić, A., Mueller, K., Merkle, P., Fehn, C., Kauff, P., Eisert, P., & Wiegand, T. (2006). 3D video and free viewpoint video - Technologies, applications and MPEG standards. *Proceedings of IEEE ICME*, Canada, (pp. 2161-2164).

Smolic, A. (2011). 3D video and free viewpoint video – From capture to display. *Pattern Recognition, 44*(9), 1958–1968. doi:10.1016/j.patcog.2010.09.005

Smolic, A., & McCutchen, D. (2004). 3DAV exploration of video-based rendering technology in MPEG. *IEEE Transactions on Circuits and Systems for Video Technology, 14*(3), 348–356. doi:10.1109/TCSVT.2004.823395

Smolic, A., Mueller, K., Stefanovski, N., Ostermann, J., Gotchev, A., & Akar, G. (2007). Coding algorithms for 3DTV – A survey. *IEEE Transactions on Circuits and Systems for Video Technology, 17*(11), 1606–1621. doi:10.1109/TCSVT.2007.909972

So-In, C., Jain, R., & Tamimi, A.-K. (2009). Scheduling in IEEE 802.16e mobile WiMAX networks: Key issues and a survey. *IEEE Journal on Selected Areas in Communications, 27*(2), 156–171. doi:10.1109/JSAC.2009.090207

Son, N., & Jeong, S. (2008). An effective error concealment for H. 264/AVC. In IEEE *8th International Conference on Computer and Information Technology Workshops* (pp. 385-390).

Soomro, A., & Cavalcanti, D. (2007). Opportunities and challenges in using WPAN and WLAN technologies in medical environments. *IEEE Communications Magazine, 45*(2), 114–122. doi:10.1109/MCOM.2007.313404

SopCast. (2010). *SopCast home page*. Retrieved from http://www.sopcast.org/

Sorbier, F. D., Takaya, Y., Uematsu, Y., Daribo, I., & Saito, H. (October 2010). *Augmented reality for 3D TV using depth camera input*. IEEE VSMM 2010, Seoul, Korea.

Sorwar, G., Murshed, M., & Dooley, L. S. (2007). A fully adaptive distance-dependent thresholding search (FADTS) algorithm for performance-management motion estimation. *IEEE Transactions on Circuits and Systems for Video Technology, 17*(4), 429–440. doi:10.1109/TCSVT.2006.888816

Standard, 8.-2. I. (2009). *802.16-2009 IEEE standard for local and metropolitan area networks part 16: Air interface for broadband wireless access systems*. IEEE.

Starck, J., Kilner, J., & Hilton, A. (2008). Objective quality assessment in free-viewpoint video production. *IEEE Proceedings of 3DTV08*, (pp. 225–228).

Stauffer, C., & Grimson, W. (1999). Adaptive background mixture models for real-time tracking. In the *Proceedings of the IEEE Conference on Computer Vision and Pattern Recognition* (CVPR), Vol. 2, (p. 252).

Steiner, M., En-Najjary, T., & Biersack, E. W. (2007). A global view of Kad. In *Proceedings of 7th ACM SIGCOMM Conference on Internet Measurement IMC'07*. San Diego, CA, USA.

Stewart, J., Yu, J., Gortler, S., & Mcmillan, L. (2003). A new reconstruction filter for undersampled light fields. *Eurographics Symposium on Rendering, ACM International Conference Proceeding Series*, (pp. 150–156).

Stiemerling, M., & Kiesel, S. (2010). Cooperative P2P video streaming for mobile peers. *2010 Proceedings of 19th International Conference on Computer Communications and Networks* (ICCCN), (pp. 1-7).

Stockhammer, T. (2011). Dynamic adaptive streaming over HTTP – Design principles and standards. In *Proceedings of the Second Annual ACM Conference on Multimedia Systems* (pp. 133-144).

Stockhammer, T., & Bystrom, M. (2004). H. 264/AVC data partitioning for mobile video communication. In *IEEE International Conference on Image Processing* (pp. 545-548).

Stockhammer, T., Kontopodis, D., & Wiegand, T. (2002). Rate-distortion optimization for JVT/H.26L video coding in packet loss environment. In *Proceedings of Packet Video Workshop 2002*. Pittsburg, PA.

Stockhammer, T., Hannuksela, M. M., & Wiegand, T. (2003). H. 264/AVC in wireless environments. *IEEE Transactions on Circuits and Systems for Video Technology, 13*(7), 657–673. doi:10.1109/TCSVT.2003.815167

Stockhammer, T., & Zia, W. (2007). Error-resilient coding and decoding strategies for video communication. In van der Schaar, M., & Chou, P. A. (Eds.), *Multimedia over IP and wireless networks* (pp. 13–58). Burlington, MA: Academic Press. doi:10.1016/B978-012088480-3/50003-5

Stoica, I., Morris, R., Liben-Nowell, D., Karger, D. R., Kaashoek, M. F., & Dabek, F. (2003). Chord: A scalable peer-to-peer lookup protocol for Internet applications. *IEEE/ACM Transactions on Networking, 11*(1), 17–32. doi:10.1109/TNET.2002.808407

Stoykova, E., Alatan, A., Benzie, P., Grammalidis, N., Malassiotis, S., & Ostermann, J. (2007). 3D time varying scene capture technologies - A survey. *IEEE Transactions on Circuits and Systems for Video Technology, 17*(11), 1568–1586. doi:10.1109/TCSVT.2007.909975

Streamcast Networks. (2008). *Morpheus home page* (Web archive). Retrieved from http://web.archive.org/web/*/http://morpheus.com

Sullivan, G. J., & Ohm, J.-R. (2010). Recent developments in standardization of high efficiency video coding (HEVC). In *Proceedings of SPIE Applications of Digital Image Processing XXXIII, 7798*, paper no. 7798-30.

Sullivan, G. J., Topiwala, P., & Luthra, A. (2004). *The H.264/AVC advanced video coding standard: Overview and introduction to the fidelity range extensions*. Presented at the SPIE Conference on Applications of Digital Image Processing XXVII, 2004.

Sullivan, G. J., & Wiegand, T. (2005). Video compression - From concepts to the H.264/AVC standard. *Proceedings of the IEEE, 93*(1), 18–31. doi:10.1109/JPROC.2004.839617

Sullivan, G., & Wiegand, T. (1998, November). Rate-distortion optimization for video compression. *IEEE Signal Processing Magazine, 15*(6), 74–90. doi:10.1109/79.733497

Sun, H., & Zdepsky, J. (1994, February). Error concealment strategy for picture header loss in MPEG compressed video. In *Proceedings of SPIE Conference of High-Speed Networking and Multimedia Computing* (Vol. 2188, pp. 145-152).

Sun, Q., Lu, Y., & Sun, S. (2010). A visual attention based approach to text extraction. *2010 20th International Conference on Pattern Recognition* (ICPR), (pp. 3991-3995).

Sun, Z., & Sun, J. (2008). Tracking of dynamic image sequence based on intensive restraint topology adaptive snake. *2008 International Conference on Computer Science and Software Engineering*, Vol. 6, (pp. 217-220).

Sun, H., & Kwok, W. (1995, April). Concealment of damaged block transform coded images using projections onto convex sets. *IEEE Transactions on Image Processing, 4*(4), 470–477. doi:10.1109/83.370675

Sun, J., Zheng, N. N., & Shum, H. Y. (2003). Stereo matching using belief propagation. *IEEE Transactions on Pattern Analysis and Machine Intelligence, 25*, 787–800. doi:10.1109/TPAMI.2003.1206509

Suresh, K. V., Kumar, G. M., & Rajagopalan, A. N. (2007). Super-resolution of license plates in real traffic videos. *IEEE Transactions on Intelligent Transportation Systems, 8*(2), 321–331. doi:10.1109/TITS.2007.895291

Su, X., & Dhaliwal, S. K. (2010). Incentive mechanisms in P2P media streaming systems. *IEEE Internet Computing, 14*(5), 74–81. doi:10.1109/MIC.2010.119

Tachikawa, K. (2003). A perspective on the evolution of mobile communications. *IEEE Communications Magazine, 43*(10), 66–73. doi:10.1109/MCOM.2003.1235597

Tai, H.-M., Long, M., He, W., & Yang, H. (2002). An efficient region of interest coding for medical image compression. *Proceedings of the Second Joint Annual Fall Meeting of the Biomedical Engineering Society*, Vol. 2, (pp. 1017- 1018).

Tamura, H., Mori, S., & Yamawaki, T. (1978). Textural features corresponding to visual perception. *IEEE Transactions on Systems, Man, and Cybernetics, 8*, 460–473. doi:10.1109/TSMC.1978.4309999

Tan, E., Guo, L., Chen, S., & Zhang, X. (2001). CUBS: Coordinated upload bandwidth sharing in residential networks. In *Proceedings of the 17th IEEE International Conference on Network Protocols* (ICNP'09). IEEE, Oct. 2009, (pp. 193-2002).

Tan, Y. H., Lee, W. S., Tham, J. Y., Rahardja, S., & Lye, K. M. (2009). Complexity control and computational resource allocation during H.264/SVC encoding. In *Proceedings of the Seventeenth ACM international conference on Multimedia*, Beijing, China, (pp. 897-900).

Tan, D. M., & Wu, H. R. (2006). Perceptual image coding. In Wu, H. R., & Rao, K. R. (Eds.), *Digital image quality and perceptual coding*. Boca Raton, FL: CRC Press.

Tang, Y., Wang, H., & Dou, W. (2004). Trust based incentive in P2P network. *Proceedings of the IEEE International Conference on E-Commerce Technology for Dynamic E-Business* (pp. 302-305). doi:10.1109/CEC-EAST.2004.71

Tanimoto, M., & Fuji, T. (2003). *Ray-space coding using temporal and spatial predictions*. ISO/IEC JTC1/SC29/WG11 Document M10410.

Tan, W., & Zakhor, A. (1999). Multicast transmission of scalable video using layered FEC and scalable compression. *IEEE Transactions on Circuits and Systems for Video Technology, 11*(3), 373–386. doi:10.1109/76.911162

Tan, W., & Zakhor, A. (2001, March). Video multicast using layered FEC and scalable compression. *IEEE Transactions on Circuits and Systems for Video Technology, 11*(3), 373–386. doi:10.1109/76.911162

Taubman, D. S., & Marcellin, M. W. (2002). *JPEG2000: Image compression fundamentals, standards, and practice*. Boston, MA: Kluwer. doi:10.1007/978-1-4615-0799-4

Taylor, I. J., & Harrison, A. (2009). *From P2P and grids to services on the web: Evolving distributed communities* (2nd ed.). Springer Publishing Company, Incorporated.

Technical, E. B. U. (2010). *Peer-to-peer (P2P) technologies and services*. Geneva, Switzerland: Author.

Teh, Y. W., Jordan, M. I., Beal, M. J., & Blei, D. M. (2006). Hierarchical dirichlet processes. *Journal of the American Statistical Association, 101*(476), 1566–1581. doi:10.1198/016214506000000302

Tekalp, A. M. (1995). *Digital video compression*. Prentice Hall PTR.

Telea, A. (2004). An image inpainting technique based on the fast marching method. *Journal of Graphics Tools, 9*(1), 23–34. doi:10.1080/10867651.2004.10487596

Teo, K. H., Tao, Z., & Zhang, J. (2007). The mobile broadband WiMAX standard. *IEEE Signal Processing Magazine, 24*(5), 144–148. doi:10.1109/MSP.2007.904740

Test Sequence Download Page, M. P. E. G.-F. T. V. (n.d.). *Free-viewpoint TV*. Retrieved from http://www.tanimoto.nuee.nagoya-u.ac.jp/~fukushima/mpegftv/

Thang, T. C., Bae, T. M., Jung, Y. J., Ro, Y. M., Kim, J.-G., Choi, H., & Hong, J.-W. (2005). *Spatial scalability of multiple ROIs in surveillance video*. JVT-O037, Busan, KR, 16-22 April, 2005.

Thomos, N., Argyropoulos, S., Boulgouris, N., & Strintzis, M. (2005). Error-resilient transmission of H. 264/AVC streams using flexible macroblock ordering. In *Second European Workshop on the Integration of Knowledge, Semantic, and Digital Media Techniques* (pp. 183-189).

Thompson, G., & Chen, Y. R. (2009). IPTV: Reinventing television in the internet age. *IEEE Internet Computing, 13*(3), 11–14. doi:10.1109/MIC.2009.63

Tran, D. A., Hua, K., & Do, T. (2003). ZIGZAG: An efficient peer-to-peer scheme for media streaming. In *Proceedings of IEEE INFOCOM*.

Triantafyllidis, G. A., Tzovaras, D., & Strintzis, M. G. (2002). Blocking artifact detection and reduction in compressed data. *IEEE Transactions on Circuits and Systems for Video Technology, 12*(10), 877–890. doi:10.1109/TCSVT.2002.804880

Tsai, R., & Huang, T. (1984). Multiframe image restoration and registration. *Advances in Computer Vision and image Processing, 1*, 317-339.

Tseng, B. L., & Anastassiou, D. (1995). *Perceptual adaptive quantization of stereoscopic video coding using MPEG-2's temporal scalability structure*. Paper presented at the International Workshop on Stereoscopic and Three Dimensional Imaging 1995, Santorini, Greece.

TU Delft - Tribler. (2010). *Tribler project home page*. Retrieved from http://tribler.org/trac/wiki

Turk, M. A., & Pentland, A. (1991). Face recognition using eigenfaces. In the *Proceedings of the IEEE Computer Vision and Pattern Recognition Conference* (CVPR), (pp. 586-591).

Turletti, T., & Huitema, C. (1996). *RTP payload format for h.261 video streams*. United States: RFC Editor.

Tu, Y.-C., Sun, J., Hefeeda, M., & Prabhakar, S. (2005). An analytical study of peer-to-peer media streaming systems. *ACM Transactions on Multimedia Computing. Communications and Applications, 1*(4), 354–376.

TVU networks. (2010). *TVU networks home page*. Retrieved from http://www.tvunetworks.com/

UUSee. (2010). *UUSee home page*. Retrieved from http://www.uusee.com/

van der Schaar, M. (2007). Cross-layer wireless multimedia. In van der Schaar, M., & Chou, P. A. (Eds.), *Multimedia over IP and wireless networks* (pp. 337–408). Burlington, MA: Academic Press. doi:10.1016/B978-012088480-3/50013-8

van der Schaar, M., Krishnamachari, S., Choi, S., & Xu, X. (2003). Adaptive cross-layer protection strategies for robust scalable video transmission over 802. 11 WLANs. *IEEE Journal on Selected Areas in Communications, 21*(10), 1751–1763. doi:10.1109/JSAC.2003.815231

Varsa, V., Hannuksela, M. M., & Wang, Y. K. (2001). *Non-normative error concealment algorithms*. VCEG-N62, 14th Meeting: Santa Barbara, CA, USA, 21-24 September, 2001.

Vaughan-Nichols, S. (2004). Achieving wireless broadband with WiMAX. *Computer, 37*(6), 10–13. doi:10.1109/MC.2004.1266286

Vermaak, J., Doucet, A., & Perez, P. (2003). Maintaining multi-modality through mixture tracking. In the *Proceedings of the Ninth IEEE International Conference on Computer Vision* (ICCV'03), Nice, France.

Vermeirsch, K., Dhondt, Y., Mys, S., & de Walle, R. V. (2007). Low complexity multiple description coding for H.264/AVC. In *Eighth International Workshop on Image Analysis for Multimedia Interactive Services, WIAMIS '07* (p. 61). doi: 10.1109/WIAMIS.2007.55

Vetro, A., Su, Y., Kimata, H., & Smolic, A. (2006). *Joint multi-view video model*. Joint Video Team, Doc. JVT-U207, Hangzhou, China.

Vetro, A., Wiegand, T., & Sullivan, G. J. (2011). Overview of the stereo and multiview video coding extensions of the H.264/AVC standard. *Proceedings of IEEE, Special Issue on "3D Media and Displays", 99*(4), 626–642.

Vetro, A., Tourapis, A. M., Muller, K., & Chen, T. (2011). 3D-TV content storage and transmission. *IEEE Transactions on Broadcasting, 57*(2), 384–394. doi:10.1109/TBC.2010.2102950

Vezhnevets, M. (2002). Face and facial feature tracking for natural human-computer interface. In *International Conference on Computer Graphics between Europe and Asia* (GraphiCon-2002), (pp. 86-90).

Vijverberg, J., Loomans, M., Koeleman, C., & deWith, P. (2009). Global illumination compensation for background subtraction using Gaussian-based background difference modelling. In the *Proceedings of the Sixth IEEE International Conference on Advanced Video and Signal Based Surveillance* (AVSS) (pp. 448 –453).

Viola, P., & Jones, M. (2001a). Rapid object detection using a boosted cascade of simple features. In the *Proceedings of the IEEE Computer Vision and Pattern Recognition Conference* (CVPR).

Vlasic, D., Peers, P., Baran, I., Debevec, P., Popovic, J., & Rusinkiewicz, S. (2009). Dynamic shape capture using multi-view photometric stereo. *ACM Transactions on Graphics, 28*(5). doi:10.1145/1618452.1618520

Vlavianos, A., Iliofotou, M., & Faloutsos, M. (2006). BiTos: Enhancing bittorrent for supporting streaming applications. In *Proceedings of the 9th IEEE Global Internet Symposium*, Apr. 2006.

VQEG. (2000). *Final report from the video quality experts group on the validation of objective models of video quality assessment*. Retrieved from http://www.vqeg.org

VQEG. (2007). RRNR-TV group test plan draft version 2. Retrieved from http://www.vqeg.org

VSRS. (n.d.). *View synthesis reference software*. Retrieved from http://wg11.sc29.org/svn/repos/MPEG-4/test/trunk/3D/view_synthesis/VSRS

Vukobratovic, D., Stankovic, V., Sejdinovic, D., Stankovic, L., & Ziong, Z. (2008). Expanding window Fountain codes for scalable video multicast. In *Proceedings of IEEE International Conference on Multimedia and Expo*, (pp. 77–80).

Wah, B. W., Su, X., & Lin, D. (2000). A survey of error concealment schemes for real-time audio and video transmissions over the Internet. In *IEEE International Symposium on Multimedia Software Engineering* (pp. 17-24).

Waitzman, D., Partridge, C., & Deering, S. E. (1988). *Distance vector multicast routing protocol*. Request for Comments IETF. Retrieved from http://www.ietf.org/rfc/rfc1075.txt

Wallach, D. S. (2003). A survey of peer-to-peer security issues. In *Proceedings of the Mext-NSF-JSPS International Symposium on Software Security – Theories and Systems (ISSS'02), LNCS 2609*, (pp. 42–57). Tokyo, Japan, Nov. 2003. Springer.

Wang, B., Kurose, J. F., Shenoy, P. J., & Towsley, D. F. (2004). Multimedia streaming via TCP: An analytic performance study. In *Proceedings of ACM Multimedia Conference* (pp. 908-915).

Wang, D., & Liu, J. (2006). *A dynamic skip list based overlay network for on-demand media streaming with VCR interactions*. IEEE International Conference on Multimedia & Expo (ICME), Toronto, ON, Canada, July 9-12, 2006.

Wang, H., & Suter, D. (2005). A re-evaluation of mixture-of-gaussian background modeling. In the *Proceedings of the IEEE International Conference on Acoustics, Speech, and Signal Processing*, (pp. 1017-1020). Philadelphia, PA, USA.

Wang, H., Leng, J., & Guo, Z. M. (2002). *Adaptive dynamic contour for real-time object tracking*. In Image and Vision Computing New Zealand (IVCNZ2002), Dec. 2002.

Wang, J.-M., Cherng, S., Fuh, C.-S., & Chen, S.-W. (2008). Foreground object detection using two successive images. *IEEE Fifth International Conference on Advanced Video and Signal Based Surveillance, AVSS '08*, (pp. 301-306).

Wang, M., & Li, B. (2007). *Lava: A reality check of network coding in peer-to-peer live streaming*. In IEEE INFOCO, Anchorage, Alaska, May 2007.

Wang, Y., & Lucey, S. (2008). Enforcing convexity for improved alignment with constrained local models. In the *Proceedings of the IEEE Computer Vision and Pattern Recognition Conference* (CVPR).

Wang, Y., Casares, M., & Velipasalar, S. (2009). Cooperative object tracking and event detection with wireless smart cameras. In *Proceedings of the 2009 Sixth IEEE International Conference on Advanced Video and Signal Based Surveillance* (AVSS '09), Washington, DC, USA, (pp. 394-399).

Wang, Z., Bovik, A. C., & Lu, L. (2002). Why is image quality assessment so difficult. *Proceedings IEEE International Conference in Acoustics, Speech and Signal Processing*, Vol. 4, (pp. 3313-3316).

Wang, M., & Li, B. (2007). R^2: Random rush with random network coding in live peer-to-peer streaming. *IEEE Journal on Selected Areas in Communications*, 25(9), 1655–1666. doi:10.1109/JSAC.2007.071205

Wang, Y., Wenger, S., Wen, J., & Katsaggelos, A. K. (2000, July). Error resilient video coding techniques. *IEEE Signal Processing Magazine*, 17(4), 61–82. doi:10.1109/79.855913

Wang, Y., & Zhu, Q. F. (1998, March). Error control and concealment for video communication: A review. *Proceedings of the IEEE*, 86(5), 974–997. doi:10.1109/5.664283

Wang, Y., Zhu, Q. F., & Shaw, L. (1993). Maximally smooth image recovery in transform coding. *IEEE Transactions on Communications*, 41(10), 1544–1551. doi:10.1109/26.237889

Wang, Z., & Bovik, A. (2006). *Image quality assessment*. New York, NY, USA.

Wang, Z., Bovik, A. C., Sheikh, H. R., & Simoncelli, E. P. (2004). Image quality assessment: from error visibility to structural similarity. *IEEE Transactions on Image Processing*, 13(4), 600–612. doi:10.1109/TIP.2003.819861

Wang, Z., Lu, L., & Bovik, A. C. (2004). Video quality assessment based on structural distortion measurement. *Signal Processing Image Communication*, 19(2), 121–132. doi:10.1016/S0923-5965(03)00076-6

Wang, Z., Sheikh, H. R., & Bovik, A. C. (2003). Objective video quality assessment. In Furht, B., & Marqure, O. (Eds.), *The handbook of video databases: Design and applications* (pp. 1041–1078). CRC Press.

Wan, S., & Izquierdo, E. (2007, May). Rate-distortion optimized motion-compensated prediction for packet loss resilient video coding. *IEEE Transactions on Image Processing, 16*(5), 1327–1338. doi:10.1109/TIP.2007.894230

Watson, A., Yang, G. Y., Solomon, J., & Villasenor, J. (1997). Visibility of wavelet quantization noise. *IEEE Transactions on Image Processing, 6*(8), 1164–1175. doi:10.1109/83.605413

Wei, Z., & Zhou, Z. (2010). An adaptive statistical features modeling tracking algorithm based on locally statistical ROI. *2010 International Conference on Educational and Information Technology* (ICEIT), Vol. 1, (pp. 433- 437).

Welch, G., & Bishop, G. (1995). *An introduction to the Kalman filter. Technical report tr95-041*. University of North Carolina at Chapel Hill.

Wen, J. H., Li, C. Z., & Yan, N. W. (2012). Cross-diamond search algorithm for motion estimation based on projection. *Advanced Materials Science and Information Technology, 433-440*, 3713-3717.

Wenger, S. (2003). H. 264/AVC over IP. *IEEE Transactions on Circuits and Systems for Video Technology, 13*(7), 645–656. doi:10.1109/TCSVT.2003.814966

Wheatstone, C. (1838). On some remarkable, and hitherto unobserved, phenomena of binocular vision. *Philosophical Transactions of the Royal Society of London, 54*, 196–199.

Wicker, S. (1995). *Error control systems for digital communication and storage*. Upper Saddle River, NJ: Prentice Hall.

Widmer, J., Denda, R., & Mauve, M. (2001). A survey on TCP-friendly congestion control. *IEEE Network, 15*(3), 28–37. doi:10.1109/65.923938

Wiegand, T., & Sullivan, G. (2003). *Final draft ITU-T recommendation and final draft international standard of joint video specification* (ITU-T Rec. H.264 ISO/IEC 14 496-10 AVC). In Joint Video Team (JVT) of ITU-T SG16/Q15 (VCEG) and ISO/IEC JTC1/SC29/WG1, Annex C, Pattaya, Thailand, Mar. 2003, Doc. JVT-G050.

Wiegand, T., Farber, N., Stuhlmuller, K., & Girod, B. (2000, June). Error-resilient video transmission using long-term memory motion-compensated prediction. *IEEE Journal on Selected Areas in Communications, 18*(6), 1050–1062. doi:10.1109/49.848255

Wiegand, T., Sullivan, G. J., Bjontegaard, G., & Luthra, A. (2003). Overview of the H. 264/AVC video coding standard. *IEEE Transactions on Circuits and Systems for Video Technology, 13*(7), 560–576. doi:10.1109/TCSVT.2003.815165

Wiegand, T., Zhang, X., & Girod, B. (1999). Long-term memory motion-compensated prediction. *IEEE Transactions on Circuits and Systems for Video Technology, 9*(1), 70–84. doi:10.1109/76.744276

Winkler, S. (2005). *Digital video quality – Vision models and metrics*. Wiley. ISBN 0 470 02404 6

Witten, H., Neal, M., & Cleary, G. (1987). Arithmetic coding for data compression. *Communications of the ACM, 30*(6), 520–540. doi:10.1145/214762.214771

Witterman, R., & Zitterbart, M. (2001). *Multicast communication: Protocols and applications*. San Francisco, CA: Morgan Kaufmann.

Wu, C., Li, B., & Zhao, S. (2008). Exploring large-scale peer-to-peer live streaming topologies. *ACM Transactions on Multimedia Computing Communivations and Applications, 4*(3), 1-23. New York, NY: ACM. doi: http://doi.acm.org/10.1145/1386109.1386112

Wu, H. R., & Rao, K. R. (Eds.). (2006). *Digital video image quality and perceptual coding*. Boca Raton, FL: CRC/Taylor & Francis.

Wu, Y., Chou, P. A., & Kung, S. Y. (2005, November). Minimum-energy multicast in mobile ad hoc networks using network coding. *IEEE Transactions on Communications, 53*(11), 1906–1918. doi:10.1109/TCOMM.2005.857148

Wu, Y., Chou, P. A., Zhang, Q., Jain, K., Zhu, W., & Kung, S. Y. (2005). Network planning in wireless ad hoc networks: A cross-layer approach. *IEEE Journal on Selected Areas in Communications, 23*(1), 136–150. doi:10.1109/JSAC.2004.837362

Xiang, G. (2009). Real-time follow-up tracking fast moving object with an active camera. *2nd International Congress on Image and Signal Processing, CISP '09*, (pp. 1-4).

Xiao, X., Zhang, Q., Shi, Y., & Gao, Y. (2011). How much to share: A repeated game model for peer-to-peer streaming under service differentiation incentives. *IEEE Transactions on Parallel and Distributed Systems, 99*, 1. doi:doi:10.1109/TPDS.2011.167

Xie, L. Y., Su, X. Q., Zhang, S., & Xu, Z. G. (2012). A Novel adaptive fast motion estimation algorithm for video compression. In the *Proceedings of International Conference in Electrics, Communication and Automatic Control*, (pp. 241-250).

Xie, Y., & Han, G.-Q. (2005). ROI coding with separated code block. *Proceedings of 2005 International Conference on Machine Learning and Cybernetics*, Vol. 9, (pp. 5447-5451).

Xie, S., Li, B., Keung, G. Y., & Zhang, X. (2007). Coolstreaming: Design, theory, and practice. *IEEE Transactions on Multimedia, 9*(8), 1661–1671. doi:10.1109/TMM.2007.907469

Xiph.Org Foundation. (2011). *Theora specification.* Retrieved September 21, 2011, from http://theora.org/doc/Theora.pdf

Xu, D., Chai, H.-K., Rosenberg, C., & Kulkarni, S. (2003). Analysis of a hybrid architecture for cost-effective streaming media distribution. In *Proceedings of SPIE/ACM MMCN*.

Xu, D., Liu, J., Liu, Z., & Tang, X. (2004). Indoor shadow detection for video segmentation. In the *Proceedings of the IEEE International Conference on Multimedia and Expo, 2004*, Vol. 1, (pp. 41-44).

Xu, L., Ma, S., Zhao, D., & Gao, W. (2005). Rate control for scalable video model. In *Proceedings of the SPIE, Visual Communications and Image Processing*, Vol. 5960, (p. 525).

Xue, Z., Loo, K.-K., & Cosmas, J. (2008). Bandwidth efficient error resilience scheme for wavelet based video transmission. *2008 IEEE International Symposium on Broadband Multimedia Systems and Broadcasting*, (pp. 1-6).

Xue, Z., Loo, K.-K., Cosmas, J., Tun, M., Feng, L., & Yip, P.-Y. (2010). Error-resilient scheme for wavelet video codec using automatic ROI detection and Wyner-Ziv coding over packet erasure channel. *IEEE Transactions on Broadcasting, 56*(4), 481–493. doi:10.1109/TBC.2010.2058371

Xu, J.-B., Po, L.-M., & Cheung, C.-K. (1999). Adaptive motion tracking block matching algorithms for video coding. *IEEE Transactions on Circuits and Systems for Video Technology, 9*, 1025–1029. doi:10.1109/76.795056

Yamamoto, K., Kitahara, M., Kimata, H., Yendo, T., Fujii, T., & Tanimoto, M. (2007). Multiview video coding using view interpolation and color correction. *IEEE Transactions on Circuits and Systems for Video Technology, 17*, 1436–1449. doi:10.1109/TCSVT.2007.903802

Yang, B., & Hector, G.-M. (2002). Efficient search in peer-to-peer networks. In *Proceedings of the 22-th IEEE International Conference on Distributed Computing Systems.*

Yang, H., & Rose, K. (2005, March). Rate-distortion optimized motion estimation for error resilient video coding. In *Proceedings of ICASSP '05* (Vol. 2, pp. 173-178). Philadelphia, PA.

Yang, H., & Rose, K. (2006, May). Generalized source-channel prediction for error resilient video coding. *Proceedings of ICASSP '06*, Vol. 2, (pp. 533-536).

Yang, J., Everett, M., Buehler, C., & Mcmillan, L. (2002). A real-time distributed light field camera. *Proc. of the 13th Eurographics Workshop on Rendering*, (pp. 77–86).

Yang, J., Zhong, Y., & Zhang, S. (2003). An efficient interest-group based search mechanism in unstructured peer-to-peer networks. In *Proceedings of the International Conference on Computer Networks and Mobile Computing*, (pp. 247-252).

Yang, H. (2007, July). Advances in recursive per-pixel end-to-end distortion estimation for robust video coding in H.264/AVC. *IEEE Transactions on Circuits and Systems for Video Technology, 17*(7), 845–856. doi:10.1109/TCSVT.2007.897116

Yang, H., & Rose, K. (2010, January). Optimizing motion compensated prediction for error resilient video coding. *IEEE Transactions on Image Processing, 19*, 108–118. doi:10.1109/TIP.2009.2032895

Yang, M.-H., Kriegman, D. J., & Ahuja, N. (2002). Detecting faces in images: A survey. *IEEE Transactions on Pattern Analysis and Machine Intelligence, 24*(1), 34–58. doi:10.1109/34.982883

Yao, J., Duan, Y., & Pan, J. (2006). Implementation of a Multihoming Agent for Mobile On-board Communication. In *Proceedings of VTC, 2006.*

Yao, Z.-W., & Xu, X. (2010). Dynamic region of interest extract method for JPEG2000 coding. *2010 International Conference on Computer and Communication Technologies in Agriculture Engineering* (CCTAE), Vol. 2, (pp. 150-153).

Yatawara, Y., Caldera, M., Kusuma, T. M., & Zepernick, H.-J. (2005). Unequal error protection for ROI coded images over fading channels. *Proceedings Systems Communications, 2005*, 111–115.

Yiu, W., Chan, S. Xiong, Y., & Zhang, Q. (2005). *Supporting interactive media on-demand in peer-to-peer networks.* Technical report, 2005.

Yoo, H.-W. (2002). Visual information retrieval system via content-based approach. *Pattern Recognition, 35*(3), 749–769. doi:10.1016/S0031-3203(01)00072-3

Yoon, H., Kim, J., Tan, F., & Hsieh, R. (2008). On-demand video streaming in mobile opportunistic networks. [Washington, DC: IEEE Computer Society.]. *Proceedings of PERCOM, 08*, 80–89.

You, W. (2010). *Object detection and tracking in compresses domain.* Retrieved from http://knol.google.com/k/wonsang-you/object-detection-and-tracking-in/3e2si9juvje7y/7#

You, W., Sabirin, M. S. H., & Kim, M. (2007). *Moving object tracking in H.264/AVC bitstream. MCAM 2007, LNCS* (*Vol. 4577*, pp. 483–492). Heidelberg, Germany: Springer.

You, W., Sabirin, M. S. H., & Kim, M. (2009). Real-time detection and tracking of multiple objects with partial decoding in H.264/AVC bitstream domain. In Kehtarnavaz, N., & Carlsohn, M. F. (Eds.), *Proceedings of SPIE* (pp. 72440D–72440D, 12). San Jose, CA: SPIE. doi:10.1117/12.805596

Yuan, L., & Mu, Z.-C. (2007). Ear detection based on skin-color and contour information. *2007 International Conference on Machine Learning and Cybernetics*, Vol. 4, (pp. 2213-2217).

Zakhor, A. (2002). Iterative procedures for reduction of blocking effects in transform image coding. *IEEE Transactions on Circuits and Systems for Video Technology, 2*(1), 91–95. doi:10.1109/76.134377

Zang, Q., & Klette, R. (2004). Robust background subtraction and maintenance. In the *Proceedings of the 17th International Conference on Pattern Recognition,* (ICPR), Vol. 2, (pp. 90-93).

Zeinalipour-Yazti, D., Kalogeraki, V., & Gunopulos, D. (2004). Information retrieval in peer-to-peer networks. *The IEEE CS and the AIP, 6*(4), 20–26.

Zeng, W., Du, J., Gao, W., & Huang, Q. (2005). Robust moving object segmentation on H.264/AVC compressed video using the block-based MRF model. *Real-Time Imaging, 11*(4), 290–299. doi:10.1016/j.rti.2005.04.008

Zhang, B., Jamin, S., & Zhang, L. (2002). Host multicast: A framework for delivering multicast to end users. In *Proceedings Twenty-First Annual Joint Conference of the IEEE Computer and Communications Societies INFOCOM 2002 IEEE* (Vol. 3, pp. 1366-1375). doi: 10.1109/INFCOM.2002.1019387

Zhang, C., Chen, X., Chen, M., Chen, S.-C., & Shyu, M.-L. (2005). A multiple instance learning approach for content-based image retrieval using one-class support vector machine. *IEEE International Conference on Multimedia & Expo*, (pp. 1142-1145).

Zhang, H., Bruce, C., Brian, L., & Victor, L. (2004). A multi-agent approach for peer-to-peer-based information retrieval systems. In *Proceedings of the International Joint Conference on Autonomous Agents and Multiagent Systems*, (pp. 456-464).

Zhang, M., Luo, J.-G., Zhao, L., & Yang, S.-Q. (2005). A peer-to-peer network for live media streaming using a push-pull approach. In *Proceedings of ACM International Conference on Multimedia*.

Zhang, M., Zhao, L., Tang, Y., Luo, J.-G., & Yang, S.-Q. (2005). Large-scale live media streaming over peer-to-peer networks through global internet. In *Proceedings ACM Internaitonal Conference on Multimedia, P2PMMS Workshop*.

Zhang, R., Regunathan, S. L., & Rose, K. (2001, November). End-to-end distortion estimation for RD-based robust delivery of pre-compressed video. In *Proceedings of 35th Asilomar Conference on Signals, Systems and Computers* (Vol. 1, pp. 210-214).

Zhang, T., Liu, C., Wang, M., & Goto, S. (2009). Region-of-interest based H.264 encoder for videophone with a hardware macroblock level face detector. *IEEE International Workshop on Multimedia Signal Processing, MMSP '09* (pp. 1-6).

Zhang, W., Fang, X. Z., & Yang, X. (2006). Moving cast shadows detection based on ratio edge. In the *Proceedings of the 18th International Conference on Pattern Recognition* (ICPR), Vol. 4, (pp. 73-76).

Zhang, X., Liu, J., Li, B., & Yum, Y.-S. P. (2005). Cool-Streaming/DONet: A data-driven overlay network for peer-to-peer live media streaming. *Proceedings of the 24th Annual Joint Conference of the IEEE Computer and Communications Societies (INFOCOM)*, (pp. 2102-2111).

Zhang, D., Wang, F., Shi, Z., & Zhang, C. (2010). Interactive localized content based image retrieval with multiple-instance active learning. *Pattern Recognition*, *43*(2), 478–484. doi:10.1016/j.patcog.2009.03.002

Zhang, J., Liu, L., Ramaswamy, L., & Pu, C. (2008). PeerCast: Churn-resilient end system multicast on heterogeneous overlay networks. *Journal of Network and Computer Applications*, *31*(4), 821–850. doi:10.1016/j.jnca.2007.05.001

Zhang, R., Regunathan, S. L., & Rose, K. (2000, June). Video coding with optimal inter/intra-mode switching for packet loss resilience. *IEEE Journal on Selected Areas in Communications*, *18*(6), 966–976. doi:10.1109/49.848250

Zhang, X., Chen, S., & Sandhu, R. (2005). Enhancing data authenticity and integrity in P2P systems. *IEEE Internet Computing*, *9*(6), 42–49. doi:10.1109/MIC.2005.124

Zhang, Y. (2009). *WiMAX network planning and optimization*. CRC Press. doi:10.1201/9781420066630

Zhang, Y., & Chen, H.-H. (2007). *Mobile WiMAX: Toward broadband wireless metropolitan area networks*. Auerbach Publications. doi:10.1201/9780849326400

Zhang, Y., Gao, W., Lu, Y., Huang, Q., & Zhao, D. (2007, Apr.). Joint source-channel rate-distortion optimization for h.264 video coding over error-prone networks. *IEEE Transactions on Multimedia*, *9*(3), 445–454. doi:10.1109/TMM.2006.887989

Zhang, Y., Jiang, G., Yu, M., Yang, Y., Peng, Z., & Chen, K. (2010). Depth perceptual region-of-interest based multiview video coding. *Journal of Visual Communication and Image Representation*, *21*(5-6), 498–512. doi:10.1016/j.jvcir.2010.03.002

Zhang, Z. (2000). A flexible new technique for camera calibration. *IEEE Transactions on Pattern Analysis and Machine Intelligence*, *22*, 1330–1334. doi:10.1109/34.888718

Zhanwu, X., & Miaoliang, Z. (2006). Color-based skin detection: Survey and evaluation. In the *Proceedings of the 12th International Multi-Media Modelling Conference*.

Zhao, Q., & Tao, H. (2005). Object tracking using color correlogram. In the *Proceedings of the 2nd Joint IEEE International Workshop on Visual Surveillance and Performance Evaluation of Tracking and Surveillance*, (pp. 263-270).

Zhao, B. Y., Huang, L., Stribling, J., Rhea, S. C., & Kubiatowicz, A. D. (2004). Tapestry: A resilient global-scale overlay for service deployment. *IEEE Journal on Selected Areas in Communications*, *22*(1), 41–53. doi:10.1109/JSAC.2003.818784

Zhao, T., & Nevatia, R. (2004). Tracking multiple humans in complex situations. *IEEE Transactions on Pattern Analysis and Machine Intelligence*, *26*(9), 1208–1221. doi:10.1109/TPAMI.2004.73

Zheng, J.-M., Zhou, D.-W., & Geng, J.-L. (2007). ROI progressive image transmission based on wavelet transform and human visual specialties. *International Conference on Wavelet Analysis and Pattern Recognition, ICWAPR '07*, Vol. 1, (pp. 260-264).

Zhou, Y., Gu, L., & Zhang, H. (2003). Bayesian tangent shape model: Estimating shape and pose parameters via Bayesian inference. In the *Proceedings of the IEEE Conference on Computer Vision and Pattern Recognition (CVPR)*, (pp. 109-116).

Zhou, W., & Bovik, A. C. (2002). Bitplane-by-bitplane shift (BbBShift) - A suggestion for JPEG2000 region of interest image coding. *Signal Processing Letters, 9*(5), 160–162. doi:10.1109/LSP.2002.1009009

Zhu, C. (1997, Mar.). *RTP payload format for H.263 video streams*. IETF draft.

Zhu, C., Wang, Y. K., Hannuksela, M., & Li, H. (2006). Error resilient video coding using redundant pictures. In *IEEE International Conference on Image Processing* (pp. 801–804).

Zhu, Q., Avidan, S., Yeh, M., & Cheng, K. (2006) Fast human detection using a cascade of histograms of oriented gradients. In the *Proceedings of the IEEE Conference on Computer Vision and Pattern Recognition* (CVPR).

Zhu, Y., Yang, X., & Hu, Y. (2005). Making search efficient on Gnutella-like P2P systems. In *Proceedings of the International Parallel Distributed Processing Symposium*, (p. 56a).

Zhuang, S. Q., Zhao, B. Y., Joseph, A. D., Katz, R. H., & Kubiatowicz, J. D. (2001). Bayeux: An architecture for scalable and fault-tolerant wide-area data dissemination. In *Proceedings of the 11th International Workshop on Network and Operating Systems Support for Digital Audio and Video, NOSSDAV '01* (pp. 11-20). New York, NY: ACM. doi: http://doi.acm.org/10.1145/378344.378347

Zhu, C., Chau, L.-P., & Lin, X. (2002). Hexagon-based search pattern for fastblock motion estimation. *IEEE Transactions on Circuits and Systems for Video Technology, 12*(5), 349–355. doi:10.1109/TCSVT.2002.1003474

Zhu, C., Lin, X., Chau, L., & Po, L.-M. (2004). Enhanced hexagonal searchfor fast block motion estimation. *IEEE Transactions on Circuits and Systems for Video Technology, 14*(10), 1210–1214. doi:10.1109/TCSVT.2004.833166

Zhu, S., & Ma, K.-K. (2000). A new diamond search algorithm for fast block-matching motion estimation. *IEEE Transactions on Image Processing, 9*, 287–290. doi:10.1109/TIP.2000.826791

Zinger, S., Ruijters, D., & de With, P. H. N. (2009). *iGLANCE project: Free-viewpoint 3D video*. 17th International Conference on Computer Graphics, Visualization and Computer Vision (WSCG). Plzen, Czech Republic.

Zinger, S., Do, L., & de With, P. H. N. (2010). Free-viewpoint depth image based rendering. *Journal of Visual Communication and Image Representation, 21*(5-6), 533–541. doi:10.1016/j.jvcir.2010.01.004

Zink, M., & Mauthe, A. (2004). P2P streaming using multiple description coded video. *Proceedings 30th Euromicro Conference, 2004* (pp. 240-247). doi: 10.1109/EURMIC.2004.1333377

Zitnick, C., Kang, S., Uyttendaele, M., Winder, S., & Szeliski, R. (2004, August). High-quality video view interpolation using a layered representation. *ACM Transactions on Graphics, 23*(3). doi:10.1145/1015706.1015766

Zitov, B., & Flusser, J. (2003). Image registration methods: A survey. *Image and Vision Computing, 21*(11), 977–1000. doi:10.1016/S0262-8856(03)00137-9

Zvikhachevskaya, A., Markarian, G., & Mihaylova, L. (2009). Quality of service consideration for the wireless telemedicine and e-health services. *Wireless Communications and Networking Conference*, Budapest, Hungary, (pp. 1-6).

About the Contributors

Reuben Farrugia received the first degree in Electrical Engineering from the University of Malta, Malta, in 2004, and the Ph.D. degree from the University of Malta, Malta, in 2009. In 2004 he was employed a Research Engineer with the Department of Communications and Computer Engineering of the University of Malta. His research work included wireless network modeling and resilient video coding. In January 2008 he was appointed Assistant Lecturer with the same department and is now a Lecturer. His research interests are in video coding and image processing.

Carl James Debono received his B.Eng. (Hons.) degree in Electrical Engineering from the University of Malta, Malta, in 1997 and the Ph.D. degree in Electronics and Computer Engineering from the University of Pavia, Italy, in 2000. Between 1997 and 2001 he was employed as a Research Engineer in the area of Integrated Circuit Design with the Department of Microelectronics at the University of Malta. In 2000 he was also engaged as a Research Associate with Texas A&M University, Texas. In 2001 he was appointed Lecturer with the Department of Communications and Computer Engineering at the University of Malta and is now a Senior Lecturer. He is currently the Deputy Dean of the Faculty of ICT at the University of Malta. Dr. Debono is a Senior Member of the IEEE and served as chair of the IEEE Malta Section between 2007 and 2010. He is the IEEE Region 8 Conference Coordination sub-committee chair for 2012. His research interests are in wireless systems design and applications, multi-view video coding, resilient multimedia transmission, and modeling of communication systems.

* * *

Ali Alinejad received the PhD degree from the Faculty of Science, Engineering and Computing, Kingston University, London, U.K., in 2012. Since 2003, he has been a Lecturer at Islamic Azad University, Islamshahr Branch, Islamshahr, Iran. His current research interests include broadband wireless access, m-health, and cross layer optimization in 4G wireless networks. Mr. Alinejad is a research member of the Medical Information and Network Technologies Research Centre (MINT), Kingston University, and a student member of the IEEE Engineering in Medicine and Biology Society.

Muhammad Altaf received his BSc degree from the University of Engineering and Technology, Peshawar, Pakistan in 2001 and his MSc degree in Computer System Engineering from the National University of Science and Technology, Rawalpindi, Pakistan in 2004. He subsequently obtained his PhD from the University of Essex, UK in 2010. He is now an Assistant Professor and head of department in the Faculty of Engineering, Attock Campus, COMSATS Institute of Information Technology, Pakistan. His research interests are video compression and video streaming over wired and wireless networks.

Carlos T. Calafate is an Associate Professor in the Department of Computer Engineering at the Technical University of Valencia (UPV) in Spain. He graduated with honors in Electrical and Computer Engineering at the University of Oporto (Portugal) in 2001. He received his Ph.D. degree in Computer Engineering from the Technical University of Valencia in 2006, where he has worked as an Assistant Professor since 2005. He is a member of the Computer Networks research group (GRC). His research interests include mobile and pervasive computing, security and QoS on wireless networks, as well as video coding and streaming.

Vinod Chandran holds a PhD in Electrical and Computer Engineering from Washington State University in 1990. He also has Master's Degrees in Electrical Engineering from Texas Tech University, USA, and Computer Science from Washington State University, USA, and a B. Tech in Electrical Engineering (Electronics) degree from the Indian Institute of Technology, Madras, India. He joined the Queensland University of Technology, Brisbane, Australia in 1993 and is currently a Professor in the School of Engineering Systems at the Queensland University of Technology, Brisbane, Australia. He has co-authored over 150 papers and has supervised 12 PhD students to completion as the principal supervisor. His research interests span signal, speech and image processing with applications mainly to biometrics and biomedical systems.

Jiann-Jone Chen received the B.S.E.E and M.S.E.E degrees from National Cheng-Kung University, Tainan, Taiwan, in 1989 and 1991, respectively, and the Ph.D. degree in Electronic Engineering from National Chiao-Tung University, Hsinchu, Taiwan, in 1997. From 1999 to 2002, he was with ITRI Computer & Communication Laboratories, Hsinchu, Taiwan. He joined the Electrical Engineering Department of National Taiwan University of Science & Technology, Taipei, Taiwan, in August 2002. Dr. Chen received the ISI Classic Citation Award in 2001. He has conducted researches in video encoding, media streaming, image indexing, and image/video processing. His research interests include various topics in digital image processing and multimedia communications.

Alessandra M. Coelho D.Sc. degree from the Instituto Politécnico do Rio de Janeiro (IPRJ)/Universidade Estadual do Rio de Janeiro, Brazil in 2012; an M.Sc. degree from the Centro Federal de Educação Tecnológica de Minas Gerais, CEFET/MG, Brazil in 2006; and a B.Sc. in computer science from the Centro de Ensino Superior de Juiz de Fora, Brazil in 1998. She currently works at Federal Institute of Education, Science and Technology of Southeast of Minas Gerais as a full-time college professor. Her interests include optimization, remote sensing, image processing, inverse problems, computer architectures, photogrammetry, algorithms and operating systems.

Simon Denman received the B. Eng (Electrical) and B. IT degrees from the Queensland University of Technology (QUT) in 2003. He completed a PhD at QUT in the area of object tracking for intelligent surveillance in 2009. He is currently a Research Fellow with the Speech, Audio, Image and Video Technology (SAIVT) group at QUT. Dr. Denman's current research interests include object tracking and soft biometrics, crowd surveillance, event detection, and using intelligent surveillance to extract operational measures.

Peter H. N. de With graduated in Electrical Engineering (MSc., IR.) from the University of Technology in Eindhoven. In 1992, he received his Ph.D. degree from the University of Technology Delft, The Netherlands. He joined Philips Research Labs Eindhoven in 1984, where he became a member of the Magnetic Recording Systems Department and set-up the first DCT-based compression systems. From 1985 to 1993, he was involved in several European research projects on SDTV and HDTV recording. He was the leading video compression expert for the DV camcorder standard from 1989-1993. In 1994, he became a member of the TV Systems group at Philips Research Eindhoven, where he was leading the design of advanced programmable video architectures and a senior TV systems architect. In 1997, he was appointed as full Professor at the University of Mannheim, Germany, at the faculty Computer Engineering and heading the chair on Digital Circuitry and Simulation. Between 2000 and 2007, he was with LogicaCMG in Eindhoven as a principal consultant and distinguished business consultant and simultaneously, he is Professor at the University of Technology Eindhoven, at the faculty of Electrical Engineering, heading the chair on Video Coding and Architectures as part of the Dept. on Signal Processing Systems.

Luat Do obtained his MSc degree in Electrical Engineering at the Eindhoven University of Technology (TU/e), Eindhoven, The Netherlands in 2009. In September 2009, he joined the Video Coding and Architectures group at the TU/e as a PhD. student and is currently working on free viewpoint interpolation algorithms which is a part of the iGlance project.

Vania V. Estrela is a Professor in the School of Engineering at the Universidade Federal Fluminense since 2010. She earned a B.S. degree at the Universidade Federal do Rio de Janeiro (UFRJ), Rio de Janeiro (RJ), Brazil, in Electrical and Computer Engineering (ECE); an M.Sc. from the Instituto Technological Aeronautics (ITA), Brazil; an M.Sc. in ECE at the Northwestern University, USA; and a Ph.D. in ECE from the Illinois Institute of Technology (IIT). She taught at DeVry University and, later, at DePaul University, both in Chicago; for the Universidade Estadual do Norte Fluminense (UENF), and for the Universidade Estadual da Zona Oeste (UEZO), Brazil. She was a Visiting Professor at the Universidade Estadual do Rio de Janeiro (UERJ) from 2004 to 2010. Her research interests include image processing, multimedia, inverse problems, machine learning, remote sensing and instrumentation. Some of her pet causes are technology transfer (specially to/from BRICS), Engineering/Math education, environmental issues and digital inclusion. She is a Member of IEEE, OSA, and American Institute of Physics; an Editor for the International Journal of Image Processing (IJIP); and a reviewer for Springer, IET and Elsevier journals, ELCVIA and IJIP.

Martin Fleury holds a first degree from Oxford University, UK and an additional Maths/Physics based bachelor degree from the Open University, Milton Keynes, UK. He obtained an MSc in Astrophysics from QMW College, University of London, UK in 1990 and an MSc from the University of South-West England, Bristol in Parallel Computing Systems in 1991. He holds a PhD in Parallel Image-Processing Systems from the University of Essex, Colchester, UK. He is currently a Visiting Fellow at the University of Essex, UK, having previously worked as a Senior Lecturer at the University of Essex. Martin has authored or co-authored around two hundred and forty five articles on topics such as document and image compression algorithms, performance prediction of parallel systems, software engineering, reconfigurable hardware, and vision systems. His current research interests are video communication over wireless networks. He is also an external examiner for the Arab Open University in Kuwait and the Open University in the UK.

Clinton Fookes is an Associate Professor in the School of Electrical Engineering & Computer Science in the Science & Engineering Faculty of the Queensland University of Technology in Brisbane, Australia. He holds a BEng (Aerospace/Avionics), an MBA and a PhD in the field of computer vision. Clinton actively researches in the fields of computer vision and pattern recognition including biometrics, intelligent surveillance, airport security and operations. Clinton has attracted over $11.5M of cash funding for fundamental and applied research from external competitive sources and has published over 100 internationally peer-reviewed articles. He is a member of professional organisations including the IEEE. He is also an Australian Institute of Policy and Science Young Tall Poppy and an Australian Museum Eureka Prize winner.

Mohammad Ghanbari became an IEEE Fellow in 2001 for his pioneering work on scalable video. He has registered for eleven international patents on various aspects of video networking. Amongst his various books he is the author of "Standard Codecs: Image Compression to Advanced Video Coding" published by the IET press in 2011 in its 3rd edition. Prof. Ghanbari has authored or co-authored about 500 journal and conference papers, a good number of which have had a fundamental influence in this field. Prof. Ghanbari now divides his time between the University of Essex, UK and Sharif University, Iran.

Dan Grois received the B.Sc. degree at the Electrical and Computer Engineering Department, Ben-Gurion University (BGU), Beer-Sheva, Israel, 2002. He received the M.Sc. degree at the Communication Systems Engineering field (at the Electro-optics Unit), BGU, 2006, and the Ph.D. degree at the Communication Systems Engineering Department, BGU, 2011. Starting from 2011, Dan is a senior post-doctoral researcher at the Multimedia Lab, Communication Systems Engineering Department, BGU. Dan has a significant number of academic publications presented at peer-reviewed international conferences and published by IEEE and Elsevier scientific journals, Wiley publisher, et cetera. In addition, Dan is a referee of top-tier conferences and international journals, such as the *IEEE Transactions in Image Processing, Journal of Visual Communication and Image Representation,* Elsevier, *IEEE Sensors, SPIE Optical Engineering,* et cetera. Dan is a member of the ACM and a Senior Member of the IEEE. Dan's research interests include image and video coding and processing, video coding standards, region-of-interest scalability, computational complexity and bit-rate control, network communication and protocols, computer vision, and future multimedia applications and systems.

Ofer Hadar received the B.Sc., the M.Sc. (cum laude), and the Ph.D. degrees from the Ben-Gurion University of the Negev, Israel, in 1990, 1992, and 1997, respectively, all in Electrical and Computer Engineering. From August 1996 to February 1997, he was with CREOL at Central Florida University, Orlando, FL, as a Research Visiting Scientist, working on the angular dependence of sampling MTF and over-sampling MTF. From October 1997 to March 1999, he was Post-Doctoral Fellow in the Department of Computer Science at the Technion-Israel Institute of Technology, Haifa. Currently he is a faculty member at the Communication Systems Engineering Department at Ben-Gurion University of the Negev. His research interests include: image and video compression, routing in ATM networks, flow control in ATM networks, packet video, and transmission of video over IP networks and video rate smoothing and multiplexing. Hadar also works as a consultant for several hi-tech companies such as, EnQuad Technologies Ltd in the area of MPEG-4, and Scopus in the area of video compression and transmission over satellite networks. Hadar is a member of the SPIE and a Senior Member of the IEEE.

Yo-Sung Ho (M'81-SM'06) received both B.S. and M.S degrees in Electronic Engineering from Seoul National University (SNU), Korea, in 1981 and 1983, respectively, and Ph.D. degree in Electrical and Computer Engineering from the University of California, Santa Barbara, in 1990. He joined Electronics and Telecommunications Research Institute (ETRI), Korea, in 1983. From 1990 to 1993, he was with Philips Laboratories, Briarcliff Manor New York, where he was involved in development of the advanced digital high-definition television (AD-HDTV) system. In 1993, he rejoined the technical staff of ETRI and was involved in development of the Korea direct broadcast satellite (DBS) digital television and high-definition television systems. Since 1995, he has been with the Gwangju Institute of Science and Technology (GIST), where he is currently a Professor in the Information and Communications Department. His research interests include digital image and video coding, image analysis and image restoration, advanced coding techniques, digital video and audio broadcasting, 3D television, and realistic broadcasting.

Robert S. H. Istepanian received the Ph.D. degree from the Department of Electronic and Electrical Engineering, Loughborough University, Leicestershire, U.K., in 1994. He is currently a Professor of Data Communications at Kingston University, London, where he is also the founder and Director of the Medical Information and Network Technologies Research Centre (MINT) Since then, he has held several academic and research academic posts in U.K. and Canada including senior lectureships in the Universities of Portsmouth, Portsmouth, U.K., and Brunel University,Middlesex, U.K. He was also an Associate Professor in the University of Ryerson, Toronto, ON, Canada, and an Adjunct Professor at the University of West Ontario, ON. He is widely recognized as the founder of the concept of mobile health (m-health). He was the 2008 Leverhulme distinguished Visiting Fellow at the Centre for Global ehealth Innovation, University of Toronto, Toronto, and the University's Health Network. He is the author or coauthor of more than 170 refereed journal, conference papers an chapter books, and has edited three books in the areas of mobile communications for healthcare (m-health). Prof. Istepanian is an investigator and coinvestigator of several Engineering and Physical Sciences Research Council and European Union (UN) research grants on m-health and e-health projects. He leads several EU-Information Society Technologies and e-Ten projects in the areas of mobile healthcare. He was on several IEEE Transactions and international journals' editorial boards including *IEEE Transaction on Information Technology in Biomedicine* (1997–2011), *IEEE Transactions on Nanobioscience*, and *IEEE Transactions on Mobile Computing, International Journal of Telemedicine and Applications*, and *Journal of Mobile Multimedia*.

Harilaos Koumaras was born in Athens, Greece in 1980. He received his BSc degree in Physics in 2002 from the University of Athens, Physics Department, his MSc in Electronic Automation and Information Systems in 2004, being scholar of the non-profit organization Alexander S Onassis, from the University of Athens, Computer Science Department and his PhD in 2007 at Computer Science from the University of Athens, Computer Science Department, having granted the four-year scholarship of National Centre of Scientific Research "Demokritos". In 2003 he joined the Media Networks Lab at the National Centre of Scientific Research "Demokritos" and participated in numerous EC-funded and national funded projects with presentations and publications at international conferences, scientific journals and book chapters. His research interests include objective/subjective evaluation of the perceived quality of multimedia services, video quality and picture quality evaluation, video traffic modeling, digital terrestrial television and video compression techniques. Currently, he is the author or co-author of 50 scientific papers in international journals, technical books and book chapters, numbering 112 non-self citations. He is an editorial board member of the *Telecommunications Systems Journal* and a reviewer of the *IEEE Network magazine*, the *EURASIP Journal of Applied Signal Processing*, the *IEEE Transactions on Image Processing,* and the *IEEE Transactions on Broadcasting.* Dr. Koumaras is a member of IEEE, SPIE and National Geographic Society.

Fabrice Labeau is an Associate Professor in the Electrical and Computer Engineering department at McGill University, Montreal, Quebec, Canada. He received the Electrical Engineer degree in 1995 from Université Catholique de Louvain, Belgium, and the Diplôme D'études Spécialisées en Sciences Appliquées, orientation Télécommunications also from UCL in 1996. From 1996 to 2000, he was with the Communications and Remote Sensing Laboratory of UCL. From January to March 1999, he was a visiting scientist to the Signal and Image Department (TSI) of ENST Paris. He received a Ph.D. degree in September 2000 from UCL. His research interests include signal processing applications to e-health and energy management, multirate processing, joint source channel coding, data compression, and error-control coding. He was part of the organizing committee of ICASSP 2004 in Montreal and is/ was Technical Program Committee co-chair for the IEEE Vehicular Technology Conference in the Fall of 2006 and 2012, and the IEEE International Conference on Image Processing 2015. He is a Senior Member of IEEE.

Cheon Lee (S'06) received his B.S. degree in Electronic Engineering and Avionics from Korea Aerospace University (KAU), Korea, in 2005 and M.S. degree in Information and Communication Engineering at the Gwangju Institute of Science and Technology (GIST), Korea, in 2007. He is currently working towards his Ph.D. degree in the Information and Communications Department at GIST, Korea. His research interests include digital signal processing, video coding, 3D video coding, 3D television, and realistic broadcasting.

Frank Lin received the B. Eng (Electrical) and B. IT degrees from the Queensland University of Technology (QUT) in 2003. He completed a PhD at QUT in the field of computer vision, focusing on super resolution for improved face recognition in 2008. Dr. Lin currently works as a Software Engineer with Zap Technology.

Kourtis Michail-Alexandros was born in Athens, Greece in 1989. He received his BSc degree in Computer Science from the Athens University of Economics and Business(AUEB). He is currently a MSc student at AUEB and pursuing his PhD at the Department of Informatics and Telecommunications at the University of Athens. From early 2010 until today he is a Research Associate at the Institute of Informatics and Telecommunications, at NCSR Demokritos. My research interests include: video and picture quality, study of video coding standard H.264/AVC, benchmarking and analysis of the novel HEVC / H. 265, objective and subjective evaluation of the perceived quality of multimedia services, novel approaches on temporal video quality assessment methods, QoS, and QoE.

Sandro Moiron graduated in Electrical Engineering in 2005 from the Polytechnic Institute of Leiria and received an M.Sc. degree in 2007 from the University of Coimbra, Portugal. He completed a PhD degree at the University of Essex, UK in 2011 in the area of transcoders for video communication. He is a Research Engineer at the Instituto de Telecomunicações in Portugal and also now works as an engineer specializing in compressed video at VMware, London, UK. His research interests include video coding, transcoding, error resiliency, and compressed-domain signal processing.

Jânio Monteiro is an Adjunct Professor in the Higher Institute of Engineering, at the University of Algarve (UALG), in Portugal. He graduated in Electrical and Computer Engineering at the University of Oporto (Portugal) in 1995. He received his M.Sc. and Ph.D. degrees in Electrical and Computer Engineering from the Technical University of Lisbon respectively in 2003 and 2010. He is a researcher of the INESC-ID and INOV institutes. His research interests include coding and transmission of scalable and multi-view video, as well as peer-to-peer networks.

Yannick Morvan received his M.S. in Electrical Engineering from the Institut Superieur d'Electronique et du Numerique (ISEN), France in 2003. During his undergraduate studies, he worked, in 2002, at Philips Research on embedded image processing software and, in 2003, at Philips Medical Systems on X-ray image quality enhancement algorithms. In 2004, he joined, as a Ph.D. candidate, the Signal Processing Systems group at the Eindhoven University of Technology in The Netherlands. During his Ph.D. project, he was involved in a joint project of Philips Research and the Eindhoven University of Technology about the development of a multi-camera video acquisition and compression system for 3-D television. In 2007, one of his papers on multi-view video coding obtained a Best Paper award nomination at the Picture Coding Symposium in Lisboa, Portugal. In 2008, Yannick Morvan became 3D Imaging Scientist at Philips Healthcare, Best in The Netherlands.

Manzur Murshed received the B.Sc.Eng. (Hons.) degree in Computer Science and Engineering from Bangladesh University of Engineering and Technology (BUET), Dhaka, Bangladesh, in 1994 and the Ph.D. degree in Computer Science from the Australian National University, Canberra, Australia, in 1999. He is currently an Associate Professor and Head of Gippsland School of Information Technology, Monash University, Australia where his major research interests are in the fields of video technology, wireless communications, information theory, distributed coding, and security and privacy. He has so far published 160+ refereed research papers with 1,900 (approx.) citations and received around $1 million research grants, including two prestigious Australian Research Council Discovery Project grants in 2006 and 2010 on video coding & communications and a large industry grant in 2011 on video conferencing for medical general practitioners. To date he has successfully supervised 11 PhDs and is currently supervising five PhD students. He is an Associate Editor of *IEEE Transactions on Circuits and Systems for Video Technology*, an Editor of *International Journal of Digital Multimedia Broadcasting*, and a Guest Editor of an annual special issue series of *Journal of Multimedia*. He received a University Gold Medal from BUET in 1994, the inaugural Early Career Research Excellence award from the Faculty of Information Technology, Monash University in 2006, and the Vice-Chancellor's Knowledge Transfer commendation award from the University of Melbourne in 2007.

Mário S. Nunes graduated with the Electronics Engineer degree in 1975, PhD degree in Electronics Engineer and Computers in 1987, and the Aggregation degree in the same area in 2006, all from the Instituto Superior Técnico, Technical University of Lisbon, Portugal. He is now Full Professor at Instituto Superior Técnico, where he teaches in telecommunications and networking areas in graduate and postgraduate courses. He has been responsible for the INESC participation in several European projects, namely RACE, ACTS and IST programs in the areas of fixed and wireless networks. Since 2001 he is Director of INESC Inovação, where he is scientific coordinator of the Telecom Area. He is author of two books and submitted 10 patents. He is a Senior Member of IEEE.

Sunday Nyamweno is an Analyst with the New Broadcast Technologies department of CBC/Radio-Canada. He received his BEng degree in 2002 from McMaster University (Hamilton, Ontario, Canada), his M.Sc. (with distinction) from the University of Leeds (Leeds, UK) in 2004, and his PhD in Electrical Engineering from McGill University (Montreal, Quebec, Canada) in 2012. His interests are mainly focused on signal processing applications for broadcasting, colour science, multimedia streaming, video quality analysis, and next generation transcoding solutions.

Charalampos Z. Patrikakis was born in Greece in 1970. He received his Dipl.-Ing. and his Ph.D from the Electrical Engineering and Computer Science Department of NTUA, Greece. He is an Assistant Professor at the Dept of Electronics of the TEI of Piraeus and a Senior Research Associate of the Institute of Communications and Computer Systems, working on research projects. He has participated in more than 27 national, European, and international programs, in 12 of which he has been involved as technical coordinator or principal researcher. He has more than 100 publications in chapters of books, international journals, and conferences, and has 2 contributions in national legislation. He is a member of the editorial committee of more than 50 international journals and conferences, and has acted as editor in the publication of special issues of international journals, conference proceedings volums and coedited two books. He is a senior member of IEEE and councelor of the IEEE student department of TEI of Piraeus.

Nikolaos Papaoulakis received the degree and Ph.D of Electrical and Computer Engineer from the Electrical Engineering and Computer Science School of NTUA, in the area of RRM in Wireless Networks. He is currently working in the field of heterogeneous networking regarding the converge use of mobile and fixed networks in both National and European projects as a research associate of the Telecommunications Laboratory of ICCS. He has participated in several European Union projects. His main research interests are in the area of heterogeneous and ad-hoc mobile networking, radio resource management on GSM, UMTS, WLAN, WiMax networks, and terrestrial and hierarchical Digital Television Broadcasting DVB-T. He has performed a large number of publications and journals, book chapters, conferences and standardization bodies. He has received the Best Paper Award on the 15th IST Mobile and Wireless Summit 2006, 4-8 June 2006, Greece, Myconos, for his work entitled "Congestion Avoidance". Dr. Papaoulakis has participated in the task force of NATO, for the creation of a technical report for "Awareness of Emerging Wireless Technologies: Ad-hoc and Personal Area Networks Standards and Emerging Technologies." He was councilor of the Telecommunication Minister and author of the laws regarding the identification of prepaid mobile phone and DVB service framework. Since September of 2002 is member of the Administrative and Decision board of the Greek Telecommunication and Post Regulator, the Hellenic Telecommunication and Post Commission.

Goran Petrovic is a researcher in the Saarland University. He performs research on video streaming in the Telecommunications Lab. Currently he is finishing his PhD project in the Eindhoven University of Technology. His PhD project is conducted in the Video Coding and Architectures Research group, Signal Processing Systems department, Electrical Engineering. His research interests include streaming in wireless networks, IP-television, and 3D video streaming.

Nada Y. Philip received the Ph.D. degree from the Faculty of Computing, Information System and Mathematics, Kingston University, London, U.K., in 2008. She is currently a Lecturer at Kingston University, where she is also a research staff with the Medical Information and Network Technologies Research Centre (MINT). She is also Honorary Tutor at St. George's University of London, London. She is the author or co-author of more than 20 journal and conference papers. Her research interests in e-health and m-health include medical quality of service and experience, medical video streaming optimization, internet of things, and mobile applications for disease management and support.

Nadia N. Qadri received her Master's of Engineering (Communication Systems and Networks) and Bachelor's of Engineering (Computer Systems), from Mehran University of Engineering and Technology, Jamshoro, Pakistan in 2004 and 2002, respectively. From 2006 to 2010 she took a PhD at the University of Essex, UK, where she was awarded her doctorate with the title P2P Video Streaming in Mobile and Vehicular Ad Hoc Networks. She has more than ten years of teaching and research experience at renowned universities of Pakistan viz. Mehran University of Engineering & Technology, Fatima Jinnah Womens University and COMSATS Institute of Information Technology. She is currently an Associate Professor in charge of the Telecommunication Engineering Program at COMSATS Wah Cantt Campus in Pakistan. Her research interests include video streaming for mobile ad hoc networks and vehicular ad hoc networks, along with P2P streaming.

Ramdas Bangalore Satyan received his PhD in Electrical Engineering at McGill University, Montreal, Canada in 2011. He is currently working as a video research engineer at eBrisk Video Inc. His work involves design and development of algorithms for the next generation video coding technologies and standards. His research interests include video coding, error resilience in video coding and multimedia communication. He received his Bachelor of Engineering in Electronics and Communication from R.V. College of Engineering Bangalore, India in 2003. After receiving his Bachelor's, he worked as a Systems Engineer for two years designing and implementing GPS receiver algorithms on DSP chipsets.

Rui Santos Cruz graduated with the Electrical Engineer degree in 1982, MSc. in Electrical and Computer Engineering in 2005 and is pursuing the PhD in Information Systems and Computer Engineering all from the Instituto Superior Técnico, Technical University of Lisbon, Portugal. He is Assistant Professor at Instituto Superior Técnico, where he teaches Networking and Computer Engineering in graduate and postgraduate courses and a researcher at INESC-ID/INOV, where he participated in some European projects, namely the My-eDirector and SARACEN projects. During the course of his professional career in the industry, he was involved in the analysis, design, development, and deployment of computer and communication systems and data and telecommunications networks as senior staff engineer, manager and director. He is a senior member of IEEE and chairs the IEEE Portugal section. He is also a Professional Member of ACM.

Golam Sorwar received B.Sc.(Hons) degree in Electrical and Electronic Engineering in 1994 from Bangladesh University of Engineering and Technology (BUET), Bangladesh, M.Sc. degree in Electrical, Electronic and Systems Eng. in 1998 from National University of Malaysia, Malaysia, and Ph.D. degree in Information Technology from Monash University, Australia in 2003.He is currently a Lecturer at Southern Cross Business School at Southern Cross University, Australia, where his major research interests are in the fields of multimedia signal processing and communication, electronic health and telemedicine applications. He has published more than 45 peer-reviewed, book chapters, journal articles and conference papers. He is a member of Institute of Electrical and Electronics Engineering (IEEE), Australian Computer Society (ACS), and Institute of Engineers of Bangladesh (IEB), Bangladesh.

Sridha Sridharan received the BSc degree in Electrical Engineering and the MSc degree in Communication Engineering from the University of Manchester Institute of Science and Technology (UMIST), UK. He obtained the PhD degree in the area of Signal Processing from the University of New South Wales (UNSW), Sydney, Australia. He is currently a full Professor in the School of Electrical Engineering & Computer Science in the Science & Engineering Faculty of the Queensland University of Technology (QUT), and the leader of the Research Program in Speech, Audio, Image, and Video Technology (SAIVT) at QUT.

Chun-Rong Su was born in Taipei, Taiwan on November 8, 1982. He received the B.S. and M.S. degrees in Electrical Engineering from Southern Taiwan University, Tainan, Taiwan, and National Taiwan University of Science and Technology, Taipei, Taiwan, in 2005 and 2007, respectively. He is currently pursuing the Ph.D. degree in Electronics Engineering in National Taiwan University of Science and Technology. His research interests include image indexing, digital image processing, and image/video encoding.

Andreas Unterweger received his Master's-equivalent Diploma degree in Information Technology and Systems Management (with distinction) from the Salzburg University of Applied Sciences in 2008 and his Master's degree in Computer Science (with distinction) from the University of Salzburg in 2011. He is currently pursuing his Ph.D. degree in Computer Science at the University of Salzburg where he specializes on selective video encryption. In addition, he is an External Lecturer at the Salzburg University of Applied Sciences, teaching Microcontroller Programming and Applied Mathematics in the Bachelor's degree program. His current research interests include real-time video coding and selective video encryption.

Svitlana Zinger received the M.Sc. degree in Computer Science in 2000 from the Radiophysics faculty of the Dnepropetrovsk State University, Ukraine. She received the Ph.D. degree in 2004 from the Ecole Nationale Superieure des Telecommunications, France. Her Ph.D. thesis was on interpolation and resampling of 3D data. In 2005 she was a postdoctoral fellow in the Multimedia and Multilingual Knowledge Engineering Laboratory of the French Atomic Agency, France, where she worked on creation of a large-scale image ontology for content based image retrieval. In 2006-2008 she was a postdoctoral researcher at the Center for Language and Cognition Groningen and an associated researcher at the Artificial Intelligence department in the University of Groningen, the Netherlands, working on information retrieval from handwritten documents. She is currently a postdoc at the Video Coding and Architectures Research group in the Eindhoven University of Technology.

Index

CPSIA information can be obtained at www.ICGtesting.com
Printed in the USA
BVOW052336041212

306976BV00007B/89/P

9 781466 626607